Addison Wesley 7

Science & Technology

Authors

Kyn Barker
York Region District School Board,
Ontario

Steve Campbell
Richmond School Board,
British Columbia

Gary Greenland
Toronto District School Board,
Ontario

Douglas Hayhoe
Toronto District School Board,
Ontario

Doug Herridge
Faculty of Education,
York University, Ontario
York Region District School Board,
Ontario

Kathy Kubota-Zarivnij
Faculty of Education,
York University, Ontario
Toronto Catholic District School Board,
Ontario

Shelagh Reading
Calgary Board of Education,
Alberta

Lionel Sandner
Saanich School Board,
British Columbia

Beverley Williams
Annapolis Valley Regional
School Board, Nova Scotia

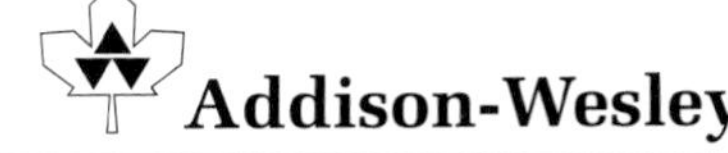

Addison-Wesley

An imprint of Addison Wesley Longman Ltd.

Don Mills, Ontario • Reading, Massachusetts
Harlow, England • Glenview, Illinois
Melbourne, Australia

Coordinating Editor
Cecilia Chan

Project Coordinator
Jeff Siamon

Editors and Writers
Julie Bedford
Jonathan Bocknek
Julie Czerneda
Jackie Dulson
Klaus Richter
Yvonne Van Ruskenveld
John Yip-Chuck

Production Editors
Jane Clark
Ellen Davidson

Indexer
Chris Blackburn

Research Manager
Louise MacKenzie

Researchers
Christy Hayhoe
Keith Lennox
Kendra McKnight

Design
Word & Image Design Inc.

Classroom Consultant
Lynn Short, Toronto District School Board, Ontario

Acknowledgment
Addison Wesley Longman and the authors of *Addison Wesley Science and Technology Grade 7* would like to thank the teachers and consultants who reviewed and field-tested this material.

ISBN 0-201-61394-8

This book contains recycled product and is acid-free.
Printed and bound in Canada.

ABCDEF – BP – 04 03 02 01 00 99

CONTENTS

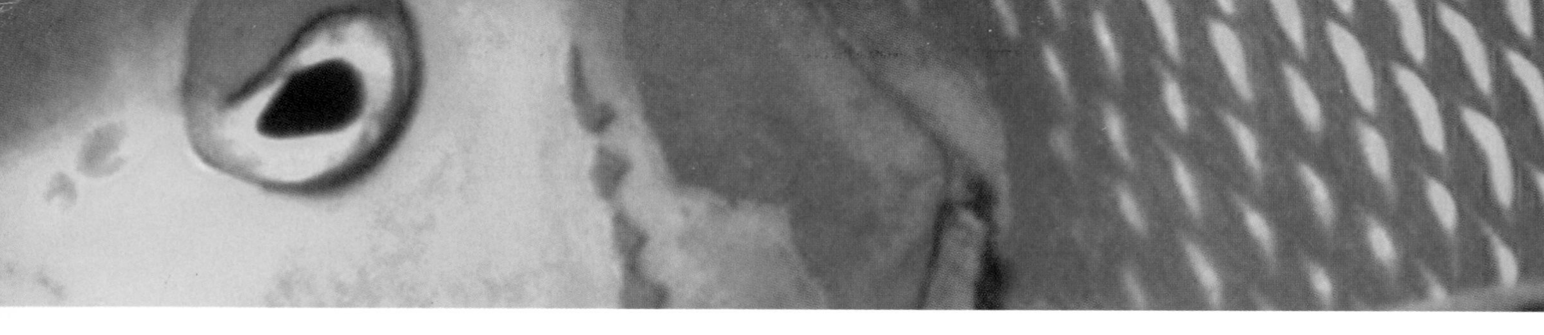

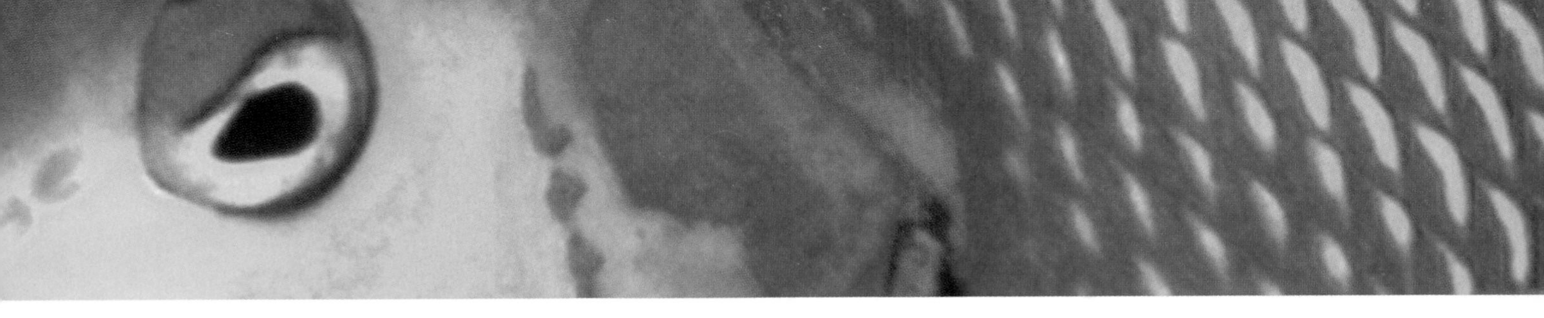

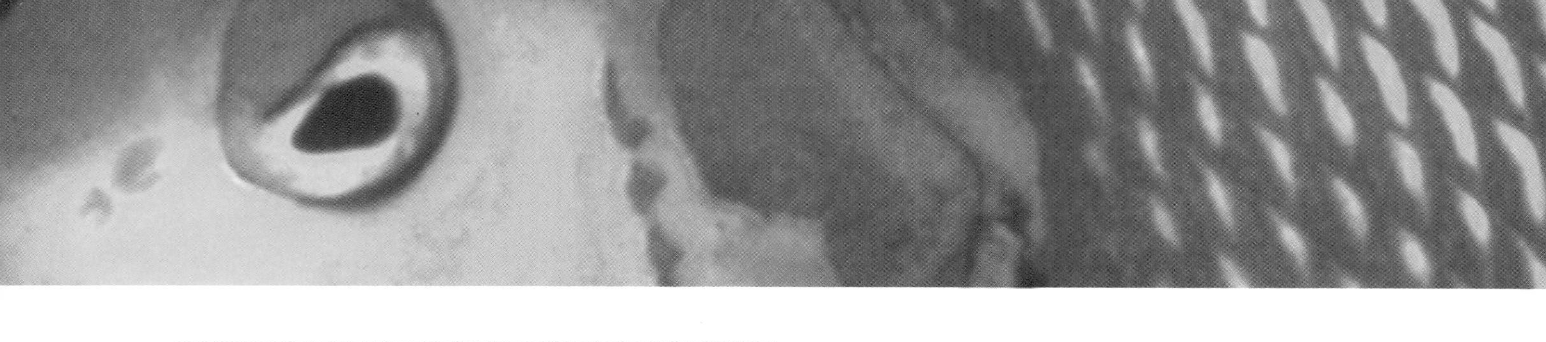

Chapter 4 Structures 237

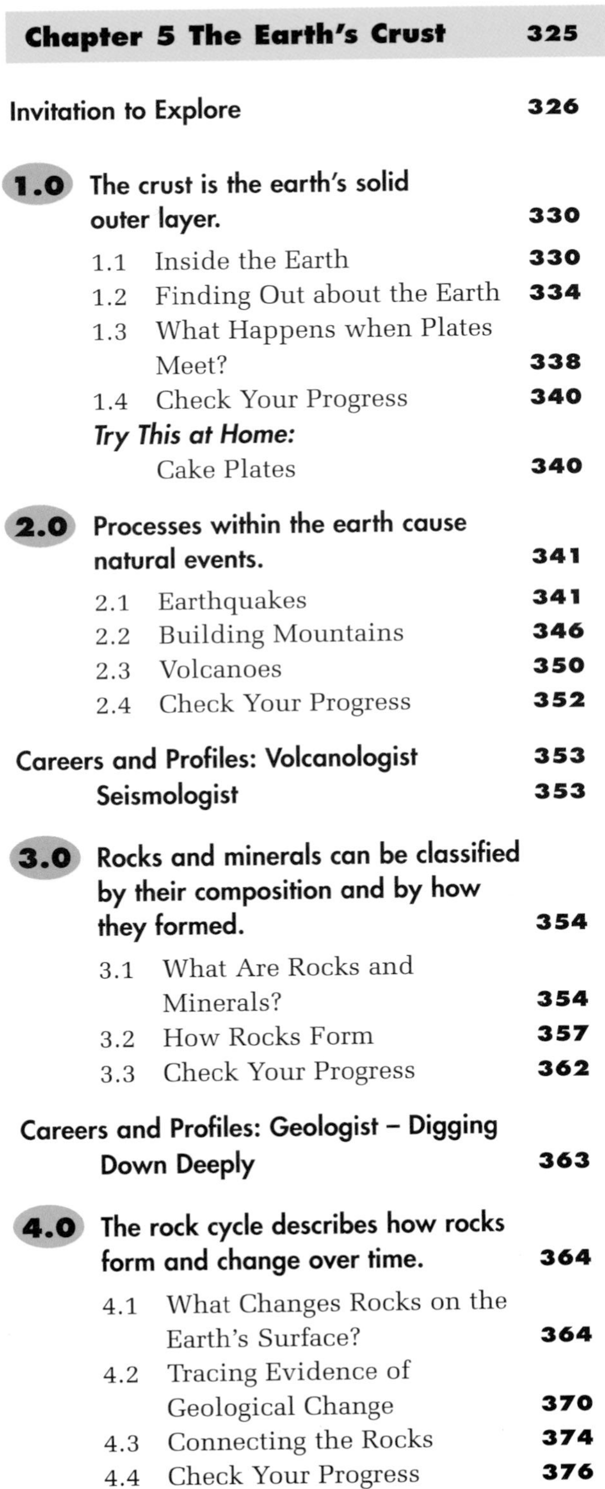

Introduction

Welcome to Addison Wesley Science and Technology!

You are about to begin a journey exploring Ecosystems, Mixtures, Heat, Structures, and The Earth's Crust.

You'll be investigating the natural phenomena of the world around you and technological responses of our society to this world. As you do so, we help you by

- building on your own experience of scientific phenomena,
- providing you with examples of scientific achievement that people like yourself have undertaken,
  and
- providing you with different types of activities that suit different types of thinkers.

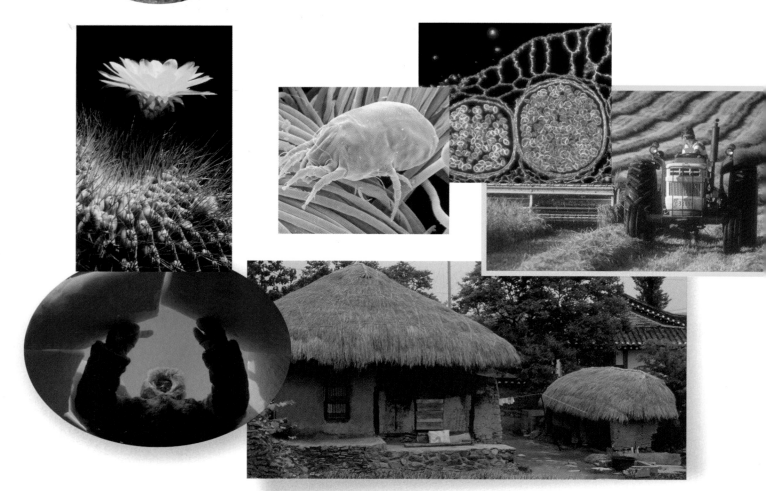

A Look at a Chapter of Addison Wesley Science and Technology

1 Chapter Introduction

This section of the page provides a quick overview of what you'll be doing.

The list of Big Ideas provides a road map to the learning of the chapter. The number beside the Big Idea identifies a section of the chapter, so you can use this framework to help you connect the knowledge and skills in each chapter.

Chapter 1

ECOSYSTEMS

habitat

Our planet is teeming with life. The largest living thing would take up more than one-third of the length of a football field. The smallest are so small that there could be 10 billion of them in just a spoonful of soil.

Believe it or not, you have a lot in common with all living things. It doesn't matter if they're large or small. It doesn't matter if they live in the ocean, deep in the soil, or out in your schoolyard. In fact, your life—all life—depends on and is connected with other living things.

In this chapter, you will consider these and other ideas about living things. You will find out how all living things are related. You're invited to explore!

BIG Ideas

bioinvasion

1.0 Ecosystems are made up of living and non-living things.

2.0 Ecosystems are interactions of biotic and abiotic components.

3.0 Ecosystems are made up of producers, consumers, and decomposers that interact to form food webs.

4.0 Matter and energy are necessary for all ecosystems.

5.0 Natural changes can cause changes in ecosystems.

6.0 Human activities can change ecosystems.

7.0 Technologies have been developed to manage wastes that humans generate.

decomposers

2 Invitation to Explore

A real-world example about the topic of the chapter will allow you to

- draw on what you already know about the topic,
- share your ideas about the topic with others,
- think about some of the implications of the topic for our society,
- ask questions before you begin the chapter of study.

Invitation to Explore

1 ECOSYSTEMS

EarthNews On-line Journal

Netsite:

Home Page | Search | Support | Software

EarthNews On-line Journal

CONTENTS

Home
Last Month's Issue
Back Issues
Feature Articles
Search
Subscribe!
Contact Us
FAQs

The Birth of an Island

Reykjavik, Iceland

Imagine inviting people to a party and then waiting years, maybe even decades, for your guests to arrive. That's what it's like for scientists pacing the shores of one of earth's newest islands, Surtsey, off the coast of Iceland.

The "guests" are the life forms slowly beginning to live on this barren island. Scientists have been waiting and watching for 30 years.

First, it was the mosses. Then came the sea sandwort, a relative of the cactus, which makes its home on the shores of many Arctic islands and land masses. Over time, grasses, flies, and a number of ocean birds, many of them gulls, followed these sturdy pioneers.

But back on a cold November day in 1962, the island of Surtsey was just beginning. That's when the crew of a fishing boat first noticed the rotten-egg smell of sulphur compounds. They also saw the ocean surface bubbling like water in a pot.

About 6.5 km away, deep down in the ocean, a small underwater volcano was erupting. Plumes of ash shot as high as 9 km into the air the next day.

It took four years before the volcanic activity finally stopped. When it had, earth's newest land form — named Surtsey, after the Norse god of fire — occupied an area of nearly 3 km².

2 Invitation to Explore

According to this Web page, Surtsey was just a barren rocky surface in the beginning. Now there are different plants and animals living on this island. The nearest living things are 18 km away on another island. How do you think life appeared on Surtsey?

infoBIT

Iceland: Surtsey Island

Surtsey Island

With a partner or in a small group, brainstorm ways that these living things could find their way to Surtsey.

- plants
- insects
- birds

If you can think of any ways to test your ideas, try them!

Which of these animals could survive on Surtsey?

Invitation to Explore 3

The **Focus Your Thoughts** section will help you to draw conclusions and put together your thoughts before you start work on the chapter itself.

A short activity will require you to solve a particular problem and think about what you already know about similar situations.

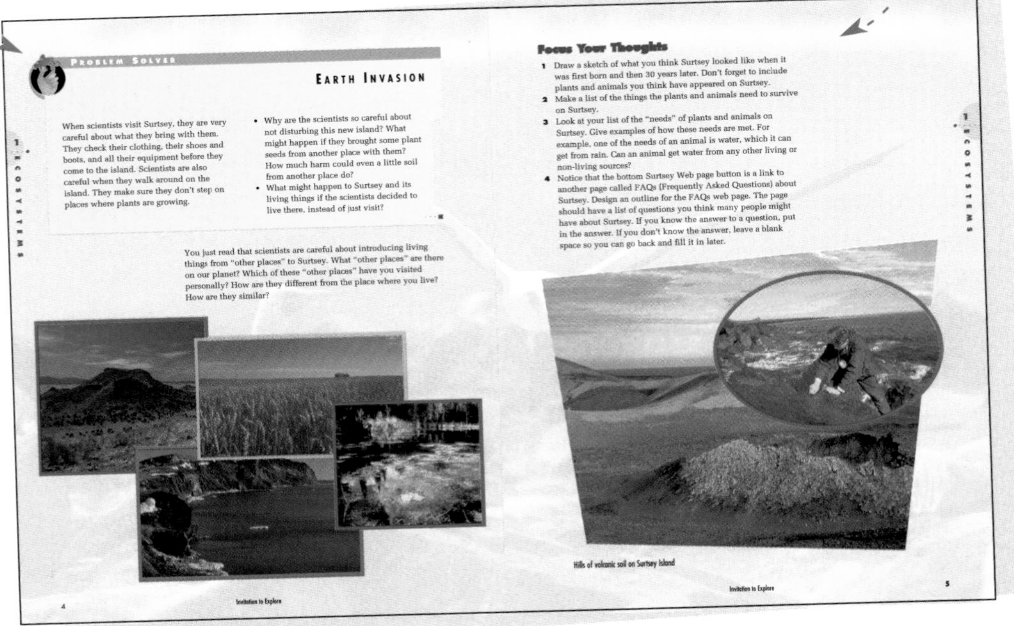

Problem Solver

Earth Invasion

When scientists visit Surtsey, they are very careful about what they bring with them. They check their clothing, their shoes and boots, and all their equipment before they come to the island. Scientists are also careful when they walk around on the island. They make sure they don't step on places where plants are growing.

- Why are the scientists so careful about not disturbing this new island? What might happen if they brought some plant seeds from another place with them? How much harm could even a little soil from another place do?
- What might happen to Surtsey and its living things if the scientists decided to live there, instead of just visit?

You just read that scientists are careful about introducing living things from "other places" to Surtsey. What "other places" are there on our planet? Which of these "other places" have you visited personally? How are they different from the place where you live? How are they similar?

4 Invitation to Explore

Focus Your Thoughts

1. Draw a sketch of what you think Surtsey looked like when it was first born and then 30 years later. Don't forget to include plants and animals you think have appeared on Surtsey.
2. Make a list of the things the plants and animals need to survive on Surtsey.
3. Look at your list of the "needs" of plants and animals on Surtsey. Give examples of how these needs are met. For example, one of the needs of an animal is water, which it can get from rain. Can an animal get water from any other living or non-living sources?
4. Notice that the bottom Surtsey Web page button is a link to another page called FAQs (Frequently Asked Questions) about Surtsey. Design an outline for the FAQs web page. The page should have a list of questions you think many people might have about Surtsey. If you know the answer to a question, put in the answer. If you don't know the answer, leave a blank space so you can go back and fill it in later.

Hills of volcanic soil on Surtsey Island

Invitation to Explore 5

3 Chapter Sections

Each section has a **Big Idea** as a heading. This Big Idea is a key concept that you should remember when the chapter is done.

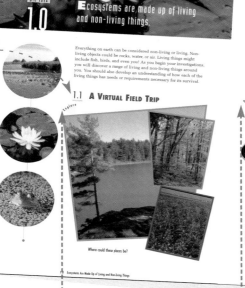

Each Big Idea section is broken down into smaller sections. Each small section explains an aspect of the Big Idea.

When you see the **Explore** icon, you'll be asked to draw upon what you already know before you begin the content of the small section.

When you see the **Develop** icon, you know that you will find activities that investigate a part of the Big Idea in depth.

At the end of every small section, you'll see a **Communicate** icon, and know that you have a chance to test your understanding of the section and further develop your thinking.

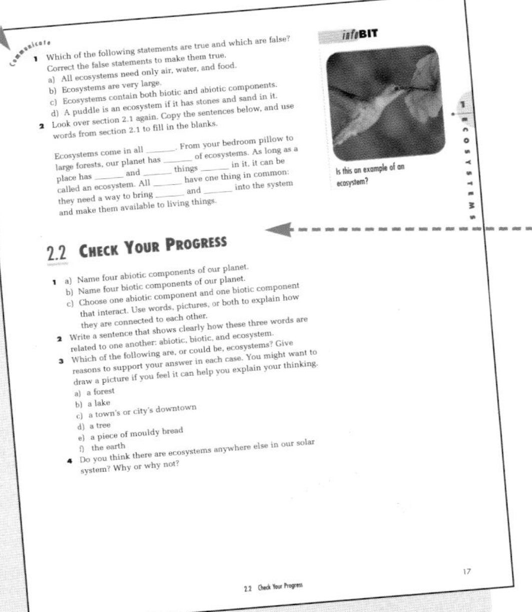

Communicate

1 Which of the following statements are true and which are false? Correct the false statements to make them true.
a) All ecosystems need only air, water, and food.
b) Ecosystems are very large.
c) Ecosystems contain both biotic and abiotic components.
d) A puddle is an ecosystem if it has stones and sand in it.

2 Look over section 2.1 again. Copy the sentences below, and use words from section 2.1 to fill in the blanks.

Ecosystems come in all ______. From your bedroom pillow to large forests, our planet has ______ of ecosystems. As long as a place has ______ and ______ things ______ in it, it can be called an ecosystem. All ______ have one thing in common: they need a way to bring ______ and ______ into the system and make them available to living things.

infoBIT

Is this an example of an ecosystem?

2.2 Check Your Progress

1 a) Name four abiotic components of our planet.
b) Name four biotic components of our planet.
c) Choose one abiotic component and one biotic component that interact. Use words, pictures, or both to explain how they are connected to each other.

2 Write a sentence that shows clearly how these three words are related to one another: abiotic, biotic, and ecosystem.

3 Which of the following are, or could be, ecosystems? Give reasons to support your answer in each case. You might want to draw a picture if you feel it can help you explain your thinking.
a) a forest
b) a lake
c) a town's or city's downtown
d) a tree
e) a piece of mouldy bread
f) the earth

4 Do you think there are ecosystems anywhere else in our solar system? Why or why not?

17

2.2 Check Your Progress

At the end of each Big Idea section, you can check your understanding of the Big Idea.

4 Activities

Critical thinking activities in *Addison Wesley Science and Technology* are of three kinds.

An **Investigator** activity provides a chance for you to work in a lab setting to develop the scientific skills of observing, measuring, experimenting, and much more. Investigators encourage you to explore the material phenomena found in our world.

Develop
Food Chains for Producers and Consumers

Investigator

Energy Pathway

Before you start...
You know that plants, through photosynthesis, provide a way for the sun's energy to enter ecosystems. What happens to that energy? Does it disappear or get used by other living things? Discuss your thoughts with your partner or other classmates.

The Question
What pathway does energy follow in ecosystems, and what happens to that energy?

Materials & Equipment
- *your notes you recorded about the living things in your schoolyard*

Procedure
1 Review the results of your schoolyard survey in the Investigator activity in section 1.1. Think about all the living things you recorded. Group the living things into possible food chains. Draw these food chains.
2 Pick an ecosystem photo from earlier in this chapter. Or if you want, find a picture of an ecosystem that appeals to you. Identify as many food chains as you can that you think might exist in that ecosystem. Include living things that you can see in the photo, as well as any others that you think would live in that ecosystem.

continued on next page

27

1.3 Food Chains

5.1 Natural Changes in Ecosystems
Explore
A forest once stood here. That was before the thunderstorm. Lightning pierced the sky, striking and igniting one of the taller trees. The fire jumped from treetop to treetop until the entire forest was burning. The photo above shows all that's left.
Do you think there's anything living here in this barren-looking, desolate scene? Could anything ever live here again?

Problem Solver

To Change or Not To Change

Imagine what the forest scene in the photo looked like before the fire. Make a sketch in your Science Journal to show what you're imagining. What kinds of living things populated this scene? What abiotic and biotic components of the forest ecosystem supported them? Where are the living things now?

How do you think this scene will look a few years from now? Will it be any different? What could make it different? Use a sketch to record your impressions. Add labels to clarify your ideas.
How will this scene look 20 years from now? 50 years from now? 100 years or more from now?

46

5.0 Natural Changes Can Cause Changes in Ecosystems

Problem Solver activities are open-ended activities with very little set-up. There is no one correct solution. With Problem Solvers, you need to be creative in your thinking.

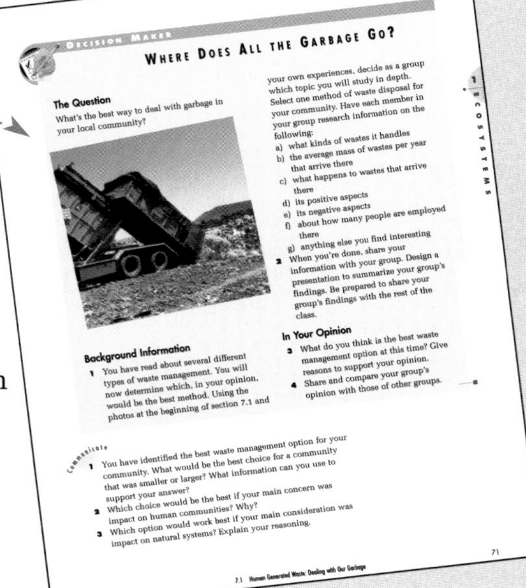
Decision Maker

Where Does All the Garbage Go?

The Question
What's the best way to deal with garbage in your local community?

Background Information
1 You have read about several different types of waste management. You will now determine which, in your opinion, would be the best method. Using the photos at the beginning of section 7.1 and your own experiences, decide as a group which topic you will study in depth. Select one method of waste disposal for your community. Have each member in your group research information on the following:
a) what kinds of wastes it handles
b) the average mass of wastes per year that arrive there
c) what happens to wastes that arrive there
d) its positive aspects
e) its negative aspects
f) about how many people are employed there
g) anything else you find interesting
2 When you're done, share your information with your group. Design a presentation to summarize your group's findings. Be prepared to share your group's findings with the rest of the class.

In Your Opinion
3 What do you think is the best waste management option at this time? Give reasons to support your opinion.
4 Share and compare your group's opinion with those of other groups.

Communicate
1 You have identified the best waste management option for your community. What would be the best choice for a community that was smaller or larger? What information can you use to support your answer?
2 Which choice would be the best if your main concern was impact on human communities? Why?
3 Which option would work best if your main consideration was impact on natural systems? Explain your reasoning.

71

7.1 Human-Generated Waste: Dealing with Our Garbage

Decision Maker activities present issues or questions related to your life. You may need to develop an opinion based on the evidence and make a decision. When you present your decision to your teacher and classmates, you may have to be persuasive.

5 Project and Chapter Review

The **Project** at the end of each chapter presents a hands-on opportunity for you to demonstrate what you've learned. You'll work both in groups and individually. The Project requires you to apply the skills and knowledge that you've acquired to a new situation.

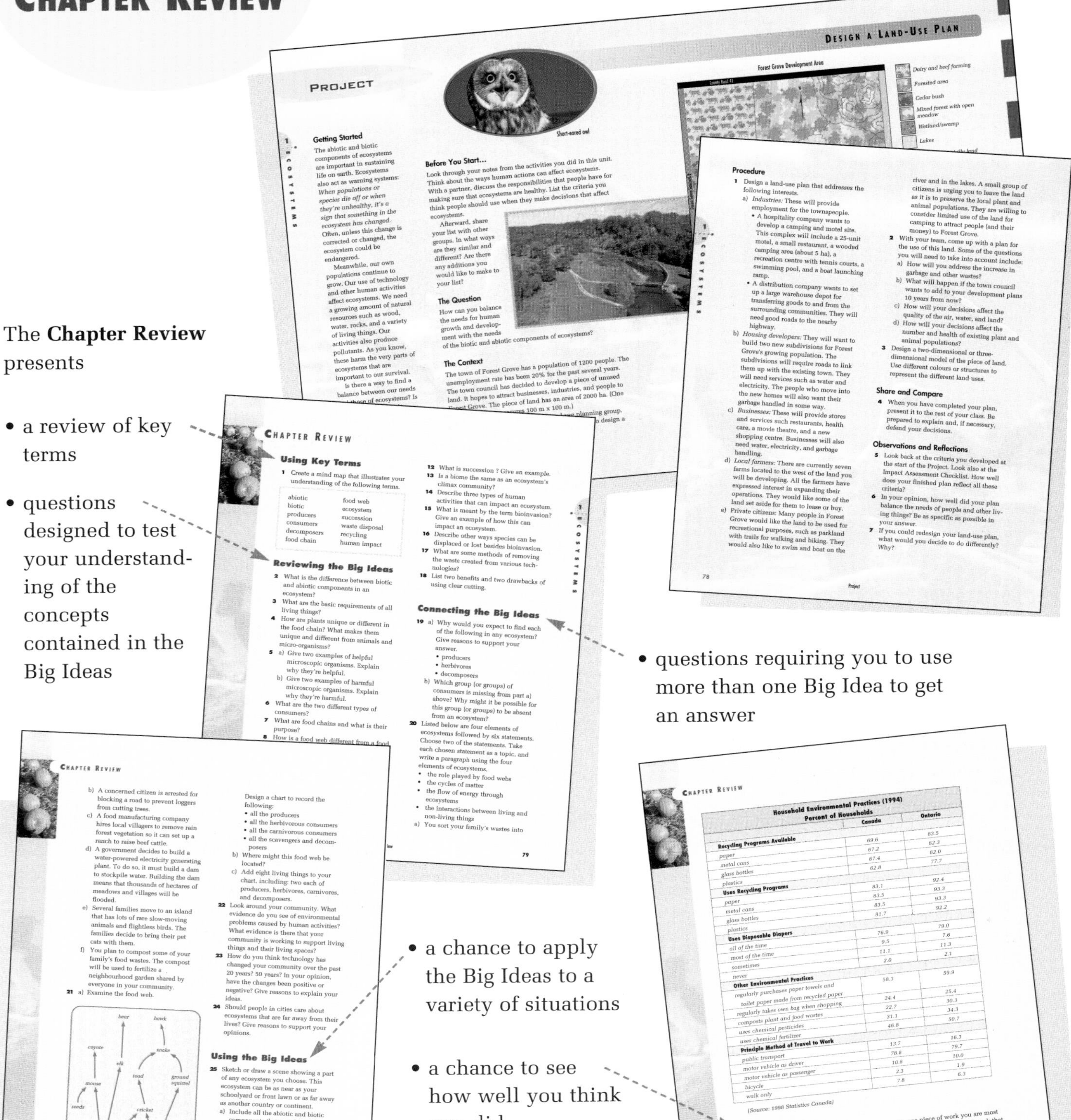

The **Chapter Review** presents

- a review of key terms
- questions designed to test your understanding of the concepts contained in the Big Ideas
- questions requiring you to use more than one Big Idea to get an answer
- a chance to apply the Big Ideas to a variety of situations
- a chance to see how well you think you did

6 Other Features

Experiment on Your Own

This is your chance to design your own experiment to check out a hypothesis or to solve a problem.

Science World

In this feature, there's an example of a real-world situation or application of the topics you're studying.

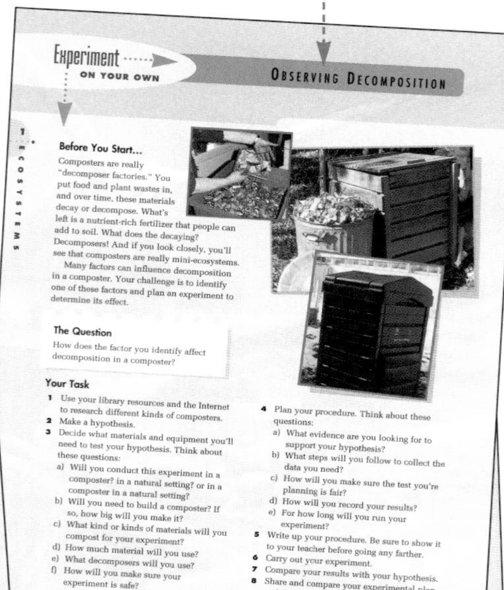

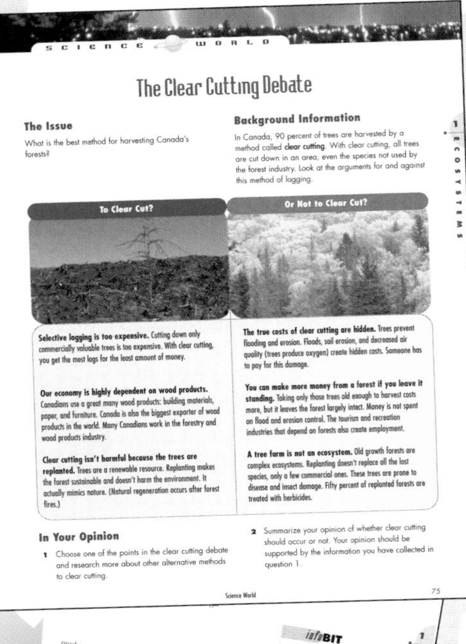

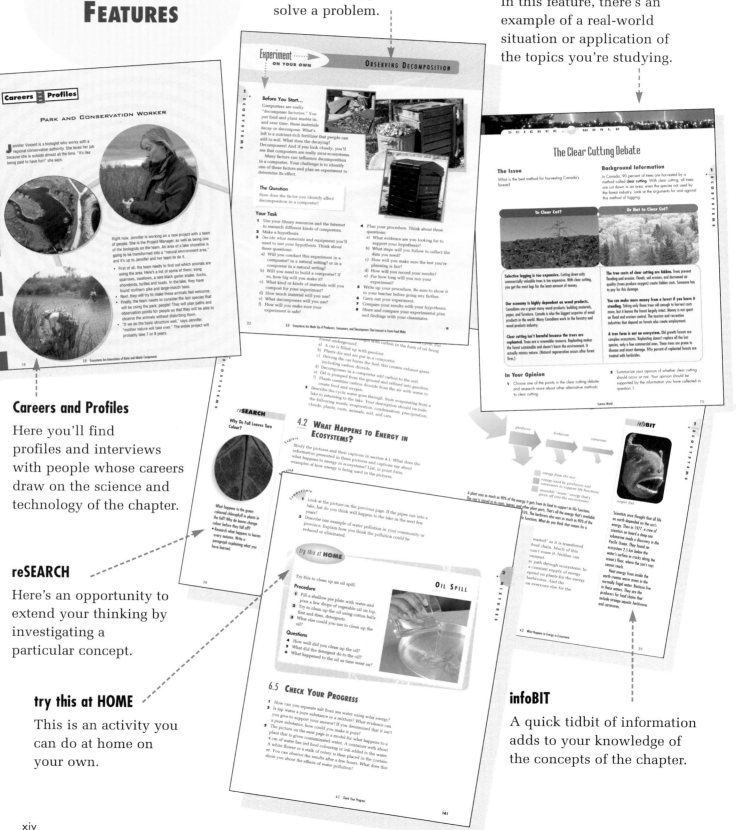

Careers and Profiles

Here you'll find profiles and interviews with people whose careers draw on the science and technology of the chapter.

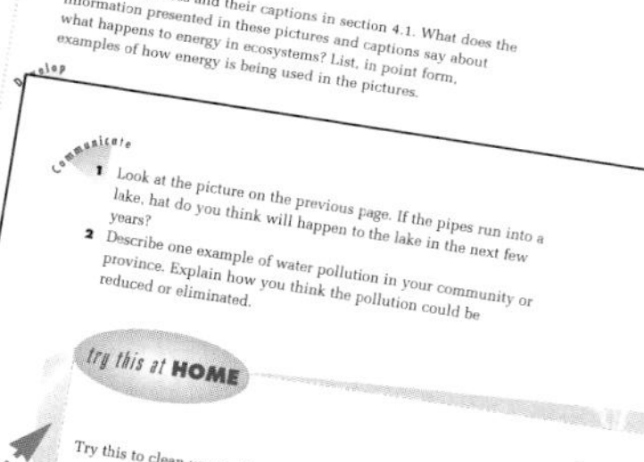

reSEARCH

Here's an opportunity to extend your thinking by investigating a particular concept.

try this at HOME

This is an activity you can do at home on your own.

infoBIT

A quick tidbit of information adds to your knowledge of the concepts of the chapter.

The Big Ideas of Science and Technology

There is much to learn in the science and technology you are studying this year. The Big Ideas that organize each chapter can be used to help you develop your understanding of science and technology.

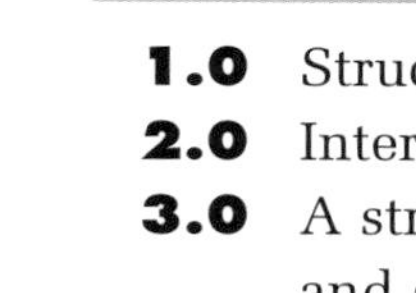

Chapter 1 ECOSYSTEMS

Our planet is teeming with life. The largest living thing would take up more than one-third of the length of a football field. The smallest are so small that there could be 10 billion of them in just a spoonful of soil.

Believe it or not, you have a lot in common with all living things. It doesn't matter if they're large or small. It doesn't matter if they live in the ocean, deep in the soil, or out in your schoolyard. In fact, your life—all life—depends on and is connected with other living things.

In this chapter, you will consider these and other ideas about living things. You will find out how all living things are related. You're invited to explore!

BIG Ideas

1.0 Ecosystems are made up of living and non-living things.

2.0 Ecosystems are interactions of biotic and abiotic components.

3.0 Ecosystems are made up of producers, consumers, and decomposers that interact to form food webs.

4.0 Matter and energy are necessary for all ecosystems.

5.0 Natural changes can cause changes in ecosystems.

6.0 Human activities can change ecosystems.

7.0 Technologies have been developed to manage wastes that humans generate.

Invitation to Explore

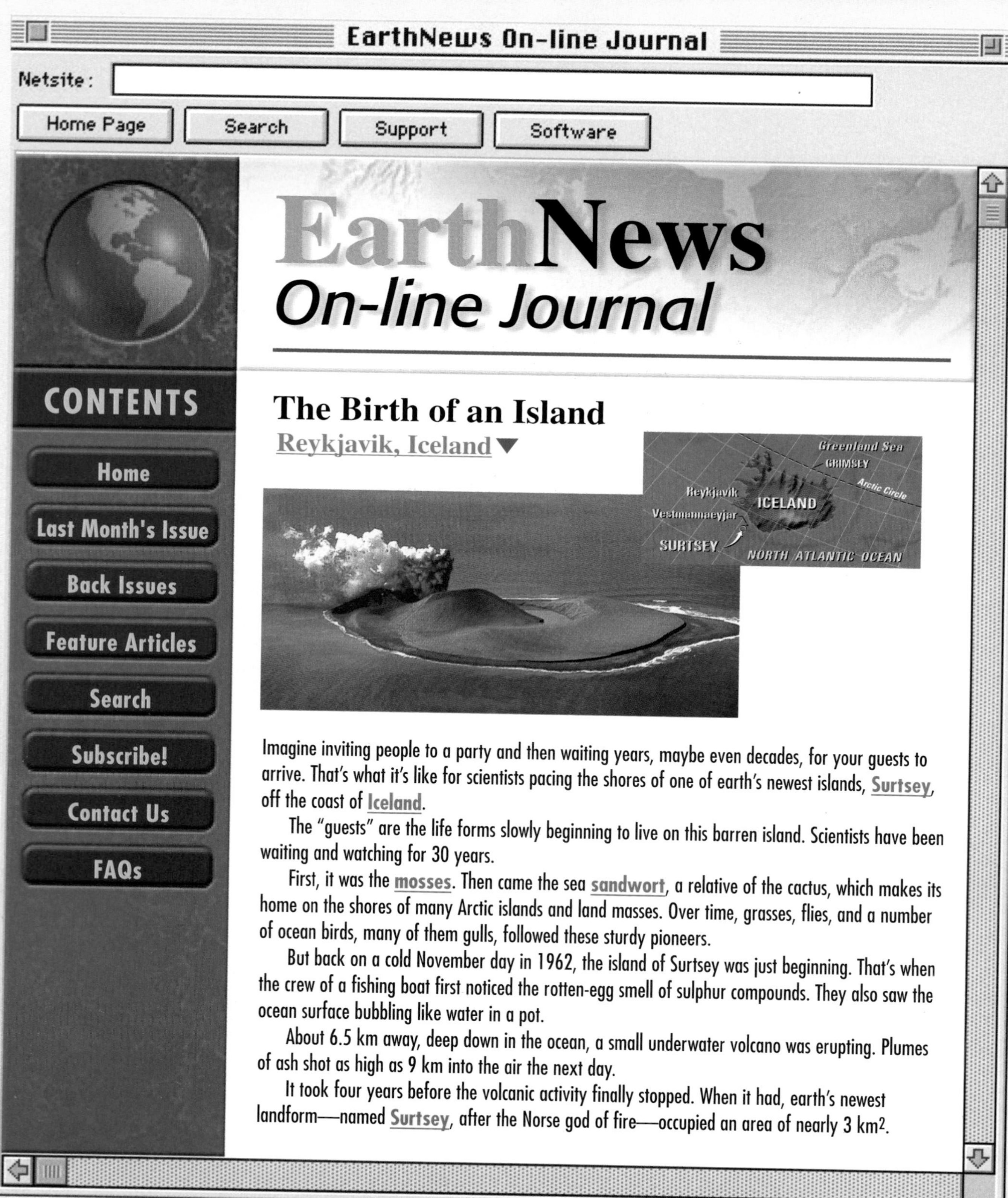

EarthNews
On-line Journal

The Birth of an Island

Reykjavik, Iceland

Imagine inviting people to a party and then waiting years, maybe even decades, for your guests to arrive. That's what it's like for scientists pacing the shores of one of earth's newest islands, Surtsey, off the coast of Iceland.

The "guests" are the life forms slowly beginning to live on this barren island. Scientists have been waiting and watching for 30 years.

First, it was the mosses. Then came the sea sandwort, a relative of the cactus, which makes its home on the shores of many Arctic islands and land masses. Over time, grasses, flies, and a number of ocean birds, many of them gulls, followed these sturdy pioneers.

But back on a cold November day in 1962, the island of Surtsey was just beginning. That's when the crew of a fishing boat first noticed the rotten-egg smell of sulphur compounds. They also saw the ocean surface bubbling like water in a pot.

About 6.5 km away, deep down in the ocean, a small underwater volcano was erupting. Plumes of ash shot as high as 9 km into the air the next day.

It took four years before the volcanic activity finally stopped. When it had, earth's newest landform—named Surtsey, after the Norse god of fire—occupied an area of nearly 3 km^2.

According to this Web page, Surtsey was just a barren rocky surface in the beginning. Now there are different plants and animals living on this island. The nearest living things are 18 km away on another island. How do you think life appeared on Surtsey?

infoBIT

Iceland: Surtsey Island

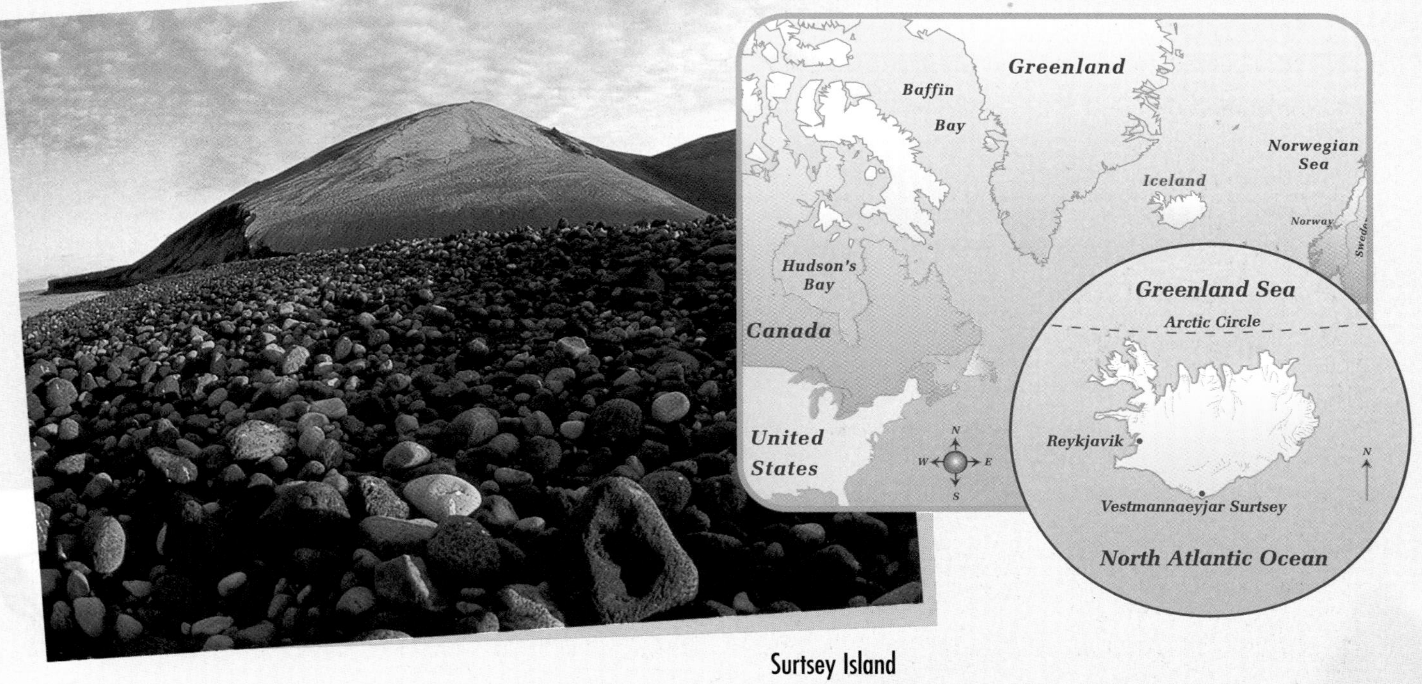

Surtsey Island

With a partner or in a small group, brainstorm ways that these living things could find their way to Surtsey.

- plants
- insects
- birds

If you can think of any ways to test your ideas, try them!

Which of these animals could survive on Surtsey?

PROBLEM SOLVER

EARTH INVASION

When scientists visit Surtsey, they are very careful about what they bring with them. They check their clothing, their shoes and boots, and all their equipment before they come to the island. Scientists are also careful when they walk around on the island. They make sure they don't step on places where plants are growing.

- Why are the scientists so careful about not disturbing this new island? What might happen if they brought some plant seeds from another place with them? How much harm could even a little soil from another place do?
- What might happen to Surtsey and its living things if the scientists decided to live there, instead of just visit?

You just read that scientists are careful about introducing living things from "other places" to Surtsey. What "other places" are there on our planet? Which of these "other places" have you visited personally? How are they different from the place where you live? How are they similar?

Focus Your Thoughts

1. Draw a sketch of what you think Surtsey looked like when it was first born and then 30 years later. Don't forget to include plants and animals you think have appeared on Surtsey.
2. Make a list of the things the plants and animals need to survive on Surtsey.
3. Look at your list of the "needs" of plants and animals on Surtsey. Give examples of how these needs are met. For example, one of the needs of an animal is water, which it can get from rain. Can an animal get water from any other living or non-living sources?
4. Notice that the bottom Surtsey Web page button is a link to another page called FAQs (Frequently Asked Questions) about Surtsey. Design an outline for the FAQs web page. The page should have a list of questions you think many people might have about Surtsey. If you know the answer to a question, put in the answer. If you don't know the answer, leave a blank space so you can go back and fill it in later.

Hills of volcanic soil on Surtsey Island

Big Idea

1.0 Ecosystems are made up of living and non-living things.

ECOSYSTEMS

Everything on earth can be considered non-living or living. Non-living objects could be rocks, water, or air. Living things might include fish, birds, and even you! As you begin your investigations, you will discover a range of living and non-living things around you. You should also develop an understanding of how each of the living things has needs or requirements necessary for its survival.

1.1 A Virtual Field Trip

Explore

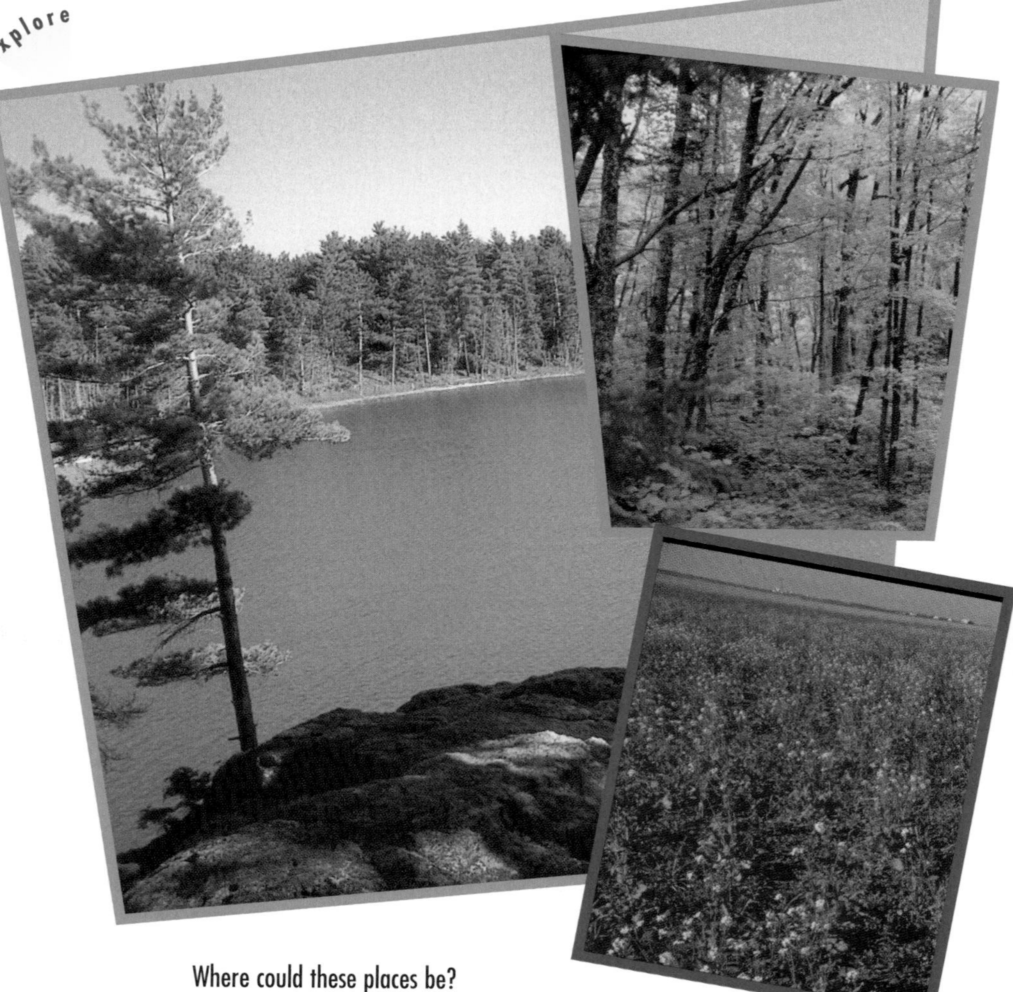

Where could these places be?

Choose one of the scenes shown in the photographs on the opposite page. Imagine walking into the scene. Record your answers to the following questions. (If you like, you can do this in the form of a brief story, poem, or song.)

- What does the air smell like?
- What sounds do you hear, and who or what is making them?
- What sights do you see?
- What sensations do you feel?
- Do you like this place? Why or why not?
- Have you visited one like it before? If so, where?
- How will this place be different three months from now? six months from now?
- In what part or parts of your province could you walk into a scene like this? Is there anywhere else like it in Canada? in the rest of the world?

Field Trip to the Schoolyard

You've played in your schoolyard and probably know it quite well. Now it's time to take a different look at the area. Somewhere out there are other living things, in the grass, around the rocks, and between the cracks in the pavement. Let's go find them.

INVESTIGATOR

How Much Do You Know about Your Schoolyard?

Before You Start...

Is your school located in the heart of a major city? Is it in the suburbs, or in a smaller city or town, or in the countryside? Regardless of where your school is located, it's probably surrounded by plants, animals, and other living things including you and your fellow humans! Some may be big enough for you to notice easily. Others may be small enough for you to have missed. Until now.

Take a moment to consider what living things make your schoolyard their home. Make a list of what living things you think are in your schoolyard. At the end of this activity, you can see how well you're aware of the life that's all around you.

The Question

What living things make their home in and around your schoolyard?

continued on next page

Materials & Equipment

- *your notebook*
- *a pen or pencil*
- *a magnifier, if available*

Procedure

1 Your class will be going outside. You'll be wandering around your schoolyard, and possibly onto neighbouring properties. As a class, create a list of "Courtesy Guidelines" that you and your classmates will agree to follow when you leave the school building.

2 Move to the schoolyard, or to another location your teacher specifies. When you get there, find a spot that you feel comfortable in. Sit down and relax. Breathe deeply for a few moments and just feel part of your surroundings.

3 Now begin to observe all around you. Use your senses of sight, hearing, and smell to help you. Whenever you observe a plant, a bird, or any other living thing, jot it down. Include a rough sketch of it if possible.

Keeping Records

4 Make a T-chart as shown below for recording your observations. In the first column of your T-chart, record the living things you observe. For each living thing record, also include a note saying where you observed it. For example, you might see a blue jay on a tree branch, or on the ground, or swooping through the air.

Living Thing I Saw	Where I Saw It
blue jay	

continued on next page

5 At some point, you'll probably want to move somewhere else to look for other living things. If you have a magnifier, be sure to use it. Many living things are quite small—so small that you'll miss them unless you look closely with a magnifier. Be sure to carefully replace anything you move or look under.

Caution!
When you decide to move from your spot, remember the "Courtesy Guidelines" that you agreed to.

6 In some cases, you may not be able to actually see a certain living thing, but you'll find evidence that it's been there. For example, perhaps you'll notice a feather, or some dried snake skin, or animal droppings. Observing evidence of living things is as good as observing the real thing. So be sure to include these in your recorded observations.

7 Continue making your observations until your teacher tells you it's time to return to the classroom.

Analyzing and Interpreting

8 How many different living things did you observe? How many of these were plants? How many were insects? How many were birds? How many were other animals?

9 Compare your answers to question 8 with those of your classmates. Did everyone in your class observe the same living things? Did you notice something nobody else did?

10 Compare your list that you made at the start of the activity with the list you have now. Are there any living things you have recorded that you didn't expect to find?

11 Think back to your observations. How many different **species** and **habitats** did you observe? Did your classmates observe the same or different ones?

Forming Conclusions

12 Design a picture, a chart, or a collage that suits this title: "The Living Things That Live in Our Schoolyard." It should summarize all the observations that you and your classmates have made in this activity.

Communicate

1 Which living things probably live full time in your schoolyard? What is it about your schoolyard that makes it a good place for these living things to live?

2 What other living things just visit or pass through your schoolyard? Where do you think they live? Why would they live there and not in your schoolyard?

1.2 What Do You Have in Common with Other Living Things?

Explore

What kinds of living things have you observed during your activities? You probably found plants such as grasses, weeds, and trees. As well, you may have encountered different kinds of insects, birds, or even mammals. Some schoolyards have been known to have a cat, dog, squirrel or raccoon travel through them. Believe it or not, you have a lot in common with these living things. With insects. With worms. And with plants.

Can you think of what you might have in common with these living things? Share your thoughts with your partner or a classmate.

Develop

The Basic Needs of All Living Things

You have basic needs that are common to all living things. As you investigate what some of these needs are, begin to develop a *virtual terrarium*, or a VT. (A terrarium is a glass or plastic box in which plants and animals are kept.) You'll create this VT on paper. It should have at least one plant and one animal in it. Be sure the design of your VT clearly shows, in pictures and words, how all the needs of the plants and animals can be met.

Living Things Need Water

About three-quarters of our planet's surface is covered with water. Water not only makes up the majority of the earth's surface, but also makes up the majority of all living things. For example, about two-thirds of your body is made up of water. About nine-tenths (or more) of a head of lettuce is water! Life cannot exist without water.

- Where do you get the water you need to survive?
- Do you have fresh water in your virtual terrarium?

Living Things Need Energy

You need energy to walk, run, breathe, eat, digest what you eat, and to grow. You need energy even when you're sitting still and relaxing. Energy keeps your heart beating, air moving in and out of your lungs, and the rest of your organs working properly. So you need energy even when you're asleep!

- Where do you get the energy you need to survive?
- Where does this energy source come from?
- How is this energy source represented in your virtual terrarium?

Living Things Need Food

You need food for the **nutrients** it provides. Nutrients include substances such as carbohydrates, fats, proteins, vitamins, and minerals. All these substances supply your body with energy and materials that you need to move, grow, and to repair and maintain the health of the billions of cells in your body. All other living things need nutrients for the same reason.

Living Things Need Oxygen

When you eat, chemical reactions take place inside your body. These reactions use oxygen to break down the food to provide you with energy. With only a few exceptions, all living things need oxygen to provide the energy they need to survive. This includes animals, plants, fungi such as mushrooms, and microscopic life forms such as bacteria.

- Where do you get the oxygen you need to survive?
- Where do living things in water get their oxygen?

*info***BIT**

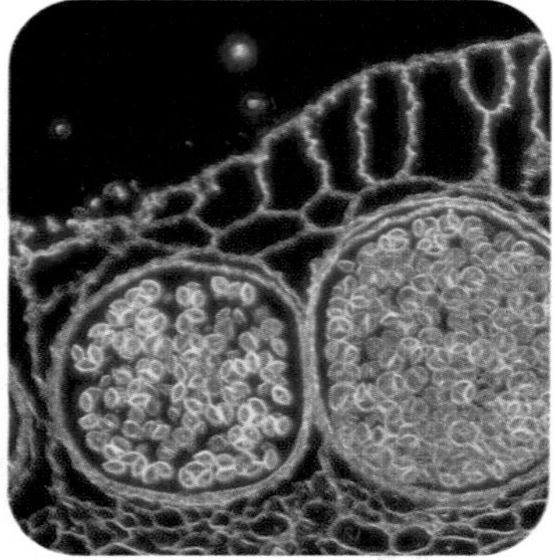

Algae are plant-like living things. They can be large, like seaweed, or so small that you need a microscope to see them. Algae are as important to the health of water environments as plants are to the health of land environments. Do you know why?

Living Things Need Suitable Living Conditions

Life can exist in some pretty harsh conditions. For example, some kinds of microscopic bacteria and algae thrive in hot springs that can reach temperatures of up to 85°C. Other kinds of life exist in the Antarctic, where temperatures can reach as low as –90°C. However, most living things live best in a more moderate range of temperatures. They often build shelters to provide safety and comfort.

- What kinds of shelters do people build?
- What kinds of shelters do other animals build?
- How will you design shelters in your virtual terrarium?

Living Things Need To Interact with Each Other and with Non-Living Things

It's easy to recognize interactions like talking to a friend, patting a dog, or waving your hand to brush away a hungry mosquito. Your life is full of interactions between you and other living things like these.

- What other examples of interactions can you think of?
- How are these interactions important to your life?
- What types of interactions do you think would occur in your virtual terrarium?

Is this an interaction?

You're always interacting with non-living things, too. Examples of non-living things include the sun, air, and water. For instance, when you breathe, you're interacting with the air.

- What other interactions do you have with non-living things?
- How are these interactions important to your life?

Communicate

1. Describe the basic needs of any living thing and use an example from your virtual terrarium to illustrate each of these needs.
2. Could you add any plants or animals to your virtual terrarium that would be beneficial to the other living things already present?

1.3 Check Your Progress

1. a) What are your basic needs for survival?
   b) In what ways are your needs the same as those of other living things?
2. Illustrate with a labelled picture how basic needs for survival are met in your own life.
3. Using your picture as a guide, identify three things in your life that you could do without and still meet your basic needs.

BIG IDEA

2.0 Ecosystems are interactions of biotic and abiotic components.

Imagine sitting quietly in a natural setting. What sensations would you have? What would you see? There certainly would be a wide variety of plants to look at. Would there be rocks, sand piles, and soil, too? Would you see animals moving around? What would you smell: flowers, pine needles, wet grass? Would you hear bird calls, the buzz of insects, rustling in the grass or bushes? The environment in which we live is composed of a wide variety of living and non-living things. Together they make up and sustain our planet.

2.1 DEFINING AN ECOSYSTEM

Explore

Any place on earth where living things interact with other living things and non-living things may be called an **ecosystem**. The living things are called the **biotic** components, or parts, of the ecosystem; the non-living things are called the **abiotic** components. The "bio" part of the word comes from a Greek word that means *life* and the "a" part means *not*; so *biotic* means *living* and *abiotic* means *not living*. With a classmate, make a list of the parts of your classroom that you would consider biotic and the parts you would consider abiotic.

Some Examples of Living and Non-Living Things

Biotic	Abiotic
pine tree	copper ore
arctic hare	gasoline
grasshopper	beach sand

reSEARCH

Coral reefs are one of the world's most incredible ecosystems. Small animals called corals build these amazing structures out of limestone produced by their bodies. Some coral reef ecosystems are home to as many as 3000 different species!

- Use your library resources or the Internet to find out more about coral reef ecosystems.

Every living thing on earth is part of an ecosystem because it is always interacting with some biotic and abiotic components. These interactions are necessary to life. They are the only way to provide everything needed to support and sustain life. All ecosystems, therefore, provide the necessities for life, including:

- energy
- water
- air (oxygen)
- carbon dioxide
- food
- suitable living conditions

Develop

What Makes up an Ecosystem?

Ecosystems can be small. For example, a puddle is an ecosystem if it supports living things and provides them with water and other abiotic components they need to survive. A puddle may not last very long, of course. But it doesn't matter if it lasts five minutes, five days, or five months. A puddle is an ecosystem as long as it has biotic components interacting with each other and with the abiotic components of the environment. A rotting log is an ecosystem, too. So is your schoolyard or a neighbourhood park.

Why is this an ecosystem?

*info***BIT**

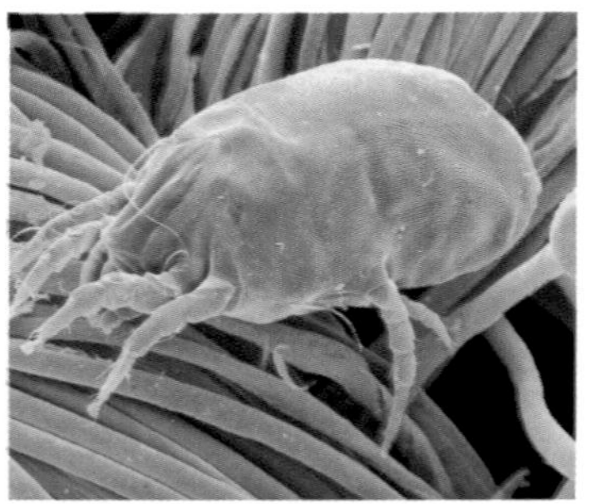

Ecosystems come in all sizes. In fact, there's an ecosystem in your bedroom! The dust in your room is made of hairs, flakes of your skin, and fibres from your clothes. Dust mites, like the one pictured above, and bacteria live in your dust and clean up your microscopic mess.

Ecosystems can also be quite large. Each of the places shown on this and the last page is an example of an ecosystem. So is a city, and so are the prairies of western Canada, and the forests of northern Canada. In fact, you can think of our entire planet as an ecosystem. Can you explain why?

Our planet has thousands and thousands of ecosystems. Some have a great deal of sunlight. Others never see light at all. Some receive lots of rain throughout the year. Others rarely receive it more than once a year. Some have rich, fertile soil that nourishes plenty of plant life. Others have loose, sandy soil that can support only a few kinds of plants.

Despite these differences, all ecosystems have one thing in common. *They need a way to bring energy and matter into the system and make them constantly available to living things.* Later in this chapter, you'll explore how energy and matter enter and move through ecosystems.

Communicate

1 Which of the following statements are true and which are false? Correct the false statements to make them true.
   a) All ecosystems need only air, water, and food.
   b) Ecosystems are very large.
   c) Ecosystems contain both biotic and abiotic components.
   d) A puddle is an ecosystem if it has stones and sand in it.

2 Look over section 2.1 again. Copy the sentences below, and use words from section 2.1 to fill in the blanks.

   Ecosystems come in all _______. From your bedroom pillow to large forests, our planet has _______ of ecosystems. As long as a place has _______ and _______ things _______ in it, it can be called an ecosystem. All _______ have one thing in common: they need a way to bring _______ and _______ into the system and make them available to living things.

infoBIT

Is this an example of an ecosystem?

2.2 Check Your Progress

1 a) Name four abiotic components of our planet.
   b) Name four biotic components of our planet.
   c) Choose one abiotic component and one biotic component that interact. Use words, pictures, or both to explain how they are connected to each other.

2 Write a sentence that shows clearly how these three words are related to one another: abiotic, biotic, and ecosystem.

3 Which of the following are, or could be, ecosystems? Give reasons to support your answer in each case. You might want to draw a picture if you feel it can help you explain your thinking.
   a) a forest
   b) a lake
   c) a town's or city's downtown
   d) a tree
   e) a piece of mouldy bread
   f) the earth

4 Do you think there are ecosystems anywhere else in our solar system? Why or why not?

Careers and Profiles

PARK AND CONSERVATION WORKER

Jennifer Vincent is a biologist who works with a regional conservation authority. She loves her job because she is outside almost all the time. "It's like being paid to have fun!" she says.

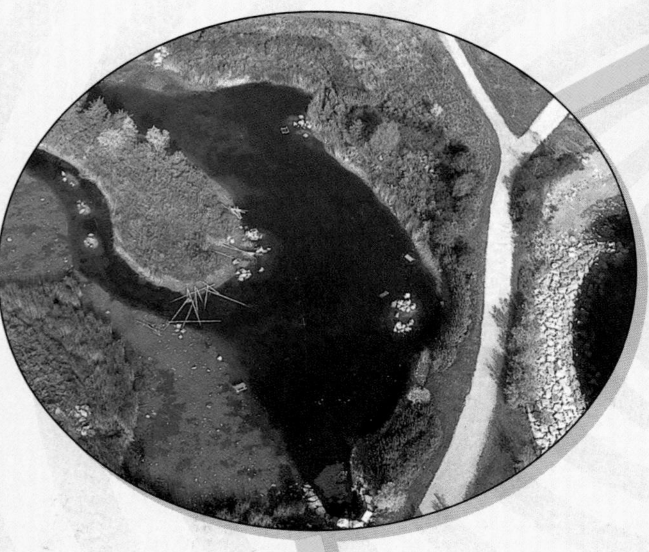

Right now, Jennifer is working on a new project with a team of people. She is the Project Manager, as well as being one of the biologists on the team. An area of a lake shoreline is going to be transformed into a "natural environment area," and it's up to Jennifer and her team to do it.

- First of all, the team needs to find out which animals are using the area. Here's a list of some of them: song sparrows, swallows, a rare black garter snake, ducks, shorebirds, turtles and toads. In the lake, they have found northern pike and large-mouth bass.
- Next, they will try to make these animals feel welcome.
- Finally, the team needs to consider the last species that will be using the park: people! They will plan paths and observation points for people so that they will be able to observe the animals without disturbing them.
- "If we do the basic structure well," says Jennifer, "mother nature will take over." The entire project will probably take 7 or 8 years.

BIG IDEA

3.0 Ecosystems are made up of producers, consumers, and decomposers that interact to form food webs.

What would you say to getting rid of some of the biting insects that attack you each spring and summer? You would probably say "yes." Actually, studying ecosystems suggests that, in fact, there is no easy way of eliminating certain species without harming the environment.

At first, it would be great to have no mosquitoes and horseflies. In a couple of years, however, you would notice some important changes. Insects are a main food source for some birds and fish. Without a steady food source, what would happen to those animals? How about the animals that feed on those fish and birds—what would happen to them? Insects also pollinate many flowers, and without them, many plants would not produce fruits and seeds. The animals that eat these fruits and seeds would suffer.

As you can see, the elements in an ecosystem seem related and dependent upon one another. It's important to understand these relationships to see how an ecosystem works.

3.1 The Components of Ecosystems

Explore

By the time you have reached Grade 7, your body mass has probably increased ten times since you were a baby.

Your body has gone through many changes. It needed energy to "fuel" all these changes. And it needed matter to supply the "stuff" that increased your size and mass. The energy and matter that your body needed came from food. Your body broke down the food into a form that it could use. Choosing the right food, then, is important, because no one food can supply your body with everything it needs.

So...how well have you performed this job lately?

Think back to the foods you've eaten over the past two days. Design a chart to list them. Include the foods you ate for breakfast, lunch, and dinner, as well as any snacks you had. Keep your list handy. You'll need it later.

Develop

You and Other Animals Are Food Consumers

Store-owners and advertisers often call people consumers. That's because people buy and use goods and services produced by companies or other people. This is the common-language meaning of the word consumer.

In science, the word consumer has another meaning. A **consumer** is any animal that has to seek out and eat, or consume, other living things for food. According to this definition, you are certainly a consumer. So is a raccoon, a cat, a moose, a bear, a hyena, a grasshopper, a seal, an elephant, and a praying mantis. In fact, *all animals are food consumers.*

Scientists often find it helpful to classify consumers based on the kinds of food they eat. Animals like cats, hyenas, seals, and praying mantises, which consume mainly animal food, are called **carnivores.** Animals like moose, elephants, and grasshoppers, which consume mainly plants and plant-like living things, are called **herbivores.** Animals like humans, bears, and raccoons, which consume other animals as well as plants for food, are called **omnivores.**

Communicate

1 Using the pictures below, classify which animals you think are herbivores, which are carnivores, and which are omnivores.

2 Refer to the food list you were asked to develop at the beginning of section 3.1.

a) Choose one food, and write its name on a fresh sheet of paper. You can draw a box around it if you like. Draw an arrow pointing to this food.

b) Decide what the source of the food was. In other words, think about what living thing was used to make or feed the food that you ate. For example, if you listed a piece of cheese, the source of the cheese might be a cow.

c) At the start of your arrow, write the food source you chose in b).

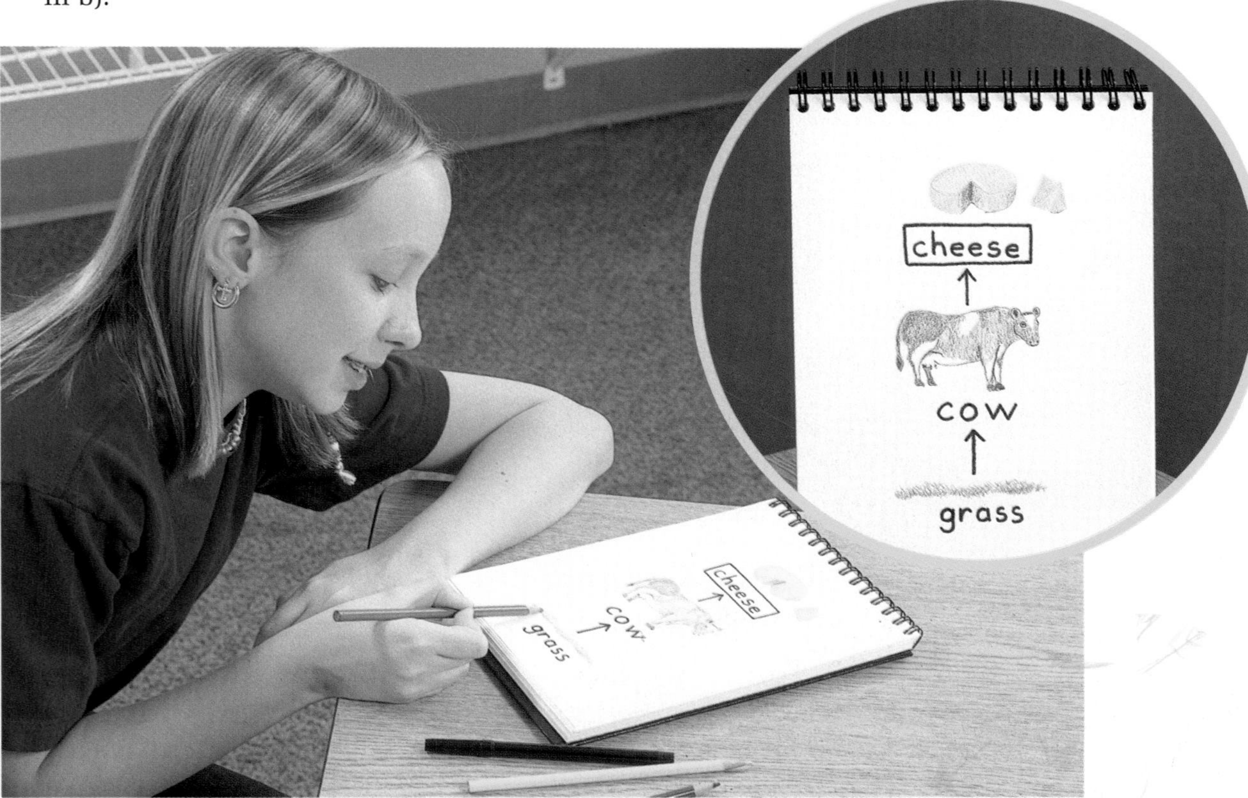

d) Draw another arrow to the food source you just wrote down. At the start of this arrow, write the food or foods used to make or feed this food source. For example, a cow is fed with grasses and grains such as oats and barley. If you aren't sure or don't know what was used to nourish the food source, put down a question mark or write "need to find out."

3 a) Choose five other foods from your food list. Repeat steps 2 a) to d).

b) When you're finished, examine the flowcharts you've made. Look for any similarities or patterns. Then write down your thoughts about this question: *What food sources do I seem to depend on for all the foods I eat?*

3.2 Producers

Explore

Compare your flowcharts in the last activity with those of others in the class. You will probably notice that all the arrows eventually start from a plant of some kind. Plants and plant-like living things play a vital role in nearly all ecosystems on earth. That's because plants can do something that you and other food consumers can't. What do you think that is?

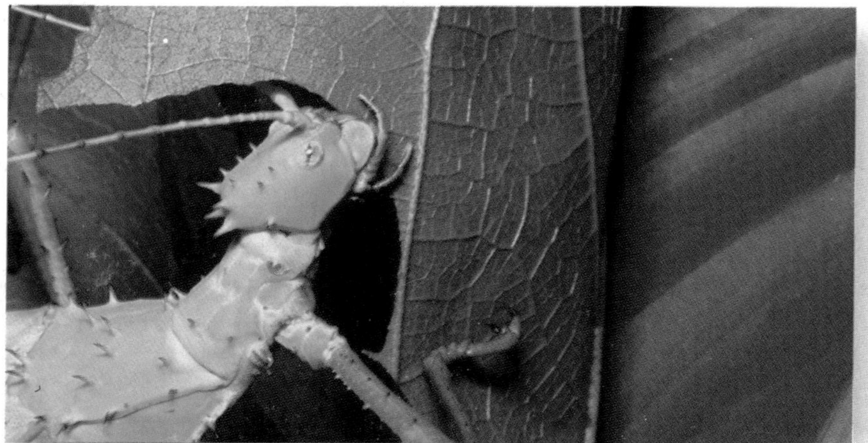

Which one is the producer?

reSEARCH

A Carnivorous Plant!

The pitcher plant eats insects such as grasshoppers and snails. Find out where it lives and how it "eats" its prey.

Develop

Food Consumers Depend on Food Producers

Animals must find food to eat to get the matter and energy they need to survive. Green plants can nourish themselves. *They can make their own food to supply the matter and energy they need to survive.*

Plants need two raw materials to make their food. They need water and carbon dioxide. However, just like animals, plants also need energy to make their food. Their energy source is the sun.

Green plants contain a substance called **chlorophyll.** This substance absorbs all colours of light except green. The green light is reflected off the plant. This explains why we see the colour green coming from living things that have chlorophyll. Chlorophyll is found mainly in the leaves and stems of plants. It absorbs light energy from the sun. Plants take in carbon dioxide and water. Inside the plant leaves, the absorbed energy is used to rearrange the particles that make up water and carbon dioxide. Two products result from this rearrangement: food and oxygen. The food is in the form of sugars and starches.

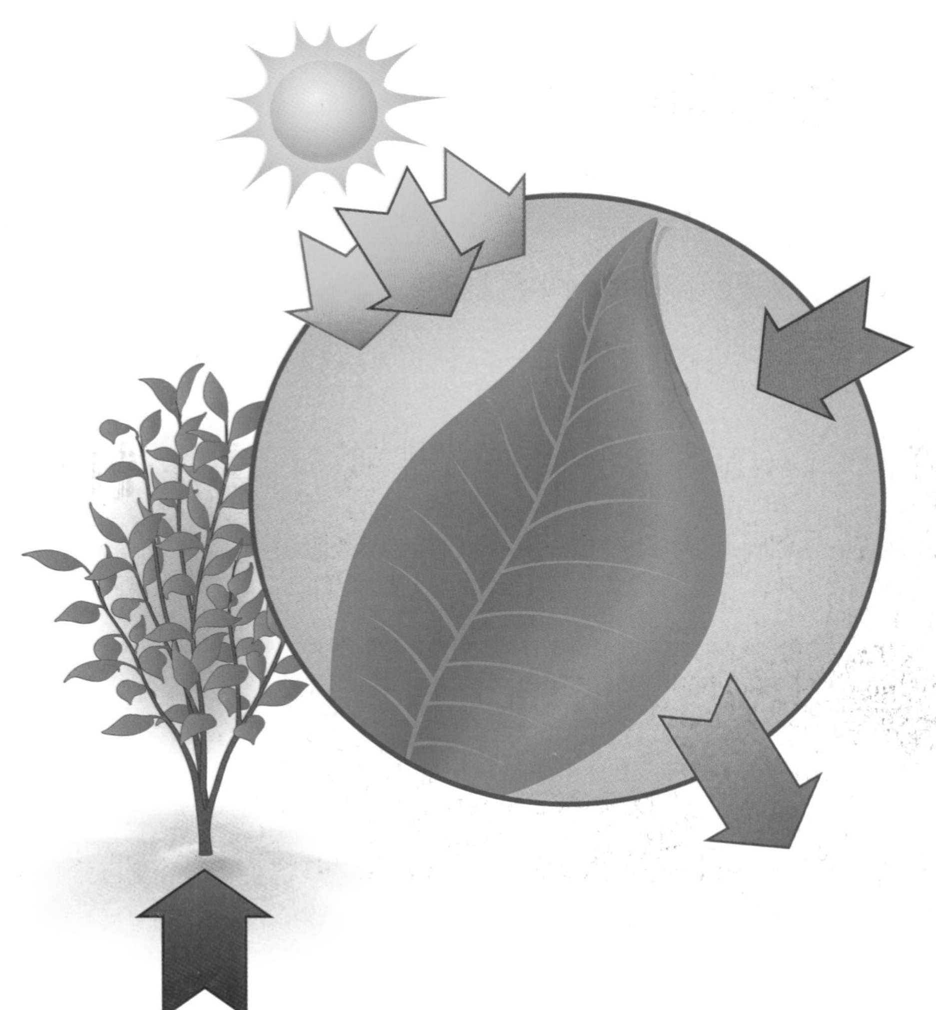

During photosynthesis, plants use sunlight, carbon dioxide, and water to make food. They also produce oxygen as a by-product. Use the diagram to answer these questions:

- Which part of the plant takes in water?
- Which part takes in carbon dioxide?
- Which part absorbs sunlight?
- Where is the oxygen released?

This whole food-making process is called **photosynthesis**. Photosynthesis is vital to your life for three main reasons.

1. Photosynthesis turns the sun's energy into chemical energy in plants that your body can use for its energy.
2. Photosynthesis provides plants with food that your body can use to function properly.
3. Photosynthesis provides the oxygen in the air that you breathe.

Photosynthesis plays an important role in ecosystems. It is the only process that allows the sun's energy to enter ecosystems in a form that other living things can use. Your life and the lives of almost all other food consumers are *totally* dependent on photosynthesis in green plants and other chlorophyll-containing living things.

Plants, through photosynthesis, produce the food and oxygen that all food consumers need to survive. That's why scientists call plants and plant-like living things **producers**.

*info*BIT

Foods Native to the Americas

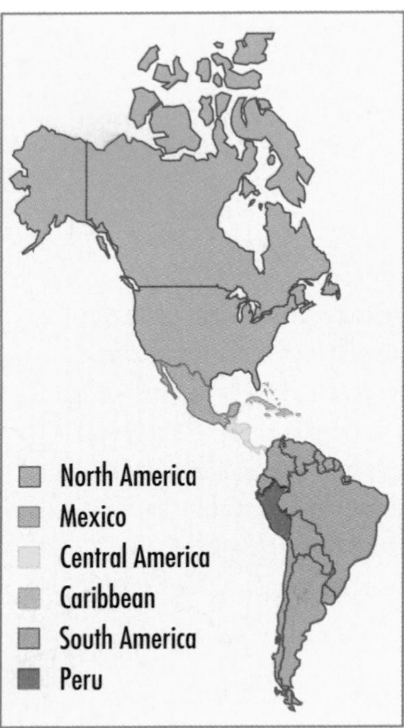

Corn
Sweet peppers
Squash, Pumpkins
Tomatoes
Cranberries
Potatoes
Peanuts
Chocolate
Turkey
Sweet potato
Avocados
Cane Sugar
Pineapples
Blueberries
Green beans
Kidney beans

diatom

flowering cactus

apple blossom

All these living things are producers. Which do you think are important for land-based ecosystems? Which are important for water-based ecosystems?

Oxygen Is More Than Just for Breathing

You've learned that photosynthesis is important for making food in plants and for producing oxygen. Food is the source of matter and energy that animals and the plants themselves need to survive. Both animals and plants need oxygen. That's right, plants need oxygen, too.

In photosynthesis, plants take in carbon dioxide and give off oxygen. The word equation below summarizes this process:

Word Equation for Photosynthesis

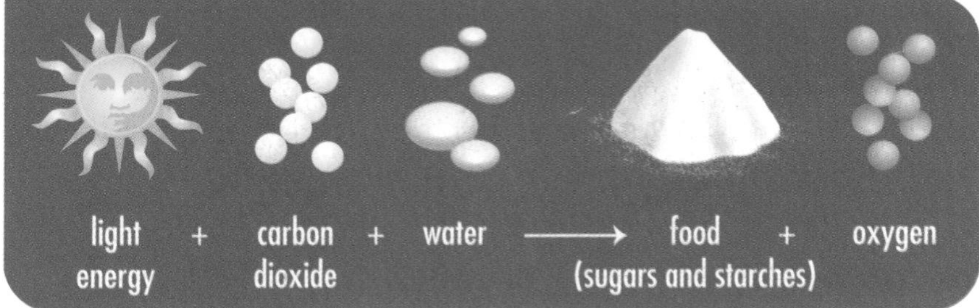

The oxygen is sometimes called a by-product or even a waste product of photosynthesis. This seems to suggest that plants don't need oxygen. But they do in another process. Nearly all living things—including plants—need oxygen to release the energy that's stored in their food. The process that's responsible for this is called **cellular respiration**. Here's a word equation that summarizes cellular respiration:

Word Equation for Cellular Respiration

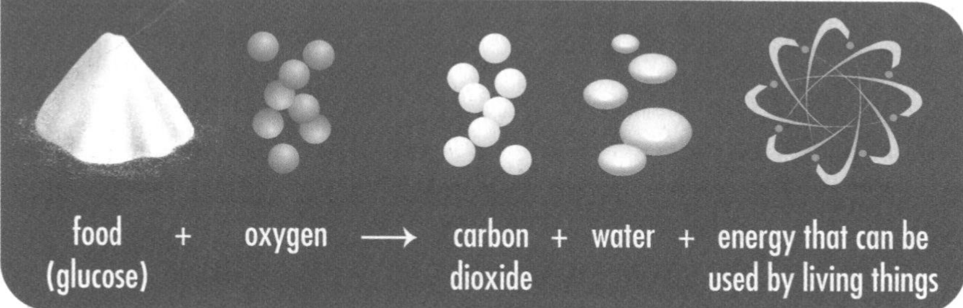

food (glucose) + oxygen ⟶ carbon dioxide + water + energy that can be used by living things

What similarities do you notice about these two word equations? Are there any differences? Write down your thoughts in your Science Journal. You'll re-examine these word equations later in this chapter.

Communicate

1 Compare the role of producers and consumers in ecosystems. How are they related? How are they different?

2 An *effect* is the result of an action or an event. A *cause* is the thing that produced the effect.
   a) What is the cause (or causes) of photosynthesis?
   b) Test the effects of photosynthesis.
   c) In a chart, describe the cause(s) and effect(s) of cellular respiration.

3 Write a poem or descriptive paragraph describing producers or what producers do in ecosystems.

*info*BIT

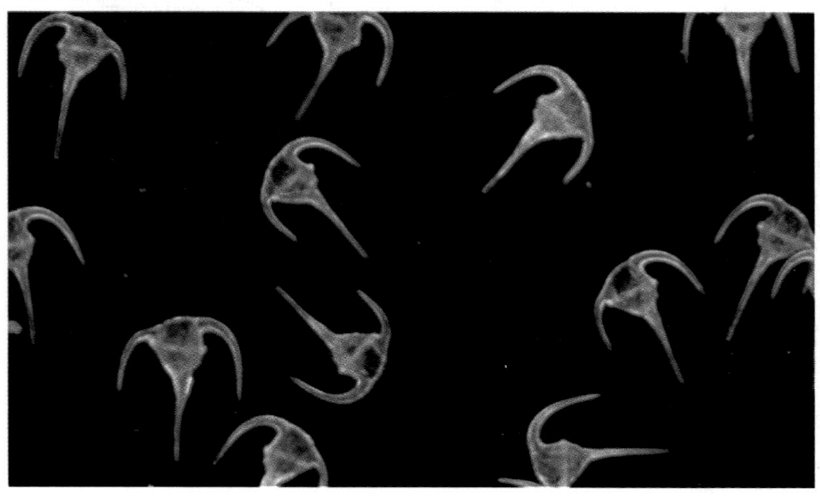

These microscopic marine plants, known as **phytoplankton**, are the main producers in the world's oceans. They are the food for almost all other marine creatures. For example, tiny shrimp-like creatures called krill mainly eat phytoplankton. The krill, in turn, form the major part of the diet of many larger creatures.

Without tiny phytoplankton, the oceans would be a barren lifeless place, where no consumers like whales, dolphins, sharks, and fish would live.

3.3 Food Chains

Explore

Scientists use a kind of flowchart called a **food chain** to show how living things are connected to each other by the food they eat. A food chain is a convenient way to show how energy moves among living things in an ecosystem.

In the flowcharts you drew earlier, you started with a consumer—yourself. You identified the food you ate and then worked backward to see what the original source of your food was. A food chain starts with the original food source: a producer. Then an arrow points to a consumer that eats that producer. In many cases, a primary consumer may, in turn, point to other secondary consumers. Here are a few examples of food chains. Notice that some food chains can be quite short, while others can be longer.

reSEARCH

Food chains are everywhere: in your backyard, in the park, even in your schoolyard. Try finding a food chain in your neighbourhood.

- Take a pencil and paper and go to your local park. Look for evidence of a food chain. Draw a simple diagram of the food chains you find. Some examples are shown below.

flower nectar	➡	butterflies
wood	➡	beetles
flower pollen	➡	insects
living plants	➡	slug
seeds	➡	ants
insects	➡	blue jay
insects	➡	spider
worms	➡	toad
nuts	➡	squirrel
small animals	➡	hawk

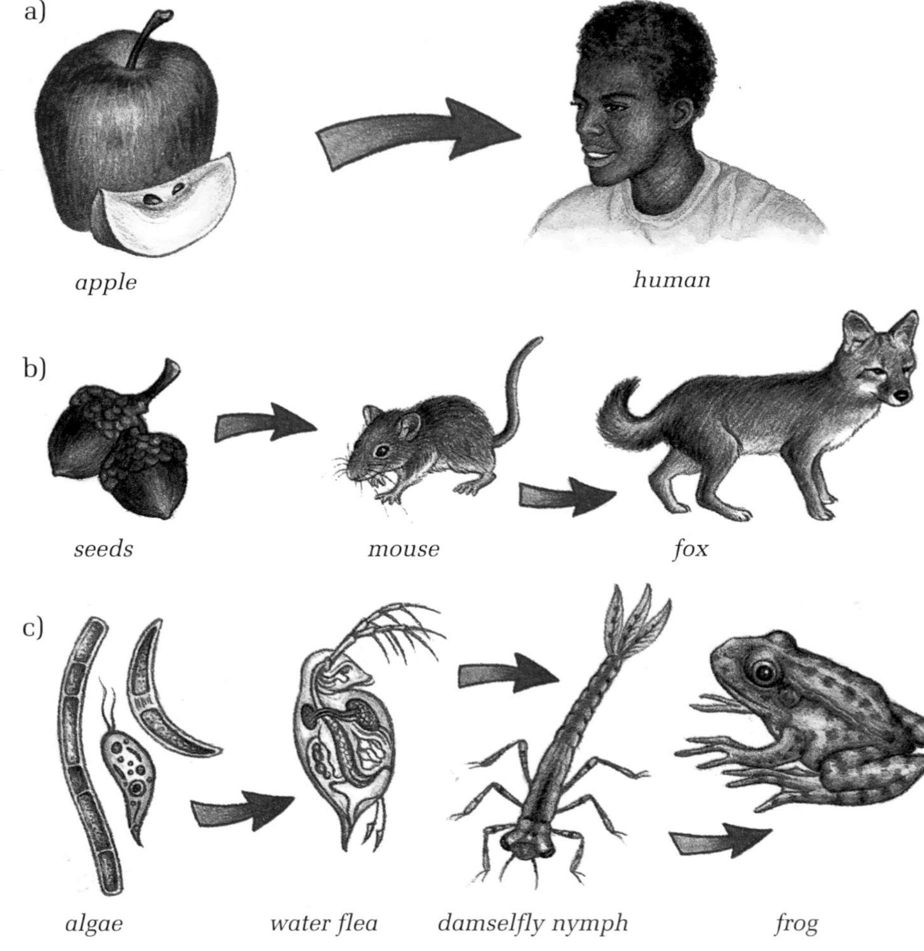

In (b) above, which is the primary consumer? Which is the secondary consumer?

Develop

Food Chains for Producers and Consumers

INVESTIGATOR

ENERGY PATHWAY

Before You Start...

You know that plants, through photosynthesis, provide a way for the sun's energy to enter ecosystems. What happens to that energy? Does it disappear or get used by other living things? Discuss your thoughts with your partner or other classmates.

The Question

What pathway does energy follow in ecosystems, and what happens to that energy?

Materials & Equipment

- *your notes you recorded about the living things in your schoolyard*

Procedure

1. Review the results of your schoolyard survey in the Investigator activity in section 1.1. Think about all the living things you recorded. Group the living things into possible food chains. Draw these food chains.
2. Pick an ecosystem photo from earlier in this chapter. Or if you want, find a picture of an ecosystem that appeals to you. Identify as many food chains as you can that you think might exist in that ecosystem. Include living things that you can see in the photo, as well as any others that you think would live in that ecosystem.

continued on next page

Analyzing and Interpreting

3 Why do all food chains start with a producer?

4 a) What kind of consumer always follows a producer in a food chain? Explain why.

b) Is there always a consumer that comes next in the food chain? Why or why not?

c) If there is a consumer that comes next, what kind could it be? Explain why.

5 How do the food chains represent the flow of energy from one living thing to another in the ecosystem?

Forming Conclusions

6 Write a summary paragraph that follows these steps.

- Recall in words what you did in this activity.
- Explain the question you were working on.
- Describe your results.
- Write one new thing you learned in this activity.

Is this a food chain?

Communicate

1 Food chains follow the pathway that energy follows as it flows through ecosystems. Do you think there's anything missing from the food chains you've been drawing? Explain your answer.

2 Do you think a food chain provides a complete picture of the way that food energy links living things together? Give reasons for your answer.

3.4 Scavengers and Decomposers—A Special Group of Consumers

Explore

All living things eventually die. As well, all consumers generate waste materials from the food they eat. Our planet would be smothered in dead bodies and waste materials if not for a special group of consumers. These consumers get the matter and energy they need from wastes and dead plants and animals. Some of these consumers are scavengers. Others are decomposers.

Scavengers are consumers that don't usually kill for their own food. Instead, they feed off the remains of living things that are killed by other consumers. Crows, ravens, and housefly larva (maggots) are examples of scavengers. Can you name some more?

Decomposers are consumers that break down (decompose) animal wastes and dead plants and animals. They also break down animal waste materials. Fungi such as mushrooms and the mould you see growing on bread, fruits, and vegetables are decomposers. So are many kinds of bacteria.

Which of the animals shown below are scavengers and which are decomposers? Explain your choice for each animal.

reSEARCH

Scientists have known about microscopic decomposers only since the late 1600s. However, people have been using certain decomposers for thousands of years. We still depend on them today to help us make foods, clean up oil spills, and manufacture medicines.

Find out about how decomposers are involved in one of the following:

- making cheese
- making vinegar
- making wine
- mining
- cleaning oil spills

1 ECOSYSTEMS

Scavengers or decomposers?

Decomposers Can Be Helpful or Harmful

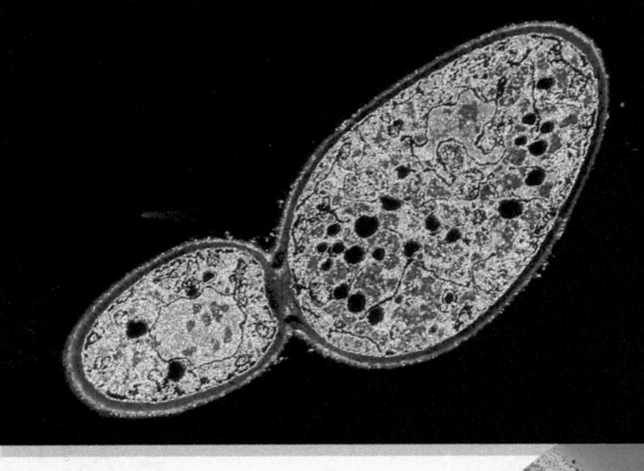

Helpful or harmful? ***Baker's yeast***—single-celled decomposers. They feed on sugars that are naturally present in foods such as grains and fruits. The carbon dioxide is a byproduct that bakers count on to make breads and pastries rise.

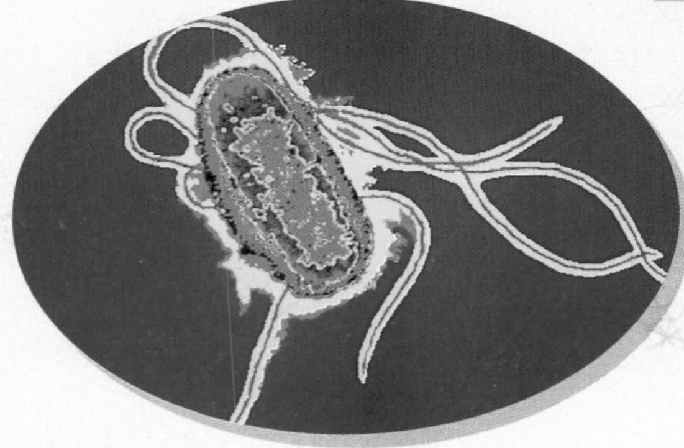

Helpful or harmful? ***E. coli*** (short for *Escherichia coli.*)—bacteria found in your large intestine. They break down nutrients in the food you eat for their own food. In the process, they manufacture several vitamins that your body needs to stay healthy.

Helpful or harmful? ***E. coli bacteria O157:H7***—a form of *E. coli* sometimes found in common food products such as ground beef, milk, and apple juice. When these decomposers break down food, they produce highly toxic chemicals that can cause food poisoning.

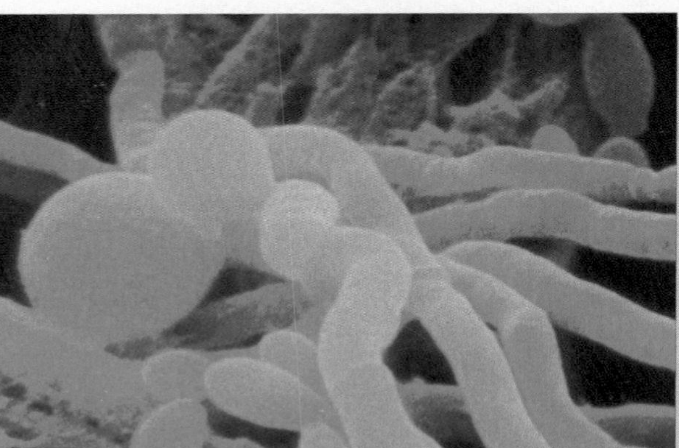

Helpful or harmful? ***Candida albicans***—a kind of yeast found in the moist mucus or mucus-producing areas of your body, such as your throat and mouth. When the body's immune system is weak, these decomposers can grow and reproduce rapidly. This results in a disease called thrush.

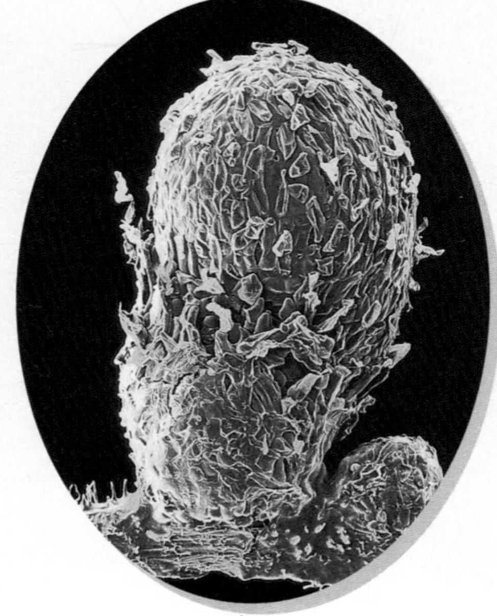

Helpful or harmful? ***Nitrogen-fixing nodules***—round swellings on some plants that are home to millions of bacteria. These micro-organisms use nitrogen for their food. In this process, they release nitrogen-containing chemicals called nitrates that the plants use.

Decomposers Are Essential to All Ecosystems

Decomposers keep us and other living things from being buried in dead bodies, feces, and urine. It's funny to think about it that way, but it's true! However, decomposers are more than just nature's "clean-up crew." Their actions mean that plants always have a supply of nutrients available to them. In fact, decomposers act like a bridge that connects the biotic components of ecosystems with the abiotic components. You will explore this important idea in the next section.

bacteria on human skin *banana slug*

Decomposers at Work

Communicate

1 Create a Venn diagram to show helpful and harmful decomposers.

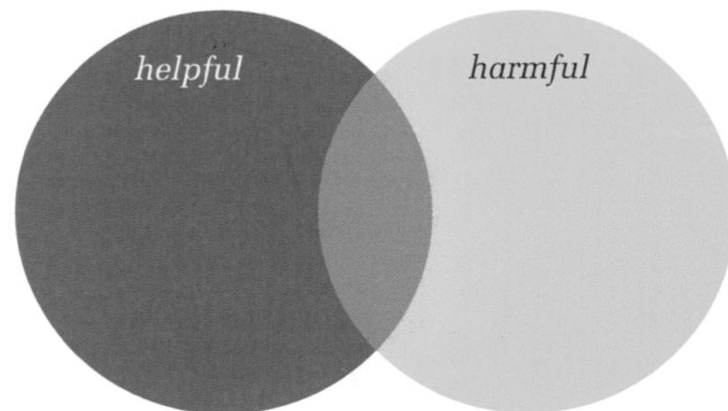

List the decomposers in the appropriate parts of your diagram. Decomposers that are both helpful *and* harmful should go in the overlapping section of the circles.

2 Scavengers and decomposers aren't often included in food chains. Can you think of a reason why? See if you can figure out a way to include them anyway. Choose three of the food chains you recorded in the Investigator activity, Food Chains for Producers and Consumers, in section 3.3. Or make up three new ones, if you want. To each food chain, add at least one scavenger or decomposer (or both).

infoBIT

For a long time, scientists believed that hyenas were exclusively scavengers. That's because people often saw hyenas scavenging during the day. Now thanks to Hans Kruuk, a Danish researcher, science has a different view. He discovered that hyenas do hunt for their food but only at night. In fact, hyenas are skillful, cunning hunters. But they're always ready and willing to scavenge a free meal if they have the chance.

Experiment ON YOUR OWN

OBSERVING DECOMPOSITION

Before You Start...

Composters are really "decomposer factories." You put food and plant wastes in, and over time, these materials decay or decompose. What's left is a nutrient-rich fertilizer that people can add to soil. What does the decaying? Decomposers! And if you look closely, you'll see that composters are really mini-ecosystems.

Many factors can influence decomposition in a composter. Your challenge is to identify one of these factors and plan an experiment to determine its effect.

The Question

How does the factor you identify affect decomposition in a composter?

Your Task

1. Use your library resources and the Internet to research different kinds of composters.
2. Make a hypothesis.
3. Decide what materials and equipment you'll need to test your hypothesis. Think about these questions:
   a) Will you conduct this experiment in a composter? in a natural setting? or in a composter in a natural setting?
   b) Will you need to build a composter? If so, how big will you make it?
   c) What kind or kinds of materials will you compost for your experiment?
   d) How much material will you use?
   e) What decomposers will you use?
   f) How will you make sure your experiment is safe?
4. Plan your procedure. Think about these questions:
   a) What evidence are you looking for to support your hypothesis?
   b) What steps will you follow to collect the data you need?
   c) How will you make sure the test you're planning is fair?
   d) How will you record your results?
   e) For how long will you run your experiment?
5. Write up your procedure. Be sure to show it to your teacher before going any farther.
6. Carry out your experiment.
7. Compare your results with your hypothesis.
8. Share and compare your experimental plan and findings with your classmates.

3.5 Check Your Progress

1 a) Think of a park or natural setting. Name two producers, two herbivorous consumers, and two carnivorous consumers you would find in this ecosystem.

b) Explain how these living things are related to one another.

c) Would you expect to find scavengers and decomposers in a park ecosystem? Why or why not?

2 The list below shows typical producers and consumers you would find in a pond ecosystem.

a) The list is in alphabetical order. Reorganize it to make two lists: one showing all the producers and the other, all the consumers. (If you aren't sure what some of these living things are, make an inference, or look them up in a reference such as an encyclopedia.)

algae
bladderwort
bullrush
deer
dragonfly
duckweed
fish
fox
frog
heron
mosquito
reed sweet grass
roundworm
spider
toad
water flea
water horsetail
water lily
wolf

b) Construct as many food chains as you can using the living things in your lists.

reSEARCH

A common decomposer you probably see whenever it rains is the earthworm. Earthworms are an important part of many ecosystems. Use print or electronic resources to find out why. Write a report, design a poster, or prepare a multimedia presentation to share your discoveries.

3 How do you think the number of producers in an ecosystem compares with the number of herbivores? (In other words, are there more producers than herbivores, or fewer?) How do you think the number of carnivores compares with the number of herbivores? Give reasons to support your answers.

4 Prepare a chart similar to the one shown below in your Science Journal. Complete parts a) to c).

Ecosystem	a) Carnivore b) What it eats c) What, if anything, eats it?	a) Herbivore b) What it eats c) What, if anything, eats it?	a) Omnivore b) What it eats c) What, if anything, eats it?
A prairie grassland	*a)* *b)* *c)*	*a)* *b)* *c)*	*a)* *b)* *c)*
The Arctic	*a)* *b)* *c)*	*a)* *b)* *c)*	*a)* *b)* *c)*
A desert	*a)* *b)* *c)*	*a)* *b)* *c)*	*a)* *b)* *c)*
A pond	*a)* *b)* *c)*	*a)* *b)* *c)*	*a)* *b)* *c)*
An ocean	*a)* *b)* *c)*	*a)* *b)* *c)*	*a)* *b)* *c)*
A forest	*a)* *b)* *c)*	*a)* *b)* *c)*	*a)* *b)* *c)*

a) For each ecosystem, write an example of a carnivore, a herbivore, and an omnivore that lives in it.

b) For each animal you list in a), write two living things that it eats.

c) For each animal you list in a), decide if there are others that eat it. If there are, give an example.

American badger

pronghorn

striped skunk

What does it eat? What, if anything, eats it?

BIG IDEA

4.0 Matter and energy are necessary for all ecosystems.

Both matter and energy are abiotic components. Both are required for ecosystems. Together they influence all areas of the ecosystem. In this section, you will investigate how water, carbon, and energy interact in all ecosystems.

4.1 WHAT HAPPENS TO MATTER IN ECOSYSTEMS?

Explore

Study the following pictures on this and the next page. What does the information presented in these pictures and captions say about what happens to matter in ecosystems? Write a paragraph that summarizes what you think these pictures are telling you.

Sunlight, soil, and water from the abiotic environment provide plants with what they need to grow and live their lives.

Plants serve as food for herbivores. The herbivores can sometimes serve as food for other consumers.

continued on next page

Plants and animals grow, reproduce, produce wastes, and in time, die.

Scavengers and decomposers feed on the wastes and remains. This process breaks down once-living matter into smaller, simpler particles. In time, even solid skeletons are broken down.

Skeletons are made up of chemicals such as calcium, phosphorus, and carbon. These chemicals (minerals) are nutrients that other living things (such as plants) need to survive. Mineral nutrients are non-living, so they are part of the abiotic environment.

Develop

Water and Carbon Cycles

You are made up of matter. So are all living things and non-living things. The matter that makes up all living and non-living things on earth has been here for several billion years. On occasion, a meteorite or a comet has struck our planet. When this happens, matter from outer space is added to our planet. For the most part, though, all the matter that exists here today has been here for a long, long time.

So where does the matter that living things need come from? Matter continually moves from the abiotic environment (non-living things) to the biotic environment (living things) and back to the abiotic environment. The over-and-over-again movement of matter is referred to as a **cycle**.

There are many cycles of matter in nature. In each of these cycles, matter is used by living things and then returned to the abiotic environment to be used again by living things. The diagrams on the facing page show two important cycles of matter: the **water cycle** and the **carbon cycle**.

reSEARCH

There are cycles of matter for other substances living things need, such as nitrogen, iron, phosphorus, and sulphur. Choose one of these substances to investigate further. Find out why the substance is important for living things and how it is cycled in nature. Present your findings in the form of a diagram similar to the water cycle or carbon cycle diagrams.

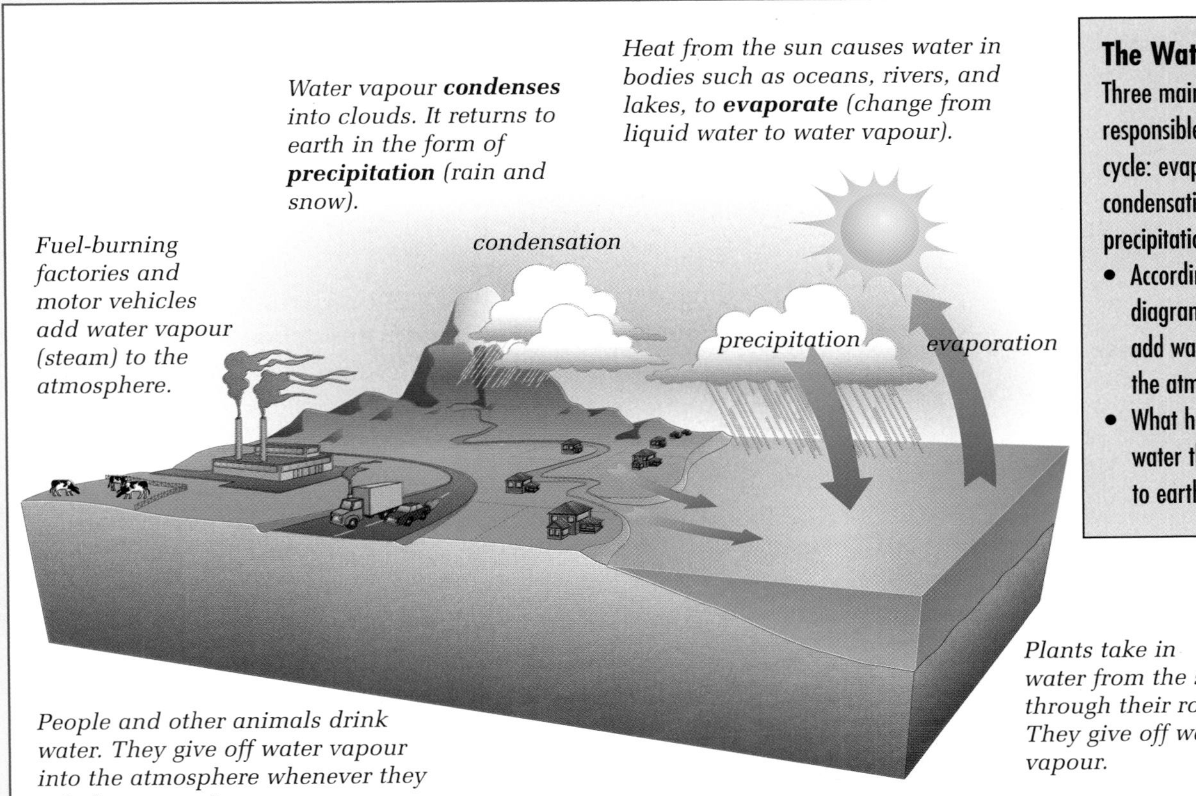

Water vapour **condenses** into clouds. It returns to earth in the form of **precipitation** (rain and snow).
Heat from the sun causes water in bodies such as oceans, rivers, and lakes, to **evaporate** (change from liquid water to water vapour).
Fuel-burning factories and motor vehicles add water vapour (steam) to the atmosphere.
condensation
precipitation
evaporation
Plants take in water from the soil through their roots. They give off water vapour.
People and other animals drink water. They give off water vapour into the atmosphere whenever they exhale or perspire.

The Water Cycle

Three main processes are responsible for the water cycle: evaporation, condensation, and precipitation.

- According to this diagram, what sources add water vapour to the atmosphere?
- What happens to the water that falls back to earth?

Living things use oxygen in combination with food to release the energy they need to survive (this is called cellular respiration). This process gives off carbon dioxide as a byproduct. Living things on land add carbon dioxide mainly to air. Living things in bodies of water add carbon dioxide mainly to water.

Plants take in carbon dioxide from the atmosphere and water from the soil. Photosynthesis transforms these substances into food and oxygen.

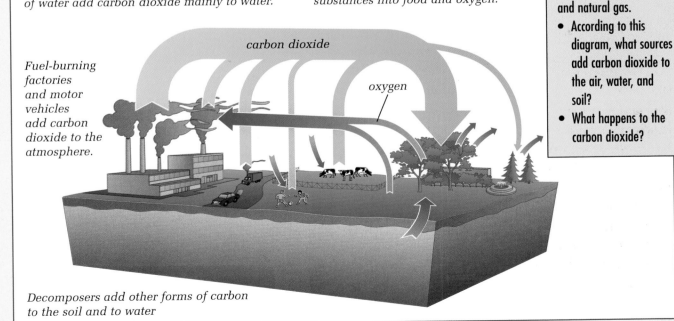

carbon dioxide

Fuel-burning factories and motor vehicles add carbon dioxide to the atmosphere.

oxygen

Decomposers add other forms of carbon to the soil and to water

The Carbon Cycle

The carbon substances may, over millions of years, change to become fuels such as coal, oil, and natural gas.

- According to this diagram, what sources add carbon dioxide to the air, water, and soil?
- What happens to the carbon dioxide?

Communicate

1 The following statements have to do with the carbon cycle. Put them in order. Hint: Begin with carbon in the form of oil being found underground.
   a) A car is filled up with gasoline.
   b) Plants die and are put in a composter.
   c) Driving the car burns the fuel; this creates exhaust gases including carbon dioxide.
   d) Decomposers in a composter add carbon to the soil.
   e) Oil is pumped from the ground and refined into gasoline.
   f) Plants combine carbon dioxide from the air with water to create food and oxygen.

2 Describe the cycle water goes through, from evaporating from a lake to returning to the lake. Your description should include the following words: evaporation, condensation, precipitation, clouds, plants, roots, animals, soil, and cars.

reSEARCH

Why Do Fall Leaves Turn Colour?

What happens to the green-coloured chlorophyll in plants in the fall? Why do leaves change colour before they fall off?

- Research what happens to leaves every autumn. Write a paragraph explaining what you have learned.

4.2 What Happens to Energy in Ecosystems?

Explore

Study the pictures and their captions in section 4.1. What does the information presented in these pictures and captions say about what happens to energy in ecosystems? List, in point form, examples of how energy is being used in the pictures.

Develop

Does Energy Cycle Through Ecosystems as Well?

You have seen that matter is constantly recycled, or used over and over again, through ecosystems. Is energy recycled in the same way? Near the end of section 3.2, you compared the word equations for photosynthesis and cellular respiration.

Word Equation for Photosynthesis

light energy + carbon dioxide + water ⟶ food (sugars and starches) + oxygen

Word Equation for Cellular Respiration

food (glucose) + oxygen ⟶ carbon dioxide + water + energy that can be used by living things

At first glance, it looks as though photosynthesis and cellular respiration are the reverse of each other. However, there's an important difference. Look carefully at the energy part of each word equation. Photosynthesis uses light energy. However, cellular respiration results in a different kind of energy. This energy is used by living things to function and grow. It isn't available to ecosystems in the same way as light energy. Use this diagram to help you understand why this energy isn't cycled through ecosystems.

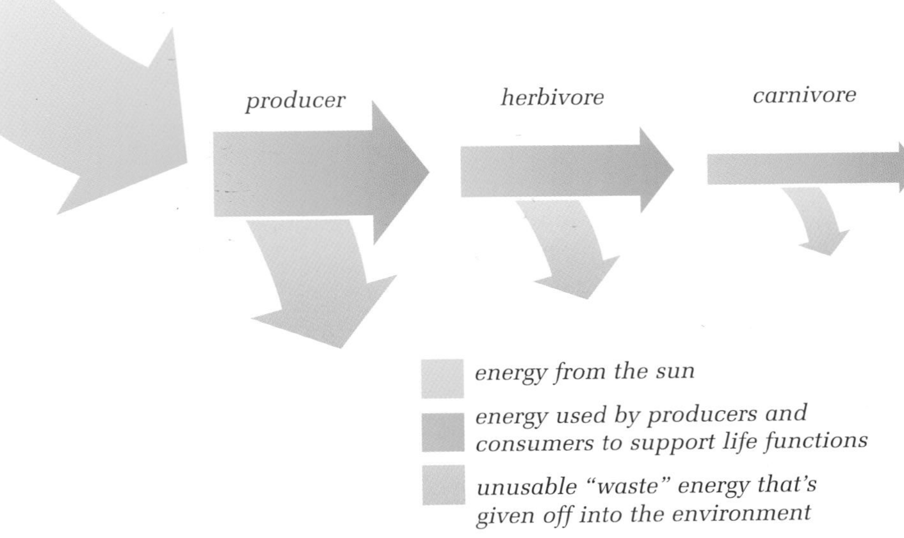

A plant uses as much as 90% of the energy it gets from its food to support its life functions. The rest is stored in its roots, leaves, and other plant parts. That's all the energy that's available to a herbivore that eats the plant: about 10%. The herbivore also uses as much as 90% of the energy from its plant food to support its life functions. What do you think that means for a carnivore that eats the herbivore?

As you can see, a lot of energy is "wasted" as it is transferred from one living thing to another in a food chain. Much of this "wasted" energy is body heat. Plants can't reuse it. Neither can animals. It just escapes into the environment.

Energy, therefore, follows a one-way path through ecosystems. In all ecosystems, producers depend on a constant supply of energy from the sun to survive. Herbivores depend on plants for the energy they need. Carnivores depend on the herbivores. And the scavengers and decomposers depend on everyone else for the energy they need.

*info*BIT

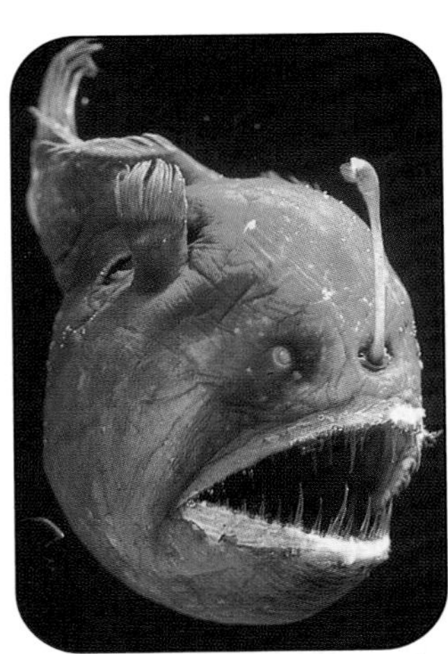

angler fish

Scientists once thought that all life on earth depended on the sun's energy. Then in 1977, a crew of scientists on board a deep-sea submarine made a discovery in the Pacific Ocean. They found an ecosystem 2.5 km below the water's surface in cracks along the ocean's floor, where the sun's rays cannot reach.

Heat energy from inside the earth creates warm areas in the normally frigid water. Bacteria live in these waters. They are the producers for food chains that include strange aquatic herbivores and carnivores.

Communicate

1 What is the difference between the energy used in photosynthesis and the energy used in cellular respiration?
2 Why is energy in cellular respiration wasted?
3 In terms of the flow of energy through an ecosystem, which is the correct order for each of the following situations?
a) rabbit, sun, rose, wolf, earthworm
b) mushroom, grass, cow, sun, human
c) seaweed, sea urchin, otter, sun, bacteria

infoBIT

Food webs are made up of a wide variety of living things. If you were to count the number of organisms in a typical food web and graph the results, this is what the graph might look like.

Number of Organisms

1 carnivore
10 omnivores
100 herbivores
1000 primary producers

- Suppose that one type of organism was to disappear from an ecosystem. Which type do you think would have the greatest impact on the other organisms? the least impact?

4.3 Food Webs

Explore

So far in this chapter, you have been using food chains to help you understand how all living things are connected with one another and with the abiotic components of their environment. However, food chains are simplified ways of showing these interactions. In real ecosystems, there are usually many carnivores, many more herbivores, and many, many more producers. And there are countless decomposers.

In real ecosystems, there can be dozens, hundreds, or even thousands of different food chains. Each living thing may be a part of many food chains. Many of these food chains are linked. If you link up all the possible food chains in an ecosystem, you get a **food web.**

Develop

Food Webs and Ecosystems

INVESTIGATOR

If This Affects That, and That Affects This, Then...

Before You Start ...

In this activity, you will play the role of an abiotic or biotic component of a typical forest ecosystem. You will explore how changes in either the abiotic or biotic components affect the members of the food web. As you will see, these changes can have a great effect on living things in an ecosystem.

The Question

How do abiotic and biotic components in the forest ecosystem affect the food web?

continued on next page

Materials & Equipment

- *30–40 m length of strong string or yarn, or light rope*
- *"forest identity" cards*

Procedure

1. Your teacher will hand out a forest identity card to everyone in your group. When you get your card, quietly think about your new identity and how you fit into a forest ecosystem. Think of a part of the forest (abiotic or biotic) that depends on or uses you. Think of a part of the forest that you depend on or use.
2. Form a circle around your teacher. One person will be chosen to hold one end of the string. Let's say the person is you.
3. Announce your identity to everyone in the forest circle. If you like, say something about why you're important to the forest and how you feel about your vital role. Ask if there's anyone in the circle who depends on you or whom you depend on. Those people should raise their hands.
4. Select a classmate who has raised her or his hand. Hang on to the end of the string, and ask your teacher to take the rest of it to the person.
5. This person then repeats steps 3 and 4.
6. Continue making connections this way until everyone in the circle is connected. It's okay if you're connected more than once. Remember that connections can be made between abiotic and biotic parts of the forest, as well as between biotic and biotic parts.

continued on next page ·····➤

7 Once everyone is connected, find the person who is water. Pretend that there's a drought this year, so there's very little water for the forest. The water person should tug gently on the string. Do you feel the tug? Does anyone else in the circle?

8 Repeat step 7 for each of these situations.
   a) Disease has killed the foxes.
   b) Too many trees have been cut down.
   c) The air has become heavily polluted with dirt, dust, and smelly chemicals.

9 If you like, make up some of your own situations to try out. When you've finished, answer the following questions.

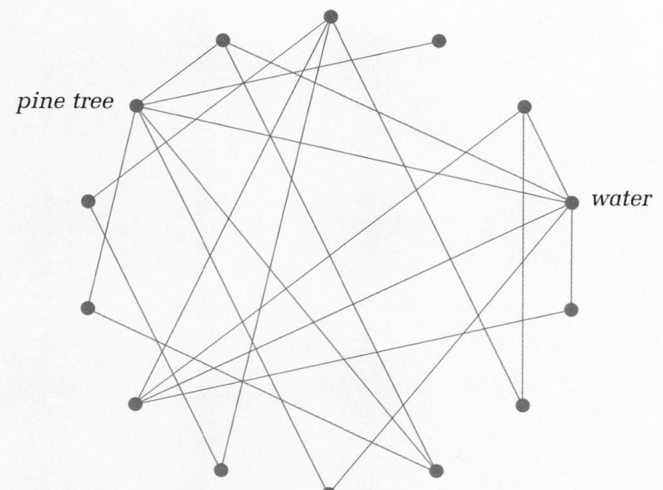

Analyzing and Interpreting

10 When the water person tugged on the string, how many people felt it? Did this surprise you? Why or why not?

11 In the other situations, how many people felt the tug? Again, did this surprise you? Why or why not?

12 a) Make a sketch of the forest ecosystem that you were part of in this activity (see the partially completed diagram). You might want to use different colours for some of the connections. If you like, add any other living things that you want to include.
   b) Label all the biotic and abiotic components. Then draw lines to connect all biotic parts of the ecosystem into a food web.

Forming Conclusions

13 Summarize this activity by answering the following:
   a) What do you think are the most important things about food webs?
   b) What did you learn about food webs that you didn't know before?
   c) What is one thing about food webs you would like to know more?

Communicate

1 a) In what ways could a tree be connected to a mushroom?
   b) In what ways could a fox be connected to a fern?
   c) In what ways could you be connected to a tree? to a mushroom? to a fox? to a fern?

2 Compare a forest food web with a food web in a desert. How are the food webs different? How are they similar?

3 Compare a forest food web with a food web in any other ecosystem you choose. How are they different? How are they similar?

4.4 CHECK YOUR PROGRESS

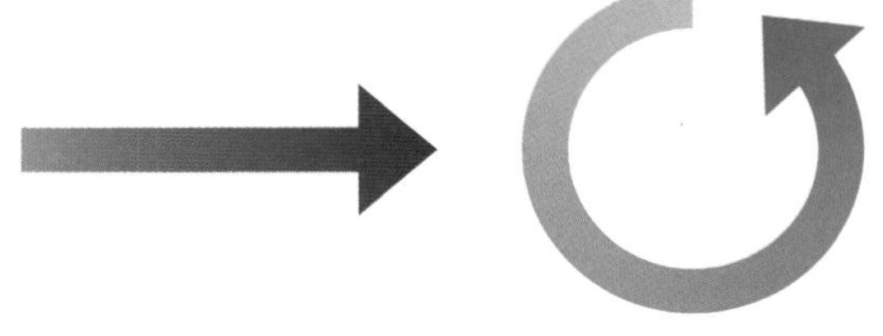

1 a) Which of the arrows at right describes the path that energy moves in ecosystems?

b) Which describes the path that matter moves in ecosystems?

c) Give reasons to explain your answers to a) and b).

2 This picture shows a typical food web.

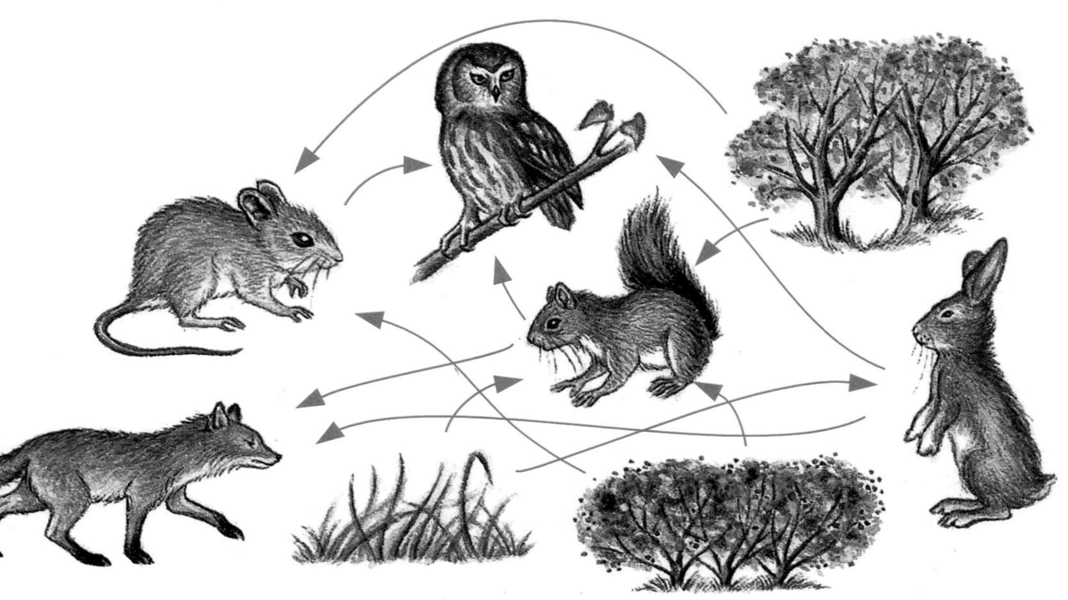

a) Name an ecosystem in which you would find a food web like this.

b) Identify at least three food chains in this food web.

c) Why does a food web give a more realistic picture of the interactions in an ecosystem?

d) Does a food web give a complete picture of the interactions in an ecosystem? Why or why not?

3 Describe a change in an ecosystem that would effect plants and animals living there. What are the positive and negative effects of this change?

4 What would happen if matter in the abiotic environment wasn't recycled? How do you know?

5 What would happen if an ecosystem's supply of sunlight was removed? How do you know?

6 Look back at the diagram of the carbon cycle in section 4.1. Why does burning fossil fuels add carbon to the planet's ecosystems?

7 Compare and contrast the similarities and differences of the carbon and energy in ecosystems.

Careers and Profiles

NATURALISTS—OUR ENVIRONMENTAL WATCHDOGS

Do you want to know more about preserving and protecting the natural environment? If so, you become a naturalist. These are people interested in protecting endangered species, preserving animal habitats, reducing pollutants that affect ecosystems, and other environmental issues.

While many naturalists have a background in science, some are just concerned citizens. Here are two examples of people who didn't start out studying science but who had a great influence on the environment.

Jack Miner (1865–1944) was a farmer who became one of Canada's first naturalists. He set up bird sanctuaries and did research on bird migration.

Even though Jane Goodall (1934–) had no formal science training, she has become world famous for her research on chimpanzees. She later received a Ph.D. from Cambridge University in England without first having earned an undergraduate degree.

ETHNOBOTANISTS

The inner bark of the red-osier dogwood shrub is used to heal sores and swellings.

Canadian ethnobotanist, Nancy Turner, works with plant specialists like Mary Thomas, a Shuswap elder.

What do leukemia, high blood pressure, diabetes, multiple sclerosis, and cerebral palsy have in common? They've all been treated with drugs that have originally come from plants. In fact, about one-quarter of today's prescription drugs have been developed from plants.

There are probably even more cures in ecosystems just waiting to be discovered. Unfortunately, finding them is very difficult and costly. That's where an ethnobotanist comes in. Ethnobotanists study native cultures to find out how natives use plants. They work closely with plant specialists and elders of native communities.

Big Idea

5.0 Natural changes can cause changes in ecosystems.

These two animals once roamed our planet. Now they're both gone. The last *Tyrannosaurus rex* died about 65 million years ago. A dramatic, natural change in its ecosystem may have led to its death.

The last Great Plains Lobo Wolf died around the year 1926. A dramatic change in its ecosystem caused by humans led to its death.

Ecosystems are always changing. Sometimes these changes are natural. Drought or floods can cause massive, long-term changes to ecosystems. Sometimes these changes are the result of human activity. Building dams and clearing forests can cause great, long-term changes to ecosystems.

What kinds of changes do you think drought, floods, dams, and forest-clearing cause? How do these changes affect living things?

5.1 Natural Changes in Ecosystems

Explore

A forest once stood here. That was before the thunderstorm. Lightning pierced the sky, striking and igniting one of the taller trees. The fire jumped from treetop to treetop until the entire forest was burning. The photo above shows all that's left.

Do you think there's anything living here in this barren-looking, desolate scene? Could anything ever live here again?

Problem Solver

To Change or Not To Change

Imagine what the forest scene in the photo looked like before the fire. Make a sketch in your Science Journal to show what you're imagining. What kinds of living things populated this scene? What abiotic and biotic components of the forest ecosystem supported them? Where are the living things now?

How do you think this scene will look a few years from now? Will it be any different? What could make it different? Use a sketch to record your impressions. Add labels to clarify your ideas.

How will this scene look 20 years from now? 50 years from now? 100 years or more from now?

All Things Change

Everything changes. You may not notice it, but you are not exactly the same as you were one day ago. Tomorrow you will be different again. Change is always happening, everywhere inside you and around you. All things change, including ecosystems.

To talk about changes in ecosystems, you need to understand some science terms we haven't yet used. These words are **species**, **population**, and **community**. Use the pictures and captions in the box to think about the meanings of these words.

blue shark *mute swan*

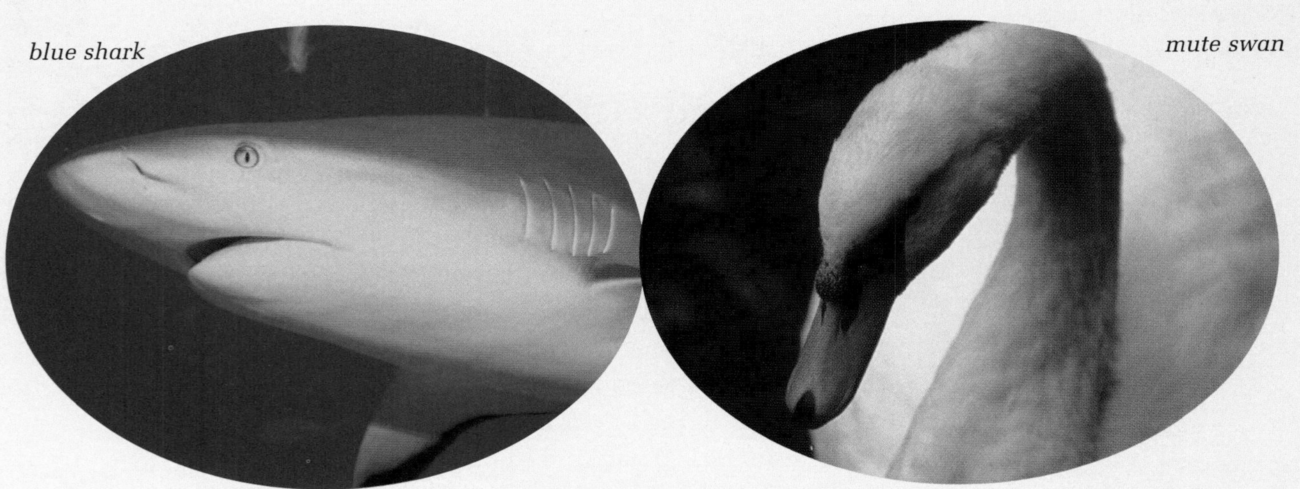

Sharks and swans are members of different species. Living things of the same species are able to reproduce and have young that are also able to reproduce. The young usually look very similar to the parents.

A population is all the individuals of the same species that live in a certain place at the same time. In this lawn, all the grass plants make up the lawn's grass population. What other populations do you see in this photo?

All the populations of different species that live and interact in the same place form a community. This photo shows a forest community. What populations do you see? What other kinds of communities have you visited? What communities are you part of?

Communicate

1 Explain in your own words the meaning of these terms: species, population, and community.

2 Match the words in the left column with the terms in the right column.

flock of birds	species
grizzly bear	population
school of fish	community
pond	
ant	

reSEARCH

Before there was a city of Toronto, the area was made up of different habitats and species. Now the most noticeable species is humans.

Research the early history of your community. What was the natural land like? What species lived there?

1 ECOSYSTEMS

5.2 The Fight for Survival: Competition

Explore

You probably have been involved in some type of competition in your life. Whether it is running a race or designing a school logo, a competition involves more than one person trying to reach the same goal. All living things compete with all other living things in their community. They compete for resources like food, water, and space to live. Because there is a limit to how much there is of each resource, all living things are always trying to get their share of these resources. What kind of resources do you compete for?

The next activity will give you a chance to be part of a competition between two species as they gather food.

Develop

Competing for Food

INVESTIGATOR

Survival in the Field

The Question

How does competition between two species affect their numbers and health?

Materials & Equipment

(for a group of 10 students)

- *4 plastic spoons*
- *4 forks with centre tines removed*
- *100 g of sesame seeds*
- *10 small Styrofoam balls*
- *10 10-cm pieces of string*
- *10 toothpicks*
- *a timing device*

continued on next page

Procedure

1. You are about to be part of a simulation of species competing for the same resource: food. There are two species, the *forks* and the *spoons*. In your group, assign four people to be spoons, four to be forks and one person to be the recorder for each species.
2. The recorders randomly spread out the materials in a 10 m by 10 m area called the community.
3. The task for the members of the two species is to collect one food item from the community within 20 seconds. Members who cannot collect a food item and return to the recorder in this time period are considered to have died from starvation. A fork or spoon who brings back more than one food item will be considered to have died from over-eating. Only members who collect one food item can go on to the next round. A food item is one pile of sesame seeds, one ball, one string, or one toothpick.
4. Begin Round 1 by having all the forks and spoons line up on one edge of the community. When your teacher tells you to start, go into the community and collect one food item. When you get your food item, come back to your recorder to have your item recorded. Any fork or spoon who is unable to collect food or who has collected too much cannot continue into the next round.
5. Repeat step 4 until no forks or spoons are left. Make sure each food item you collected is recorded at the end of each round.

Keeping Records

6. To record what each fork and spoon collected in each round, draw the following table on a clean sheet of paper.

Species	Round 1	Round 2	Round 3	Round 4	Round 5
Fork 1					
Fork 2					
Fork 3					
Fork 4					
Spoon 1					
Spoon 2					
Spoon 3					
Spoon 4					

continued on next page

Analyzing and Interpreting

7 Create a line graph that shows how many spoons and how many forks competed against each other in each round.

8 Using the graph, can you describe a trend that shows which species was more successful in the competition for food? What information can you use to support your conclusion?

9 Create a bar graph for forks and spoons that shows what type and how much food each species collected in each round.

10 Was there a preferred food at any time for each of the species?

11 Was there a food that you thought limited the survival of a species? Or was there a food that only one species could use to survive?

Forming Conclusions

12 Using the information you collected from this activity, describe how you think competition for food might affect the number and health of the forks and spoons in this activity.

Communicate

1 In the Investigator activity, you explored one factor that can affect who will populate ecosystems: competition for food. Other factors include:

- predation (living things eating or hunting other living things for food)
- weather
- natural disasters such as floods, fires, and landslides
- human activities

How do you think these factors affect populations and communities in ecosystems?

2 The following graph shows the populations of the snowshoe hare and the lynx over a period of time. Why do you think the populations peak and crash at different times?

*info*BIT

A **population cycle** describes the relationship of two or more species in an ecosystem. The lynx–snowshoe hare graph illustrates an example. But these cycles don't just happen between only two species. Many animals are connected to the lynx and snowshoe hare population cycle in a less dramatic way: great horned owls, red-tailed hawks, coyotes, red and flying squirrels.

lynx

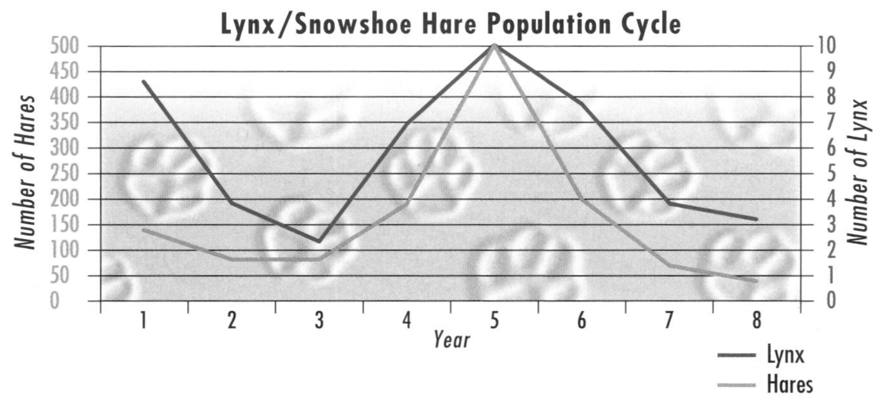

Competition between Three or More Species

Getting Started

In the last activity, you examined competition involving only two species. It was a very small community. However, it's rare to find ecosystems that are so small. There may be hundreds or even thousands of populations in an ecosystem. In the experiment below, you will work with just a few populations to observe what happens when several species compete in an ecosystem.

The Question

How does competition affect the number of plant populations in an ecosystem?

Your Task

1. Make a hypothesis that will allow you to determine how three or more species of plants will be affected by competition if they are competing for the same resources. (A **hypothesis** is a possible answer to a question or a possible explanation of a situation.)

2. Decide what materials and equipment you'll need to test your hypothesis. For example, you might ask:
   a) How many populations will you experiment with?
   b) Will you grow the plants from seeds or work with seedlings?
   c) How many containers will you need?
   d) How much soil will you need?
3. Plan your procedure. Ask yourself questions such as:
   a) What evidence are you looking for to support your hypothesis?
   b) What steps will you follow to collect the data you need?
   c) Is the test you're designing fair? How do you know?
   d) How will you record your results? For example, do you need a data chart? a graph? both? neither?
   e) How long will you run your experiment?
4. Write up your procedure. Be sure to show it to your teacher before going any further.
5. Carry out your experiment.
6. Compare your results with your hypothesis. Did your results support it? If not, what possible reasons might there be?
7. Share and compare your experimental plan and findings with your classmates. Did anyone plan an experiment exactly like yours? similar to yours? completely different from yours? How do your results compare with theirs?

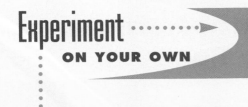

5.3 Succession: How Ecosystems Change Over Time

Explore

Have you ever noticed how bare patches on the ground don't often stay that way? Sooner or later, you will see new plants growing where there used to be just soil. Scientists call the first species that arrive **pioneer species**. Even though the abiotic conditions may be harsh, these pioneers find a way to live there. They also "pave the way" for populations of other species to enter the community and establish themselves. As time goes on, many of the pioneer species may get "crowded out" by the new arrivals. These, in turn, may be replaced by other, still newer arrivals.

This process of change can take a long time. It may take decades, centuries, even thousands of years. Scientists have been observing enough of these changes to notice a pattern. They can usually tell which species came first and which came later just by looking at an ecosystem. This predictable pattern of change in ecosystems is called **succession**.

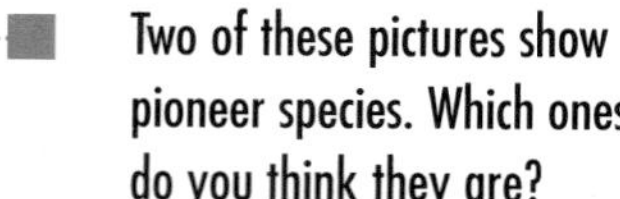

Two of these pictures show pioneer species. Which ones do you think they are?

Develop

Changes in Populations in Ecosystems

You can predict how populations in ecosystems will change, too. The next activity will help you do this.

INVESTIGATOR

Exploring Succession

The Question

What kinds of succession are there, and how do they affect ecosystems?

Procedure

1. Read the following draft Web page article on succession in ecosystems.

continued on next page

EarthNews On-line Journal

Netsite:

Home Page | Search | Support | Software

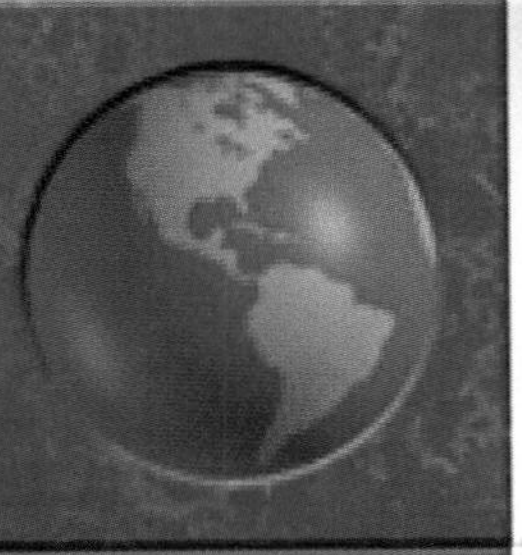

EarthNews On-line Journal

CONTENTS

- Home
- Last Month's Issue
- Back Issues
- Feature Articles
- Search
- Subscribe!
- Contact Us
- FAQs

What is Succession?

Succession happens because of one or more of the following factors:

- competition between species
- human activities changing the community
- environmental changes

Lichen

Growing Grass

Young Forest

Climax Forest

There are two types of succession to consider when observing communities.

Primary succession occurs when a new community begins to form in an area where no community existed before. The process begins with the colonization of the area by pioneer species. These plants are suited to grow in barren, rocky areas. Over time, they help to break down the rocks into soil. An example of a pioneer plant would be lichen.

Over time, other species of plants begin to grow in the community. Grassy areas are replaced by trees with shallow roots. As more soil builds up, larger trees become established. In time, a generally stable community of a diverse number of species is formed. This is called a climax community. Unless disturbed by natural or human forces, a climax community can exist for many generations.

Secondary succession occurs when a community has been destroyed or disturbed. A farmer's field, a vacant lot in the city, even a strip mine are examples of where this type of succession could occur.

Island Succession involves plants and animals reaching newly created land. The plants and animals that reached the island of Surtsey are examples of this type of succession. Usually this type of succession is very slow. Colonization happens when winds carry seeds, plants, or birds to the island.

continued on next page

Keeping Records

2 This Web page is under "construction." You will need to design two more pages that can be linked to this page. As you read the article, begin to think about what information you will put on these two pages. For example, one page may include terms that are boldfaced and another may show examples of succession in your community.

Analyzing and Interpreting

3 Which living things seem to be the pioneer species in all ecosystems? Suggest a reason to explain this.

4 Describe the key stages to the development of a climax community.

Forming Conclusions

5 Based on your discoveries, state your opinion about the following statement: *Eventually, all ecosystems stop changing.*

What examples of succession can you find in this scene?

Communicate

1 What is the difference between primary and secondary succession?

2 Give an example each of a pioneer species and a species of a climax community.

3 Over many years, the following plants and animals appeared in an area where a forest fire occurred. In what order do you think they appeared?

- fireweed
- birch tree
- mouse
- bear
- grass

5.4 Biomes: The Products of Succession

Explore

The end result of succession is usually a climax community of living things that is fairly stable. Some populations will die out or move away. Others may move in to take their place. But, by and large, the producers of the community stay pretty much the same. However, this situation can change when humans become involved.

When you hear people talking about tropical forests, grasslands, and deserts, they're talking about ecosystems with well-defined climax communities. Scientists have another way of talking about these ecosystems. They call them biomes. A **biome** is a large area with a definite climate that supports certain vegetation. Use the map of world biomes to help you understand this definition.

A simplified outline of the world's major biomes

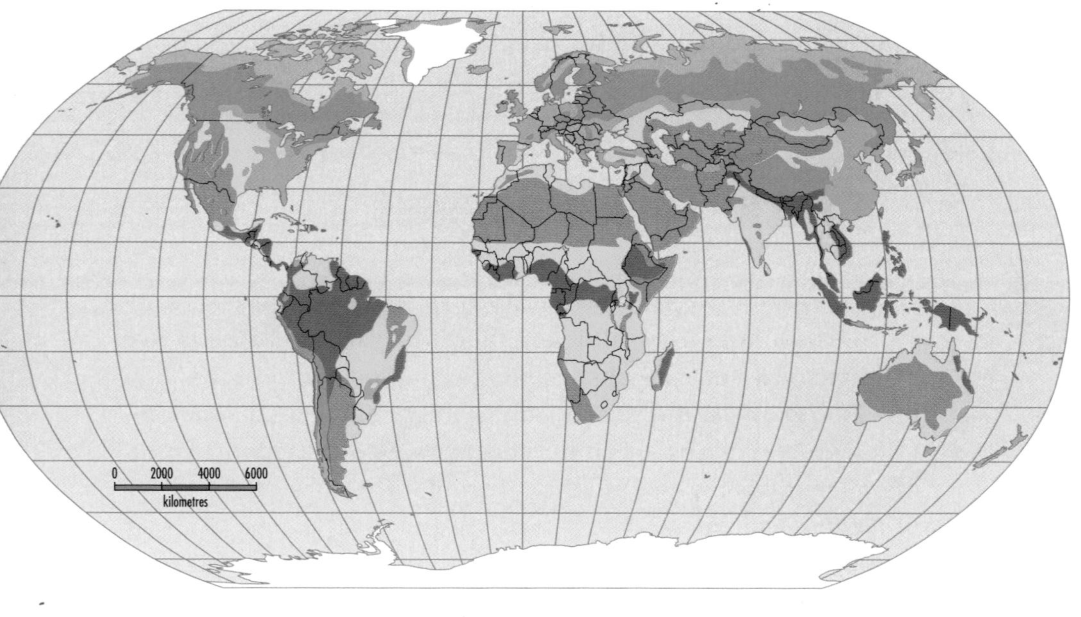

LEGEND:

***Tundra**: Climate is very cold and dry.*

***Boreal Forest**: Climate is cold in winter and cool in summer.*

***Temperate Deciduous Forest**: Climate is cold in winter and hot in summer. Both seasons have lots of precipitation (snow and rain).*

***Grassland**: Climate is cold in winter and hot in summer. Both seasons have some precipitation.*

***Desert**: Climate is very dry, with hot daytime temperatures and low nighttime temperatures.*

***Tropical Rain Forest**: Climate is very hot and wet all year long.*

Can you match each picture with the correct biome?

grey wolf *black-tailed prairie dog* *striped skunk* *keel-billed toucan* *arctic hare* *sun scorpion*

Develop: Canadian Biomes

PROBLEM SOLVER

WHAT BIOMES DO WE HAVE IN CANADA?

- Sketch or trace a map of Canada. Then use your knowledge of Canadian climate to infer what biomes we have and where they are.
- Use different colours to mark these biomes on your map.
- Use an encyclopedia or another information resource to check your results.

Communicate

1 How is a biome different from a community?
2 How many biomes did you find for Canada? Which one takes up the most area? Which one do you think has the greatest number of species? the least number of species?
3 What biome do you live in? What observations or information can you use to support your answer?

reSEARCH

Which of these biomes covers the most area in Canada?

5.5 CHECK YOUR PROGRESS

1 a) Whether they're started naturally or by people, fires change forests all the time, affecting their ecosystems. Name at least three other natural changes that can affect ecosystems.
   b) Choose one and describe how it might affect an ecosystem.
2 Use words, pictures, or both to describe how these four words are related: species, population, community, ecosystem.
3 a) What is succession?
   b) Look back at the Surtsey news article at the beginning of this chapter. Surtsey started as a barren mass of rock. Over time, however, it began to support life. What form of life first established itself there? What other living things followed? Is this a pattern you would have expected? Why or why not?
4 a) What is a biome?
   b) Do you think a biome is the same thing as an ecosystem? Why or why not?
5 Agree or disagree with this statement: *Some biomes are more important than others.*

BIG IDEA

6.0 Human activities can change ecosystems.

Abiotic factors often cause ecosystems to change. For example, some sand dunes can move as much as 30 m in a year. What abiotic factors do you think could cause a sand dune to move? Abiotic factors can cause ecosystems to change in size, too. What abiotic factors could cause a desert to increase in size?

Below is a scene from the world's largest desert, the Sahara in Africa. It covers an area of more than 9 000 000 km^2. And it's growing. From 1950 to 1975, its border extended 100 km to the south.

In the case of the Sahara, abiotic factors aren't responsible for the desert's dramatic change. Biotic factors are. In fact, it's one particular biotic factor: humans. What human activities do you think are responsible for the Sahara's increase in size? Can you think of places in Canada where human activities have changed, or are changing, ecosystems? What about other places around the world? How do these changes affect living things?

What do you think will happen to this ecosystem?

6.1 The Impact of Technology

Explore

People—like all living things—need food, water, air, shelter, and living space to survive. We, like all living things, find what we need from the ecosystems in which we live. In this way, then, we're no different from other living things.

However, humans *do* have a bigger impact on ecosystems than any other living thing. There are several reasons for this.

1. We are part of communities in every biome on the planet. No other species inhabits as many different ecosystems.
2. We invent and use technology to alter the ecosystems in which we live. Several other species, such as chimpanzees, use simple tools. However, there is little or no impact of these non-human tools on ecosystems.
3. There are so many of us. Our population is more than five billion and growing.

The following chart shows a sample of the ways that we use plants or plant materials to meet our needs. Take some time to look them over. For each example, try to provide another example.

What examples of technology can you find in this picture?

We Use Plants To Provide Us With	Examples
food	*growing wheat to make flour*
drinks	*growing coffee beans to make coffee*
fuels	*burning logs in fireplaces*
chemical products	*using plants of all kinds to make medicines, dyes, cosmetics, pesticides, cleaners*
raw materials	*cutting down trees for lumber, paper, and using plant-parts for making fabrics*
pleasure	*growing gardens for their beauty*
information	*studying plants in the wild, in "captivity," and in the laboratory*

Coffee beans

*info*BIT

The Dirty Thirties

Imagine a dust cloud so high, it could blot out the sky and nearly bury a house. That's what happened in the Canadian prairies during the 1930s. The Prairie provinces were hit with hot, dry weather. For years, farmers had used their land with little care for the health of the soil. Drought caused this poor soil to become dry and less productive.

When the hot winds of the 1930s came, they lifted up this dry soil and created giant dust storms. At times the dust was so heavy it was impossible to drive alongside open fields. Visibility was often reduced to just a few metres. Roads, fences, and even houses were partly buried by the drifting sand.

To make matters worse, the desert-like conditions offered the perfect environment for grasshoppers. They reproduced rapidly until hundreds of thousands of square kilometres were covered in grasshoppers. They flew in clouds that darkened the sky. These hungry grasshoppers destroyed everything in sight.

Develop

How Does Technology Change Ecosystems?

Now you are starting to develop an understanding of how technology impacts ecosystems. It's time to investigate this impact in more detail.

PROBLEM SOLVER

PLANT TECHNOLOGY CHALLENGES

1 In order to put plants to use, people usually have to use some form of technology.

For example, growing a garden might only require a single technological tool: a small shovel. In most cases, though, the technology is more complex. Your first challenge is to pick one way people use plants from the list on the previous page and discover the technology or technologies linked to that use.

2 Your second challenge is to find out the impact of the technologies you discovered. That is, how the technologies affect:

a) the community of which the plants are a part
b) the ecosystem of which the plants are a part
c) the ability of certain species to survive
d) the ability of people to earn money to support themselves, their families, and their lifestyles
e) the Canadian economy

Communicate

1 In what ways do our lives and lifestyles depend on technologies?

2 In what ways do our lives, lifestyles, and technologies affect ecosystems?

Careers and Profiles

NATURE'S OWN FOOD

Cassandra Bassett owns and operates a 4-ha (hectare, 1 ha = 10 000 m^2) farm on Hornby Island, just off the coast of British Columbia. "We grow garlic, strawberries, apples, plums, pears, asparagus, artichokes... you name it, we grow it," says Bassett. This is not an ordinary farm, however. Her farm is 100% organic, which means Bassett grows her food without using synthetic chemicals.

Conventional farms use large amounts of

- insecticides to kill insects
- herbicides to kill weeds
- fertilizers to help plants grow.

These chemicals make farms more productive, but they can also harm the environment if used improperly.

Instead of using these chemicals on her farm, Bassett takes an "ecosystem approach":

Pests
Bassett plants certain crops close to one another. "On the coast the carrot rust fly is a very bad pest," says Bassett. To keep this insect away, she always plants her carrots next to her onions because the carrot fly stays away from onions.

Weeds
Bassett covers the ground between her crops with big pieces of black plastic. This blocks the sunlight, thus preventing weeds from growing.

Fertilizer
Bassett nourishes her crops with compost and manure. This decayed organic matter also replaces soil that washes away in the rain. Soil erosion can be a major problem on conventional farms, because organic matter isn't added to renew the topsoil.

Does Bassett think organic farming is a good career choice? "If you expect to get rich then I would say no," she says. "If you expect to be incredibly fulfilled and feel good about what you've accomplished then I'd say yes."

6.2 The Impact of Human Activities

Explore

The human populations on earth are very large, and they continue to grow. This means we need more and more space to live. We need more and more land to grow and raise living things for food. We need more and more energy sources such as coal and oil to fuel our technologies. We need more and more raw materials such as wood, rocks, and minerals to build our homes, our industries, and our vehicles. Each human "need" has an impact on ecosystems and the living things that populate them—including ourselves.

We regularly pollute the air, water, and soil on which all life depends. These pictures show a few examples of ways we have changed or polluted our own planet. Have you seen or heard of other examples like these? In what other ways do we pollute our planet?

This hydro-electric project is located on the La Grande river which flows into James Bay in northern Québec. The top picture shows the river before the dam was built for the plant, and the bottom picture shows the site seven years later. The dam is nearly 3 km long and now contains the reservoir which extends over 2835 km^2. In what ways do you think the environment was changed to build the electricity-generating plant? What effects would these changes have had on living things?

Before

After

Each year, people throw away great amounts of garbage. Potato chip bags, fruit pits and peels, bottles, and paper and plastic of all kinds make up the majority of this litter. Who do you think pays to have the garbage collected? How would living things be affected if we left the garbage where it lay?

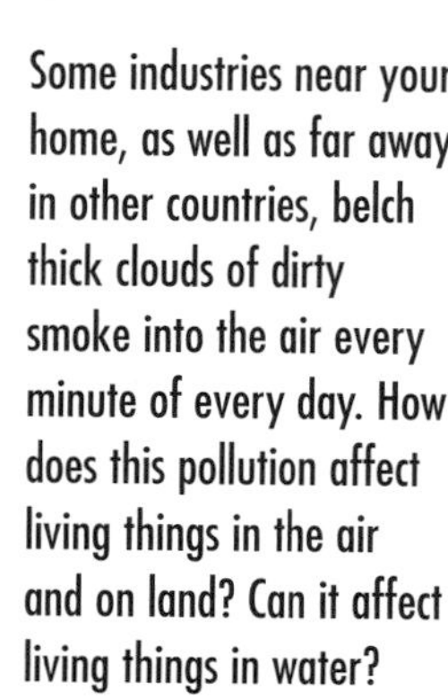

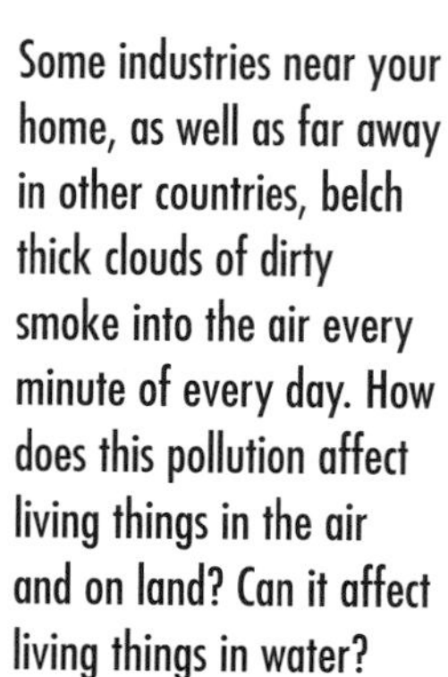

Some industries near your home, as well as far away in other countries, belch thick clouds of dirty smoke into the air every minute of every day. How does this pollution affect living things in the air and on land? Can it affect living things in water?

Develop

Human Impact on Ecosystems: Chemical Use

Here's what can happen when humans interfere with an ecosystem they don't understand.

1 In the 1950s, humans try to rid Borneo of malaria-carrying mosquitoes by spraying them with DDT.
2 The DDT also gets on cockroaches.
3 The geckos, which eat the cockroaches, suffer nerve damage and move more slowly.
4 Cats, who normally eat rats, switch to the slow-moving, easier-to-catch geckos. Cats die from DDT poisoning.
5 With fewer cats to catch the rats, the rats multiply quickly. They move out of the jungle and into the villages.
6 Fleas, piggy-backing on the rats, carry a bacteria which causes plague.
7 Plague spreads to humans.

While DDT has now been banned in most of the world, there are other pesticides that threaten species. Migrating birds are very vulnerable because they visit so many localities. A recent example is the case of the Swainson's hawks. Many of these birds of prey summer in Saskatchewan and Alberta. They winter in Argentina and Brazil.

Mysteriously, in just a few short years, between five and ten percent of the world's population of Swainson's hawks died. That translated into thousands of deaths to the 100 000 birds that summer in Canada. The reason is that Argentinian farmers used a pesticide to kill grasshoppers. What farmers didn't realize is that the hawks eat grasshoppers.

Now, thanks to environmentalists in North America and Argentina, alternatives to using pesticides are being explored.

Communicate

1 Describe three ways humans can impact or change an ecosystem.
2 Identify one example of human impact on an ecosystem that you could help to lessen. Describe what you could do to lessen this impact.
3 Why does introducing a chemical to kill an small insect have an impact on humans?

reSEARCH

Many pollution-related problems have world-wide effects. Pick one of the following environmental problems. Find out what scientists know about it, what they think they know, and their prediction of the effects on living things and ecosystems in the future.

- the greenhouse effect
- global warming
- acidic precipitation (commonly called acid rain)

6.3 Bioinvasion

Explore

Many of the plants and animals that you may think are common to Canada actually have come from somewhere else. The European settlers introduced plants and animals from their home countries. Some well-meaning naturalists introduced other species, and still others were accidentally introduced.

Scientists call this species introduction **bioinvasion**. Because many of these new species were stronger than the native species or had no natural enemies, they quickly multiplied. Their effects on ecosystems and on other living things have been dramatic.

Alien Invasion!

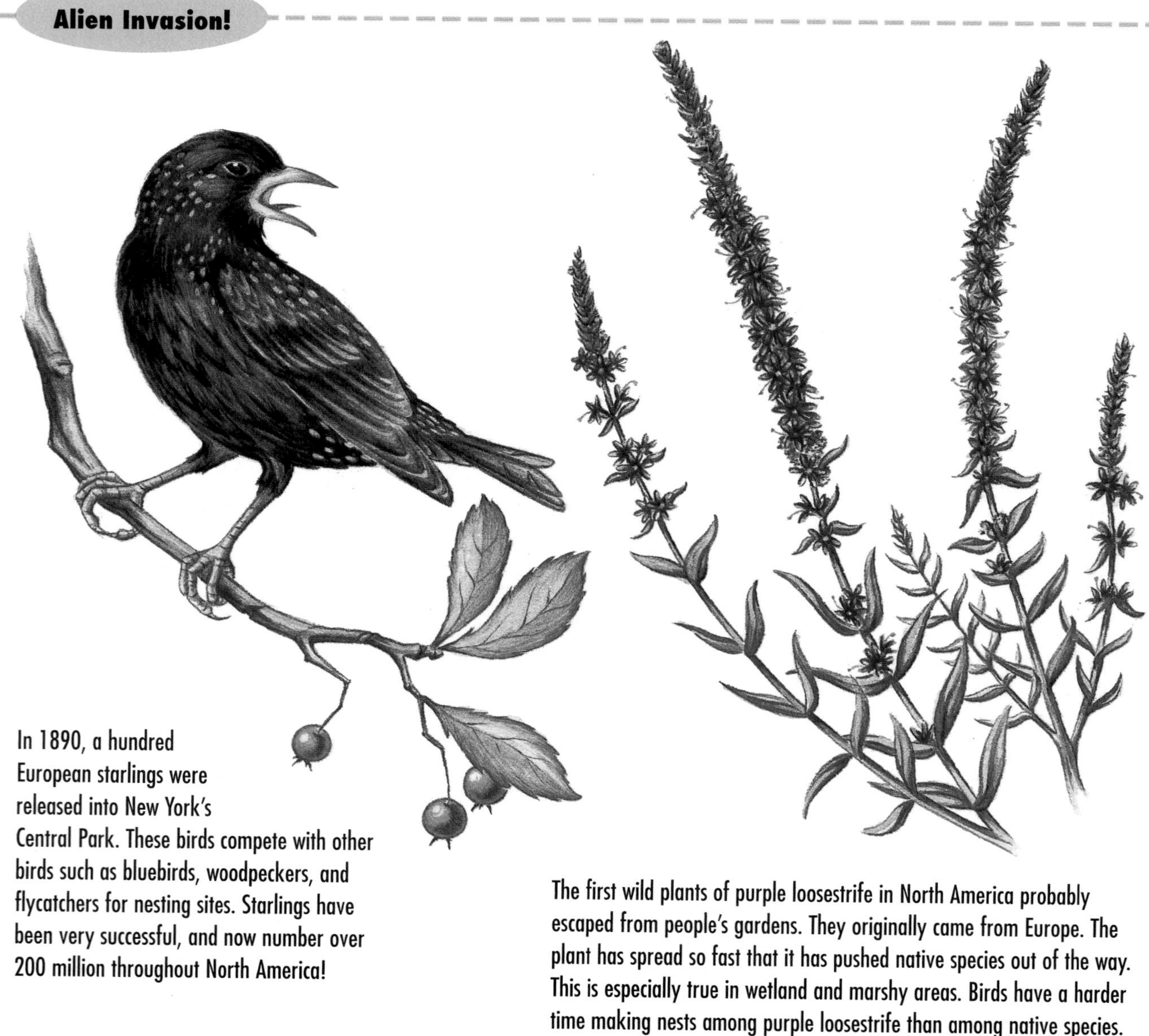

In 1890, a hundred European starlings were released into New York's Central Park. These birds compete with other birds such as bluebirds, woodpeckers, and flycatchers for nesting sites. Starlings have been very successful, and now number over 200 million throughout North America!

The first wild plants of purple loosestrife in North America probably escaped from people's gardens. They originally came from Europe. The plant has spread so fast that it has pushed native species out of the way. This is especially true in wetland and marshy areas. Birds have a harder time making nests among purple loosestrife than among native species.

The first horses were brought to North America in the early 1500s by the Spanish explorers. The French introduced horses to Québec in 1660. Many of these horses escaped and became wild. At one time, there were almost 15 million wild horses in North America!

Zebra mussels were first noticed in the Great Lakes in 1988. They probably travelled over here on a ship from Europe. By 1994, there were as many as 93 000 mussels/m^2 in some rivers near the Great Lakes.

House sparrows were also purposely released in New York's Central Park over 100 years ago. They compete for food and nesting sites with many native birds.

More than one quarter of Canada's plant species are not native.

- Research three more common plants and animals that are not native to Canada.
- Why are some of these alien species so successful in North America? Why are some species a threat to these ecosystems?

Develop

Where Have All the Species Gone?

Many species of plants and animals are in danger of being eliminated from our planet completely. Many others are already extinct. Human activity and bioinvasion are largely responsible for this situation. The chart below outlines some of the 55 plants and animals in Canada that are extinct, endangered, or threatened.

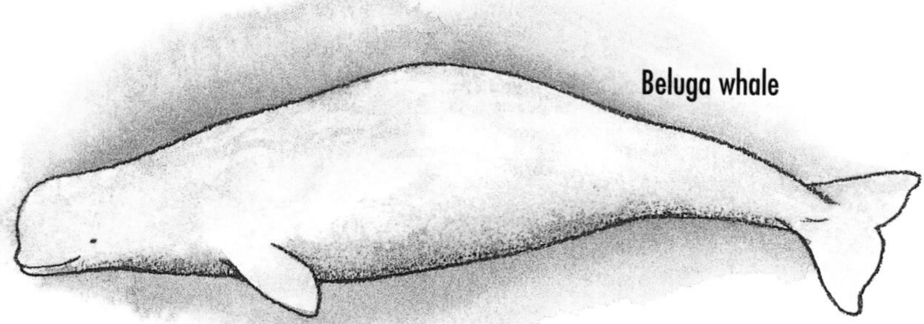

Beluga whale

Extinct, Endangered, or Threatened Plants and Animals in Canada		
Extinct	***Endangered***	***Threatened***
• *Dawson's caribou* • *sea mink* • *great auk* • *Labrador duck* • *passenger pigeon*	• *eastern cougar* • *sea otter* • *bowhead whale* • *right whale* • *beluga whale* • *whooping crane* • *eastern prickly pear cactus* • *Arcadian whitefish*	• *wood bison* • *pine martin* • *burrowing owl* • *eastern massasauga rattlesnake* • *ginseng*

Labrador duck

Whooping crane

Ginseng

Communicate

1. Create a poster or picture that describes the present state of endangered or threatened species in Canada.
2. Do you think that species that are endangered or threatened should be saved? Write a short paragraph explaining your view on this question.

6.4 Check Your Progress

1 a) All living things have an effect on ecosystems as they go about their daily lives. Give three examples to show this.
b) Give three reasons why people change ecosystems.
c) Which has a bigger impact: human changes to ecosystems or changes caused by other living things? Explain your answer.

2 In what ways do the following human activities affect ecosystems?
a) clearing farmland to build a new housing development
b) cutting down trees to make paper and building materials
c) transporting crude oil across the ocean
d) burning logs in a fireplace
e) growing an apple orchard to sell the apples
f) harvesting rare plants to make new medicines from the chemicals they contain

3 a) In what ways do we pollute our planet? What are some reasons for this pollution?
b) What is the impact of our pollution on ecosystems?

4 Why have some species become endangered or extinct in North America?

Will the grizzly bear be extinct in Canada someday?

*info***BIT**

North American Species Before and After Europeans Arrived

Before 1492	60 million bison	100 000 grizzly bears	150 000 bald eagles	massive flocks of millions of passenger pigeons	1500 whooping cranes
After	541 in 1891 today about 200 000	less than 2000 in Canada and the U.S. 31 000 in Alaska	10 000 in Canada and the U.S. 40 000 in Alaska	extinct since 1940	22 in 1940 158 today

Bison or buffalo

Bald eagle

BIG IDEA

7.0 Technologies have been developed to manage wastes that humans generate.

As long as there have been people on our planet, they have produced waste material. Long ago, all these wastes were biodegradable. Scavengers and decomposers were able to break them down. This would return important nutrients to the environment as part of the cycle of matter. Our use of technology has changed these natural cycles. For example, how have the following materials affected ecosystems?

- new materials such as glass and plastic
- fuel-burning technologies such as fireplaces and engines

In what other ways has technology had a negative effect on ecosystems? Are there ways in which we use technology to help ecosystems?

7.1 Human Generated Waste: Dealing with Our Garbage

Explore

Much of our garbage used to be poured into open pits. They were called "dumps" because people just dumped their garbage there. Dumps were smelly and unattractive-looking. Sometimes, they would catch on fire, polluting the air with sooty, foul smoke. Rainwater often washed dangerous chemicals and disease-causing bacteria away from the dumps and into local water systems.

Today, in North America, we've done a great deal to clean up our act. Our garbage is directed to one or more of the places shown in these pictures. Are any of these garbage solutions found in your community?

Recycling depot

Composting

Sanitary landfill

Incineration

Household hazardous waste operation

Waste transfer station

Develop

What to Do with All the Garbage

In Belleville, Ontario, residents have been keeping track of how much household waste they produce each year. Let's take a look inside their homes and see what this waste consists of. Shown below are the kinds and masses of materials that a typical household in Belleville disposed of in one year.

glass (e.g., pop bottles, beer bottles, liquor bottles, containers, light bulbs)	58.3 kg
plastic (e.g., bottles, containers, wrap, bags, toothbrushes, foam meat trays, toys)	56.5 kg
metal (e.g., pop cans, beer cans, paint containers, aerosol containers, aluminum foil, nails)	35.2 kg
paper (e.g., junk mail, packaging, magazines, catalogues, phone books)	79.6 kg
newspaper	130.7 kg
cardboard (e.g., cereal boxes, corrugated cardboard)	64.5 kg
polycoat (e.g., milk cartons)	4.3 kg
textiles	12.8 kg
ceramics	2.0 kg
multilayer packaging (e.g., tetra-paks)	4.1 kg
sanitary products (e.g., diapers)	50.4 kg
pharmaceutical and cosmetic waste, including containers	1.3 kg
footwear, luggage, and handbags	4.7 kg
appliances	1.9 kg
hazardous wastes (e.g., aerosols, paint)	3.9 kg
animal waste, including kitty litter	32.7 kg
treasure (e.g., repairable items like lamps, radios, etc.)	32.5 kg
bulky items (e.g., mattresses, furniture)	9.3 kg
building materials	45.0 kg
floor sweepings	1.5 kg
kitchen organics	176.2 kg
yard waste (e.g., leaves, house plants, grass clippings)	151.9 kg

Now, let's see how much of the waste can be recycled. Make a two-column chart. On one side of the chart, list the materials that can be recycled and their masses. If only part of the material can be recycled, estimate the mass. On the other side of the chart, list the materials that cannot be recycled and their mass. Again, estimate the mass if necessary. What percentage of the waste can be recycled? What percentage cannot be? What could people do with the waste that cannot be recycled?

In the next activity, you'll choose a waste management method to study in depth.

*info***BIT**

Estimating

When you don't know an exact number or an exact amount of something, you have to estimate it. This means you'll make a reasonable guess at what it should be. For example, some of the paper waste may be recyclable. You can use your own experiences or the views of your classmates to make an estimate of how much of the 79.6 kg you think could be recycled.

DECISION MAKER

WHERE DOES ALL THE GARBAGE GO?

The Question

What's the best way to deal with garbage in your local community?

Background Information

1 You have read about several different types of waste management. You will now determine which, in your opinion, would be the best method. Using the photos at the beginning of section 7.1 and your own experiences, decide as a group which topic you will study in depth. Select one method of waste disposal for your community. Have each member in your group research information on the following:

a) what kinds of wastes it handles
b) the average mass of wastes per year that arrive there
c) what happens to wastes that arrive there
d) its positive aspects
e) its negative aspects
f) about how many people are employed there
g) anything else you find interesting

2 When you're done, share your information with your group. Design a presentation to summarize your group's findings. Be prepared to share your group's findings with the rest of the class.

In Your Opinion

3 What do you think is the best waste management option at this time? Give reasons to support your opinion.

4 Share and compare your group's opinion with those of other groups.

Communicate

1 You have identified the best waste management option for your community. What would be the best choice for a community that was smaller or larger? What information can you use to support your answer?

2 Which choice would be the best if your main concern was impact on human communities? Why?

3 Which option would work best if your main consideration was impact on natural systems? Explain your reasoning.

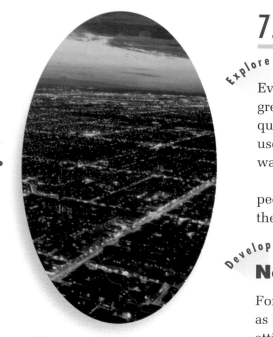

What examples of energy use can you find in this picture?

7.2 Have We Learned from the Past?

Explore

Every moment of every day, our human communities draw upon great quantities of energy and materials. We also generate great quantities of wastes. In the past, we didn't think much about our use of matter and energy. Nor did we worry about the impact our wastes and activities had on ecosystems.

Fortunately, our attitudes have changed. All over the planet, people are thinking about the effects they have on ecosystems. And they're changing the way they use matter and energy.

Develop

New Attitudes for a New Age

For thousands of years, humans have treated the earth's ecosystems as if they were limitless storehouses of matter and energy. These attitudes, however, have not helped to preserve our natural environment. Instead, they have created vast deserts, permanently destroyed thousands of plant and animal species, and polluted some of the resources we need for our survival.

The Canadian economy depends a great deal on many of these natural resources. For example, the mineral and forest industries directly employ 4% of Canada's workforce. What might happen to the way Canadians live if these resources were used up? What new attitudes must people develop to make sure that future generations will have the same standard of living that we have today?

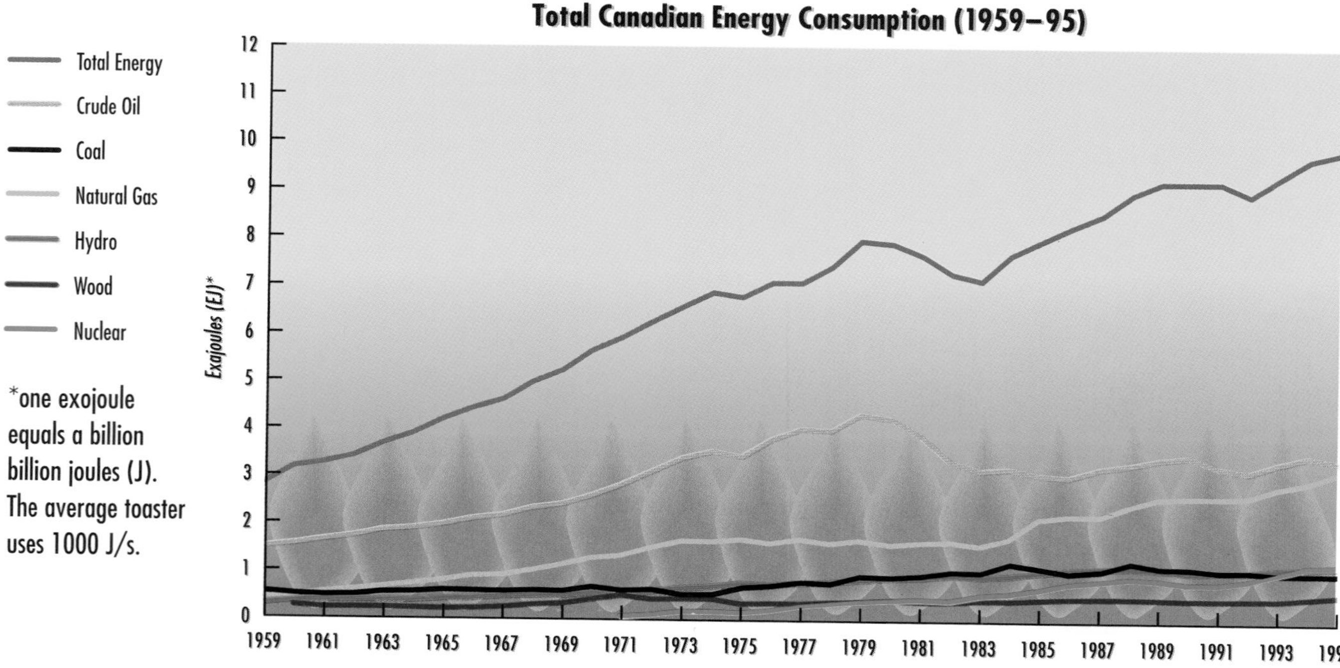

THINKING ABOUT SUSTAINABLE DEVELOPMENT

Using renewable resources in a way that doesn't use them up is called **sustainable development**. Farming and forestry are two industries that can be made sustainable.

Mining and petroleum production use non-renewable resources. These industries are not sustainable.

Brainstorm a list of products that come from the forest.

- How would reducing the number of forest products you use help to sustain our forests?
- What forest products could you live without?

- Brainstorm a list of products that use minerals products (copper, iron, etc.).
- Suggest ways in which people could reduce the amount of minerals mined in Canada.

Communicate

1 The following article identifies a successful recycling program in Whitby, Ontario. Create a one-page poster that could be used to illustrate the success of this project. Your poster should have at least one graph, one picture, and a short description of project.

1 ECOSYSTEMS

The Region of Durham

WHITBY, ONTARIO—Recycling really works in the Regional Municipality of Durham. In 1996 alone, residents set out 20 957 t (tonnes) of recyclables in their curbside blue box program, saving about 173 kg of waste per household from going to a landfill. Residents of apartments and townhouse units got into the act, too, by recycling over 1480 t. A central compost facility took in over 8000 t of leaf-and-yard waste from residents, while other materials were collected at four Waste Management Facilities in the region.

The Region of Durham Works Department generated almost 1.3 million dollars in revenue from selling 13 500 t of old newspapers, 3900 t of glass bottles and jars, 1900 t of metal cans and plastic pop bottles and 3600 t of old cardboard. Residents received recycling information on Regional Waste Reduction Programs through special displays in shopping malls, promotional and educational information distributed on the radio, on buses, in bus shelters, in train stations and through newsletters.

7.3 Check Your Progress

1 What are the different ways in which humans dispose of their waste? Provide a short description or drawing of each one.
2 Which methods of waste disposal can you personally be responsible for in your community? Which methods require the assistance of others? Are there any methods that cannot be done in your community?
3 In your opinion, what is the greatest cost and the greatest benefit to recycling? to disposing of waste?
4 How would each of the following activities help to reduce the amount of waste going into a landfill?
   - taking a lunch to school in reusable containers
   - donating old clothes to a local charity
   - putting rechargeable batteries into a Walkman
   - taking a cloth bag shopping or reusing a plastic shopping bag
5 What other things could you do to reduce the amount of waste thrown out at your school?
6 In any issue, there are two or more points of view. Read "The Clear Cutting Debate" on the following page. List what you learned about the different points of view in this debate.

The Clear Cutting Debate

The Issue

What is the best method for harvesting Canada's forests?

Background Information

In Canada, 90 percent of trees are harvested by a method called **clear cutting**. With clear cutting, all trees are cut down in an area, even the species not used by the forest industry. Look at the arguments for and against this method of logging.

To Clear Cut?

Selective logging is too expensive. Cutting down only commercially valuable trees is too expensive. With clear cutting, you get the most logs for the least amount of money.

Our economy is highly dependent on wood products. Canadians use a great many wood products: building materials, paper, and furniture. Canada is also the biggest exporter of wood products in the world. Many Canadians work in the forestry and wood products industry.

Clear cutting isn't harmful because the trees are replanted. Trees are a renewable resource. Replanting makes the forest sustainable and doesn't harm the environment. It actually mimics nature. (Natural regeneration occurs after forest fires.)

Or Not to Clear Cut?

The true costs of clear cutting are hidden. Trees prevent flooding and erosion. Floods, soil erosion, and decreased air quality (trees produce oxygen) create hidden costs. Someone has to pay for this damage.

You can make more money from a forest if you leave it standing. Taking only those trees old enough to harvest costs more, but it leaves the forest largely intact. Money is not spent on flood and erosion control. The tourism and recreation industries that depend on forests also create employment.

A tree farm is not an ecosystem. Old growth forests are complex ecosystems. Replanting doesn't replace all the lost species, only a few commercial ones. These trees are prone to disease and insect damage. Fifty percent of replanted forests are treated with herbicides.

In Your Opinion

1 Choose one of the points in the clear cutting debate and research more about other alternative methods to clear cutting.

2 Summarize your opinion of whether clear cutting should occur or not. Your opinion should be supported by the information you have collected in question 1.

PROJECT

Short-eared owl

1 ECOSYSTEMS

Getting Started

The abiotic and biotic components of ecosystems are important in sustaining life on earth. Ecosystems also act as warning systems: *When populations or species die off or when they're unhealthy, it's a sign that something in the ecosystem has changed.* Often, unless this change is corrected or changed, the ecosystem could be endangered.

Meanwhile, our own populations continue to grow. Our use of technology and other human activities affect ecosystems. We need a growing amount of natural resources such as wood, water, rocks, and a variety of living things. Our activities also produce pollutants. As you know, these harm the very parts of ecosystems that are important to our survival.

Is there a way to find a balance between our needs and those of ecosystems? Is it possible to maintain healthy ecosystems and still have growth that consumes space and other natural resources?

Before You Start...

Look through your notes from the activities you did in this unit. Think about the ways human actions can affect ecosystems. With a partner, discuss the responsibilities that people have for making sure that ecosystems are healthy. List the criteria you think people should use when they make decisions that affect ecosystems.

Afterward, share your list with other groups. In what ways are they similar and different? Are there any additions you would like to make to your list?

The Question

How can you balance the needs for human growth and development with the needs of the biotic and abiotic components of ecosystems?

The Context

The town of Forest Grove has a population of 1200 people. The unemployment rate has been 20% for the past several years. The town council has decided to develop a piece of unused land. It hopes to attract businesses, industries, and people to Forest Grove. The piece of land has an area of 2000 ha. (One hectare, or 1 ha, measures 100 m x 100 m.)

Imagine you are a member of a land-use planning group. Forest Grove's town council has hired your team to design a plan to develop this land.

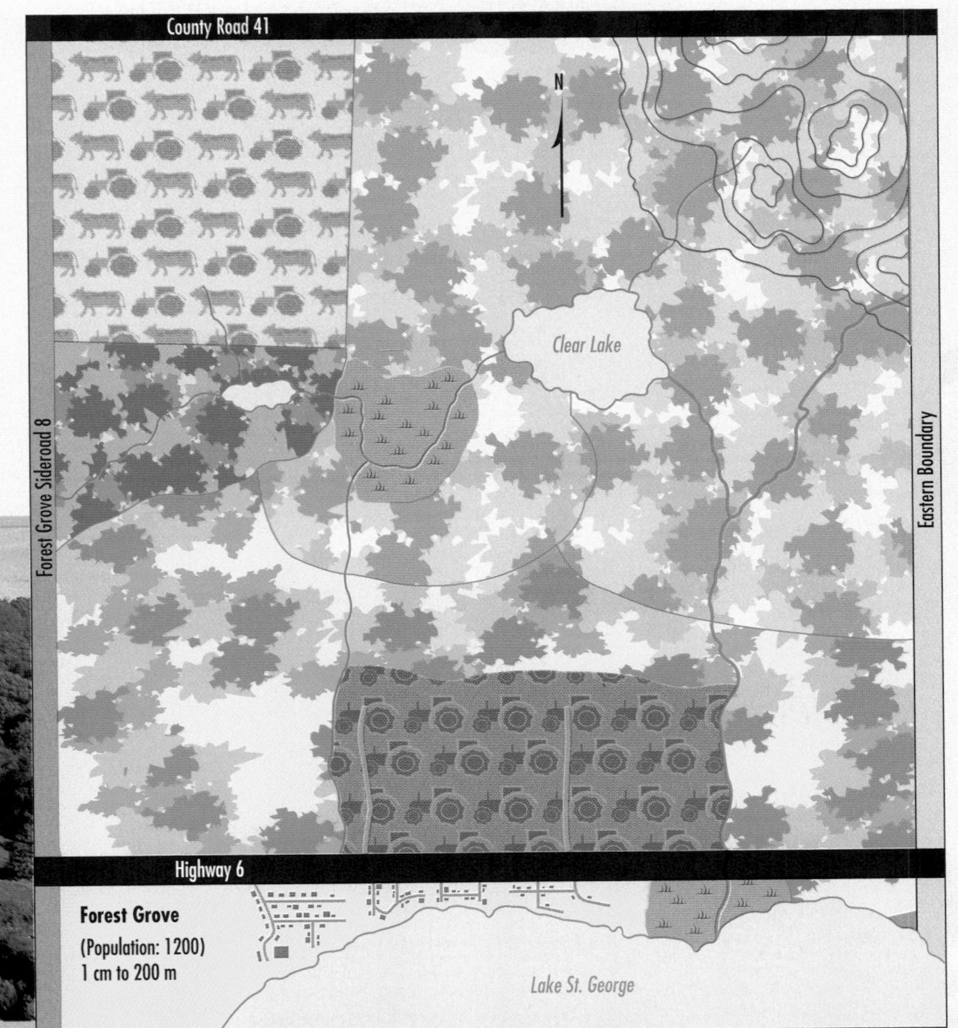

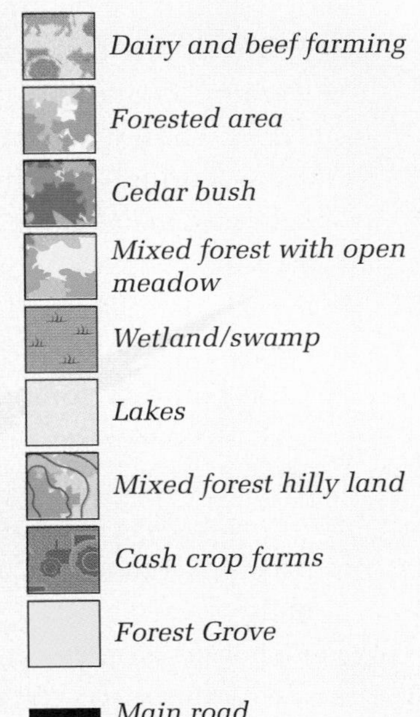

The map shown here outlines the various features of the land. Study it closely. Many different groups of people have ideas for developing this land. You will have to decide which ideas to use, which to ignore, and which to change. Use the Impact Assessment Checklist to help you evaluate your plans.

Impact Assessment Checklist

In what ways can your plans:

- ☐ *allow opportunities for more growth and development in the area?*
- ☐ *minimize the effects of growth and development on the habitats of the area?*
- ☐ *minimize the effects of growth and development on the living things of the area?*
- ☐ *deal with pollution and other negative effects to the area?*
- ☐ *balance the need for preserving natural ecosystems with the needs of people and their families?*

continued on next page

Procedure

1 Design a land-use plan that addresses the following interests.

a) *Industries:* These will provide employment for the townspeople.
- A hospitality company wants to develop a camping and motel site. This complex will include a 25-unit motel, a small restaurant, a wooded camping area (about 5 ha), a recreation centre with tennis courts, a swimming pool, and a boat launching ramp.
- A distribution company wants to set up a large warehouse depot for transferring goods to and from the surrounding communities. They will need good roads to the nearby highway.

b) *Housing developers:* They will want to build two new subdivisions for Forest Grove's growing population. The subdivisions will require roads to link them up with the existing town. They will need services such as water and electricity. The people who move into the new homes will also want their garbage handled in some way.

c) *Businesses:* These will provide stores and services such restaurants, health care, a movie theatre, and a new shopping centre. Businesses will also need water, electricity, and garbage handling.

d) *Local farmers:* There are currently seven farms located to the west of the land you will be developing. All the farmers have expressed interest in expanding their operations. They would like some of the land set aside for them to lease or buy.

e) Private citizens: Many people in Forest Grove would like the land to be used for recreational purposes, such as parkland with trails for walking and biking. They would also like to swim and boat on the river and in the lakes. A small group of citizens is urging you to leave the land as it is to preserve the local plant and animal populations. They are willing to consider limited use of the land for camping to attract people (and their money) to Forest Grove.

2 With your team, come up with a plan for the use of this land. Some of the questions you will need to take into account include:

a) How will you address the increase in garbage and other wastes?

b) What will happen if the town council wants to add to your development plans 10 years from now?

c) How will your decisions affect the quality of the air, water, and land?

d) How will your decisions affect the number and health of existing plant and animal populations?

3 Design a two-dimensional or three-dimensional model of the piece of land. Use different colours or structures to represent the different land uses.

Share and Compare

4 When you have completed your plan, present it to the rest of your class. Be prepared to explain and, if necessary, defend your decisions.

Observations and Reflections

5 Look back at the criteria you developed at the start of the Project. Look also at the Impact Assessment Checklist. How well does your finished plan reflect all these criteria?

6 In your opinion, how well did your plan balance the needs of people and other living things? Be as specific as possible in your answer.

7 If you could redesign your land-use plan, what would you decide to do differently? Why?

Chapter Review

Using Key Terms

1 Create a mind map that illustrates your understanding of the following terms.

abiotic	food web
biotic	ecosystem
producers	succession
consumers	waste disposal
decomposers	recycling
food chain	human impact

Reviewing the Big Ideas

2 What is the difference between biotic and abiotic components in an ecosystem?

3 What are the basic requirements of all living things?

4 How are plants unique or different in the food chain? What makes them unique and different from animals and micro-organisms?

5 a) Give two examples of helpful microscopic organisms. Explain why they're helpful.

b) Give two examples of harmful microscopic organisms. Explain why they're harmful.

6 What are the two different types of consumers?

7 What are food chains and what is their purpose?

8 How is a food web different from a food chain?

9 Describe the difference between how matter and energy cycle through a food web.

10 Identify three ecosystems that you have walked through in the past few days. Explain how you know they are ecosystems.

11 Identify natural factors that can alter the living conditions in ecosystems.

12 What is succession ? Give an example.

13 Is a biome the same as an ecosystem's climax community?

14 Describe three types of human activities that can impact an ecosystem.

15 What is meant by the term bioinvasion? Give an example of how this can impact an ecosystem.

16 Describe other ways species can be displaced or lost besides bioinvasion.

17 What are some methods of removing the waste created from various technologies?

18 List two benefits and two drawbacks of using clear cutting.

Connecting the Big Ideas

19 a) Why would you expect to find each of the following in any ecosystem? Give reasons to support your answer.

- producers
- herbivores
- decomposers

b) Which group (or groups) of consumers is missing from part a) above? Why might it be possible for this group (or groups) to be absent from an ecosystem?

20 Listed below are four elements of ecosystems followed by six statements. Choose two of the statements. Take each chosen statement as a topic, and write a paragraph using the four elements of ecosystems.

- the role played by food webs
- the cycles of matter
- the flow of energy through ecosystems
- the interactions between living and non-living things

a) You sort your family's wastes into

recyclables and non-recyclables.

b) A concerned citizen is arrested for blocking a road to prevent loggers from cutting trees.

c) A food manufacturing company hires local villagers to remove rain forest vegetation so it can set up a ranch to raise beef cattle.

d) A government decides to build a water-powered electricity generating plant. To do so, it must build a dam to stockpile water. Building the dam means that thousands of hectares of meadows and villages will be flooded.

e) Several families move to an island that has lots of rare slow-moving animals and flightless birds. The families decide to bring their pet cats with them.

f) You plan to compost some of your family's food wastes. The compost will be used to fertilize a neighbourhood garden shared by everyone in your community.

21 a) Examine the food web.

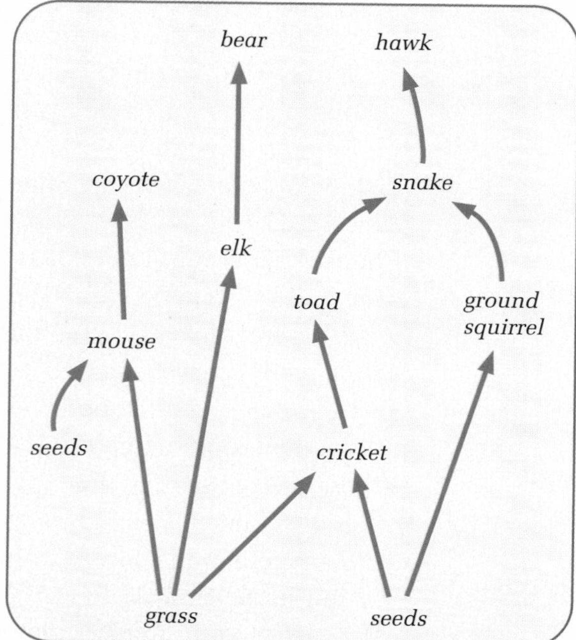

Design a chart to record the following:

- all the producers
- all the herbivorous consumers
- all the carnivorous consumers
- all the scavengers and decomposers

b) Where might this food web be located?

c) Add eight living things to your chart, including: two each of producers, herbivores, carnivores, and decomposers.

22 Look around your community. What evidence do you see of environmental problems caused by human activities? What evidence is there that your community is working to support living things and their living spaces?

23 How do you think technology has changed your community over the past 20 years? 50 years? In your opinion, have the changes been positive or negative? Give reasons to explain your ideas.

24 Should people in cities care about ecosystems that are far away from their lives? Give reasons to support your opinions.

Using the Big Ideas

25 Sketch or draw a scene showing a part of any ecosystem you choose. This ecosystem can be as near as your schoolyard or front lawn or as far away as another country or continent.

a) Include all the abiotic and biotic components that you think are important. Add labels to identify all the features that you've included and the reason why you included them. Remember, you must include yourself in this ecosystem.

b) What do you and other living things need to survive?
c) How do living things depend on one another, and why?

26 In 1944, soldiers from the U.S. Army moved a herd of 29 reindeer to a remote island in the Arctic. Then the soldiers left. The only other consumers on this island were arctic foxes and voles (voles are mouse-like animals). There were numerous producers including grasses and plant-like living things called lichens, which reindeer love to eat.

In 1957, scientists visited the island. They discovered that the number of reindeer had increased to 1350. They also observed that there were fewer producers on the island. However, there were still plenty for the reindeer to feed on.

In 1963, scientists visited again. The reindeer now numbered 6000. The producers were nearly gone. One year later, when scientists arrived once more, they discovered that most of the reindeer had died. Only 42 remained.

a) Sketch a food web to show how you think the biotic components of this island ecosystem were related.
b) What you think happened to the reindeer, and why?
c) What abiotic or biotic conditions might have led to a different ending to this story? Explain your answer.

27 Is a city an ecosystem? Why or why not?

28 A population of noisy crows has moved into your neighbourhood. They're chasing away the local birds, and their wastes are fouling the streets and rooftops. Which of the following actions would you support, and why?
a) Spray the area with a powerful chemical that's known to kill crows.
b) Leave the crows alone and put up with the inconvenience.
c) Hire a company to catch the crows and move them to another area.

29 Use the data in the chart on the next page to answer the following questions.
a) Which activities probably have a positive impact on ecosystems? Which probably have a negative impact?
b) In which cases did Ontarians perform "better" than the rest of Canada? Suggest a reason that could explain this.
c) In which cases did Ontarians perform "worse" than the rest of Canada? Suggest a reason that could explain this.
d) How would your family rate against the Ontario data? against the Canadian data?
e) The data in this chart were collected in 1994. If a new survey were done today, how do you think the results would be different? Why?

Household Environmental Practices (1994) Percent of Households		
	Canada	**Ontario**
Recycling Programs Available		
paper	69.6	83.5
metal cans	67.2	82.3
glass bottles	67.4	82.0
plastics	62.8	77.7
Uses Recycling Programs		
paper	83.1	92.4
metal cans	83.5	93.3
glass bottles	83.5	93.3
plastics	81.7	92.2
Uses Disposable Diapers		
all of the time	76.9	79.0
most of the time	9.5	7.6
sometimes	11.1	11.3
never	2.0	2.1
Other Environmental Practices		
regularly purchases paper towels and toilet paper made from recycled paper	58.3	59.9
regularly takes own bag when shopping	24.4	25.4
composts plant and food wastes	22.7	30.3
uses chemical pesticides	31.1	34.3
uses chemical fertilizer	46.8	50.7
Principle Method of Travel to Work		
public transport	13.7	16.3
motor vehicle as driver	78.8	79.7
motor vehicle as passenger	10.6	10.0
bicycle	2.3	1.9
walk only	7.8	6.3

(Source: 1998 Statistics Canada)

Self Assessment

28 Look back on the work you did during the course of this chapter. Identify one piece of work you feel you worked hard on, one piece of work you are most proud of, and one piece of work that you think you could do better next time. Explain why you chose each one.

Chapter 2

MIXTURES

solvent

Everything is made of matter: from cars to sinks, hairbrushes to fingernails. Matter is everything that you can see, touch, smell, breathe, and eat. You use it, eat it, live in it, and breathe it. In fact you are matter! However, matter is not all the same. It can be a pure substance or a mixture of different kinds of substances. Some mixtures are mechanical mixtures while others are solutions.

In this chapter, you will investigate the different kinds of matter, especially matter that makes up mixtures. You will learn how to distinguish between different kinds of mixtures and how to separate mixtures into pure substances. You will do many activities to help you understand and explore different mixtures.

BIG Ideas

unsaturated

1.0 The amount of matter is measured in two ways: volume and mass.

2.0 Mixtures can be classified into two types: mechanical mixtures and solutions.

3.0 Components of mechanical mixtures and solutions can be separated.

4.0 All matter is made up of tiny particles.

5.0 Solutions are used in a variety of technological situations.

6.0 Water, the universal solvent, must be used responsibly.

7.0 Mixtures of raw materials can be processed to make useful things.

distillation

Invitation to Explore

Sick of seeing stains in your sink?
Grossed out by grimy grease?
New!
NOW, Spit & Polish IS HERE!
Guaranteed to dissolve all stains and to power away grease.
Just rinse with water!
All your dirt and cares will go down the drain and out of your life forever.
New! Spit & Polish
HOUSEHOLD CLEANER
THE ALL PURPOSE CLEANER
Guaranteed to dissolve all stains and to power away grease.
Just rinse with water!
All your dirt and cares will go down the drain and out of your life forever.
Brought to you by the makers of Elbow Grease.
The dirt does the disappearing because we do the dissolving!

According to this advertisement, the cleaner will dissolve dirt and grease. How do cleaners work and why can they get rid of grease? Why can't this kind of dirt be cleaned away with plain old water? The advertisement claims that the cleaner, plus water, will rinse away dirt forever. Is it true that once you rinse water down the drain, you never see it again?

MIX IT UP

In this activity, you will investigate the characteristics and interactions of pure substances and mixtures. You will also be developing your laboratory skills by using a variety of scientific equipment.

Work in groups to observe the interactions between various types of matter. There will be eight stations to visit. The order you visit the stations is not important. At each station, carefully observe what happens.

Here are some of the materials you will use:

- test tubes to hold the various materials
- a test-tube rack to hold the test tubes upright
- rubber stoppers to seal the test tubes
- stirring rods to stir the different materials
- measuring spoons to place the solid into the liquid in the test tube

Procedure

Follow the same procedure at stations 1 to 6. At stations 7 and 8, the procedures are slightly changed.

1. Pour the liquid into a clean test tube to a depth of three fingers (about 10 mL).
2. Using a clean measuring spoon, add one scoop of the solid to the liquid in the test tube.
3. Put the stopper in the test tube. Hold the stopper with your thumb, turn the tube upside down, and shake it.
4. Record what you observe at each station in a chart.
5. Make sure you wash your test tube and spoon before leaving each station. Place the test tube upside down in the rack to dry.

Stations

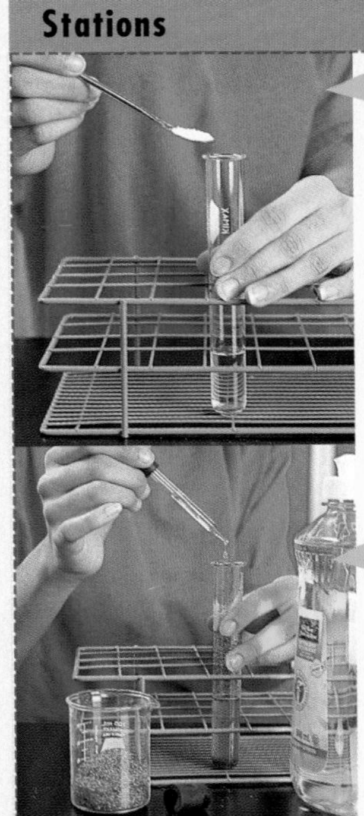

1. *Mix salt with room-temperature water.*
2. *Mix sugar with room-temperature vinegar.*
3. *Crush an antacid tablet into powder. Mix the powder with room-temperature water.*
4. *Mix pepper with room-temperature water, then add a drop of dish soap.*
5. *Mix flour with room-temperature water.*

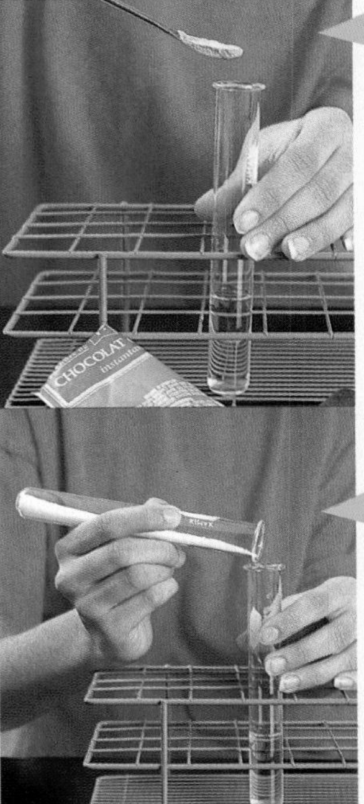

6. *Mix one scoop of dry chocolate powder with room-temperature water. Next, mix another scoop of the powder with hot water.*
7. *Prepare two test tubes, one with cold water and one with hot water. Add some juice crystals to each test tube. Don't shake!*
8. *Prepare two test tubes in a rack, one half full of sugar, one half full of hot water. Carefully add all the sugar to the water, stirring with the stirring rod as you do. Do you end up with a full test tube?*

continued on next page

2 MIXTURES

Questions

Look over your observations and notes before you answer the following questions:

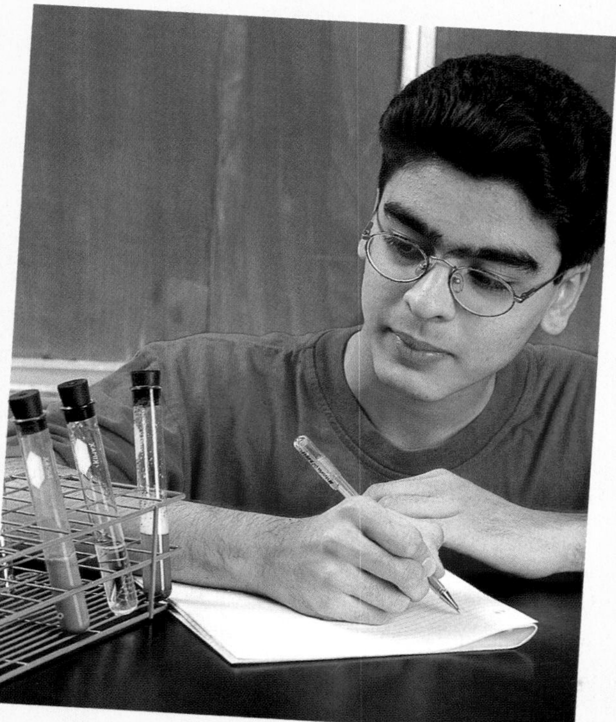

1 In which cases did the solid totally disappear, leaving a clear liquid? What do you think happened to the solid in these cases? Did it disappear or leave the liquid? How do you know?
2 In which cases can you still see the solid in the liquid? Why do you think it didn't disappear?
3 Did the solids react in one way in the hot water and differently in the cold water? If they did, can you explain why?
4 In which case did a chemical reaction take place between a solid and water? How do you know?
5 Did the half test tube of sugar and half test tube of water add up to one full test tube? Explain what you think happened.

Focus Your Thoughts

1 Match the following words with the best description: solid, liquid, gas, **physical change**, **chemical change**.
   a) combination of two or more materials into a new material
   b) ice
   c) ripping a piece of paper into small pieces
   d) soda pop
   e) a person breathing air
2 Is the advertisement at the beginning of this chapter true or is it misleading? The ad states that Spit and Polish will dissolve stains and make grease disappear. Describe a method you could use to prove or disprove the claims of this ad.
3 Give an example or description for these words:
   a) mixture
   b) solution
   c) pure substance

BIG IDEA 1.0

The amount of matter is measured in two ways: volume and mass.

Think about what you did this morning. You probably got up, brushed your teeth with toothpaste, had a glass of juice or milk, and maybe made yourself a bowl of cereal with milk on it. In other words, you used, drank, and prepared various mixtures. And that was just this morning! You are constantly coming into contact with mixtures. But how do you measure the amount of your mixtures?

1.1 MEASURING VOLUME

Explore

If you have ever made a cake or cooked something from a recipe, you will know that sometimes you need to add a certain amount of liquid, such as water, milk, or vegetable oil. What type of measuring device did you use? You may have used a spoon or cup that holds a particular amount of liquid. This amount of liquid is called the **volume** of liquid. A milk carton is an example of a container that comes in several common volumes, such as 250 mL (millilitres), 500 mL, or 1 L (litre).

Measuring volume is an important skill to develop. This skill will help you in future activities both in and out of science class. In the next Investigator activity, you will be using a long cylindrical container called a **graduated cylinder** to measure volume. When you get your equipment, look at the side of the cylinder. What do the numbers along the side represent? Why are there so many little lines between each of the numbers?

*info***BIT**

The volumes of solids and gases can also be measured. A solid sugar cube has a volume of about 1 cm^3 (read as "one cubic centimetre").

Develop

Using a Graduated Cylinder to Measure Volume

In the next activity, you will learn to read a graduated cylinder to measure volume accurately.

INVESTIGATOR

2 MIXTURES

What's the Volume?

The Question

How do you accurately measure volume?

Materials & Equipment

- *water*
- *2 100-mL graduated cylinders*

Procedure

1 Predict what measurement you would get if you added 40 mL of water to 40 mL of water.

2 Pour 40 mL of water into a graduated cylinder. Be sure to read the measurement at the lowest part of the curved surface of the water, which is called the **meniscus**. Make sure that your eye is directly opposite this curve.

3 Pour 40 mL of water into another graduated cylinder. Again, remember to read the volume at the lowest part of the meniscus.

4 What volume would you get if you combined the two 40 mL volumes of water?

5 Add the contents of the first graduated cylinder to the second graduated cylinder. Read the resulting volume.

6 Try steps 1 to 5 using varying amounts of water: 20 mL and 60 mL; 30 mL and 50 mL.

Keeping Records

7 Record your observations and include a diagram of what a meniscus looks like.

Analyzing and Interpreting

8 How did your predictions compare with the actual results?

9 What happened to the total volume when you mixed the different amounts of water?

10 How accurately do you feel you can measure the volume of a liquid in a graduated cylinder?

Forming Conclusions

11 Describe the steps that are necessary to make accurate measurements of volume.

Communicate

1 Why must you read the volume of liquid from the bottom of the meniscus?

2 What is a common measurement unit for volume?

3 What are two other devices that can be used to measure volume?

1.2 Science Safety in the Class

Explore

Before you begin your study of what mixtures are, there are some safety rules and basic lab skills you need to develop. The illustration below shows a science class performing an experiment. Unfortunately, some of the students are not following proper safety procedures. Work with a partner to identify as many inappropriate actions as you can. After you identify them, suggest a better, safer way to perform each action. After you have finished, share your observations with the class.

Develop

Laboratory Rules and Safety

You will be doing many activities in this chapter. A "Caution!" note will tell you if you need to take special care. Are there any other lab safety rules you would add for your own protection and that of your classmates? Are there any rules for behaviour in the lab that must be followed? Following are important lab safety rules. (See also Toolbox 1 at the back of this book.)

*info*BIT

Household Warning Labels

Warning — Corrosive

Danger — Poison

Caution — Flammable

Caution — Explosive

Lab Safety Rules

1. Read all written instructions before doing an activity.
2. Listen to all instructions and follow them carefully.
3. Wash your hands carefully after each activity and after handling chemicals.
4. Wear gloves, an apron, or safety goggles as required.
5. Think before you touch. Equipment may be hot and substances may be dangerous.
6. Smell a substance by fanning the smell toward you with your hand. Do not put your nose close to the substance.
7. Do not taste anything in the lab.
8. Tie back loose hair and roll up your sleeves.
9. Never pour liquids into containers held in your hand. Place a test tube in a rack before pouring substances in it.
10. Clean up any spilled substances immediately as instructed by your teacher.
11. Never look into test tubes or containers from the top. Always look through the sides.
12. Never use cracked or broken glassware. Make sure you follow your teacher's instructions when getting rid of any broken glass.
13. Label any container you put chemicals in.
14. Report all accidents and spills immediately to your teacher.
15. If there are **WHMIS** (Workplace Hazardous Materials Information System) safety symbols on any chemical you will be using, make sure that you understand all the symbols. See Toolbox 1 at the back of this book.

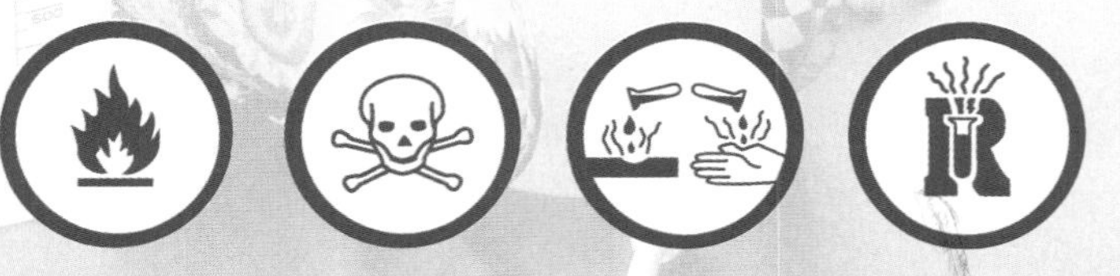

Communicate

1. Which of the safety rules did you already know? Which ones were new to you?
2. Make a chart of WHMIS symbols. For each symbol, list two or three substances or items for which the symbol applies (flammable: fireworks, gasoline, etc.).

1.3 Measuring Mass

All objects contain matter and are said to have **mass**. You have mass, your pencil has mass, even air has mass. Mass is commonly measured in kilograms and grams. A chicken egg has a mass of about 60 g. A thumbtack has a mass of about 1 g and an average North American person has a mass of about 68 kg.

Measuring mass is an important skill for many scientific activities. What are some of the ways of measuring mass that you know of? How would you measure your own mass? How would you find the mass of a big truck? What about the mass of the earth? All these objects can be measured in a variety of ways. In the next Investigator activity, you will estimate and then measure the mass of a variety of objects.

Finding the Mass of Common Substances

In the next investigation, you'll be using a triple beam or electronic balance to determine the mass of a variety of objects.

infoBIT

The mass of the earth is 6×10^{24} kg. This is written out in full as the number six with 24 zeros after it.
6 000 000 000 000 000 000 000 000 kg

2 MIXTURES

INVESTIGATOR

What's the Mass?

The Question

How accurately can you measure the mass of solids and liquids?

Materials & Equipment

- *100-mL beaker*
- *graduated cylinder*
- *variety of objects of different masses*
- *triple beam or electronic balance*
- *paper*
- *sugar or salt*
- *water*
- *vinegar*

Procedure

1. Make a prediction about what the mass of each object is. Record your estimates.
2. Use the balance to measure the mass of each object.
3. To measure the mass of sugar or salt, take a piece of paper and fold it so that there is a trough in the middle. Find the mass of the paper. Add the substance slowly to the paper. Record the mass of the paper and the substance. How do you find the mass of the substance alone?
4. To measure the mass of water, first find the mass of an empty beaker. (Make sure that it is dry.) Using a graduated cylinder, add 10 mL of water to the beaker. Find the total mass of the beaker with the water.

continued on next page

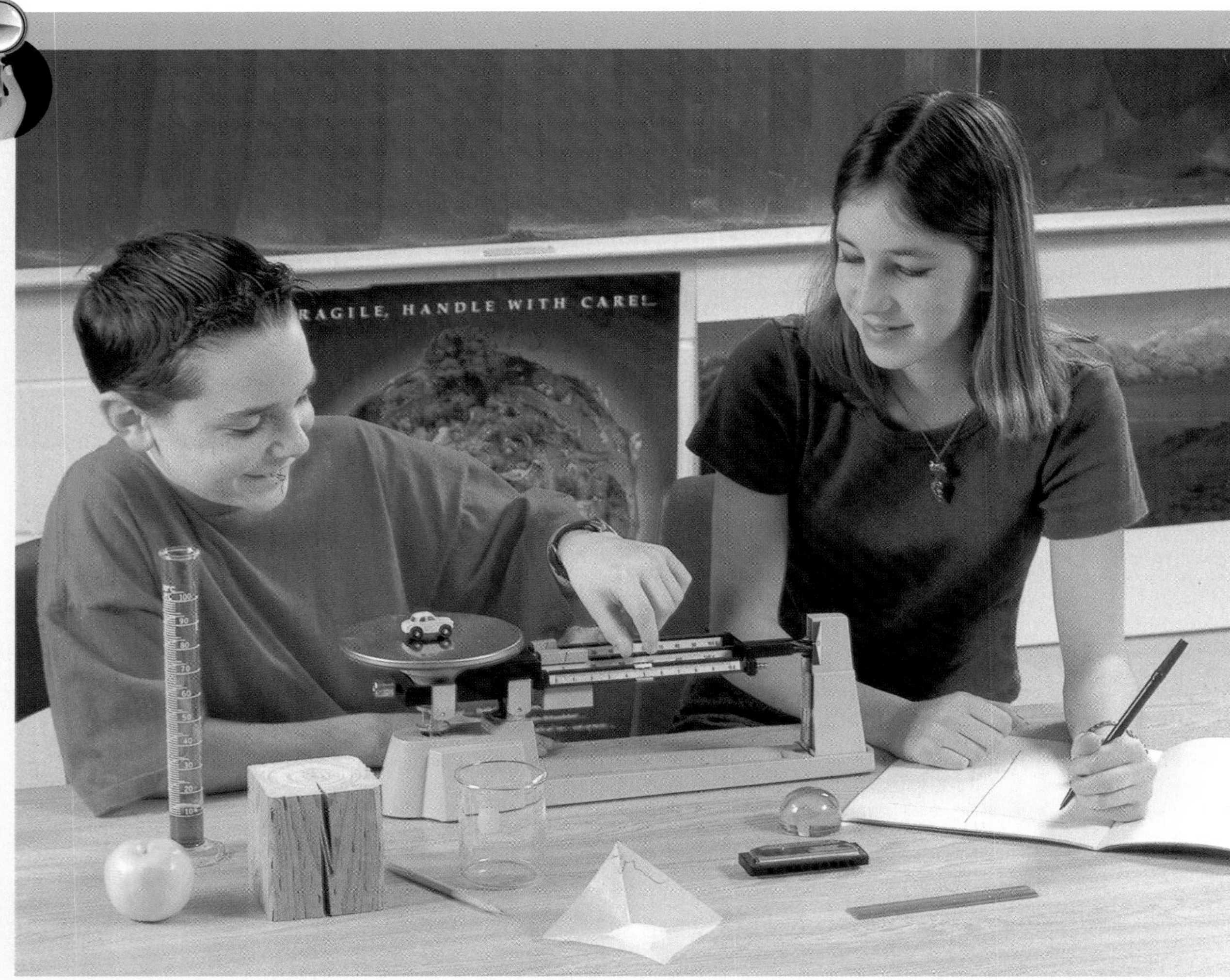

5 How could you measure the mass of 10 mL of vinegar?

Keeping Records

6 Write down your measurements in a table.

Analyzing and Interpreting

7 Why did you have to include the mass of the paper when you were measuring the mass of the substance?

8 Why did you have to include the mass of the beaker when measuring the mass of the water?

9 What is the mass of 10 mL of water?

Forming Conclusions

10 Describe the differences between the process of measuring the mass of a solid and the mass of a liquid.

You now have an understanding of volume and mass. In the next activity, you will investigate how they can be related when mixing certain substances.

PROBLEM SOLVER

THE VOLUME AND MASS MIX-UP

What happens to the volume and mass of substances when they are mixed together? For example, suppose you were to add 25 g of sugar to 200 g of warm water (40°C). If you then measured the mass of this sugar and water mixture, would it equal 225 g? Why not find out?

Procedure

- Plan an investigation where you add a certain mass of sugar to a mass of warm, 40°C water.
- Be careful to make the correct measurement before and after mixing.
- Repeat your experiment, keeping your variables constant.

Questions

- What happens to the total mass when you add the sugar to the water?
- What happens to the total volume?
- What conclusions can you make about combining sugar and water?
- What questions do you have that can't be answered by your conclusions?

Communicate

1 What is the difference between mass and volume?
2 Why is cereal sold by mass and not by volume?
3 Can you think of a faster way to determine the mass of a given volume of water than the way described in the Investigator activity?

1.4 CHECK YOUR PROGRESS

1 Describe how you make a measurement of an unknown volume of liquid.
2 What labels would you expect to find on containers of the following materials?
   a) smoke detector
   b) bleach
   c) paint thinner
   d) unknown bacteria
3 Describe the process for getting rid of broken glass in your class.
4 What protective measures must be taken when working around an open flame?
5 Explain how measuring the mass of a solid is different from measuring the mass of a liquid.

*info*BIT

Here is a riddle: *Is it possible for you to lift two times your body weight?* The answer: *Yes. If you were to lift that weight on the moon, it would definitely be possible!*

- The moon's force of gravity is about 1/6 that of the earth's. Can you explain the answer to the riddle?

Big Idea

2.0 Mixtures can be classified into two types: mechanical mixtures and solutions.

2 MIXTURES

In the last section, you studied some of the basic skills needed to determine the volume and mass of substances. You have also reviewed how to conduct safe experiments. In this section, you will investigate ways to classify matter. You will also explore the differences between pure substances and various types of mixtures.

Look at the items pictured on this page. Every one is made up of matter.

2.1 What's Matter?

Explore

All the pictures have at least one thing in common. They are examples of **matter**. Could you identify which examples are solids, liquids, or gases? There is another way, however, that scientists classify matter. Take a look at the following diagram.

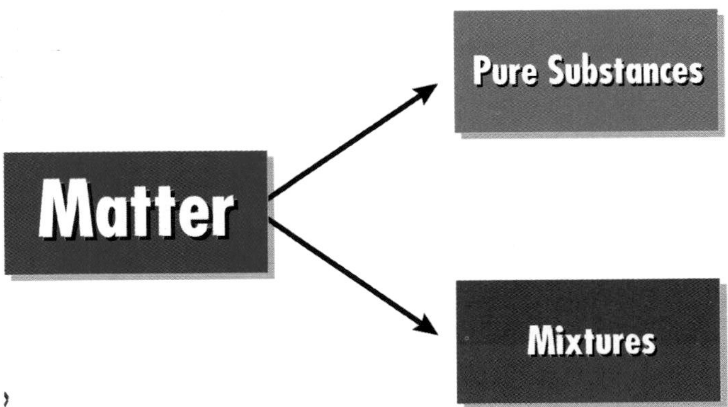

All matter is either a pure substance or a mixture. A **pure substance**, such as sugar, has only one kind of matter in it. A **mixture**, like soil, is a combination of different substances.

Go on an identifying mission.

- Look around your classroom or home and identify twenty of the most interesting things you can see. Try to find a variety of solids, liquids, and gases if you can.
- Classify each thing as either a pure substance or a mixture. Make a third grouping for materials that you are not sure about.
- Write down your observations. Compare your results with those of your classmates and discuss any differences.
- Could you tell the pure substances and mixtures apart? How?
- Which were the hardest things to classify?
- Were there some things that did not seem to you to be either a pure substance or a mixture?

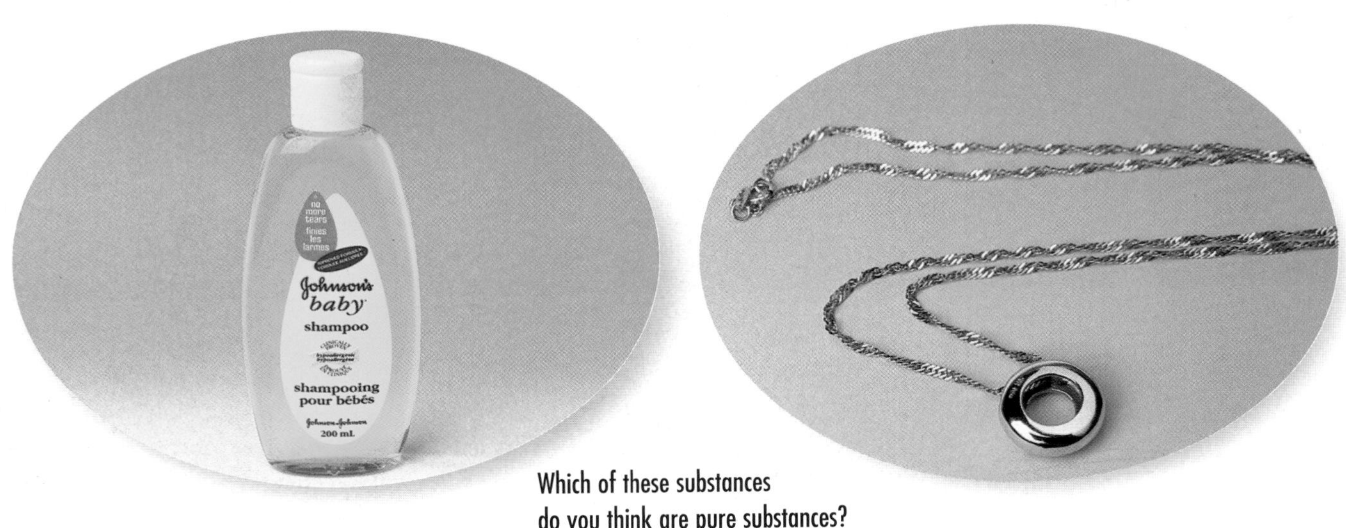

Which of these substances do you think are pure substances?

Develop

Examining How Matter is Classified

Look at the list of items that you identified as being pure substances. You may have listed a copper penny as being a pure substance. You would probably be correct, because copper pennies minted before 1997 are made up of just one substance, copper. Other common pure substances include sugar, water, salt, aluminium, and oxygen gas.

Pure Substances

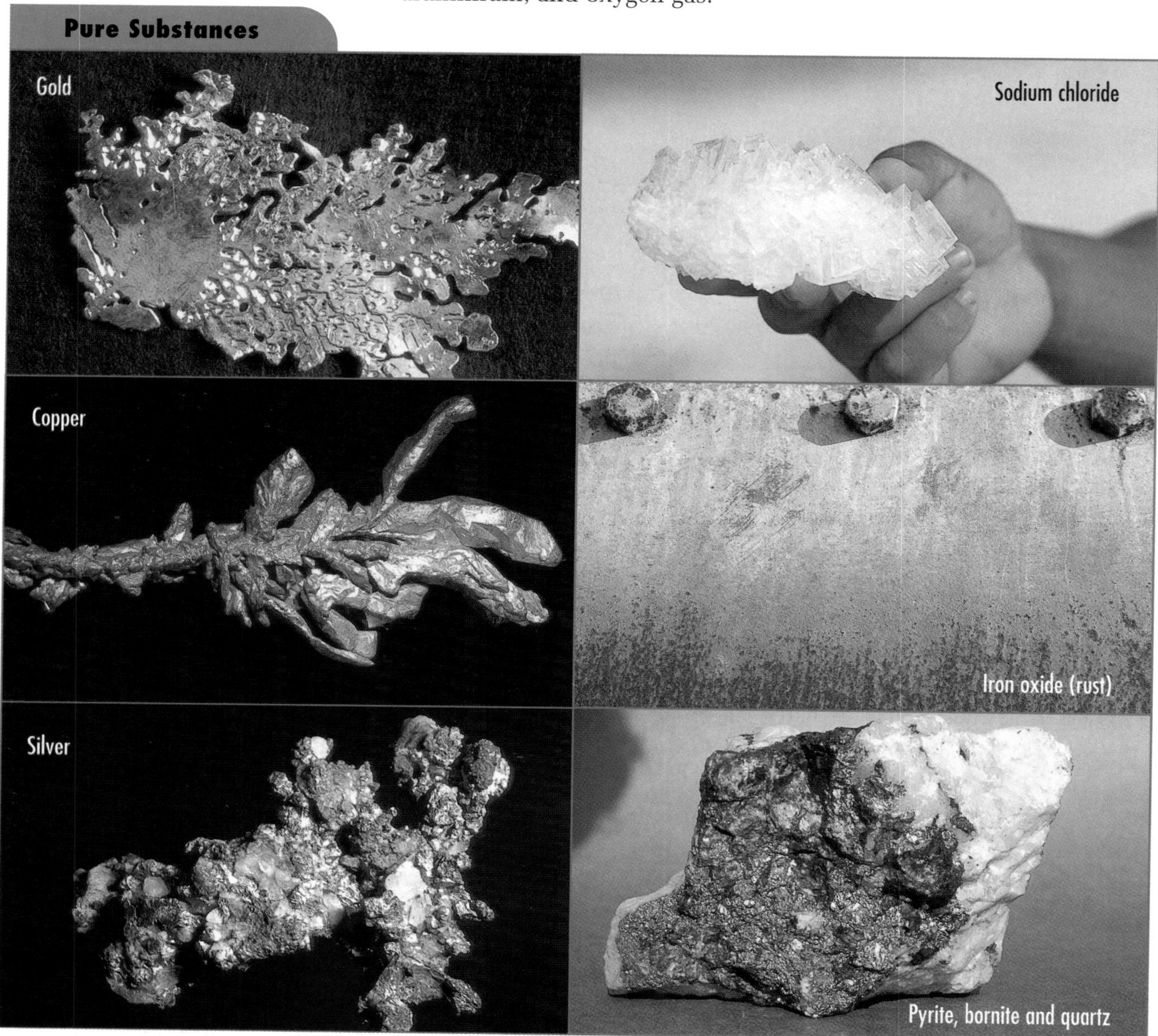

Mixtures

Look at the list of items that you identified as being mixtures. Can you classify these items further? There are two common classifications for mixtures—mechanical mixtures and solutions.

In a **mechanical mixture**, you can see all the different parts. Soil is a mechanical mixture. Sometimes this type of mixture is also called a **heterogeneous mixture**. There are other mixtures, such as vinegar, in which you cannot see the different parts. These mixtures are called **solutions**. A solution is a **homogeneous mixture**. As you will see, it is not easy to tell a solution from a pure substance.

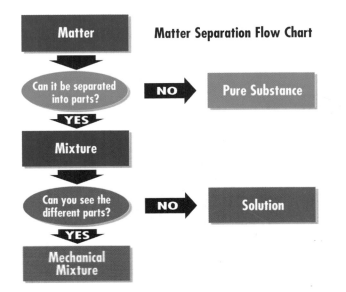

*info*BIT

Heterogeneous means made up of dissimilar, or varied, parts. A heterogeneous mixture does not have a uniform composition.

Homogeneous means made up of similar parts. A homogeneous mixture has the same composition throughout.

Matter Separation Flow Chart

Matter

Can it be separated into parts? → NO → Pure Substance

YES

Mixture

Can you see the different parts? → NO → Solution

YES

Mechanical Mixture

Communicate

1. What is the difference between a mixture and a pure substance?
2. What substances do you think are used in this airplane?
3. How can you tell the difference between a heterogeneous mixture and a homogeneous mixture?
4. Below are some pictures of various examples of matter. Create a flowchart that could be used to classify the examples as either a heterogeneous mixture, a homogenous mixture, or a pure substance.

2.2 Getting the Right Mix

Explore

You can probably think of some examples of mechanical mixtures made from solids mixed with other solids and solids mixed with liquids. What other kinds of mechanical mixtures are possible? Why are each of the following pictures called a mixture?

Mechanical Mixtures

Develop

Creating a Mechanical Mixture

Now it's your chance to try to create a mechanical mixture using two liquids.

PROBLEM SOLVER

FLOATING COLOURS

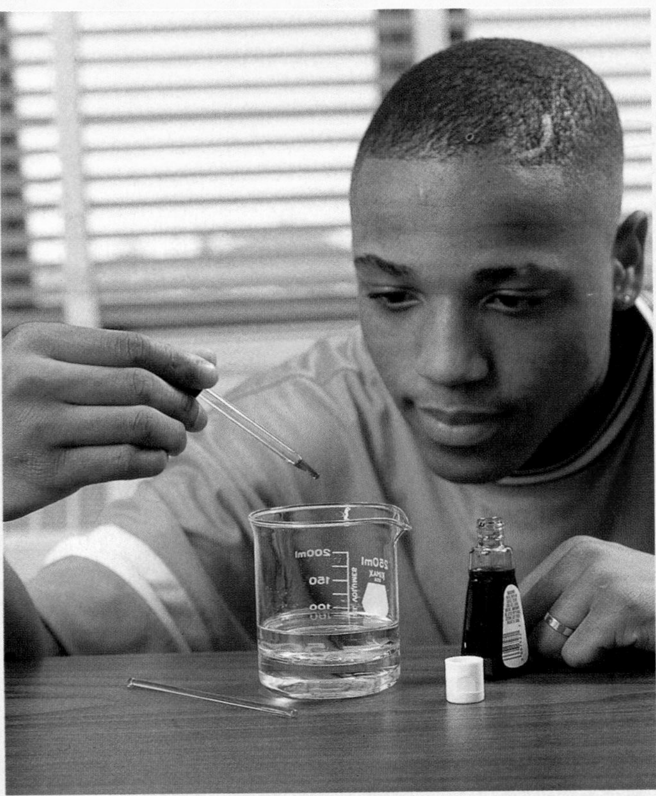

Can you make a mechanical mixture using two liquids?

1 Add 25 mL of water to a small beaker or test tube. Slowly add 25 mL of oil to the water.
2 Add 3 drops of food colouring to the beaker. Look at the beaker at eye level. What happens to the food colouring?
3 Push the drops of food colouring through the oil layer to the water layer using a stirring rod, spoon, or pencil. Watch what happens to the food colouring.
   a) Was the mixture that you produced a mechanical mixture? Why or why not?
   b) What happened to the food colouring when it reached the water?
4 Add a few drops of detergent to your mixture. Stir well. What happens to your mixture?

Communicate

1 a) Explain the difference between a mechanical mixture and a solution.
   b) How is a pure substance different from a mechanical mixture or a solution?
2 Give an example of a mechanical mixture made up of:
   a) two or more liquids
   b) two or more solids
   c) solids and gases
   d) a liquid and a solid
3 Is soda pop a mechanical mixture or a solution? Explain your answer.

2.3 Solutions

Explore

Drink a glass of juice or a can of pop. Think of the blood circulating through your veins or the air pumping through your lungs. While these two ideas are very different, they have one thing in common—they involve mixtures called solutions. Solutions are created when two or more substances are mixed together, just as a mechanical mixture is. However, a solution looks like only one substance. In the next activity, you will look at the ink in a marker pen and decide if it's a solution. Look back at your list of 20 things that you made in section 2.1. Are any of them solutions? Were some of the things you had trouble classifying solutions?

The pictures on the next page all appear to show a liquid, but is each a mixture or a pure substance? Which one is a pure substance? Is there any way you could test your guess to find out if you're right? Share and compare your ideas with your classmates.

*info*BIT

What's in Some Solutions and Common Mixtures?

Shampoo is a solution. It contains some form of *lauryl sulphate,* a gentle soap to clean your hair. Other common ingredients are: *lecithin* to give you shiny hair, *lauramide DEA* to give lots of suds, *animal protein* to fix split ends, and *glycol stearate* to get rid of tangles.

Toothpaste is a solution that contains water, *sodium fluoride* to strengthen your teeth against cavities, and *silica* as an abrasive (like sandpaper) to clean your teeth.

Lipstick is a solution with more than 25 ingredients!

Nail polish is a solution of *colour particles* and *lacquer* (varnish) dissolved in either *acetone* or *ethyl acetate.* The acetone or ethyl acetate evaporates as your nail polish dries, leaving the lacquer and colour particles on your nails.

Cookie batter is a mixture of flour, sugar, eggs, butter, and water. It's not a solution, because if you look closely, you'll still see the grains of sugar and streaks of butter.

Pasta is a solution of flour and eggs in water.

Coffee and **tea** are both solutions of caffeine in water, along with many other natural chemicals. Coffee contains alcohol and acetone (used as nail polish remover) in very small quantities.

Which substances are mixtures? Which substances are solutions?

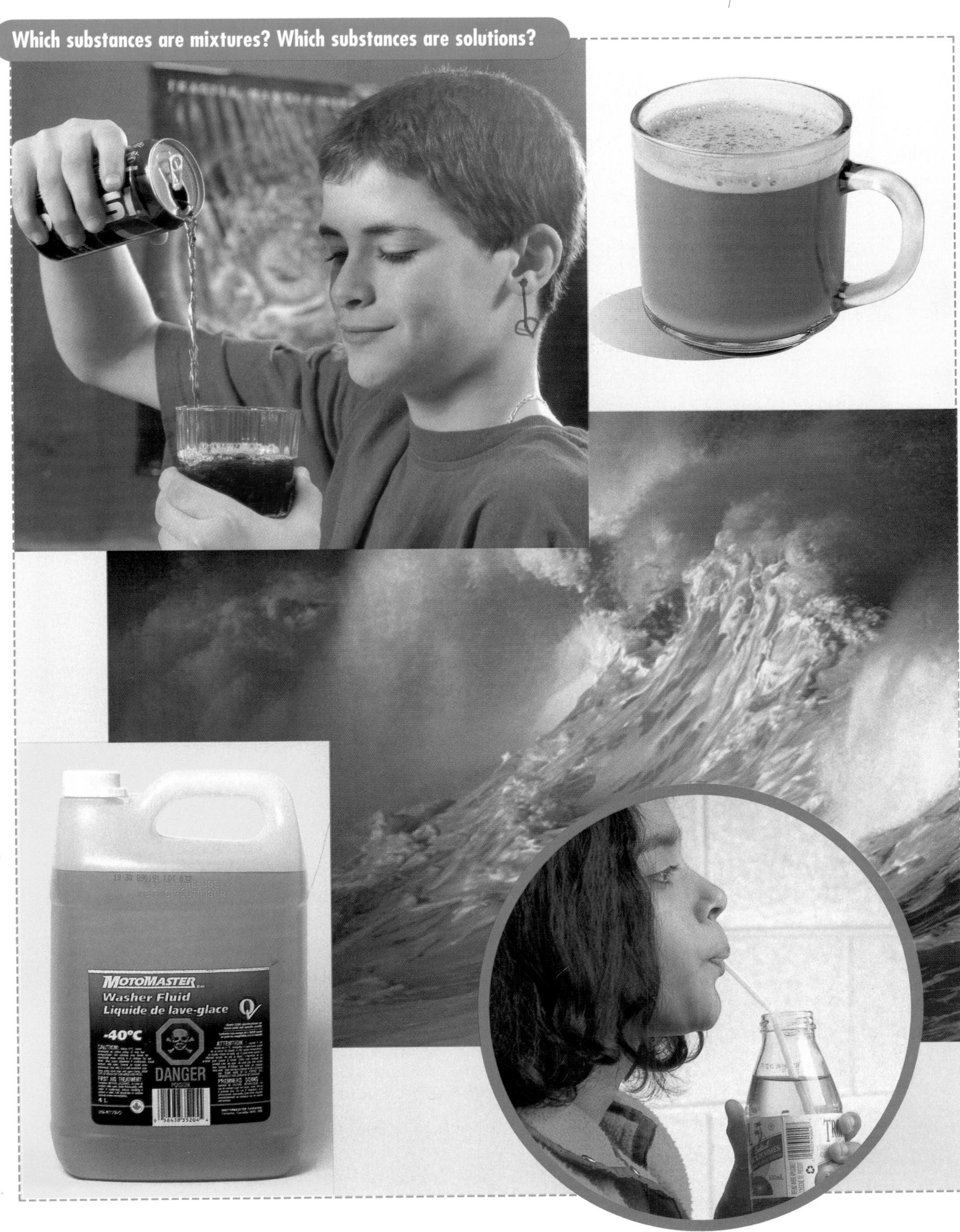

*info***BIT**

Chromatography comes from the Greek words for colour, *chroma*, and writing, *graphikos*. Chromatography means "writing in colours."

Develop

Paper Chromatography

One method of determining whether a liquid is a pure substance or a solution is to perform a **paper chromatography** test. You can observe the results very quickly—sometimes the outcomes are very interesting!

INVESTIGATOR

LOOKING FOR THE SOLUTION

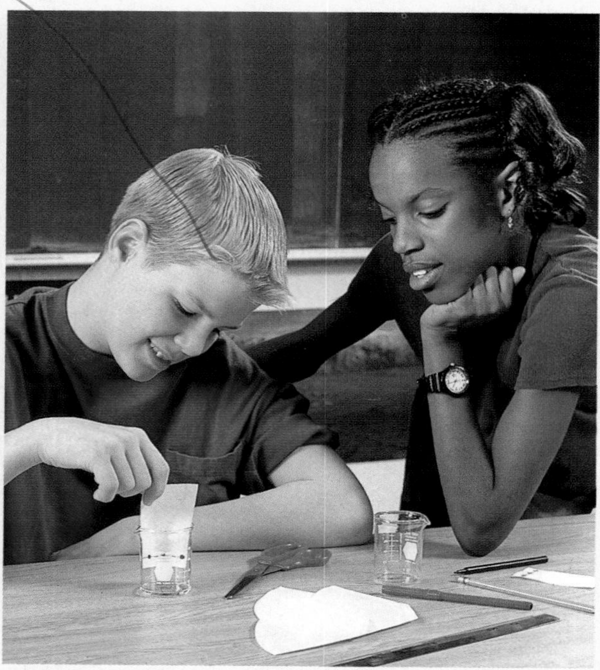

The Question

Is the black ink in a marker pen a pure substance or a solution?

Materials & Equipment

- *filter paper or coffee filters*
- *250-mL beaker*
- *black, water-soluble marker pens*
- *paper towels*
- *water*

Procedure

1. Cut a strip of filter paper to fit the width of a beaker.
2. Using a pencil, draw a horizontal line 1 cm from one end of the paper.
3. Pour some water into the beaker to a maximum depth of about 0.5 cm.
4. Put large dots of black ink on the filter paper along the horizontal line. Make sure that the dots aren't too close to each other.

continued on next page

5 Curve the paper so that it can stand up by itself in the beaker. Be sure the bottom edge is level with the bottom. The line of dots should be just above the water. *Do not* allow the water to touch the line of dots.

6 The water will move up the paper. When the colour reaches the top, take the paper out and place it on a towel. Allow it to dry.

Keeping Records

7 Record your observations. Be sure to include or draw your strip of paper. This is called a *chromatogram*.

Analyzing and Interpreting

8 What happened to the original colour of the black dot?

9 Why did the colour spread out?

10 Is the ink in a marker a solution or a pure substance? Why?

11 What would happen if you used coloured markers? Try it and find out.

Forming Conclusions

12 Explain what you think happened to the ink.

As you have seen, you can make a solution by dissolving one substance in another. The substance that dissolves is called the **solute**. The substance that does the dissolving is called the **solvent**.

try this at **HOME**

MAKING ROCK CANDY

Procedure

1 Bring 250 mL of water to a rolling boil and remove from stove. Very slowly add 500 mL of sugar. Stir until it is all dissolved.

2 Pour the sugar solution into a 500-mL glass jar. Cut a slit in a piece of paper and insert a piece of cotton string into the slit. Put the paper on the jar to cover it so that the string hangs into the jar and sugar solution.

3 Record your observations every day for a week. Then, pull out the string and dry what you have collected.

Questions

- What substance did you collect?
- What do you think happened to the sugar and water?
- Is the result a mixture or a solution?

Communicate

1 Which substance was the solute and which was the solvent in the Paper Chromatography Investigator activity?

2 What is the solute in a solution of fruit punch? What is the solvent?

3 What practical uses other than criminal investigations can you think of that would require chromatography?

*info***BIT**

Crime Stoppers

Crime investigators use chromatography to spot fake documents. In a recent case, a greedy man changed the dollar amount on a will from "$1000" to "$10000" by simply writing in an extra "0." By comparing the ink from the different digits, investigators determined that the ink from one of the zeros came from a different pen. The man was charged and convicted of forgery.

2.4 CHECK YOUR PROGRESS

1 Give an example of a pure substance. Why is it a pure substance?

2 What are some examples of mechanical mixtures? Why are they mechanical mixtures?

3 What is the definition of a solution?

4 The ink used in a pen is a solution. You know this from the Paper Chromatography Investigator activity. The different substances that made up the ink solution dissolved in the water and moved up the filter paper at different rates. Not all solutions are made by dissolving a solid solute in a liquid solvent. Some solutions can be made by dissolving a solid in another solid. For example, steel is made from a solution of hot, molten (liquid) carbon and molten iron, which then cools down to a solid.

a) Can you think of examples of solutions made by combining different states of matter? Make a chart like the one shown below, and fill it in with an example of each combination of substances.

Substance	Substance	Solution Made	Other Examples
solid	*liquid*	table syrup	
solid	*solid*	steel	
liquid	*liquid*	perfume	
liquid	*gas*	tap water	

b) Which combination of substances was the most difficult to think of as a solution?

c) Which combination was the easiest?

d) Can you identify the solute and the solvent for each of your examples?

e) In the example above, what gas do you think is dissolved in tap water? How could you prove your answer?

Careers and Profiles

Chocolate Maker

It's a job but somebody's got to do it! Imagine mixing big batches of chocolate liquor with milk, sugar, and cocoa butter. Naturally you'd have to taste the result at each stage to make sure the solution was just right. Well, that's what you would do if you were a chocolate maker. Chocolate treats are actually solutions. Different ingredients in the solutions determine the types of chocolate:

Chocolate Mixer

- **White Chocolate:** cocoa butter, milk, sugar
- **Semi-Sweet Chocolate or Dark Chocolate:** chocolate liquor, cocoa butter, sugar
- **Milk Chocolate:** chocolate liquor, cocoa butter, sugar, milk

Each ingredient has a job to do. Together, they make chocolate!

- Chocolate liquor is a dark brown liquid from the cocoa bean. It gives chocolate its rich taste.
- Cocoa butter also comes from the cocoa bean, but it is a yellow fat like butter. It makes chocolate melt at exactly the temperature of your mouth: 37°C.

Soft-Drink Manufacturer

Or why not start up a soft-drink company? First, you'll experiment with different combinations of water, sugar and flavourings to make a syrup. Flavours come from fruits and berries, as well as from tree bark, herbs, and roots. Once you've got exactly the right taste, this syrup will be your own secret formula! Soft-drink companies never, ever tell anyone their secret syrup formulas, so you'll have to make sure yours is locked up safely.

Next, you'll carefully purify the water for your drink. Then, you'll mix your secret syrup with the right amount of water. So far, your drink has been a solution, since the sugar and flavourings dissolve in water.

The last step is pumping your water and syrup solution into a machine called a carbonator. In this machine, carbon dioxide gas is mixed into your solution under very high pressure. Now your drink is a mixture of a gas and a liquid! The drink goes straight from the carbonator into the bottle or can, which is then sealed so the gas won't escape.

What's in a soft drink? There's lots of carbon dioxide gas, 86% extra-purified water, 10% sugar, and about 4% flavourings.

BIG IDEA

3.0 Components of mechanical mixtures and solutions can be separated.

Mechanical mixtures and solutions

What does the gasoline in your family's car have in common with your nylon jacket and a plastic chair? Well, all these substances came from a mixture that had been separated into its parts. The crude oil that is extracted from the ground is a mixture of many substances. Using a process called **fractional distillation**, these substances, which include gasoline and petrochemicals (used to make nylon and other plastics), are separated. As you can see, it is sometimes important to be able to separate mixtures. But you would not expect to use the same method to separate gold from rocks as you would to separate salt from water. Or would you?

3.1 SEPARATING MECHANICAL MIXTURES

Explore

Knowing that something is a mixture is only half of the story. Sometimes you start with a mixture, but you want the separate parts within it. So how can you separate a mixture? First, you need to know how the parts are different from each other. Then, you have to figure out a way to use those differences to separate the mixture.

Examine the photos on this page and brainstorm the ways you could separate the mixtures. Think about the properties of the substances. How are they different? Can you use these differences to separate the mixture? Would you expect to use a different method to separate a mechanical mixture than you would use to separate a solution?

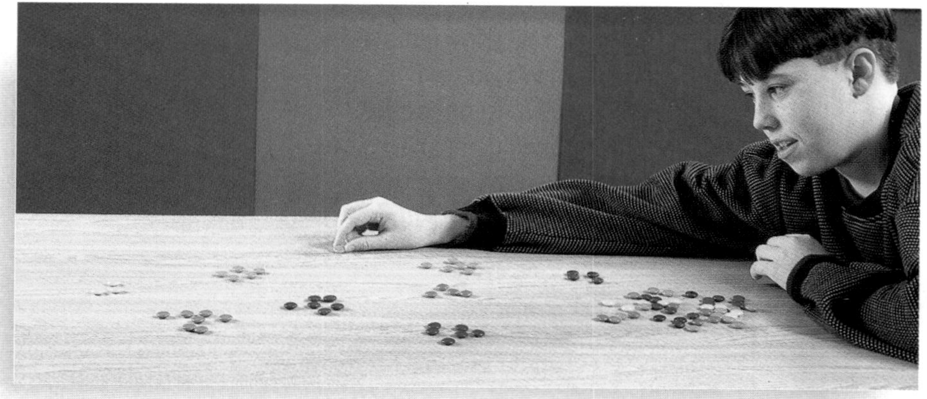

Develop

Investigating Techniques for Separating Mechanical Mixtures

Have you ever opened a box of different coloured candies and picked out, say, the red ones to eat last? By choosing one colour of the candies from the variety of colours, you are separating a mechanical mixture.

Of course not all mechanical mixtures can be separated by colour. Some mixtures are separated by using the differences in the size of their parts.

In the late 1800s, farmers in Canada separated the wheat kernels from the chaff (husks) by winnowing. When the mixture was thrown up into the air, the heavier kernels fell to the ground while the lighter chaff was blown away by the wind. This method is still used today in some parts of the world.

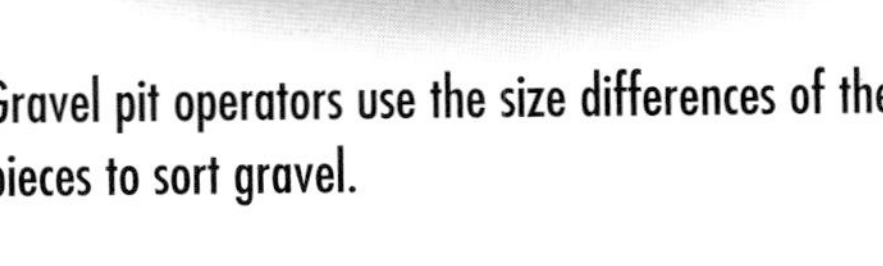

Gravel pit operators use the size differences of the pieces to sort gravel.

Separating a Magnetic Mixture

You can sometimes use one or more properties of the substances in a mixture to separate that substance out. In the next Investigator activity, you will use the property of magnetism to separate a mechanical mixture.

*info*BIT

In many recycling depots, old tin cans are separated from the rest of the garbage using a large electromagnet. The magnet latches onto the cans, but leaves the non-magnetic materials like aluminum, glass, and plastic behind.

INVESTIGATOR

2 MIXTURES

An Attractive Separation

Materials & Equipment

- *magnet*
- *iron filings*
- *sand*
- *paper*
- *containers*

The Question

How can you separate a mixture when one of its components is attracted to a magnetic substance?

Procedure

1 Mix the sand and iron filings together in a container.

2 Wrap the magnet in paper.

3 How can you use the magnet to separate this mixture?

Keeping Records

4 Write your observations in your Science Journal.

Analyzing and Interpreting

5 Why did the iron filings become separated from the sand?

6 If you didn't wrap the magnet in paper, how could you get the iron filings off the magnet?

Forming Conclusions

7 Describe what other kinds of mechanical mixtures could be separated using a magnet.

Separating a Mixture by Filtration

Air often contains dust particles. It is, therefore, a mixture of different gases and dust. Dust can irritate your nose, throat, and lungs. It can even cause damage to car engines. This explains why a car's engine has several **filters**. In the next activity, you will look at how **filtration** can separate a mechanical mixture.

INVESTIGATOR

Separating Out the Small Stuff

The Question

How can you separate sand from water?

Materials & Equipment

- *2 250-mL beakers*
- *graduated cylinder*
- *water*
- *25 mL sand*
- *filter paper (or coffee filters)*
- *funnel*
- *wash bottle*

Procedure

1. Place 100 mL of water in one beaker.
2. Add 25 mL of sand to the water in the beaker.
3. Place a filter paper cone in a funnel and place the funnel in an empty beaker.
4. Pour the sand and water mixture through the filter paper. Use the wash bottle to wash any remaining sand out of the beaker.

Keeping Records

5. Look at the filter paper and record your observations.

Analyzing and Interpreting

6. What happened to the sand and water mixture when it was poured into the filter paper? Why did this happen?

Forming Conclusions

7. Describe the process of separating a mixture using filtration.

Two Categories of Separating Mixtures

Think about how you would separate harmful weeds from a field of grass. You would probably choose a method that would destroy the weeds and leave the grass.

- Any method that separates a mechanical mixture by destroying one of its parts is called a *destructive method* of separation.
- A *non-destructive method* of separation is used when a mechanical mixture is separated and all the parts are recovered.

Communicate

1. Describe some possible ways of separating a mechanical mixture.
2. Could you use the filtration method to separate a sugar-water solution? Why or why not?

3.2 Separating Solutions

Explore

Think about a big stack of fluffy pancakes covered with real maple syrup. Have you ever wondered how the maple syrup was produced? The syrup is the result of separating a solution of sugar and water, by boiling off the water.

The sap from a sugar maple tree is about 2.5%–3% sugar. It is collected by tapping the trees with plastic pipe. Then it is boiled in an evaporator, which boils off the water. What is left is a sweet syrup that is 66.5% sugar (115 L to 190 L of sap reduces to about 3.8 L of syrup).

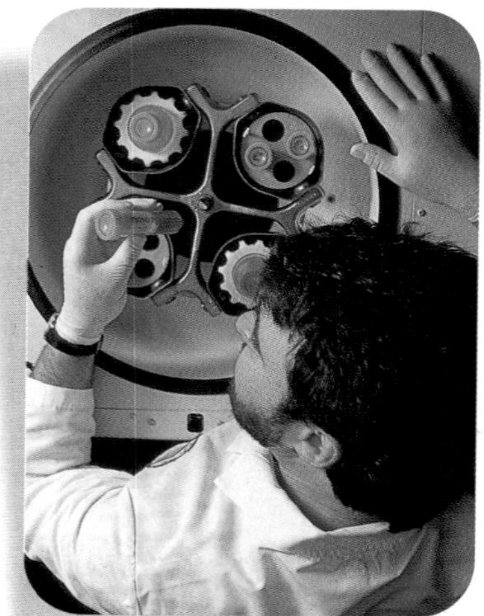

A centrifuge can be used to separate the different components found in blood.

Another way to separate tiny substances floating or suspended in liquids is to use a centrifuge. A **centrifuge** is a device that spins a set of test tubes at high speed (up to 6000 rpm). The substances that are not dissolved are "thrown" to the bottom of the test tubes.

Develop

Separating a Mixture of Salt, Sand, and Sawdust

In the next activity, you will need to apply what you know about solutions to separate salt from a mechanical mixture.

DEVELOPING A PLAN FOR A SEPARATOR

The Question

How can you separate salt from sand and sawdust, and sand from sawdust?

Materials & Equipment

- *materials and equipment for your plan*

Procedure

1 Plan an investigation in which you separate a mixture of salt, sand, and sawdust.

2 Think about these questions when planning your activity:
   a) Will you use water in this activity?
   b) Can you separate the mixture in one step or will it take many steps?
   c) What substance will be the easiest to separate? What substance will the hardest to separate?
   d) What safety measures should you take?

Keeping Records

3 Make a flowchart showing the steps involved in separating a mixture of salt, sand, and sawdust.

Analyzing and Interpreting

4 Explain in a paragraph what happened to the mixture each time a substance was separated from it.

Forming Conclusions

5 Use your flowchart to describe the differences in properties you used to make the separation in this activity.

Saving the Solvent: Distillation

Sometimes in a solution, there are not only non-dissolved substances. Some solutions are made up of more than one solvent. In these solutions, a process called **distillation** can be used to separate a solid from a liquid or one liquid in a mixture from another. How would you expect the liquids to be different from each other in order to be separated by distillation?

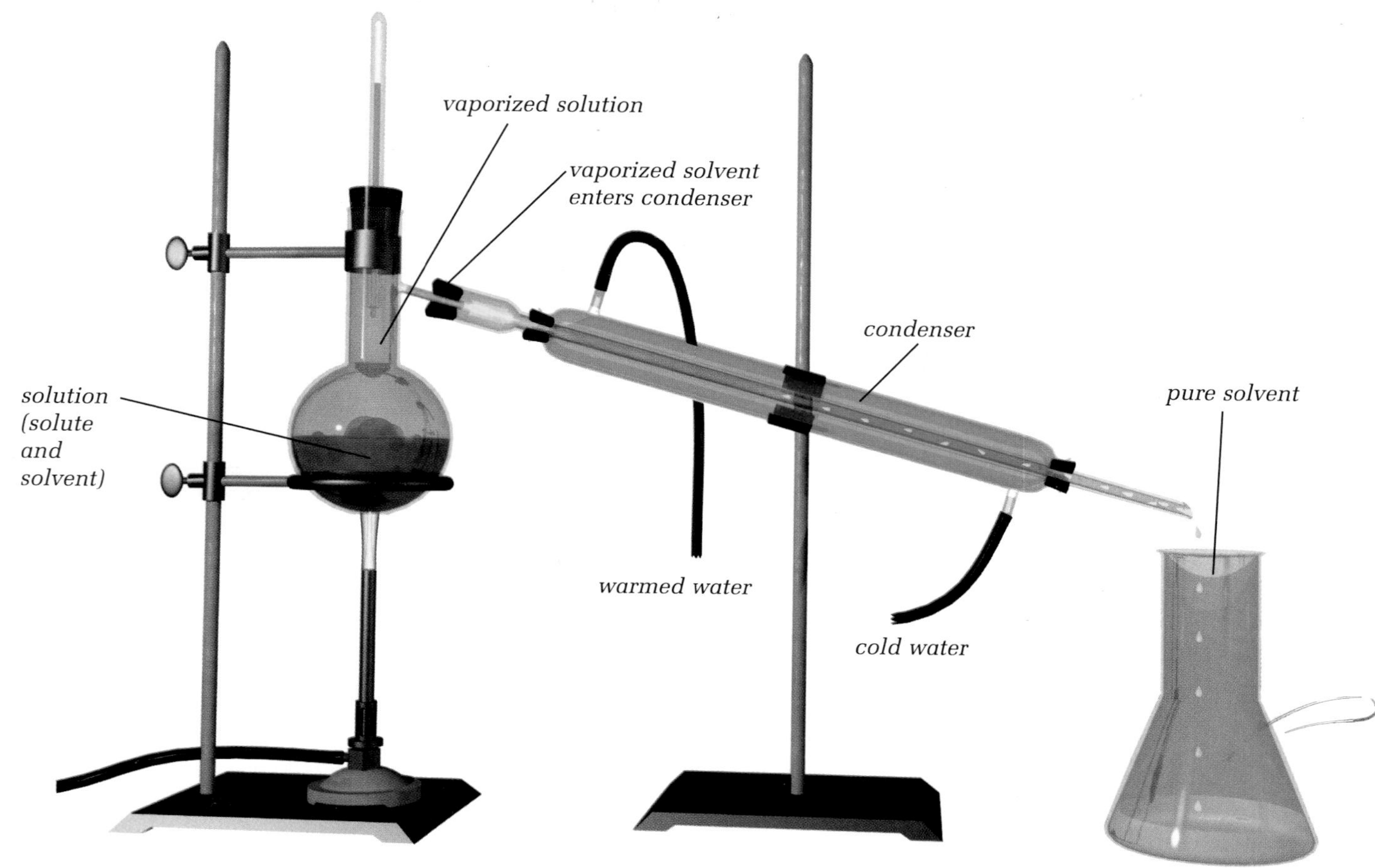

The most important commercial use of distillation is in the separation of crude oil, or petroleum. Petroleum is found in the ground as a mixture of many substances. Before it can be used as a fuel to run our cars or heat our homes, it must be separated into different liquids. Each separate liquid is called a fraction. The process is called **fractional distillation**. Fractional distillation of petroleum produces many useful substances.

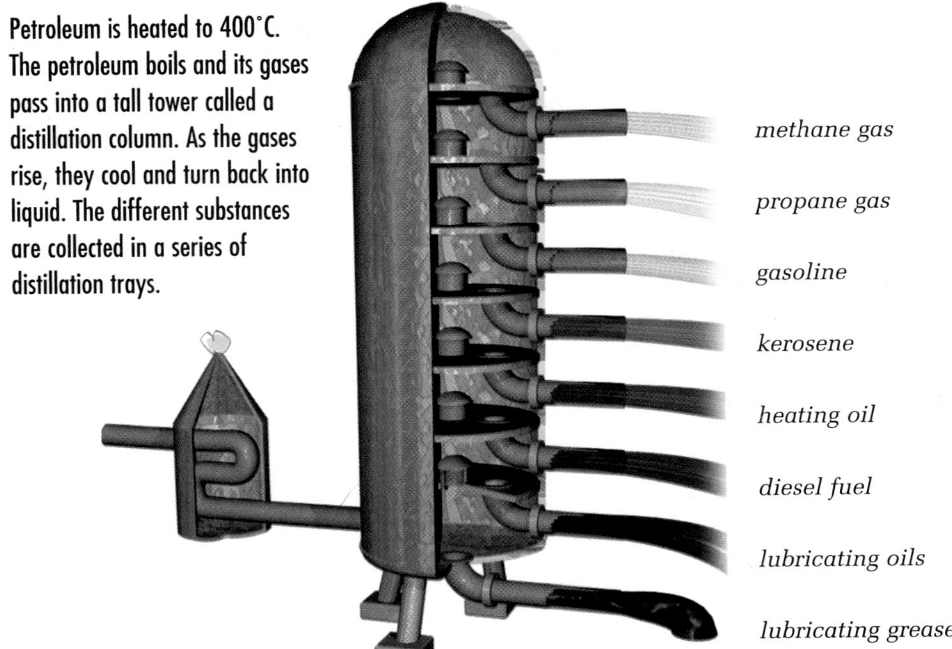

Petroleum is heated to 400°C. The petroleum boils and its gases pass into a tall tower called a distillation column. As the gases rise, they cool and turn back into liquid. The different substances are collected in a series of distillation trays.
methane gas
propane gas
gasoline
kerosene
heating oil
diesel fuel
lubricating oils
lubricating greases

Communicate

1. Could you use the distillation method to separate a sugar-water solution? Why or why not?
2. What real-life situations can you think of that might use fractional distillation to separate solutions? that might use evaporation?

3.3 Check Your Progress

1. Describe how you would separate each of the following mixtures:
   a) pencil shavings and sand
   b) white flour and white sugar
   c) a mixture of pens and pencils in a pencil case
   d) the contents of a recycling box
   e) nails and dirt
   f) three different kinds of pasta
2. For each mixture in question 1, explain what difference in properties you used to make the separation.
3. Explain three separation methods for mechanical mixtures.
4. How could you separate a salt-water solution?
5. What would happen if you distilled a sugar-water solution?
6. How could distillation be used to purify dirty water?

Big Idea

4.0 All matter is made up of tiny particles.

What is matter made of? Why is a piece of wood different from a quantity of vinegar? Why do we consider ice, water, and steam the same substance even though they don't look the same? Why are some substances naturally found in a liquid state while others only exist as a gas?

In this section, you will explore some of the answers to these questions as well as the ideas that scientists have developed to explain matter.

4.1 What's In Matter?

Explore

You are probably familiar with the three states of matter: solid, liquid, and gas. Can you think of some examples of the different states of matter that are present in the picture of the space shuttle? Write them down and share your observations with a classmate. What do all these examples of matter have in common?

What states of matter do you see in this photograph?

Develop

An Interesting Solution

You probably recall each substance can exist in any one of the three states of matter. Water can be a liquid; it can also be solid ice or gaseous steam or water vapour. In each of these states, the water has different characteristics or properties. For example, why is ice solid and hard, and water fluid and easily broken apart? Is there some way we can predict or describe these properties? The following activity will help you to develop an explanation for these differences in properties.

PROBLEM SOLVER

WHAT'S THE TOTAL VOLUME?

- Carefully measure exactly 20 mL rubbing alcohol into one graduated cylinder and exactly 20 mL of water into another. Predict what the volume of the two liquids would be if they were put together.
- Combine the two liquids and record the new volume. Is your result the same as your prediction?
- How does the volume of the water and alcohol solution compare to the total volume of the two equal amounts of water?
- Compare your results with what happened when you mixed sugar and water in the Mix It Up activity in the Invitation to Explore at the beginning of the chapter.

Communicate

1 With a partner, develop one or two possible explanations for what happened when you combined the two different liquids. Be prepared to share your ideas with the class. Remember, at this point, there are no right or wrong answers, just good ideas. As you are listening to other ideas, try to think of ways in which you could test each idea to see if it is correct.

4.2 THE PARTICLE THEORY OF MATTER

Explore

When people, including scientists, are presented with a situation for which they don't already have an explanation, they often want to find one. To begin finding an explanation, a hypothesis is created. A **hypothesis** is a possible explanation of a particular situation or phenomenon. The hypothesis is then tested through an experiment. The experiment will help to prove if the hypothesis is correct or not. After many different tests and revisions to the original hypothesis, a reasonable explanation is developed. Over time and continual testing, the explanation becomes a **theory**. The theory stands as the best explanation until some new test disproves the theory and the whole process starts over again.

Now, why did the volumes not add up when water and rubbing alcohol were put together? Scientists have developed the **Particle Theory of Matter** to describe this situation. You will study this model, and then use it in an investigation to prove or disprove your explanation of what happened.

*info***BIT**

The Particle Theory
An ancient Greek named Democritus came up with the first Particle Theory around 400 B.C. He thought that everything existing was made of tiny particles he called *atoms*. The word *atom* is Greek and means "not cuttable." Democritus believed atoms couldn't be cut into anything smaller. Today, we know that atoms are made of even smaller particles like electrons and protons.

Develop

The Four Points of the Particle Theory

The Particle Theory has four main points. Remember that these points form a model to help describe the structure of matter.

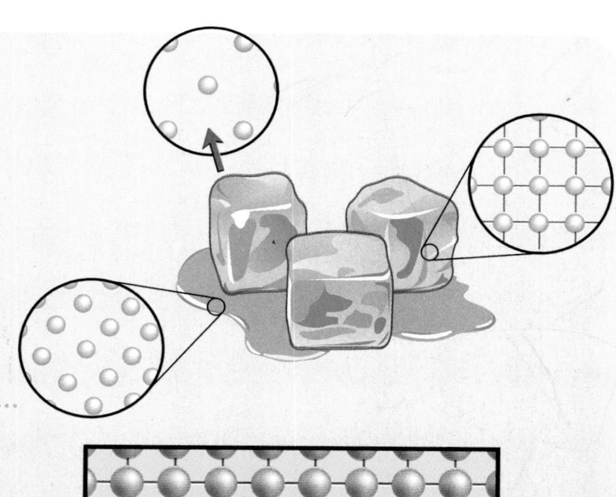

1 All matter is made up of tiny particles. Different substances have different particles.

- This means every object in any state is made up of tiny particles too small to see.
- Notice that in the diagram, there are more solid particles in a given volume than there are in the same volume of a liquid or a gas.

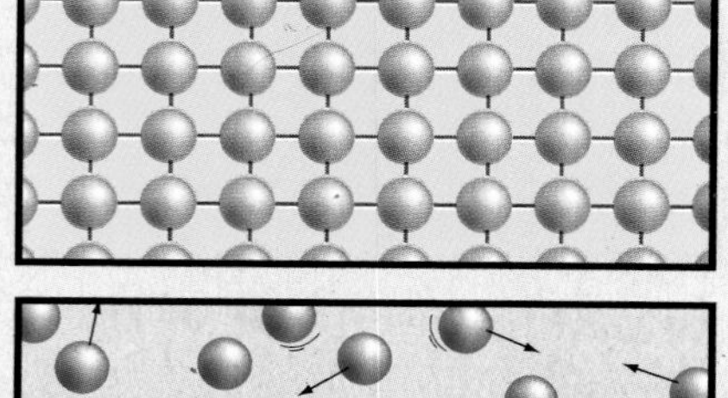

2 The tiny particles of matter are always moving and vibrating. For solids, this movement is like wiggling in one place. For liquids, the particles are sliding around and over each other. For gases, this movement means moving as far as the space they are in allows.

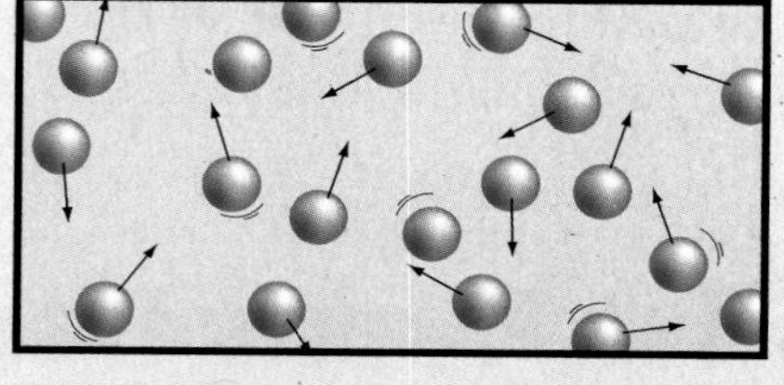

3 The particles in matter are attracted or bonded to each other.

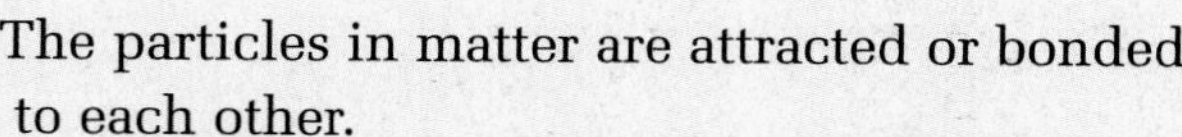

- Some particles, such as water, have more attraction for other particles, such as salt, than for each other.

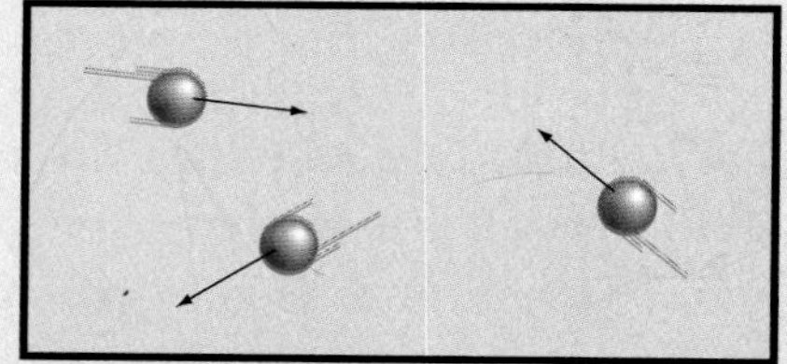

4 The particles have spaces between them.

- Notice the difference in the amount of space between particles of a solid and a gas.

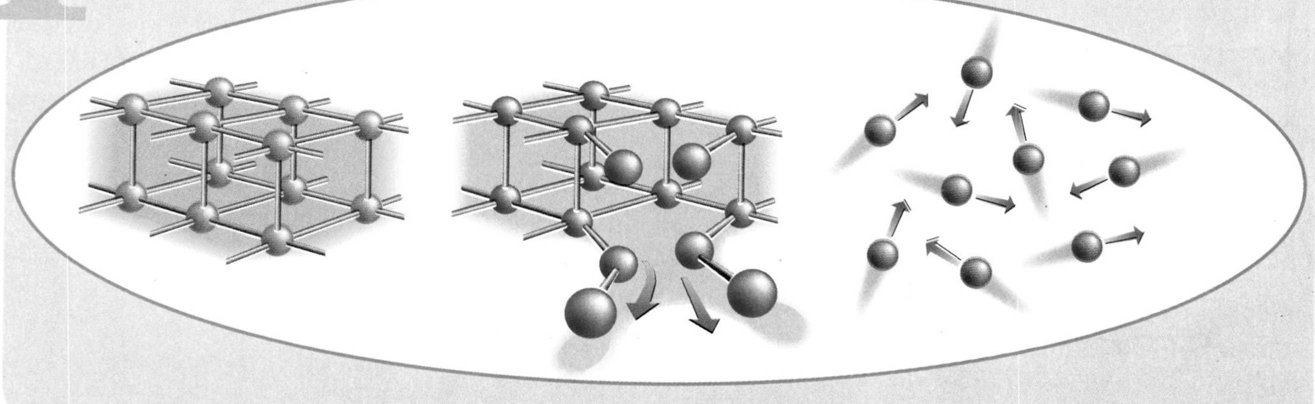

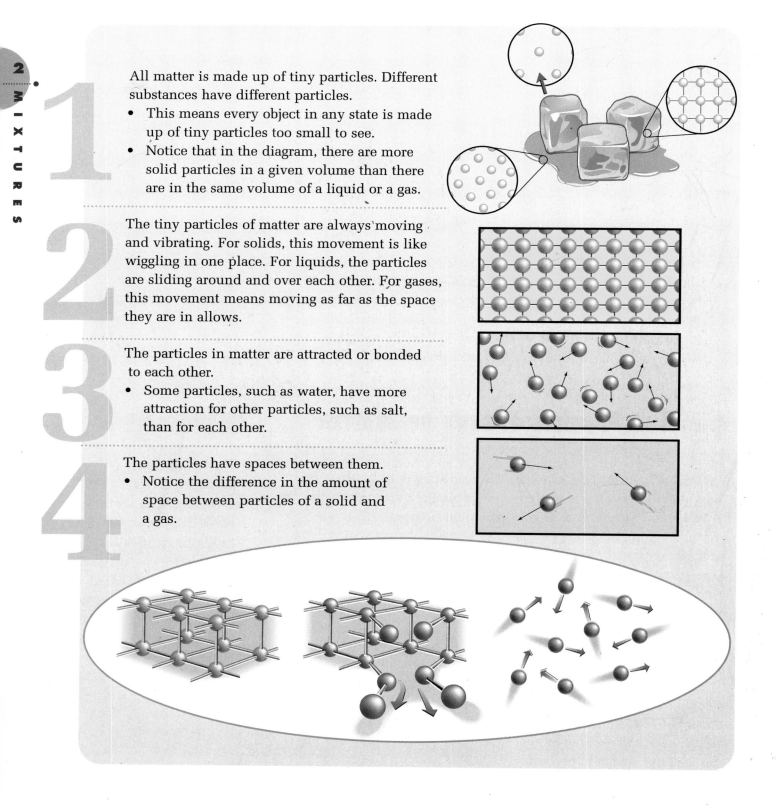

Communicate

1 When does a hypothesis become a theory?

2 The Web page below is about the Particle Theory. However, the text hasn't been added yet. In your notebook, complete the Web page, adding the information that explains each picture. Include one hyperlink topic for the text in your Web page. Write a paragraph explaining your hyperlink text.

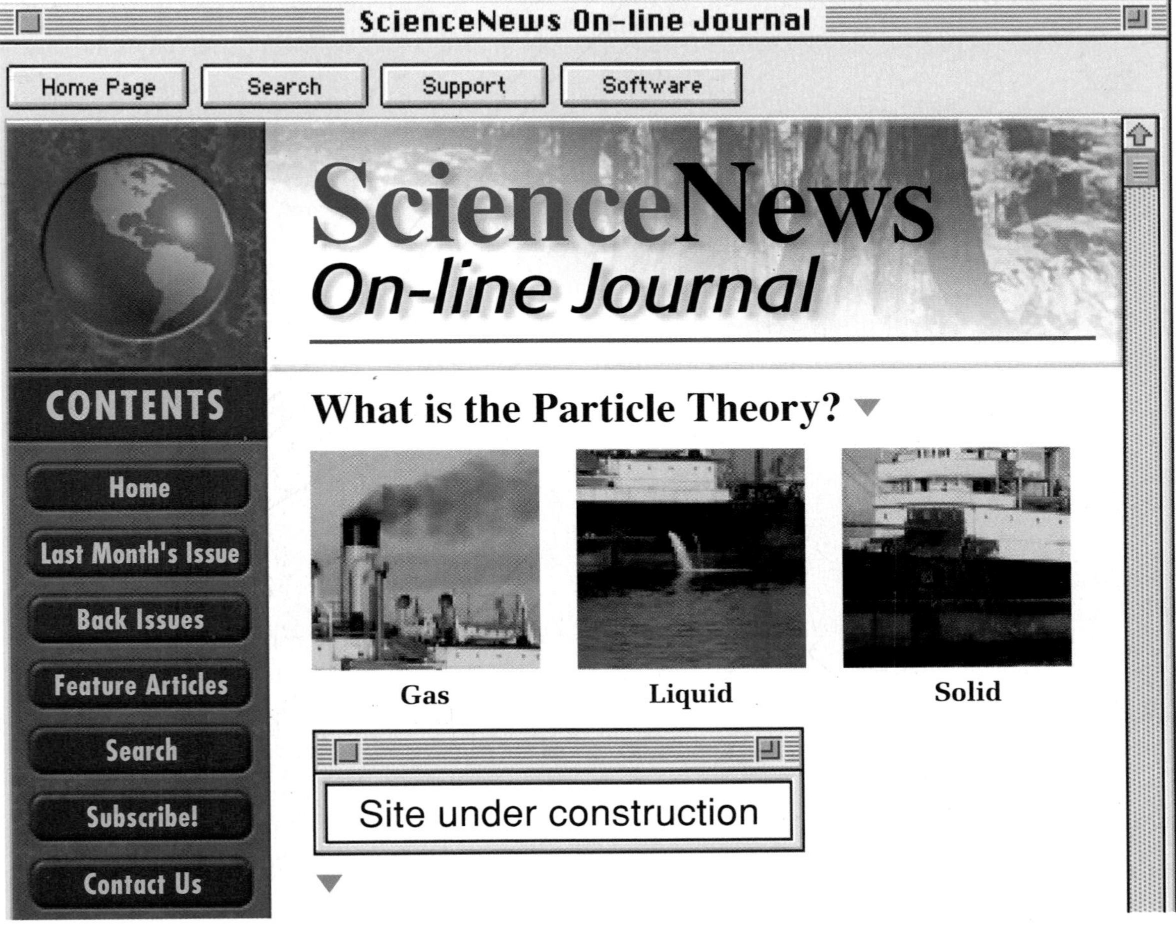

4.3 Using the Particle Theory of Matter

Explore

The Particle Theory can help you describe the interactions between substances in a variety of situations. In fact, it should help you explain why the volume dropped when you combined the water and rubbing alcohol or the sugar and water. Now, you have an opportunity to test the model in another investigation.

Develop

Investigating the Particle Theory

As you complete this activity, keep thinking about how you can use the Particle Theory to explain your observations. Remember you are using a model to help describe what you observe.

INVESTIGATOR

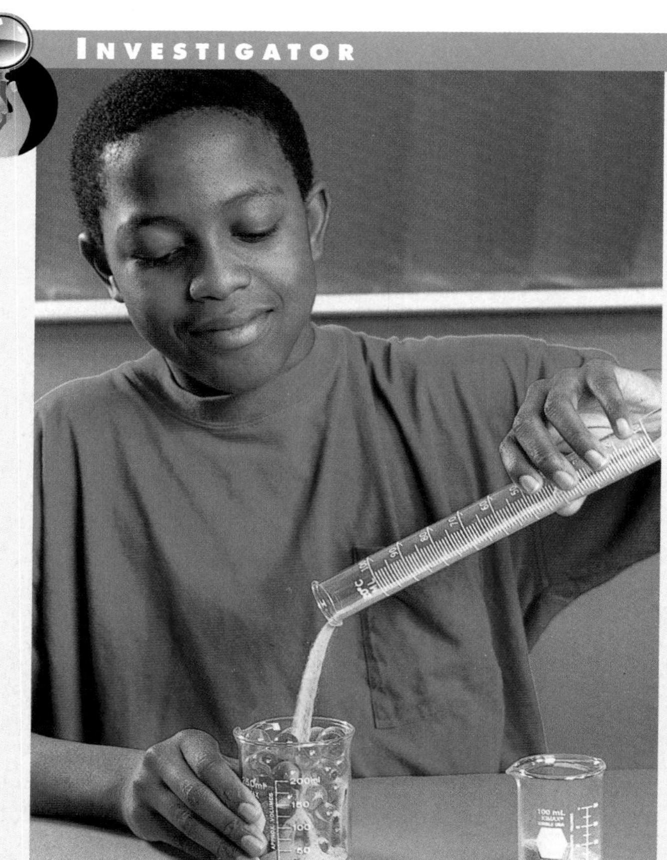

MIXING IT UP AGAIN

The Question

Can you use the Particle Theory to explain what happens when substances mix together?

Materials & Equipment

- *graduated cylinder*
- *250-mL beaker*
- *50 mL of sand (coarse or fine)*
- *250 mL of marbles*

Procedure

1 Predict what would happen to the total volume of the beaker if you mixed 50 mL of sand with a beaker full of marbles.

2 Slowly pour 50 mL of sand into a 250-mL beaker filled with marbles. What happens?

Keeping Records

3 Record your observations.

Analyzing and Interpreting

4 How did your prediction compare with the actual results?

5 Why were you able to add sand to the beaker even though it was already full of marbles?

Forming Conclusions

6 Use the Particle Theory to explain what happened when you mixed alcohol with water and when you mixed sand with marbles.

How the Particle Theory Explains Mixing Substances

Think about what happens when you add milk to a bowl of cereal. The milk fills the spaces around the pieces of cereal. If you let your cereal and milk mixture sit, what happens?

Think back to the activity you did with sand and marbles. Imagine that the marbles and sand represent particles of different sizes. The small particles (the sand) can slip into the spaces between the large particles (the marbles). This happened with the alcohol and water as well, although you could not see the different particles.

Remember the activity you did in the Invitation to Explore in which you added half a test tube of sugar to half a test tube of water? The result was not a whole test tube of sugar water for the same reason. Can you find out why?

The Particle Theory states that particles are attracted to each other. That explains why solids stay so rigid! However, particles in some substances are more attracted to particles in other substances than to themselves. For example, when salt is added to water, the salt particles break away from each other and spread around in the water. They are attracted to the water particles. This process is called **dissolving**. You will explore dissolving in the next section.

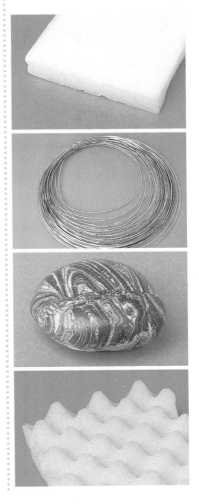

Communicate

1 Could you add marbles to a beaker filled with sand and get the same results?

2 How does the Particle Theory model explain that a substance can be solid while having spaces between its particles?

3 Why does 50 mL of water and 50 mL of sugar *not* produce 100 mL of a solution when they are mixed together?

4 How does the Particle Theory of Matter explain the decrease in volume when alcohol is added to water?

*info***BIT**

How firm or rigid a solid is depends very much on the solid. Look at the following examples of solids. What characteristics or properties make them different?

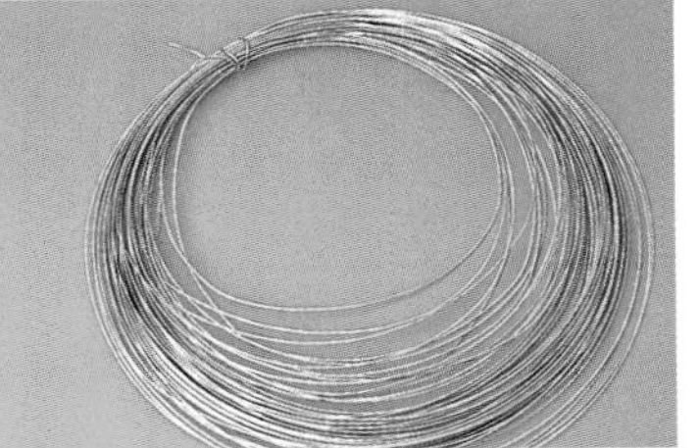

4.4 DISSOLVING

Explore

Can something dissolve without someone stirring it? To find out, fill a test tube in a rack three-quarters full with water. Let the water settle and become still. Carefully place one crystal of potassium permanganate, one juice crystal, or one drop of food colouring in the test tube. Observe the test tube for five minutes without disturbing it. What happens to the potassium permanganate, juice crystal, or food colouring? Can you explain why?

Develop

Changing the Dissolving Rate

Many solutions are made by dissolving a solid in a liquid. Think about what happens when you mix some sugar into water. It looks as though the sugar disappears. That means that sugar is **soluble** in water. But, where do the sugar particles go? How do you know where they go?

Think back to the Mix It Up activity in the Invitation to Explore at the beginning of this chapter.

- Did the flour dissolve in the water?
- Did the pepper dissolve in the water?
- Do you know the difference between a solution and a mechanical mixture?

In a solution, the particles of the solvent (water) are attracted to and cling to the particles of the solute (sugar). The solute is totally dissolved into the liquid. In a mechanical mixture, this doesn't happen. The particles of water are not as attracted to the flour particles (which are always visibly separate) as they are to other water particles.

If you place a large sugar cube in a beaker of water, you may have to wait a long time for it to dissolve completely. Most people have better things to do than to sit and watch things dissolve. Think about the times that you wanted something to dissolve in a hurry. What did you do to speed things up? Can you apply your method to the following examples?

You have 20 cans of frozen lemonade concentrate and the whole school will be arriving for a picnic in five minutes. What do you do?

Would your answer be different if you were trying to make hot chocolate for a skating party and the powder was in a large clump? How could you get the chocolate to dissolve in time?

Frozen lemonade, hot chocolate powder, and other solids dissolve in water. The Particle Theory tells us that solids are made of particles held together by forces of attraction. These forces are broken by the liquid particles moving between the solid particles. The liquid particles surround the solid particles and form stronger attractions.

Experiment ON YOUR OWN

The Disappearing Sugar Cube Race

Before You Start...

In this activity, you will be in charge of planning an experiment. Your job is to test different ways of making a sugar cube dissolve quickly. You should think about what questions to ask, how you will plan your experiment, and how you will carry it out safely. You should also consider how you can control the results of your experiment by changing one variable at a time.

The Question

How can you develop a method that will dissolve a sugar cube as quickly as possible?

Your Task

1. Make a hypothesis (remember that a hypothesis is a possible answer to a particular situation or phenomenon).
2. Decide what materials and equipment you will need to test your hypothesis.
3. Plan your investigation and carry out your experiment.
   a) Are you changing only one variable at a time? Why is this important?
4. Compare your results with your hypothesis. Were you able to support your hypothesis?
5. Share and compare your experimental plan and results with those of your classmates. Present your results in a form that clearly describes, in words, diagrams, and/or graphs, what you did.
   a) Did anyone plan an experiment exactly like yours? How do your results compare with their results?
   b) What factors had to be kept the same so that you could compare your results with those of other groups?

The Particle Theory Can Help to Explain Dissolving

In the previous activity, you discovered how you can speed up the rate at which a solute dissolves. But why do these actions affect the rate a solute dissolves? You can explain why a solute dissolves in a solvent by using the Particle Theory.

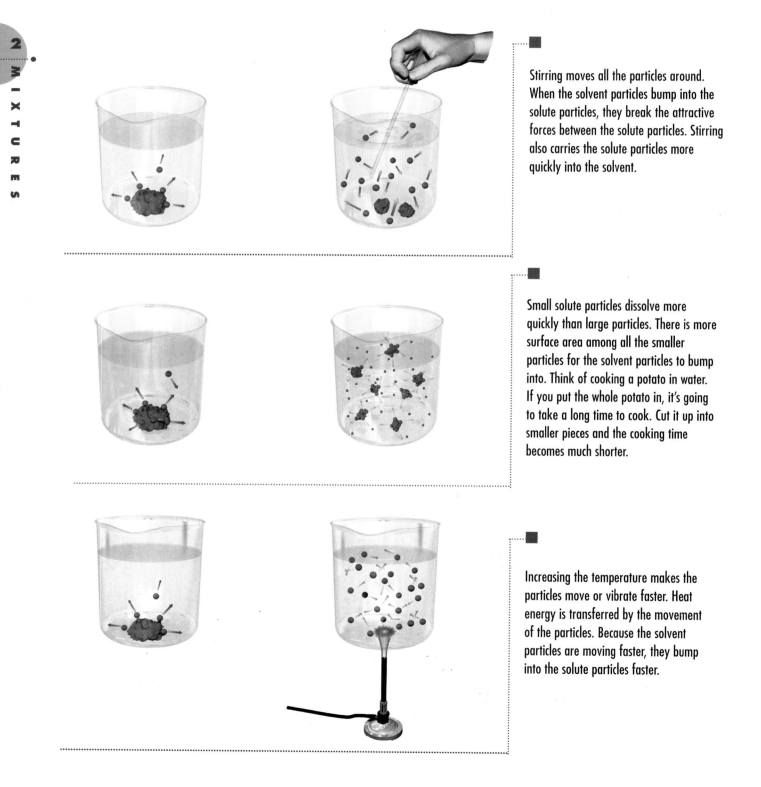

Stirring moves all the particles around. When the solvent particles bump into the solute particles, they break the attractive forces between the solute particles. Stirring also carries the solute particles more quickly into the solvent.

Small solute particles dissolve more quickly than large particles. There is more surface area among all the smaller particles for the solvent particles to bump into. Think of cooking a potato in water. If you put the whole potato in, it's going to take a long time to cook. Cut it up into smaller pieces and the cooking time becomes much shorter.

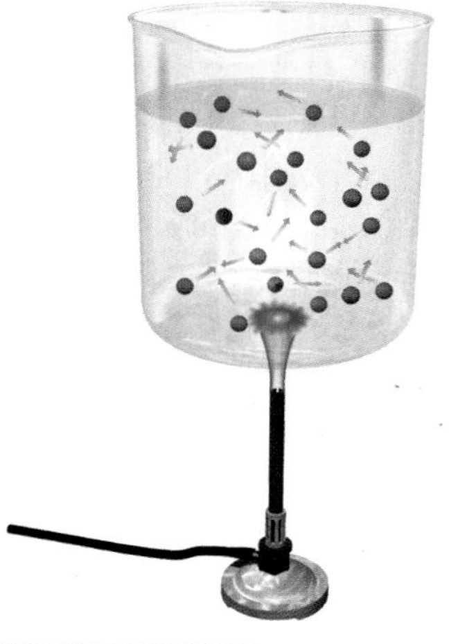

Increasing the temperature makes the particles move or vibrate faster. Heat energy is transferred by the movement of the particles. Because the solvent particles are moving faster, they bump into the solute particles faster.

1 Sketch a particle picture of pure solid gold.
2 Use the Particle Theory to explain what happens to the total volume when alcohol is mixed with water.
3 Use the Particle Theory to explain what happens when sugar is mixed with water.

4.5 Check Your Progress

1 What is the difference between melting and dissolving?
2 List three examples in which dissolving is used in your home.
3 Describe what happens to the particles of a solute when it dissolves.
4 Make a particle sketch showing instant coffee dissolving in hot water.
5 Name three ways of speeding up dissolving, and explain each using the Particle Theory.
6 Imagine eating a piece of fruit. How does your body speed up the digestion of the fruit?
7 Suppose someone spills a bucket of paint on the floor of your class. How could you use your knowledge of dissolving to help clean up the paint?
8 Some medicines are more effective if they dissolve slowly. How could you design a pill that would take longer to dissolve?
9 Suppose that you mix exactly 50 mL of water with exactly 50 mL of alcohol. Everything dissolves. Which is the solute? Which is the solvent?
10 Why is each of the following solutions? Which one is also a mixture?

BIG IDEA

5.0 Solutions are used in a variety of technological situations.

2 MIXTURES

Solutions can be anything from juice in a glass to the ocean. You have learned that when a solute (such as salt) is dissolved in a solvent (such as water), it makes a homogeneous mixture (salt water) called a solution. However, there are other terms that can be used to describe solutions.

5.1 TYPES OF SOLUTIONS

Explore

You have probably seen cans of apple juice that say "made from concentrate." But what does that mean? Concentrated apple juice is apple juice that has had most of the water taken out. Any **concentrated solution** contains large amounts of solute in a solvent. Now think of a glass of apple juice to which you have added another glass of water. You have diluted the apple juice. A **dilute solution** has small amounts of solute in a solvent.

Develop

Concentrated and Dilute Solutions

Concentrated and dilute are relative terms. They tell you whether there are small or large amounts of solute in the solvent. But they don't tell you exactly how much solute is in a certain amount of solvent. The **concentration** of a solution tells you the amount of solute (in grams) dissolved in a certain amount of solvent. For example, a solution with 50 g of solute dissolved in 100 mL of water is said to have a concentration of 50 g/100 mL. This is read as "fifty grams per one hundred millilitres."

infoBIT

Dilute: a dilute solution is one with only a few solute particles compared with the number of solvent particles.

Concentrated: a concentrated solution is one with many solute particles compared with the number of solvent particles.

PROBLEM SOLVER

THE TASTIER SOLUTION

Suppose you dissolve 10 g of juice drink crystals in 50 mL of water, and your friend dissolves 15 g of juice crystals in 100 mL of water. A second friend dissolves 6 g of the juice crystals in 25 mL of water.

- Who would have the tastiest fruit juice?
- What is the concentration of each solution?
- What would happen if you used boiling water, ice cold water, and lukewarm water?
- Would the temperature of the water affect the taste? Plan an investigation and carry it out.

Caution!
Be careful when using boiling water.

Communicate

1 What is the difference between a dilute and a concentrated solution?

2 If a solution has a concentration of 50 g per 100 mL of water, what does this mean?

3 Calculate the concentration in grams per 100 mL for the following solutions:
   a) 10 g of chocolate in 50 mL of water
   b) 3 g of sugar in 300 mL of water
   c) 5 g of maple syrup in 25 mL of water

try this at **HOME**

TASTY SOLUTIONS

The Question

Can people tell the difference between dilute and concentrated solutions?

Procedure

1 Measure 100 mL of water into each of three cups.

2 Put $\frac{1}{2}$ teaspoon of juice drink crystals into one of the cups, 1 teaspoon of juice crystals into the second cup, and $1\frac{1}{2}$ teaspoons of juice crystals into the third cup. Make sure you label each cup.

3 Stir each solution.

4 Give each solution to another family member to taste and compare. Record their reactions. Which solution do they consider to be dilute? concentrated?

5 Describe the difference between dilute and concentrated solutions.

5.2 Unsaturated and Saturated Solutions

Explore

There are still other terms that can be used to describe solutions. When you add juice drink crystals to water, you make an unsaturated solution. An **unsaturated solution** is a solution in which there is still room for more solute to dissolve. What would happen if you kept adding juice crystals? Eventually no more crystals would dissolve. If you did this you would have created a saturated solution. A **saturated solution** is a solution in which no more solute can dissolve.

Develop

Looking at Saturated Solutions

There are many everyday examples of saturated solutions. How many can you list?

INVESTIGATOR

Saturated Solutions

The Question

Can you make a saturated solution?

Materials & Equipment

- *graduated cylinder*
- *balance*
- *weighing papers*
- *water at room temperature*
- *juice drink crystals*
- *beakers*
- *stir sticks*
- *hot water*

continued on next page

Procedure

1 Measure exactly 50 mL of water into a beaker.
2 Accurately measure 5 g of juice drink crystals. Add the juice crystals to the water.
3 Stir the mixture until the juice crystals have dissolved.
4 Keep adding more juice crystals to the water, 5 g at a time, until no more juice crystals will dissolve.

Keeping Records

5 Determine the total mass of the juice crystals that you added.
6 If you repeated the activity with hot water, would you get the same answer for the saturated solution? Try it!

Analyzing and Interpreting

7 Calculate the concentration of the solution in grams of the juice crystals per 100 mL of water.
8 Did the solution become saturated with the juice crystals? How do you know?
9 Could you dissolve more juice crystals in the hot water?

Forming Conclusions

10 Use the Particle Theory to explain how a solution becomes saturated.

Communicate

1 What is the difference between a saturated solution and an unsaturated solution?
2 If a saturated solution has a concentration of 20 g per 100 mL of water, how many grams of the solute could be dissolved in 50 mL of water? in 400 mL of water?

5.3 Solubility

Explore

What could you do if you wanted to make a solution sweeter, or stronger, or saltier? In the Saturated Solutions Investigator activity, you added juice drink crystals to water until no more juice crystals would dissolve. You determined the maximum amount of solute (juice crystals) that would dissolve in that amount of the solvent (water). This maximum amount is called the **solubility** of the juice crystals in water at a certain temperature.

The solubility of any solution depends on three factors: the temperature, the type of solvent, and the type of solute. You will now investigate each of these factors.

Develop

Investigating Solubility Factors: Temperature, Type of Solvent, and Type of Solute

Which example do you think will dissolve faster:

- 50 mL of chocolate powder in cold milk?
- 50 mL of chocolate powder in hot milk?

If you said the chocolate powder and hot milk, you're correct, but do you know why? Not all solutes dissolve in solvents in the same way. And like the situation above, the temperature of the solvent has a lot to do with solubility.

PROBLEM SOLVER

WILL IT DISSOLVE?

Are some solutes more soluble in water or in oil? Try to dissolve different substances, such as juice drink crystals, petroleum jelly, sugar, and baking soda, in water and in vegetable oil. Perform "fair" tests to find out which solutes will dissolve in which solvents.

- Was the petroleum jelly more soluble in oil or in water? How do you know?
- Which substances were more soluble in oil? in water? How do you know?
- What did you do to make sure you had a fair test?

In the next activity, you will look at how temperature affects solubility.

TEMPERATURE AND SOLUBILITY

Before You Start...

You will be working in groups to investigate the solubility of different solutes. Your teacher will assign a chemical to each group. To help you focus on your task, think about what happens when you make hot chocolate. Is the hot chocolate powder more soluble (does it dissolve more easily) in hot water or in cold water? What happens to the movement of particles when they are heated? Will there be room for more solute particles in a heated solution?

The Question

What effect does the temperature have on the amount of solute that can dissolve in a fixed amount of solvent?

Materials & Equipment

- *2 beakers*
- *water*
- *thermometer*
- *hot plate or access to hot water*
- *chemical—supplied by teacher*
- *triple beam or electronic balance*

Procedure

1 Make a hypothesis on how much solute will dissolve at **room temperature** and at 50°C. Remember that you are not investigating *how fast* a solute dissolves, but *how much* solute will dissolve.
   a) What questions are answered by your hypothesis?

2 Decide what materials and equipment you'll need to test your hypothesis.

3 Plan your experiment.
   a) What variable(s) will change? What variable(s) will the stay the same?

4 Write up your procedure and show it to your teacher. Do not proceed any further until it is approved.

5 Carry out your experiment. Compare your results with your hypothesis. Were you able to confirm your hypothesis? If not, what possible reasons might there be?

Keeping Records

6 You should make sure you have recorded at least the following information: your hypothesis, your procedure, the exact temperature of both liquids, and the mass of solute you added.

Analyzing and Interpreting

7 Share and compare your experimental method and results with your classmates. How did your classmates plan their experiments?

8 What variables did each group have to keep the same in order to compare results?

Forming Conclusions

9 In a short paragraph, describe your results and how they compared with your hypothesis.

*info*BIT

Candy making goes back to the ancient Egyptians, some 3000 years ago. It is made by dissolving enough sugar in water to make a plastic-like substance. It hardens when it cools and turns into candy.

Is candy a supersaturated solution?

Supersaturated Solutions

Most solutions can dissolve more solute at higher temperatures. Think about what happens when you add sugar to hot water to make a saturated solution, and then cool it down. What happens to the sugar as the water cools? Try it and see.

Some solutes will stay dissolved in the solution as the solution cools. The cool solution contains more solute than a saturated solution. This solution is called a supersaturated solution. A **supersaturated solution** is a solution that contains more solute than it would normally be able to dissolve at a certain temperature.

Solvent Solubility

Suppose you went into a hardware store and bought a variety of nuts and bolts. When you returned home to put the nuts and bolts together, you found that not all of them would fit. Only those nuts and bolts that were the same size would fit together.

It is the same way with solutes. Some solutes "fit" with the solvent and dissolve. For example, sugar dissolves in water because the sugar particles bind with the water particles. Some solute particles do not bind with the solvent particles. These solutes are labelled as **insoluble**.

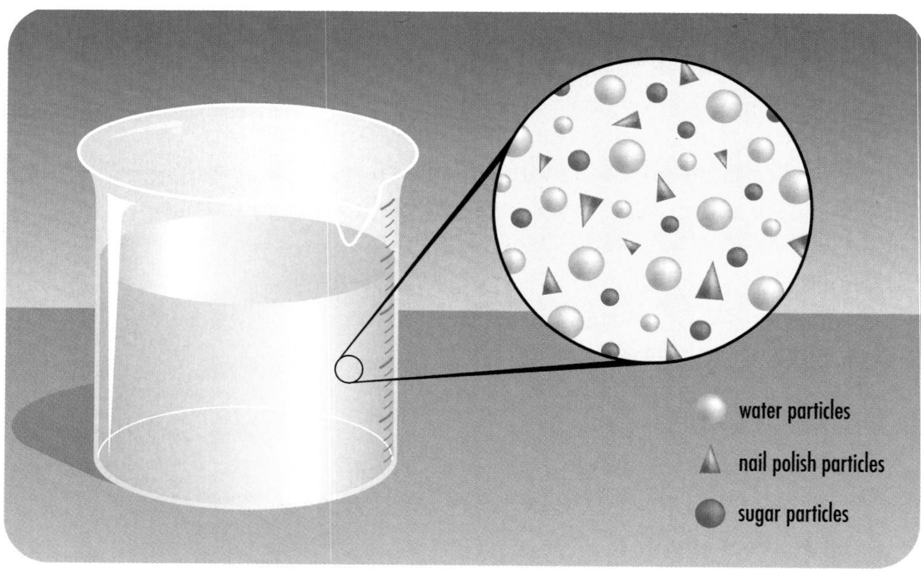

Which substance dissolves in water: nail polish or sugar?

In the next activity, you will investigate some solutes that are insoluble in water. You will also see if there are other solvents that will dissolve them.

INVESTIGATOR

Disappearing Nail Polish

The Question

Will a solute that dissolves in water also dissolve in other solvents?

Materials & Equipment

- *test tube*
- *sheet of acetate or clear mylar*
- *cotton swabs*
- *nail polish*
- *nail polish remover*
- *different coloured markers*
- *alcohol (ethanol)*
- *water*
- *graduated cylinder*

Caution!
Nail polish remover should be handled with care. Make sure there is good ventilation in your work area. Wash your hands after cleaning up the activity.

Procedure

1 Look at the container of nail polish remover. Discuss the safety warnings.

2 Paint two stripes, about 4 cm long, of nail polish on a plastic sheet and allow them to dry.

3 Add about 2 mL of water to 2 mL of nail polish remover in one test tube.

4 Use cotton swabs to gently rub one stripe of nail polish with water and the other stripe with the nail polish remover mixture. Observe what happens.

5 Use different markers to make a number of lines on a plastic sheet.

6 Using a cotton swab, gently rub the lines with water and then with alcohol. Observe what happens.

Keeping Records

7 Record your observations in a table similar to the one shown below:

Solute	Solvent	Result of mixing

Analyzing and Interpreting

8 What were the safety concerns about the nail polish remover and alcohol?

9 What safety steps were taken for each solvent?

10 What factors had to be kept the same for a fair comparison? How was this done?

11 Did all the solutes dissolve in water? Explain why or why not.

Forming Conclusions

12 Use your results from this Investigator activity to agree or disagree with the following two statements.

a) A solute that dissolves in water always dissolves in other solvents.

b) There are solvents that will dissolve solutes that won't dissolve in water.

When a substance does not dissolve in another substance, it is because the particles of the first substance do not attract the particles of the second substance. For example, water particles and oil particles do not attract each other. Can you think of other solutes that do not dissolve in water, but will dissolve in other solvents?

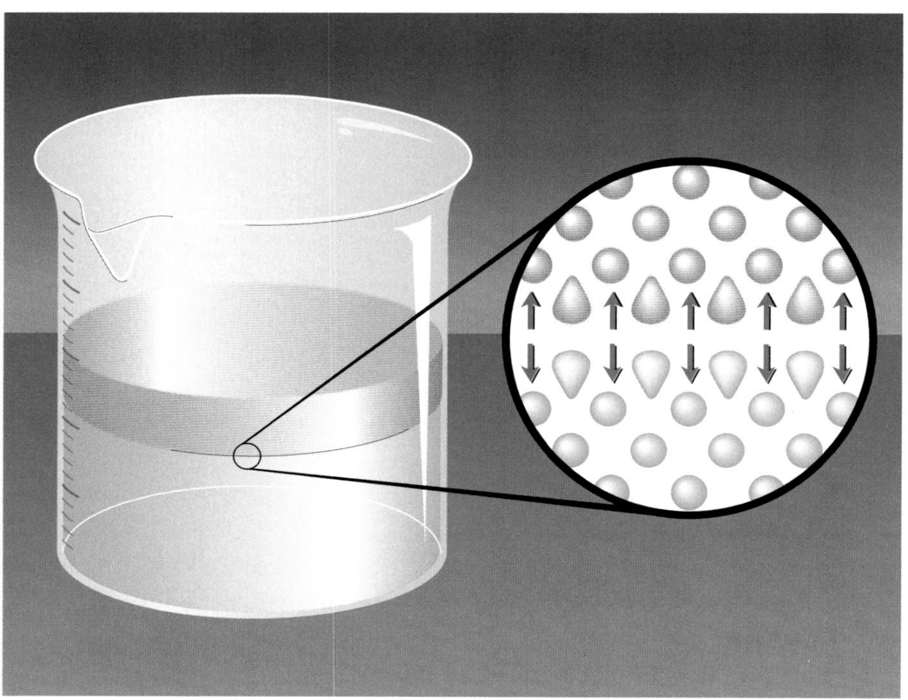

Communicate

1 Which of the following combinations will produce a solution?

Solute	Solvent
juice drink crystals	*oil*
juice drink crystals	*water*
baking soda	*oil*
petroleum jelly	*water*
petroleum jelly	*oil*

2 What three factors affect solubility?

3 Anita makes rock candy by stirring 100 mL of sugar into 50 mL of boiling water. After allowing the mixture to sit for a few days, she noticed that crystals had formed. She collected the crystals with a spoon and washed them with cold water to remove the sticky syrup. Finally, she set them in a warm place to dry. Did Anita make a solution?

4 Why are some substances insoluble in water? Give an example.

5.4 CHECK YOUR PROGRESS

1 Use the Particle Theory to explain what happens to the solubility of a solute as temperature is increased.

2 The Particle Theory says that there are spaces between the particles. What might happen to the spaces as temperature increases? Why?

3 For the substances in the chart below, answer the following questions.

Solubility in 100 mL of Water		
Substance	***at 0°C***	***at 100°C***
sodium chloride	*35 g*	*39 g*
calcium acetate	*37.4 g*	*29.7 g*
sodium carbonate decahydrate	*21 g*	*421 g*

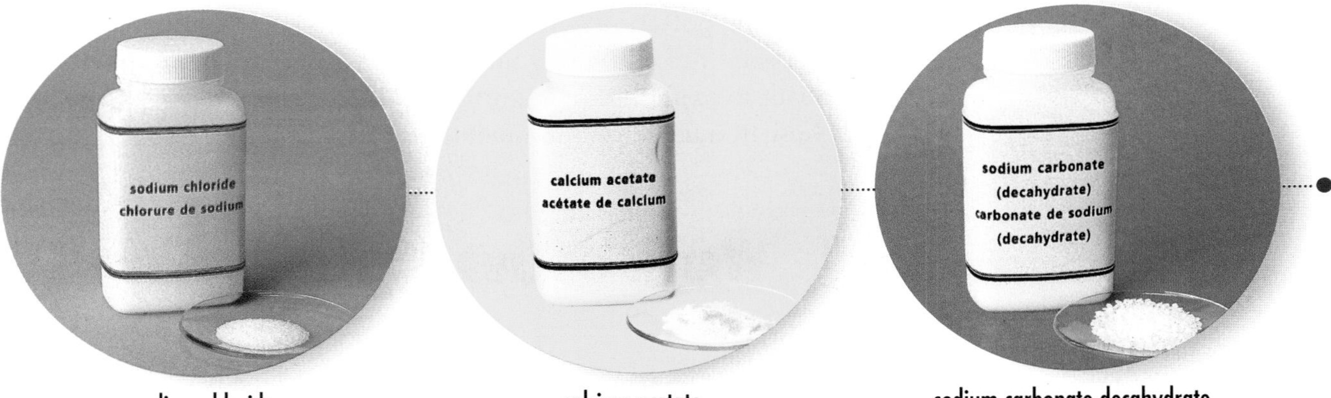

sodium chloride　　calcium acetate　　sodium carbonate decahydrate

a) Which substance is the most soluble at 100°C?

b) Which substance is the most soluble at 0°C?

c) Which substance showed the most change in solubility as the temperature increased?

d) According to the chart, 421 g of sodium carbonate decahydrate would dissolve in 100 mL of water at 100°C. Predict what would happen if you made a saturated solution of sodium carbonate decahydrate at 100°C, and then cooled the solution to 0°C.

4 You probably noticed that there were symbols on some of the solvent containers. Describe what each symbol means. What safety precautions did you take when you saw these symbols?

5 What does insoluble mean? Name some substances that are insoluble in water.

6 Draw a particle sketch comparing what happens when nail polish mixes with water to what happens when nail polish mixes with nail polish remover.

Big Idea

6.0 Water, the universal solvent, must be used responsibly.

Water, water everywhere!

Water is the most common substance on earth; it covers over 70% of the earth's surface. Your body is two-thirds water. All living things need water to survive. But do you ever stop and think about how important water really is?

Most of the water on earth is salt water. Less than 1% of all the earth's water is available as fresh water in lakes, rivers, and under the ground. Unfortunately, this fresh water is subjected to pollution. Much of the pollution comes from the manufacturing of goods, the use of pesticides and herbicides, and untreated waste products. You are about to explore the properties of water, how people use water, and how human activities affect the quality of water.

6.1 Water in Our World

Explore

Water: you drink it, shower in it, and swim in it. It is used for cooking and bathing, as well as for washing cars and clothes. It is delivered to agricultural crops by irrigation, and it is used in many kinds of manufacturing. For all of us, water is an important resource.

Water is called the universal solvent. Many substances can dissolve in water to form drinks, cleaning fluids, and other mixtures. Water also helps dissolve food and carry it around your body. In ecosystems, water carries dissolved minerals into plants and animals. But where does water come from?

Develop

The Water Cycle

The earth has always had the same amount of water. The water that existed when the dinosaurs were on earth is the same water you use today; it is recycled over and over as part of the water cycle. You get most of your water from this cycle.

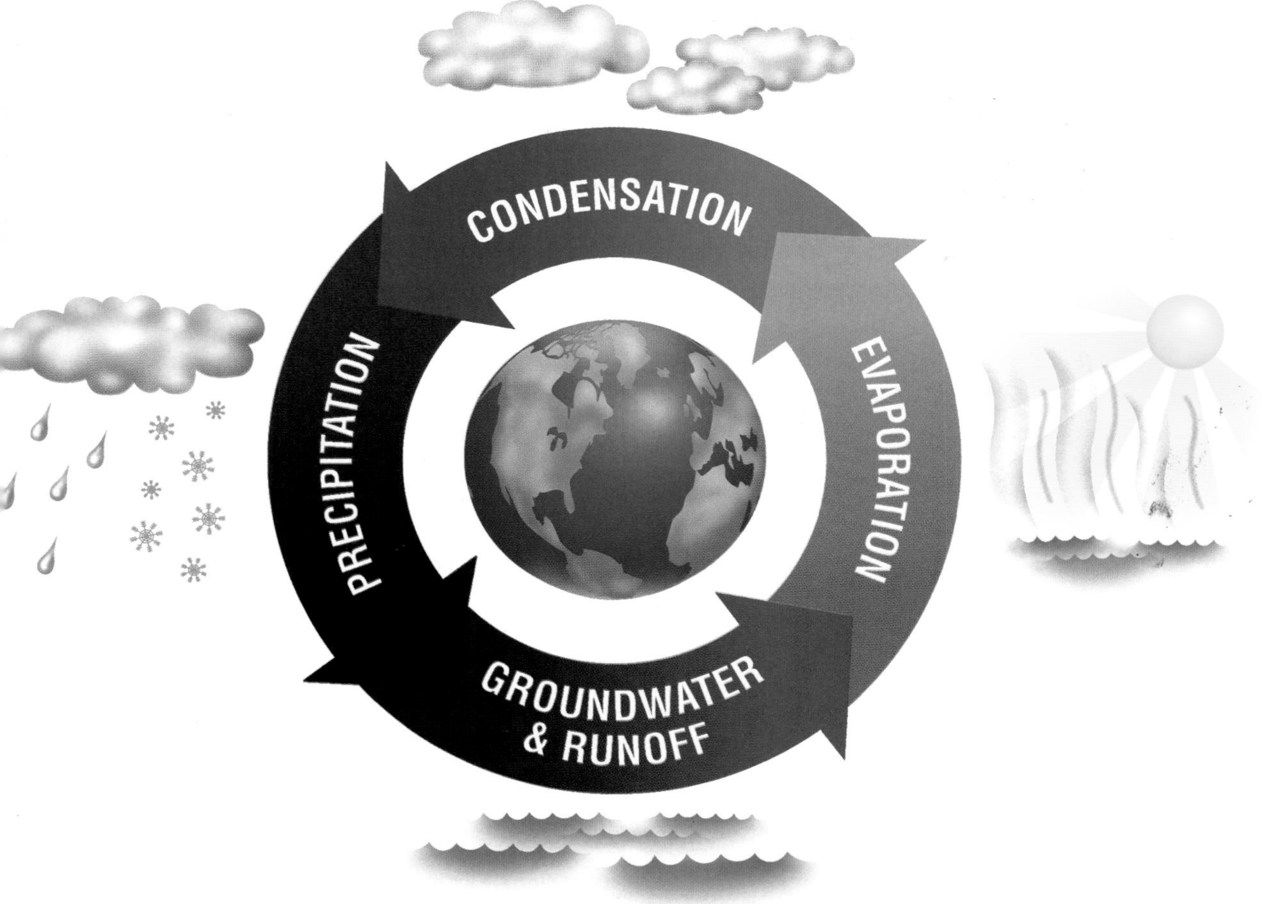

CONDENSATION

EVAPORATION

GROUNDWATER & RUNOFF

PRECIPITATION

When water drains from your sink, it ends up in rivers, lakes, or the sea. It evaporates in the heat of the sun to form water vapour (**evaporation**). The vapour may be carried high in the air until it cools enough to condense into clouds of water droplets and ice (**condensation**). The water then falls back to the earth as rain and snow (**precipitation**).

Pure water is rarely found in nature. Sea water contains about 3.5% salt, most of which is sodium chloride (table salt). Even fresh water contains dissolved substances, such as carbonates and sulphates. Rainwater may contain dissolved gases, such as sulphur dioxide, which produce acid rain. One of the reasons that water pollution is a big problem is that water is such an excellent solvent.

Precipitation

Communicate

1 Use the Particle Theory of Matter to explain each of the following:
   a) water as it evaporates
   b) water as it condenses to snow
   c) water from melting snow

2 Create a poster or write an "infomercial" that illustrates the many uses of water.

6.2 HUMAN USE OF WATER

Explore

The average volume of water people use daily varies from country to country. Use the activities in the table below to calculate about how much water your family would use in a day.

Daily Water Use for the Average Household (1993)

Average Water Usage By Country	
Country	**litres/person/day**
United States	*710*
Canada	*528*
Japan	*429*
France	*319*
United Kingdom	*277*
Egypt	*166*
India	*50*
Sri Lanka	*27*

Average Canadian Water Usage		
Activity	**litres /person /day**	**% of total**
Toilet Flushing	*140*	*26.5*
Showers and Baths	*122.5*	*23.2*
Drinking and Cooking	*17.5*	*3.3*
Laundry and Dishes	*70*	*13.3*
Lawn watering/car washing	*178*	*33.7*
Total	*528*	*100%*

How does your family compare with the Canadian average? with the other countries in the table?

All this water that we use comes from rivers, lakes, reservoirs, and wells. If you live in a city or town, the water is pumped through a network of pipes to your faucets. Along the way, it undergoes a series of treatments:

- First, the water must be cleaned. The water is usually pumped into reservoirs where the solid debris settles to the bottom.
- The water is then filtered through gravel and sand to remove smaller impurities.
- Then, it is treated with chlorine to kill germs.
- Finally, the clean water is pumped to you.

In the next activity, you will look at filtering water.

*info***BIT**

Desalting Sea Water

Many areas in the world do not have access to fresh water. However, as the picture at left shows, it is possible to convert salt water to fresh water. What would be some of the advantages and disadvantages of this conversion? What process is used to remove the salt?

Another way to get large quantities of fresh water might be to tow an iceberg to an area that needs water. Do you think that this idea would work? Can you think of any other ideas for obtaining fresh water for areas in need?

Develop Water Quality

In the next Investigator activity, you will use and determine the effectiveness of a chemical process for cleaning water.

INVESTIGATOR

CLEANING WATER

The Question

How well can you clean water?

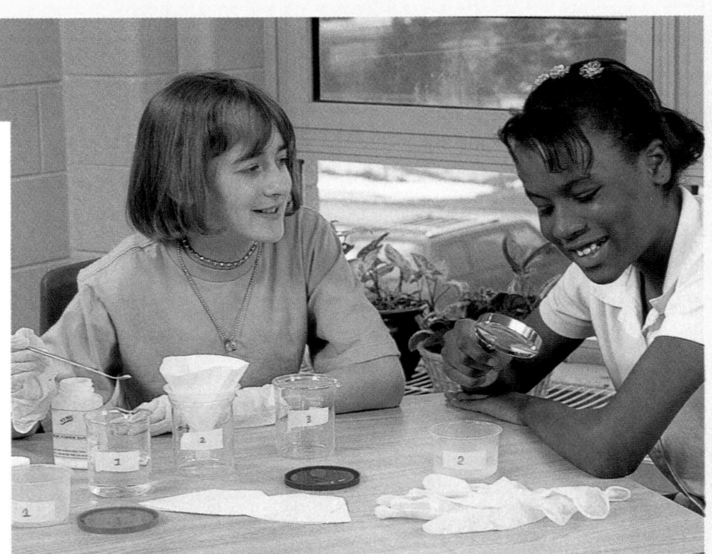

Materials & Equipment

- *clean containers*
- *clean beakers or jars for water samples*
- *filter paper and funnel*
- *magnifying glass*
- *a variety of water samples (from puddles, a lake, a pond)*
- *potassium aluminum sulphate (alum powder)*
- *scoopula*

Caution!
Do *not* taste the water samples.

Procedure

1. Collect water samples from different sources. Use a magnifying glass to look closely at each one. Compare the samples.
2. Make a filter-paper cone and fit it into a funnel. Place the funnel into a clean beaker.
3. Pour a water sample into the funnel. Collect the filtered water in the beaker. Using a new piece of filter paper and a clean beaker, repeat filtering each of the water samples.
4. Add a few crystals of potassium aluminum sulphate to each filtered water sample. Observe what happens. Then, pour each water sample through another clean filter.

Keeping Records

5. Record your observations before and after filtering each water sample.

Analyzing and Interpreting

6. How did your filtered water samples compare with the original samples?
7. How did the filters you used for the different water samples compare?
8. What did the potassium aluminum sulphate do to the water samples?
9. Describe your treated samples and compare them with tap water.

Forming Conclusions

10. Describe the process you used to clean your water. Is the filtered water clean enough to drink? Why or why not?
11. Compare the quality of the different samples. Which would be the best for drinking water? the worst? Explain why.

*info***BIT**

Drinking Water
Drinking water is never pure—without dissolved substances. The water you drink probably contains:
Tap Water: minute amounts of iron, lead, benzene, ammonia, chlorine, and sometimes even arsenic. None of these substances are in amounts that are dangerous to health.
Bottled Water: calcium, magnesium, and potassium. The dissolved substances in bottled water vary from brand to brand.

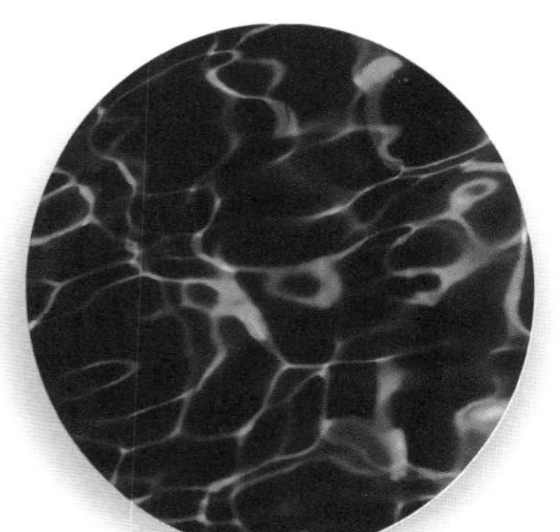

Communicate

1. List and explain two ways you and your family could reduce water use.
2. Plan an investigation to determine how much water your family uses in a day.
3. How clean is snow? How could you find out?
4. You need water to live. Although you can go without eating for about 30 days, you can only survive without water for three days! So what would you do if you were stranded somewhere with no clean water to drink?

6.3 Water Characteristics

Explore

When we talk about the type and amount of minerals in water, we say that the water is hard or soft. Calcium minerals especially tend to make water hard. **Hard water** leaves a chalky feel on your hands when it dries. It is also difficult to make soap lather in hard water. With **soft water**, it is very easy to make soap suds.

Develop

Testing for Water Hardness

In the next activity, you will test the water hardness in your area.

INVESTIGATOR

How Hard Is Your Water?

The Question

Is your tap water hard?

Procedure

1. Pour identical amounts of distilled and tap water and other water samples into each jar.
2. Put one drop of soap solution in the distilled water, screw on the lid, and shake it. Add one drop of soap solution at a time until you make suds. Note how many drops of soap solution you need to make the distilled water sudsy.

Materials & Equipment

- *tap water*
- *distilled water*
- *other water samples (rain, melted snow, etc.)*
- *dropper*
- *liquid soap*
- *screw-top jars for the water samples*
- *Epsom salts*
- *measuring spoon*
- *250-mL beaker*

continued on next page

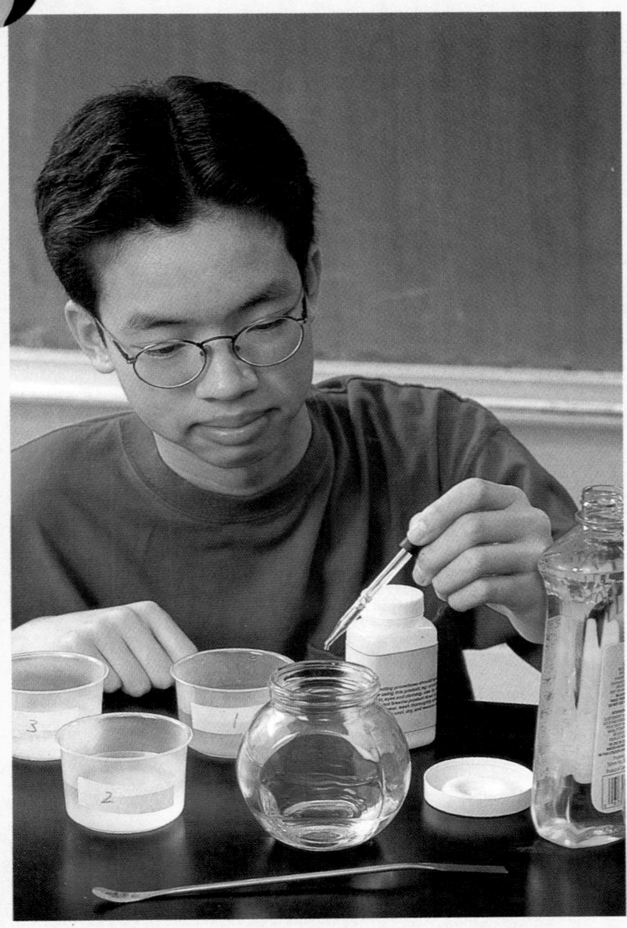

3 Repeat the test with tap water and water from other sources.

4 Pour 100 mL of distilled water into a beaker. Add 1 teaspoon of Epsom salts and stir until the salts have dissolved.

5 Add two drops of soap solution to the distilled water and Epsom salt mixture and stir. Observe what happens.

6 Repeat steps 4 and 5 using distilled water and 2 teaspoons of Epsom salts.

7 Keep adding additional teaspoons of Epsom salts until you cannot produce suds.

Keeping Records

8 Record the number of drops of soap solution it takes to make the different water samples produce suds.

9 Compare the amount of suds against the amount of Epsom salts added to the distilled water.

Analyzing and Interpreting

10 Is the water in your area hard? How do you know?

11 What effect did the Epsom salts have on the sudsing ability of the soap?

Forming Conclusions

12 How can you make hard water soft? Why would you want to do this?

Communicate

1 Explain how you would solve the following problems. Try to give as many possible answers as you can.
   a) Your washing machine is producing too many soap bubbles.
   b) Every time you wash your hands, there seems to be no way to get all the soap off.
   c) The dish detergent you use doesn't seem to make many soap bubbles.

6.4 Water Pollution

Explore

Only 1% of all the water on earth is available as fresh water. So what happens if we pollute this water? Wastes and other pollutants are continually dumped into our fresh water supplies where they are dissolved. Industries are the greatest source of **pollution**. In North America, many industries are located on the shores of the Great Lakes as well as rivers draining into the lakes. Some manufacturing facilities use fresh water to carry away such wastes as mercury, lead, sulphur, oil, and petrochemicals.

How clean is this water?

Some cities and towns discharge untreated or partially-treated sewage into the waterways. Precipitation drainage carries contaminants from roads into waterways, as well as pesticides and fertilizer residues from farms. Oil spilled accidentally or flushed from tankers and offshore rigs can destroy beaches and kill bird, fish, and plant life. Did you know that 1 L of spilled oil can contaminate up to 2 000 000 L of water? Trash, solid industrial wastes, and sludge formed during sewage treatment are all commonly dumped into the oceans, as well.

Develop

Water Pollution in Canada

All water pollutants are hazardous to people, as well as to other life forms. Along many shores, shellfish can no longer be eaten because of contamination by these wastes. Dysentery, salmonella, and hepatitis are among the diseases transmitted by untreated sewage in contaminated drinking water. Beaches have been ruined for swimmers by industrial wastes and municipal sewage. There are ways, however, to help prevent these types of situations from occurring.

Problem Solver

Pollution Poster

Create a poster that will inform people about a potential pollution problem in Canada. Your poster should address one of the following areas:

- Manufacturing pollutants: sources and characteristics
- Agricultural pollutants: sources and characteristics
- Household chemicals: sources, regulations for safe use and disposal
- Community waste (such as sewage and trash): sources and environmental considerations related to their disposal

When you have completed your poster, present it to the class.

Communicate

1. Look at the picture on the previous page. If the pipes run into a lake, hat do you think will happen to the lake in the next few years?
2. Describe one example of water pollution in your community or province. Explain how you think the pollution could be reduced or eliminated.

try this at HOME

OIL SPILL

Try this to clean up an oil spill.

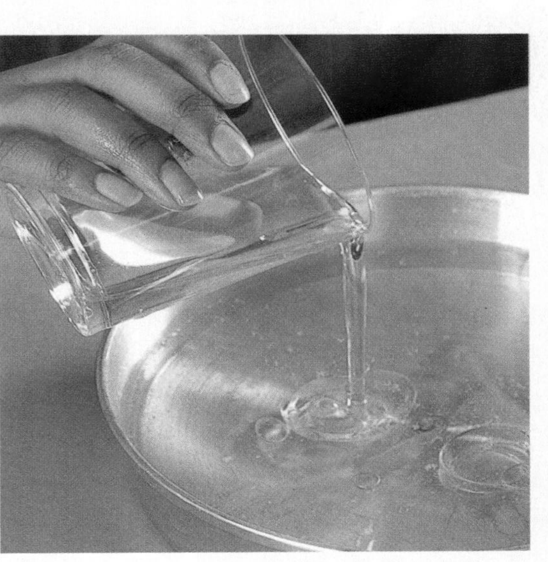

Procedure

1. Fill a shallow pie plate with water and pour a few drops of vegetable oil on top.
2. Try to clean up the oil using cotton balls first and then, detergents.
3. What else could you use to clean up the oil?

Questions

4. How well did you clean up the oil?
5. What did the detergent do to the oil?
6. What happened to the oil as time went on?

6.5 CHECK YOUR PROGRESS

1. How can you separate salt from sea water using solar energy?
2. Is tap water a pure substance or a mixture? What evidence can you give to support your answer? If you determined that it isn't a pure substance, how could you make it pure?
3. The picture on the next page is a model for what happens to a plant that is given contaminated water. A container with about 4 cm of water has red food colouring or ink added to the water. A white flower or a stalk of celery is then placed in the container. You can observe the results after a few hours. What does this show you about the effects of water pollution?

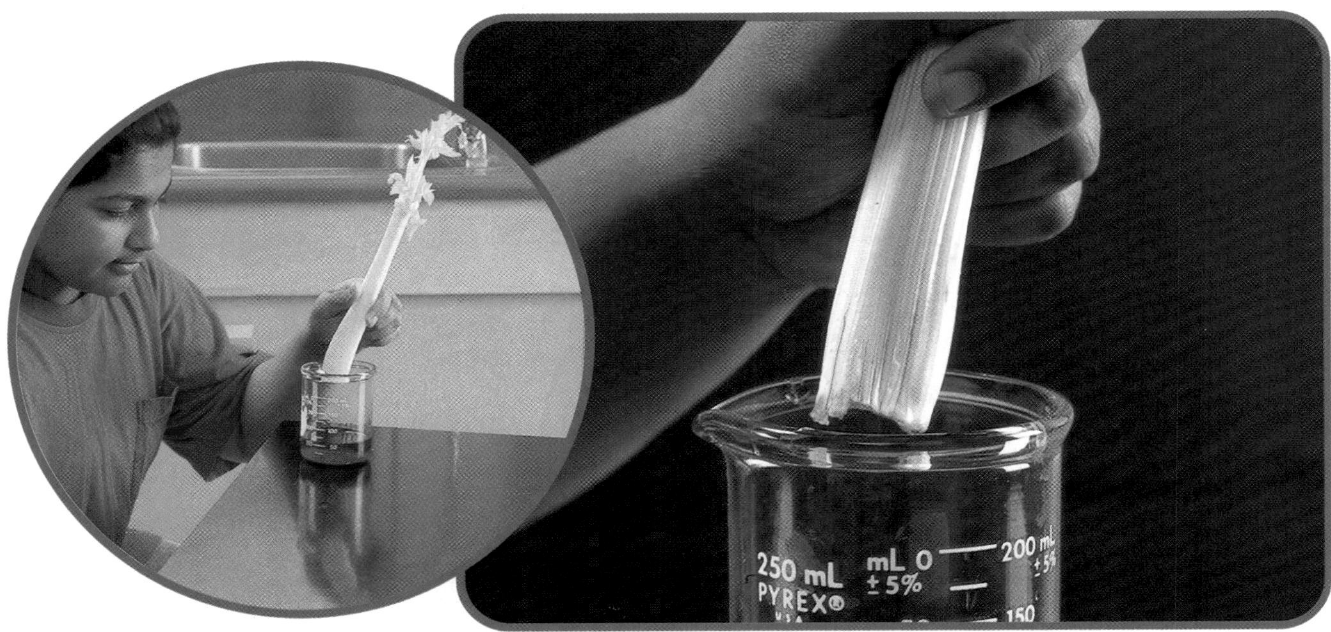

4 Water pollution can be difficult to eliminate because it is often linked to many causes and events. Choose one of the situations listed below. List all the related events and causes that could be related to these examples of water pollution. Offer one possible solution to the problem. The first one has been done for you.

a) The water in a lake used for drinking water is polluted with minerals and a film of oil and paint thinner. No motor boats are allowed on the lake. The nearby community has no disposal depot for household hazardous wastes. So the waste disposal site includes used paint, oil, gas, and household cleaners. These hazardous chemicals from the waste disposal site get into the water system and eventually into the lake. <u>One possible solution</u>: *Collect hazardous household wastes separately and deliver them to a waste treatment plant.*

b) A pulp and paper mill has been discharging pollutants into a river for over ten years. Now, all the well water in the area is contaminated.

c) An oil tanker hits a rock a few kilometres from a public beach. The tanker loses millions of litres of oil, polluting the coastline.

d) Fish in a northern wilderness lake have begun to die mysteriously. There is fear that in a few years, the fish will disappear.

e) Every time it rains heavily in a community, a nearby lake becomes polluted.

Careers and Profiles

The Nose Knows

"If you want a perfume that smells like an orange, with a top note of an apple, and in an hour smells like an apricot, I could make it for you," says Russell Berger. Berger is a trained perfumer, otherwise known in the perfume industry as a "nose." He's trained to tell the difference between hundreds of different fragrances and fragrance blends. Berger has been designing new perfumes for many years and recently designed a fragrance called "Me" for his wife. He also designs personal fragrances for celebrities.

Russell Berger testing fragrance samples at his company, Liage International Inc.

To create a perfume, Berger begins with three basic ingredients:

- **Essential oils:** aromatic oils extracted from plants. They are used to give perfume its fragrance. A single perfume will have 5 to 25 different essential oils blended together.
- **Fixative:** an oil that evaporates very slowly. It is mixed with the essential oils and traps them, causing them to evaporate more slowly. This makes the fragrance last longer.
- **Alcohol:** a solvent used to dilute the essential oils, thus preventing the fragrance from being too powerful.

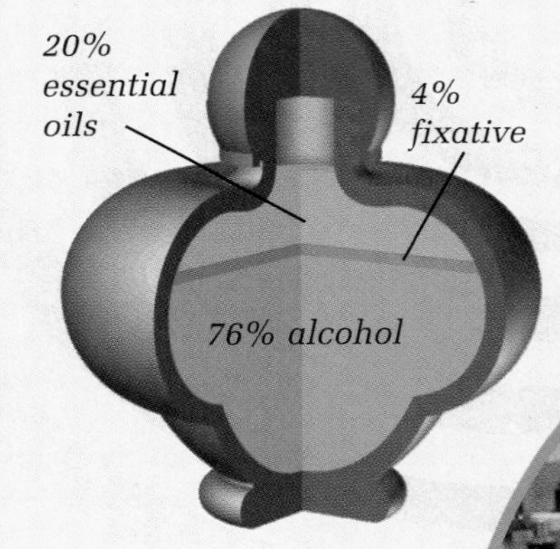

The different essential oils in perfume evaporate at different rates. This causes a perfume's fragrance to change over time. These changes are called "notes."

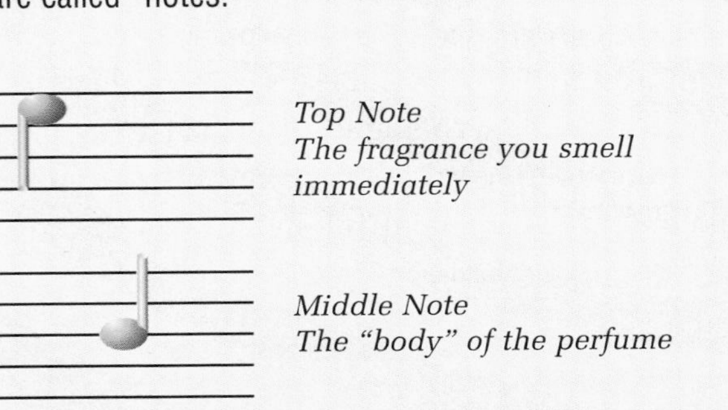

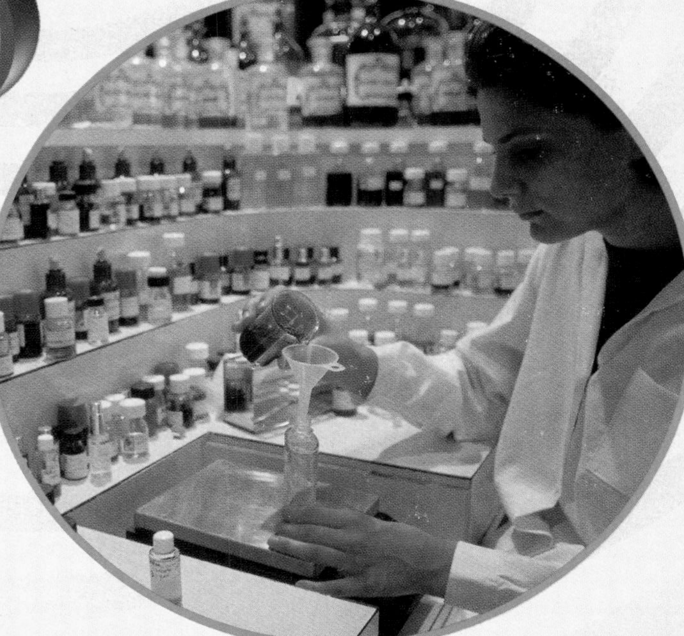

When designing a new perfume, the perfumer uses many essential oils to create different "notes."

BIG IDEA

7.0 Mixtures of raw materials can be processed to make useful things.

2 MIXTURES

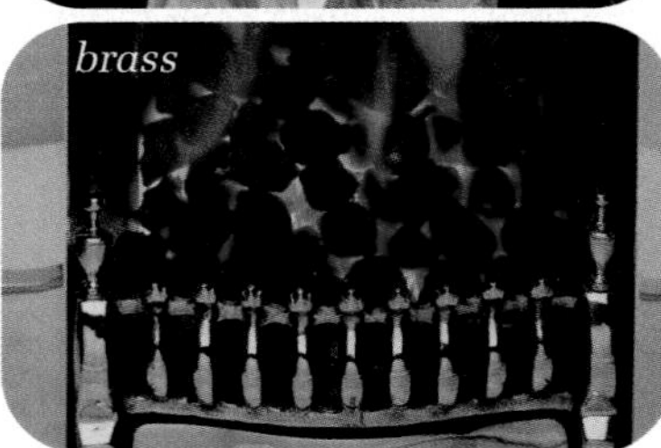

These metals are called **alloys**. They are really solutions of two or more natural metals.

There are all sorts of manufactured products made from mixtures. You may be surprised to find out that some of these products have very different properties from the original **raw materials**. In the next section, you will find out about super-cooled liquids that look like solids and about raw materials that, when combined, make some of the strongest materials in the world. You will also investigate some of the environmental problems that go with producing, using, and disposing of these products.

7.1 Products Manufactured From Mixtures

Explore

Thousands of years ago, people began to mix substances together to make more useful materials. Raw materials such as sand, soda, and limestone, can be collected and processed to produce different materials, such as glass. Let's look at how some manufactured products are made from mixtures.

Develop

A Mix of Ingredients

Making Glass

You are surrounded by glass, from the bottles that contain your drinks to the windows that you look through. **Glass** is a unique material that looks like and behaves as a solid, but has many of the properties of a liquid. Scientists regard glass as a super-cooled liquid. Glass is a manufactured material made by heating a mixture of substances that can include sand, carbonates, and limestone. Other substances can be added to give the glass colour or special qualities. Although these materials are plentiful and cheap, the energy needed to heat them is expensive.

Glass is made in a tank furnace. The raw materials—sand, carbonates, and limestone—are fed into one end and molten glass at 1000°C is produced at the other. This molten glass can be made into flat sheets, blown by automated machines into containers, or pressed into different shapes.

Glass is used to make containers, mirrors, and windows. It deteriorates only a little over time and doesn't contaminate its contents. Glass can even be spun into fibres, which are stronger than steel, and used in fibre optics to transmit light and information. Glass for bottles or windows is made of 75% sand, 15% carbonates, and 10% lime (from limestone). Recycled glass is sometimes added to help the melting process and may make up 50% of the total mixture.

Most glass containers are disposable—they are made to be thrown out. This creates an environmental problem because smashed pieces of glass are dangerous and glass does not break down easily. However, today, many towns and cities recycle glass to sell back to the manufacturers who use it to produce new glass.

Making Steel

Steel is a very strong metal. It is used to make building materials, food cans, cutlery, and ocean liners. **Steel** is a mixture of iron (from iron ore), carbon, and small quantities of other substances.

*info***BIT**

People have been making glass for over 6000 years. At first, highly coloured glass was used to glaze pottery for decoration. The Egyptians used glass for jewellery, and around 1500 B.C., they produced the first glass bottles. These bottles were used for holding perfume and oils.

Egyptian glass, 1500 B.C – 1300 B.C.

How Steel Is Made

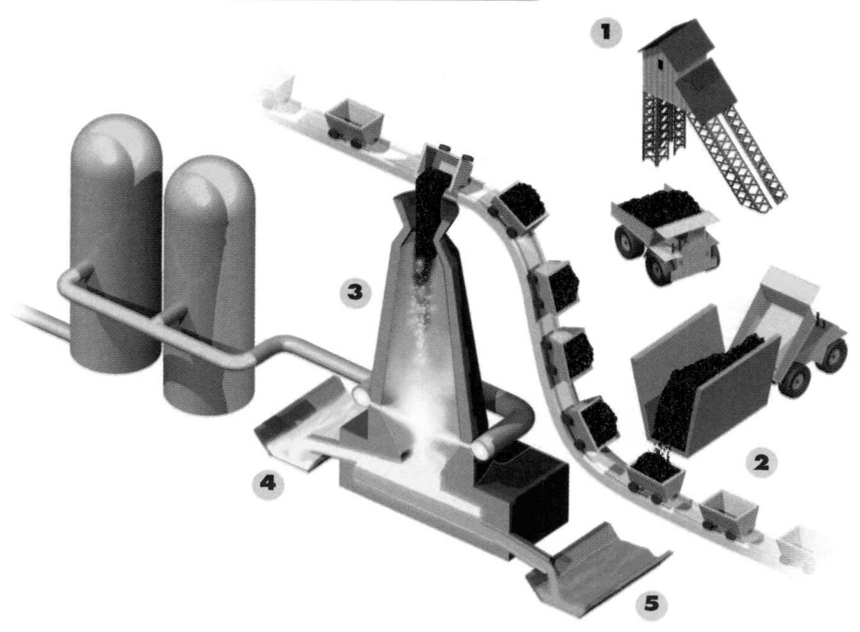

1 Iron ore is mined from the ground.
2 It is put into a blast furnace and mixed with limestone and **coke** (a type of coal).
3 At about 1650°C, the coke mixes with the iron ore to make liquid iron, called **pig iron**.
4 The limestone mixes with unwanted substances to make **slag** (waste matter).
5 The pig iron contains about 4% carbon.

The iron is processed to remove impurities to make steel (which should contain about 2% carbon or less).

Communicate

1. List three raw materials used to make glass.
2. What are three characteristics of glass that make it a useful mixture in our lives? Give an example of how one characteristic is used in a product.
3. What is the difference between pig iron and steel? Are both of these materials pure substances or mixtures? How do you know?
4. List at least two other mixtures that are made into manufactured products.

7.2 Cleaning Our World

Explore

While you are eating a hamburger, a glob of grease falls and lands on your pants. You hope that laundry detergent will be able to get the grease stain out. But what is it about detergents that gives them their special cleaning powers?

A **detergent** is a substance that cleans away dirt. Most detergents are liquids or powders that can dissolve in water. **Soap** is a type of detergent. Generally, the word detergent refers to synthetic detergents, which have a different composition than soap. Detergents and soaps contain a cleaning agent called a surfactant. **Surfactants** are particles that attach themselves to dirt and oil particles, and pull them into the water to be rinsed away.

How Detergent Works

Dirt and grease on fabric

The mixture of water, detergent, and clothes is agitated in the washing machine. Dirt breaks off from the clothes.

Detergent surrounds the dirt particles so they can't re-attach to clothes.

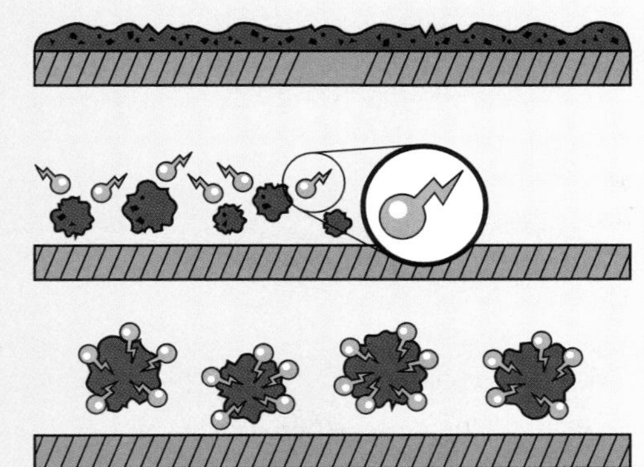

In the past, manufacturers added chemicals called phosphates to detergents. **Phosphates** increased the number of suds that the detergent produced and made the suds last longer. However, phosphates caused damage to the environment by polluting the water. Today, most detergents do not include phosphates.

Develop

What Cleans Best?

The best cleaners have the ability to dissolve dirt and grease. In the next activity, you will look at different solvents and their cleaning abilities.

INVESTIGATOR

CLEANING SOLVENTS

The Question

Can you remove stains from clothing using different solvents?

Procedure

1. Pour 50 mL of water into one beaker, 50 mL of rubbing alcohol into another beaker, and 50 mL of vinegar into a third beaker. Label the beakers.
2. Mark each piece of fabric with mud, lipstick, and chocolate.

Materials & Equipment

- *3 250-mL beakers*
- *water (at room temperature)*
- *rubbing alcohol (at room temperature)*
- *vinegar (at room temperature)*
- *graduated cylinder*
- *3 identical pieces of fabric*
- *mud*
- *lipstick*
- *chocolate*
- *laundry detergent*
- *pair of forceps or tweezers*

continued on next page

3 Place one piece of soiled fabric into each of the three beakers. Swirl the fabric around in each solution using the forceps. Leave for at least 10 min. Look at the stains.

4 Add some laundry detergent to the beaker containing water. Use the forceps to move the fabric around in the solution.

Keeping Records

5 Make a chart of your observations.

Analyzing and Interpreting

6 Did the mud dissolve in each solvent? Explain.

7 Did the lipstick dissolve in each solvent? Explain.

8 Did the chocolate dissolve in each solvent? Explain.

9 Did the detergent help the water dissolve the stains?

Forming Conclusions

10 Describe the results from your investigation and conclude which solvent did the best cleaning job for each type of stain and which was the worst. Support your conclusions with your data. Also, include one new thing you learned in this activity that you didn't know before.

*info***BIT**

Ingredients in a typical laundry detergent:

Ingredient	What It Does
surfactant	*cleans clothes*
filler	*stops detergent from clumping*
suspension agent	*stops dirt from re-attaching to material*
bleach	*removes stains*
fragrance	*adds scent*

Ingredient	What It Does
builder	*softens water to help surfactant clean*
corrosion inhibitor	*prevents washer from rusting*
enzyme	*removes protein stains*
optical whitener	*adds brightness*
colouring agent	*gives detergent colour*

Non-toxic Cleaners

Cleaners that contain toxic or hazardous chemicals can be damaging to your skin, as well as to the environment. You can make cleaners using some common household ingredients. Are these natural cleaners as effective as cleaners that contain toxic or hazardous chemicals?

PROBLEM SOLVER

HOME-MADE CLEANERS

Make your own cleaners and test them against store brands. To make an all-purpose cleaner, mix 50 mL of baking soda, 125 mL of vinegar, and 4 L of water in a spray bottle.

> **Caution!**
> **Read the caution labels on the cleaners you use. It is dangerous to mix certain cleaners.**

- Decide what your cleaner will clean.
- Develop a plan to make a sample amount of your cleaner. Make a sample.
- What are some advantages and disadvantages of home-made cleaners?
- Create a fair test that investigates the differences between a home-made and a store-bought cleaner.

Long ago, people cleaned their teeth with a powder made from marble. Today, most toothpastes still contain powdered minerals, such as bauxite, as well as other substances. These substances include a binder made from wood pulp (to keep the paste mixed), a detergent (made from chemicals) to clean your teeth, fluoride (a chemical to help keep your teeth strong), colouring, and flavouring (made from plants such as mint).

What's in Toothpaste?

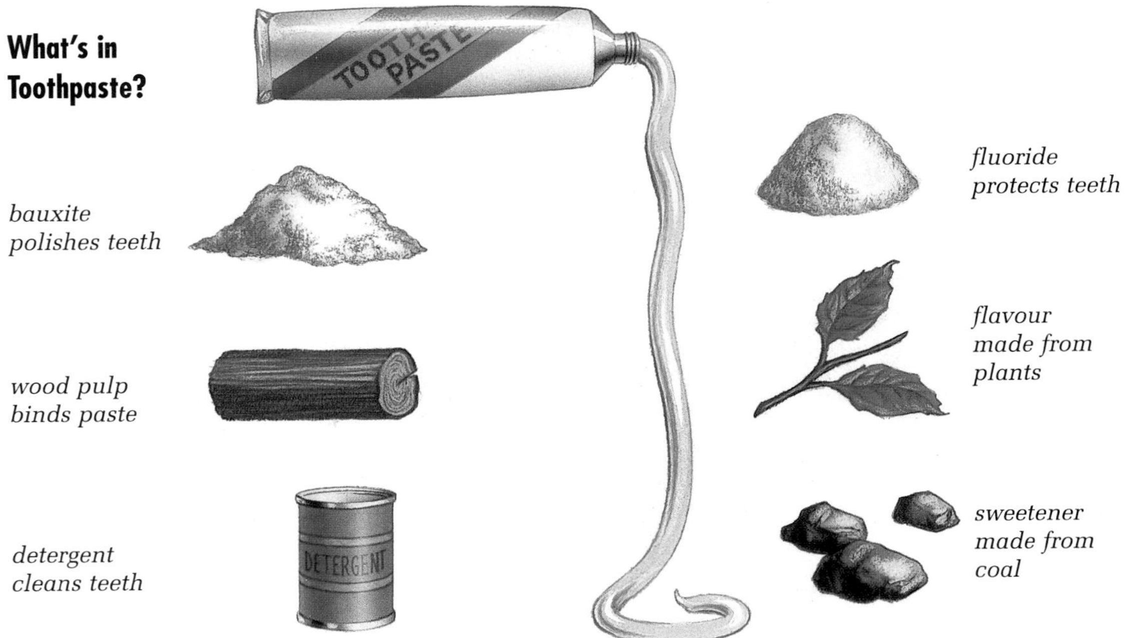

Communicate

1 Describe one thing you learned about cleaners that you didn't know before.
2 Describe the results of the fair test you developed for Home-made Cleaners. Which type of cleaner cleaned best?
3 The following statements were taken from advertisements for laundry detergents. What ingredients are being emphasized?
   a) "Now brighter and whiter than ever"
   b) "Cleans your washing machine as it cleans your clothes"
   c) "Removes the toughest stains"
   d) "Now in new ocean mist scent"

7.3 WASTE AND THE ENVIRONMENT

Explore

Nature is very good at reusing and recycling natural waste materials. Just think about what happens to fallen leaves and dead plants. Although people are very good at producing waste, they aren't as good at recycling it. Some forms of the waste humans produce can be used again, but most are dumped as garbage. Many of the substances that are thrown away as waste are not **biodegradable**. This means that they do not break down, as leaves and dead plants do.

Waste materials that are dumped and do not decompose can cause pollution. Other waste materials produce pollutants when they decompose. There are many sources of waste that affect the environment, including trash, industrial waste, air pollution, agricultural waste, and sewage.

What do you think of when you hear the word pollution?

- List some environmental problems that concern you.
- Give some specific examples of how these problems affect your daily life.

These were once new cars!

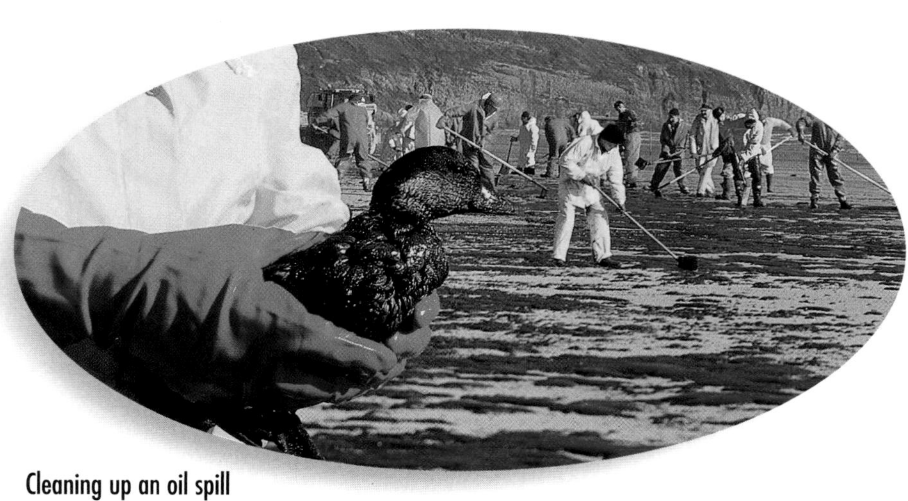

Cleaning up an oil spill

Develop

Examining Different Types of Waste

People produce a variety of different types of waste: industrial waste, air pollution, agricultural waste, and sewage.

Industrial Waste

Industries are responsible for creating large amounts of waste. These industries include food processing, mining, petrochemical and plastic production, and the manufacture of consumer goods. Industries depend on raw materials, such as iron, water, and wood, to manufacture goods. The manufacturing processes produce waste products, which may be toxic. Toxic wastes can harm the environment and people.

What are these bags waiting for? They are what's left over when PVC (polyvinyl chloride) material is incinerated. Every kilogram of incinerated PVC produces 2 to 3 times that amount of waste!

About 10–20% of industrial waste is considered to be hazardous. Hazardous wastes contain such chemicals as cyanide, asbestos, and mercury. By law, they must be recorded and taken to special treatment facilities. But some hazardous wastes are illegally dumped, ending up in landfill sites, lakes, or oceans.

Air Pollution

During hot, hazy summer days, have you ever heard warnings about poor air quality? Many of the pollutants in the air come from the burning of fossil fuels (coal, gasoline). Air pollution can cause smog and acid rain.

The major air pollutants are sulphur dioxide, nitrogen oxides, and carbon monoxide. Once in the atmosphere, sulphur and nitrogen oxides dissolve in water droplets to produce sulphuric acid and nitric acid. These acids fall to the ground in rain and snow. Acid rain changes the **pH** of water. But what does pH mean? Read the infoBIT and do the next activity to find out.

*info*BIT

Beluga whales grow to be about 4 m in length. In the St. Lawrence River, the beluga's food supply (fish, shrimp, snails, crabs, and worms) has become contaminated with industrial waste. As a result, there are only about 500 beluga whales left in this area.

*info*BIT

The pH scale is a measure of how acidic or basic a solution is. The scale goes from 0 to 14. The difference between each number is equivalent to an increase of *ten times* the strength. (For example, a pH of 3.0 is ten times more acidic than a pH of 4.0.)

An acidic solution can have a pH between 0 and 6.

Orange juice can have a pH of around 3.7.

Water is usually considered to be neutral or to have a pH of about 7.0.

A basic solution has a pH between 8 and 14.

Chlorine bleach is near the end of the scale with a pH of 12.6.

INVESTIGATOR

How Acidic Is the Rain?

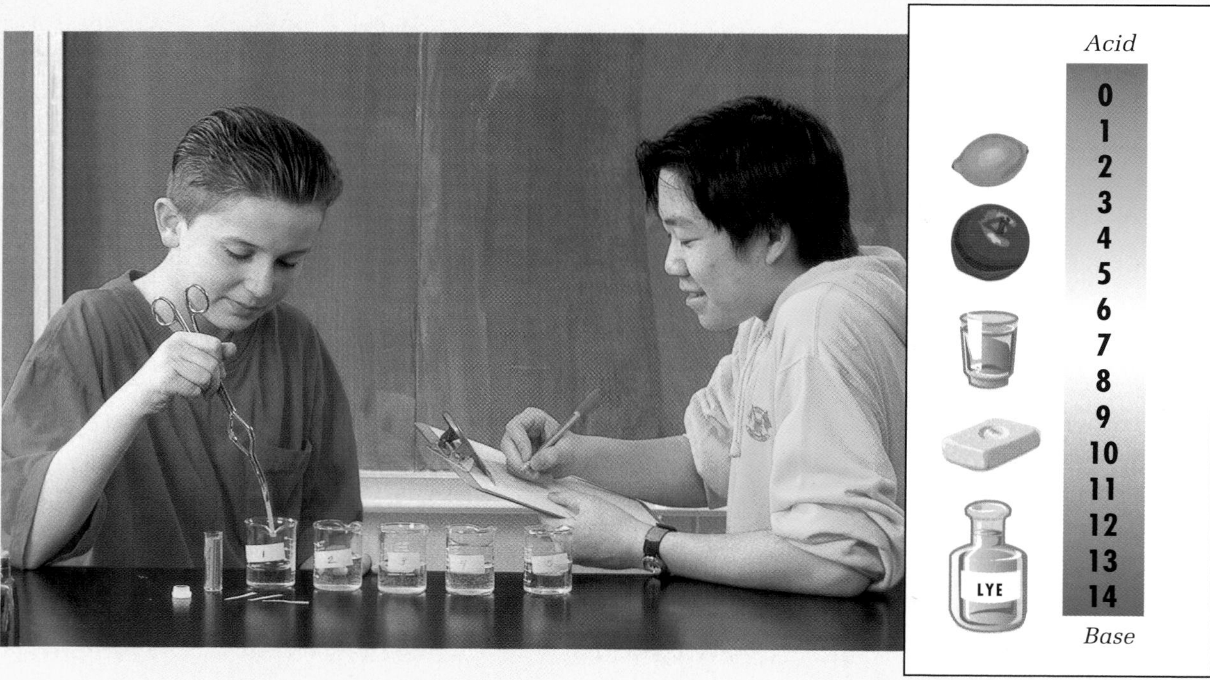

The Question

What is the pH of different water samples?

Materials & Equipment

- *250-mL beakers*
- *different water samples (rain water, tap water)*
- *distilled water*
- *vinegar*
- *litmus paper (pH test strips)*
- *tongs*

Procedure

1. Collect different samples of water in beakers. If you can, include a beaker of rain water or snow. Label your beakers.
2. Pour a mixture of half tap water and half vinegar into one of the beakers. Label all the beakers.
3. Use tongs to dip a strip of litmus paper into each beaker.

Keeping Records

4. Record what happens to the litmus paper in each beaker.

Analyzing and Interpreting

5. What did the colour of the litmus paper tell you about the water samples?
6. What happened when you tested rain water? Why?
7. What is the pH of distilled water? Why?

Forming Conclusions

8. Present your results in a table or short description. Using the results, explain why you think your water samples may or may not be polluted.

Agricultural Waste

Livestock on farms produce a lot of waste. Large amounts of manure cannot be recycled naturally, so the waste is kept in pits and later spread on the fields. However, if it is spread too thickly, the waste may be washed off into rivers and streams, causing water pollution.

A manure spreader

Fertilizer for the home garden

Some farmers use pesticides and fertilizers containing nitrogen to make crops grow rapidly and to produce large harvests. The fertilizer is broken down by the soil to produce nitrates, which are used by plants. However, too much fertilizer produces too much nitrates that can be washed away by rain, like manure, into the ground water or into rivers.

Too much nitrates in water cause plants and algae to grow uncontrollably. In time, these plants will choke out most other living things.

Sewage

Between 1832 and 1854, over 20 000 people in London, England died from cholera. Cholera is caused by drinking water that contains sewage. **Sewage** is the waste that goes down the sink, the drain, and the toilet. In most areas, sewage is collected in sewers and drains that lead to sewage treatment plants. At a sewage treatment plant, the wastes are separated and the liquids are cleaned and returned to the water cycle. The solids are processed to form sludge, which may be dumped in landfill sites, in the ocean, or used to enrich soil for non-food crops.

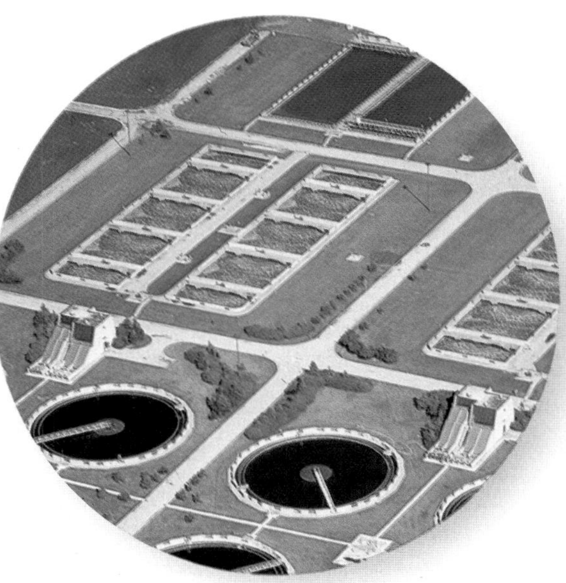

A modern sewage treatment plant

Good News

People have begun to realize how seriously pollution can harm the earth. You know that your health and enjoyment of life depends on a healthy environment. Much is being done to clean up the environment. Environmental information is becoming widely available, and different countries are working together to develop strict guidelines for the control of wastes. Industries are also becoming more environmentally responsible.

Communicate

1 What are three waste threats to our environment?
2 There are many simple, practical ways you can help protect the environment. Find out what effect you and those around you have on the environment. Think about an environmental concern that you may have. Brainstorm ways in which you could make a difference to the problem you identified.

7.4 CHECK YOUR PROGRESS

1 Choose a product you use. What substances do you think go into making it? Where would these substances come from?
2 What properties give detergents their ability to clean things?
3 How can a detergent clean grease off clothes?
4 If you had a beaker of water, a beaker of rubbing alcohol, and a beaker of vinegar, describe how you would construct a fair test to determine which liquid was the best cleaner.
5 What is the difference between toothpaste used in the past and toothpaste today. Were both types of toothpaste mixtures?
6 What are the different types of pollution and how do they impact our environment?
7 How can learning about pH help you understand acid rain?

*info***BIT**

In the 1960s, Lake Erie was declared a "dead lake." Pollution from cities and farms caused weeds and algae to grow out of control. Fish populations, once one of the richest in the Great Lakes, were at an all-time low. Today, after a huge environmental clean-up, the fish are back and the lake has never looked better.

Sewage Treatment: A Mix of Solutions

Every community produces a great amount of sewage. This is a mixture of all sorts of "nasty" stuff: human waste, bits of food, toxic and non-toxic chemicals, and just plain dirt. But one part of the mixture is very valuable—it's the water!

There is only a certain amount of water on earth. As you know, it moves in what is called the water cycle. Unfortunately, as people use water during this cycle, they also pollute it. Water is polluted by sewage, by industrial chemicals, and by pesticides from farms.

- What can we do to clean the water we've polluted?
- How can we separate the water from the rest of the mixture?

There are three levels of sewage treatment that communities use: primary treatment, secondary treatment, and tertiary treatment.

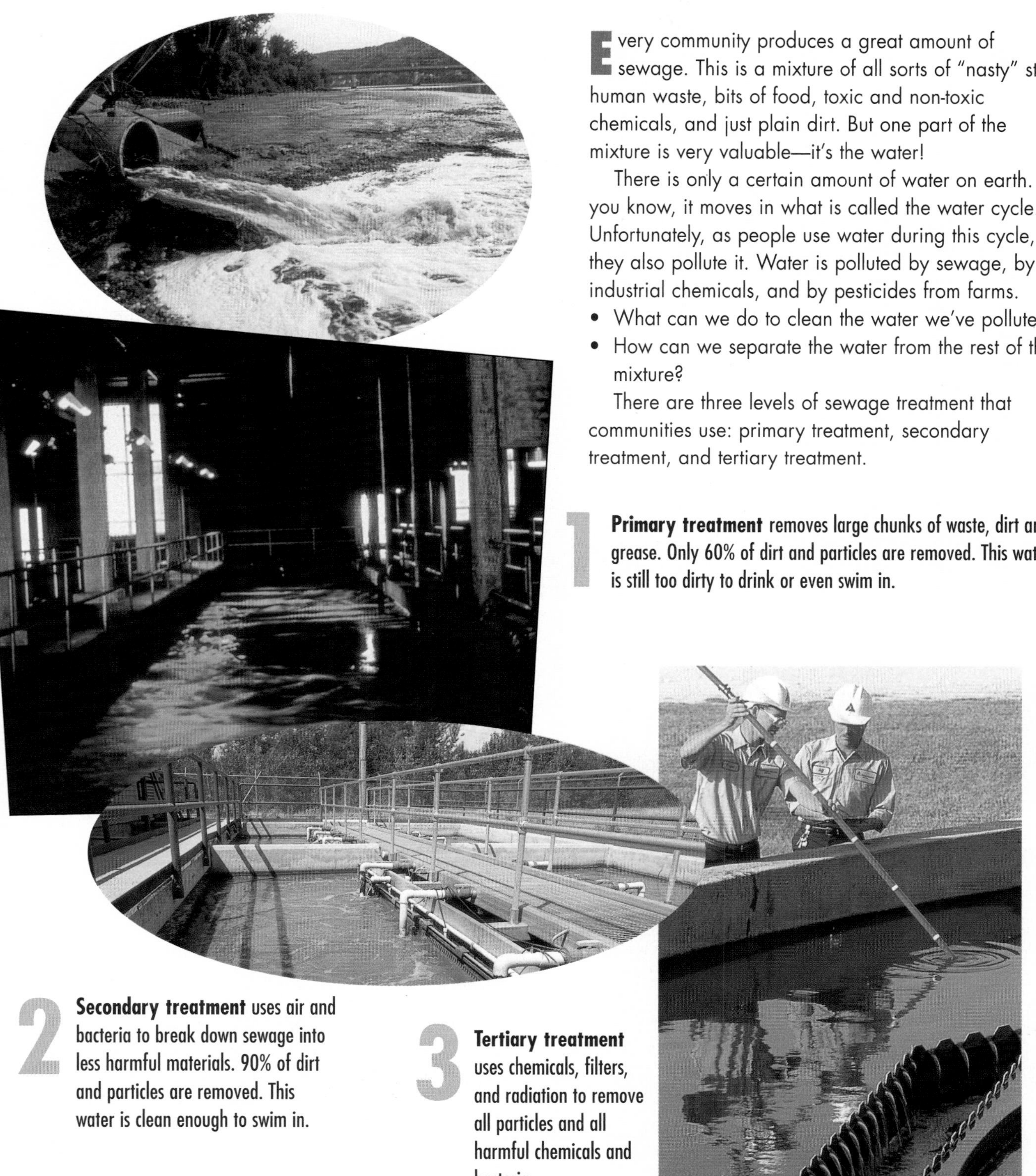

1 **Primary treatment** removes large chunks of waste, dirt and grease. Only 60% of dirt and particles are removed. This water is still too dirty to drink or even swim in.

2 **Secondary treatment** uses air and bacteria to break down sewage into less harmful materials. 90% of dirt and particles are removed. This water is clean enough to swim in.

3 **Tertiary treatment** uses chemicals, filters, and radiation to remove all particles and all harmful chemicals and bacteria.

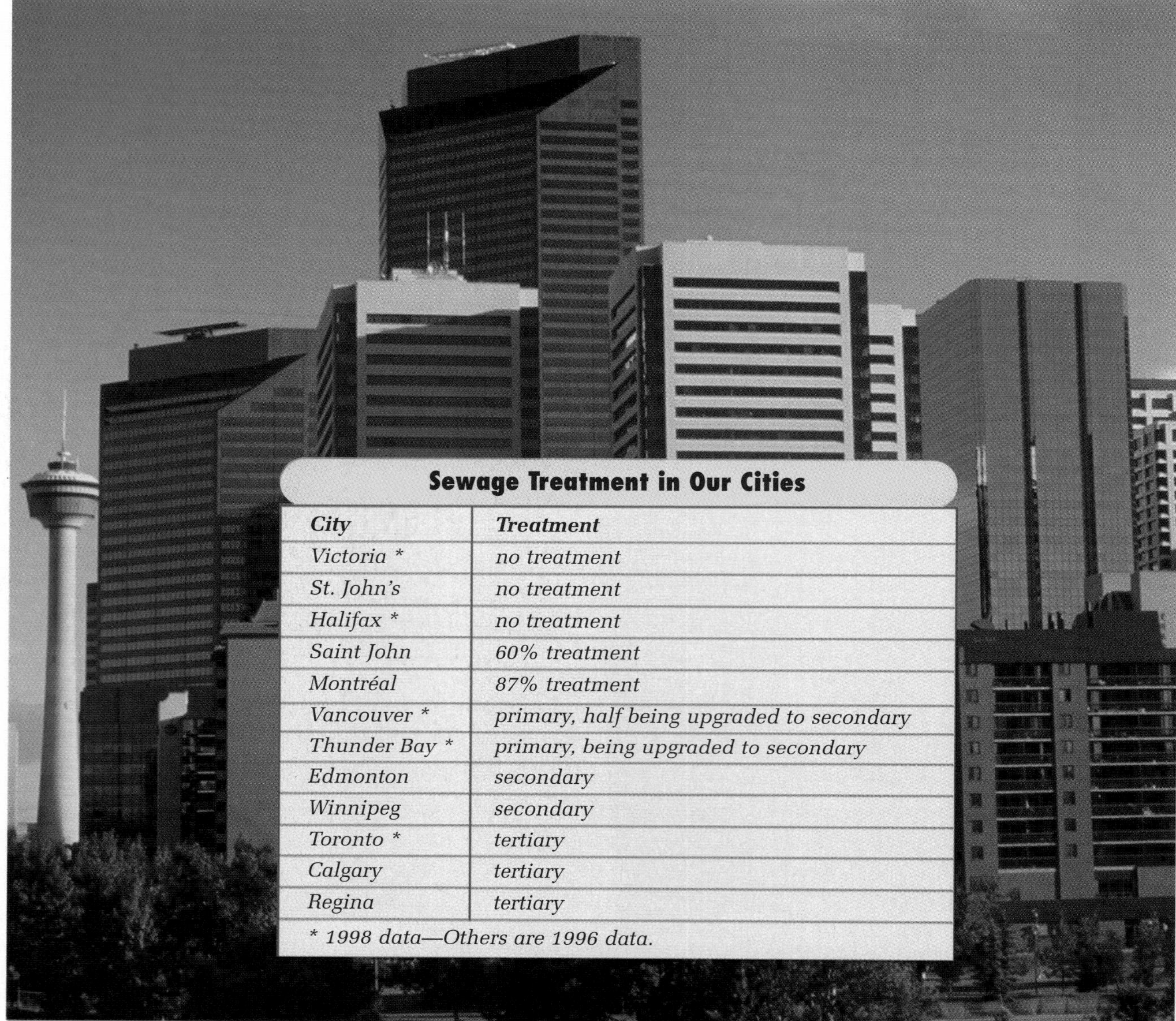

Sewage Treatment in Our Cities

City	*Treatment*
*Victoria **	*no treatment*
St. John's	*no treatment*
*Halifax **	*no treatment*
Saint John	*60% treatment*
Montréal	*87% treatment*
*Vancouver **	*primary, half being upgraded to secondary*
*Thunder Bay **	*primary, being upgraded to secondary*
Edmonton	*secondary*
Winnipeg	*secondary*
*Toronto **	*tertiary*
Calgary	*tertiary*
Regina	*tertiary*

** 1998 data—Others are 1996 data.*

In Your Opinion

1. Work in a group of four to develop reasons supporting each of the following options. (Each group member chooses a different option.)

Four Sewage-Treatment Options:
- **a)** No treatment
- **b)** Primary treatment
- **c)** Secondary treatment
- **d)** Tertiary treatment

2. Share your points of view with other members of the class. (All the people supporting "no treatment" share viewpoints, all the people supporting "primary treatment" share viewpoints, and so on.)
3. Create a presentation to convince the other members of the class that this option is the best.
4. As a class, discuss why communities must often compromise on which sewage treatment method they will use.

PROJECT

WHAT'S REALLY IN THERE?

Getting Started

During this chapter you have developed a variety of skills. These skills include how to measure volume and mass, how to use a range of techniques to separate and identify mixtures, and how to apply your understanding of matter to explain a variety of natural phenomena.

Before You Start...

Take a moment with your partner or other classmates to look over the Crime Stoppers' Report Sheet on the next page. Also, list and describe the different techniques you have used to separate both mechanical mixtures and solutions.

continued on next page ·····➤

Crime Stoppers' Report Sheet

Monday, 6:06 a.m.

Passers-by think they notice rain coming in a side door at Metro Auto Glass, off Jordon Drive. However, it is raining too hard, so they don't stop to investigate. They do call their concerns in to Crime Stoppers, who call the security company that patrols that area.

Monday, 6:14 a.m.

Allied Security arrives and discovers the glass window in the side door has been removed. They call police and the owners of Metro Auto Glass. Allied Security discovers a number of computers have been taken.

Monday, 6:23 a.m.

The owners and police arrive at about the same time. Besides the computer equipment, several sheets of auto glass and at least 20 tires have been stolen.

Just the Facts

When the police begin their investigation, they are baffled. The rain coming into the missing window has soaked the area, making it difficult to discover any clues. The police do check to see if the break-in method of removing the glass from the door has been used in other recent robberies. It hasn't.

The forensic analysts team arrives next. It's their job is to collect evidence using a variety of scientific techniques. Lasers are often used to find fingerprints. Specially made chemical sprays are also employed to find small amounts of residue left behind by the thieves. Tiny amounts of unknown material are collected and taken back to the forensic lab to be identified.

Forensic analysts identify unknown materials by performing a series of tests. This process is called *qualitative analysis.* By following an identification procedure, analysts can eventually identify unknown materials. In many criminal investigations, the information collected is very useful in solving a crime.

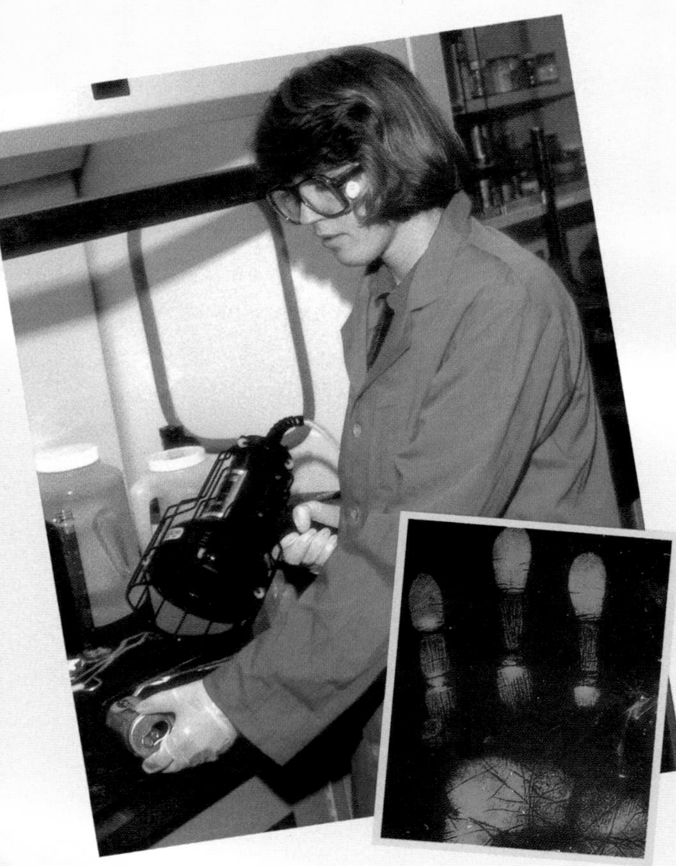

During this chapter you have developed the necessary skills to perform a qualitative analysis of an unknown mixture just as forensic analysts do. You will use the list of techniques you developed with your classmates as your guide to determining what substances are in the unknown mixture you receive from your teacher.

The Task

To identify all the substances in an unknown mixture using the proper techniques.

Materials & Equipment

- *You will need to use a variety of equipment from your previous investigations. Your teacher will help you to organize your equipment, so everyone in the class has access to it.*

Procedure

1. Review your list of techniques used to separate mixtures. Make any necessary revisions to your list before you begin the investigation.
2. Create a table that will allow you to record the results of each test you will perform.
3. Collect the sample of the unknown mixture from your teacher.
4. Using your list, perform an analysis of your unknown material to identify the substances present.
5. Record your results in a table.

Observations and Reflections

6. Summarize your results by describing what substances you think are in your mixture. Be prepared to defend your conclusions using your results.
7. How do you think you did in the investigation? Give yourself a rating on each of the following statements.

Statement	*	**	***
I used the proper techniques in this investigation.			
I remembered to follow the proper safety rules.			
My results reflect my effort.			
I worked well with others.			

* *OK, but I could have done better.*
** *I worked well and am pleased with my effort.*
*** *I worked as hard as I could and am pleased with my effort.*

Share and Compare

8. Share your results with other members of your class.

Chapter Review

Using Key Terms

1 Create a sentence that defines each of the terms below:

pure substance
mechanical mixture
homogeneous mixture
heterogeneous mixture
solution
dilute
concentrated
Particle Theory of Matter
solvent
solute
solubility
saturated
unsaturated

Reviewing the Big Ideas

2 Why is it important to measure substances accurately in the lab?

3 You see the following safety symbol on a substance. What does it mean?

4 Name five important safety rules. Explain why you should follow these rules.

5 Why is it hard to tell whether a substance is a solution or a pure substance?

6 How can you tell solutions from pure substances?

7 What is a heterogeneous mixture?

8 Name five heterogeneous mixtures you can see from where you are working.

9 What kind of mixtures can be separated using filtration? Why?

10 What kind of mixtures can be separated by distillation? Why?

11 How is distilled water made? Is distilled water pure in the scientific meaning of the word?

12 Draw a particle picture of a mechanical mixture.

13 What does a solution look like?

14 What factors affect the rate of dissolving?

15 Can a dilute solution be saturated? Can a concentrated solution be unsaturated?

16 Why is the statement "Water is the solvent in any solution" not always true? Give two examples to support your answer.

17 Think of some situations where it is important to know the concentration of a solution.

18 Explain how and why water is considered to be the universal solvent.

19 What are the major pollutants of waterways?

20 How is water cleaned and treated for drinking?

21 Give two examples of some manufactured products made from mixtures. What are their functions?

22 What are some characteristics of pollutants from agricultural systems?

23 What different types of waste are present in the environment?

Connecting the Big Ideas

24 Use the Particle Theory to explain how sugar dissolves in water.

25 Explain a mechanical mixture using the Particle Theory.

26 What type of mixture is each of the following?
  a) orange juice
  b) a brass button
  c) milk
  d) salad dressing
  e) vinegar

27 Is stirring necessary for dissolving a solute? Explain why or why not.

28 What two factors can you think of that would have little or no effect on the rate of dissolving? Why would they have no effect?

29 Why do some solutes dissolve in a particular solvent, while other solutes do not dissolve?

30 Have you ever heard a noise when you opened a cold bottle of soda pop? When you open a warm bottle of soda pop, the noise is much louder. What does this tell you about the relationship between the amount of carbon dioxide that dissolves in water and the temperature of the water?

31 Distilled water is used in some bottled drinks. Could we use distillation to purify all our drinking water? Why or why not?

32 Soda pop contains carbon dioxide. Why does a glass of soda pop go flat as it warms up?

33 Disposing of alcohol by pouring it on the ground can pollute the ground water. Is evaporating a better method of disposal?

34 Could you use soap to turn hard water into soft water?

35 Explain how laundry detergent removes a grease spot from material.

36 What is sewage pollution? How do you think it affects organisms in the water?

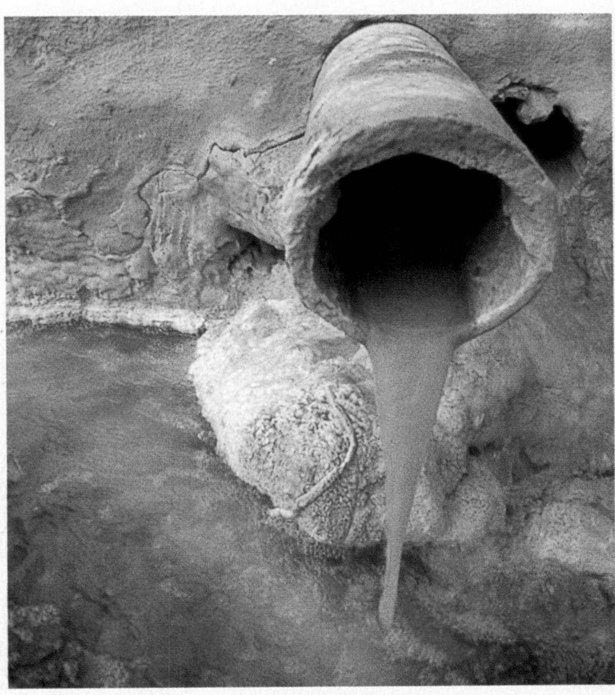

What do you think is the source of this pollution?

Using the Big Ideas

37 Which solution is more concentrated: 50 g of a substance in 200 mL of water or 10 g of the same substance in 40 mL of water? Explain. Calculate the concentration of each solution in g/100 mL of solvent.

38 The solubility of a substance at 20°C is 40 g/100 mL of water. A solution contains 30 g of solute dissolved in 100 mL of water. Is this solution saturated, unsaturated, or dilute? Explain.

39 How is salt removed from sea water to make drinking water?

40 Can you think of a mixture that is useful in one place, but is a pollutant in another place?

41 Why have many communities banned phosphates in detergents?

42 How does the filter in a vacuum cleaner work?

Self Assessment

43 Look back in your notes and identify one piece of work that you are most proud of, one piece of work you could improve on if you were to do the assignment again, and one assignment where you learned something you didn't know before. For each piece of work, describe your thoughts in a short paragraph.

Solar desalination plant in Mexico

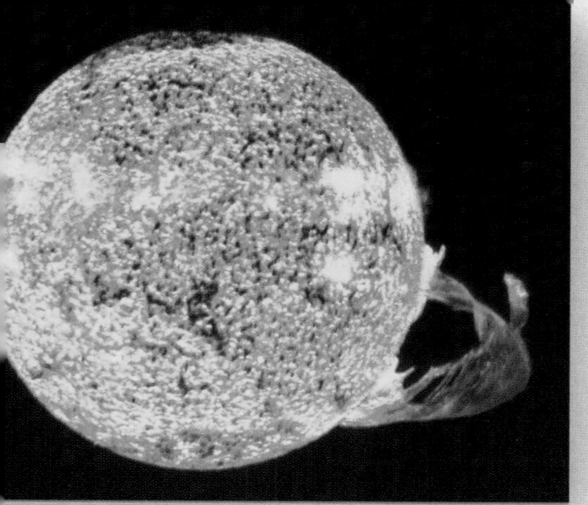

HEAT

Chapter 3

Heat. It helps keep living things alive. It creates new rocks and minerals and influences our weather systems. Too much heat can melt a bar of iron into a bubbling liquid. Too little heat can plunge our planet into an ice age. It can be as hot as the sun, or without it, as cold as outer space.

In this chapter, you will begin to investigate the nature of heat and how it can change substances. You will have many chances to explore its effects and uses in everyday life.

BIG Ideas

1.0 Heat can cause matter to change.

2.0 The Particle Theory can be used to explain volume and state changes in matter.

3.0 The amount of heat energy in an object depends on its temperature, mass, and composition.

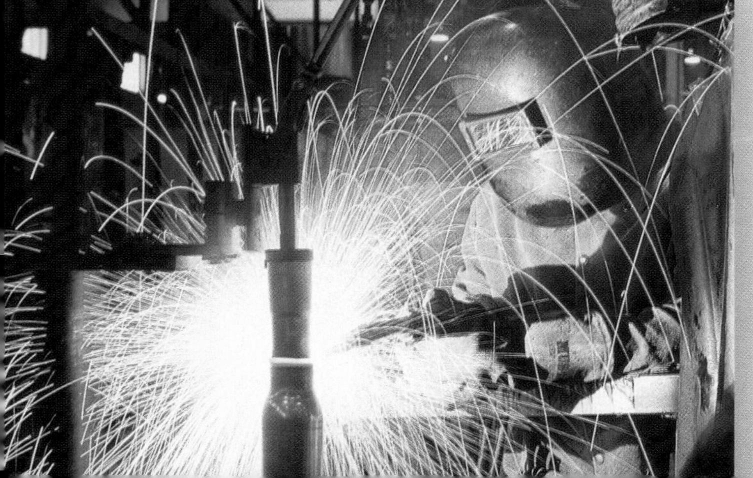

4.0 Heat energy is transferred in different ways.

5.0 Heat energy is related to other forms of energy.

6.0 Technologies that use heat energy have benefits and costs to society and the environment.

Invitation to Explore

Survival at sea

HALIFAX—A search-and-rescue helicopter helped save three sailors adrift in the frigid waters off the coast of Nova Scotia early this morning.

Waves up to five metres and 80 km/h winds made rescue efforts difficult.

"It was like being in an out-of-control roller coaster," one of the rescued sailors said.

The rescuers credit the insulated floater coats the sailors were wearing for saving their lives. "Without the coats, they wouldn't have lasted more than a few minutes in the frigid waters," SAR Tech Captain Alan Moreau explained.

The sailors had been in the water for nearly an hour before they were safely on board the helicopter.

According to this news article, the rescued sailors were exposed to "frigid waters" for nearly an hour. How cold is "frigid," do you think?

INVESTIGATOR

Is it hot? Is it cold?

What do you think would happen if you place one of your hands in a bucket of cold water and the other hand in a bucket of warm water? Within seconds, your hands would probably start to feel the temperature changes.

Your hands have many nerves that can detect the change in temperature. They send electrical signals to your brain telling you your hand is in cold or warm water. You can experience the way these nerves detect such changes by doing the following exploration.

- Stick one hand in a bucket of cold water and the other hand in a bucket of warm water. Try to keep both hands in the water for a minute.
- While you are waiting, predict what you think your hands will feel like if you place them into a bucket of water at room temperature.
- Take both hands out of the buckets and place them into a bucket of water at room temperature. Wait another minute and describe to a classmate how your two hands feel.
- Was your prediction correct? Can you explain what happened?

You have read and explored two situations involving heat. The sea rescue involved sailors in cold water wearing insulated floater suits. The buckets of water allowed you to see how the human body detects different temperatures. Look at the picture below. What do you think the object in the picture is and how could it be related to heat?

This object is an insulated tent designed for use by firefighters as a fire shelter. If firefighters become trapped in a forest fire, they can wrap themselves inside the tent for protection. It works by reflecting away 95% of the heat from the flames, keeping the air inside cool enough to breathe safely.

In the sea rescue and the fire tent, materials were used to insulate a person from the heat escaping or coming into the body. In your Investigator activity, you experienced the effect of heat on your hands when you placed them in the buckets of water. Both these situations are clues to the characteristics of heat.

- With a partner, identify what you think are two or three key characteristics of heat.
- Compare your answers with another group and share the results with the class.

Focus Your Thoughts

1 Based on your readings, explorations, and discussions, list what you think are the key characteristics of heat. Beside each characteristic, put a plus sign or question mark:
   - a plus sign means "I am sure this is a key characteristic"
   - a question mark means "key characteristic I am not sure about at this time"

2 Below is a list of words whose definitions you may or may not know. Sort these words into groups and predict how you think each group represents one of the key features of heat you have explored so far. For example, you may take the words cold, hot, and insulated, and label them "Protection from heat." If you have some words that do not fit into any of the groups, you may put them into other groups and create another heat-related label for them.

Insulated	Hot	Cold
Change of State	Temperature	Heat
Expand	Contract	Steam
Energy	Mass	Conduction
Convection	Radiation	Matter
Particle Theory	Thermometer	
Celsius	Ice	

3 Using one of your groupings, draw and label a picture of a situation outside of school that involves heat.

4 Look at the pictures on this page. For each, create a title that explains what it has to do with the idea of heat.

BIG IDEA

1.0 Heat can cause matter to change.

3 HEAT

You have observed many changes in matter caused by heat in your life. Some of these changes you have experienced yourself; for example, when you add ice cubes to a warm drink or when you use boiling water to make hot chocolate. Some changes you may not have actually seen, but have experienced the results of the change; for example, when you hang your clothes out to dry in the sun or put water in the freezer to make ice cubes. Now you will have an opportunity to explore different ways that heat affects matter.

1.1 STATES OF MATTER

Explore

In the activity that follows, you'll try to find ways to change ice to water as fast as you can.

PROBLEM SOLVER

A "COOL" HEAT CHALLENGE

Melt an ice cube as fast as you can. *But wait!* Before you start, here are three rules you must follow:

- You can only use whatever is on or at your desk right now.
- You must keep and collect as much of the melted ice as possible. (Decide how you'll collect the water.)
- You can't put it in your mouth! Record your time in seconds.

When you've finished, jot your answers to these questions on a piece of paper or in your Science Journal.

- What strategies did you use to melt the ice cube?
- How did you decide on them?
- Did any strategies work better than others? Why might that be?
- If you could try this again, what would you do differently and why?
- If the rules changed, and you could use anything you wanted to melt the ice cube, what would you use? How would it change your results?

Develop

How Does Heat Affect State of Matter?

When you melt ice, or any other substance, you change it from one form to another. You probably know that matter can exist in three forms: solid, liquid, and gas. These three forms of matter are often called **states of matter**. One way that heat can affect matter is by causing a **change of state**.

Three States of Matter

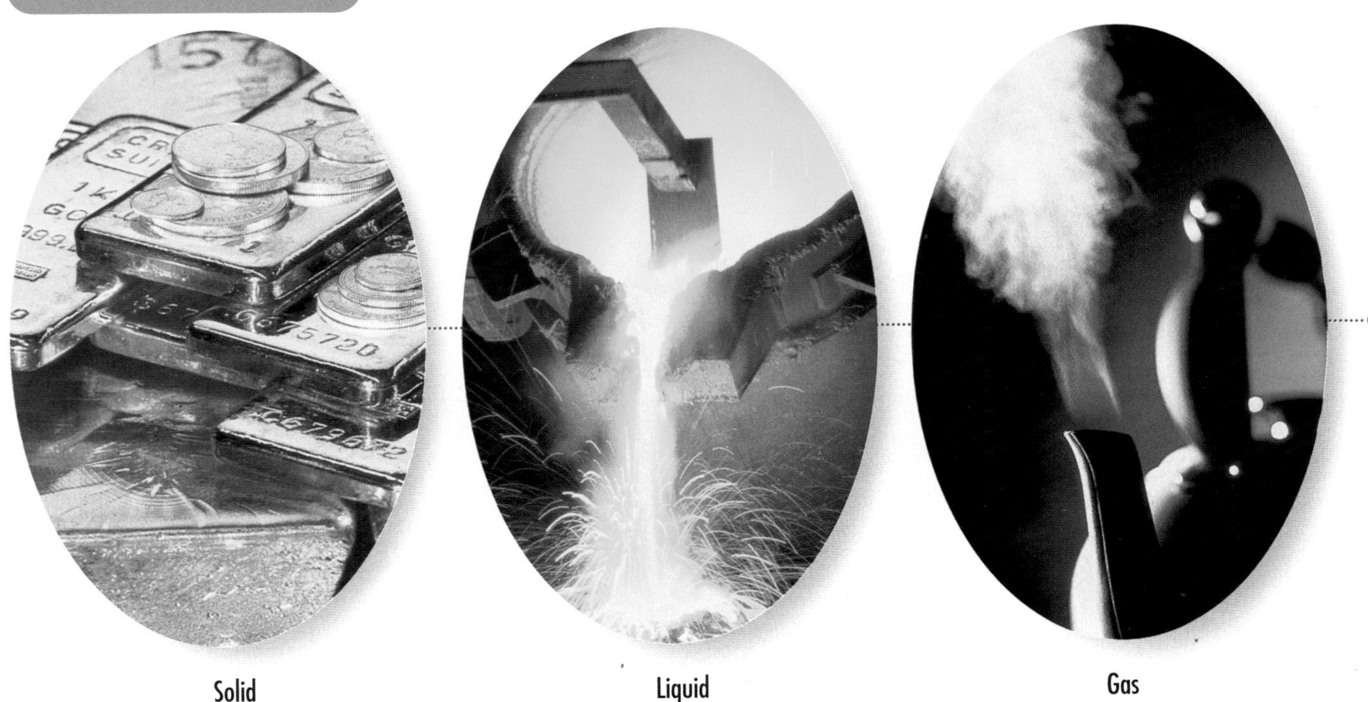

Solid

Liquid

Gas

No doubt you are familiar with the changes of state involving water.

- Ice is water in the solid state.
- If enough heat is added to ice, it changes to become a liquid. Ice melts (changes state from a solid to a liquid) at a temperature of 0°C. The **melting point** of ice is 0°C.
- If enough heat is added to liquid water, it will change state to become a gas. Liquid water boils (changes state from a liquid to a gas) at a temperature of 100°C. The **boiling point** of water is 100°C.

Removing heat from matter can also cause a change of state. For example, in nature, we only find oxygen in its gas state. If enough heat is removed from oxygen gas, it will condense into liquid oxygen. **Condensation** happens at a very low temperature for oxygen: –183°C. For liquid oxygen to change to the solid state, even more heat must be removed. Liquid oxygen freezes at –218°C. The **freezing point** of oxygen is –218°C.

Communicate

1 In the diagram below, where do you place the following terms: melting, freezing, boiling, and condensation?

ice ⇌ water ⇌ steam

2 Below are pictures of three pure substances. Their melting points and boiling points are listed. Use these data to answer the questions below each picture.

Sulphur
- *changes from the solid state to the liquid state at a temperature of 113°C*
- *changes from the liquid state to the gas state at a temperature of 445°C*

Mercury
- *changes from the solid state to the liquid state at a temperature of –39°C*
- *changes from the liquid state to the gas state at a temperature of 357°C*

Chlorine
- *changes from the solid state to the liquid state at a temperature of –101°C*
- *changes from the liquid state to the gas state at a temperature of –35°C*

In nature, sulphur is most often found in the solid state. What happens to the state of sulphur when the temperature changes from 20°C to 100°C? from 100°C to 120°C?

In nature, mercury is most often found in the liquid state. It is the only metal existing in liquid state at room temperature. In what state is mercury at –50°C? –20°C? 200°C? 400°C?

In nature, chlorine is most often found in the gas state. What would you have to do to make chlorine gas change into a liquid? to make solid chlorine change into a liquid?

3 Make a table or graph that illustrates the melting and boiling points of the three substances shown above.

1.2 Heat Can Affect the Volume of Liquids and Gases

Explore

When you wake up at 7:00 a.m., you look at the **thermometer** outside the window and see the temperature is 12°C. Later at school, you check the class thermometer and see the temperature is 20°C. You also notice both thermometers are similar and wonder what the liquid in the thermometer is. In fact, how can a liquid be used to make a thermometer? What liquids can be used?

Some interesting facts about the history of the thermometer are shown below.

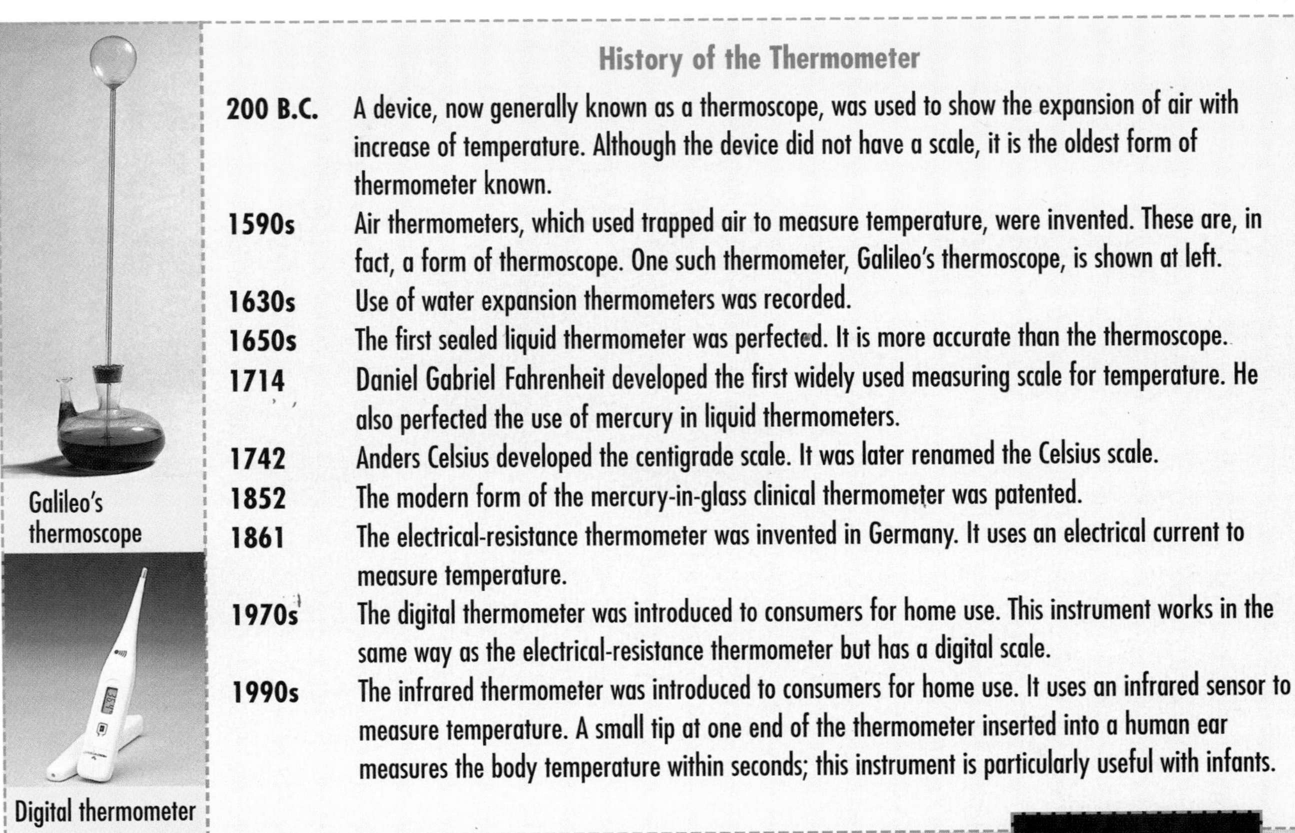

History of the Thermometer

200 B.C.	A device, now generally known as a thermoscope, was used to show the expansion of air with increase of temperature. Although the device did not have a scale, it is the oldest form of thermometer known.
1590s	Air thermometers, which used trapped air to measure temperature, were invented. These are, in fact, a form of thermoscope. One such thermometer, Galileo's thermoscope, is shown at left.
1630s	Use of water expansion thermometers was recorded.
1650s	The first sealed liquid thermometer was perfected. It is more accurate than the thermoscope.
1714	Daniel Gabriel Fahrenheit developed the first widely used measuring scale for temperature. He also perfected the use of mercury in liquid thermometers.
1742	Anders Celsius developed the centigrade scale. It was later renamed the Celsius scale.
1852	The modern form of the mercury-in-glass clinical thermometer was patented.
1861	The electrical-resistance thermometer was invented in Germany. It uses an electrical current to measure temperature.
1970s	The digital thermometer was introduced to consumers for home use. This instrument works in the same way as the electrical-resistance thermometer but has a digital scale.
1990s	The infrared thermometer was introduced to consumers for home use. It uses an infrared sensor to measure temperature. A small tip at one end of the thermometer inserted into a human ear measures the body temperature within seconds; this instrument is particularly useful with infants.

Galileo's thermoscope

Digital thermometer

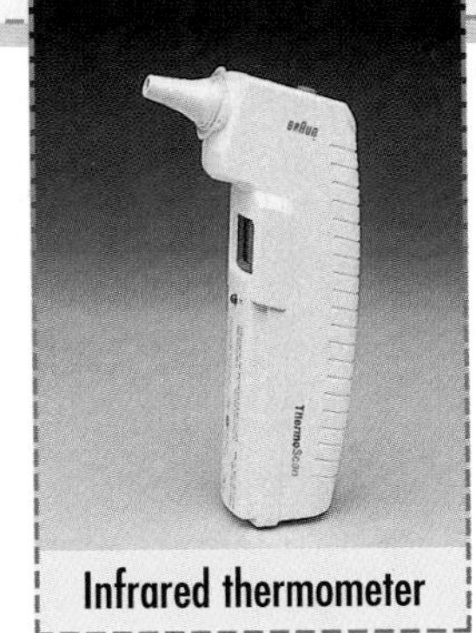

Infrared thermometer

A liquid that was once commonly used in thermometers is mercury. Mercury is poisonous and is now rarely used. Alcohol is the liquid now commonly used. The use of a liquid in a thermometer demonstrates one of the key characteristics of heat. Adding heat to matter causes it to **expand**, that is, the volume increases. Removing heat from matter causes it to **contract**, that is, the volume decreases. The volume of the liquid in a thermometer therefore changes when heat is added to or removed from the thermometer. By knowing how much it changes, a temperature scale can be put on the thermometer.

Develop

How Does Heat Affect Volume of a Gas?

You've read about how heat affects a liquid. In the next Investigator activity, you'll see how heat affects a gas. The gas you'll be looking at is the air in a pop bottle.

INVESTIGATOR

GROWING BALLOONS

The Question

What effect does heat have on the volume of air?

Caution!
You'll be using scalding hot water in this activity. Take care not to spill it.

Materials & Equipment

- *2 identical balloons*
- *2 identical, empty, 2-L plastic pop bottles*
- *2 retort stands and clamps*
- *2 dish pans or deep containers large enough for the pop bottles to be placed inside*
- *water* • *kettle* • *oven mitts*

Procedure

1. Boil some water in a kettle.
2. Place a dish pan or deep container on each retort stand.
3. Stand a bottle in each pan and clamp it to the retort stand at its neck.
4. Blow up both balloons to stretch them and then let them deflate.
5. Place a balloon over the opening in the neck of each bottle.
6. Carefully pour hot water into one of the pans so that the water fills up around the bottle but does not overflow.
7. Pour cold tap water into the other pan to fill up around the bottle as in step 6.
8. Let the bottles sit in the water for 10 min. Observe what happens.
9. Wearing oven mitts, carefully remove the bottles and place them on a counter. Again observe what happens.

Keeping Records

10. Record the changes to the two balloons.

Analyzing and Interpreting

11. What happened to the balloon over the bottle that was surrounded by hot water? by cold water?
12. What happened to the balloons as they sat on the counter after the bottles were taken out of the water?

Forming Conclusions

13. Write a summary statement that answers the question: "What effect does heat have on the volume of air?" Your summary should include the words volume, expand, contract, heat, and gas.

Communicate

1. In your own words, describe the effect on the volume of a gas when you add heat and remove heat. Provide an example from your experiences outside of school.
2. Go back to your grouping of words you completed in the Invitation to Explore. Make changes to the words in the groups or titles of the groups using what you've now learned about heat.
3. It snowed the night before and it's very cold. You have just bought some balloons for a birthday party. As you walk home, you notice the balloons have gotten smaller and look a bit wrinkled. Are the balloons wrecked? Should you return them to the store or continue to head home? Explain what you think happened to the balloons.

*info*BIT

Steam Cars

Steam-powered automobiles were popular in the late 1800s. Some cars could go very fast: in 1906, one car was clocked at 205 km/h! However, by the 1930s, because the internal combustion engine had become popular, steam cars had all but disappeared.

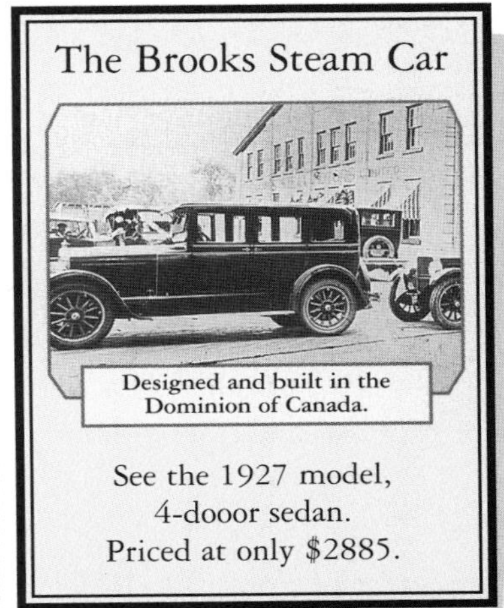

The Brooks Steam Car
Designed and built in the Dominion of Canada.
See the 1927 model,
4-dooor sedan.
Priced at only $2885.

1.3 Heat Can Affect the Volume of Solids

Explore

You have had an opportunity to investigate how heat brings about changes in state and in the volume of liquids and gases. Now it is time to investigate how heat affects a solid. Before you begin, work with a partner to develop an explanation for what happened in the following situations.

1. A large slab of concrete is used for the base of an outdoor skating rink. After the first winter, it is noticed that the concrete has many cracks in it. It appears the concrete will have to be replaced.
2. A metal bolt fits easily and comfortably inside a metal nut. The bolt is left outside in the hot sun for an hour. You find it hard to hold, but you find it even harder to fit inside the nut now. It seems too large to fit into the hole.

Keep your explanations for the two situations above in your mind. As you collect more information, you may need to revise your explanations.

Develop

Expansion and Contraction in Solids

In the next Investigator activity, you will have an opportunity to explore how adding and removing heat affects a solid.

INVESTIGATOR

How Long Is It Really?

The Question

What will happen to a copper wire when it is heated and cooled?

Materials & Equipment

- *2 retort stands*
- *about 130 cm of thin copper wire*
- *a paper clip*
- *oven mitts or a candle holder*
- *a steel nut (not galvanized) or any mass of 20–25 g*
- *a candle*
- *matches*
- *aluminum foil*
- *a metre stick*
- *safety goggles*

Procedure

1. Wind and tie the copper wire around the two retort stands. Set the stands apart so that the copper wire is taut. There should be about 1 m of wire.
2. Place a sheet of aluminum foil on a table top so that it is under the wire.
3. Carefully bend part of the paper clip into a hook shape. Hang the hook from the middle of the copper wire. (See picture.)
4. Hang the nut on the open end of the paper clip.

Caution!
Don't forget to follow the safety rules when working with an open flame.

5 Measure the distance from the bottom of the nut to the aluminum foil on the table. Record this distance in a chart like the one shown at right.

6 Carefully light the candle. Use a candle holder or oven mitts to hold it on an angle so that the wax will drip onto the foil.

7 Using the candle, heat a portion of the wire for about 5 min.

8 After 5 min of heating, measure the distance from the nut to the foil again. Record this distance in your chart.

9 Carefully blow out the candle and let the wire cool.

10 After about 10 min of cooling, measure the distance from the nut to the aluminum foil again. Record this distance.

Keeping Records

11 Record the distance from the bottom of the nut to the aluminum foil in your chart.

Distance of Nut from Table Top (mm)		
Step 5	*Step 8*	*Step 10*

Analyzing and Interpreting

12 How did the distance from the nut to the aluminum foil change as heat was added to the wire (*when it was heated*)?

13 How did the distance from the nut to the aluminum foil change as heat was removed from the wire (*when it was cooled*)?

Forming Conclusions

14 Write a summary statement that answers the question: "What will happen to a copper wire when it is heated and cooled?" Include a diagram to help your explanation.

Communicate

1 Using your own words, complete the following sentences.
   - Adding heat to a solid causes ...
   - Removing heat from a solid causes ...
   - The copper wire stretched when heated because ...

2 During the Explore part of this section, you had to provide an explanation for two situations involving heat being added or removed from a solid. Revise your explanation based on the last investigation. Rewrite your explanation based on what you have learned.

3 Below are four pictures, each with a short description of the situation and some questions. Using your understanding of heat and its effects on matter, suggest some answers to the questions.

Train tracks span great distances. Spaced many metres apart are small gaps between the rails. What's the purpose of these gaps? What might happen if the gaps weren't there?

Workers set up these electrical cables during the summer. You'll notice that the cables are not stretched tightly. They sag. What is the advantage of leaving some slack when installing electrical cables like these? What might happen if the cables were installed tightly with no slack?

Did you ever notice that sidewalks are made of slabs with gaps between them? What is the advantage of leaving these gaps? What might happen if the slabs were placed right up against each other?

Pop and juice bottles are never filled all the way to the top. What is the advantage of leaving some space in these bottles? What might happen if the bottles were filled completely?

try this at **HOME**

HOMEMADE HOT-AIR BALLOONS

Do you have a hair dryer, a plastic bag, and some paper clips at home? If you do, you can make a hot-air balloon with the help of a friend.

Procedure

1. Find the largest plastic bag you can, for example, a large garbage bag. If you have more than one bag, you can split the bags along a seam and join them together to make a very large one.
2. Check for any holes in the bag, and seal them with tape if there are. You're halfway to making your hot-air balloon!
3. Using paper clips, gather parts of the open edge of the bag to make the opening smaller, about 10 cm in diameter. Spread the paper clips evenly around the opening.
4. You will probably want to do the next three steps inside, but you can go outside if there is no wind and power is available for your hair dryer.
5. Ask your friend to hold a hair dryer so that the hot-air nozzle is pointed upward. Make sure that the air intake vent of the hair dryer is not blocked. This will prevent the hair dryer from overheating.
6. Turn the hair dryer on to its highest heat setting. Be very careful when handling the hair dryer.
7. Gently bring the open end of your bag over the hair dryer, keeping it at least 10 cm away from the nozzle. Hold the bag in place until it appears to be full of hot air. Turn off the hair dryer. Release the bag and observe.

Things to Think About

- Did your balloon go straight up or was it a crooked flight?
- What could you add to your balloon to give you more control over its flight? Look at the picture of the hot-air balloon above for some possible ideas.
- Would using different types of bags make any difference?
- Could you use more than one hair dryer?
- Would using different heat settings on the hair dryer make a difference to the flight of your balloon?
- Can you design your hot-air balloon so that it could carry an object like a pen or small toy into the air?

1.4 Check Your Progress

1 Look back at your grouping of terms you did in the Invitation to Explore at the beginning of this chapter. Would you change any of these groups based on what you now know about heat? Make your changes using arrows to show which words you would move from one group to another.

2 Name five ways you can use heat in your life. Be as specific as possible in your answer.

3 Create a chart or a web diagram to show some of the ways that heat affects matter.

4 Why do you think we find oxygen only in its gas state in nature? (Hint: Think about the temperatures at which it changes state.)

5 Abbi tried, without success, to open a brand-new jar of jam. The lid was sealed too tightly. After running the lid under the hot-water tap for a short while, she was able to open the lid. Explain what happened.

6 There's only one substance on our planet that you can easily find in all three states throughout the year. Which one is it? Explain how you decided.

7 At the end of each winter, roads are usually filled with cracks and potholes. Why do you think this happens after a cold winter, rather than a hot summer?

8 Examine the photographs below, and think about the information in the captions. Why did the chip bag inflate? What expanded? What caused the inflating?

This bag of chips was stored in a cool place before it was put here on a very hot, sunny day. Notice how crinkled the bag looks.

It's been an hour or so since the chip bag was exposed to the sun's heat. Notice that the bag has changed. It looks as if someone has inflated it!

Big Idea

2.0 The Particle Theory can be used to explain volume and state changes in matter.

Think of butter melting in a pan. You know that heat causes matter to change state, and in this case, the solid butter is melting to form liquid butter. But consider for a minute:

- How can you explain what is happening to the structure of the butter?
- What is the heat doing to the butter that makes it change state?

What do you think is happening to the structure of the matter when it changes from the solid state to the liquid state?

2.1 Main Ideas of the Particle Theory of Matter

Explore

All matter is made up of extremely tiny particles.

They are much too small to see except with powerful, magnifying instruments, called electron microscopes.

The tiny particles of matter are always moving and vibrating.

This movement involves a form of energy known as kinetic energy. Each particle of matter has **kinetic energy**—energy of movement.

Adding heat to matter makes the particles move around faster and vibrate faster.

Faster-moving things have more kinetic energy. So adding heat increases the kinetic energy of the particles.

The particles have space between them.

This is *empty* space not filled with air. Different states of matter have different amounts of space between the particles.

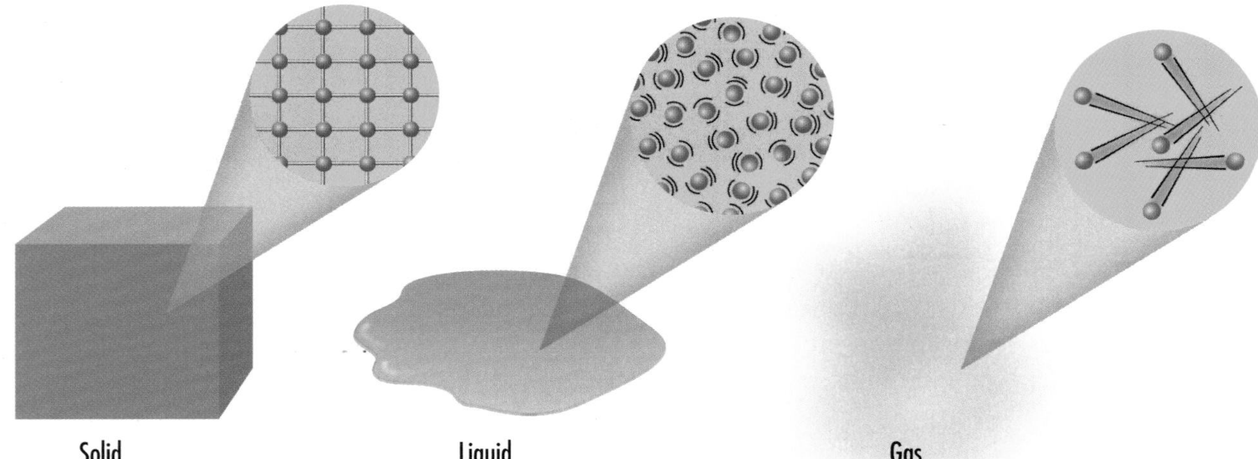

Using the information on the Particle Theory on the previous page and the diagrams above, copy and fill in the chart below with the following statements.

a) Great amount of movement; particles spread out.
b) A little farther than in a solid.
c) Fixed shape and volume.
d) Only vibrates back and forth in position.
e) Far apart.
f) Takes the shape of its container; definite volume.
g) Can move around freely; still held together by bonding forces.
h) Very close together.
i) Takes the shape of its container; no definite volume.

State of Matter	Distances Between Particles	Particle Movement	Volume and Shape
Solid			
Liquid			
Gas			

Develop

Investigating Heat and Its Effects Using the Particle Theory

Using a model can help you explain something you cannot see. You're going to have an opportunity to develop a model to explain the effect of heat on different states of matter.

INVESTIGATOR

Acting Out the Particle Theory

The Question

How can you and your classmates move and arrange yourselves to act like the particles that make up solids, liquids, and gases?

Procedure

1. You will work in groups. Each group will work in a separate area. Treat each separate area as if it's a large container.

Solid

Liquid

Gas

2. With your group, develop a way to represent a solid state of matter. Decide how to arrange yourselves and how to move to be the particles of a solid.
3. Imagine that heat is being added to you. Your solid group is becoming a liquid. Change your positions and movements to represent the particles in a liquid.
4. Now add more heat and change your positions and movements to represent gas particles.
5. Keep working together until your group is satisfied with the way you represent particles in the three states of matter. Then present one of these states to the rest of the class without saying what it is. Show yourselves changing from that state to another state.

Keeping Records

6. Draw two rectangles on a sheet of paper. The rectangles represent "containers." Use them to sketch the two states of matter your group presented. Draw arrows on you and your "fellow particles" to show your movement. Include other information about the way and the speed you (the particles) were moving.

Analyzing and Interpreting

7. As a class, judge each group's presentation. Use the following criteria to make your judgments.
   a) Was it easy to infer the state of matter?
   b) Did the group's actions accurately represent the state of matter?
   c) Did the group's actions accurately represent the kinetic energy of the particles?

continued on next page

d) Did the group's actions accurately demonstrate changes in volume?

Forming Conclusions

8 Write a paragraph that answers the question "How can you and your classmates move and arrange yourselves to act like particles that make up solids, liquids, and gases?" Include diagrams to illustrate how adding heat affects the motion of particles.

Communicate

1 Create a poster, diagram, or story that represents your understanding of the four main ideas in the Particle Theory.

2 In each of the following statements, identify which state of matter is being described:

a) particles close together, fixed shape
b) particles far apart, great amount of movement
c) particles move freely, but still held together

3 Which state of matter has the greatest kinetic energy?

2.2 How the Particle Theory Explains Volume and State Changes

infoBIT

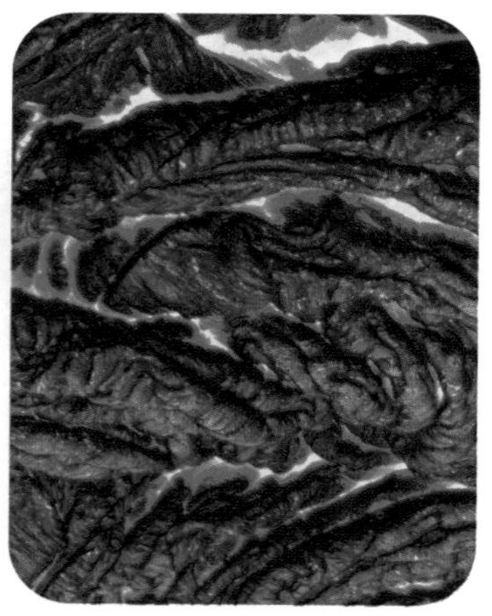

Lava is molten rock that flows out of a volcano. What change of state happens when it cools?

Explore

From your observations, you know that adding or removing heat can cause a change in state or volume of matter. Now, you can use your understanding of the Particle Theory to explain these observations. As you study the diagrams on the opposite page, consider the following two questions:

- How does the addition of heat affect the particles in a given state?
- How does the addition of heat affect the volume taken up by a given number of particles?

Develop

What Happens When You Add Heat to a Solid?

The following diagrams show what happens to the particles in a solid when you add heat to it.

1 Solid
- Solid particles are packed closely together.
- Strong electrical forces hold the particles together.
- Solids therefore have a fixed shape.
- The particles vibrate in position (shake back and forth).

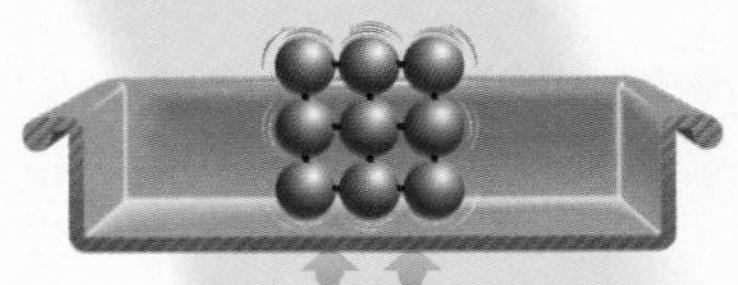

2 Heating a Solid
- Adding heat to a solid makes the particles vibrate more energetically.
- Some of the particles move farther away from one another.
- The solid expands—its volume increases.

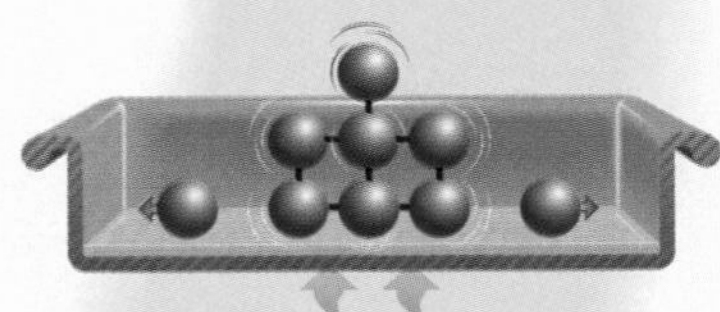

3 Melting a Solid
- As more heat is added to a solid, the particles vibrate even more.
- The particles bump against one another.
- Some of the particles break loose.
- The solid structure begins to break down—the solid melts.

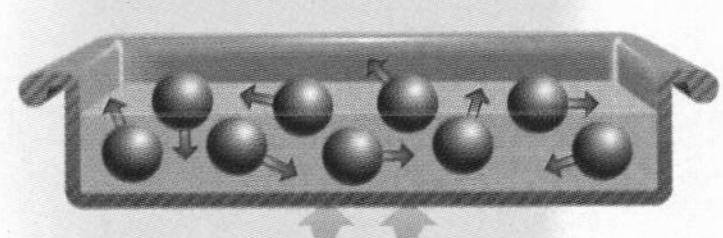

4 Liquid
- The particles have more kinetic energy to move about.
- They are farther apart than in the solid (except for water).
- The electrical forces that hold the particles together are weak.
- Liquids then take on the shape of their containers.

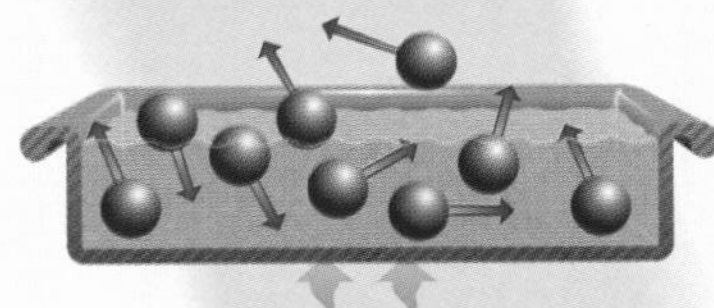

5 Heating a Liquid
- Adding heat to a liquid makes the particles move more vigorously.
- The particles move farther apart.
- The liquid expands—its volume increases.

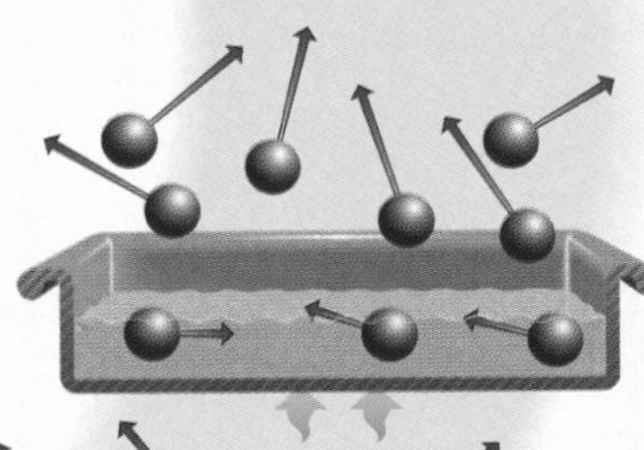

6 Boiling a Liquid
- As more and more heat is added to a liquid, the particles bump and bounce around even more.
- Some of the particles are "kicked" out of the liquid.
- The liquid boils—it changes to a gas.

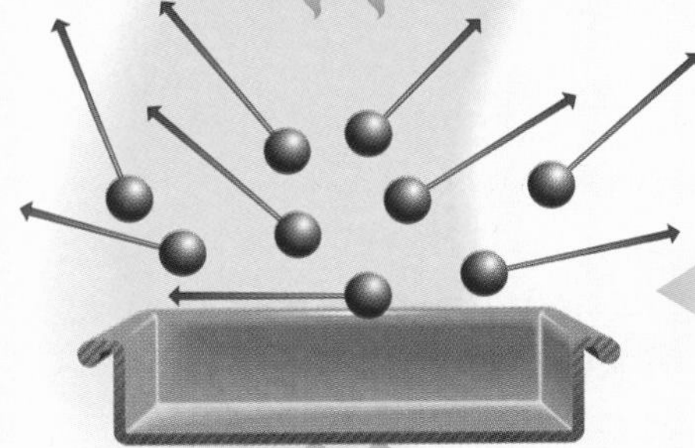

7 Gas
- Gas particles move about very quickly in all directions.
- Bumping and bouncing keep them far apart.
- Gas particles will fill up the space of any container.
- On heating, gas particles spread out even more—the gas expands.

Communicate

1. Using your own words and diagrams, describe the changes in volume, motion, and energy that gas particles experience as heat is taken away.
2. Using your understanding of the Particle Theory, explain how the addition of heat affects the particles in a solid state.
3. Use the Particle Theory to explain why the volume increases as water is heated into steam.
4. The temperature at 8:00 a.m. is –5°C. A snowdrift measures 89 cm high. The wind has stopped. The sun shines all day, and by 5:00 p.m., the snowdrift's height is only 84 cm. At no time during the day has the thermometer gone above –1°C. What do you think happened to the missing 5 cm of snow?

2.3 Check Your Progress

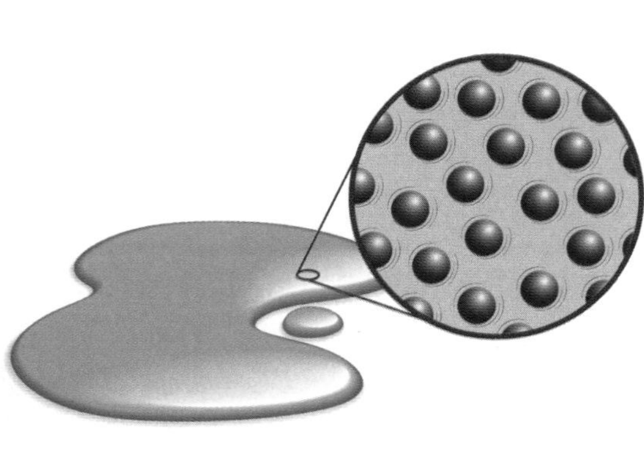

1. What does the Particle Theory say about:
   a) the way particles of matter move in a solid, a liquid, and a gas?
   b) the amount of space between particles in a solid, a liquid, and a gas?
2. a) What does the illustration to the left show? Give reasons to support your answer.
   b) Draw what will happen to the matter in the illustration as more heat is added.
   c) Draw what will happen to the matter in the illustration if heat is removed.
3. When a solid turns directly into a gas, the process is called **sublimation**. Give a common example of sublimation. How do you think the Particle Theory would explain what happens when a solid sublimates? Use words or drawings, or both, in your answer.

Experiment ON YOUR OWN

THAT CUP OF HOT CHOCOLATE!

Before You Start...

Imagine that it's a cold day. A cup of instant hot chocolate would really hit the spot, and you just can't wait. You need boiling hot water right away. How could you boil water quickly?

Here are some questions to start you thinking.

- Why does it take the living room longer to get warm than the bathroom? Does the size of the room make a difference?
- Does heat affect all objects the same way?

The Question

How can you get 250 mL of water to boil in the shortest amount of time, without using a microwave oven?

Your Task

1. Make a hypothesis. (A hypothesis is a possible answer to a question or a possible explanation about a situation.)

2. Decide what materials and equipment you'll need to test your hypothesis. Think of the answers to these questions:
   a) Will you use one or more samples of water?
   b) What kind or kinds of containers could you use?
   c) What will you use to measure the temperature?
   d) How will you ensure safety?
3. Plan your procedure. Think of the answers to these questions:
   a) What evidence are you looking for to support your hypothesis?
   b) How will you collect the data?
   c) Is the test you're planning fair? How do you know?
   d) How will you record your results?
4. Write up your procedure and show it to your teacher.
5. Carry out your experiment.
6. Compare your results with your hypothesis. Were you able to support it? If not, what possible reasons might there be?
7. Share and compare your experimental plan and findings with your classmates. How do your results compare with theirs?

BIG IDEA

3.0 The amount of heat energy in an object depends on its temperature, mass, and composition.

3 HEAT

Heat energy can cause matter to change state, or it can cause matter to expand or contract. You should now be able to explain these changes using the Particle Theory. These concepts will help you understand what determines how much heat an object can hold. To start, it is important to consider the difference between the words temperature and heat.

3.1 STUDYING HEAT AND TEMPERATURE

Explore

If heat can change matter's temperature, does that mean heat and temperature are different or the same? Many people think that heat and temperature mean the same thing. Because the two terms are often related, they can easily become confused. With a partner, think of five sentences that use the words heat and temperature to mean different things. For example, "The heat during the summer was unbearable" or "The two lawyers had a heated debate during the court trial."

While there are many different ways to use the terms heat and temperature, it is important to use them correctly. The following section will help you understand these two terms.

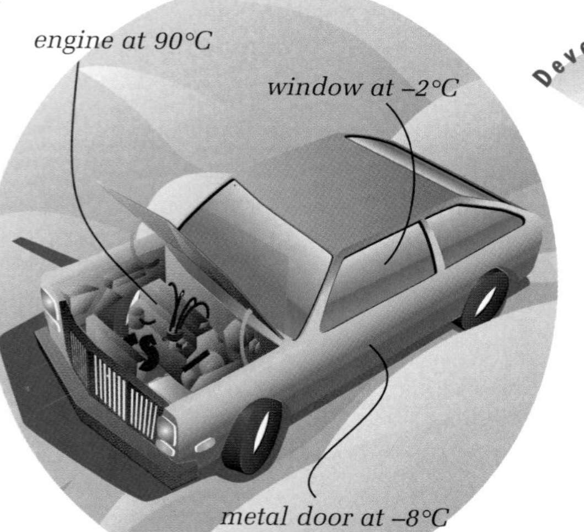

Develop

Difference between Temperature and Heat

What Is Temperature? Temperature is a measure of how hot or cold something is. For example, consider the temperatures shown in the illustration at left. The car engine is hotter than the window. Its temperature is higher than the window's. The door is the coldest. It has the lowest temperature.

The temperature of something depends on how fast its tiny particles are moving. In other words, temperature is related to the kinetic energy of the tiny particles in matter.

Matter that has faster-moving particles (*higher* kinetic energy) has a higher temperature than matter that has slower-moving particles (*lower* kinetic energy).

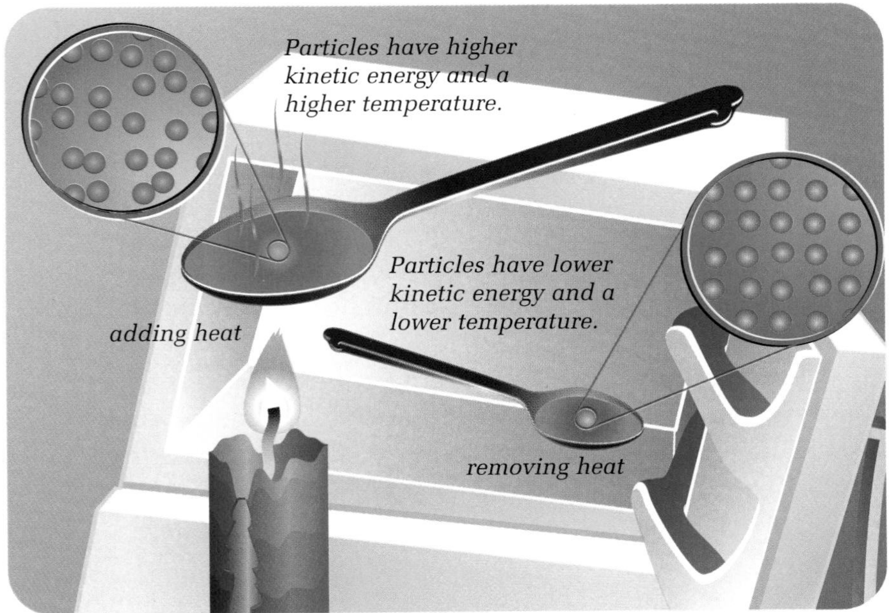
Particles have higher kinetic energy and a higher temperature.
adding heat
Particles have lower kinetic energy and a lower temperature.
removing heat

When you add heat energy to a spoonful of water (or any other kind of matter), its particles move faster. So they have a higher kinetic energy and a higher temperature. The water feels "hotter." If you remove heat energy from that water (by putting into a freezer, for example), its particles move slower. So they have a lower kinetic energy and a lower temperature. Now the water feels "colder."

Average Kinetic Energy

When scientists talk about temperature, they prefer to use terms that are more accurate than "hotter" and "colder." Here's how scientists define temperature. **Temperature** is a measure of the average kinetic energy of the particles in a substance. Why do they say average kinetic energy? Because:

- Some of the particles in any sample of matter are actually moving more energetically than others. They have more kinetic energy.
- Some of the particles are moving less energetically than others. They have less kinetic energy.
- Using the average kinetic energy gives us a better indication of the energy of the particles.

*info***BIT**

Temperature Extremes

510 million°C	Highest created in a lab
15 million°C	Centre of the sun
4000°C	Centre of the earth
1536°C	Melting point of iron
100°C	Boiling point of water
58°C	Highest ever on earth
46.5°C	Highest a person has had and survived
45°C	Highest ever in Canada
37°C	Average for human
14.2°C	Lowest a person has had and survived
0°C	Freezing point of water
–18°C	Typical refrigerator freezer
–63°C	Lowest ever in Canada
–89.2°C	Lowest ever on earth
–273.15°C	Lowest temperature possible

*info***BIT**

Time of Death

The temperature of a dead body is one of the clues investigators use to infer the time of death of a person.

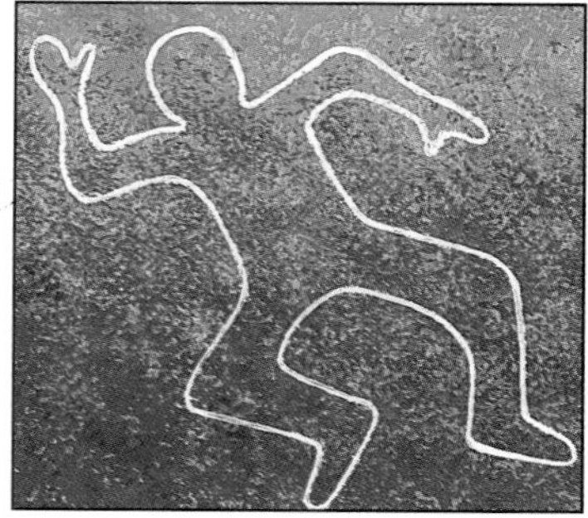

At the moment of death...

When a person dies, the body loses heat energy to the surroundings. Its temperature drops at a constant rate, about 1°C per hour under normal conditions (room temperature). Normal body temperature is 37°C. If the temperature of a corpse is 32°C, investigators infer that the person died about 5 h earlier.

What is Heat?

Heat is a form of energy. This means that it is related to other forms of energy such as:

- sound energy
- electrical energy
- light energy
- chemical energy
- mechanical energy
- nuclear energy

Like all forms of energy, heat energy has the ability to make matter move or change. And you've seen lots of evidence that heat can do that in this chapter. Since heat is a form of energy, it's more accurate—and more scientific—to call it heat energy, rather than just heat.

When scientists talk about heat energy, they need the idea of temperature to help them define it. Here's how scientists define heat energy. **Heat energy** is the energy that is transferred from matter at a higher temperature to matter at a lower temperature.

Communicate

1 Use the following two diagrams to explain the difference between heat and temperature.

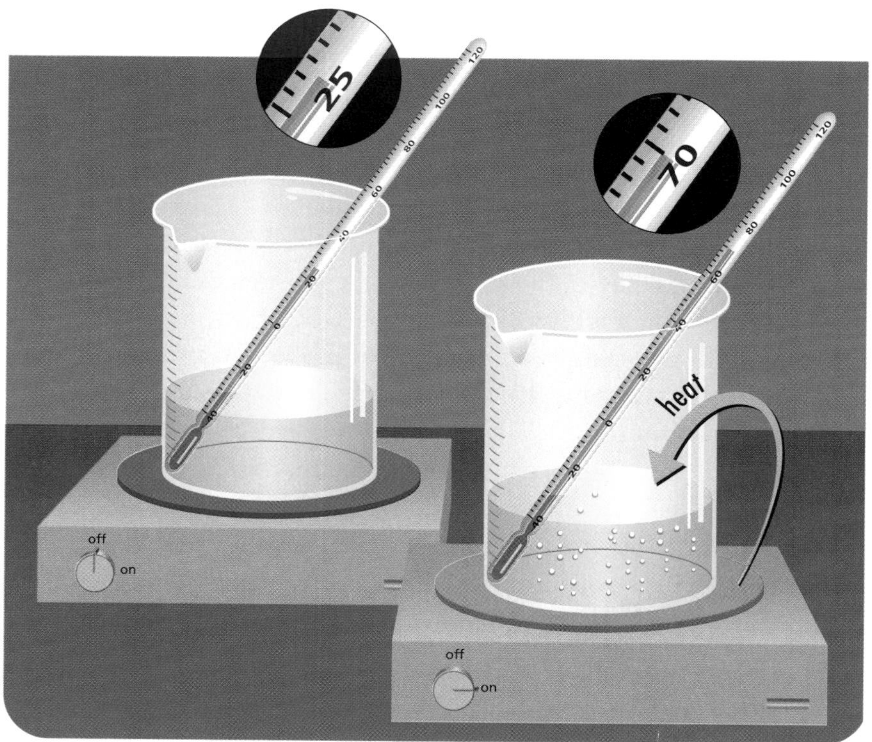

3.2 Investigating Heat Energy and Different Masses

Explore

When heat energy is added to or removed from an object, several factors can affect the rate of temperature change. Predict what factors might influence the rate of temperature change in the following situations.

- In the evening of a hot summer day, the air is cool but the sidewalk feels warm.
- A 500-mL bottle of pop freezes overnight in a freezer, but a 1000-mL bottle doesn't.

Remember your predictions, and as you work through the next activity, try to determine if your predictions are correct or if they need to be modified based on what you learn.

Develop

Rates of Temperature Change

The next activity will help you identify a factor that affects the rate of temperature change in water.

INVESTIGATOR

Time to Heat

The Question

Will 100 g of room-temperature water heat up faster than 200 g of room-temperature water?

Procedure

1. Pour 100 mL of water into one beaker and 200 mL into the other. (What's the mass of water in each case? How can you confirm it using the balance?)
2. Place both beakers on the hot plate.
3. Set up the retort stands, clamps, and thermometers as shown in the photo two pages down. Make sure that the thermometer bulbs do not touch the bottom or the sides of the beakers.
4. Read the temperature on both thermometers.
5. Turn on the hot plate. Time how long it takes for the water to reach 70°C. When the first beaker reaches 70°C, use tongs or an oven mitt to take it and the thermometer off the hot plate.
6. Keep timing until the second beaker reaches 70°C. Then turn off the hot plate.

Materials & Equipment

- *2 beakers of the same size (such as 250 mL, or 400 mL each)*
- *water at room temperature*
- *balance*
- *hot plate*
- *2 retort stands*
- *2 clamps*
- *2 thermometers*
- *timer*
- *tongs or oven mitts*
- *safety goggles*

continued on next page

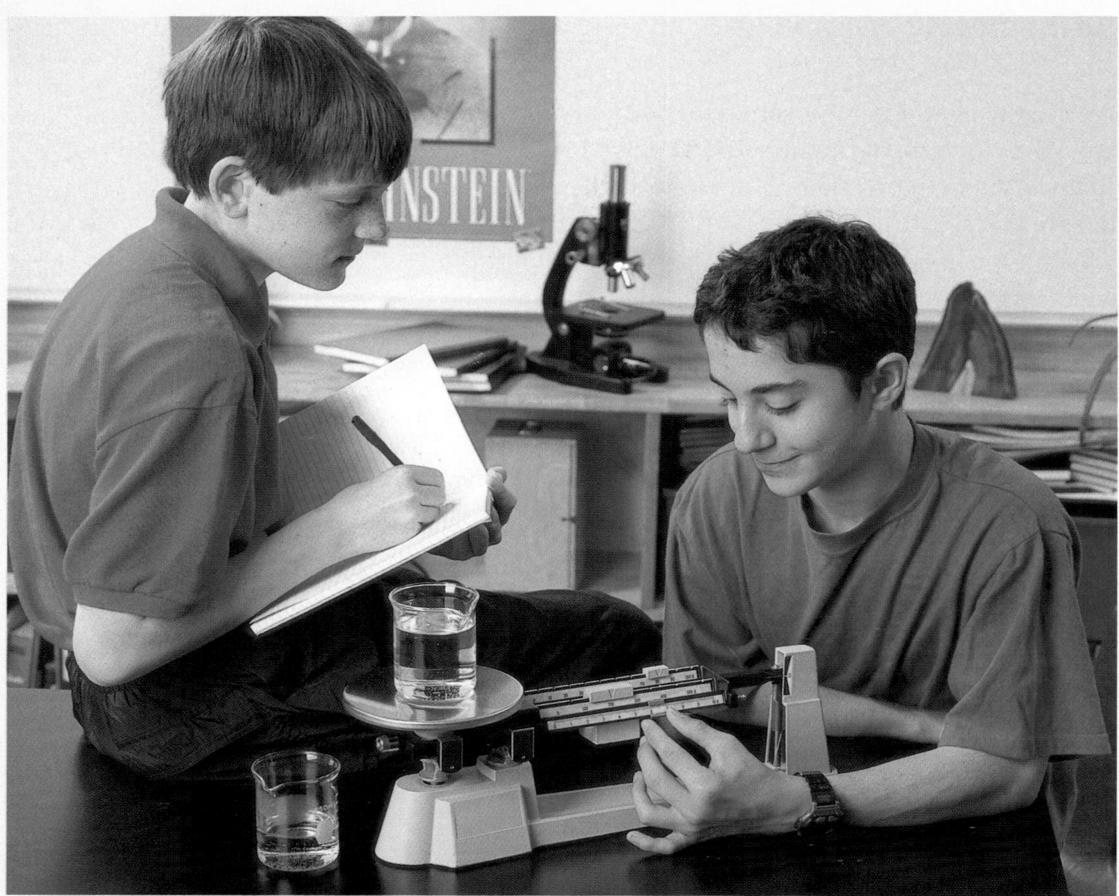

Keeping Records

7 Record your data in a chart as shown at right.

Mass of water	*Temperature at the start*	*Temperature at the end*	*Change in temperature*	*Time it took for the temperature to change*

Analyzing and Interpreting

8 Compare the 100 g of water and the 200 g of water, using these questions.

a) Were the start temperatures the same or different?

b) Were the end temperatures the same or different?

c) Were the changes in temperature the same or different?

9 a) Where did the heat energy that changed the water temperature come from?

b) How long did it take the 200 g of water to reach 70°C?

10 Which of the following statements do you agree with most? Give evidence to support your answer.

continued on next page

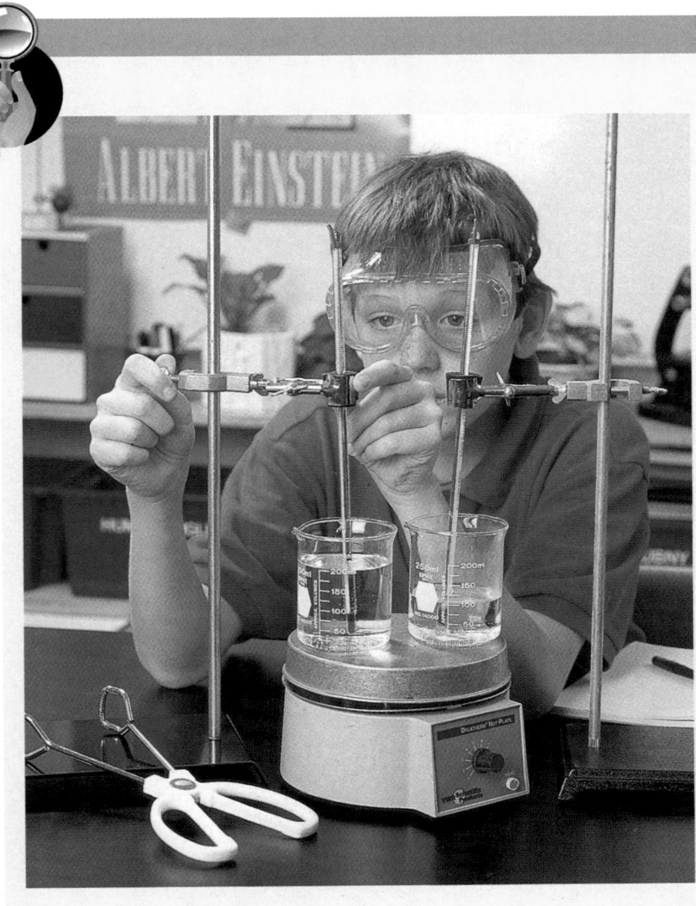

a) During the time they were heated, the 200 g of water received the same amount of total heat energy from the hot plate as the 100 g of water.
b) The 200 g of water received twice as much heat from the hot plate as did the 100 g of water.
c) The 200 g of water received half as much heat from the hot plate as did the 100 g of water.

11 For each of the statements in question 10 that you didn't choose, explain why you disagree with it.

Forming Conclusions

12 Use the data collected in this activity to demonstrate how the amount of heat an object has depends on other factors besides its temperature.

Communicate

1 In your own words, define temperature and heat energy. Provide an example of each term from your own experiences.

2 Indicate which of the following statements are true and which are false. Correct each false statement to make it true.
a) Temperature is a form of energy.
b) The average kinetic energy in a material tells you how much heat energy is in that material.
c) A thermometer measures the average kinetic energy in a given material.
d) A 100-mL cup of water and a 200-mL cup of water at room temperature will both reach boiling point at the same time if they are put on the same heating element.
e) Boiling water in a kettle requires an increase in the average kinetic energy of the water in the kettle.

3 If it takes 5 min to heat 500 mL of water, how long will it take to heat 250 mL? 1000 mL?

4 Review the predictions you made in the Explore section. Would you make any changes based on what you now know about heat energy?

3.3 Holding on to Heat Energy

Explore

Have you noticed how, on a hot summer day at the beach, barefoot people often walk across the sand and pavement very fast? Heat energy from the sun has made the sand and the pavement so hot they are almost too hot to stand on. At the end of the day as the sun sets, however, the sand is no longer hot while the pavement still feels warm. The two surfaces are now very different in how hot they feel.

Sand heats up quickly but it doesn't hold the heat energy for very long. Pavement, on the other hand, may take longer to heat up, but it keeps its heat for a longer period of time. This heat-holding ability is called **heat capacity**.

a) heat capacity of liquid water: 1.0

b) heat capacity of aluminum: 0.2

Develop

The Heat Capacity of Common Substances

Substances that hold heat energy for a long time have a large heat capacity. It takes a lot of heat energy to raise their temperature. Water is a good example. In fact, water has the second-highest heat capacity of all the natural substances on earth. (Ammonia has the highest.)

Compare water's heat capacity with the other substances in the photos. Keep in mind what the numbers mean. It takes more heat energy to change the temperature of water than to change the temperature of the other substances. In other words, other substances will get hotter more quickly than water will. They will also release their heat energy more quickly than water will.

- The heat capacity of liquid water at 1.0 is used as a standard for heat capacity. What does a number less than 1.0 tell you about a substance?
- Put these substances in order from lowest heat capacity to highest. Which of them will heat up fastest? slowest?
- Which will release heat energy fastest? slowest?

c) heat capacity of iron: 0.1

d) heat capacity of olive oil: 0.5

1 Which sample in each pair will release its heat faster?
   a) 1 L of water at 50°C
      1 L of olive oil at 50°C
   b) 100 g of aluminum at 75°C
      100 g of iron at 75°C
2 Check back to the grouping of words you made in the Invitation to Explore. Can you group any of these words under the label "heat capacity"? Explain your reasoning for this grouping.
3 What would be a better material to use to make a frying pan—aluminum or iron? Why are iron pans not usually used by people who backpack?

3.4 Check Your Progress

1 a) Use your own words to explain what temperature is.
   b) Use your own words to explain what heat energy is.
   c) What is the difference between heat energy and temperature?
2 For each of the following, give an example to show that the amount of heat energy an object has depends on:
   a) the temperature of matter
   b) the mass of matter
   c) the kind of matter
3 Explain the meaning of heat capacity as you understand it.
4 a) How much longer will it take to raise the temperature of Sample B than Sample A in the illustration below?

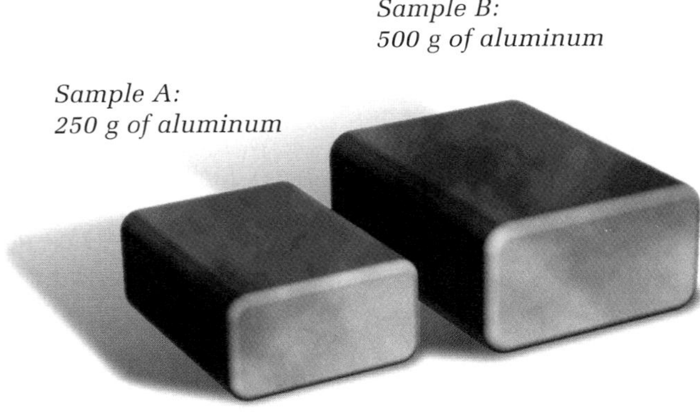

Both these samples had enough heat added to them to raise their temperatures from 15°C to 45°C.

b) How much longer will it take to raise the temperature of Sample D than Sample C?

Sample D:
1200 g of soup

Sample C:
400 g of soup

Both these samples had enough heat added to them to raise their temperatures from 17°C to 85°C.

5 a) Imagine you're standing near the shore of a large lake in mid-winter. You observe that the ground around the shoreline is frozen solid. The water of the lake is still liquid. What could you infer about the heat capacity of the shoreline soil compared with the heat capacity of the lake water?

b) Why do temperatures for coastal cities such as Vancouver tend to be milder than temperatures for inland cities such as Winnipeg? Be as specific in your answer as possible.

6 Equal masses of two different substances were heated for 10 min, using identical heat sources. The example below shows a temperature-versus-time graph that records the results. Which substance has the higher heat capacity? How do you know? Do you have enough information in this chapter to identify one or both of these substances? If so, do it. If not, explain why not.

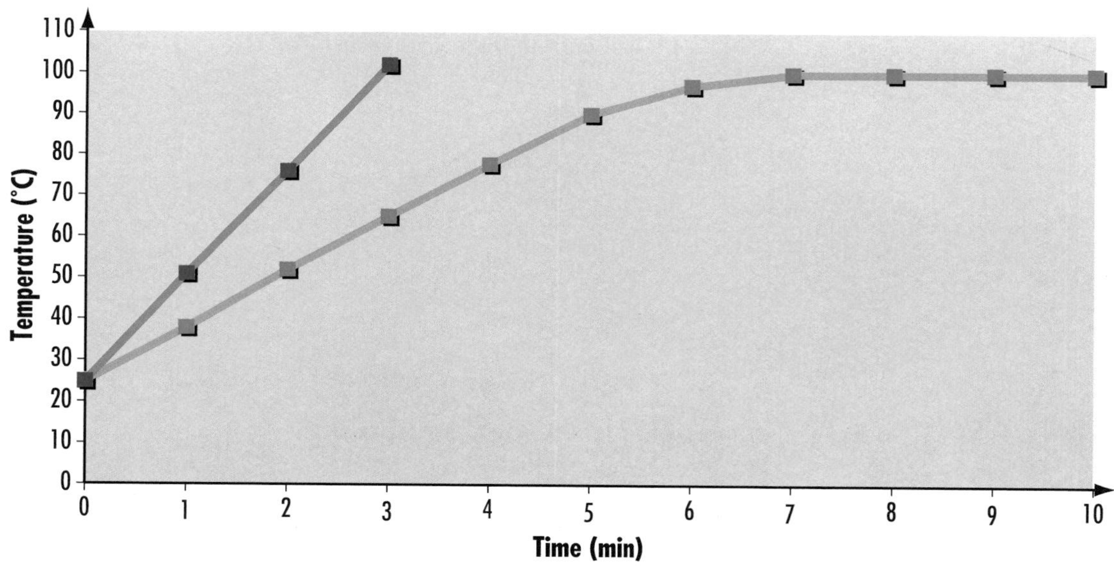

Careers and Profiles

A Scientist Who Studies Heat Energy

Mary Anne White is a professor of materials science at Dalhousie University in Halifax, Nova Scotia. She studies how well different materials conduct and retain heat. Part of her job involves the design and construction of special high-tech devices to monitor how heat flows through a particular material.

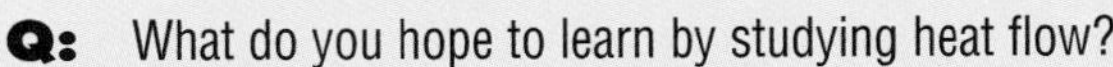

Q: What do you hope to learn by studying heat flow?

A: When we know more about how heat flows, then we could try to tailor-make new materials that have specific properties that we want them to have.

Q: What are some of the results of your research?

A: We have discovered a group of materials that store heat really well and we're using those in a solar home.

Q: How are these materials used?

A: The sunlight heats up the material and then later, when the sun is no longer shining, the material gives back the heat.

Professor White doesn't fit the common image of a scientist. She isn't the lonely mad genius locked away in a lab. She has plenty of interests outside her career. She's a caring mother of two, she plays the flute, and she loves to travel.

"I think that people don't know that much about what life as a scientist is like," says White. "They just have this idea that we're antisocial and just sit in our labs and try to blow things up." White believes this common misconception keeps many students, especially women, from choosing a career as a scientist.

"You know you don't have to be an ultra genius to make a contribution to science," she says. "Persistence and motivation, the same for many other careers, are the more important things."

Big Idea

4.0 Heat energy is transferred in different ways.

It's a hot summer day, and you want a tub of ice cream for making some refreshing ice-cream cones. The place that sells your favourite ice cream is a thirty-minute walk each way. You're afraid that it'll melt long before you get home. Unfortunately, nobody's around to drive you. You don't have access to a bike or a skateboard, and there are no buses for the route you have to take. Still, you really want that ice cream. Walking is your only option. But how will you get the ice cream back without it melting?

The pictures below offer four ways for protecting the ice cream from the sun's heat energy on your long walk home.

- Which method would you choose, and why?
- How do you think each method works?
- If you have another idea for protecting the ice cream, suggest that instead. Include reasons for rejecting the options below, and explain why your idea is a better solution.

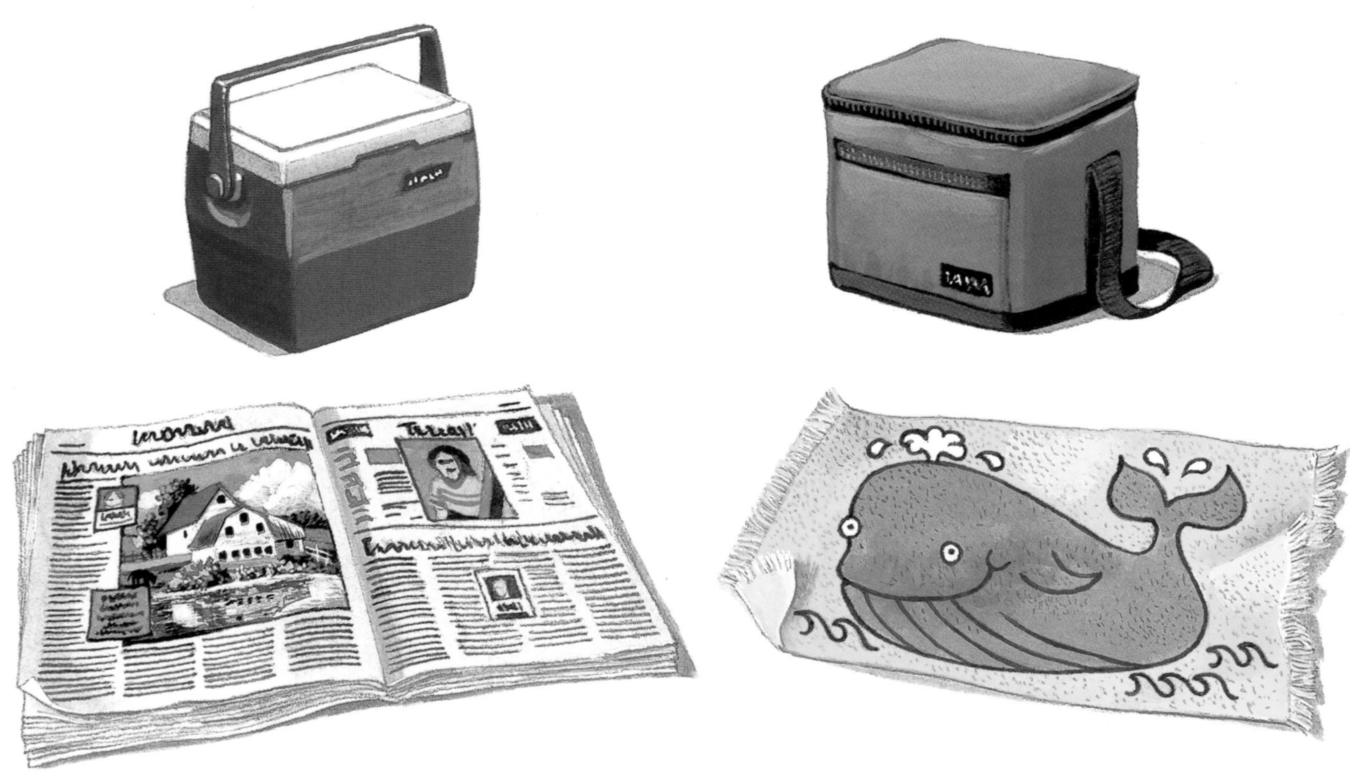

4.1 Heat Energy Can Move by Conduction

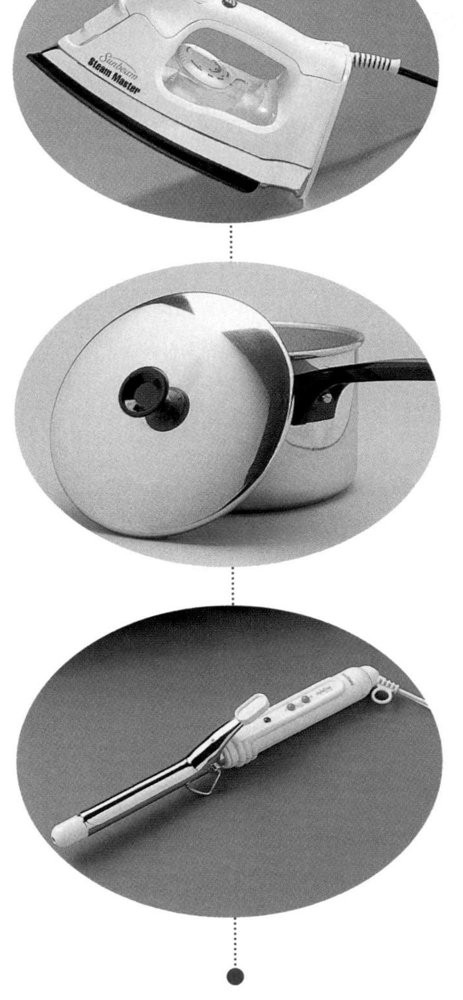

Explore

Have you ever picked a metal spoon out of a cup of hot water and been surprised how hot the spoon is? Or maybe you've almost burned your hand trying to pick up a metal tray that has just come out of the oven. In both these situations, heat energy has somehow gone from a heat source to somewhere else. Can you think of other examples where a similar situation has occurred? Perhaps a better question is, can you identify what all these situations have in common?

You may have noticed that these situations usually involve a metal material. This is no accident, as metal is considered a good conductor. A substance that lets heat energy move through it easily is called a **conductor**. You may recall that these conductors can also be used to carry electricity.

If a material is not a good conductor, that is, it doesn't allow heat energy to move through easily, it's called an **insulator**. For example, plastic, glass, and wood are good insulators, or poor conductors. People often use insulating materials to make conducting materials more useful. Look at the pictures at right and identify which parts are conductors and which parts are insulators.

Develop

Identifying Good Conductors and Insulators

Now you'll study some materials and determine which make good conductors and which make good insulators.

PROBLEM SOLVER

The Butter Test

You are doing research for a company that designs electrical appliances. These appliances generate a lot of heat, so the designers want to use some type of material that will enable the heat to move away. There is some disagreement as to which material to use. Some people want the cheapest material, others want the best conductor. You have been asked to perform the "Butter Test" on a variety of materials to determine which would be the best material based on cost and conducting ability. A description of the procedure is provided.

Your task is to make a list from the most desirable to the least desirable material to use. When completed, present your results using diagrams, charts, or graphs.

continued on next page

Procedure

The test involves placing a small amount of butter at one end of a piece of each material. Then place the other end of the material into hot water. The faster the butter melts, the better conductor the material is.

- On which material does the butter melt the fastest? the slowest?
- Which variables do you have to keep constant (or control) to make this a fair test?
- Which set-up shown will likely give more accurate results? Why? What would you have to do to the other set-up to make it a fair test?

3 HEAT

infoBIT

Fire Walking

Fire walkers walk across red-hot coals with bare feet and don't burn themselves. Can you figure out how they do it?

A Closer Look at Conduction

You have collected evidence of **conduction**—the transfer of heat energy between substances that are in contact. Use your understanding of the Particle Theory to describe how heat energy is transferred by conduction. Consider what happens when you place a piece of metal in hot water.

- The metal particles that are in the water begin to vibrate more strongly. Remember that as particles receive heat energy, they begin to vibrate more.
- The increased kinetic energy of the metal particles causes them to bump against neighbouring particles.
- This causes the neighbouring particles to vibrate more. So they start bumping against other nearby particles and, in turn, transfer some of their increased kinetic energy.
- As a result of this continuous series of particle collisions, heat energy is conducted throughout the piece of metal.

Communicate

1 Rhys tried to toast some marshmallows over a campfire using a straightened-out iron clothes hanger. About halfway through toasting his marshmallow, Rhys almost dropped the hanger into the fire because it was getting too hot. Use the Particle Theory to describe why Rhys almost burned his hand. Suggest a way he can toast the marshmallow without burning his hand.

2 Why do most frying pans come with a plastic handle but have a metal bottom?

Experiment ON YOUR OWN

DESIGN CHALLENGE: INSULATE IT!

The Situation

In section 1.1 at the beginning of this chapter, you were challenged to melt an ice cube as fast as you could. Here is an opposite challenge: *How can you stop or slow down an ice cube from melting?*

- Think about the strategies you would use.
- Review what you've learned about heat capacity, conductors, and insulators.
- How is this like the ice-cream problem in the introduction to Big Idea 4.0?

The Question

How can you make a device to prevent an ice cube from melting?

Your Ideas

1. What ideas do you have to solve the problem?
2. What materials and equipment will you need to make your device and test your ideas?
3. How will you design an experiment to test the effectiveness of your device?
4. What data will you record to show your results? How will you present them?

Construct It

5. Show your plans to your teacher. Then make and test your device. Include diagrams to explain how and why it works.

Evaluate It

6. How successfully did your device solve the problem?
7. Compare your device with others in the class. How did other people solve the problem? How successful were their devices?
8. If you had the chance to redesign your device, how would you modify it? Why?

4.2 Heat Energy Can Move by Convection

Explore

How is your bedroom heated? Do you have a radiator or an electric baseboard heater? Are there hot-air vents instead?

Maybe you've noticed that the device that supplies heat energy to your room is located on or near the floor. And it's usually only in one part of the room, near or against a wall. How, then, does it warm up your entire room? The answer involves another way that heat can move: convection. **Convection** is the transfer of heat energy that happens when heated gas or liquid particles move from one location to another.

Develop

Demonstrating Convection

The next Investigator activity will help you see how convection works.

INVESTIGATOR

Where's the Hot Air Going?

Before You Start...

Your teacher will probably demonstrate this activity, perhaps with the help of some volunteers. As you observe what happens, be on the alert for any possible fire hazards.

The Question

What happens to heated air?

Materials & Equipment

- *a smoke box*
- *a small candle*
- *a splint or an incense stick to produce smoke*
- *fire-safety equipment*

Caution!
Be sure to follow proper fire-safety procedures.

Procedure

1. Set up the smoke box as shown in the photo.
2. Slide open the plastic front cover and light the candle. Slide the plastic cover back into place.
3. Wait for a minute or so. Then light the splint or incense stick.
4. When the smoke is visible, carefully place the splint at the top of the chimney on the side without the candle.

continued on next page

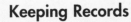

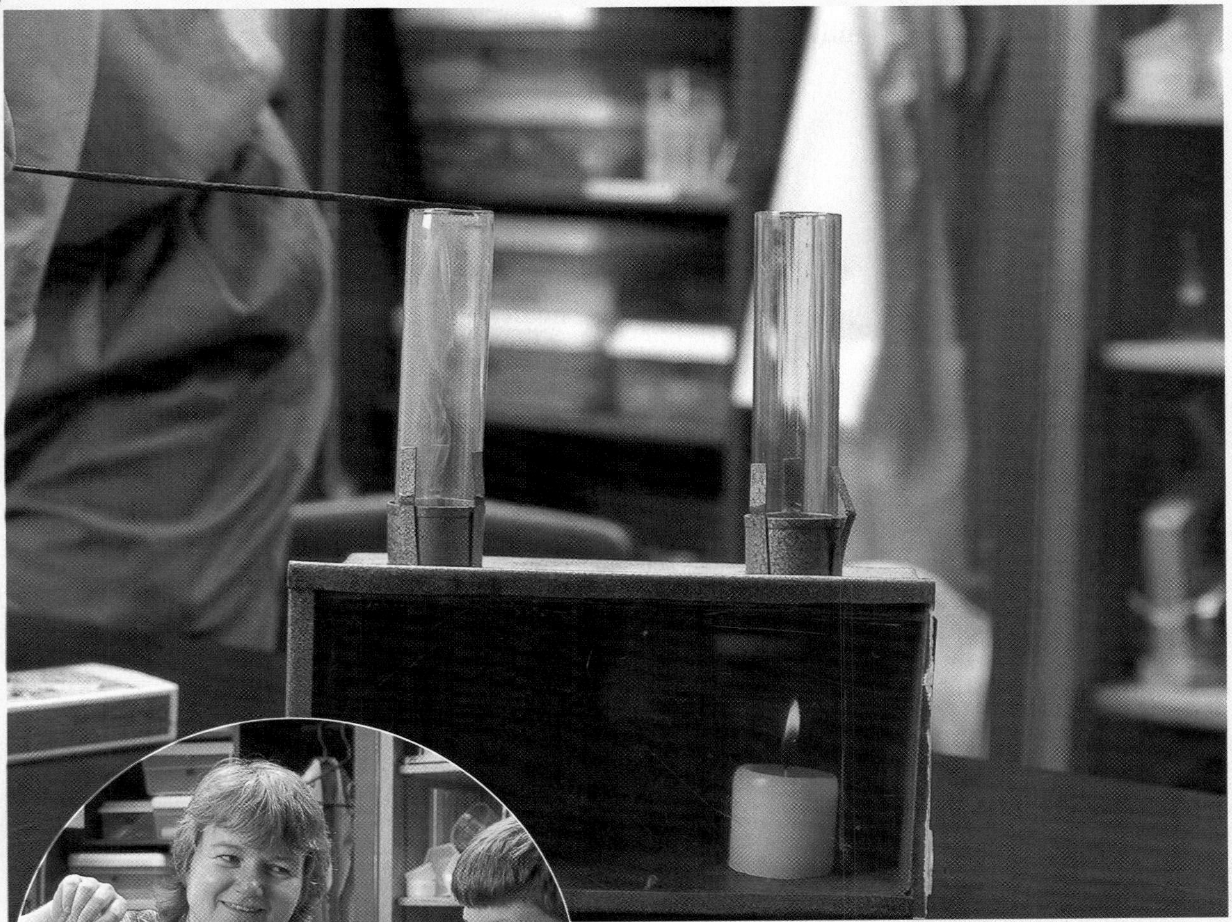

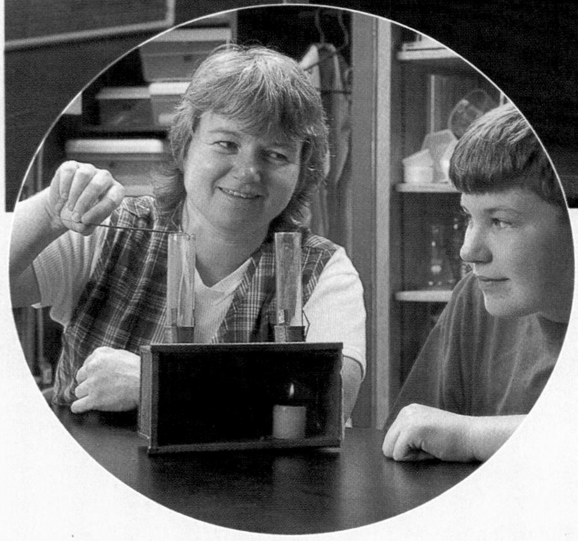

3 HEAT

Keeping Records

5 Draw the smoke box set-up when the candle is lit.

6 Draw the path of the smoke after the splint or incense stick is lit.

Analyzing and Interpreting

7 What path did the smoke from the splint or incense follow? Did you see any evidence that hot air rises? If so, what is this evidence?

8 What surprised you about the path of the smoke?

9 What effect do you think the candle's heat energy is having on the air inside the smoke box directly above the candle?

10 As the candle heats up the air above it, what do you think is happening to the rest of the air inside the box? outside the box?

Forming Conclusions

11 Using words, pictures, or both, explain what you observed in this activity.

a) Heat energy from the hot element reaches the water particles at the bottom of the pot by conduction.

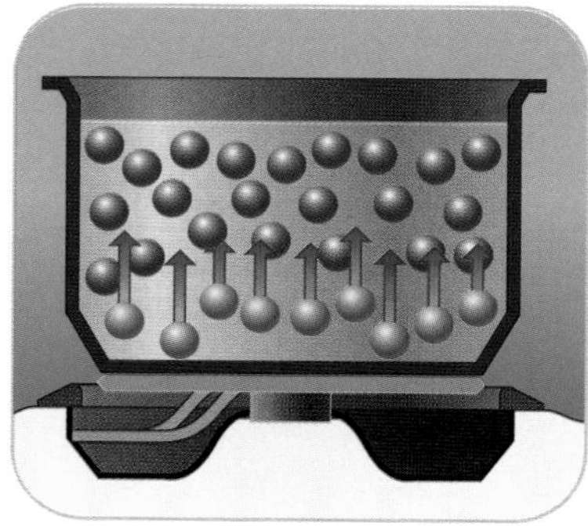

b) The heated water expands and becomes less dense. Hot particles begin to rise, pushing the cooler particles at the top to the sides.

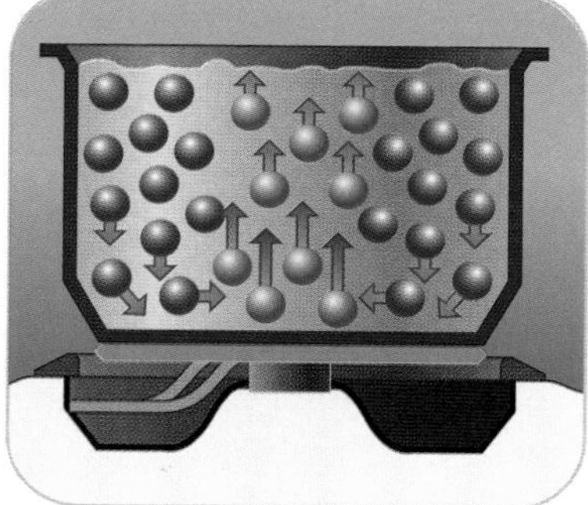

c) The cooler particles sink from the top to take the place of the rising particles.

Convection Currents

When heat energy is transferred by convection, it often moves in a circular pattern known as a **convection current**. Convection currents can form when heat energy is added to gases and liquids. Let's use a pot of water on a stove as an example.

Heat energy is first transferred to the pot's bottom by conduction. The water at the very bottom of the pot is in direct contact with the warming pot bottom. This water, in turn, gets hotter because of conduction.

The heated water particles have added kinetic energy. This causes them to move faster and to spread farther apart. In other words, the water at the bottom of the pot expands.

As the water expands, it becomes less dense and rises toward the surface. Cooler water on top sinks toward the bottom of the pot to fill the space. As this cooler water heats up, it also expands and rises, leaving space for more water from the top to sink downward.

As the water moves away from the heat source, it cools down a little. It's pushed to the sides by the warmer water rising underneath it. This sets up a circular convection current. As long as heat continues to be added, this pattern of convection currents continues to transfer heat energy throughout the water.

d) As the particles reach the bottom, they in turn are heated. The processes in a) to c) repeat continually to result in a convection current.

Communicate

1. Explain how convection heats up your bedroom.
2. Why do you think that in most homes in winter the floor is always cold?
3. Where is the cold-air-return vent located in your home? Why do you think a furnace system needs one?

4.3 Heat Energy Can Move by Radiation

Explore

How does heat energy travel from the sun to the earth? Conduction and convection both rely on the movement of particles of matter to transfer heat energy from one place to another. However, there is practically no matter between the earth and the sun.

There's a third way for transferring heat energy: radiation. **Radiation** is the transfer of heat energy (as well as other kinds of energy) in the form of radiant energy waves. The sun sends out (radiates) tremendous amounts of energy in the form of waves. These energy waves include infrared waves which are waves of heat energy.

3 HEAT

PROBLEM SOLVER

Feeling Radiation

- With the light off, take the shade off the lamp so the light bulb is easy to see. Put your hand 5 cm away from the side of the unlit light bulb. Can you feel any heat energy?
- Turn the lamp on. Put your hand 5 cm away from the side of the light bulb. Can you feel any heat energy now?
- Put a piece of cardboard between the light bulb and your hand. Can you feel any heat energy?
- Replace the cardboard with a glass pie plate or baking dish. Can you feel any heat energy?
- Can the heat energy you feel be resulting from convection or conduction? Explain.

Caution!
A lit light bulb is very hot and can cause burns. Do not touch the bulb. Do not allow the cardboard or other objects to touch the bulb.

Everyday Heat Energy and Radiation

*info*BIT

Some snakes, such as rattle snakes and boa constrictors, have infrared detectors that let them find warm-bodied prey in the dark.

All hot substances transfer heat energy by radiation. A hot object radiates (gives out) infrared waves. When these waves strike the particles of any material—such as your skin—the material's particles increase in kinetic energy. The particles move faster, so the material becomes hotter. That's why your hand feels warm when you hold it close to a hot object without touching it. The heat energy you feel is transferred to you by radiation.

When heat energy is transferred to matter by radiation, three things can happen. Matter can

- absorb the heat energy,
- reflect the heat energy,
- let the heat energy pass through it with little or no absorption or reflection.

Try to find examples of these three actions in the next Investigator activity.

INVESTIGATOR

Heating Up Different Coloured Surfaces

Before You Start...

You get into a car that has been parked in the sun on a hot, sunny day. It's hot inside—the fabric seat feels quite warm. But try touching the dashboard. It's probably so hot that it can almost burn your hand! Part of the reason for this is that the different materials absorb the sun's heat energy to different extents. Now, think about the clothing you have worn on hot, sunny days. Do you recall how you felt when you wore light-coloured and dark-coloured clothing? How do you think the different colours affect the absorption of the sun's heat energy?

The Question

How do different colours of surfaces affect the absorption of heat energy transferred by radiation?

Materials & Equipment

- *2 large test tubes*
- *test-tube rack*
- *white paper*
- *black paper*
- *scissors and tape*
- *2 thermometers*
- *sand*
- *timer*

Procedure

1. Fill each test tube with sand to the top.
2. Tape white paper around one test tube so that it's fully covered, including the top.

continued on next page

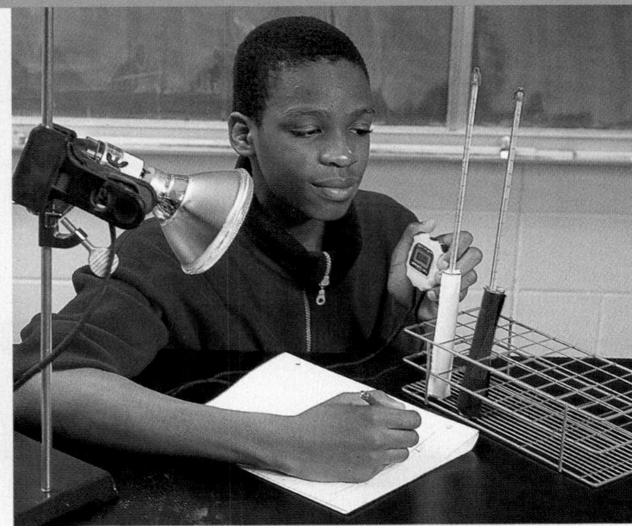

3 Cut a small hole in the top and carefully insert a thermometer about 5 cm into the sand. Gently tap the test tube to pack the sand as you insert the thermometer. Put the test tube in a test-tube rack.

4 Repeat steps 2 and 3 with the other test tube using black paper instead. Make sure that the thermometers are inserted to the same depth in the two test tubes. Put the test tube in the same rack next to the white tube.

5 Prepare a data chart similar to the one shown to record your observations.

6 Read the thermometers and record the temperature of the sand in the test tubes.

7 Place the test tubes in the rack in the sun on a window sill. If there is no sun, use a 100-W bulb as a heat source, and put the rack 20 cm in front of the bulb.

8 Predict which test tube will heat up faster in 15 min.

9 Read and record the temperature in each test tube every 3 min for 15 min.

Keeping Records

10 Record your temperature readings in your data chart.

White Tube		Black Tube	
Time (min)	*Temperature (°C)*	*Time (min)*	*Temperature (°C)*
0		*0*	
3		*3*	
6		*6*	
etc.		*etc.*	

Analyzing and Interpreting

11 Use your data to draw a graph showing how the temperature of the sand changed over time in each test tube.

12 Based on your graphs, which test tube heated up faster?

Forming Conclusions

13 Present your results in a summary paragraph. Your summary should answer the following questions:
- Which of the two test tubes absorbs more heat energy from the sun?
- What do you think your results would be if you had added a third and a fourth test tube and used orange paper and aluminum foil to cover them? Explain your reasoning.

Communicate

1 On a hot summer day, you have a choice to ride in a black car or a white car. Neither car has air conditioning. Which car would be cooler to ride in?

2 Two cartons of the same size and material have been left out in the sun all day. One carton is light green and the other is dark green. Which one will have more heat energy? Explain your reasoning.

4.4 HEAT TRANSFER AND THE EARTH

Explore

Each day, the sun provides an almost inconceivable amount of energy to our planet. It's the equivalent of the energy needed to run 375 billion cars for a year! What happens to this energy? Study the picture below and make a circle graph illustrating what happens to the energy that reaches the earth.

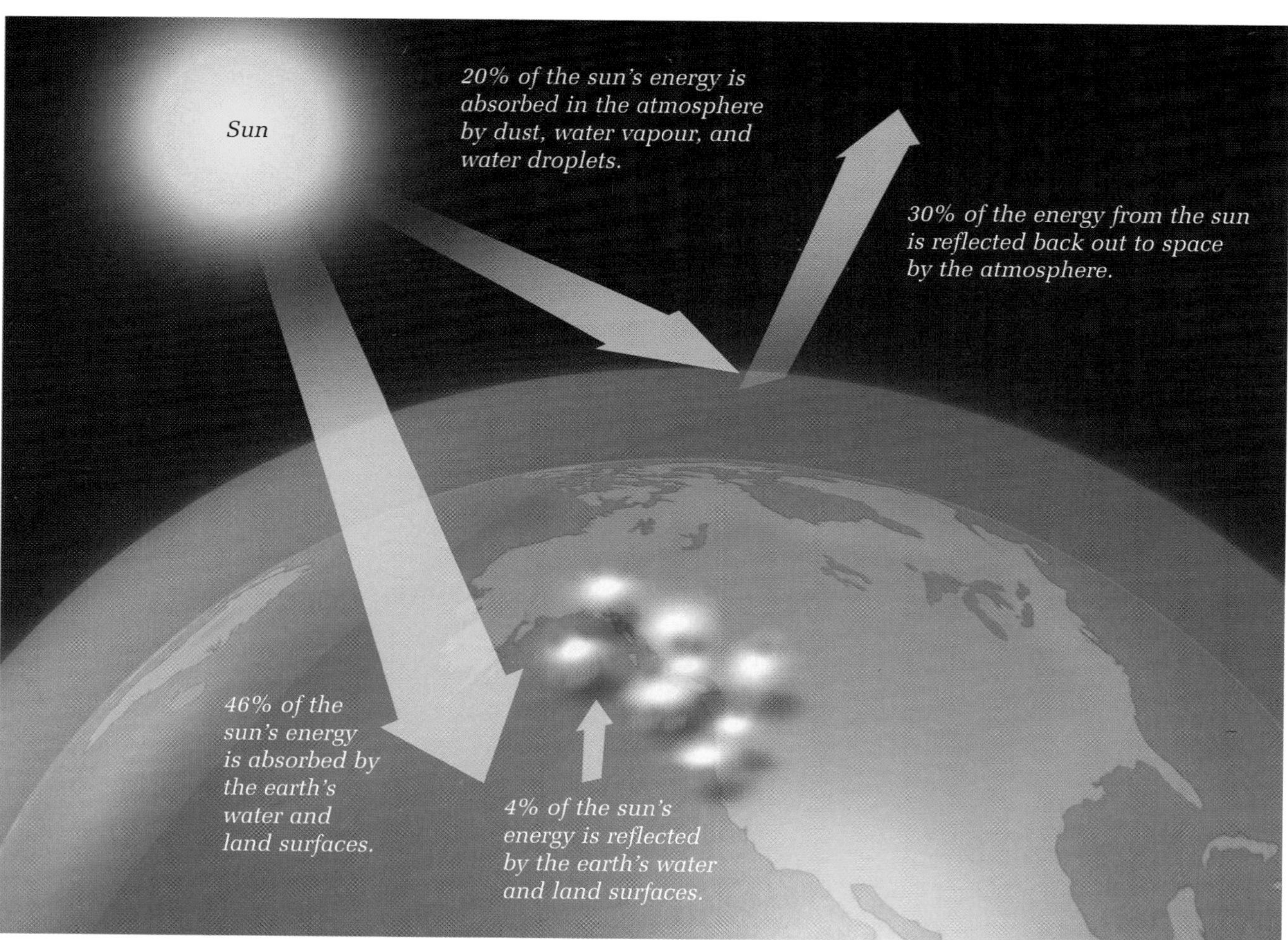

Sun
20% of the sun's energy is absorbed in the atmosphere by dust, water vapour, and water droplets.
30% of the energy from the sun is reflected back out to space by the atmosphere.
46% of the sun's energy is absorbed by the earth's water and land surfaces.
4% of the sun's energy is reflected by the earth's water and land surfaces.

Less than a billionth of the sun's total energy output reaches the earth. What do you think would happen to the plants and animals on earth if the energy reaching the earth was reduced or increased?

Develop

The Role of Heat Energy

The energy that reaches the earth not only plays a vital role for plants and animals, it is directly responsible for two natural systems that are vital to our survival: the water cycle and weather. The next activity gives you an opportunity to create a model that explains the role heat energy plays in the water cycle.

PROBLEM SOLVER

CYCLING WATER AND HEAT

A model is often used to help explain something that may be hard to understand. In this activity, you will create a model to explain the role of heat energy in the water cycle.

Using the diagram as your guide, set up a water cycle model. The cake pan contains ice cubes to keep it cold. When the water in the kettle is boiling, hold the cake pan about 10–15 cm above the spout of the kettle. Make sure you wear oven mitts when you are holding the cake pan over the steam. Observe what happens to the kettle, the water in the kettle, the steam, and the cake pan.

Combine your observations of the water cycle model with your understanding of heat to draw a diagram that illustrates the role heat energy plays in the water cycle. The diagram and notes should answer the following questions:

- How is heat energy transferred between the kettle, the water, and the cake pan?
- On earth, what plays the role of the kettle, the water in the kettle, the steam, the cake pan, and the water drops?

Creating Wind with Heat Energy

Heat energy is an important element in making rain and snow. It also has an important role to play in moving rain and snow and other weather systems from one area to another. How does heat energy do this?

Recall that different materials have different heat capacities. Remember also that water has a heat capacity higher than most other substances, which means water heats up more slowly but can hold onto heat energy longer. Earth is made up of one-third land masses and two-thirds oceans and lakes. The land masses absorb and release heat energy faster than the water. These different rates of heat energy absorption and release influence our weather.

As the land heats up faster than the water, a convection current is set up. The illustration below shows how convection currents can lead to wind that can move air and weather patterns from one area to another.

The land absorbs the sun's heat energy faster than the water does. When the land radiates some of its absorbed heat energy into the air, the warmed air begins to rise. Cooler air lying over the water moves in to take the rising air's place. In other words, a convection current forms. We call the wind that results from this convection current a *breeze*. During the day, this breeze blows from the water toward the land.

By night, the land has cooled off a great deal, but the water still contains much of its heat energy. When the water radiates some of its absorbed heat energy into the air, the warmed air begins to rise. Cooler air lying over the land moves in to take the rising air's place. This, too, is a convection current. The resulting night-time breeze blows from the land toward the water.

There are many other locations on earth where the sun's energy heats up the surface at different rates and sets up convection currents. How would the sun's energy affect the different areas listed below?

- a large forested area as opposed to a desert
- a city with pavement and concrete as opposed to a grassy meadow

When you studied ecosystems, you learned that plants are important for the survival of all living things. The sun's heat energy is very important for plant and animal life. It produces the necessary warmth for plant growth. Plants provide oxygen and form the base of all food webs. Because heat energy from the sun influences different weather patterns, there is a wide diversity of life forms. For example:

- Heat energy in the tropics is consistent and provides warmth and a great amount of rainfall. These conditions allow for tremendous growth in a wide variety of plants. The abundance of plant life, in turn, affects the number of animals that can survive in a rainforest.

- In the northern boreal forest, the weather patterns are quite different resulting in distinctly different life forms. Plants that grow in the north are adapted to the short growing season and grow quickly when there is sufficient heat. Migration and hibernation are two ways animals cope with the lack of sufficient heat energy and plant growth in the winter.

Communicate

1 Heat energy can affect the weather in a variety of other ways. Find out how heat energy is related to one of the weather events listed below. Your task is then to "weave" as many of the events as you can into a single presentation. Be creative in your presentation—you may want to use a poster, a comic strip, a mural, or a multimedia report.

breezes	monsoons
air masses	trade winds
prevailing winds	doldrums

4.5 Check Your Progress

1 a) Name three ways that heat energy can be transferred and give an example of each.
b) Which of these transfer methods needs matter for the heat energy to move through?

2 a) If you were to stir a large pot of hot boiling soup for a while, which of the following spoons would you choose to use?
- an aluminum spoon
- a stainless steel spoon
- a wooden spoon
- a plastic spoon

b) Explain the science behind your choice.

3 a) If you lived in a desert environment, which colour would you choose for clothing. Why?
b) If you lived in Canada's far north, would you choose the same colour for clothing? Why or why not?

4 What happens to the sun's energy when it reaches earth? Use the words *absorb*, *reflect*, and *pass through* in your answer.

5 How do convection currents produce breezes that blow between water and land?

6 A thermos bottle is designed to reduce the transfer of heat energy. At right is a cross section of a typical thermos. Based on your understanding of heat energy transfer, infer how a thermos keeps hot liquids hot. Then infer how it keeps cold liquids cold.

*info*BIT

The Thermos

The thermos was originally called a "Dewar Flask," because it was invented by James Dewar in 1892. At first it was used only by scientists to store chemicals at stable temperatures. Later, Reinhold Burger, a glass blower, renamed it the thermos (Greek for "heat"). He sold it to the general public as a way to keep coffee hot or lemonade cold.

A Cross Section of a Thermos Bottle

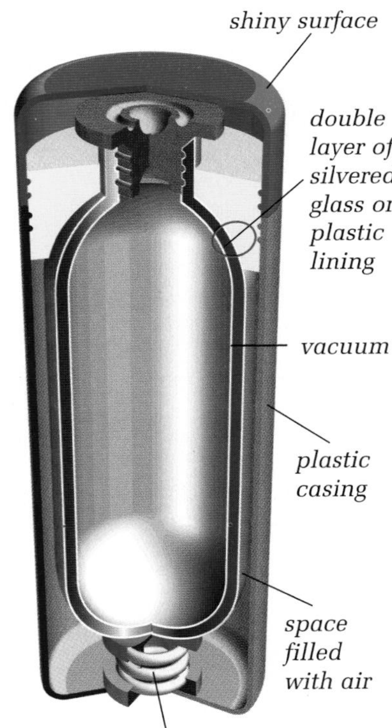

Careers and Profiles

COLD-WEATHER CLOTHING DESIGNER

Woody Blackford designs cold-weather clothing for Blackwater Designs, an outdoor-clothing manufacturer in Foymount, Ontario.

In order to design an effective winter jacket or parka, Blackford has to know about heat energy and heat transfer. A good parka, Blackford points out, keeps you warm by preventing heat transfer. When he designs a parka, he chooses materials that best prevent conduction and convection. As well, he designs the parka in layers.

Another feature of Blackford's design is that the liner is removable. That way, if you get too hot, you can wear the shell or the liner by itself.

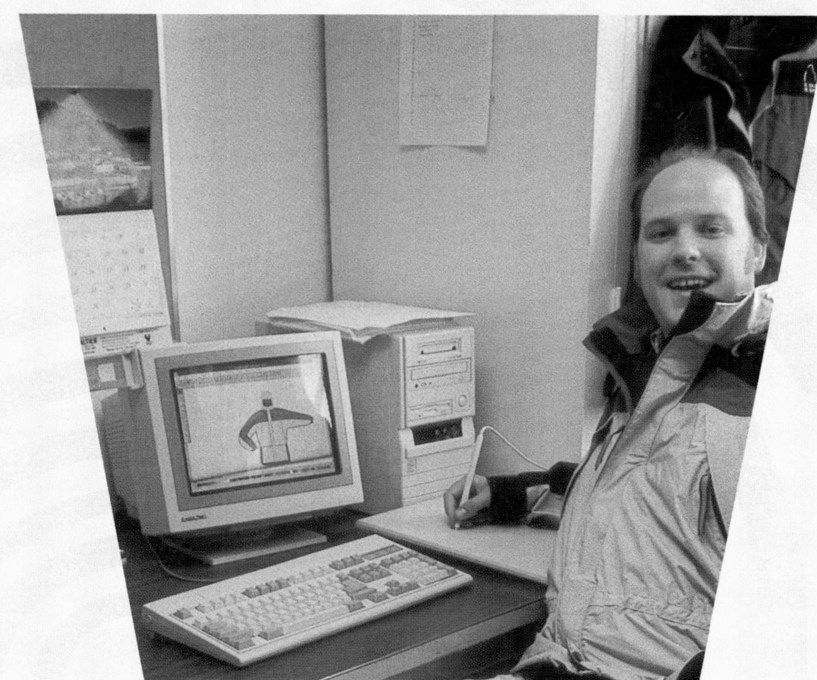

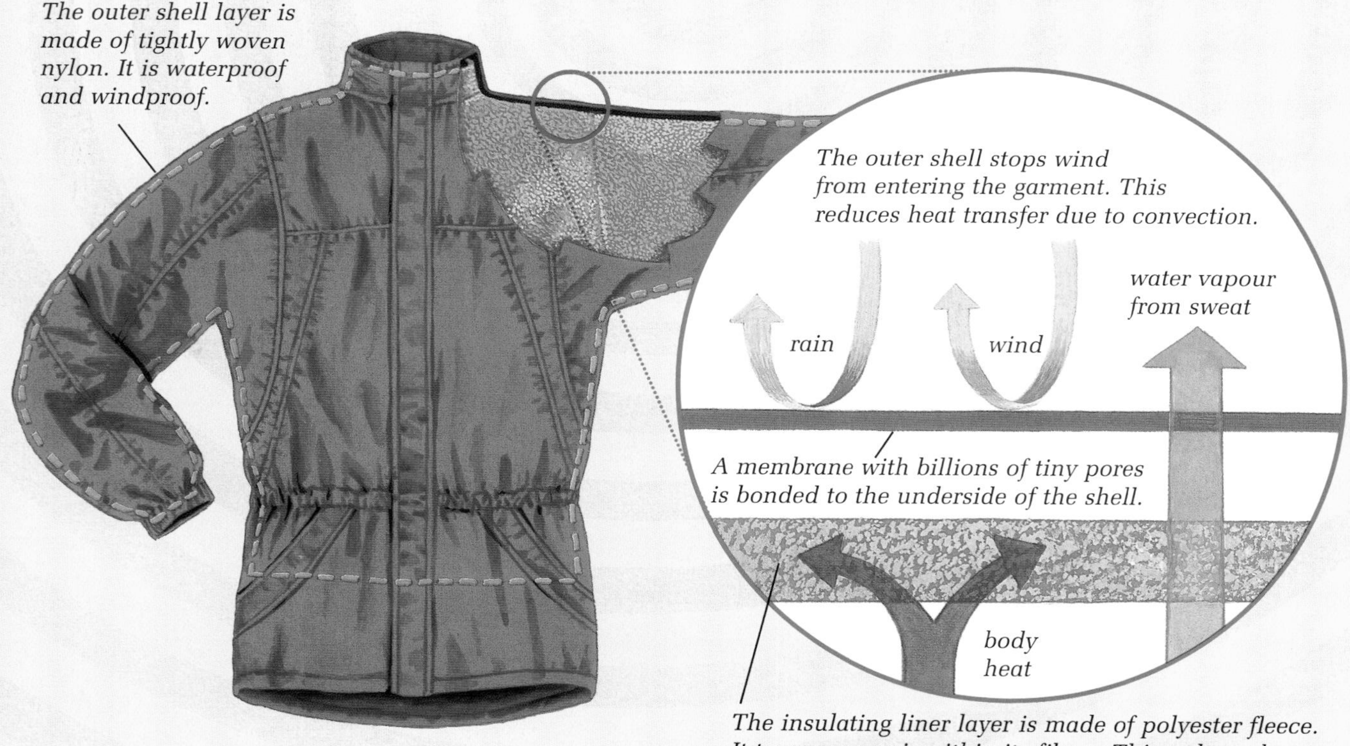

The outer shell layer is made of tightly woven nylon. It is waterproof and windproof.
The outer shell stops wind from entering the garment. This reduces heat transfer due to convection.
rain
wind
water vapour from sweat
A membrane with billions of tiny pores is bonded to the underside of the shell.
body heat
The insulating liner layer is made of polyester fleece. It traps warm air within its fibres. This reduces heat transfer due to conduction.

BIG IDEA

5.0 Heat energy is related to other forms of energy.

As you investigated the characteristics of heat energy, you have seen how heat energy can be transferred by conduction, convection, and radiation. Now you will explore how heat energy is related to other forms of energy. By examining the natural sources of heat energy, energy transformations, and methods of reducing heat loss, you will continue to develop an understanding of heat energy and learn about its relationship with other forms of energy.

5.1 NATURAL SOURCES OF HEAT ENERGY

Explore

The sun is the most important source of heat energy for all living things on earth. It provides the energy necessary to support life on our planet. There are, however, many other natural sources of heat energy. With a partner, brainstorm as many different natural sources of heat energy as you can. Place all your ideas—both words and pictures—down on a sheet of paper. This sheet of paper will become your "natural sources of heat energy place mat." Provide a real-world example of any of your natural sources if you can. Share your results with others in your class. After sharing, modify your place mat as needed.

Develop

What Natural Sources of Heat Energy Are There?

The next two pages show several other examples of natural sources of heat energy. Look at the photos and read the captions. Compare them with those listed on your natural sources of heat energy place mat. Using a different colour of pen or pencil, add or change anything on your place mat. The changes should show what new ideas you collected from the information on these pages.

*info***BIT**

Heat Shields

When the space shuttle re-enters the earth's atmosphere, the sides of the shuttle rub against air particles. This rubbing—called friction—produces enough heat energy to raise the shuttle's exterior temperature to nearly 1400°C! Heat resistant tiles are used on the space shuttle to prevent the shuttle and its crew inside from burning up. They glow red-hot on re-entry to the earth's atmosphere.

Natural Sources of Heat Energy

A volcanic eruption

A geyser

A The sun is our planet's main natural source of heat energy. Many people refer to the sun's energy as *solar energy*. "Solar" comes from an old Roman word, *sol*, which means sun.

B Our planet earth is a considerable source of heat energy. Much of this energy remains deep inside. It is called *geothermal energy*. "Geo" means earth, and "thermal" means heat. Spectacular events such as the ones shown here are evidence of this energy.

C Lightning is an example of *electrical energy*. This energy can be transformed very quickly into heat energy. The temperature of a lightning bolt may be as high as 30 000°C!

D Fires release the *chemical energy* stored inside fuel as heat energy, also *light* and often *sound energy*.

Your body is a source of heat energy. Life processes transform the chemical energy stored in the food you eat into heat energy.

At the sub-microscopic level, particles store *nuclear energy*. During nuclear reactions, this energy is released and transformed into other forms of energy such as heat energy and radiant energy. Nuclear reactions occur in stars, including our sun.

Decay is a source of heat energy. The breakdown of dead plants and animals produces heat energy. If you have ever done any composting, you have felt the heat energy produced by the decaying process.

Radioactive substances are a source of heat energy. There are only a few radioactive substances on and inside our planet. Uranium, shown here, is an example. Over time, the unstable particles of radioactive substances break up into smaller and more stable particles. When this happens, they release energy, including heat energy.

Communicate

1 Look at your natural sources of heat energy place mat and describe your thoughts on the following:
   - one thing I already knew about natural sources of heat energy before I made the place mat
   - two things I learned about natural sources of heat energy after completing the place mat
   - one thing I would like to know about natural sources of heat energy
2 Classify the natural sources of heat energy on your place mat into the following categories:
   - I regularly experience
   - I sometimes experience
   - I've never experienced
3 Name places in other parts of the world where people might experience the natural sources of heat energy that you sometimes or never experience.

*info***BIT**

A Lot of Hot Air

How can heat energy be converted into flight?

In 1782, a French papermaker named Joseph Montgolfier watched the smoke and ash from a small fire rise into the air. He wondered what would happen if he caught the rising smoke inside a bag. Would the bag rise?

The next year, he and his brother Jaques lit a fire under a large balloon made of paper and silk. The fire heated the air inside the balloon, causing it to rise high into the sky.

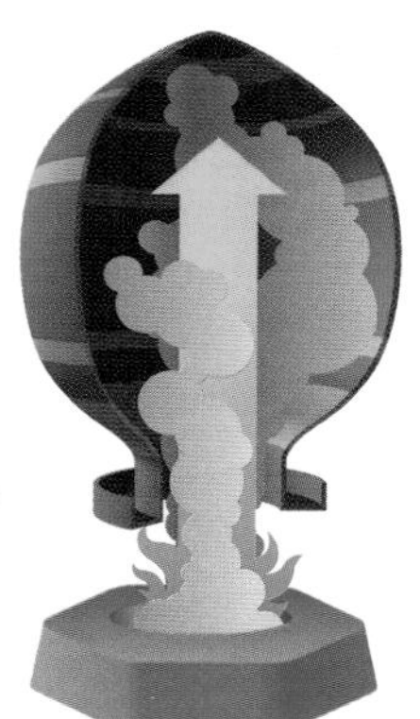

5.2 Energy Transformations and Heat Energy

Explore

You will recall that changing energy from one form to other forms is called **energy transformation**. All energy transformations result in heat energy. When you turn on a light switch, not only will you see light, you'll also feel some heat if you hold your hand near the light bulb. You are changing electrical energy into light energy and also heat energy. In fact, a light bulb gives out more heat energy than it does light energy! Of the electrical energy that goes into a light bulb, 95% changes into heat energy; only 5% changes into light energy.

Following are some pictures that show energy being transformed. In each transformation, heat energy is always given off. Try to identify the form of energy being transformed, and to what, in each picture. A list of the different forms of energy is provided to help you.

Forms of energy:

chemical energy
heat energy
electrical energy
nuclear energy
mechanical energy
sound energy
radiant energy

Develop

All Energy Transformations Result in Heat Energy

Any device that transforms energy from one form to another is an energy converter. A motor vehicle such as a car, truck, or bus is an energy converter. It transforms chemical energy from fuel into mechanical energy that moves the vehicle wheels. A portable CD player is an energy converter that transforms chemical energy from batteries into electrical energy, mechanical energy, and sound energy.

Energy converters can be much larger than these examples suggest. For example, the power plant that generates the electricity you use at home is also an energy converter. Depending on where you live in Canada, you may depend on thermal power plants, nuclear power plants, or hydroelectric power plants to generate electrical energy. All of these plants and mechanisms transform one type of energy into another. In many cases, heat energy is produced as a by-product of the transformations.

- Think of the CD player described earlier. Have you ever felt a CD player after it has been on for a while? It has been producing heat energy and feels warm to the touch.
- Think of your computer. Electrical energy is transformed into light and sound energy, but heat energy is also produced. As in many other situations, this heat energy is not used.

*info*BIT

A Greek inventor named Hero designed this model energy converter nearly 2000 years ago. What energy transformations are involved? Do you see any similarities between this energy converter and others you've seen in this chapter or in your life experiences?

- Many factories use machines to manufacture useful products. The machines also produce heat energy that is released into the atmosphere.

You can see from these examples that:

- all energy transformations result in heat energy,
- the resulting heat energy is not always used — it only warms up the surroundings.

That is why scientists say that heat energy is the final form of energy transformations.

Communicate

1 Look at the machines and mechanisms below. Work with a partner and list the different transformations that take place.

2 Which mechanisms produce heat energy as a by-product?

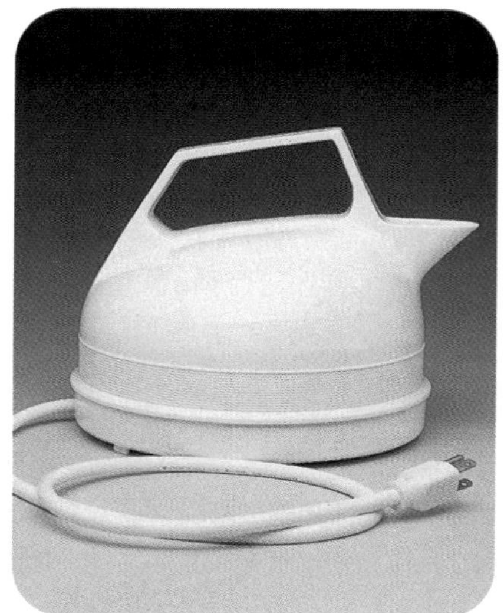

Electric kettle

Refrigerator

Lawn mower

Electric stove

Nuclear power plant

Circular saw

5.3 Reducing Loss of Heat Energy

Explore

A thermal power plant generating electricity produces a number of unwanted energy transformations. Little or none of the unwanted forms of energy can be used. They're considered "waste" energy. What happens to it? Many people talk about energy being "lost" when energy transformations result in unusable forms of energy. In fact, energy can't be created or destroyed. It can only be transformed into other forms.

Scientists have also discovered another important fact about energy. Whenever energy is transformed from one form to another, heat energy is also the result. Whether it's usable or not, and whether we want it or not, heat energy always results when energy is transformed. Every time energy is converted from one form to another, some energy is wasted as unusable heat energy. Because of this fact, scientists consider heat energy to be the final form of all energy transformations.

Develop

Reducing "Wasted" Heat Energy

We can't stop this wasted heat energy from being produced. However, we can, and do, try to reduce the amount of heat energy that's wasted during energy transformations. The next Investigator activity will help you think about how.

INVESTIGATOR

Reducing Friction

Before You Start...

Mechanical systems like turbines, engines, and bicycle gears have moving parts that rub against one another. This constant rubbing, called **friction**, results in lots of wasted heat energy. The more you can reduce this wasted heat energy, the more efficient the mechanical system can be.

In this activity, you will think about ways to reduce the heat energy that results from friction when you rub your hands together. You will then use your experiences to infer how technologists design mechanical systems to reduce friction and increase their efficiency.

The Question

How can you reduce friction when you rub your hands together?

continued on next page

Materials & Equipment

- *cooking oil (olive oil, corn oil)*
- *hand cream or lotion*
- *several round pencils*
- *a cup of water*
- *a pair of gloves*
- *materials to clean up afterward*

Procedure

1 Hold your hands tightly together. Rub them back and forth quickly.

2 Describe what you feel to a classmate.

3 Choose one of the materials to put on or between your hands and repeat the rubbing.

4 Repeat step 3 with the other materials. Record the effect the material has on the friction between your hands.

Keeping Records

5 Design a chart to rank the materials in order from most effective to least effective in terms of how well they reduce friction.

Analyzing and Interpreting

6 Work with a partner and compare your results. Compose your own explanation of how the different materials affect the friction between your hands.

Forming Conclusions

7 Based on your data and observations, describe different ways you can reduce friction. Your description should rank the different ways from excellent to poor. Don't forget to use your Investigator activity data to defend your ranking.

Communicate

1 Based on your experiences, suggest one way to reduce friction in these situations:
   a) a car engine in which metal rubs constantly against other metals
   b) a heavy cardboard box that needs to be moved down the hall
   c) an electric fan that rotates alternately clockwise and counterclockwise
   d) a high-speed drill boring into a piece of metal
   e) two gears on a bicycle

2 How is friction useful in the following situations:
   a) the hand brakes on a 21-speed bicycle
   b) special shoes for running on ice

5.4 Check Your Progress

1. Give five examples of sources of heat energy that you have experienced in the past day.
2. In what ways is heat energy related to other forms of energy?
3. What device uses this energy transformation?
   sound energy ⟶ kinetic energy
   Draw a picture to record your answer. (Hint: It could be more than one device. It could also be natural or technological.)
4. Identify the energy transformation taking place in the photo below. Be sure to include all the forms of energy that result.

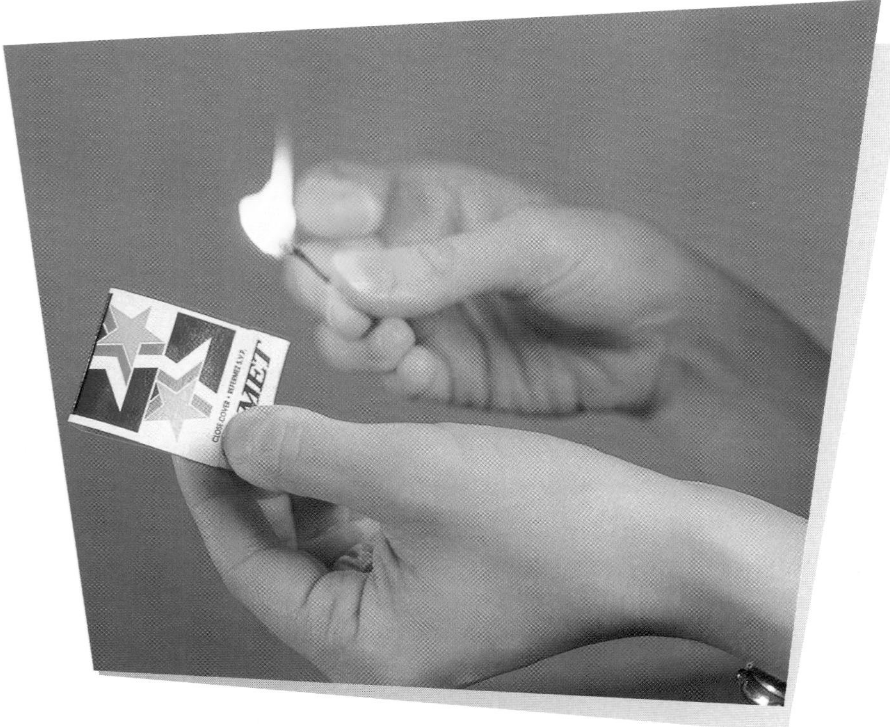

5. From a scientist's point of view, why is it incorrect to talk about "losing heat" and "heat loss"? Why do you think people often use this phrasing anyway?
6. How does friction reduce the efficiency of mechanical systems? Name two ways to deal with this problem.
7. Why do scientists consider heat energy to be the final result of all energy transformations? Explain using examples from this chapter.

*info*BIT

Your body functions best when your internal temperature is 37°C. If it rises, your body's cooling system transfers the excess heat energy outside your body. You sweat!

A part of your brain (called the *hypothalamus*) is your body's temperature regulator. In a way, it acts like a thermostat. When your body temperature rises too high, your brain signals your skin's sweat glands to produce sweat.

Heat energy from inside your body is transferred (by conduction) to the watery sweat on your skin. This heat energy causes the sweat to evaporate, which has a cooling effect.

Big Idea

6.0 Technologies that use heat energy have benefits and costs to society and the environment.

3 HEAT

From fibreglass insulation for houses to fireplaces to keep us warm, we use various heat technologies in our lives. In many situations, we take the use of heat energy for granted. Now it's time to investigate different uses of heat energy. You will have opportunities to consider different heating-system technologies, study a virtual dissection, find out what R-value means, and decide if cogeneration is a good idea, plus much more!

6.1 Heating-System Technologies

Explore

Keeping warm in Canada has always been a challenge. Early settlers were unprepared for Canada's cold winters. They had to learn how to produce and maintain a warm living environment throughout the winter months.

Most homes, schools, and buildings have technological systems to control indoor temperatures. Usually, this means keeping the inside at or near 20°C. We call this "room temperature." It seems to be our modern standard for comfortable living conditions.

If you were living 100 years ago, the technology that heated your home probably would have looked similar to the examples on the next page.

*info*BIT

Early Heating Technology Time Line

- 7000 B.C. — Humans create fire
- 100 B.C. — Romans develop central heating
- A.D. 1200 — Chimneys first appear in Europe
- 1300s — Fireplaces with chimneys are built into the walls of buildings
- 1700s — Cast-iron stoves
- late 1700s — Central heating
- 1800s — Forced-air heating
- 1906 — Electric heaters

fireplace

Franklin Stove

Fireplaces are one of our oldest heating technologies. The Franklin Stove is a dual-purpose heating system designed by the American inventor and politician, Benjamin Franklin (1706–1790). With the door in front opened, it served as a fireplace. With the door closed, it served as a cooking stove.

Today, two main technologies help us achieve and maintain room temperature—or any other temperature we choose. There are local heating systems and central heating systems.

- *Local heating systems* provide heat energy for only one room or a small part of a building. Fireplaces, wood-burning stoves, and space heaters are common local heating systems. (A space heater is a small portable heating device. It can run on fuel or electricity.)
- *Central heating systems* provide heat energy from a single, central location. The heat energy is transferred through a network of pipes, ducts, and openings (vents) to different places in a home or building.

Which of these systems provide heat energy for your home? How is it controlled?

Develop

How Do We Control Heating Systems?

When a fireplace becomes too hot or not hot enough, you can adjust the damper. This device is a movable plate that regulates the amount of air that's exposed to the fire. If you want to slow down the fire, you close the damper to reduce the amount of airflow. If you want to build it back up, you open the damper to allow more airflow.

Most modern heating systems make use of a thermostat to control or regulate temperature. ("Thermo" means *heat* and "stat" means *maintain*.) A **thermostat** makes automatic adjustments to temperature by switching a heating system on or off. Find out how it works in the next activity.

PROBLEM SOLVER

THERMOSTAT: WHAT'S INSIDE

This diagram shows the inside of a typical thermostat.

- Use this diagram to infer and explain how a thermostat works. Here are three tips if you need help:
  a) Metals expand when they are heated and contract when they cool down.
  b) Not all metals expand and contract at the same rate.
  c) An electrical conductor allows the passage of an electrical current.
- Name five devices in which you would expect to find thermostats.

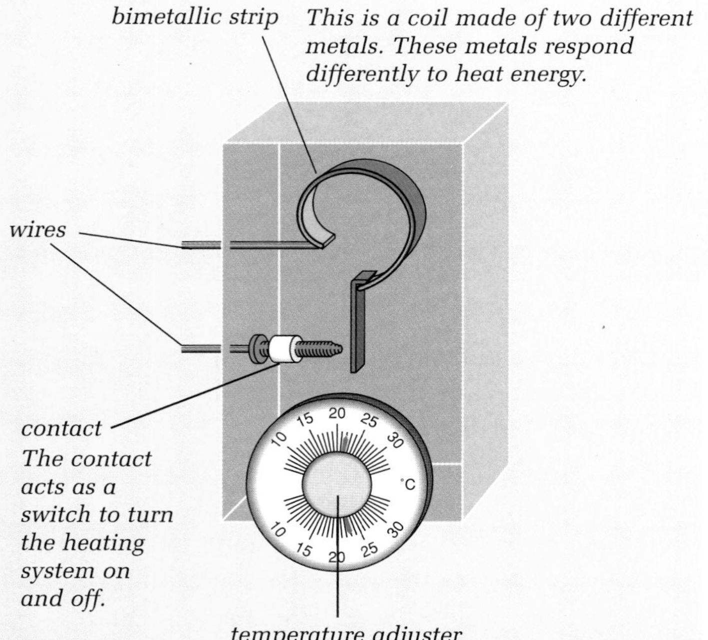

bimetallic strip
This is a coil made of two different metals. These metals respond differently to heat energy.
wires
contact
The contact acts as a switch to turn the heating system on and off.
temperature adjuster
°C

*info*BIT

Substances that insulate differ in the amount of heat energy transfer they're able to stop. Every insulator is assigned a number called an **R-value.** This value is a measurement of its ability to stop or restrict heat energy transfer.

Substances that have a higher R-value are better insulators than substances with a lower R-value. For example, you know that glass is a good insulator. But glass has a lower R-value than fibreglass. So fibreglass is a better choice to use for insulation.

Average Heat Loss in a House

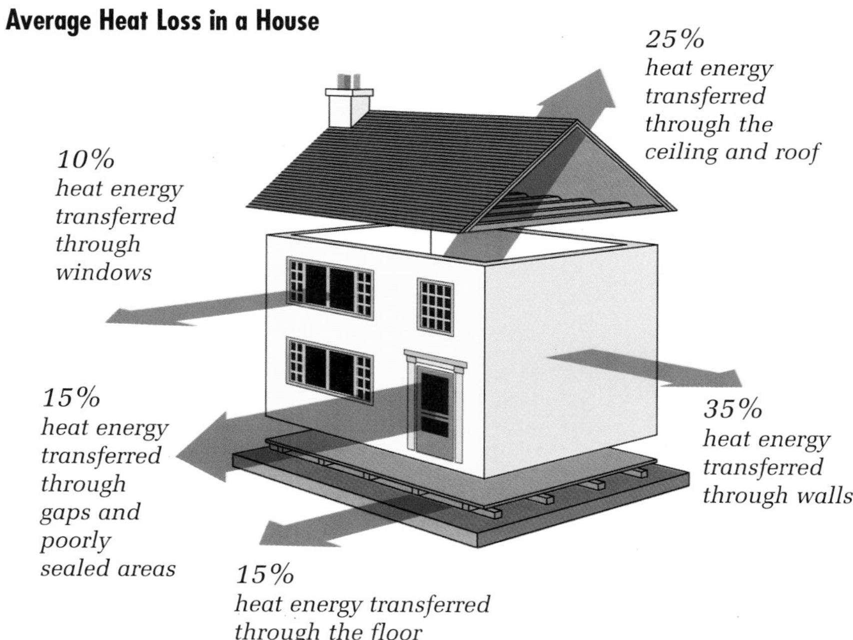

Where does wasteful heat energy transfer happen in this house? Why does it happen in these places? How would you reduce it?

As you know, heat energy is always transferred from objects at a higher temperature to objects at a lower temperature. This poses a challenge for maintaining comfortable temperatures in our homes all year long. When it's hotter inside our homes than it is outside—as it usually is in winter—the inside heat energy naturally moves outside. When it's cooler inside than it is outside—as it usually is in summer—the outside heat energy naturally moves inside. Both these problems can be solved using the same material: insulation.

Insulation is any substance that limits the transfer of heat energy. In the Experiment on Your Own in section 4.1, you tried to keep an ice cube from melting. What type of insulation did you use?

For buildings, walls made of solid stone make good insulation. They do not allow heat energy to pass through them very well. However, the walls must be extremely thick and that would not be practical. Here are some more practical insulating materials that are commonly used.

Fibreglass

Styrofoam

*info***BIT**

How can you tell where a house is "losing" most of its heat energy?

Contractors use an infrared coloured photograph called a thermogram. The colour shows the type of heat loss.

- white/yellow: the greatest heat loss
- pink/purple: the next greatest heat loss
- green/blue: the least heat loss

Communicate

1 Examine these two heating systems. Copy a larger version of each one into your Science Journal. (Either draw it freehand, scan it into a computer, or use drawing software.)

- Identify all the places where heat energy is transferred by conduction, convection, and radiation throughout the system.
- Pick one of these other heating systems: radiant heating, active solar heating, or passive solar heating. Do research so you can add labels and captions to communicate how each works.

Forced-Air Heating

- Air is heated by burning fuel in a furnace.
- The heated air travels through ducts (pipe-like passageways) to registers in different rooms. (Registers are panels or grates in the wall near the floor or in the floor itself.)
- A blower helps pull returning air back to the furnace.
- The filter helps trap dust, hairs, and other fine particles before the air returns to the furnace.

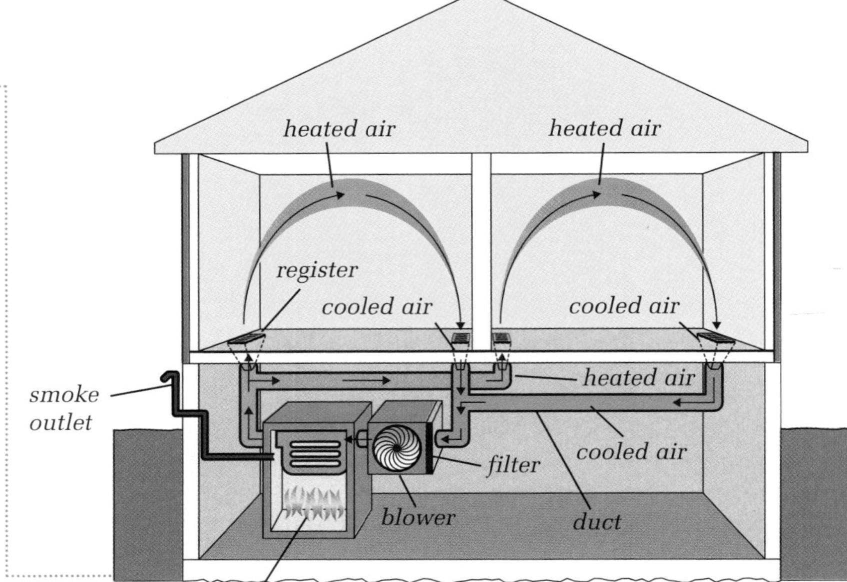

Hot-Water Heating

- Water is heated by burning fuel in a furnace or boiler.
- A pump forces the heated water through a network of pipes that lead to metal radiators.
- The hot water heats the radiators which then warm the air in the room.
- As the water cools, it is returned to the boiler and heated up again.

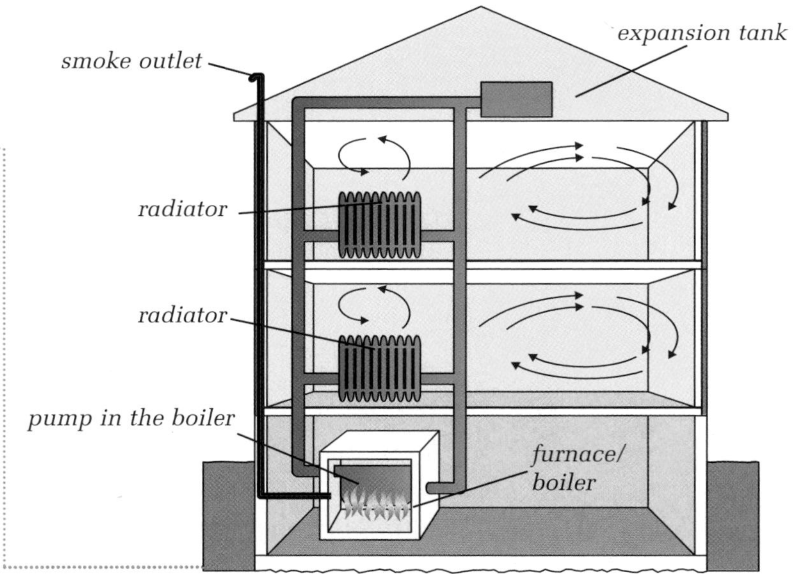

2 Describe what you would do to a house to help conserve energy and explain your decision.

6.2 The Costs of Relying on Heat Energy

Explore

Every time you turn up the thermostat or switch on an electrical appliance, you are using an energy resource. It costs money to use energy resources. The more energy you need to warm your home or run a computer, the more money it costs. Who pays? You and your family do. In fact, you pay with more than money, as you will see.

One way of keeping track of the benefits and costs is to make a "+/–" chart. The "+" refers to the benefits and the "–" refers to the costs. As you read the rest of this section, make a "+/–" chart. Afterwards, work with a partner to add any more benefits or costs you can think of that relate to the use of an energy source.

reSEARCH

Air pollution is linked to several threats to the environment and living things. These threats include acid rain, the greenhouse effect, and global warming. Pick one of these to explore.

- How is air pollution involved?
- What effects does it have?
- What are people doing about it?

Environmental Costs of Relying on Heat Energy

More than 72% of Canada's energy needs are supplied by fossil fuels: coal, oil, and natural gas. Burning fossil fuels releases soot and ashes and gases such as carbon dioxide, carbon monoxide, sulphur dioxide, and nitrogen oxides.

Thermal and nuclear power plants produce large amounts of unwanted heat energy. Great volumes of cool water are used to absorb this wasted heat energy. This **thermal pollution**, as it's been called, raises water temperatures, affecting fish and other members of aquatic ecosystems.

reSEARCH

All technologies have both advantages and disadvantages. Pick one, two, or all of the following alternative energy resources to explore. What are their advantages? What are their disadvantages? Which, if any, is the most promising energy resource for our future? Which, if any, is the most practical?

- solar energy
- wind energy
- tidal energy
- energy from hydrogen
- geothermal energy
- energy from nuclear fusion

Economic Costs of Relying on Heat Energy
For example, businesses and industries waste a great deal of heat energy. In the past, little was done to reclaim or reduce this waste heat. Now, many businesses and industries have started to adopt safer, environmentally responsible practices.

Costs to Society of Relying on Heat Energy
What if we used up all our remaining energy resources? What if using energy resources became so expensive that only wealthy people could afford it? What if it became so expensive that even they couldn't afford it?

Develop

Heat Energy Is All Around You

Whenever a decision is made, both the benefits and costs must be considered. You have just read about some of the costs of using energy to the environment, economy, and society. They must be considered when we rely on energy to heat our homes, run our televisions, and cook our food.

You will now have an opportunity to decide if your community should build a new energy facility called *energy cogeneration* by analyzing its benefits and costs.

REUSING HEAT ENERGY

The Issue

Your community is looking for an efficient way to generate more electricity from existing sources. Some people want to build a bigger electricity producing site. Others are arguing to use alternative forms of energy production. While no one can agree on what is the best answer, everyone does agree that a type of energy production called cogeneration is worth investigating.

Your task is to determine the costs and benefits of cogeneration and prepare a summary for everyone in your community to read. You are expected to clearly describe the benefits and costs of cogeneration. Then you must use this information to support your decision to use or not use cogeneration in the community.

Background Information

You know that all energy transformations result in wasted heat energy. When electricity generators transform fuel into electrical energy, they waste as much as two-thirds of the energy stored in the fuel.

Wouldn't it be nice if we could make use of at least some of this wasted energy? Well, we can!

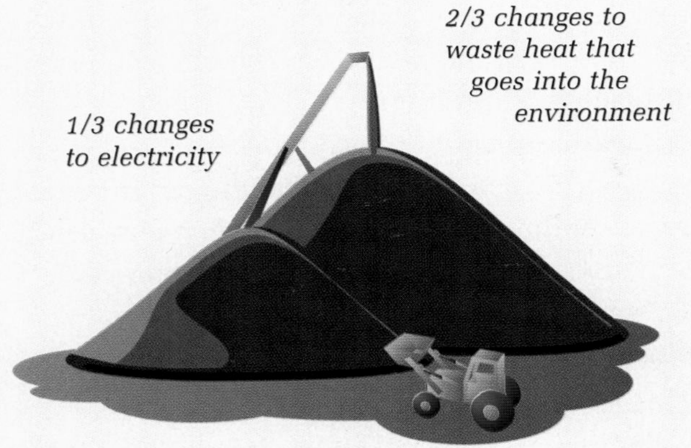

The technology for doing this is called **cogeneration**. It involves generating two or more forms of energy from the same energy converter. Usually, cogeneration includes generating electrical and heat energy.

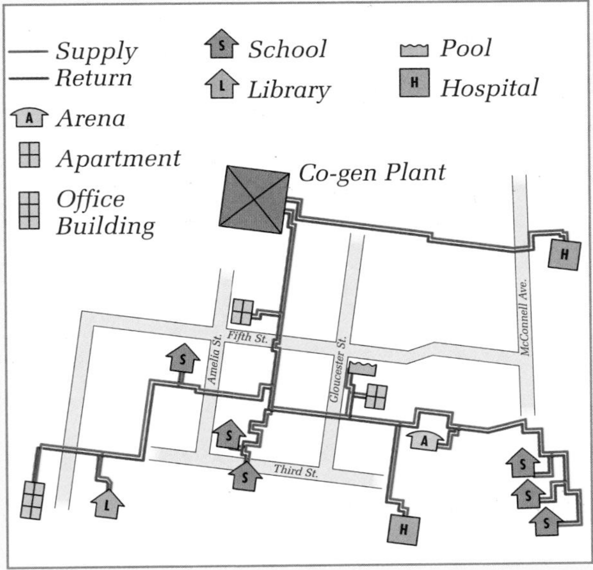

The electricity generating plant in Cornwall, Ontario, uses its waste heat to heat part of the local community. Hot water is pumped through 10 km of underground pipes.

Cogeneration makes sense, because:

- It makes good use of heat energy that would otherwise be wasted.
- It can reduce the costs of generating electrical energy, as well as the costs of heating buildings.
- It reduces air pollution because two forms of energy are generated at the same time, rather than individually.
- It reduces thermal pollution of bodies of water.

continued on next page

So who's using cogeneration technology? Great Britain, Denmark, and several other European countries have been reusing heat energy since the 1980s. Several Asian and East Asian countries (for example, China and India) are investigating this technology.

There are well over 100 universities across North America—including the Universities of Toronto and Western Ontario—that use and support cogeneration technology.

Your Opinion

In your own words, explain why adopting cogeneration does or does not make sense for your community. Remember your explanation should highlight benefits and costs and be clear for everyone to understand. You may wish to make a poster, handout, or short report.

Communicate

1 With a partner or in a small group, brainstorm a list of other ways people might use wasted heat energy.

2 Identify situations in your own life where you think heat energy is wasted. List these situations and suggest ways to reduce and conserve this wasted heat energy.

6.3 CHECK YOUR PROGRESS

1 a) What is the difference between a local heating system and a central heating system?
   b) Give one example of a place you would use each of these heating systems.

2 Explain what a thermostat is and how it works.

3 Agree or disagree with these two statements, and explain why.
   a) It's easier and cheaper to maintain comfortable temperatures inside a well-insulated building.
   b) Insulation can warm up cold things.

4 In what ways does burning fossil fuels affect the environment?

5 Where does thermal pollution occur, and why is it a concern?

6 a) What do people mean when they talk about "conserving" energy?
   b) Name two things that you personally can do to conserve energy.
   c) Name two things that industries can do to conserve energy.
   d) Name two things that society can do to conserve energy.

The Great Heat Treasure Hunt

What do you think of when you see smoke stacks pumping out black clouds of smoke?

If you lived fifty or more years ago, you would have probably thought it was a beautiful sight! Smoke and smoke stacks were the signs of modern civilization. They meant progress, wealth, and a healthy economy.

But wait! How could smoke be a sign of anything healthy? For the answer you have to go back to the past.

Woodcutters in England around the early 1700s

Fire Power

People first learned to harness heat energy by burning wood. This dramatically changed the way they lived. They used the new heat source to cook their food, keep warm, make their tools and pottery, and give them light.

Then two events happened that changed the nature of society. Both took place in England in the 1700s.

The Fuel Wood Crisis

Wood was England's main source of fuel. Great amounts were used to turn (or smelt) iron ore into metal. Iron was in great demand for tools, weapons, and parts for ships and carriages. But by the early 1700s, England had cut down most of its forests.

Suddenly there was an energy crisis. Wood prices soared. Many iron smelters were forced to close down. Huge quantities of wood had to be imported from North America.

Then, in the mid-1700s, Abraham Darby figured out how to smelt iron using coal instead of wood. Almost overnight, England's fuel wood problem was solved. In just a few years, coal had become the most widely used fuel for creating heat.

The Industrial Revolution

Once coal began to be used, inventors from around the world started experimenting with ways of controlling and using the heat from this new resource. Probably one of the most important developments came in 1769. James Watt perfected a steam engine. Inside Watt's engine, the heat from burning coal turned water into steam. The steam was used to move a piston which could be used to do work.

James Watt (1736–1819) improved the steam engine.

Manchester, a 19th-century English factory town

By the early 1800s, coal-fired steam engines powered factories, locomotives, ships, and cotton mills. People who were needed to operate the new machines moved from farms into cities to work in factories. Many traditional skills once performed by hand were now done by machine.

Historians call this time the Industrial Revolution. And a revolution it was. Factories replaced water-powered mills. Farmland was transformed into strip mines and row housing. Hundreds, thousands, then tens of thousands of inventions were created each year, but not without cost to people and the environment: air, water, and soil pollution; loss of farmland; and overcrowding in cities.

In Your Opinion

1. Research Canadian factory towns and cities during the mid-1800s. What social and environmental effects did the Industrial Revolution have in Canada?
2. List examples of how electronic technology has changed society. How do these changes compare with those of the Industrial Revolution?

This land once grew a variety of crops. If all the farmland is used for cities, where will people get their food?

PROJECT

DESIGN AN ENERGY-EFFICIENT BUILDING

Getting Started

People want homes, restaurants, and business places designed to conserve as much energy as possible. At the same time, they want all the modern conveniences and comforts. These modern conveniences often require the use of energy. Some of them can use energy in an efficient manner; for example, low-wattage light bulbs. Some of them can use a lot of energy; for example, a hot water heater set at a very high temperature.

Imagine you are an architect or engineer who is designing a building. Your job is to make sure the building conserves as much heat energy as possible. You will use the information you have learned in this chapter to complete such a task.

There are probably buildings in your community that have been designed to be an energy-conserving or energy-efficient structure. The pictures on the right show examples of how to make a building more energy efficient or conserve energy. Look at the pictures and see if you can answer these questions:

- Do any of the buildings generate their own energy?
- Do any of the buildings use environmental conditions to heat or cool the building?
- What do you think is the purpose of the trees around the farm in inset A?
- Name a feature in inset B that helps to keep heat out.
- What direction do you think the windows in inset C most likely face?

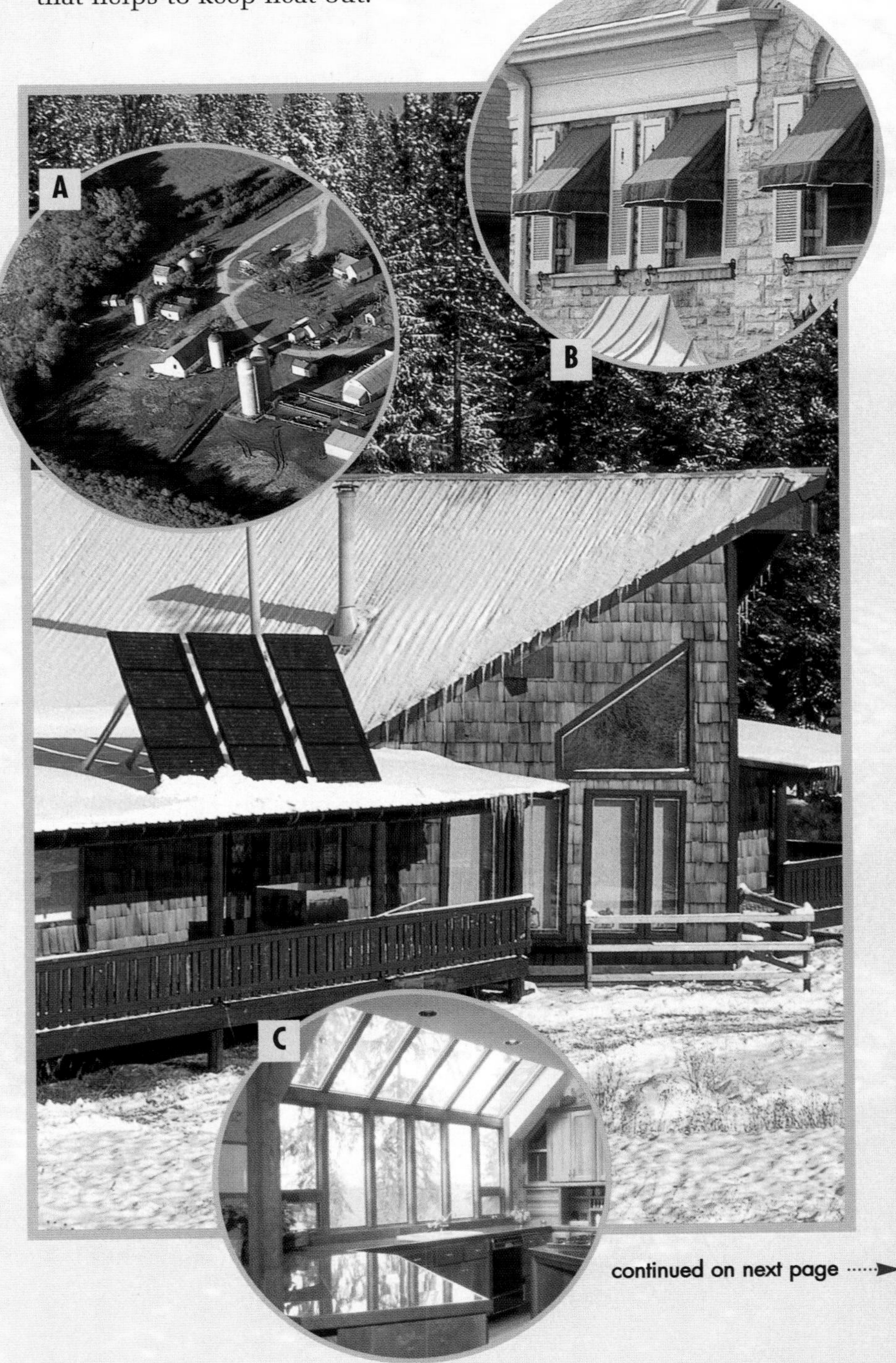

continued on next page

During the course of this chapter, you have developed some ideas about heat energy. When you go to the next page, you will have an opportunity to apply your understanding of heat energy. Your task is to make informed judgments about making a building more energy efficient and find ways to conserve heat energy.

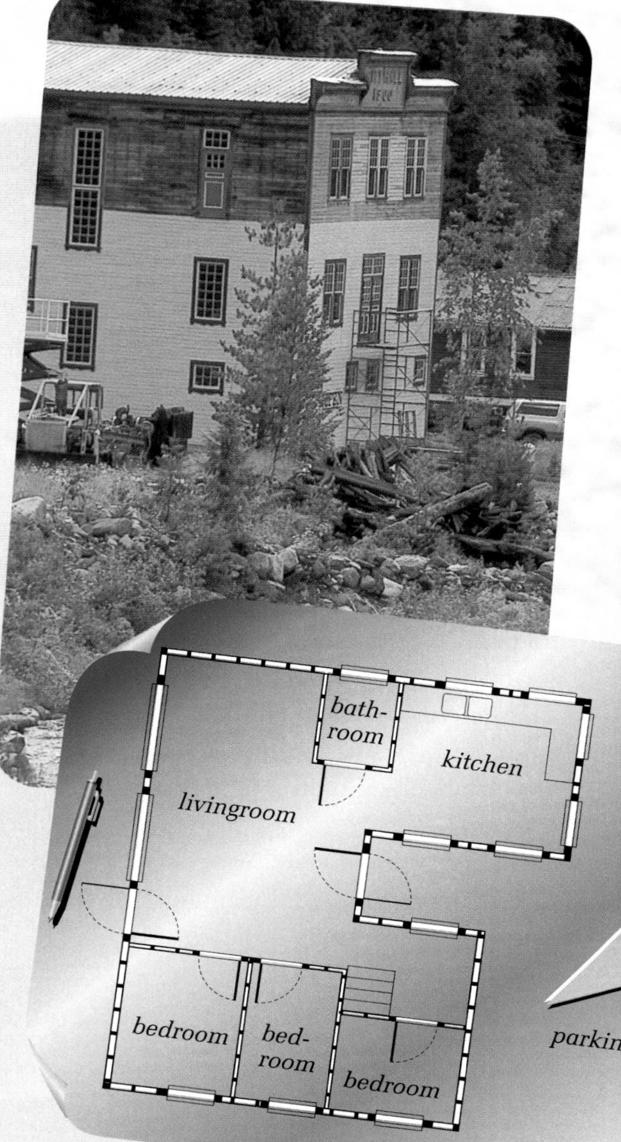

Before You Start...

You're a member of a team of thermal energy consultants. A thermal energy consultant is someone who uses an understanding of heat energy to provide information to people who need it. The assignment you must complete for your company is described below. Remember you can use any information you have collected during this chapter. While there is no one correct answer to the assignment, your team's recommendations need to include supporting scientific information.

The Question

To: Thermal Energy Consultant Team
From: James Joules – President and CEO *NRG 4 U*

Our company has been asked to submit recommendations for renovations to the building in the supplied picture. The building is located just outside the National Park. It is part of a small town that has many tourists all year. The weather is usually sunny and there are hot springs nearby. There are three options for the use of the building. It may become:

- a restaurant,
- a shop for clothes and/or sports equipment, or
- a lodge for outdoor enthusiasts.

While the weather is sunny, it gets very cold for most of the winter. As a result, the owners are especially concerned about making the building comfortable for all users but also inexpensive to operate.

Your job is to review the existing building and complete the following two tasks. First, decide how the building should be used. Second, give recommendations on how heat energy can be conserved in the building and how the building can be made more energy efficient.

Your recommendations should address the following questions:

1. Should the colour of the building be considered in the new design?
2. How should the building be heated?
3. Can the heating system be designed to minimize energy transfer between the walls?
4. How can the heating system be controlled?
5. Are there any potential heat pollution problems with the design?
6. What can be done by the owners to conserve heat energy after the building has been redesigned?

Procedure

1. Get your team together and decide what use you'll recommend for the building. Record your decision.

2. Brainstorm features of your building that you think are important for energy conservation or efficiency. Make sure you record all your thoughts. You can discard unusable ideas later.
3. Look at the results of your brainstorming. As a team, decide which ideas are worth developing further. Use the following questions to help you make your decisions.
   a) How will the features you design affect the heating of the building?
   b) Which features would be fairly simple to put into practice? Which ones will need some researching or further thought?
   c) What materials would you need to build the features you have identified? Can you get these materials easily and at a reasonable cost?
4. Reach an agreement on which features you will design into the building. Assign one or more features to individual members or small groups on your team.
5. Describe each feature and sketch it into the plans of the building. You will have to make sure each feature works with the other features. This will require meeting with the other team members to make sure all the features work together.
6. As a team, review your design. Once you agree on the design, write your report of recommendations.
7. Assign the task of describing each feature and how it works in the building to each team member. As a team, decide how you will present the information. You may want to use a report, poster, or some type of multimedia presentation.

Share and Compare

8. a) Share your team's design with your class. As you watch other teams' presentations, make a table with the following headings:

Features Other Teams Used That We Used	Features We Should Have Used	Features Used by Others but We Won't Use

   b) Complete and add this table to your report.

Observations and Reflections

9. Include your answers to the following questions in your report.
   a) Which design in the class do you think is the most effective in conserving energy? Which do you think is the most interesting? Explain your decisions.
   b) Which design feature or features in the class do you think are the least effective at using less heat energy? Which do you think is the most interesting? Explain your decisions.
   c) If you had a chance to redesign your building, what changes would you make? Give reasons for your answer.

CHAPTER REVIEW

Using Key Terms

1 Write a sentence that defines each of the terms below.

- temperature
- heat energy
- Particle Theory
- average kinetic energy
- conduction
- convection
- radiation
- cogeneration

Reviewing the Big Ideas

2 Describe what would happen in each situation and explain why.

a) A cube of ice is left on the kitchen table.

b) An inflated balloon is left outside in the sun.

c) Water is dripping from the roof of a building and the temperature falls below freezing.

d) A metal lid on a jam jar is stuck, and you blow hot air on it using a hair dryer.

3 a) What happens to the particles in a substance when heat energy is added to it?

b) What happens to the particles in a substance when heat energy is removed from it?

c) Describe the changes that could occur to a substance when heat energy is added to it or removed from it.

4 Agree or disagree with the following statements. Give evidence to support each of your decisions.

a) Temperature measures the amount of heat energy in a substance.

b) If you keep adding heat energy to boiling water, its temperature will increase.

c) If you keep adding heat energy to boiling water, the kinetic energy of its particles will increase.

d) The distance between particles of matter in the liquid state is halfway between the distances between the particles in solids and gases.

e) The amount of heat energy an object has depends on the kind of matter it is, the amount of matter it has, and its temperature.

5 Which contains more heat energy: a 14-L pot filled with boiling water or a large lake in which the water temperature is 14°C? Explain your reasoning.

6 Explain the similarities and differences between conduction, convection, and radiation.

7 What is the difference between a conductor and an insulator of heat?

8 What are the natural sources of heat energy? Give examples of each source.

9 Describe the energy transformations that occur when a hand dryer, found in many public washrooms, is turned on.

10 Explain how heating is controlled in a house and identify ways of conserving heat energy.

11 A thermostat is used to control the temperature in a home. Explain how it would work to control an air-conditioning system.

Connecting the Big Ideas

12 Choose two of the following statements. For each, explain the role that heat energy, temperature, and the Particle Theory plays.

a) At a restaurant, you have a pitcher of your favourite pop with a few ice cubes in it, but the pop in the pitcher isn't that cold.

b) You and your friends want to cook a big pot of spaghetti, but it's taking a long time for the water to boil.

c) A cup of hot chocolate is hot when its temperature is about 50°C. An oven is hot when it reaches 220°C.

d) A candle's flame can burst a balloon without touching it.

e) A metal cup with hot tea in it can burn your lip. A ceramic mug with the same tea in it only feels warm. (Ceramic mugs are made from clay that has been hardened in an oven.)

13 The illustration below shows several different shapes of frozen water. Each was made using exactly the same volume of liquid water.

a) List the shapes in order from the one you think will melt first to the one you think will melt last.

b) Is your answer to part a) a prediction? Why or why not?

c) What kind of test would you design to find out the accuracy of your answer to part a)?

14 Choose two of the following statements. For each, explain the role that energy transfer, energy transformations, and technology plays.

a) About 5% of the electrical energy that goes into a regular light bulb is transformed into light energy. The rest is transformed into heat energy.

b) The electrical cord from a home appliance is made from copper wires that are covered with plastic or rubber.

c) A hand-held electric sanding machine feels very warm after it's been running for a few minutes.

d) The air temperature inside a greenhouse is higher than the air temperature outside the greenhouse.

e) Scientists believe that average worldwide temperatures have increased over the past 100 years, mainly because of burning fossil fuels.

15 a) A summer day temperature inside a wooden shack is 20°C, and the air temperature outside the shack is 29°C. A winter day temperature inside the shack is 20°C, and the air temperature outside the shack is 8°C. In which case would you expect there to be more heat energy transfer? Why?

b) Is there any information missing from part a) that could affect your answer? Explain.

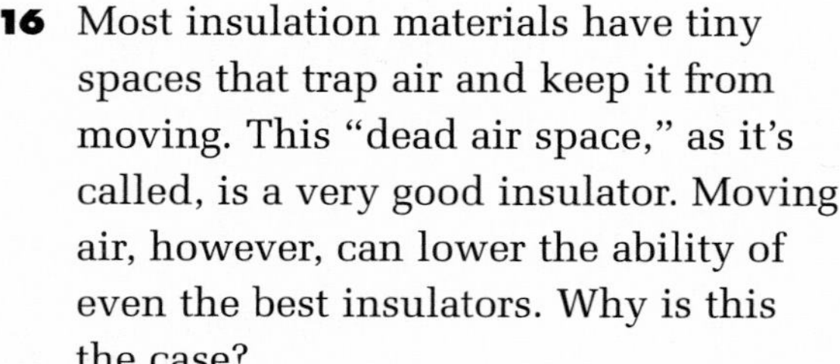

16 Most insulation materials have tiny spaces that trap air and keep it from moving. This "dead air space," as it's called, is a very good insulator. Moving air, however, can lower the ability of even the best insulators. Why is this the case?

Using the Big Ideas

17 One evening, Denise cleared the snow from the driveway, and then left her shovel resting on a snowbank. The shovel has a metal blade and a wooden handle. The temperature outside stayed at –15°C for the rest of the evening and all night long. In the morning, Denise went to retrieve the shovel. She touched the wooden handle with her bare hand. Then she touched the metal blade. "Wow!" she yelped in surprise. "That blade is much colder than the handle. I'll bet it's at least ten degrees colder." What do you think of Denise's observation? Explain why you do or don't agree with her.

18 a) Could a landslide or an avalanche be a source of heat energy? Why or why not?

b) Could a landslide or an avalanche be an energy resource? Why or why not?

19 a) You feel cold when heat energy is being transferred out of your body. From what parts of your body do you think this heat energy transfer occurs?

b) What could you do to minimize this heat energy transfer?

c) In terms of heat energy transfer, are there any similarities between you and a building? Give reasons to support your answer.

20 Industries produce a lot of waste heat energy. What do you think are some of the ways people could use this waste heat energy? What would be the advantages and disadvantages of using this heat energy?

Self Assessment

21 What are the key ideas of this chapter?

22 Which of the key ideas did you already know before you started this chapter?

23 Which of the key ideas did you learn during the course of this chapter?

24 Which of the key ideas do you still have questions about?

25 What is one idea or thing that surprised you during the course of this chapter?

Chapter 4 STRUCTURES

function

Structures have a job to do. They must resist the forces acting against them. An *inuksuk* must stand in place to mark important locations for Arctic travellers. A roof must stay in place in spite of a heavy load of snow, protecting whatever it covers. A bridge must support the load of hundreds of vehicles and withstand all the forces that nature throws at it.

In this chapter, you will investigate the forces that act on and within structures. You will explore the shapes and materials that allow structures to withstand these forces. As you build and test your own structures, you will learn about the relationship between design and function. You will have chances to apply what you learn in order to better understand how the structures you use every day are able to do their job.

BIG Ideas

design

1.0 Structures can be classified in different ways.

2.0 Internal and external forces act on structures.

3.0 A structure's strength and stability are determined by its characteristics.

4.0 Designing and making products involve more than meeting a specific need.

construct

Wind Challenge!

The Challenge

- Build the tallest free-standing structure.
- It must stand up to the wind for 60 s without moving.
- The wind will be provided by a fan blowing at its lowest speed at a distance of 1 m from your structure.
- Only materials listed below can be used.
- Building time limit: 10 min

Materials

- *newspaper*
- *uncooked spaghetti*
- *bamboo skewers*
- *plastic straws*
- *Lego® Blocks*
- *a fan*
- *masking tape*
- *cellophane tape*
- *marshmallows*

How would you meet this wind challenge? You probably realize that some methods and materials are better than others for making your structure strong and stable. Now, you will gather some ideas about what makes structures stable and strong. You will then have an opportunity to put your ideas into action.

Look at the shape and size of each structure. Compare them with the CN Tower on the previous page. What do these structures have in common? Why are they built this way?

Think about which position is more stable: standing with your feet close together or standing with your feet wide apart. (Try it!) How does this relate to the shape of towers? Think about all the different tall structures you may have seen in your community. Brainstorm ideas with your classmates about designing and constructing a tall structure which can withstand the wind. Record your design ideas in your Science Journal.

Take a look at this construction scene. What do all of the objects shown have in common? Discuss your ideas with a classmate and record your ideas.

All of these objects are structures. A **structure** can be described as anything that provides support. It is made from one or more parts. For example, parts of a steel fence include posts, fencing, and steel clamps. Parts of a bird's nest include bits of grass, twigs, and feathers the bird connects together.

What do you notice about the structures in this illustration? They are all being pushed or pulled by something else. In other words, they are being acted on by a force. How many examples of forces can you find in the scene? Why is it important that these structures are able to resist the forces acting on them?

In the next activity, you will build a tall structure that can support an egg or golf ball and can resist the pushing force of a wind.

TAKE THE CHALLENGE

Caution!

Before starting any construction project, be sure you know the answers to these questions:

1. **What special safety precautions should you take?**
2. **Where do you store any tools when you have finished using them?**
3. **How should you dispose of any waste or unused materials?**

Before You Start...

Look at the Wind Challenge poster. Think about the features that are important in towers. What ideas can you use to help you create a tall and stable structure? What materials will you use? What's the best design and building plan for your choice of materials?

Materials & Equipment

- *a timer*
- *an egg or a golf ball*
- *materials listed on the Wind Challenge poster*

Identifying the Problem

Using the materials in the Wind Challenge, build the tallest free-standing structure that can support an egg or golf ball and withstand the wind from the fan for 60 s.

continued on next page

4 STRUCTURES

Designing and Building

1 Use the materials to build your structure.
2 Decide how you will know if your structure is stable and as tall as possible.

Keeping Records

3 What data will you collect about your structure? You might want to measure the structure's height, width, and mass, or record the quantity of materials used (for example: number of straws, number of newspaper sheets).
4 What other types of data could you collect?

Testing and Evaluating

5 Compare your structure with the structures that your classmates have designed and built.
6 Why are some structures more able to resist the wind? That is, why are they more stable than others?
7 What is the overall range of structure heights? Which structure is the tallest? the shortest?
8 How much material was used to create your structure?
9 What two-dimensional shapes did you use most often? least often?
10 Compare the area of the bottom of your structure with the area of the top of your structure.

Forming Conclusions

11 Suggest improvements that you could make to your structure.

Congratulations! You've just completed your first design challenge. Was it as easy as you thought? You designed your tower to withstand a wind for 60 s. Imagine designing, building, and testing real-life structures, like tall buildings in your neighbourhood. If these structures fall down, people could be hurt. Obviously, it is very important that real-life structures be strong and stable.

The terms strength and stability are commonly used by structural designers, engineers, architects, and builders. The **strength** of a structure is the capacity (or how much of a load) the structure can support. In other words, strength is the load of its own materials and any additional load that is applied to it. The **stability** of a structure is the ability of the structure to maintain its position.

Strength and stability allow structures to resist the forces acting on them. Throughout this chapter, you will be investigating, designing, building, and evaluating a variety of structures according to their strength and stability.

Focus Your Thoughts

1 Look at the structures on this page. What do they have in common? They are all designed to be strong and stable in all sorts of weather conditions.
- How long do you think these structures will look and perform as they do when they are first built?
- Rank the structures according to the number of years you think each will last, starting with the one that you predict will stay strong and stable the longest and ending with the one you think will fail first.

2 Based on your readings, explorations, and discussions, list the features that make different structures strong and stable.

3 How do different forces affect the strength and stability of structures?

BIG IDEA

1.0 Structures can be classified in different ways.

4 STRUCTURES

There are many types of structures. In fact, every object, natural and human-made, is a structure. Structures differ in a variety of ways. Some structures are found in the natural world and some are made by people. Some structures are stronger than others. Some structures are more stable. But how can you compare different structures? For example, is a mushroom stronger than an umbrella? Is a log across a river more stable than an iron bridge? How would you decide? Let's explore how the design and characteristics of a structure relate to its structural strength and stability.

1.1 COPYING NATURE

Explore

Look at the pictures on this and the next page. Decide which structures are natural and which structures are made by people.

Match a natural structure with a human-made structure that is similar in design (has the same shape). Compare the structures in the pair. How else are they similar besides the design? How are they different? For example, you can match a bat's wing with an airplane

wing because they are similar in design. Besides being similar in design, the bat's wing and the airplane wing are similar in **function:** they both provide a means to fly. They differ in material and the way in which they are constructed. Match other pairs of structures from the pictures. Make a table to record the similarities and the differences in each pair.

Decide whether your comparisons support this statement: "A structure's design depends on its function." If they do not support this statement, write a new statement that will better describe what you have found.

Develop

Classifying Structures

Take another look at the structures shown on the previous pages. Can you classify these structures according to some of the following characteristics?

- their purpose or function
- how they work
- types of materials used to make them
- the shapes of their parts
- whether they were rigid or non-rigid
- whether they were symmetrical or asymmetrical (not symmetrical)

For example, you might classify these structures by function. Some structures might function to produce movement (for example, a bat wing). Other structures might function as shelter (for example, a sod house). Some structures might function to produce both movement and shelter (for example, an airplane). You can use a Venn diagram to show this classification.

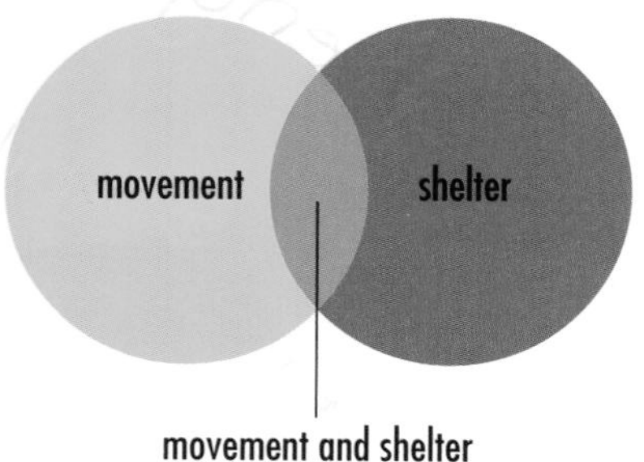

Communicate

1 What characteristics did your classmates use for their classifications? Share your ideas with your classmates and add their ideas to your own sorting list.

2 Why is it is important to understand the different ways that structures can be classified?

3 Can you use the various classifications to help you understand why some structures are stronger or more stable than other structures?

1.2 Classifying Structures by Design

Explore

Did you know that you can also classify structures according to their design? There are three basic designs of structures: solid structures, frame structures, and shell structures. How would you sort the structures shown on the previous pages according to design?

Develop

Different Structural Designs

There are three different types of structural designs: solid, frame, and shell.

Solid structures, sometimes called **mass structures**, are usually made from a solid piece of some strong material. A hockey puck is an example of a solid structure. A solid structure has little or no space inside and relies on its own mass to resist the forces that act upon it.

Large solid structures are often built from brick, concrete, mud, or stone. Why do you think these materials are used to construct solid structures? Examples of solid structures include stone arches, bridges, dams, and monuments.

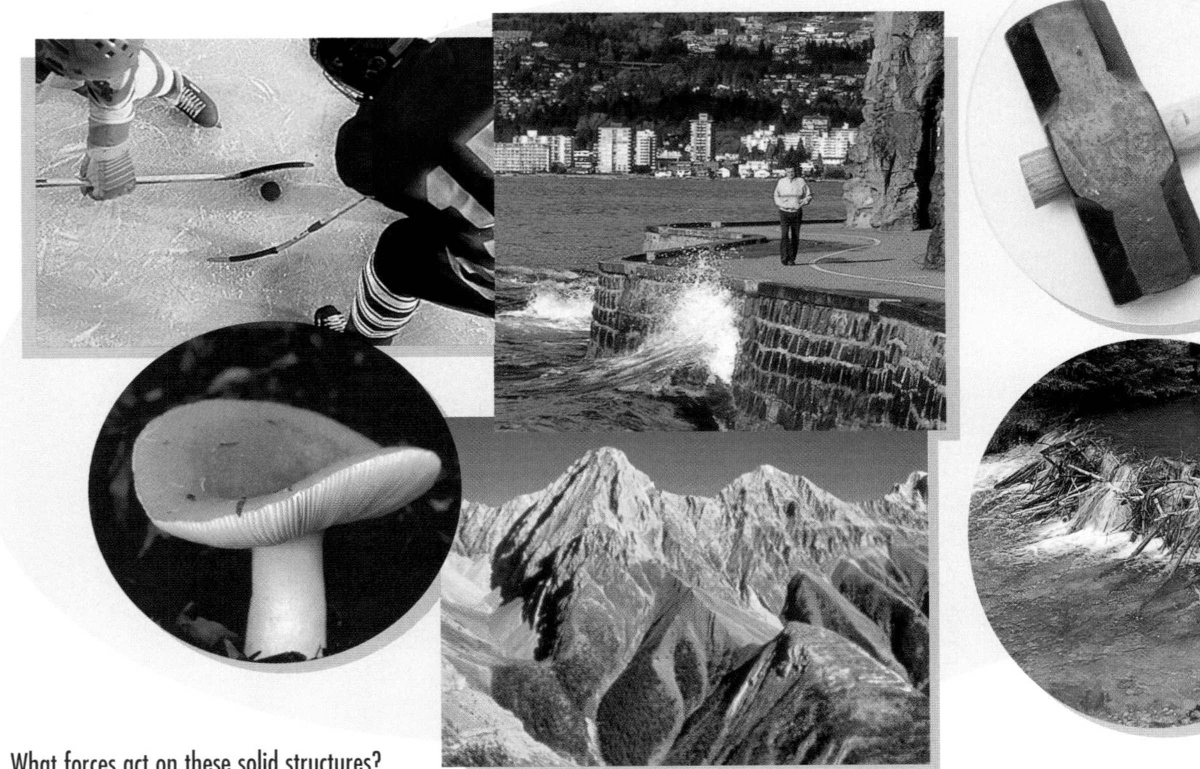

What forces act on these solid structures?

reSEARCH

Stonehenge is a prehistoric, megalithic (meaning large rocks) monument on the Salisbury Plain in England. The structure is enclosed by a circular ditch 91 m in diameter and was built over 3000 years ago. Although there are many theories, the purpose of Stonehenge remains a mystery. Many other megalithic structures have been discovered, some in North America.

- Use the Internet to learn more about North American megaliths, their shape and possible function.

Frame structures have a rigid arrangement, or framework, made up of parts fastened together, called structural components. Your skeleton is a frame structure made up of your bones, tendons, and joints. A frame structure can be arranged in two dimensions, as a door frame or a fence. A frame structure can also be organized in three dimensions, as the frame for a music stand or the framing wood for a house. Other examples of frame structures include suspension bridges, bicycle frames, bus shelters, and others shown in the pictures below. Like solid structures, frame structures are built to resist forces that act on them.

What forces act on these frame structures?

*info*BIT

Today, most buildings are frame structures. For most houses, lumber is used for framing. In malls, and in office, apartment, and industrial buildings, reinforced concrete and steel are used for framing. Can you explain why?

Shell structures have a moulded shape that provides strength and rigidity. A hollow ball is an example of a shell structure. Early shell structures were made with ice, sod, clay, small stones, straw, and wood. They were strong, but heavy. Today, with a variety of new building materials available, shell structures can be constructed to be strong and light. Examples of shell structures include egg cartons, plastic containers, car bodies, and others shown in the pictures below. Like solid and frame structures, shell structures are built to resist forces that act on them.

What forces act on these shell structures?

*info***BIT**

Is It a Frame, a Shell, or Both?

When you were classifying structures, did you notice that some structures could be classified as a combination of structural designs? For example, a tent can be considered to be a frame structure (because it has poles forming a frame) *and* a shell structure (because the metal frame is covered with material to create a shell).

Communicate

1 How are structures classified according to design?
2 What type of structure is the telephone pictured here? How do you know? How could you check your reasoning?

4 STRUCTURES

reSEARCH

Create an illustrated time line that describes a variety of structures (solid, frame, and shell) from different cultures in the past and present. Collect your information from books, encyclopedias, videos, museums, or the Internet.

1.3 Considering Design and Function When Building Structures

Explore

You should now be able to classify structures based on their design and function. Knowing something about both of these is important when you have to design an object or device. For example, designing a long-lasting durable chair is not good if it is not comfortable. With everything that is desired, consideration must be given to both structure and design. Sometimes an improvement on an existing structure can include many other elements and other times it may only include one or two. For example, how would you modify your desk to make it more functional? Illustrate your ideas in a rough sketch and share it with your classmates.

Develop

Designed to Function

Now it's time to apply your knowledge and skills of structural function and design.

SOLID, FRAME, OR SHELL?

Caution!
Refer to the safety precautions in the Take the Challenge activity in Invitation to Explore.

Before You Start...

The upcoming winter carnival in your community needs volunteers for many tasks. One task is to design temporary structures to be used as tables by visitors to the carnival. These tables will be left outdoors during the carnival and have to withstand being covered in snow as well as supporting whatever people choose to put on top.

Imagine you are one of the volunteers looking for the best way to make these tables. You will work in a group. Your group will choose a structure type, design and build a model, and compare it with other groups. Your class will then decide on the type that best suits the purpose.

Building a Solid Structure

Identifying the Problem

Can you build a solid structure that can support a load, using Plasticine or modelling clay?

continued on next page

Designing and Building

1 Use a diagram to help you plan your design. Label your diagram to show all of the components of your structure.
2 Include the materials you will use.
3 Once you are satisfied with your design for your structure, proceed to build it.

Testing and Evaluating

4 When you are done, examine your structure. How do you know that it is a solid structure?
5 a) Check the height and perimeter of your solid structure.
b) Record your measurements in a chart. Don't forget to measure the perimeter at the top, middle, and bottom of your structure. Why do you think measurements should be made at more than one place?
6 Test your structure's ability to support a load. Record your results.

Forming Conclusions

7 What material would you use to make a full-sized version of your structure? What are its advantages? disadvantages?

Building a Frame Structure

Identifying the Problem

Can you build a frame structure that can support a load, using cardboard or straws, and masking tape?

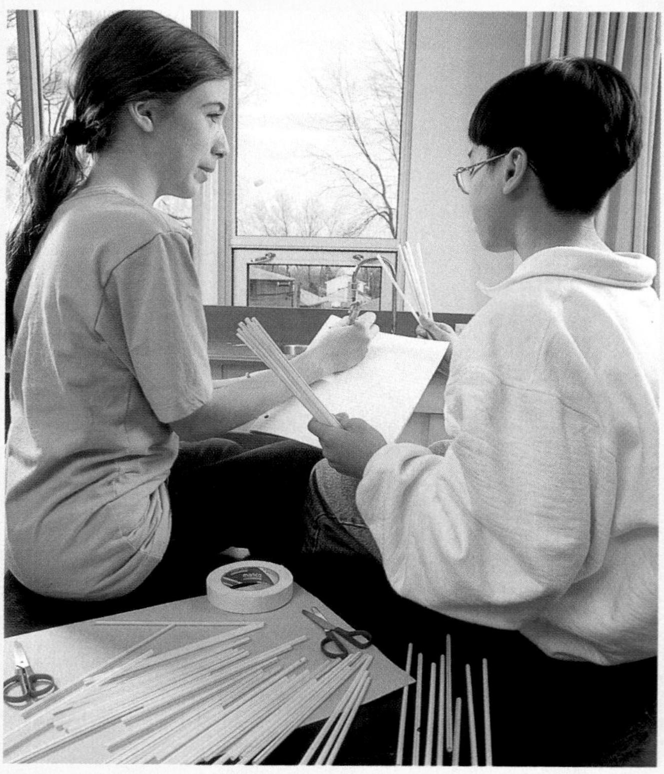

Designing and Building

1 Use a diagram to help you plan your design. Label your diagram to show all of the components of your structure.
2 Include the materials you will use.
3 Once you are satisfied with your design for your structure, proceed to build it.

Testing and Evaluating

4 When you are done, examine your structure. How do you know that it is a frame structure?
5 a) Check the height and perimeter of your frame structure.
b) Record your measurements in a chart. Don't forget to measure the perimeter at the top, middle, and bottom of your structure. Why do you think measurements should be made at more than one place?

6 Test your structure's ability to support a load. Record your results.

Forming Conclusions

7 What materials would you use to make a full-sized version of your structure? State any advantages and disadvantages for using these materials.

8 What changes would you have to make to turn your frame structure into a solid structure?

Building a Shell Structure

Identifying the Problem

Can you construct a shell structure that can support a load, using paper and tape?

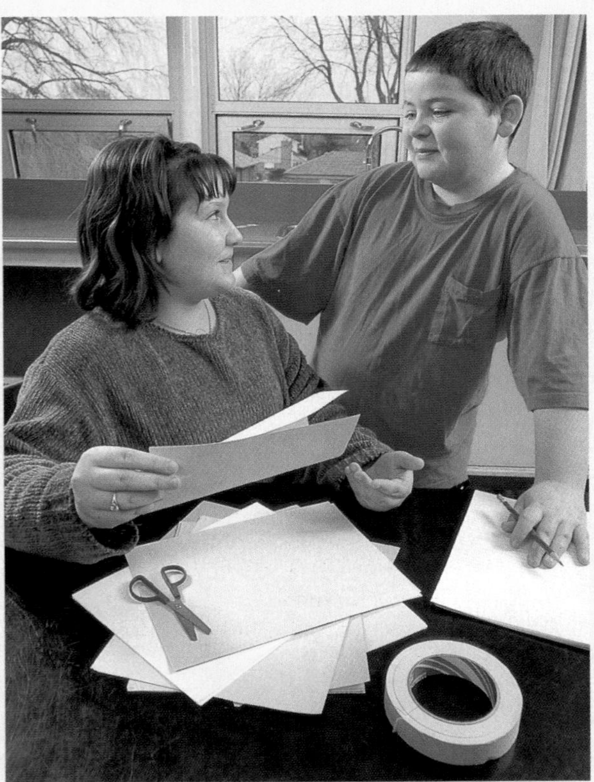

Designing and Building

1 Use a diagram to help you plan your design. Label your diagram to show all of the components of your structure.

2 Include the materials you will use.

3 Once you are satisfied with your design for your structure, proceed to build it.

Testing and Evaluating

4 When you are done, examine your structure. How do you know that it is a shell structure?

5 a) Check the height and perimeter of your shell structure.

b) Record your measurements in a chart. Don't forget to measure the perimeter at the top, middle, and bottom of your structure. Why do you think measurements should be made at more than one place?

6 Test your structure's ability to support a load. Record your results.

Forming Conclusions

7 What materials would you use to make a full-sized version of your structure? What are the advantages and disadvantages of these materials?

8 What changes would you have to make to turn your shell structure into a solid structure or a frame structure?

Comparing Results

Each group will present its model table design to the class and describe the test results. Once all groups have presented their findings, the class will vote on the structure type that would make the best temporary table for a winter carnival.

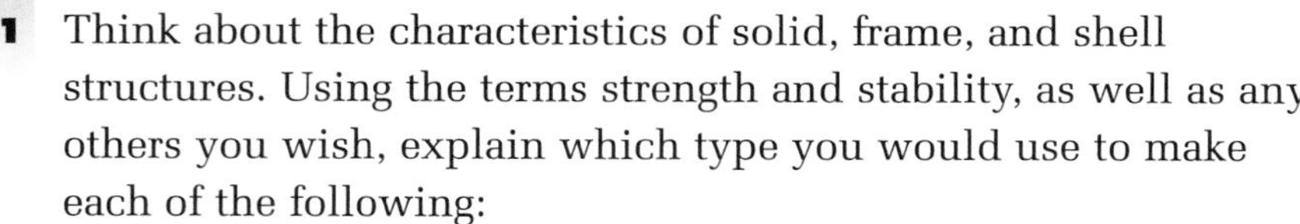

1 Think about the characteristics of solid, frame, and shell structures. Using the terms strength and stability, as well as any others you wish, explain which type you would use to make each of the following:

a) a bridge to carry trains over a deep valley
b) a rain shelter in a public garden
c) a stand to hold a guitar
d) a stand to hold a large plant
e) a child's playhouse

1.4 Check Your Progress

1 Give three examples of human-made structures that are copies of natural structures in design and function. Also name those natural structures.

2 Describe some of the different ways of classifying structures. Give examples for each classification.

3 Make a three-column chart with these headings: solid, frame, and shell. Use your chart to classify each of the illustrated structures on this page by putting the name of the structure in the column that best describes it. If any can be classified as being more than one type, explain why this is so. Put the name of that structure in all of the columns that apply.

4 Choose a structure in your classroom.

a) Identify its basic structural design.
b) Describe its function.
c) Explain how its design supports its function.

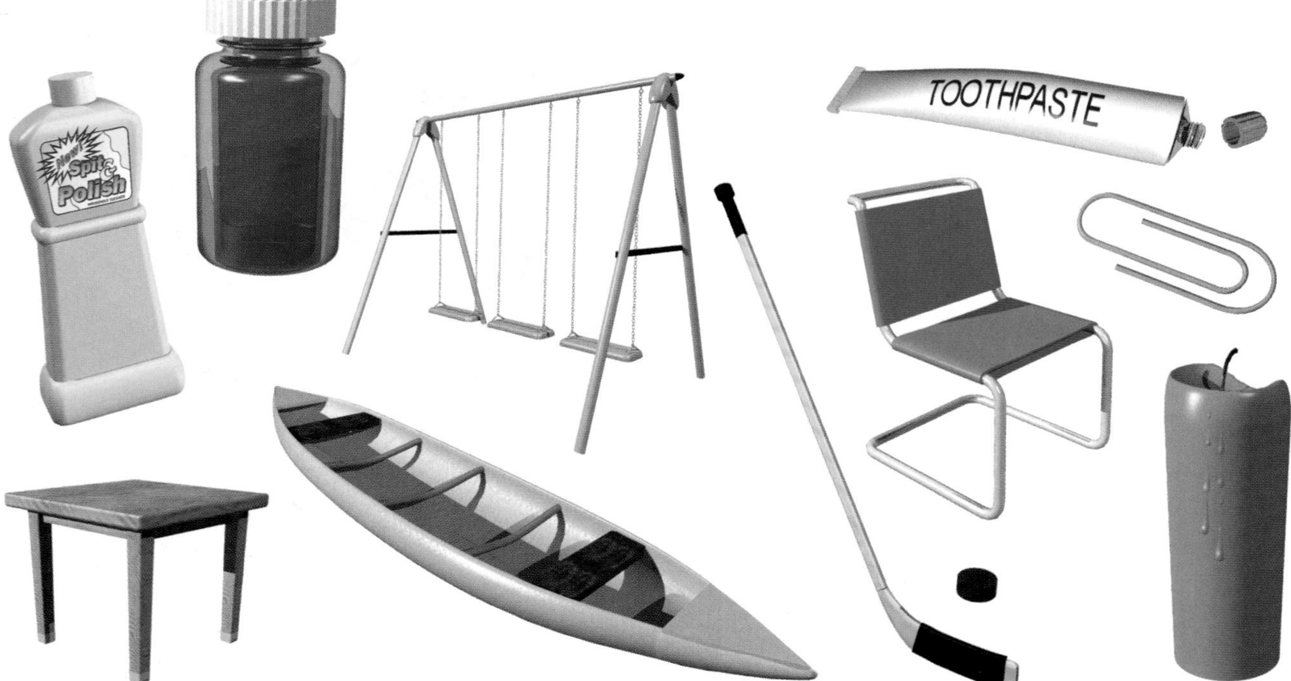

Careers and Profiles

DESIGNING FOR THE ENVIRONMENT

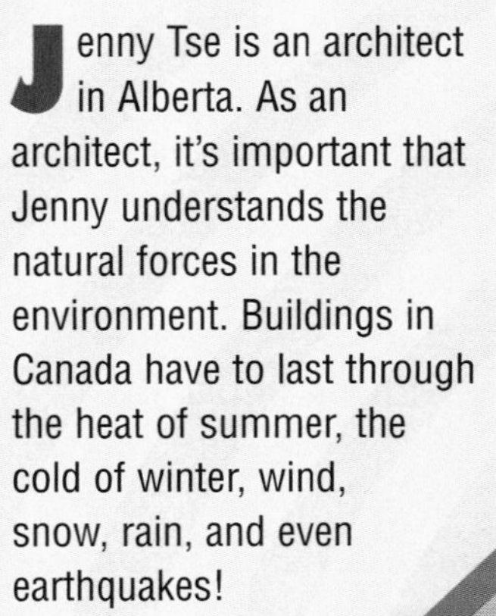

Jenny Tse is an architect in Alberta. As an architect, it's important that Jenny understands the natural forces in the environment. Buildings in Canada have to last through the heat of summer, the cold of winter, wind, snow, rain, and even earthquakes!

Jenny Tse was trained in Hong Kong and moved to Canada in 1969.

How does Jenny plan a house? First, she starts drawing designs. These drawings show her ideas about the shape of the house and the arrangement of the rooms. If Jenny's clients like her design, she makes working drawings of the house. These are very detailed drawings that tell the builder how to construct the house. When construction starts, Jenny has to check the construction site often to make sure the builder is following her design and instructions. Then, finally, she hands the new house over to its new owners, who hopefully live happily ever after.

Jenny's job changes all the time and gives her lots of challenges—but she still says, "I love it! Students who want to be architects should be creative and love to work with people," says Jenny. "An architect's life is exciting, but you will learn a lot, too!"

Hong Kong, China

"In Hong Kong, the weather is always warm and there is not much space for building. It was a fun and interesting adjustment to adapt myself to cold climate design." Jenny says. "For example, in the Arctic region, buildings are put on stilts. This stops the building's heat from escaping into the ground, which will melt the permafrost and cause the building to collapse."

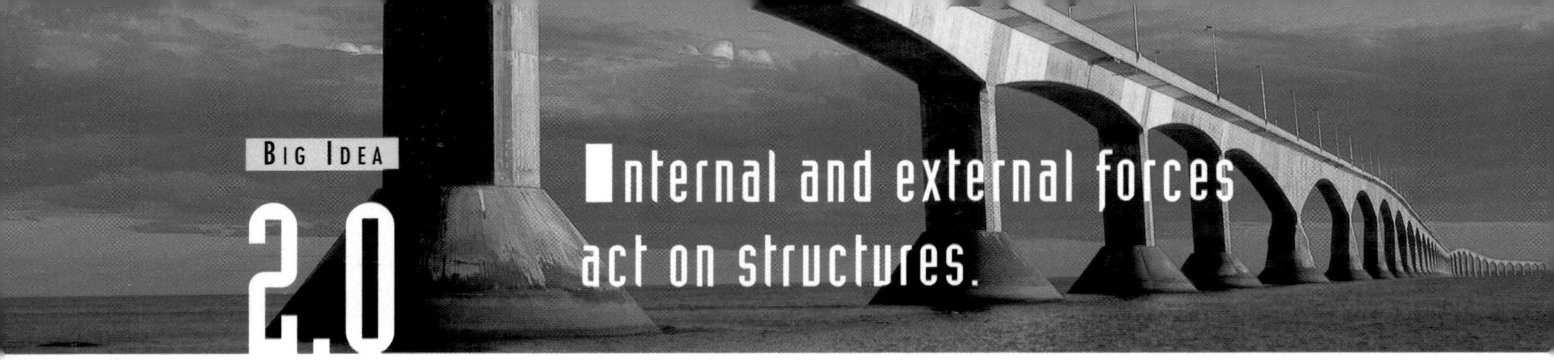

BIG IDEA

2.0 Internal and external forces act on structures.

A brand new hockey helmet is hammered against a steel anvil at almost 15 km/h. A car is driven into a brick wall at 25 km/h. These shattering events are all in a day's work for the people who test how well these and other structures withstand the forces acting on them. A helmet must be strong enough to protect a player's head against the types of collisions encountered during a game. A car bumper must protect the front of a car against damage during impact. By testing with events that make structures fail, designers learn how to make better structures.

What causes a structure to fail? Think about the Wind Challenge at the beginning of this chapter. Did all the towers stand upright? When a wind was added, did some towers fail to stand? The wind was a force acting on the structure. Forces cause structures to fail, but what is a force?

A **force** is a push or pull that acts on an object. In this section, you will look at all of the forces that can act on a structure, beginning with a force acting on you right now: gravity. You will identify forces as internal or external. You will also explore the differences between the stress, fatigue, and failure of structures.

- An **external force** is applied from outside an object. For example, the force supplied by the moving stick is about to act on the puck. This is an external force.
- An **internal force** is one that acts within an object or from something attached to the object. For example, it is the force supplied by the player's muscles which move the player's hands.

2.1 The Force of Gravity

Explore

Think about what happens when you toss a ball up in the air. The ball travels upward a certain distance, then returns to your hand. **Gravity** is the force that brings the ball back to your hand and keeps your feet on the ground. It acts by pulling objects toward the ground. The larger the object's mass, the greater the pull.

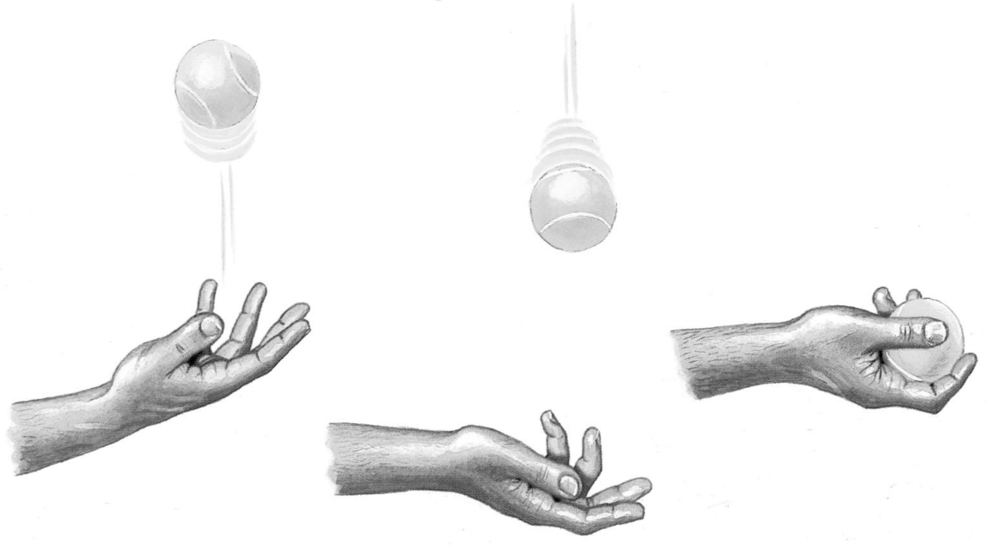

The earth's gravity is an external force that constantly acts on you and everything else on earth. In previous activities, you have seen how a wind—an external force—could make a structure fall over. Why is it possible for structures to be stable when the force of gravity acts on them all the time? You'll find out why.

Why does it feel easier to go downstairs than upstairs?

These athletes take symmetry very seriously. Why?

reSEARCH

The effect of gravity becomes less and less as objects move away from the earth. Find out how far away a spacecraft leaving the earth would have to travel before it would escape the pull of the earth's gravity.

Develop

Centre of Gravity

When you built a tower and used a fan to provide a wind, it was easy to see exactly where the force was acting on the tower. Where does gravity act? If you hold your arms out straight for a few minutes, you can tell that gravity is acting on both of your arms. In fact, gravity acts on every part of your body or every part of a building, all of the time.

What happens if you were to stand on one foot for a while? To keep balanced, you might use your arms or lean to one side. Gravity is having an effect on the **stability** of your body. How can you predict this effect on a structure? Scientists have discovered that, even though gravity acts on all parts of a structure, you can think of gravity as pulling the structure downward through a point within the structure. This point is called the **centre of gravity**. The location of the centre of gravity of a structure determines the structure's stability.

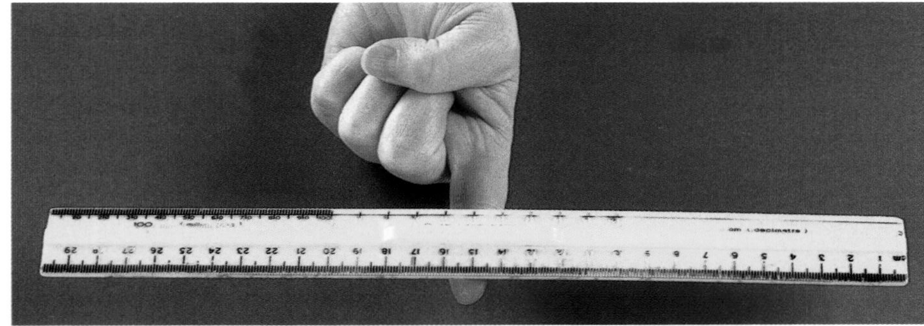

Have you ever tried to balance a ruler on your finger? Try it now! Where do you have to place your finger to get the ruler to balance? This point on the ruler is the centre of gravity. When you place your finger under the ruler's centre of gravity, the ruler stops wobbling and becomes **stable**, or balanced.

Because of **symmetry**, the mass of the ruler is distributed evenly on both sides of your finger. The force of gravity pulls vertically downward on all parts of the ruler around the centre point, where your finger is supporting it. The ruler is stable in this position. However, if your finger is not placed under the centre of the ruler, then gravity pulls on one side more than the other. Similarly, for the gymnast shown here to hold a stable position on the balance beam, the forces of gravity on all parts of her body in the air must be balanced around her hands on the beam. In the centre picture on the opposite page, the athletes form a stable arrangement in the air. The forces of gravity acting on the athletes and chairs are balanced on all sides of the support at the bottom.

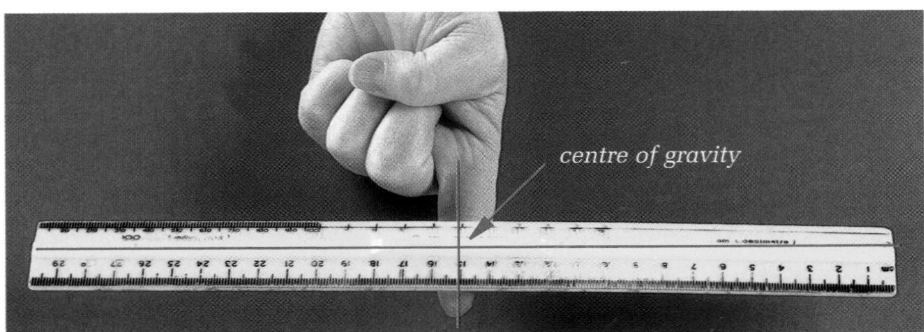

The centre of gravity for this ruler has been marked. What do you notice about its location on the ruler? It divides the ruler into two equal parts that look the same. This is the definition of symmetry. What do you predict about the centre of gravity for symmetrical structures? You will have a chance to test your prediction in the next Problem Solver activity.

PROBLEM SOLVER

MAKING A STABLE SIGN

A sign maker has seven identical cubes to make a letter "F." The letter must stand upright so it can be seen from a distance.

- Predict how the sign maker can make an upright "F" structure. Record your prediction as a drawing.
- Using seven cubes and your drawings, test your prediction.
- Using your seven cubes, make as many structures of different letters or shapes as you can. Draw each arrangement of cubes that gives you an upright stable structure.
- Using 21 cubes, make as many structures of different shapes as you can. Make a drawing of each stable structure.
- What pattern can you find in the bases and heights of the stable structures?
- What can you conclude about the centre of gravity of these structures?

Think back to the tall, free-standing tower that you built at the beginning of this chapter.

- Which free-standing towers in your class were unstable? Why were those structures unstable?
- What is the relationship between the size of a structure's base and the distribution of the structure's mass?
- How would you describe the relationship you have observed between a structure's centre of gravity and its stability?

INVESTIGATOR

WINNING AGAINST GRAVITY

STRUCTURES

Identifying the Problem

Which arrangement of structural parts creates the tallest and most stable solid structure?

Materials & Equipment

50 uniform blocks consisting of:

- *cubes*
- *rectangular prisms*
- *cylinders*
- *hexagonal prisms*
- *trapezoidal prisms*

Designing and Building

1 Build as many different structures as possible, using the same number of blocks. Begin by building different structures with 10 blocks, then 20 blocks, then 50 blocks.

2 Test the stability of each structure.

Keeping Records

3 Record your observations in a chart. Draw each structure that you create. On your drawing, point out whether the structure was stable or not.

Testing and Evaluating

4 Examine your drawings of each of your structures. Locate the centre of gravity.

5 Draw a vertical line through the centre of gravity. What do you notice?

6 Does the number of blocks affect the stability of structures?

Forming Conclusions

7 Summarize your findings about how the size of the base and height of the structure, the position of the structure's centre of gravity, and the stability of the structure relate to each other.

Communicate

1 Copy the following sentences. Fill in the blanks using the words below. (Hint: You can use the same word more than once.)

centre | gravity | stable | internal | external | symmetry

a) An ____________ force is one that acts on a structure. An example of this kind of force is ____________.
b) A structure that can be divided into two equal portions that look the same has ____________.
c) If a structure can resist the forces acting on it, it is ____________.
d) The ____________ of ____________ is the point where the force of gravity appears to act on a structure.

2 a) List four different solid or frame structures with which you are familiar. Draw an outline of each structure.
b) On each drawing, mark the position of the structure's centre of gravity. How do you know where to mark this position? What further information do you need in order to confirm your prediction?
c) For each structure, describe how its centre of gravity affects how stable the structure is.

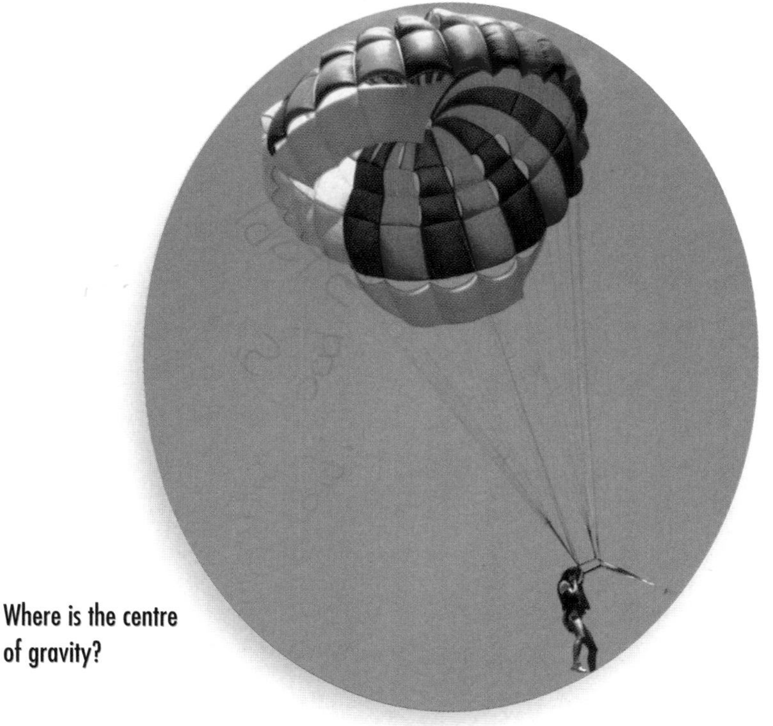

Where is the centre of gravity?

3. Describe how you can determine any structure's centre of gravity. Justify why your strategies are reasonable.
4. Think of a symmetrical shell structure and determine its centre of gravity and lines of symmetry. How do you know that your findings make sense?

try this at **HOME**

BACKPACK POSTURE

You may have heard news reports about how some students are harming their backs by carrying too much in their backpacks. The problem relates to the centre of gravity.

1. Wearing your usual school clothes and shoes, stand in front of a mirror so you can see yourself from one side. Stand normally, so that you feel comfortable and balanced. Observe your posture carefully. If you were to draw an imaginary line from your shoulders to your knees, on which side of this line would your hips be?
2. Put on a backpack with your usual load for school. Repeat step 1. Has the position of your hips changed along the imaginary line? How?
3. Most backpacks are designed to hold quite a bit. Load your backpack the way you might for a day when you have a lot of homework, or must take extra shoes with you to class. Be sure the backpack can still be closed. Repeat step 1. Has the position of your hips changed along the imaginary line again? How?
4. How do the concepts of centre of gravity and structural symmetry relate to your findings? How should they be considered by backpack designers?

2.2 Types of Loads

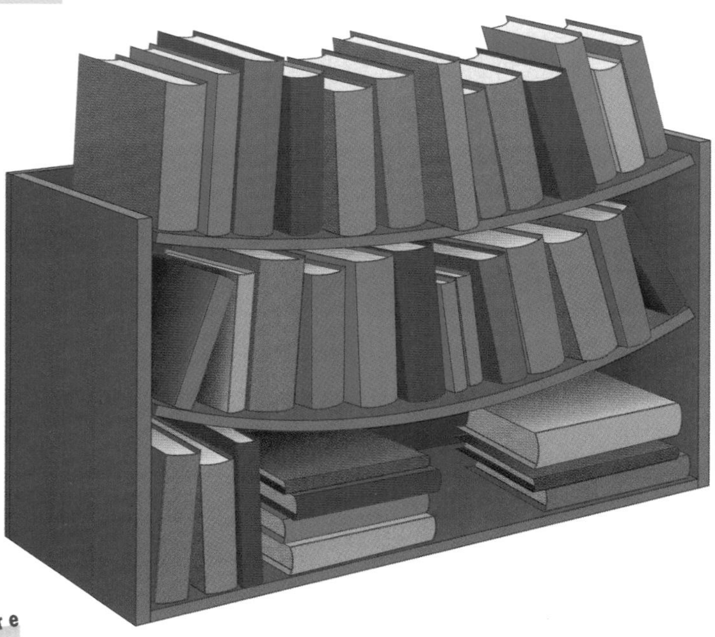

Explore

Have you ever heard the saying, "the straw that broke the camel's back?" Look at this illustration of a bookcase. What do you think might happen if you added one more book? The shelf might break under the load.

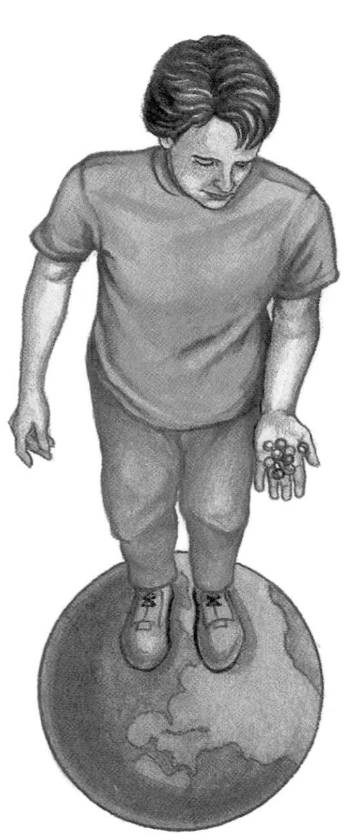

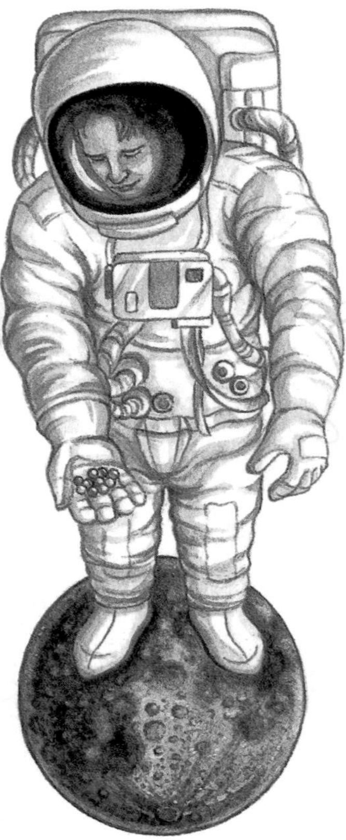

Mass, weight, and **load** are important terms which can be confusing. Here's a trick to help you remember. Think about holding a handful of identical marbles. The mass would be represented by the number of marbles in your hand. That number won't change if you took the marbles away from the earth. Their weight is due to the gravity of the earth acting on the marbles. It is how heavy the marbles feel on earth. The weight decreases farther away from the earth. The load would be the external force you feel acting on your hand as you hold the marbles. Load can be measured as the weight.

What would happen if you took the marbles to the moon, for example? The moon has less gravity, so the marbles would weigh less, but the mass would not change.

Develop

Static and Dynamic Load

The term load has a specific meaning when you are considering structures and their function. A load is an external force on a structure. The weight of the books in the example is a load on the bookcase. The force of gravity pulls down on the books and they, in turn, pull down on the bookcase. A load can be a weight, such as a car crossing a bridge, or the push of the wind blowing on a tower. There are two types of loads: *static* and *dynamic*. Look at the pictures below and make your own definitions for these terms.

The weight of a structure is called the **static load**. Some examples of static loads are the steel beams, cables, rivets, and steel plates used to create a bridge or the wood, nails, and screws used to make a bookcase. Even though these are part of the structure, the static load is an external force. Why? The reason is that gravity is acting on all the parts of the structure.

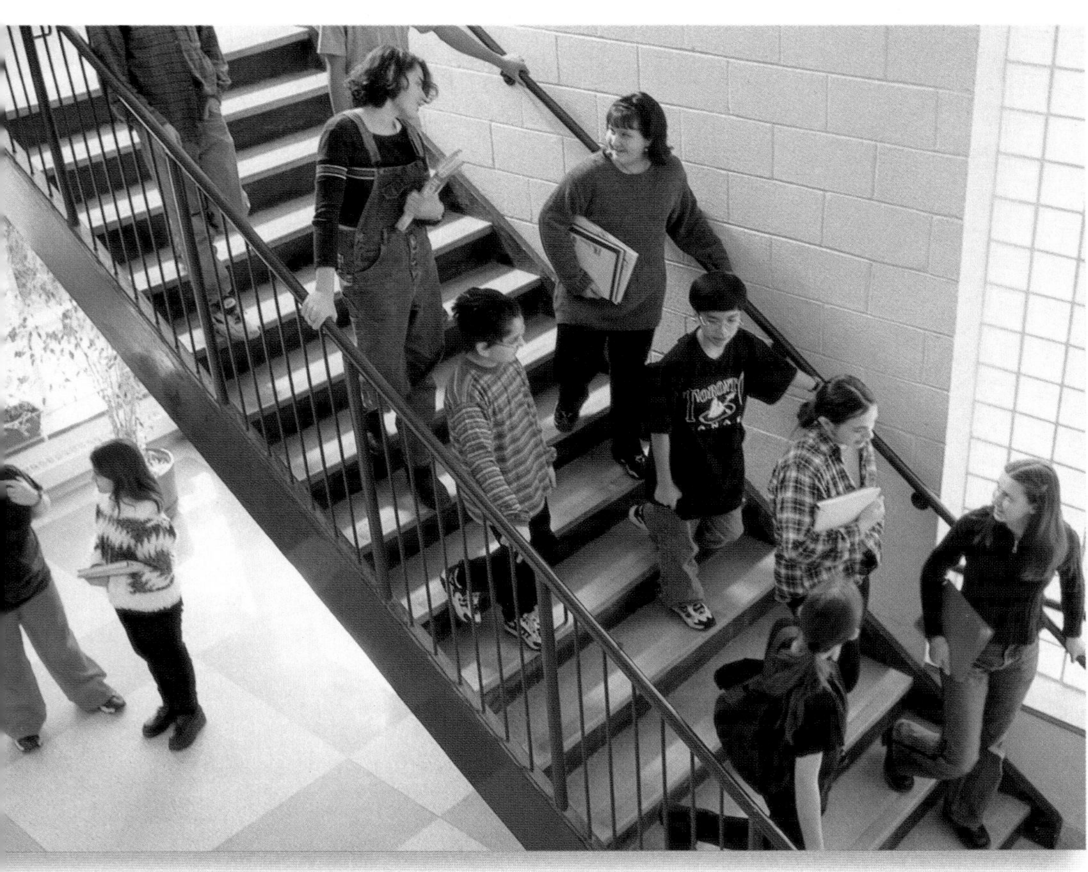

A **dynamic load** is an external force that moves or changes. These loads can change very quickly, as with a sudden gust of powerful wind or an earthquake. The weight of these students on the staircase is a dynamic load. Designers must plan their structures to resist dynamic loads, especially since these kinds of loads can be much greater than static ones.

PROBLEM SOLVER

STATIC OR DYNAMIC?

How can you identify the static and dynamic loads that act on structures? Think of three different types of structures (solid, frame, and shell) in your home, school, or neighbourhood. Sketch each structure and label the type of loads—static and dynamic—that act on it.

- What do you think is the relationship between structural stability and the load that a structure supports?

What are the static and dynamic loads for these car ramps?

Communicate

1 What is the difference between weight and mass?
2 Describe examples of static loads in your classroom.
3 Describe examples of dynamic loads in your classroom.

2.3 SUPPORTING THE LOAD

Explore

Different structures are designed to withstand different loads and forces. Think about a **bridge**. There are different types of bridges that can be built. Engineers use two conditions to decide which type of bridge will best suit a situation:

- what the bridge is crossing (for example, water or land)
- what kinds of loads the bridge will be supporting

On this and the next page are some of the different kinds of bridges. Can you figure out how their design helps support dynamic loads? Record your predictions in your Science Journal.

The **beam bridge** is the most common bridge used. A simple beam bridge is flat and is supported at its two ends. A longer beam bridge may be supported by additional piers. The piers provide vertical support.

A **truss bridge** is a lightweight, but strong bridge, made of trusses (triangle-shaped frames) along its sides.

An **arch bridge** is designed to withstand heavy loads. The load of people causes each stone in the arch to push against the stone next to it. This push is eventually transferred to the end supports, which are embedded in the ground. The ground pushes back (resists) and this resistance is passed back from stone to stone until it is pushing on the stone that is supporting the load.

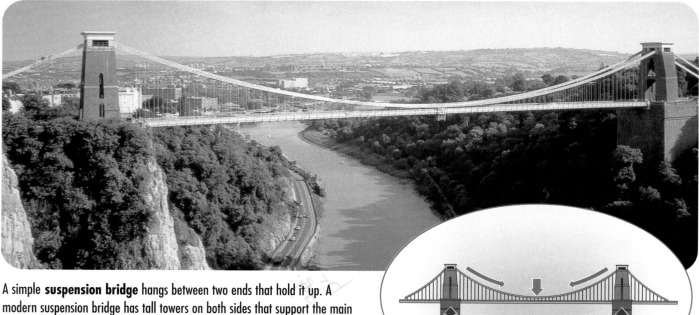

A simple **suspension bridge** hangs between two ends that hold it up. A modern suspension bridge has tall towers on both sides that support the main cables that hold up the bridge. The main cables are anchored in concrete at each end of the bridge. Smaller cables, which support the roadway, are suspended from the main cables.

Develop

How Much Load Can It Support?

In the next activity, you will design and test a bridge's performance.

INVESTIGATOR

My Bridge is Stronger Than Yours

Identifying the Problem

How can you design and build a simple beam bridge that will support the greatest possible load?

- The bridge will be 60 cm long.
- The bridge will be no more than 5 cm wide and no more than 5 cm tall.
- The bridge will span a distance of 50 cm (between two desks).
- There will be a means of fastening the test load to the centre of the bridge.

Materials & Equipment

- *cardboard*
- *wood pieces*
- *steel pieces (for example, wall shelving supports)*
- *wire*
- *aluminum foil*
- *Plasticine or modelling clay*
- *straws*
- *balance*
- *some marbles or other small heavy objects*

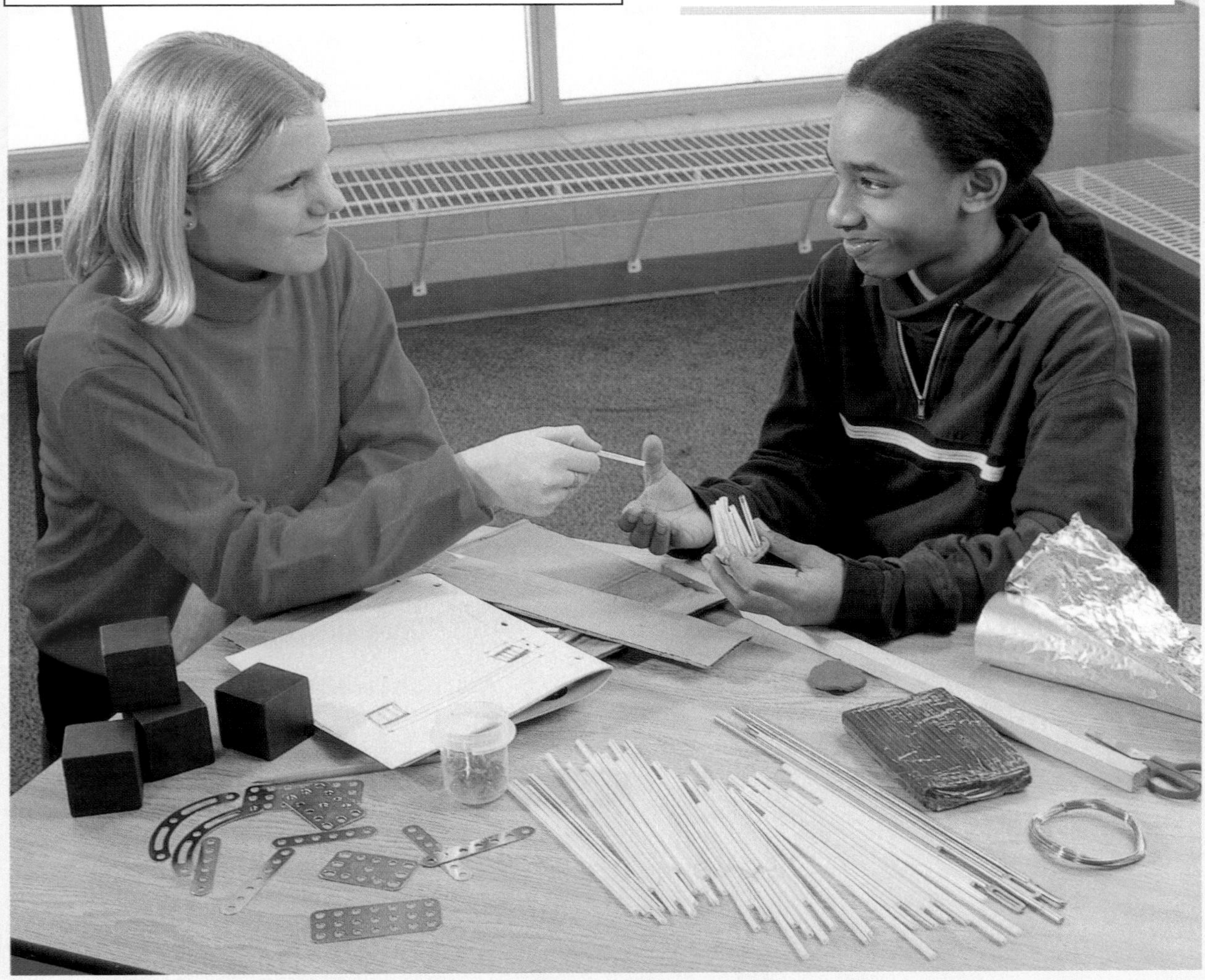

continued on next page

Designing and Building

1. Decide on the materials you will use.
2. Design and build your beam bridge to meet the parameters shown.
3. Decide how the ability of each bridge to support a load will be measured and recorded.

Caution!
Refer to the safety precautions in the Take the Challenge activity in Invitation to Explore.

Bridge Number	Static Load of Bridge	Supported Load? ✓	Dynamic Load Added	Supported Load? ✓	Maximum Dynamic Load	Supported Load? ✓

Keeping Records

4. The class results for all of the bridges will be recorded on a chart similar to the one above.

Testing and Evaluating

6. Using these results, graph the relationship between bridge mass and the mass of the maximum load the bridge can support without bending or breaking.
7. Copy each sentence, and complete using the information from your graph.
   a) The smaller the mass of a bridge, the ____________ mass it can support.
   b) The larger the mass of a bridge, the ____________ mass it can support.
   c) The relationship between bridge mass and mass supported is best described as a ____________ line.

Forming Conclusions

8. Finish this sentence: "From this test, the best way to make a beam bridge stronger is to ..."
9. Consider the different materials that were used to make the bridges. Which materials seemed to be the best choice?

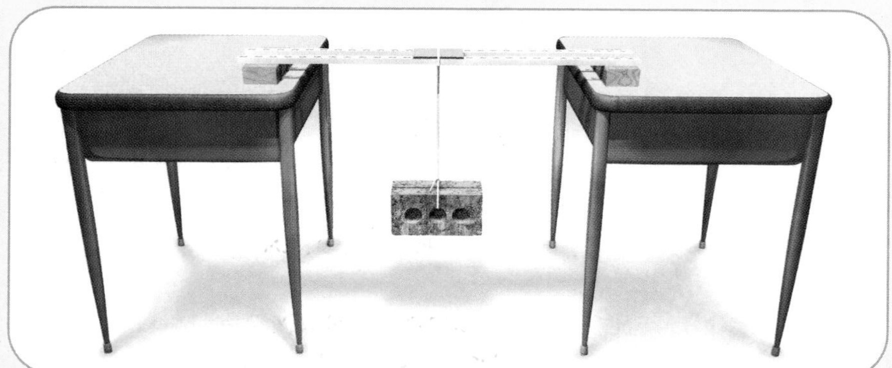

*info***BIT**

A Chart that Does the Work for You

Recording data in a chart helps you organize information in a meaningful way. Often, the next step is to take that information and sort it again. You might want to graph some variable in order to analyze your results. Wouldn't it be great if your chart could do this work for you?

	A	B
1	A1	B1
2	A2	B2
3	A3	B3
4	A4	B4
5	A5	B5
6	A6	B6

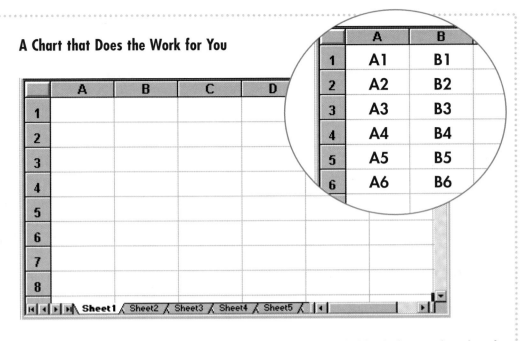

A computer ***spreadsheet*** *is like a "smart chart." You record your data by entering it into cells. Each cell holds one piece of information. The information could be a number or a word.*

Cells are identified by the letter and number of each column and row. For example, the cells in the first row would be A1, B1, C1 etc. In the first column, they would be A1, A2, A3, etc..

	A	B	C	D	E	F
1	6	8	10			
2	4.9	6.41	7.85			
3	8.2	10.8	13.3			
4	9.1	12.1	14.9			
5						
6						
7						
8						

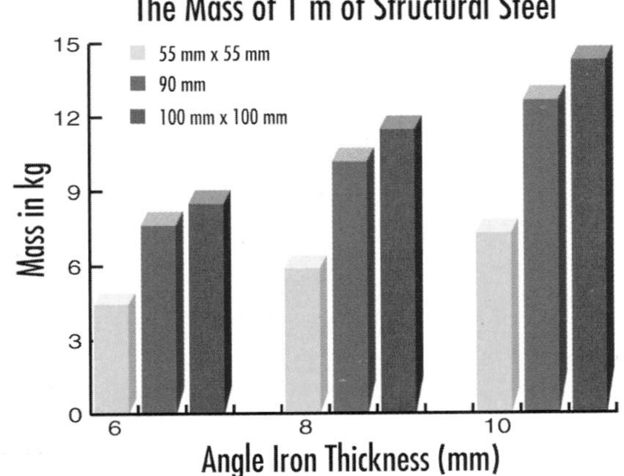

Once you have decided on the columns and rows you need and entered your data into the cells, the spreadsheet is ready to do your work. For example, you can use the menu commands to tell the spreadsheet to produce a graph.

It will use the cells you select, do any calculations you ask, then produce a graph. Changed your mind about how you want your information arranged? Highlight the cells, then point and click to move them around.

As you can see, a spreadsheet gives you a great deal of power over your data. All it takes is a bit of planning, and then entering your data carefully. Once you've done that, the chart will do the rest of your work!

Communicate

1 Describe and provide two examples of static and dynamic loads.

2 a) Use a tool to apply pressure to a toothpick that rests on two small blocks. As you apply more pressure (or increase the external load), what happens to the toothpick?

b) Stand another toothpick upright and use a tool to apply pressure to the top of it. (Be careful of the sharp point!) What happens to the toothpick?

c) Describe the forces that are acting on the toothpick in both demonstrations.

3 Make a three-column chart. In the first column, list the different types of bridges. In the second column, describe how each type of bridge supports a load. In the third column, rank each type of bridge by how well you think it would support a heavy load over a long distance.

a) Which type did you rank as the strongest? Why?

b) What other factors might need to be considered when deciding on the type of bridge to build?

4 A bridge has a total mass of 1000 t (tonnes). It is designed to support cars and trucks with a total mass of 10 000 t. A rope bridge has a mass of 50 kg, and is designed to support people with a total mass of 1000 kg. How does the performance of the first bridge compare with that of the second?

*info***BIT**

Arch Support

Although the Egyptians and the Greeks invented the arch, it wasn't until the Romans developed it that the arch became an important part of a building's structure.

try this at **HOME**

TABLE TOP RAMP

Your design for a structure to act as a temporary table during your community's winter carnival has been accepted. However, one table must be used to display the prize for the carnival raffle: a mini-van! The table will need to have a ramp attached to allow the vehicle to be driven on top. How can you modify your design to make it possible for your table to hold such a load? How should the ramp be constructed?

- Based on the class results, which type of structure will you use to make the table to hold the van?
- Brainstorm the factors that might affect how well the structure could support a greater load. How will you test the ability of this table to support the dynamic load of the van?

2.4 INTERNAL FORCES

Explore

What do you think will happen next in the situations pictured here?

Why does this structure stay together in the first place?

Some forms of exercise rely on resisting internal forces in order to produce strength and stability.

Develop

Compression, Tension, Shear, and Torsion

If you press the palms of your hands together firmly, you can feel the force your muscles are exerting. This is an example of an internal force. **Internal forces** are those forces that one part of a structure exerts on other parts of the same structure. In other words, internal forces are forces that act within a structure. Internal forces can be classified by the direction in which they act:

- **compression**— a squeeze together
- **tension**— a pull apart or stretch
- **shear**— a push in opposite directions
- **torsion**— a twist

Pressing the palms of your hands together models a force of compression. Now try using your hands to model a force of tension, shear, and torsion.

Let's look at the different types of internal forces.

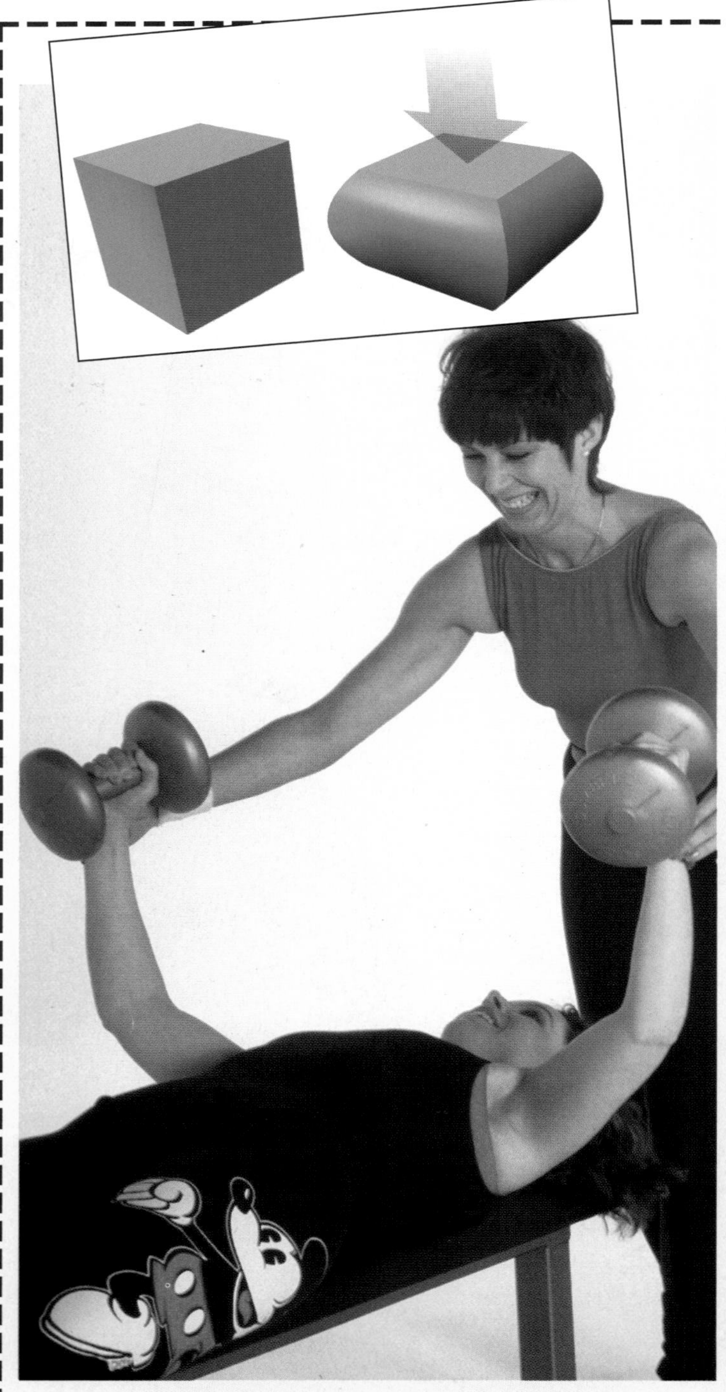

Compression is a force that acts to push objects together. How is this person using compression to exercise? Structures with parts that must resist compression include chairs, shelves, and columns. Which parts of these structures do you think are resisting compression? Think of some other examples.

Tension is a force that acts to pull things apart. How is this person using tension to exercise? Structures with parts that must resist tension include suspension bridges, hydro towers, and running shoes. Which parts of these structures do you think are resisting tension?

Shear is a force that acts to push parts that are in contact with each other in opposite directions. As the pole vaulter exerts force on the pole, where is the shear force? Structures with parts that must resist shear include doors, airplanes, and scissors.

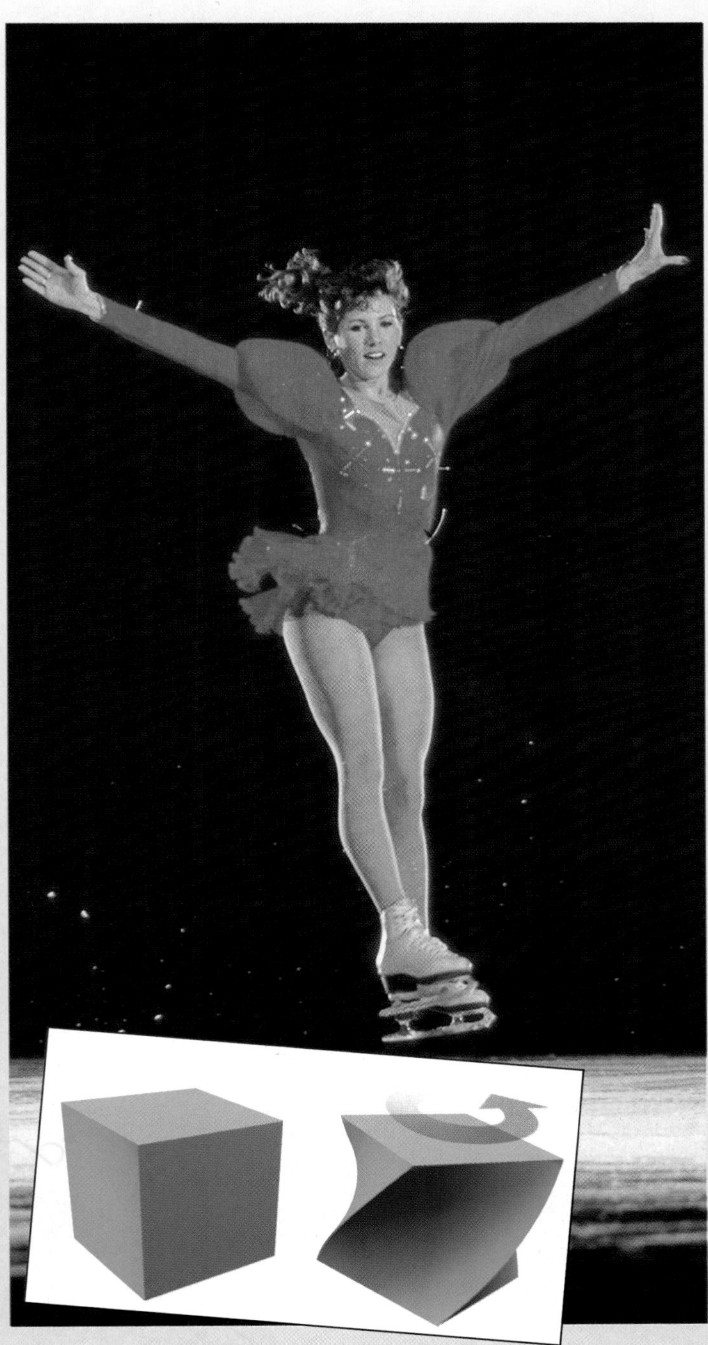

Torsion is a force that acts to twist parts of a structure. (This twisting is sometimes called *torque.*) Any parts of a structure that move can cause torsion which may affect other parts. How do you think torsion is affecting this skater? Structures with parts that must resist torsion include bicycles, fans, and cars.

Communicate

1 Think of any frame structure. Draw this structure and show how the different internal forces act within the structure.
2 Describe and provide examples of the following structural forces:

a) compression b) tension
c) shear d) torsion

2.5 Relating Internal and External Forces

Explore

Look at the structure of the truck.

- What external forces are acting on the truck?
- Which types of internal forces are acting on the truck?
- How do you think each of the internal forces might be affected by the external forces? Record your predictions.

Develop

More Than One Force

When you plan a fair test of a structure's performance, you consider only one factor, or force, acting on the structure at a time. This lets you see the effect of that force. However, in real life, a structure must resist combinations of forces. In fact, some kinds of internal forces occur together. They are called **complementary forces**. For example, compression and tension act together. Have you ever tried bending a stick until it breaks? Bending produces compression on one side of the stick and tension on the opposite side.

If you could see inside a structure that is supporting a load, you would be able to observe compression and tension acting together on that same structural part. Can you tell where each force acts on a structure? Test your prediction during the next activity.

PROBLEM SOLVER

COMPLEMENTARY FORCES

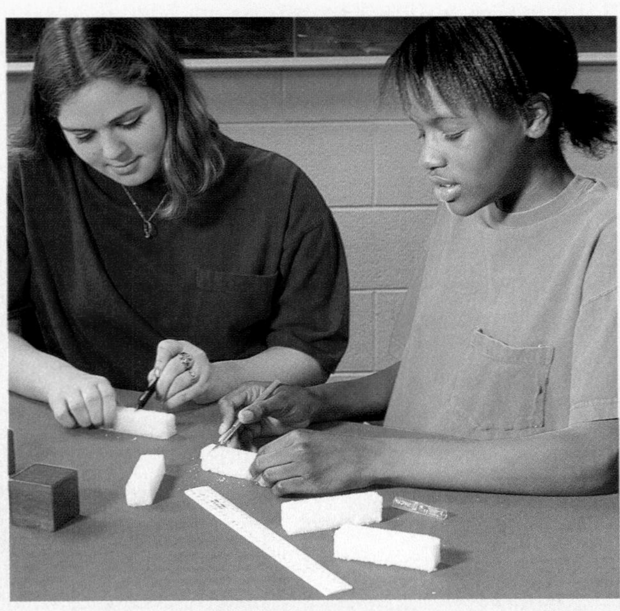

1 Take a strip of Styrofoam measuring about 2 cm by 3 cm by 10 cm. Make several, equally-spaced cuts (about 0.5 cm deep) on both the top and bottom of the Styrofoam.
2 Place the Styrofoam on two supports of the same size, such as wood blocks or text books.
3 Press your finger in the middle of the Styrofoam.
4 What happens to the top and bottom of the Styrofoam? Can you see two different forces acting on the Styrofoam?
5 Where is the compression force acting? Where is the tension force acting? Record your results in a drawing.

Like a stick, a beam may bend under the stress of a heavy load. If the load is too great, the beam will break. This break would be the result of the beam's failure to resist either compression or tension. By examining where a break happens on a beam, engineers could find out how to improve the structure. For example, if it failed first along on the upper surface, the beam should be designed to be stronger here to resist compression. If it failed first along the lower surface, what design change would you recommend? What reasons can you give for your design change?

Six days of freezing rain damaged this hydro tower in Montreal. What forces caused it to collapse?

Communicate

1 Copy the following sentences and complete them using the correct term.
   a) When you stretch an elastic band, you are applying a force of ___________.
   b) When you twist an elastic band, you are applying a force of ___________.
   c) When you bend back the peel of a banana, you are applying a force of ___________.
   d) As you bend back the peel of a banana, a ___________ force is acting on the inside of the peel and a ___________ force is acting on the outside of the peel.

2 Identify the internal and external forces that act on the earth beneath a glacier. Draw a sketch and use arrows to show these forces.

reSEARCH

Concrete is strong under compression, but weak under tension. Steel frames are strong under tension, but weak under compression. Find out how builders combine concrete and steel to make very strong structures.

2.6 More About Force

Explore

You know that a force can be defined as a push or a pull in a given direction. When a force acts on an object, the object tends to move away from the force. This movement depends on how massive the object is. For example, you can send a volleyball soaring over a net with one push of your hands but the same push would barely move a car. The actual effect of a force on a structure depends on three things:

- the magnitude, or size, of the force
- the direction of the force
- the location where the force is applied (the point and plane)

The stronger the force (or magnitude), the more effect it will have on a structure. You need to also consider how massive the structure is, since the same force will have a greater effect on a smaller structure.

The direction of a force is an important consideration in designing a structure. When you examine this view of a dam, what clues tell you about the direction of the force it must withstand?

The location where a force acts on a structure, the point and plane, can be very important. For example, these sailors constantly adjust their sails in order to capture the greatest amount of the wind's force at a proper angle. If they choose the right angle, the force will move the boat forward. If they choose the wrong angle, the force will tip the boat into the water.

Develop

Structural Stress, Fatigue, or Failure

It's critical that structures be designed and built to withstand all forces. This bridge was so badly designed that it fell down before it was even finished!

NATIONAL HERALD

August 29, 1907

Bridge Collapses!

QUÉBEC CITY—Five hundred and fifty metres and nearly 19 million kilograms of twisted steel collapsed this morning killing at least 75 people. There were an estimated 86 men working on the bridge at the time of the tragedy.

The Québec Bridge, as it was called, was to have the longest span of any cantilever bridge in the world. But its construction had been plagued by lack of money, delays, and design changes that were not tested or tried. The original design called for a span of 490 m but it was lengthened to 550 m to get the piers completely out of the water.

"They never recalculated the stresses when they lengthened the span," a source that wished to remain anonymous told the Herald. "Those beams began bending and buckling as soon as they were put in. They couldn't support those kinds of loads."

The effect of all of the forces acting on a structure at one time is called **structural stress**. A strong, stable structure is able to resist this stress without harm or failure. In the case of the Québec Bridge, the combination of external and internal forces weakened the steel beams. When structural stress causes this kind of damage to a material, it is called **structural fatigue**.

Structural fatigue happens when too much force is continually applied to a structural part. These ongoing forces leave the structure weak. They could even lead to **structural failure** as in the case of the Québec Bridge. Structural failure also happens when a structure has reached its limit in supporting a load.

A structure needs strength and stiffness to avoid structural failure:

- The *strength of a structure* is defined by the load at which it fails. For example, suppose it takes a load of 10 kg to collapse a bridge you have built. The strength of your bridge would be 10 kg.
- The *stiffness of a structure* is its ability to withstand changing shape under a load. For example, if your bridge starts to bend under a 7-kg load, that is a measure of its stiffness.

INVESTIGATOR

A Force to Consider

The Question

What is the effect of the location and direction of a force acting on a structure?

Materials & Equipment

- *straws*
- *tape*
- *spring scale*
- *small object to act as load*

Procedure

1. Using straws and tape, construct a simple bridge across a gap of 50 cm between tables or other supports. Tape the bridge to the tables or supports to hold it in place.

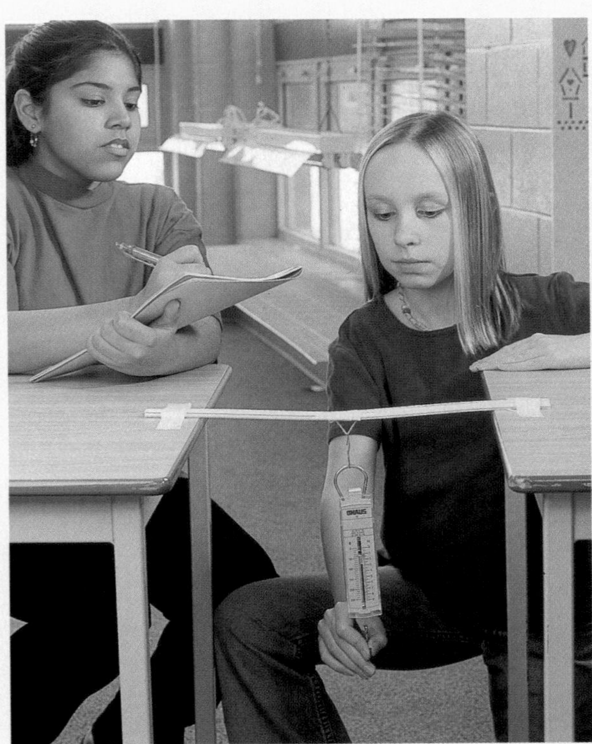

2. Place a load on your bridge.
3. Use a spring scale to pull down on the bridge as follows until the bridge just begins to bend. Then release the scale.
   a) Pull straight down at the centre of the bridge.
   b) Pull straight down at one end of the bridge, close to the support.
   c) Pull down at a 45° angle from the centre.
   d) Pull down at a 45° angle from one end.

Keeping Records

4. Observe what happens and record the force on the scale when the bridge begins to bend in each case.

Analyzing and Interpreting

5. What was the difference between pulling straight down from the centre of the bridge and pulling straight down from one end of the bridge?
6. What was the difference between pulling straight down from the centre and pulling at a 45° angle? Was this result the same at the end of the bridge?

Forming Conclusions

7. What do you conclude about the importance of knowing where a force will act on a structure?
8. From your results, determine the weakest point on your bridge. What does this suggest about where a bridge should be tested for the maximum dynamic load it can support?

Experiment ON YOUR OWN

Build a Working Model of a Drawbridge

Before You Start...

You are now familiar with the different types of structural forces, the characteristics of structural stability, and the nature of structural stress, fatigue, and failure. Let's use your knowledge to design and construct a bridge that will not only withstand external forces but will also have moving parts.

Identifying the Problem

1 Design a bridge with either one or two movable sections.

2 Decide what materials and equipment you will need to build your structure. For example:
   a) What kind of building materials will you use?
   b) How will you lift and lower the movable sections?
   c) How will you test your structure for wind resistance?

3 Design your procedure. For example:
   a) How will you collect your data?
   b) Is the test you are designing fair? How do you know?
   c) How will you record your results?

4 Write up your procedure and your design. Show it to your teacher.

5 Build your drawbridge.

Testing and Evaluating

6 Now perform various "stress" tests on your bridge.

7 Test the raising and lowering of your movable sections.

8 Share and compare your experimental design and findings with your classmates. How do your results compare with theirs?

9 How would you improve your design?

Communicate

1 The effect of a force on a structure depends on three factors. What are these three factors?
2 Which of the factors would you consider most important when designing each of the following structures?
   a) a kite
   b) a lighthouse
   c) a backpack
   d) a bridge
3 Make a flowchart to connect the following events, beginning with the one that happens first. You can connect more than one event to another. You can use an event in more than one place. (Hint: you will first have to put these events in the correct order.)
   - The bridge structure experiences structural stress.
   - A freight train loaded with iron ore passes over the bridge.
   - The bridge collapses.
   - The beams of the rail bridge bend slowly.
   - The rail bridge carries 10 trains a day over the valley.
   - The beams of the rail bridge give way.
   - The bridge is experiencing structural fatigue.
   - A rail bridge was built here 30 years ago.
   - The bridge is experiencing structural failure.
4 Your family is visiting your grandparents' farm. It has been a couple of years since your last visit. One of the changes is in you: you have grown quite a bit.
   a) Your parents warn you not to try climbing into the treehouse, although this was your favourite place when you were small. Why?
   b) Suggest how you could reassure your parents that the treehouse is safe for you to use.
   c) If you find out that it isn't, what could you do? Use the terms: dynamic load, static load, force, fatigue, and structural failure at least once in your answer.

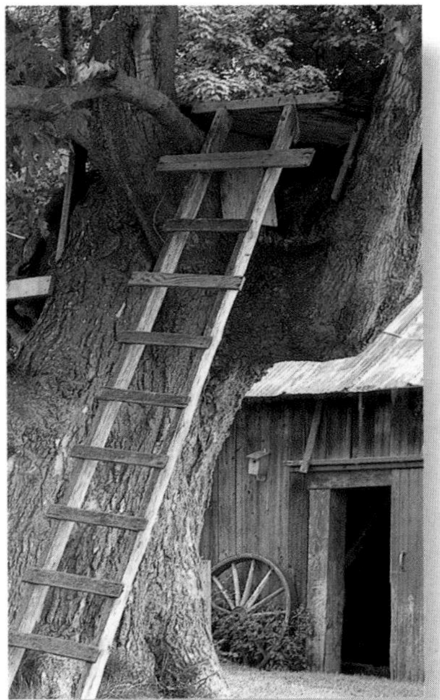

try this at **HOME**

MAKE A CAN CRUSHER

You want to make room in your family's recycling box for more aluminum cans. To do this, you decide to crush the empty cans so each one takes up less space.

1 Test an empty can to find out the type and direction of force which works best.
2 Design and make a device which will apply this force to empty cans.

2.7 CHECK YOUR PROGRESS

The Leaning Tower of Pisa

1 Write a definition in your own words for each of the following terms:
   a) force
   b) external force
   c) internal force
   d) gravity
   e) structural stress
   f) structural failure
   g) structural fatigue
2 Explain how compression and tension act together by describing what happens to your arm when you pick up a book.
3 Why do you think astronauts practise building techniques underwater that they will need to use in space?
4 What is the difference between shear and torsion? Give an example of each.
5 What is the difference between a structure's strength and its stiffness?
6 How can a structure remain standing for several years, then suddenly collapse?
7 The Leaning Tower of Pisa is a famous landmark. The tower has been gradually tipping to one side for years. There is concern that if it tips a little more, it will suddenly fall. Explain why this would happen.
8 A local marina wants to suspend a sign from a bridge. There are two choices. It could hang straight down from cables, or it could hang between two cables at 45° angles from the bridge. Which arrangement do you recommend? Why?

reSEARCH

If you were on this bridge, would you be able to admire the view? — probably not. Most modern bridges in Canada are designed with tall barriers that prevent water from running off the surface of the bridge. Instead, this water is collected into a storm drain and piped away from the bridge. Find out why bridges no longer have open railings on either side.

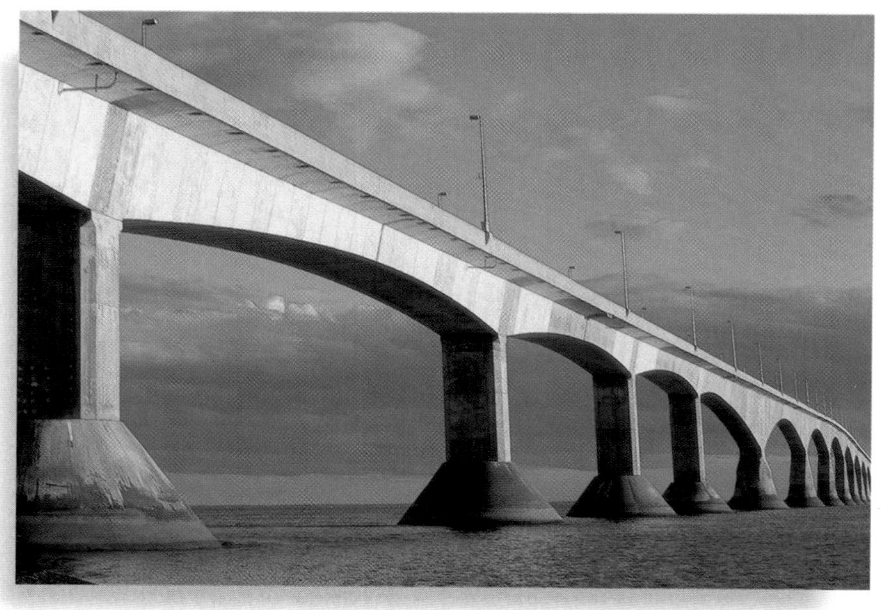

Big Idea

3.0 A structure's strength and stability are determined by its characteristics.

Have you ever wondered why some structures stay strong and stable for longer periods of time than other structures? Look at the illustrations of the Seven Ancient Wonders of the World. Some took many years to complete, so the dates shown are approximate. Which of these structures are still standing today?

350 B.C.—The marble Temple of Artemis at Ephesus

350 B.C.—The marble Mausoleum of Halicarnassus

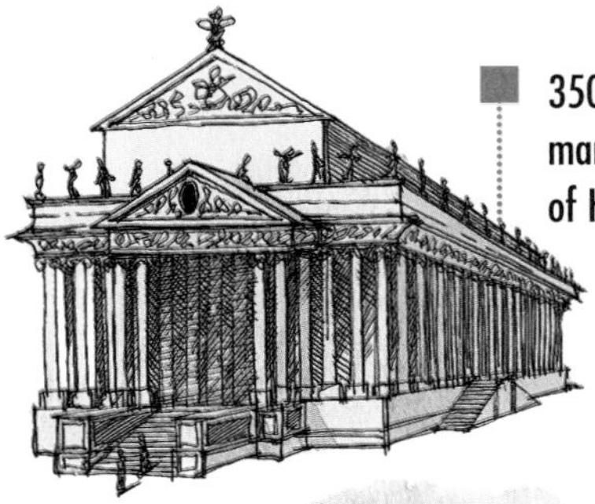

290 B.C.—The Colossus of Rhodes. This was a huge bronze statue of the sun god, Helios. It stood more than 35 m high overlooking Rhodes Harbour in Greece.

297 B.C.—The Pharos of Alexandria

2500 B.C.—The Pyramids of Egypt, at Giza

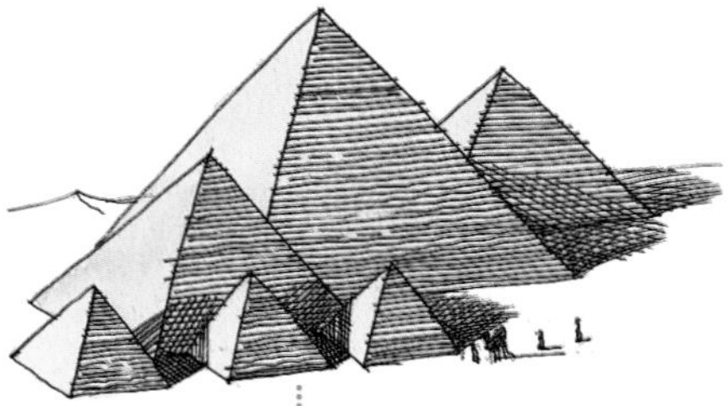

560 B.C.—The Hanging Gardens of Babylon. These beautiful gardens were created in the middle of the desert.

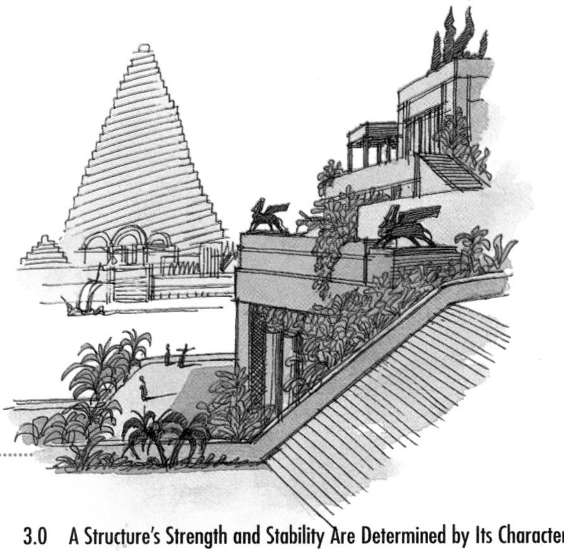

430 B.C.—The Statue of Zeus at Olympia. It was made of ivory and gold and stood 12 m high.

Today, only one of the original 127 columns in the Temple of Artemis still exists. Foundation remains of the Mausoleum of Halicarnassus can still be seen and some of its statues are in London's British Museum. Only the Pyramids of Egypt, at Giza still stand. What do you think contributed to their strength and stability?

3.1 Structural Shapes

Explore

Look at the following illustration. Which shapes are most common in the illustration? least common? Why do you think certain shapes are found more often than others in structures?

Develop

Two-dimensional and Three-dimensional Shapes

Think about the tower that you built at the beginning of this chapter. What shapes did you use to build your structure? You've had some opportunities to think about how the shape of a structure determines its strength. Which two-dimensional shape is the strongest: a triangle, a square, or a rectangle? Which three-dimensional shape is the strongest: a triangular prism, a rectangular prism, or a pentagonal prism? In the next activity, you will find out.

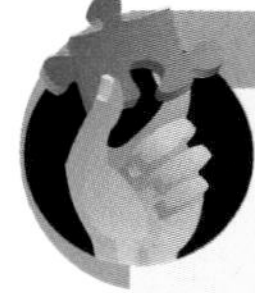

PROBLEM SOLVER

CREATING 2-D AND 3-D SHAPES

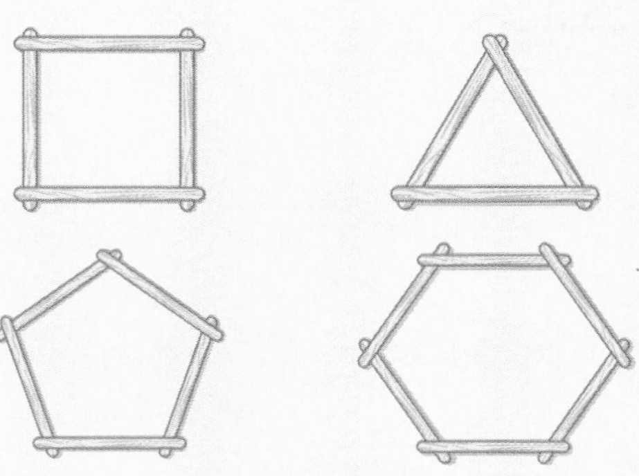

Which shapes do you think make the strongest frames?

- Using popsicle sticks, straws or pipe cleaners, assemble different two-dimensional shapes (triangle, square, rectangle) and three-dimensional shapes (triangular prism, rectangular prism, pentagonal prism). Use glue, tape, etc. to fasten the pieces.
- Test the strength of each shape by pushing on its corners.
- Which two-dimensional shape was the most rigid? Which three-dimensional shape was the most rigid?
- Why do you think some shapes are stronger than others? (Think about the forces acting on the structures.)

In the previous activity, you used popsicle sticks, straws, or pipe cleaners to make different shapes. Can you think of other ways to shape materials? What happens when you hold a piece of paper by one of its short sides? What would happen if you bent the paper in a U-shape? Test if the bent paper can support the weight of a pencil. Does changing the shape of a material change its strength? In the next activity, you will see whether or not folding paper affects the strength of the paper.

PROBLEM SOLVER

FOLDING PAPER

Can you figure out how to make only triangular paper folds on a piece of paper? Try it and see.

- Gently unfold the paper, keeping the folds intact as much as possible so that the paper is in a dome shape. Do not flatten the paper. Why is this important?
- Tape the edges of your dome to a flat surface. Test to see how strong the dome is by placing weights, or loads (such as cubes, marbles, or books) on the dome. What did you find out?
- Can you think of any examples of structures that use this type of shape?

Communicate

1 Identify the different two-dimensional and three-dimensional shapes in each of the following structures.

2 How can you make a two-dimensional square frame more rigid?

3 Which part of a can of soup do you think could be dented more easily, the top of the can or the side of the can? Explain your ideas.

3.2 STRUCTURAL COMPONENTS

Explore

Have you ever tried to cross a small river or stream by walking on a flat wooden plank laid across it? If the plank was weak, you probably noticed it bending. If you tried bouncing up and down, you might end up in the stream. This simple beam bridge could not withstand the structural stress. If you wanted to design a stronger bridge, what would you do differently? One approach would be to use a different material or a thicker plank. There is another way. You could use different structural components (or parts) to make your bridge. Some components are stronger than others.

Develop

Beams, Arches, and Folded Paper

Let's look at the different components that make up some structures. Try folding paper to represent each type of the following structural components.

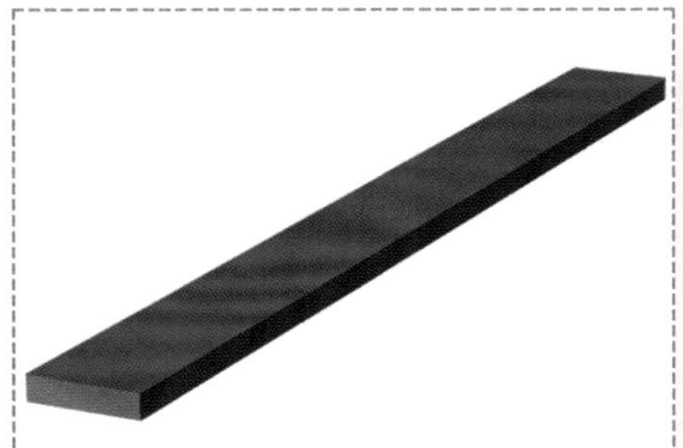

A **beam** is a flat structure that is supported at each end. If too much weight is put on a beam, it will bend in a u-shape or even break in the middle.

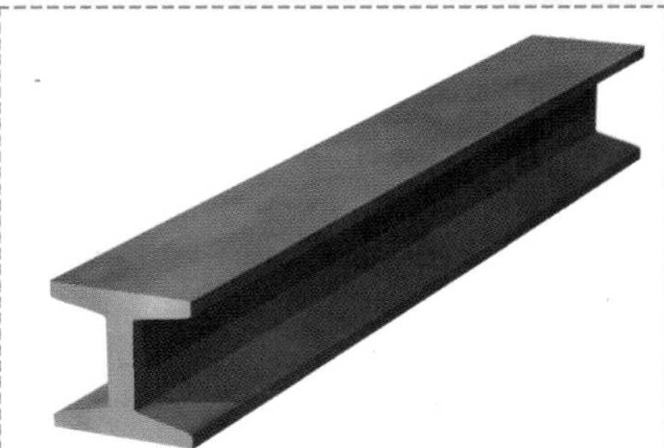

The shape of an **I-beam** gives it strength. I-beams have less mass than solid beams. Because there is less of their own mass to support, I-beams can support more of a load.

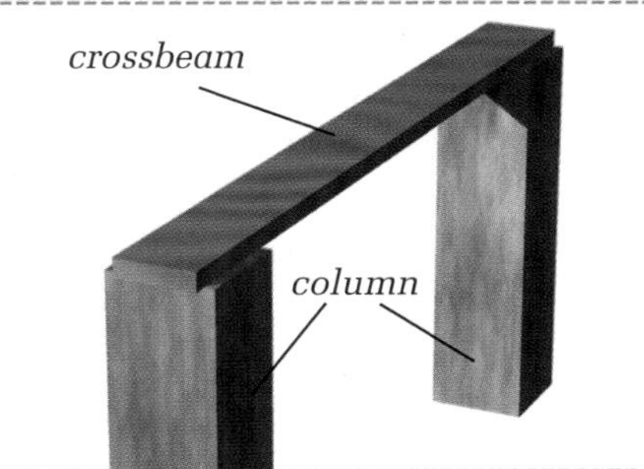

A **column** is a solid structure that can stand by itself. Columns can be used to support crossbeams.

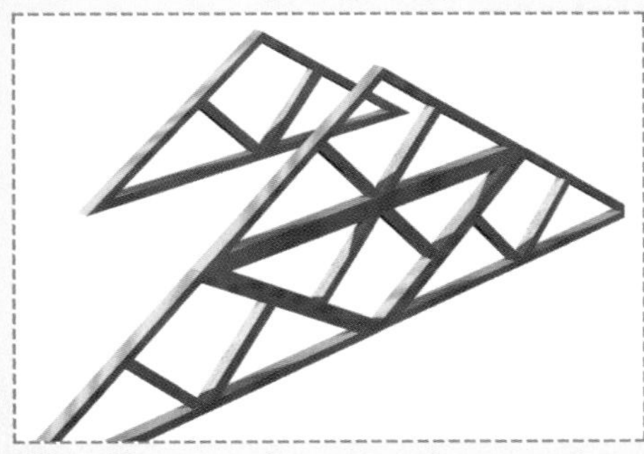

A **truss** is a framework of beams joined together. Trusses are usually in the form of interlocking triangles.

A **cantilever** is a beam that is supported only at one end. When weight is placed on the beam, the beam bends in an n-shape to resist the load.

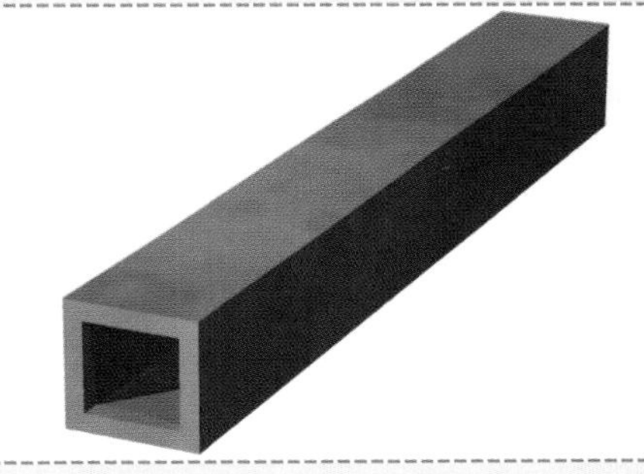

Girders, or **box beams**, are long beams in the shape of hollow rectangular prisms.

An **arch** can support a lot of weight. The force of weight on an arch is carried along the sides of the arch to its supports. This spreads out the effect of any load.

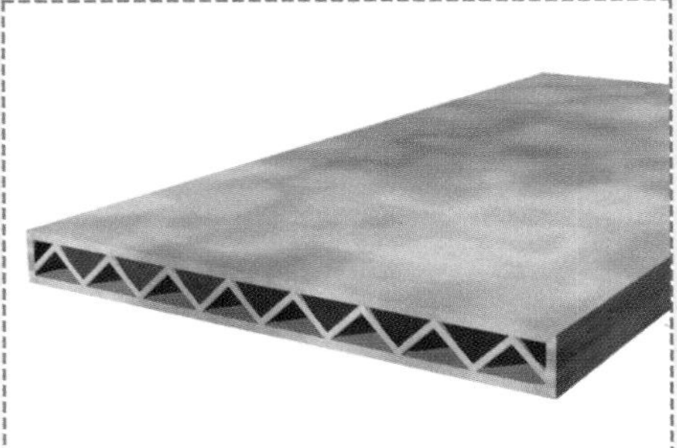

When a sheet of metal or cardboard is shaped into a series of pleats, or triangles, it is called **corrugated metal** or **cardboard**. A corrugated sheet is stronger than a flat sheet.

Now that you've created some interesting structural components, think what would happen if you combined some of them. Did you know that many bridges are made by combining the arch with triangular corrugation? Which combinations do you think are more suitable for construction? How do you know?

Communicate

1 As part of a community parks restoration project, students in a Grade 7 class have volunteered to design and build a natural bridge across a 5-m wide stream. They can only use non-living, natural materials found in the forest and a hand saw.

a) Based on your knowledge of structural components, provide some suggestions for designing and constructing the natural bridge.

b) Identify some problems that you think might happen as the bridge is being used over time and under a variety of weather conditions.

3.3 Structural Materials

Explore

In the past, people constructed shelters out of material they could find, including animal skins, mud, and sticks. Some of these shelters were large and elaborate, including multi-storey structures. Look at the materials that make up your home or your school. Name some of these materials.

The basic material of this home, a simple brick baked in the sun, has been used for thousands of years. It is durable, keeps out the heat, and is inexpensive.

This home is made from several materials. Each material was selected for its useful characteristics, for example, the tinted glass on the top floors keeps out ultraviolet radiation. Solar panels produce electricity, making the home more energy efficient.

Develop

Wood, Concrete, or Steel

Can you imagine riding a skateboard made of paper? What about a tent made from brick? It is important to choose appropriate materials for building a structure. However, sometimes the most suitable materials may not be available or may be too expensive. For example, wood is a material that is commonly used for construction, but over the years, solid wood has become more expensive. So lumber suppliers started making a variety of wood products to use instead. These products have different advantages. Some are stronger, some are lighter, and many are less expensive.

plywood

I-*beam floor joists*

particle board

These wood products are used in construction. They have several advantages over ordinary wood. For example:

- The layers of wood in the plywood add to its strength in certain directions.
- The particle board is made from waste pieces of wood. It is less expensive but not as strong, so it is used where strength isn't as important.
- The beams have been cut into shapes that provide the most strength for their mass.

Materials used to build structures are chosen because of their properties. Some of the most important properties to consider are listed on the next page. Notice that the properties can be classified into two groups. How are the two groups different?

*info***BIT**

Is it wood?

It looks like wood and withstands forces like wood. However, these deck planks are made from recycled plastic. They can be drilled and cut just like wood, but require no sanding, painting, or staining to keep them looking good.

Properties of Materials	
• ***brittleness*** *(How easily does it break?)* • ***ductility*** *(How easily can it be pulled into wire?)* • ***hardness*** • ***mass*** • ***plasticity*** *(How easy is it to shape?)* • ***resistance to heat*** • ***resistance to water***	• ***strength*** • ***aesthetics*** *(appearance, texture, etc.)* • ***availability*** • ***cost*** • ***effect on the environment*** *(Can it be used safely?)* • ***disposal of waste*** *(Recycle, reuse, or pay for treatment?)*

When choosing materials for building structures such as bridges, houses, roads, and tunnels, the material's strength, appearance, and cost, are important considerations. Plastics, wood, concrete, and steel are some of the common materials used for such structures.

Think back to the tower you built for the Wind Challenge in the Invitation to Explore. Which materials did you use to create your structure? What materials would have been better to make your structure stronger, taller, and more stable? The next activity will test and compare some different materials.

INVESTIGATOR

Choosing a Material for Strength and Stability

The Question

Which material(s) will improve the strength and stability of a tall, free-standing tower?

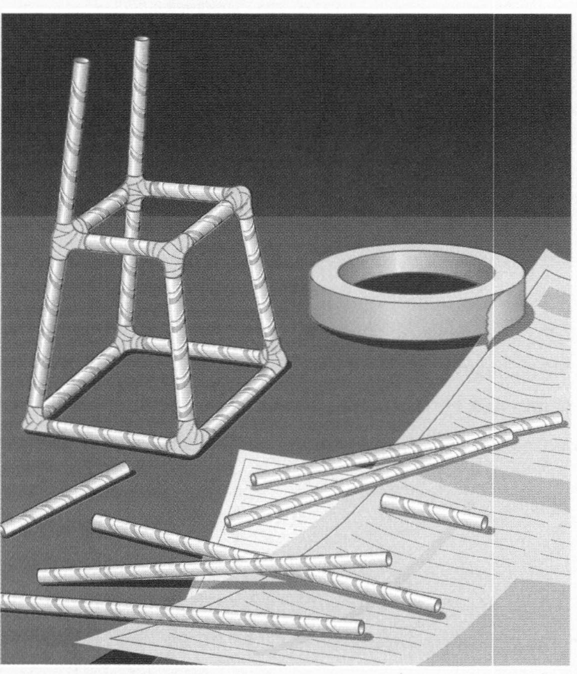

Materials & Equipment

- *uncooked spaghetti*
- *newspaper*
- *plastic straws*
- *bamboo skewers*
- *masking tape*

Procedure

1. As a class, identify and record the properties that might affect the strength and stability of a tower.

continued on next page

2 Predict which materials will be the most suitable for building a tall, free-standing structure that supports the greatest load.

3 Record the properties of your chosen materials. How will you test the materials you have chosen for internal and external forces?

4 Using your chosen materials, construct a tower using the illustrated model as your design.

5 As a class, decide how you will test for internal and external forces affecting the towers in order to compare the properties of the different building materials.

Keeping Records

6 Record your observations and the test results in a chart like the one shown.

Analyzing and Interpreting

7 How did you determine which material to use in building your tower? Explain.

8 Were there any other material properties that should have been investigated? How do you know?

9 Which materials most resisted the internal and external forces acting on your structure?

Forming Conclusions

10 How do you know that your tests were fair, that is, valid and reliable?

11 What material properties do you think are the most important in real life for building tall, free-standing structures that can support the greatest mass? Why?

Property	Findings			
	Material 1	Material 2	Material 3	Material 4
strength	need to use many pieces bound together			
water resistance				
mass				
(any other properties you choose to compare)				

Communicate

1 Identify and describe a structure in your classroom, school, home, or neighbourhood. How do the properties of the materials used in this structure help it to function? How do the properties help it to resist internal and external forces?

2 What should you look for when choosing materials for a design and construction project?

3 Debate this claim: "Almost any material can be used to build any structure."

4 A dam is used to hold back water in a local river in order to generate electricity, but it is beginning to need expensive repairs. Several experts have been asked to provide advice to the designers of the new dam, including:

- a person from the marina upstream from the dam
- a freshwater ecologist
- a local fishing guide
- a drinking water expert from the city downstream
- a person representing the power company
- a person representing a local group wishing to open a biking trail and to use the new dam as a bridge

a) Choose one of these individuals. Think about what you, as that person, might want included in the design of the new dam.
b) Write down or draw your ideas. Compare your ideas with those of a classmate who has chosen a different individual. How could both of your ideas be included in the new design?

3.4 BUILDING A STRUCTURE

Explore

You have looked at how the shapes and materials of structural components affect the strength and stability of a structure. But, without some kind of organization, structural components are nothing more than a pile of parts.

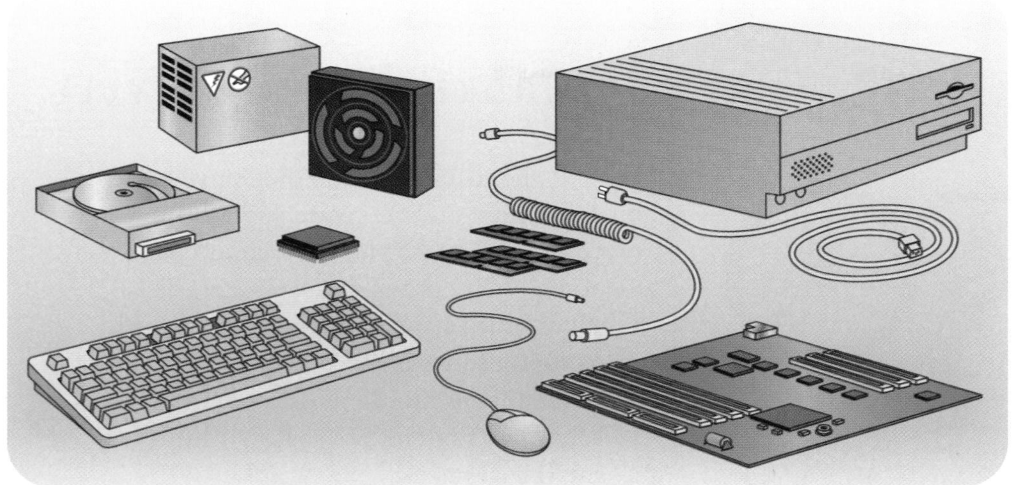

What has to happen before this structure is ready to use?

Picture a heap of toothpicks and a bottle of glue. You can arrange these materials to make a variety of structures. For example, you could create a toothpick bridge model. Brainstorm some different structures you could build with toothpicks and glue. How would you arrange and build these different structures?

Develop

Putting Parts Together

Now imagine these materials: lumber, nails, a door, hinges, and a door knob. These materials can be arranged to make a garden shed. But they could also be arranged to create a playhouse, a piece of furniture, or even a boat (although it may not float!). However, these materials could not be arranged to make a bicycle or an airplane wing. Why do you think that is?

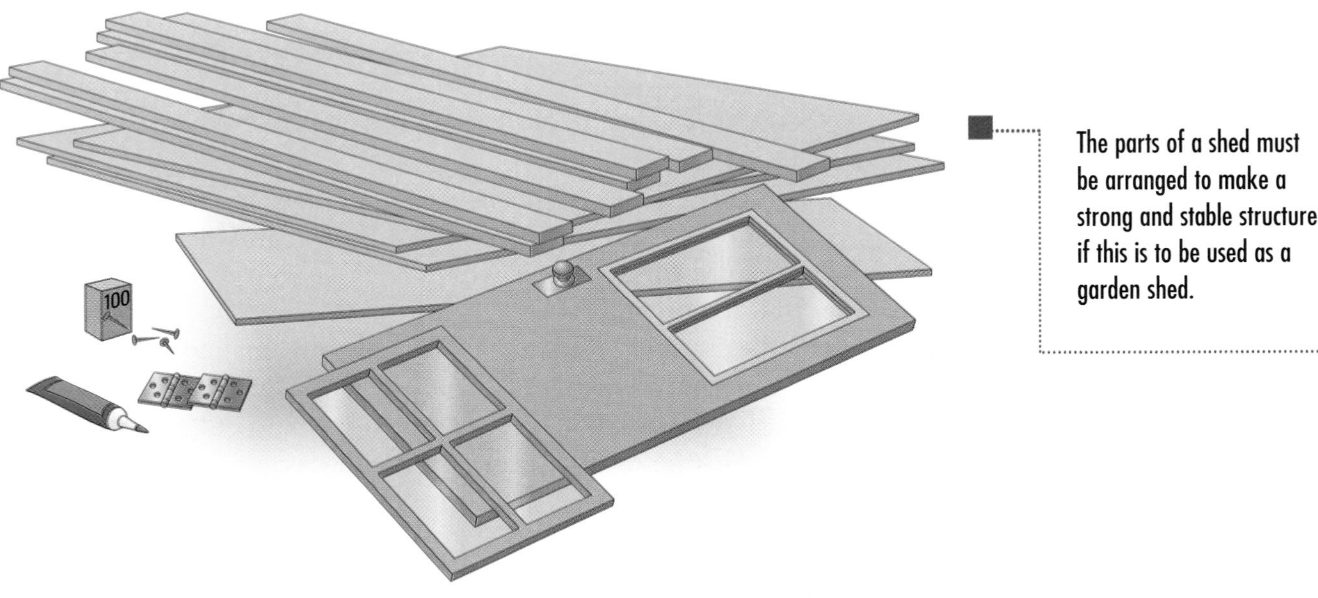

The parts of a shed must be arranged to make a strong and stable structure if this is to be used as a garden shed.

PROBLEM SOLVER

LOOKING AT A BICYCLE

Look at the different parts of a bicycle. If you did not know that the parts came from a bicycle, how could you arrange the parts together? Write down a few design ideas.

- What other structures could you build using these parts?
- What shapes are the most common?
- What parts could be separated into smaller parts?
- What forces would you have to consider if you were designing a bicycle?

So far, you have learned a great deal about the "nuts and bolts" of designing and building structures. In the remaining sections of this chapter, you will explore the sources of structures you use every day. You will see how other factors beyond strength and stability are considered by designers and manufacturers. You will meet some inventors. Along the way, you will explore what really happens from idea to product and beyond.

Communicate

1 Structures that are sold "ready-to-assemble" usually come with instructions. Look over your drawings for a structure you have designed in this chapter.

a) Write a set of instructions to help someone else make the same structure.

b) How easy was it to write these instructions? What problems, if any, did you find?

c) Let one of your classmates read your instructions. Ask this person if he or she feels able to go ahead and build the structure without your help. Ask for suggestions to improve your instructions.

2 Read the assembly instructions that come with a model, tool, or other device. Are they understandable? What did you find most helpful? What else would you need to know in order to build the structure?

3.5 Check Your Progress

1 Research how wasps build their nests. What materials do wasps use? What is the advantage of these materials? (Hint: think about their properties.)

2 Look at the photo of a brick wall. What shape are the bricks? Why are the bricks in the wall not stacked directly on top of each other?

3 The method of house construction shown in the photo below uses thin pieces of wood. It is sometimes called "stick building." Why are these "sticks" able to support the heavy load of the walls and roof as well as external forces?

4 Describe four different structural components using a labelled drawing. Answer the following questions:
   a) For each, give an example of a structure in which you would use this component.
   b) For each, what is the advantage of including this component in a structure?
   c) If all of these components were of the same mass, which one would be the strongest? Why?
5 Research one of the various steps in constructing a house. Sketch or describe what happens at the different stages.

6 Use some rope (3.5 m), thick sticks or dowels (total length of 3 m), scrap pieces of wood, thick cardboard, and newspapers to design a chair that you can sit on. What two-dimensional and three-dimensional shapes are in your structure?

Careers and Profiles

Roller-Coaster Designer

Roller-coaster designers use computer programs to design coasters. These programs help them change factors like the height and steepness of the coaster to get the fastest and safest ride possible.

Once the design is ready, a small scale model of the coaster is built, probably around one-eighth of the actual size. The designers test this model to make sure it is safe and works well. Next, a full-sized model is built and tested. Finally, the roller coaster is completed. It is set up in an amusement park and ready to go!

- What forces do you think are acting on the roller coaster shown?

Building Inspector

Building inspectors make sure buildings are safe for people to live and work in. When a building is under construction, a city building officer will come to check that the builders are following proper safety rules.

- The structure and foundation of the building have to be strong enough to hold up the weight it will be carrying.

- Tall buildings have to be stiff enough to resist the force of strong winds.
- Buildings in earthquake zones have to be sturdy enough to withstand an earthquake.

If your family buys a house, you might hire a home inspector to examine it. The inspector will check that the structure, heating, plumbing and electricity in the house are all safe and working well.

Building inspectors need to understand how structures work. They also need to understand the forces like wind and gravity that act on a building. In Canada, for example, roofs have to be strong enough to hold up the weight of snow that builds up during the winter.

BIG IDEA

4.0 Designing and making products involve more than meeting a specific need.

The ***inuksuk*** pictured at the beginning of this chapter is strong and stable. The people who built it knew it would be able to resist the forces acting against it. But why did they build it? It's a symbol "expressing joy and much happiness" for any traveller who encounters it. There are different types of *inuksuit*, each serving a slightly different function.

Some *inuksuit* point in the direction where traditionally caribou herds have been hunted.

Some *inuksuit* act as sight lines, pointing to special places beyond the horizon.

All structures are designed and built for a reason. A sculpture may be built to express the artist's emotions. A home is built to provide safe, sheltered living space. You have learned to consider the shape and materials used to make a structure able to withstand the forces that act on it. Now it is time to examine *why* certain things are made as they are.

Think about a hospital building and a toaster. Both are structures. Both have been designed and built to meet people's needs. The hospital is larger and more complex, involving far more people in its construction. Yet, like the hospital, the toaster was once an idea, then a design, and finally a finished structure. How are people's needs met from ideas to finished products? In this section, you will look at how products are developed and manufactured. You will begin by investigating the sources of new ideas.

4.1 You Need a What?

Explore

Have you ever thought about all the products that you use? If you were to make a list, you could probably classify each product as being food, clothing, shelter, transportation, education, or entertainment. Products are designed to meet people's basic needs for food, clothing, and shelter, as well as to make life easier. Can you think of other reasons why products are developed?

The first electron microscope was developed in Germany in 1933. However, its resolution wasn't any better than an optical microscope. Then in 1938, two University of Toronto students, James Hillier and Albert Prebus, improved the design. Their microscope could see objects thousands of times smaller than anything science had ever seen.

Today, the electron microscope is a common laboratory tool in biology, physics, chemistry, and medicine. Many remarkable discoveries can be attributed to its use.

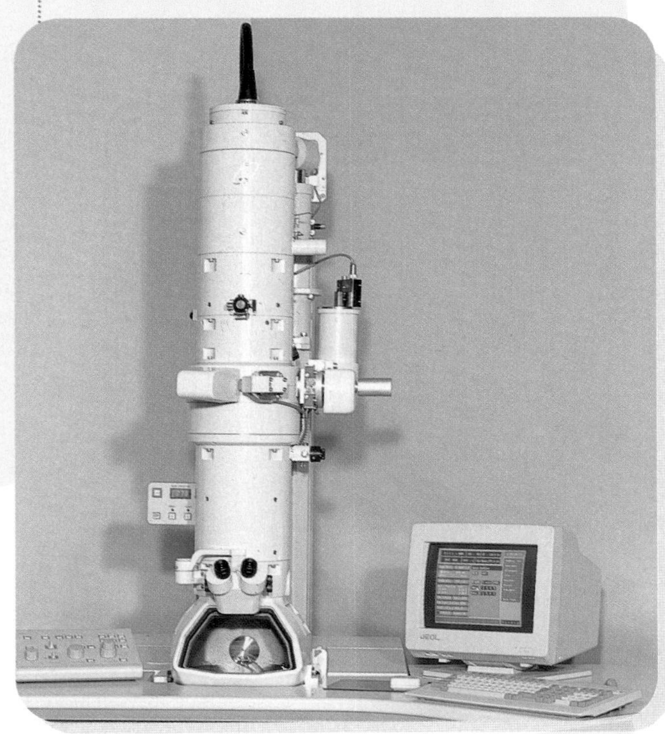

Quills (goose feathers) were used as pens from the 5th century until 1830 when pens with steel nibs replaced them.

In 1938, Ladislao Biro invented the ballpoint pen after he became frustrated with the fountain pen. This advanced version can write upside down or be used in space.

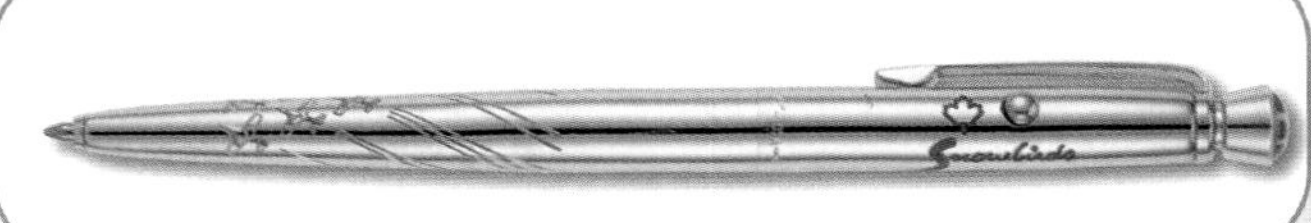

In 1922, at the age of fifteen, Joseph Armand Bombardier designed and built a motorized sleigh. Over the years he refined the design which eventually became the modern skidoo in 1959.

Bombardier's invention gave rise to an entire industry.

In 1876, Alexander Graham Bell invented the telephone, a device for communicating sound using wires in an electric circuit.

Today's cellular phones communicate sound using signals transmitted from satellites and communication towers to locations around the world.

Develop

The Perfect Solution

Have you ever had a great idea for a product? Have you ever looked at something and asked yourself "Why didn't I think of that?" Products are created to satisfy some need or to improve an existing product. Sometimes products may even be created by accident. However, every product, from a zipper to a computer, started as an idea in someone's head. And every product has some story to tell about how it came to be.

Think about the zipper on your coat. Did you know that the zipper started out as a way to fasten shoes? In 1893, Whitcomb Judson patented a slider device that he had invented to make it easier to close high-button shoes. Unfortunately, Judson's invention did not work well. In 1913, Gideon Sundback, one of Judson's workers, improved on Judson's design. However, it was not until 1923, when the B. F. Goodrich Company decided to sell galoshes (rubber boots) with hookless fasteners, that the product became popular. Because the galoshes could be fastened with a single zip of one hand, the fasteners were soon called *zippers*.

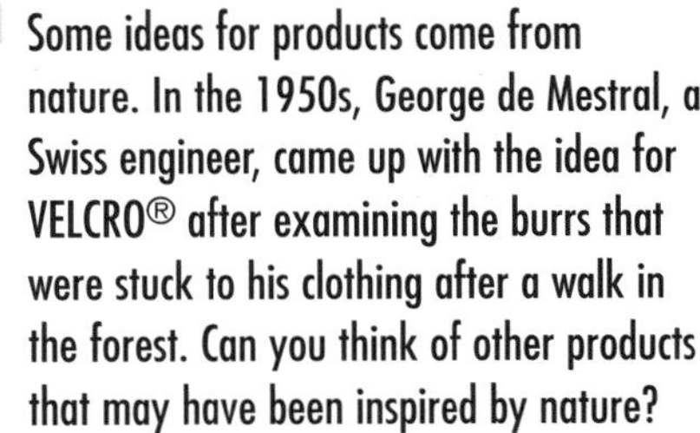

Some ideas for products come from nature. In the 1950s, George de Mestral, a Swiss engineer, came up with the idea for VELCRO® after examining the burrs that were stuck to his clothing after a walk in the forest. Can you think of other products that may have been inspired by nature?

Most new products come from identifying a need and then thinking of ways to satisfy that need. For example, in 1886, Josephine Cochrane patented her invention to wash dishes and started a company to manufacture dishwashers. She was inspired to invent the dishwasher because she was tired of dishes being broken while they were washed. Cochrane saw a need and invented a product to satisfy that need.

PROBLEM SOLVER

ROOM FOR IMPROVEMENT

1 Brainstorm ideas for a new product. Your ideas could be a way to improve an old product or you could come up with an idea for an entirely new product. To help you focus your thoughts, you should identify a need and think about how your product would satisfy that need.

2 After you've come up with an idea, start thinking about a design for your product. List all of the factors you want to consider. Here are some questions to get you started:
- Does my product need to last for a long time?
- Does it need to be attractive?
- Is it environmentally friendly?
- Do I want to make this an inexpensive or expensive product?

3 Present your design as a scale drawing, with labels and any details you wish to include.

You've been thinking about how ideas for a product are developed. However, coming up with the idea for a new product is only the first, and perhaps the easiest, step. A successful product needs a market. In other words, people have to need or want your product for it to be successful. How do you think that information on what people want or need is collected?

Communicate

1 Look at the photos showing several products. Choose a product and research how it was invented. Find out who invented the product and how important or popular it has proven to be.

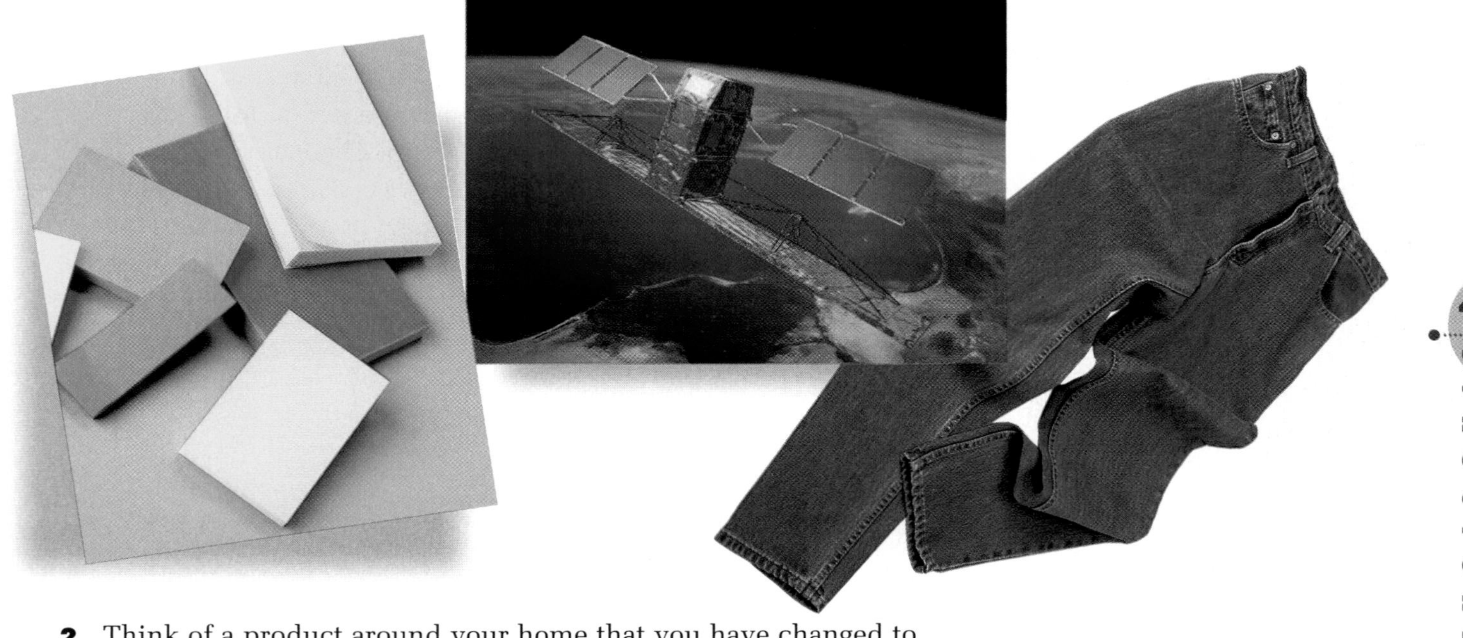

2 Think of a product around your home that you have changed to make it more personal. Why and how did you change the product?

4 STRUCTURES

4.2 Market Research

Explore

Imagine that you have an idea for a new type of backpack. Your new backpack will revolutionize how students carry their things to school. You believe it could be a great success. When you talk to manufacturers about making your design, they ask to see your market research. You are willing to do it. But what exactly is market research?

Market research involves gathering and evaluating data about what people like or don't like. Market research can also give you information about the economy, whether there is a need for your product, and what people would be willing to pay for your product.

Do you try on a new pair of running shoes before buying them? If you do, you are doing a kind of research.

Develop

Research and Surveys

Research is a very important step in developing products. For example, an inventor with a new idea will do research to see if a similar product or invention already exists. This is done by conducting a patent search. A **patent** is a legal document that is used to prove the ownership of an idea or product. No one can copy, make, or sell a patented idea or product without the owner's permission.

*info*BIT

Holiday Lights

In 1917, there was a terrible fire in New York City caused by candles that had been placed on a Christmas tree. At the time, the Sadacca family had a novelty business selling wicker cages with imitation birds in them that lit up. Their son Albert, who was 15, suggested that his family begin making electric lights for Christmas trees. The lights were not popular, however, until after Albert thought of painting the bulbs different colours. One boy's idea had started a new industry!

After the patent search, the research has just begun. To develop an idea into a product, a designer might need to research the types of materials available or find out about different building techniques. There may be tests to perform. There are government regulations about safety or other factors to consider. However, before investing time and effort into a new product, the most important type of research you need to carry out is market research. *Will anyone want what you plan to make?*

Cobblers once made shoes by hand.

Market research was developed during the Industrial Age, early in the 20th century. Before then, if you wanted a particular product, such as shoes, you would go directly to the person who made the product. This person, the cobbler, would make a pair of shoes just for you. Today, manufacturing industries are able to make products for millions of customers. Manufacturers need to know what is best to produce—products that will sell.

Market research is a process of asking questions or finding out information about the market, the competition, and potential customers. From this information, manufacturers can determine whether anyone will buy their new product. If there is no interest in a product, manufacturers will not be interested in producing it. How do you think that market research would be carried out for a new product? In the next activity, you will do a little market research of your own.

PROBLEM SOLVER

WHAT DO YOU LIKE?

1 Design a **survey** form you could use to get information about what other students like or don't like about their backpacks. Keep these considerations in mind:
   - Does your form allow people to respond in privacy?
   - Will your questions provide answers that can be graphed or otherwise analyzed? Why is this important?
   - Is there a way for people to give you extra information?
   - How will you make sure your survey is completed by people who might buy a new backpack? Why does this matter?

2 Make your survey form using a computer with word processing software. Keep your form to a single page.

3 If you have permission from your teacher, use your survey form to find out what other students would like in a new design of backpack. Present your findings to the class.

Communicate

1 Angela Blades has an idea for a new type of in-line skates. What research information does she need to gather before she presents her idea to a manufacturing company? Where would she obtain this information?

2 How do you think market research is used to predict the success or failure of new television programs?

reSEARCH

It's All in the Computer

A computer **database** is a collection of **data**. The most common databases supply information on population characteristics, manufacturing statistics, and health statistics.

Customers who use debit or credit cards are entering information about their purchases into store databases each time they swipe their cards at a store. The database is used to help the store stock more of what its customers have bought.

You may have entered information into a library database when you borrowed books using a library card with a barcode on the back.

4.3 Making a Product

Explore

Think about all the things you can see in your classroom. Think about how you arrived at school this morning. Think about what you are going to eat for dinner. What do all these things, your desk, your school bus, most of your food, have in common?

Which items being used by the students in this illustration have been manufactured? Manufacturing is the process by which raw materials are assembled into finished products. Most manufacturing has changed over the years from hand-and-tool production by individual workers into automated production in modern factories.

Develop

Manufacturing

Suppose you have developed a great idea for a new product. You have researched the market and found that there are no other patents for similar products. By doing market research, you have also found out that there will be a demand for your product. Now you need to start making, or **manufacturing**, your product.

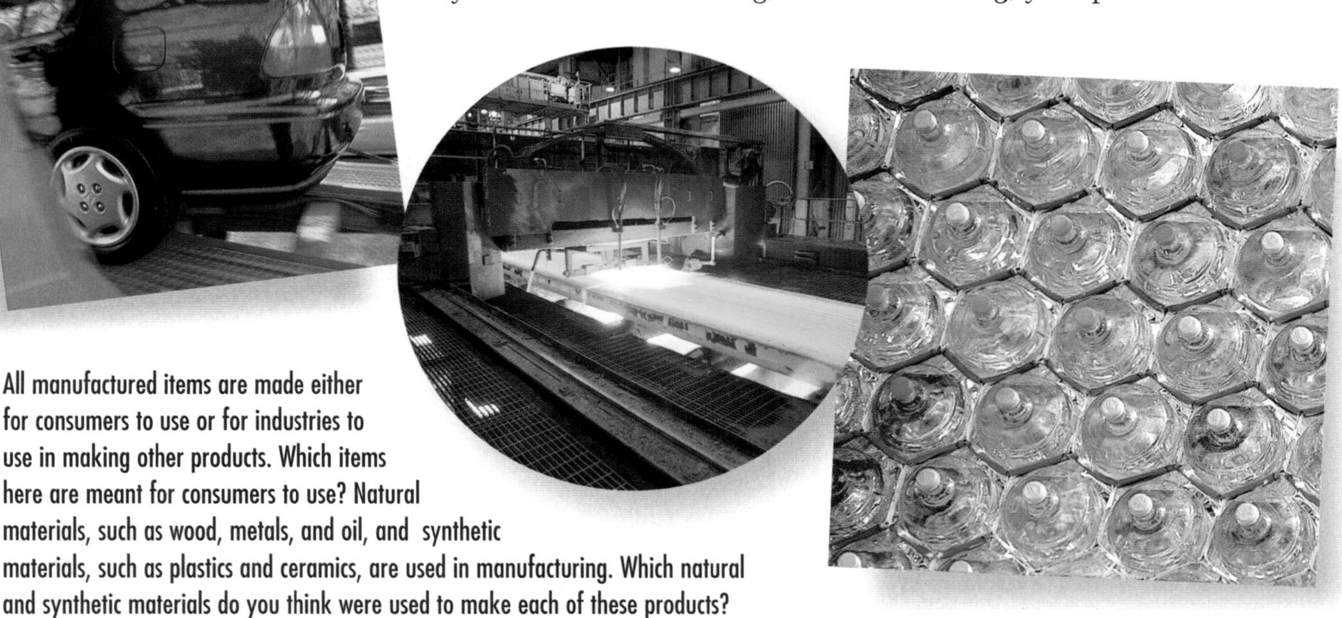

All manufactured items are made either for consumers to use or for industries to use in making other products. Which items here are meant for consumers to use? Natural materials, such as wood, metals, and oil, and synthetic materials, such as plastics and ceramics, are used in manufacturing. Which natural and synthetic materials do you think were used to make each of these products?

There are many steps involved in the manufacturing process. Let's look at how paper is manufactured.

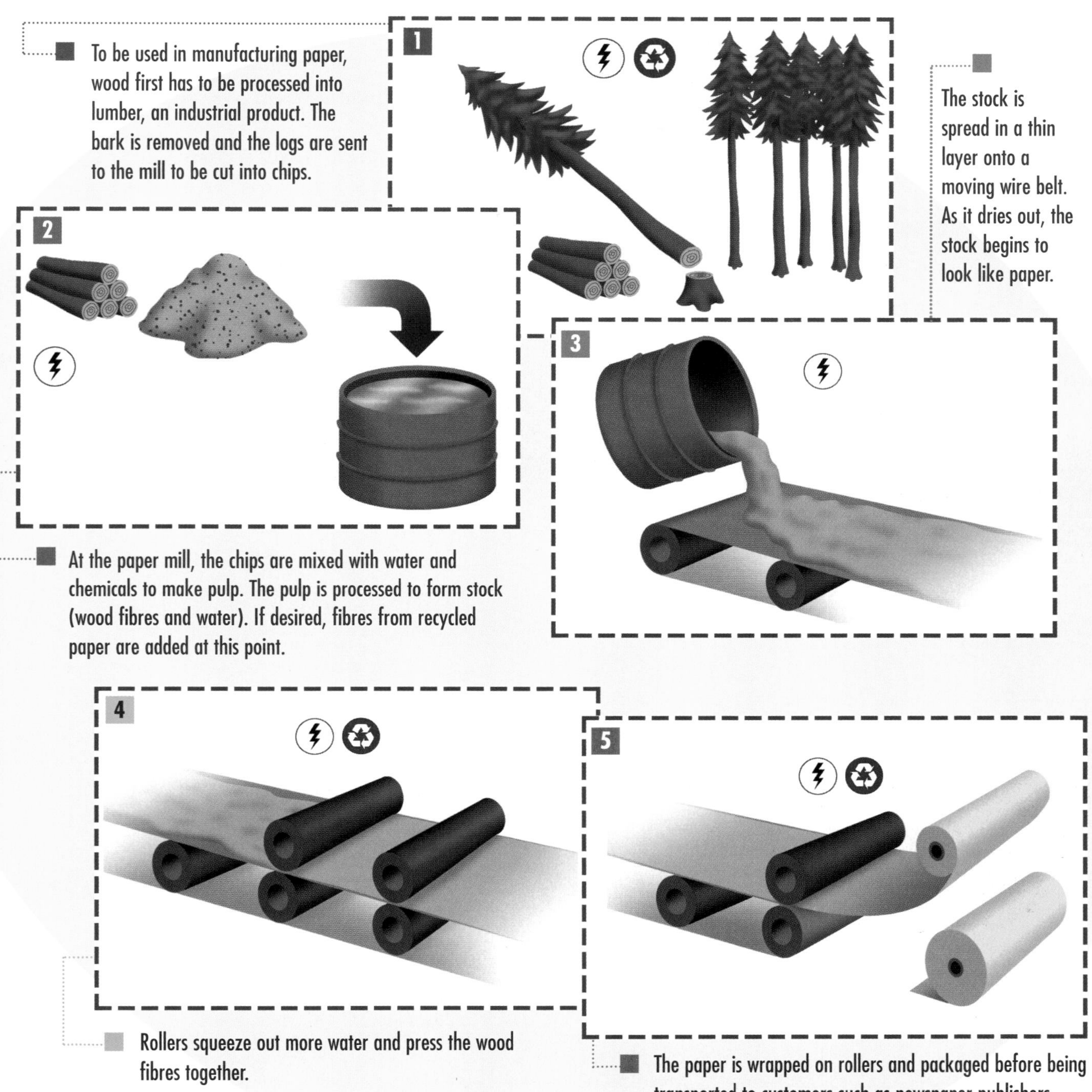

1
To be used in manufacturing paper, wood first has to be processed into lumber, an industrial product. The bark is removed and the logs are sent to the mill to be cut into chips.
2
At the paper mill, the chips are mixed with water and chemicals to make pulp. The pulp is processed to form stock (wood fibres and water). If desired, fibres from recycled paper are added at this point.
3
The stock is spread in a thin layer onto a moving wire belt. As it dries out, the stock begins to look like paper.
4
Rollers squeeze out more water and press the wood fibres together.
5
The paper is wrapped on rollers and packaged before being transported to customers such as newspaper publishers.

- The lightning bolts mark steps which require energy.
- The recycle symbols mark steps where waste materials must be removed and handled.
- Why must these two factors be considered when calculating the cost of paper?

Computer Technology

Computers have become commonplace in Canadian homes, allowing more people to work from their homes as well as offering entertainment. In the same way, computer technology has been changing manufacturing. Today, much of the manufacturing process is computer controlled, a development known as **Computer-Integrated Manufacturing** (CIM).

For example, designers use **Computer-Aided Design**, or CAD, software to produce two-dimensional and three-dimensional technical drawings. These drawings can be analyzed and redesigned by computer. Before this technology was available, designers might have to build and test several different prototypes of a new product before being satisfied. Many of these tests can now be done using the CAD software, saving time and expense. In the next activity, you will practise using CAD software.

PROBLEM SOLVER

DESIGNING WITH CAD SOFTWARE

How do you prepare a technical drawing using CAD software?

1. Using CAD software, copy this drawing. Be as accurate as you can and include a scale.
2. Once you are satisfied with your drawing, make a copy under a different file name. This will let you save your original work. Use this copy to experiment with changes to the bicycle. Save any changes you like under a new file name before experimenting further.
3. What are the advantages to designing a product using a computer? What are the disadvantages?

Computers are also used to control the operation of machines during production. Using computers to manufacture a product is called **Computer-Aided Manufacturing** (CAM). In CAM, engineers use computers for planning manufacturing processes, controlling manufacturing operations, testing finished parts, and managing entire plants. CAD is linked with CAM through a database shared by design and manufacturing engineers. Let's look at how CIM can help produce a product.

This auto manufacturer uses the latest in Computer-Integrated Manufacturing technology. It all starts with a designer using CAD software to develop an idea for a new car. The result will be a pattern for all the components of the car. This pattern will be sent to the suppliers.

Computer databases keep track of parts and other materials. Orders are sent automatically over the Internet to suppliers all over the world to make sure the manufacturer has all the parts it needs at the right time.

Quality control inspectors check the product at several points in the manufacturing process. Any adjustments that need to be made are fed into the computer control systems.

These machines, or robots, perform their tasks under computer control.

The car dealer keeps a database listing the price of different options as well as an inventory. If a customer wants a type of vehicle this dealer doesn't have in stock at the moment, the database allows the dealer to find one at another dealer and arrange for it to be delivered.

Communicate

1 What is manufacturing?
2 List three ways in which computers can be used in Computer-Integrated Manufacturing. What is the advantage of each? Are there any disadvantages?
3 Why must a manufacturer consider the cost of energy in developing a new product?

reSEARCH

- What are the raw materials used to make a car?
- Where do they come from?
- Why do the car manufacturers choose these materials?

4 STRUCTURES

4.4 MANUFACTURING AND THE ENVIRONMENT

Explore

People have been concerned about the effects that manufacturing processes have on the environment. Some manufacturing processes involve the use of hazardous chemicals that can harm the environment. As well, air and water pollution can be problems during some manufacturing processes. Even waste products connected with manufacturing can affect the environment.

You are probably familiar with recycling materials. Recycling helps reduce the need for raw materials. Using recycled materials can help manufacturers save money or even make a profit. For example, because there is such a high demand for paper that contains recycled paper, Canadian paper manufacturers use what is recycled in Canada as well as importing old newspaper from the United States.

Manufacturers can reuse materials to make new products. For example, most appliances and cars contain steel which came from scrapped cars, rail lines, or other waste parts.

Develop

Getting Rid of Waste Materials

Manufacturing produces a great deal of waste material. At one time, much of this material was thrown away. Recycling and improved production methods have reduced the amount of waste material.

PROBLEM SOLVER

REDUCING THE AMOUNT OF WASTE FROM A CONSTRUCTION PROJECT

- Make a three-column chart with these headings:

Type of Waste	The Ideal Way to Dispose of It	What Actually Happens

continued on next page

- List the waste items from the illustration, in the first column. Add any others you can think of from your projects.
- In the next column, state the ideal way to dispose of each type of waste. Which methods would best protect the environment? Would you recycle, reuse, or dispose of each type?
- Investigate your school's recycling and waste-handling procedures. In the last column, record what you find out about what actually happens to each type of waste.
- Make suggestions on how to improve your school's methods of disposing of construction waste. Try to be practical. For example, if your school is unable to recycle a certain material, is there any other place that would?

Communicate

1 The radio in the photograph doesn't use batteries. It doesn't have a plug for electricity. Instead, a few turns of the crank provide enough power for about 30 minutes of operation. More products like this are being made. Why would such devices be popular?

4.5 Improving Designs

Explore

You've been looking at how a product is created and manufactured. When you go to a store, have you ever noticed how many different kinds, or designs, of the same products are for sale? For example, if you want to buy a bicycle, you will find that there is a wide selection to choose from. All the bicycles perform the same function: they are used to get you from point A to point B. The difference is their design.

Design is also important in **packaging**. Packaging serves several functions. The most important is to protect whatever is inside, from keeping food clean and fresh to preventing breakage during shipping. It also acts as advertising. When you go to a store, do you sometimes buy a product because you like the packaging? Advertisers certainly hope so! The next time you are shopping, pay attention to the packaging used for a particular kind of product. See if you can see a trend or a pattern to the package design.

The main objective when designing a product is to make it work or function. Once the product functions properly, changes can be made to the design to make the structural parts lighter, or thinner, or cheaper. Let's look at a case study.

Develop

Rocky Mountain Bicycles

In 1978, two men in a Vancouver bike store modified a Nishiki road bike by adding wide tires, straight handlebars, and thumb shifters. This was the first "mountain bike" experience for the future "Rocky Mountain Bicycles" founders. In 1982, the "Sherpa," their first Rocky Mountain bike, was produced.

*info*BIT

In 1817, German engineer Karl von Drais introduced the Draisine, or "running machine."

In 1861, Frenchman Pierre Michaux added pedals to the front wheel. Ten years later, James Starley in England improved efficiency by increasing the size of the front wheel. The bike became known as the "penny-farthing."

The design of modern bicycles takes advantage of new light materials to reduce the weight of the bicycle. How does being light and strong affect a structure's performance?

- Since the bicycle was invented, many changes in design have taken place over the years. Can you think of reasons why the design of the bicycle has changed?

How Rocky Mountain Bicycles Makes Bikes

Before you make a new bicycle, you have to know what kind of bike people want. By doing market research, the company determines which bicycles are popular and which features, such as straight handlebars, are favoured by customers.

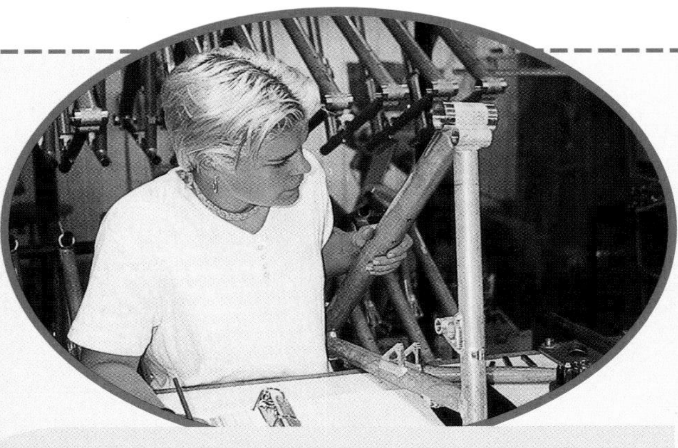

At Rocky Mountain Bicycles, the most important criteria for materials are strength, weight, and cost. Some of the materials that have the best strength-to-weight ratios are expensive and limited to only high-end bikes. Aluminum, which costs less, also has excellent strength-to-weight properties and is used to make mid- to high-end frames. Steel is generally used for mid-to low-end frames because of its generally low cost.

The traditional shape for a bicycle is basically two triangles. Hollow tubes are generally used because they provide the best strength and stiffness against forces for a given weight.

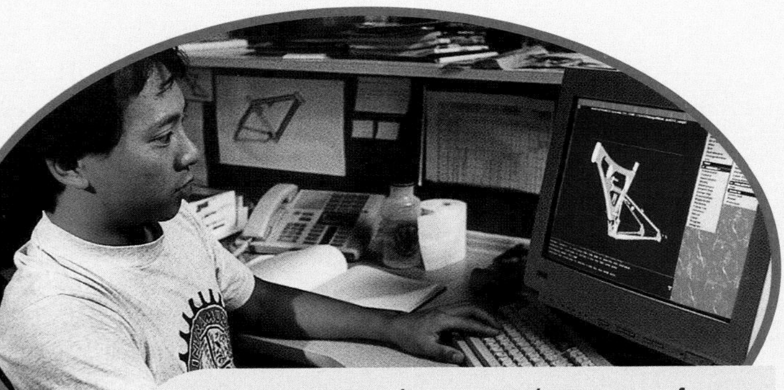

Rocky Mountain Bicycles uses CAD/CAM systems for all of its bike designs. This allows other departments in the company, such as marketing, to approve the design before an actual bike is built.

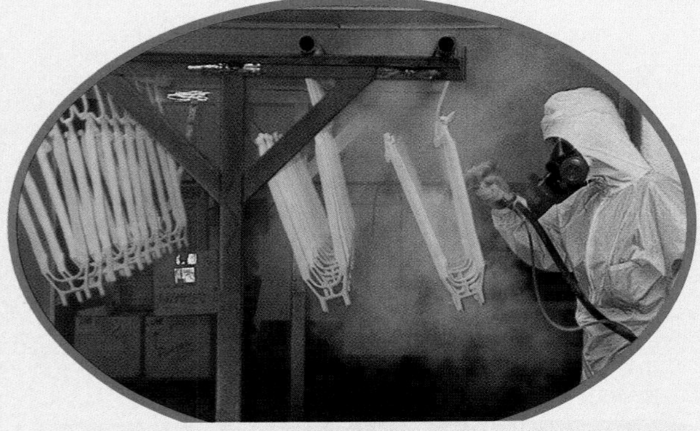

New techniques in painting use non-toxic chemicals that produce little waste. Extra material and rejected frames are cut up and recycled. Even the cardboard used for packaging is made from recycled material.

Rocky Mountain Bicycles uses a combination of trade shows, advertising in bike magazines, promotions, Web sites, and sponsorships to promote its products. It also encourages trade magazines to test and evaluate its product. However, word of mouth is the best advertisement.

A Touch of Beauty

The glint of the sun on the massive shoulder of an *inuksuk*, the gleaming paint on a new bicycle, the smooth feel of fine furniture are all things we appreciate as part of the beauty of structures. Sometimes there is a conscious effort to make a design beautiful, or aesthetically pleasing. **Aesthetics** is the study of beauty and is an important part of products people use every day, from clothing to buildings where they live and work.

Even if aesthetics hasn't been considered, the appearance of a well-made object may have a special appeal to people who see it. It is at this moment that the work of the designer, the engineer, and the builder, approaches that of the artist. Beautiful structures perform their function while enriching the lives of those who make and use them.

Communicate

1. It would be more efficient to make one style of shoe for everyone. Why are there so many styles available?
2. Advertising is all around you. What structures in your community are used for advertising? What features do these structures have in common? Why?
3. a) Write down three reasons why an item might need packaging.
   b) What are some disadvantages to packaging?
   c) Think of an example of a product you use that is sold packaged, but doesn't need to be. Think of another example of a product you use that you would only buy if sold packaged.
4. Make a flowchart to show the major steps in designing, making, and selling a new kind of bicycle. Circle any steps that require energy. Put a star beside any steps that produce waste. Underline any steps that involve research.
5. When a bicycle gets old and falls apart, who is responsible for disposing of the bicycle in an environmentally friendly way—the store that sells the bicycle or the buyer?

4.6 Check Your Progress

1. Why are products developed?
2. What is market research and why is it important?
3. What is aesthetics? List three products or structures which you consider beautiful. Explain why this beauty is important to their function.

4 Your community has enough money to build one type of recreation facility. Everyone agrees to choose the facility that serves the most people. No one seems to agree on which facility that would be.

a) Design a survey to find out which structure would serve the most people: a curling rink, an ice rink, an indoor swimming pool, or an indoor track.

b) How would you know if your results reflected a broad cross-section of the population?

5 Product packaging is designed to attract attention, to get you to recognize one packaged product from among thousands. Explain what makes a product's packaging appealing to you. When you buy something new, do you consider the packaging or the merits of the product?

What makes a bestseller: what's on the book or what's between its covers?

6 Research how one of the products below is manufactured.

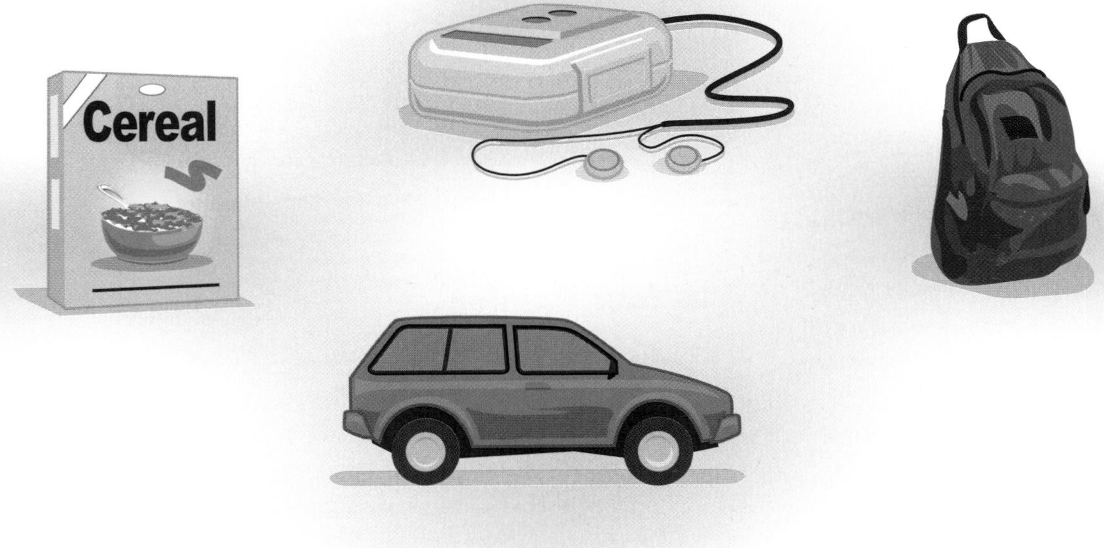

Preserve or Destroy?

Buildings were once built to be used for centuries. But today there are thousands of abandoned structures in North America: homes, offices, factories, warehouses, railroad stations—even abandoned shopping malls and plazas. To some, these rundown structures are eyesores that should be torn down and replaced with modern buildings. To others, they are things of beauty and heritage that should be preserved.

What are your views in the debate?

Why Preserve?

- Many old buildings have historical value.
- Many old buildings are beautiful and have architectural value.
- Demolishing old buildings to replace them with new ones is a waste of materials and resources.

Why Demolish?

- Many old buildings don't meet modern building codes or the needs of modern tenants.
- Old buildings that sit abandoned because they don't meet modern standards will decay in time.
- As a compromise, sometimes a part of the old building is used as a facing (or facade) for the new building.

A Compromise

Some people believe the best way to save an old building is to renovate, bringing it up to modern standards. However, there are several major concerns with this approach:

- Any renovation job, no matter how carefully done, will destroy some of the building's original character.
- Renovating is often more expensive than demolishing and rebuilding from scratch.
- Some people argue that a building can't be saved simply as an empty monument. It must have a use that generates cash.

This abandoned home was built in the 1890s.

Now it's been carefully renovated into a two-family residence.

In Your Opinion

1. For each of the concerns listed above, give an opinion that supports renovation.
2. Choose an abandoned structure in your area. What would you do with this structure: preserve, renovate, or demolish it? Give reasons for your choice.

PROJECT

THE CRAZY GADGET DESIGN CHALLENGE!

Getting Started

Each of these unusual-looking products is available in a store. Each was designed to perform a certain useful function.

- What do you think is the function of each product?
- How did you decide?

Before You Start...

Look through your notes from the activities you did in this chapter. You have learned how to design structures to withstand forces of various types. You have also learned about turning an idea into a successful new product. Now, here is your challenge: *take what you have learned and create something which moves, stands, and is fun to use.*

Answers

pencil eraser vacuum
wind chime direction finder
face cooling system

continued on next page ······➤

Developing the Process

How can you design and build an interesting gadget or device that everyone wants to use?

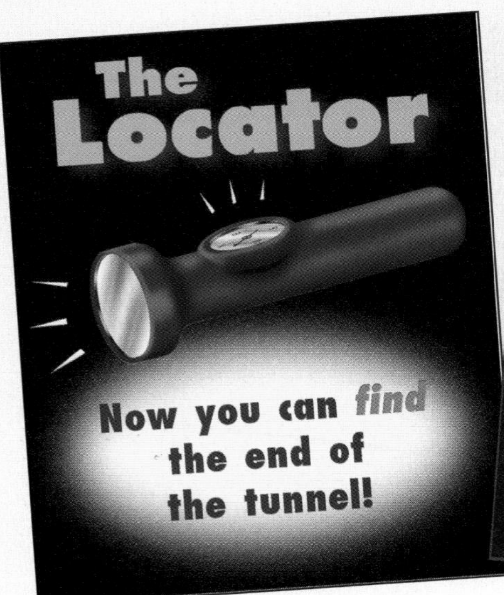

The Locator
Now you can find the end of the tunnel!

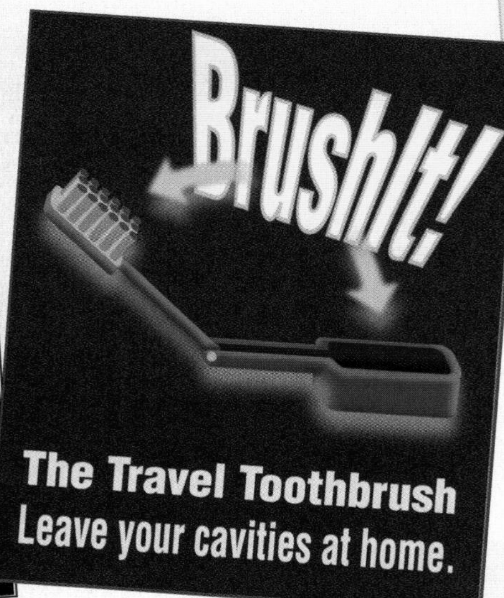

BrushIt!
The Travel Toothbrush
Leave your cavities at home.

Magifork

Eat a whole plate of spaghetti in one bite!

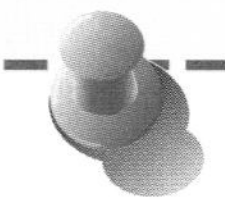

Criteria for your Crazy Gadget

Here are the criteria for your "gadget":

- ✔ It must have a name and a function. The illustrations above will give you some ideas.
- ✔ It must be safe to use.
- ✔ You must dispose of any waste materials properly.
- ✔ Record any energy you used to make your gadget.

This flowchart gives you an idea of how you could proceed with this project. Make any changes you feel necessary.

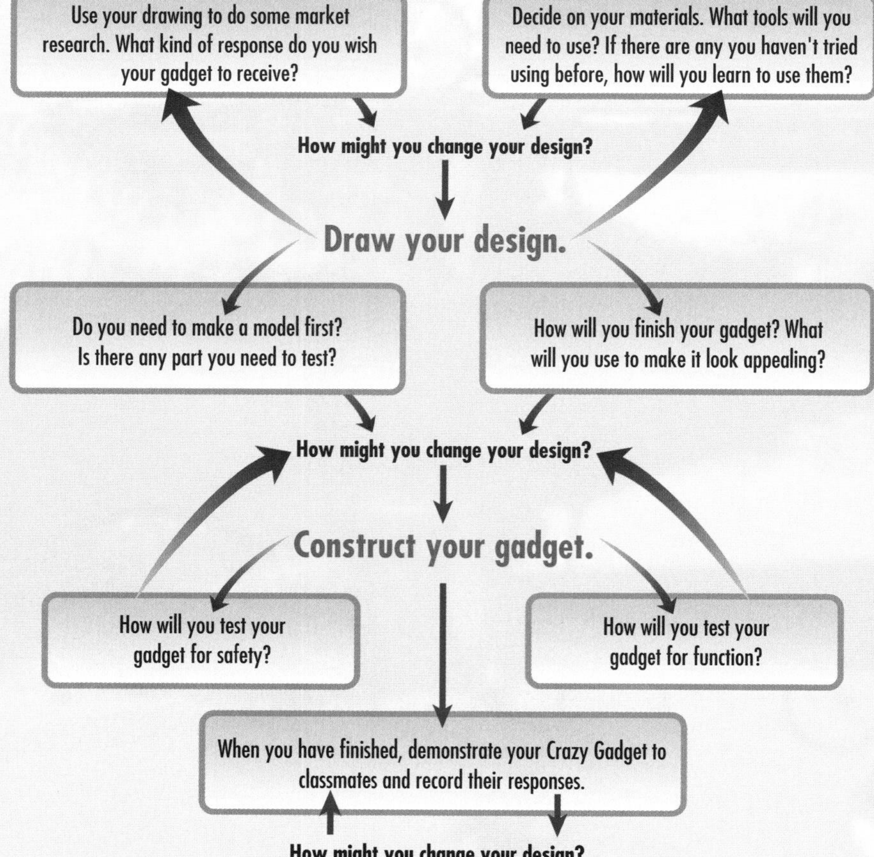

Use your drawing to do some market research. What kind of response do you wish your gadget to receive?
Decide on your materials. What tools will you need to use? If there are any you haven't tried using before, how will you learn to use them?
How might you change your design?
Draw your design.
Do you need to make a model first? Is there any part you need to test?
How will you finish your gadget? What will you use to make it look appealing?
How might you change your design?
Construct your gadget.
How will you test your gadget for safety?
How will you test your gadget for function?
When you have finished, demonstrate your Crazy Gadget to classmates and record their responses.
How might you change your design?

How helpful was your market research? What was the response of your classmates to your gadget? After looking at your classmates' gadgets, what new ideas do you have to improve yours?

Record Keeping

- ❑ Did you save all of your drawings and notes in a folder?
- ❑ Did you record the materials you used as well as any tools?
- ❑ Did you prepare a flowchart showing how you made your gadget? include any changes you made along the way and why they were necessary?
- ❑ Did you identify and describe the structural forces that were acting on the structure?

Testing and Evaluating

1. Estimate the amount of force acting on parts of the structure. Explain how you developed your estimates.
2. Identify the structural parts and explain how each part contributed to the overall purpose and design of your structure.
3. What part of this challenge did you find most difficult? Why? How did you overcome or deal with this problem?
4. What part of this challenge did you find most successful? Why?
5. Compare your final product to your original idea. Explain any changes.

Forming Conclusions

6. Describe the production of your gadget in terms of energy cost, environmental effects, and time.
7. How could you improve any of these factors if you were to build another gadget?
8. Exchange your gadget with others in your class. Can they figure out what your gadget is and what it does?

Chapter Review

Using Key Terms

1 Create a concept map of the following terms. Remember to use a couple of words or a short sentence between the terms to show how you connected these terms.

centre of gravity
complementary forces
dynamic and static load
frame, solid, and shell structures
manufacturing
market research
stability
strength
structural fatigue
structure

Reviewing the Big Ideas

2 Classify a castle, an igloo and a recreational vehicle on the basis of function.

3 Make a Venn diagram to compare the design and function characteristics of ice skates and in-line skates.

4 What is the difference between solid, frame, and shell structures?

5 What is the centre of gravity and why is it important to consider when designing a structure?

6 Why are most large structures symmetrical?

7 What are the different types of bridges that can be used to support a load? Use a labelled diagram to illustrate the similarities and differences between them.

8 Give an example of a dynamic and a static load. How are these two examples the same and how are they different?

9 Describe the four different types of internal forces.

10 A container is needed to hold a collection of fifty music CDs. The container should have easy access to all discs and should be able to withstand being dropped. What shape would you use? Why?

11 What types of beams can you identify in this structure?

12 Why do you think houses in Ontario have more brick in them than houses in British Columbia?

13 What types of careers could you pursue that are related to structures? Which one seems the most interesting to you? Why is this?

14 If you have an idea for an invention, what are the steps you would have to consider to get the product ready to sell to people?

15 How can computers help in the manufacturing of a product?

16 What are some actions you can take to help protect the environment when you are building a structure or producing something?

Connecting the Big Ideas

17 If you were to design a picnic table, would you pay more attention to the function or the design characteristics? Why?

18 What structural shapes and materials would you use to build a observation tower in a bird sanctuary?

19 From your experiences, what do you think is the best type of structure to hold up a large mass? What evidence can you provide to support your opinion?

20 How does your body respond to the four internal forces? Give an example for each.

21 A broken beam in a frame structure was found to crack along the lower surface first. How could you redesign the beam to account for this problem?

22 Describe what forces are acting on this bridge, what the result is and what you think will happen. Your description should include the words dynamic load, internal forces, external forces and structural fatigue.

23 You have the choice of building a bicycle storage shed with either wood or concrete bricks. Create a chart that demonstrates the benefits and costs of using each type of material. Your chart should include the information on the type of structure, shape of the structure and the type of material to be used. Once you have completed your chart, select a material and describe why you chose it using the information you collected.

24 Market research involves collecting information from people. This information helps you make decisions about how you will sell the product you are making. Listed below are several different ways market surveys can be collected. Identify the advantages and disadvantages of each method:

a) interviewing people
b) telephoning people at home
c) electronically monitoring people's spending habits
d) asking people's opinions in focus groups

Using the Big Ideas

25 a) What do you think might happen to this crane if it tried to pick up the load?

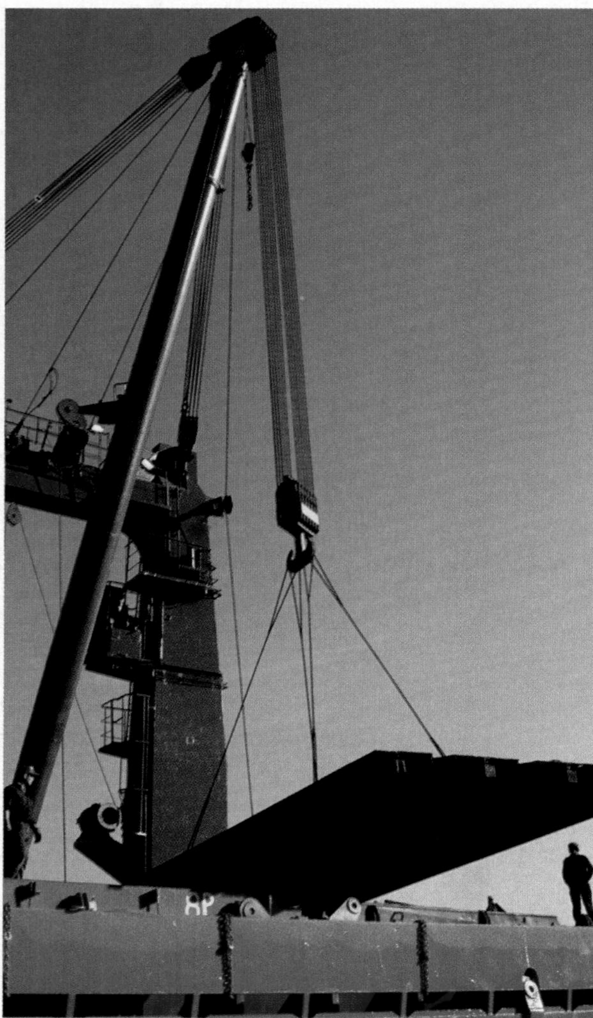

b) How could you modify the crane to get it to lift the load?

26 Your class is creating a time capsule to be opened by students at your school in 100 years. In the time capsule will be a letter from each person in your class and an object that represents something important to each person. Your task is to design a structure to hold these materials and identify a place to store the structure.

27 You have been asked to design a short foot bridge across a muddy section of the schoolyard. Develop the plans needed to build this structure. You should have a diagram of the structure, a list of materials, and a brief description of how to assemble the bridge.

Self Assessment

28 Think back on everything you did during this chapter, from the Wind Challenge, to designing signs, to learning about how new bikes are developed. Use your thoughts to answer the following questions:

- The most surprising part of the Structures chapter for me was:
- During my study of structures, the toughest thing was:
- I solved this by:
- I would like to find out more about:
- I still have a question about:
- My advice to someone starting this chapter would be:
- What I liked most about structures was:

29 Create a poem or picture that illustrates three things you will remember about this chapter.

THE EARTH'S CRUST

Chapter 5

land use

The first astronauts described the earth as a "blue pearl in space." But our world isn't an island of shining calm floating in space. It's a planet of constant motion and change. Intense heat from deep inside the earth creates volcanoes that gush lava. Huge plates moving across its surface cause earthquakes that shake and split the ground. Mountains grow toward the sky. Weather and water wear them down and carry them away.

In this chapter, you will discover the powerful forces that shape our earth. You'll find out what the earth's surface is made of and why it's important to us. And you'll see how humans can determine what effect they'll have on their home planet. You're invited to join the earth exploration expedition.

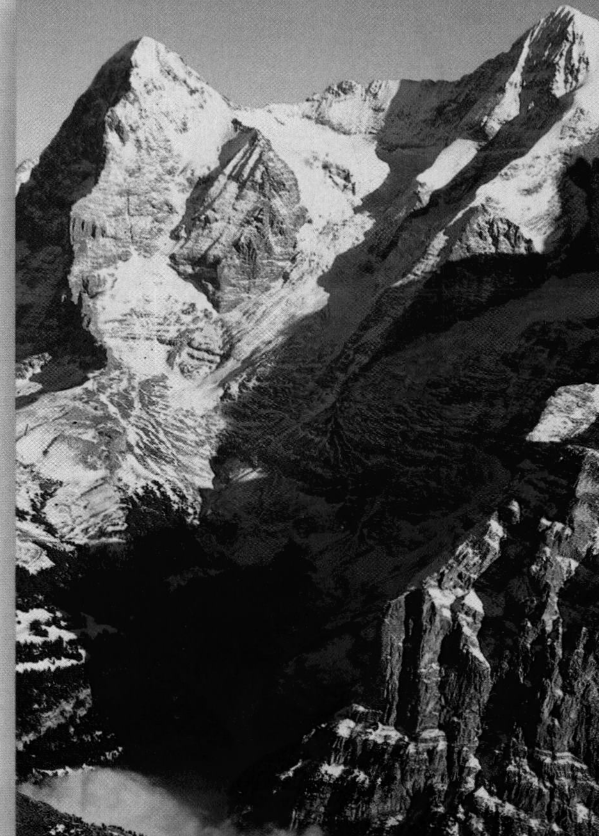

weathering

BIG Ideas

1.0 The crust is the earth's solid outer layer.

2.0 Processes within the earth cause natural events.

3.0 Rocks and minerals can be classified by their composition and by how they formed.

4.0 The rock cycle describes how rocks form and change over time.

5.0 Knowing the characteristics of soil can help you understand how it can be used and conserved.

6.0 We can make informed decisions about how our actions might affect the landscape.

tectonics

Invitation to Explore

Earth-Shattering Events
COLLECTOR'S CARDS
Mountain blows its top! On May 18, 1980, Mount St. Helens in Washington State exploded. Gas and ash shot 19 km into the sky. The mountain's top collapsed—it lost 400 m of its original height!

Earth-Shattering Events
COLLECTOR'S CARDS
Shocking shock waves! At 5:46 a.m. on January 17, 1995, residents of Kobe, Japan, were thrown from their beds by a massive earthquake. Broken gas lines led to huge fires. Thousands died.

The dramatic events on these collector's cards describe the powerful forces at work within the earth. Both of these events changed the earth's surface quickly in some way.

- Where do you think earthquakes and volcanoes are most likely to happen?
- Have you ever felt an earthquake or seen a volcano?

Volcanic eruptions and major earthquakes always make the news. They happen suddenly, often destroying property and even taking lives. Events like these grab our attention, but the earth's surface is constantly changing—not just when the ground shakes or lava flows.

These changes are sometimes caused by processes that take place so deep below the surface that we can't see them. But we can see their results. Mountains form because of some of these deep processes. Other processes happen right on the surface. Rocks and other earth materials are being worn down and carried away by water and wind. Sometimes this happens quickly in landslides, but more often it happens so slowly that we don't notice.

Look at the photos below. They show situations in which rock or rock materials are being worn down. Discuss with a partner what is happening in each photo and answer these questions in your Science Journal.

- What is being worn down?
- What is wearing it down?
- Do you think this is happening slowly or quickly?
- What happens to the material that results from the wearing down process?

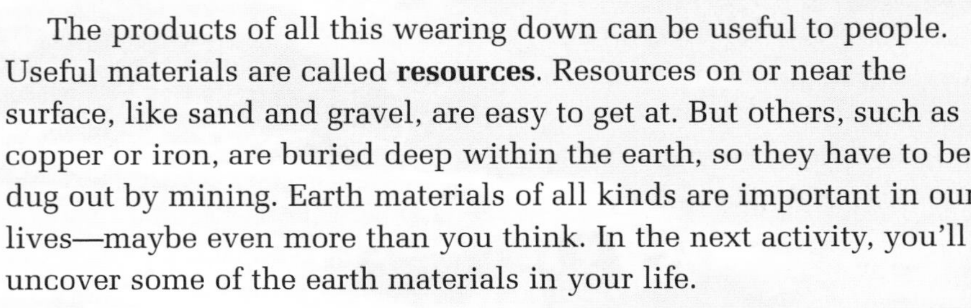

The products of all this wearing down can be useful to people. Useful materials are called **resources**. Resources on or near the surface, like sand and gravel, are easy to get at. But others, such as copper or iron, are buried deep within the earth, so they have to be dug out by mining. Earth materials of all kinds are important in our lives—maybe even more than you think. In the next activity, you'll uncover some of the earth materials in your life.

PROBLEM SOLVER

SEARCHING FOR EARTH MATERIALS

An **earth material** is anything that is made of or comes from rocks, minerals, soil, etc. Look around you right now. Do you see any rocks or minerals?

Start outside your school. If possible, stand across the street and look at the front of the school. Working with a small group, sketch what you see, and label as many things as you can that you think have earth materials in them.

- Are there any cars or trucks in front of the school? Include those in your picture.
- Are there any flower beds or lawns? What are the plants growing in?
- What is the outside of the school covered with? Is that covering made from an earth material?

For anything you're unsure about, put a question mark beside it.

Share your sketch with other groups. Did everyone notice the same things? Add anything to your sketch that your group may have missed.

Do you think you'd find as many things made of earth materials inside your classroom? With your group, look around your classroom and make a list of all the things you can see that might be made of earth materials.

Here's some information that might help you.

- Glass is made from sand.
- Steel is made from iron and other substances that come from minerals in the earth.
- Concrete is made from sand and gravel.
- Pavement (called *asphalt*) is made from sand, gravel, and heavy oil.
- Bricks are made from clay. The filler between them is made from sand and limestone.

The study of ecosystems teaches us that we are connected to all life on earth. Looking at how much we use earth materials in our lives shows another way that we depend on the earth. But our use of the earth's materials really just "scratches the surface"—the earth's surface! In this chapter, you have the opportunity to explore forces deep within the earth that affect the surface. And you'll discover how these forces interact with those on the surface to shape the planet you live on.

Focus Your Thoughts

1 Take a look around your own neighbourhood for examples of places where rocks or other earth materials, such as soil, are being worn down. Draw or take a picture of your examples. Note where you saw them and what you think is happening in each situation. With your classmates, design a poster or a Web page that combines all the examples into a display of local earth changes. As you explore the earth's crust in this chapter, add more information to your poster or Web page.

2 Look at the list of words below.

erosion	volcano	rock slide
mountain building	landslide	convection
earthquake	weathering	plate tectonics

a) Choose the words that describe processes that you think usually take place *deep within the earth.* If you can, write a one-sentence description of what the term means. If you're not sure, write what you'd like to know about it.

b) Now choose the words that describe processes that you think usually take place *on the surface of the earth.* If you can, write a one-sentence description of what the term means. If you're not sure, write what you'd like to know about it.

3 The city in this photograph is in Iceland. All the buildings in the community are heated by naturally hot water that comes from deep below the earth's surface.

a) Why do you think this water is so hot?

b) Iceland is famous for its volcanoes. Do you think there's any connection between the volcanoes and the hot water? If so, what connection?

c) What do the volcanoes and this hot water tell us about the earth's interior?

4 At the beginning of this Invitation, two collector's cards were shown from a series called "Earth-Shattering Events." Suggest another card you would add to the series that would describe another type of earth event. You don't have to name a place or date—just the type of event. What kind of a photo would you include on the card? What would the text say?

5 Review the list you made for Searching for Earth Materials.

a) Which items were manufactured from earth materials?

b) Choose three of these products and tell what you think happens to them when they are no longer useful.

Reykjavik, Iceland is heated by geothermal energy.

Big Idea

1.0 The crust is the earth's solid outer layer.

Think of the earth's long history as a story, a cross between an adventure and a mystery. The adventure part of the story is about people facing the powerful forces of the earth—earthquakes, mountain building, volcanoes—in their efforts to understand it. The mystery is about the fact that we can't easily see inside our home planet. We live on its outermost skin. How do we get inside it? How can we understand our planet better?

1.1 Inside the Earth

Explore

If a friend offered you a fruit that you had never seen before, would you take a big bite right away? You'd probably want to know something about it first. How thick is the skin? Is the inside soft or firm? You wouldn't want to break any teeth, so you'd want to know if it has anything in the centre. Does it have a stone, like a plum, or a core, like an apple? What would be the easiest way to find out the answers to your questions?

Develop

Looking into the Earth

Scientists have been investigating similar questions about the earth for a long time. How thick is its outer skin? Is the interior solid? What does the centre of the earth look like? The earth may be round, like many fruits are, but it's much too large to cut in half. Because the earth is so large, we have to use a model to help us understand its inner structure.

Using a model is a way of demonstrating an object or an idea that is difficult to see in its real form. Models are useful when something is too big or too small or too complicated for us to study easily. That's why a globe and other models are useful in studying the earth. Take a look at some possible models of the earth in the next activity and see how well they work.

THE INSIDE STORY

- You can learn a lot about the earth by looking at a globe. For example, it shows you where the equator is. What other information about the earth can you get by looking at a globe? In your Science Journal, list as many pieces of information as you can think of that you can get from a globe. Does a globe tell you anything about the interior of the earth?
- Look at the photographs on this page. Do you think that any of these items would make a good model for the interior of the earth? Give reasons for your answer.

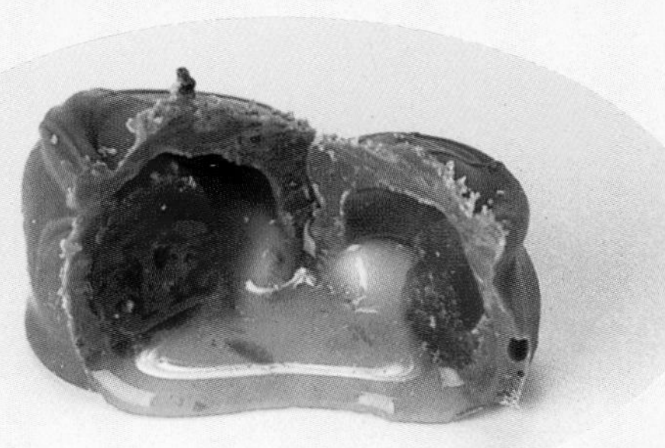

- Sketch another model for the exterior and interior of the earth. What does a model tell you about a thing or a process?

You know a lot about the earth's surface because you see it every day. But there's more to the earth than its surface. The earth is a planet made of three major layers. Imagine that you could travel deep inside it in a special vehicle. This vehicle would have to withstand very high temperatures and pressures. It would need special equipment so it could travel through both molten rock and solid rock. ("Molten" rock is another term for liquid rock.) Pack your imagination, climb into *Earth Explorer,* and begin your voyage!

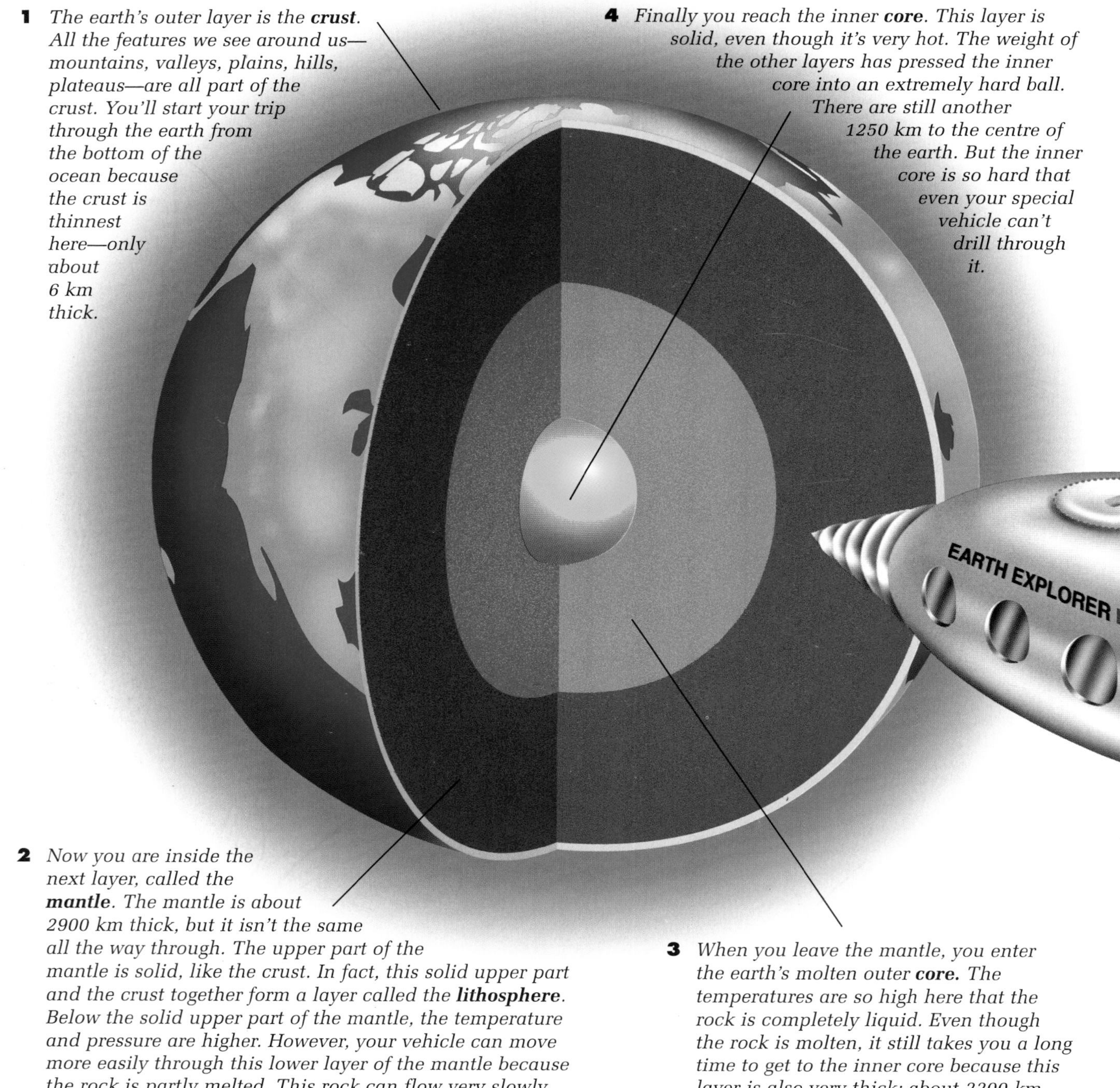

1 *The earth's outer layer is the* ***crust****. All the features we see around us—mountains, valleys, plains, hills, plateaus—are all part of the crust. You'll start your trip through the earth from the bottom of the ocean because the crust is thinnest here—only about 6 km thick.*

2 *Now you are inside the next layer, called the* ***mantle****. The mantle is about 2900 km thick, but it isn't the same all the way through. The upper part of the mantle is solid, like the crust. In fact, this solid upper part and the crust together form a layer called the* ***lithosphere****. Below the solid upper part of the mantle, the temperature and pressure are higher. However, your vehicle can move more easily through this lower layer of the mantle because the rock is partly melted. This rock can flow very slowly.*

3 *When you leave the mantle, you enter the earth's molten outer* ***core.*** *The temperatures are so high here that the rock is completely liquid. Even though the rock is molten, it still takes you a long time to get to the inner core because this layer is also very thick: about 2200 km.*

4 *Finally you reach the inner* ***core****. This layer is solid, even though it's very hot. The weight of the other layers has pressed the inner core into an extremely hard ball. There are still another 1250 km to the centre of the earth. But the inner core is so hard that even your special vehicle can't drill through it.*

What Is the Crust Made Of?

The layer of the earth that you know best is the **crust**, because you live on its surface. Plants and animals also live here. The crust is the layer we mine for minerals, such as iron ore, that we depend on for products of all kinds. Our energy supplies of oil, natural gas, and coal also come from the crust.

The crust is the thinnest layer of the earth. Its average thickness is about 50 km, but it's only about 6 km thick under the oceans. It is much thicker where it forms the continents. Under big mountain ranges like the Rocky Mountains, it can be up to 90 km thick. The total distance from the surface of the crust to the earth's centre is about 6400 km.

What do you think the crust is made of? The soil, plants, and even the oceans that we see on the surface form only a thin covering on the crust. The crust is made of solid rock. But as you can see from these photos and from your own observations of the earth's surface, rocks don't all look the same. Later in this chapter, you'll investigate the different kinds of rocks and how they form.

Marble quarry

Basalt outcrop

*info***BIT**

The Canadian Shield is the name given by geologists to the largest area of ancient crust rocks in the world. These rocks are rich in minerals such as copper, nickel, zinc, cobalt, silver, and gold. Most of Ontario is on the Canadian Shield, but the shield is much bigger than Ontario. It starts in the Arctic and extends south into the United States. It goes as far as Alberta in the west and Labrador in the east. The typical shield landscape has thin soil, bare rocks, and many lakes, ponds, rivers, and streams.

- Do you live on the Canadian Shield? How would you know?

Communicate

1 With a ruler and a pair of compasses, draw and label your own diagram of the earth's interior. Try to make your drawing to scale. For example, 1 cm could represent 500 km, or 1000 km, etc.

a) How many major layers are there beneath the earth's crust?

b) Which layer is the thickest? Which is the thinnest?

c) On your diagram, show which layers are solid and which are molten.

2 In 1864, Jules Verne wrote a book called *Journey to the Centre of the Earth*. In the book, a group of people enter the earth through a volcano. As they travel down through the earth, they see plants and animals unlike any on the surface. Finally they reach the centre. Is any of this possible? Explain your answer.

The Mediterranean Sea

1.2 Finding Out about the Earth

Explore

When you watch a TV or movie mystery, do you try to solve it along with the detective? Detectives look for clues in the connections between events and between characters. Who was near the scene of the crime? Who could have carried it out? They also look for patterns in events. Was it similar to any other crimes? Did any other similar crimes happen nearby? Investigating the earth's structure is like solving a mystery. With a partner, brainstorm what you would like to find out and where you would look for clues if you were a scientist wanting to find out more about the earth.

Develop

Clues to the Earth's Structure

Just as detectives do, scientists look for patterns and connections in their observations as they try to solve the mystery of the earth's structure and composition. Through research, scientists have collected information about the earth's surface. They have learned that the rocks that form the continents are different from those that form the ocean floors. The crust under the oceans is made of rocks that are heavier than those that form the continents.

Scientists have also studied the major features on the continents and the ocean floors. They noticed patterns in structures, such as mountains, and in events, such as earthquakes. In the next activity, you can look at these patterns for yourself.

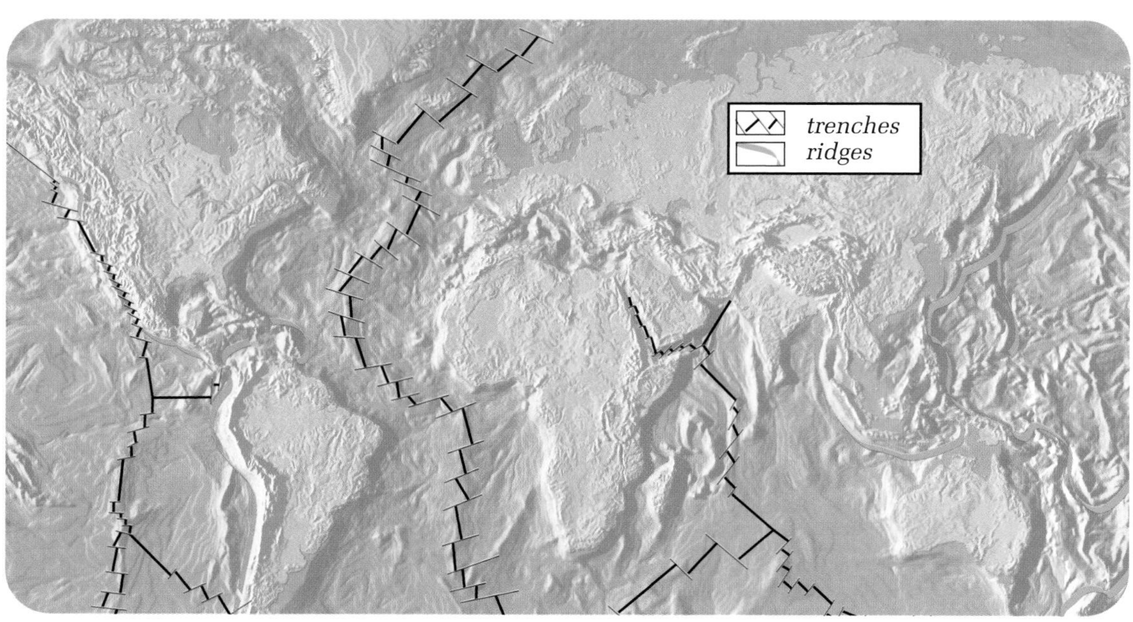

This map shows the major features scientists discovered when they surveyed the ocean floors. They found deep valleys called **trenches** and mountain chains called **ridges**.

PROBLEM SOLVER

FASCINATING PATTERNS

The map on the previous page shows the major features that scientists discovered when they surveyed the ocean floors. Make your own copy of this map. On it, use one colour of highlighter pen to show the ridges on the ocean floor and another colour for the trenches. Use a detailed map of the ocean floor from an atlas to help you. Then answer the questions below.

- How close are the trenches to the continents?
- Which are usually close to the continents: the ridges or the trenches?

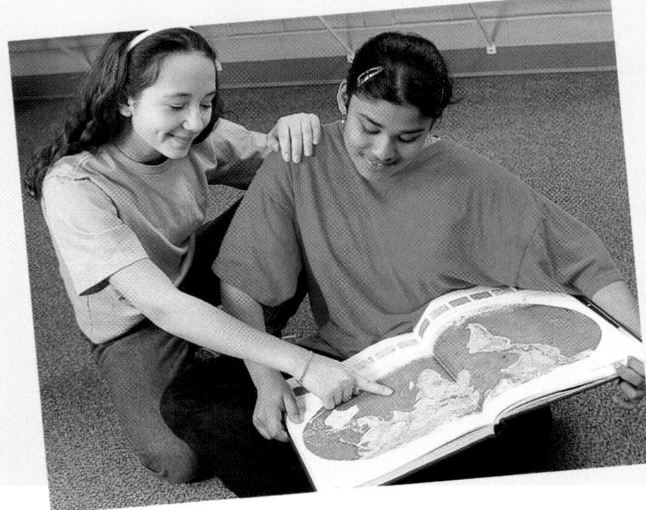

- Do you see a pattern in the position of the trenches?

Scientists also plot information about earthquakes and volcanoes on maps, adding other information about features on the earth's surface, such as the location of large mountain ranges. Plan on how to use your map to search for worldwide patterns. (This is what scientists do.)

- What features do you need to add to your map to make it more complete?
- Where will you get the information you need?
- How will you decide if there is a pattern or patterns in the data on your map?

Look carefully at all the information you've plotted on your map. Can you see any interesting patterns? Make a list of questions that you would like to have answered about this information. Work with a partner to answer as many of these questions as you can. As you work through this chapter, write down any answers you may find to the rest of your questions.

The Theory of an Active Earth

Scientists looked at the patterns like the ones you saw on your map, and they noticed two important things:

- They saw that most earthquakes and volcanoes are concentrated along narrow strips of land.
- They saw that there were very large areas with few or no earthquakes or volcanoes.

Their research showed that volcanoes were erupting along the ridges on the ocean floors, producing new oceanic crust rocks. It also showed that the ocean floor was moving away from the ocean ridges and toward the deep trenches. Scientists used all this information to develop the **Theory of Plate Tectonics**.

reSEARCH

The Internet is an excellent source of information on recent earthquakes and volcanic activity. Use one the Internet search "engines" to find up-to-date facts to add to your map.

*info***BIT**

Sometimes, important insights in science are discovered using methods other than experimentation. Alfred Wegener (1880–1930) was a scientist who studied the weather, but he was interested in everything about the earth. Looking at maps, he noticed that the coastlines of South America and Africa seemed to fit together. That was the beginning of the Theory of Plate Tectonics.

In the early 1960s, Canadian geophysicist, J. Tuzo Wilson (1908–1993) suggested another interesting theory about the earth. Volcanic islands like Hawaii were formed, he thought, by one plate moving over a fixed "hot spot" in the earth's mantle. His theory was at first rejected by the science community. Later, evidence was found to support this and other of his ideas on Plate Tectonics.

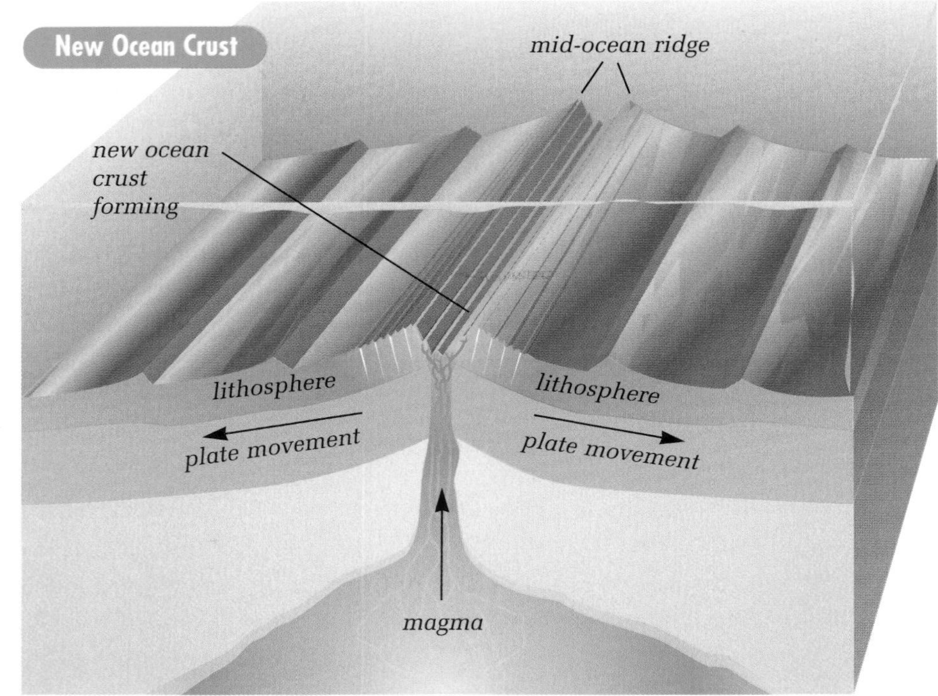

Deep under water, new crust is forming continuously from lava at mid-ocean ridges.

The Lithosphere

Earlier in this chapter, you discovered that the earth isn't just one big solid piece of rock. You learned that the earth has layers, and only some of these layers are made of solid rock. The layer that you know best—the earth's crust—is one of those layers. Look again at your diagram of the earth's interior. What is the layer below the crust called? Remember that the upper part of this layer is solid rock, like the crust. Together with the crust it forms the **lithosphere.**

According to the Theory of Plate Tectonics, the lithosphere is broken up into large areas called **plates**. Look back at your map from the last Problem Solver activity. You can see the shapes of many of these plates, outlined by the trenches and ocean ridges. The plates usually carry both continental and oceanic crust. All of these plates are moving very slowly over the surface of the earth. The next activity suggests a possible explanation of why the plates move.

Aerial view of South America and Africa

The Plates of the Earth

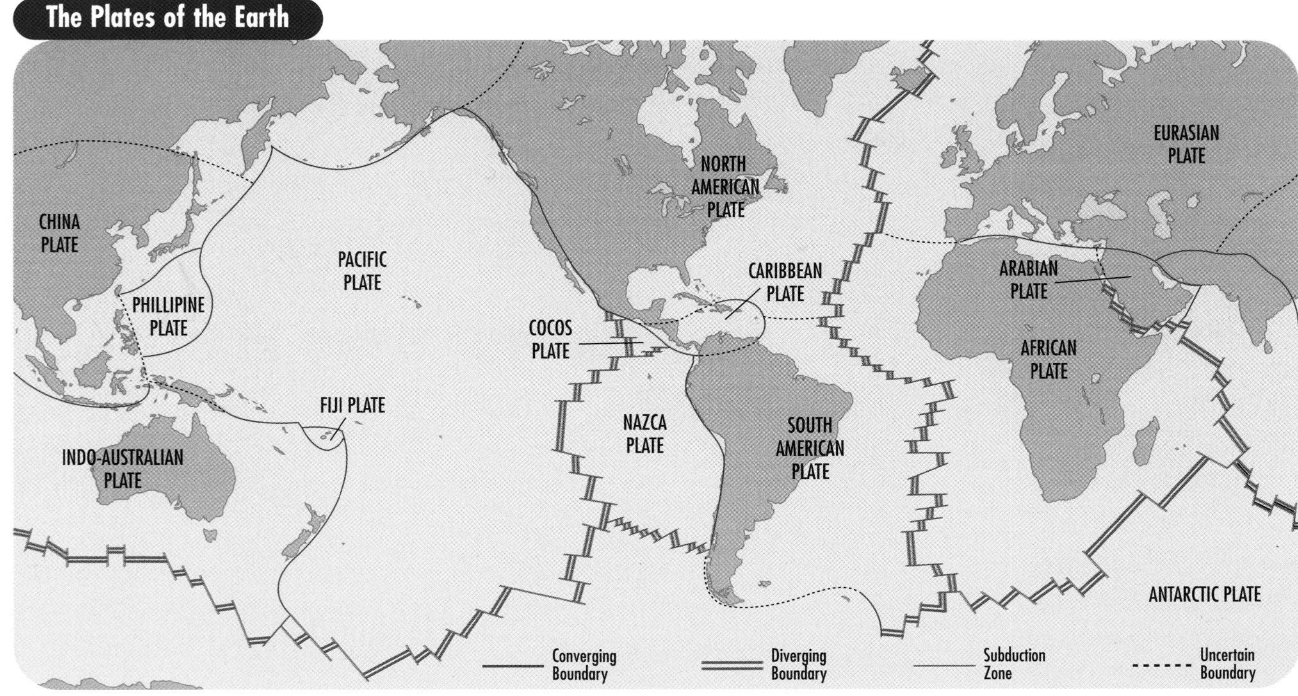

The earth's lithosphere is broken up into many large and small plates. The plates are all solid rock, but they "float" on the partly melted layer of the mantle below the lithosphere.

PROBLEM SOLVER

WHAT MAKES THE PLATES MOVE?

We can't see directly into the earth. However, through research, scientists have learned that the layer below the lithosphere isn't solid. It's likely that convection currents in this part of the mantle below the plates cause them to move. **Convection** is the transfer of heat energy that happens when a heated fluid moves from one location to another. You can learn more about convection in Chapter 3: Heat.

The pot of boiling water in this diagram is a model of the convection currents that move in the earth's interior.

- What does the water in the pot represent?
- What do you think would happen to anything floating on the surface of this water?

- The heating element on the stove causes the convection currents in the water. What do you think might cause them in the earth's mantle?

Communicate

1 Add information from the Theory of Plate Tectonics to your diagram of the earth you drew earlier. What did you add? Why?
2 What does the word *plate* refer to in the Theory of Plate Tectonics?
3 Add the outlines of the plates and their names to the map you worked on earlier in this section.

*info***BIT**

Scientists use Global Positioning System (or GPS) satellites to track the movements of the earth's plates. They receive data showing them exactly how far and in what directions the plates are moving.

1.3 WHAT HAPPENS WHEN PLATES MEET?

Explore

Think about what you've learned about the lithosphere so far. You know that it's made of plates that are always moving. But what happens at the edges of these plates? How can they keep moving if they run into each other? What happens when plates meet? The edges where plates meet are called **boundaries**. These boundaries look different depending on whether plates are moving away from each other, into each other, or alongside each other.

Develop

Movements at Plate Boundaries

The following diagrams show what happens at the different types of plate boundaries around the world. Keep your map of the plates handy as you go through this section so you can see where the different boundaries are.

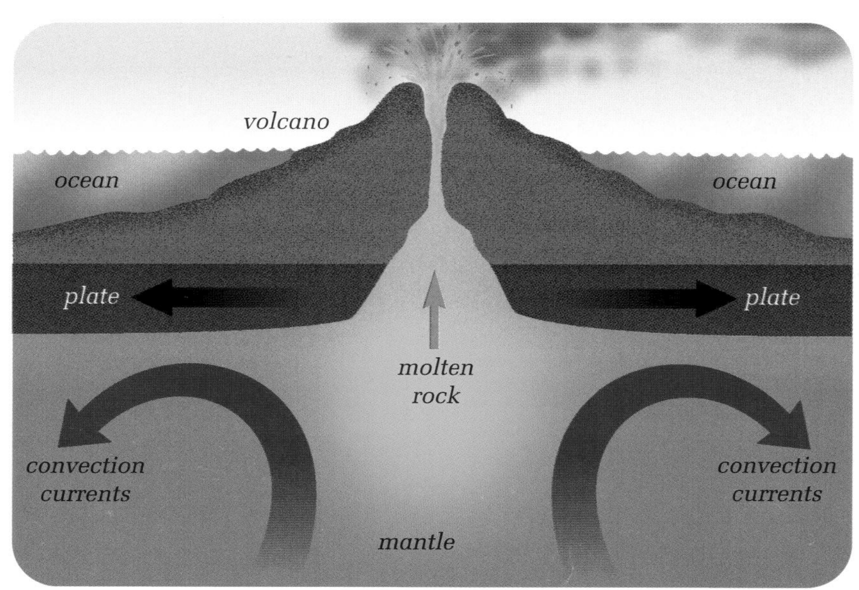

A **diverging boundary** is one where plates are moving apart. The Mid-Atlantic Ridge on the floor of the Atlantic Ocean is an example of a diverging boundary. At these boundaries, lava flows from the ridge to form new oceanic crust. Sometimes volcanoes grow tall enough that they are visible above the ocean's surface, like those that form Iceland. Look at the map on the previous page to find these boundaries.

At **converging boundaries**, plates come together. Although plates move very slowly, they are so huge that we experience the effects of their collision. We can feel the earthquakes and see the mountains, including volcanoes, that grow at or near these boundaries. There are two kinds of converging boundaries.

One kind of converging boundary happens where a trench forms. One plate carries oceanic crust, and the other one carries continental crust. As they push together, the heavier, thinner oceanic crust is forced down below the lighter, thicker continental crust. As one grinds down past the other, earthquakes rumble, and the continental crust wrinkles to form mountains. The oceanic crust moves lower into the earth and gets hotter and melts. This molten rock rises in some places to form volcanoes. Which mountain range in Canada is formed by this process?

The second kind of converging boundary happens where two plates with continental crust move up against each other. They crush together to form huge mountain ranges. Which high mountain range in Asia is being formed by this process?

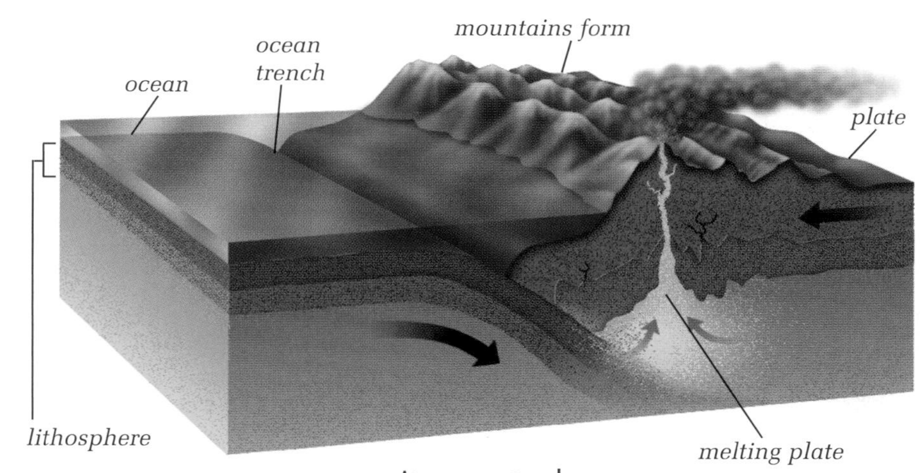

At an ocean trench

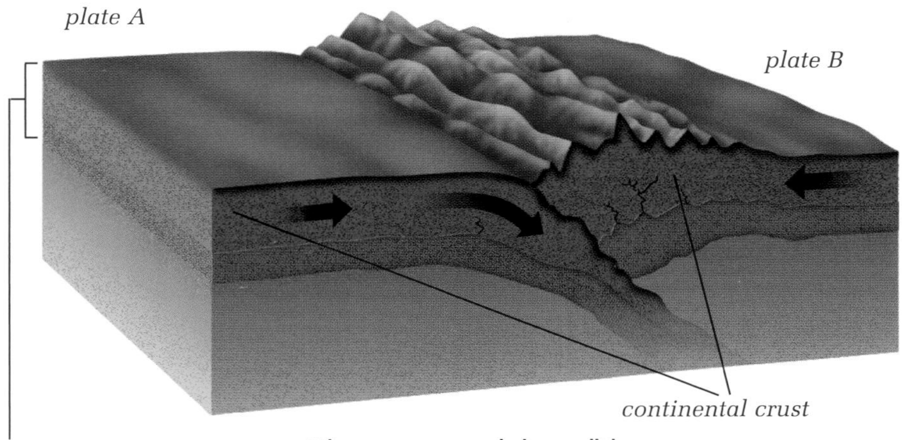

When two continental plates collide

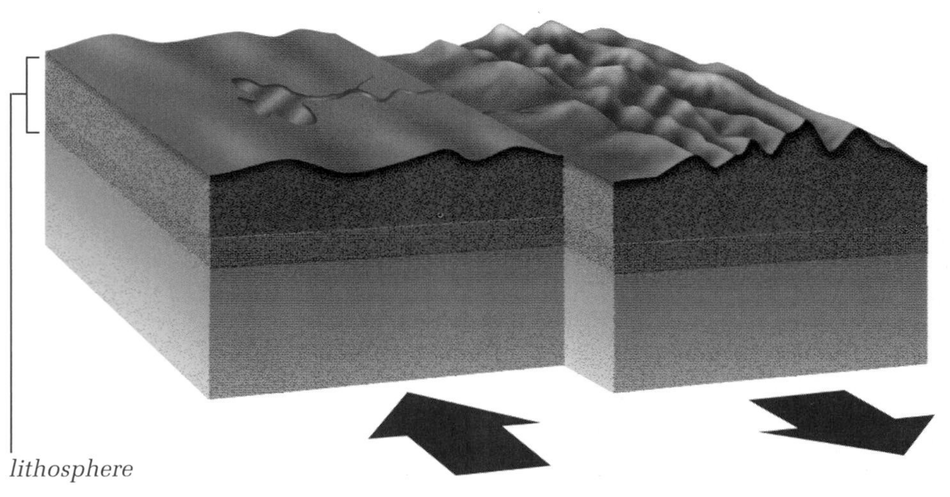

Two plates slide

The third type of boundary is a **transform boundary**. Here, plates slide along beside each other. But this sliding doesn't take place smoothly. The rocks bind and catch on each other, causing earthquakes. You can find a transform boundary along the west coast of the United States.

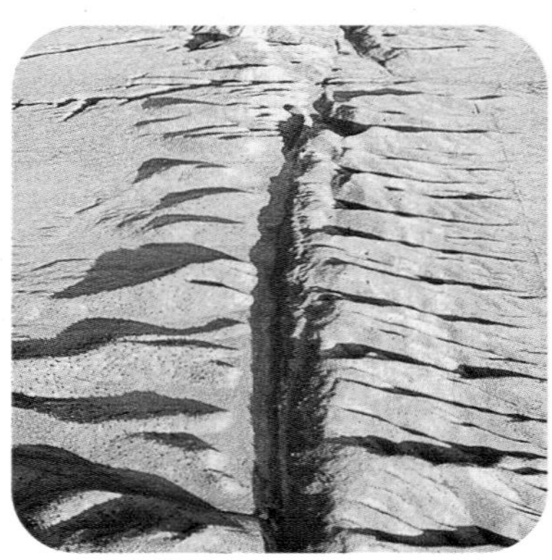

The San Andreas fault is a crack in the earth's crust that runs along part of the west coast of the United States.

Iceland is growing wider because it sits right on top of a plate boundary.

Communicate

1 Most plate boundaries are under oceans, but some can be seen on land in different parts of the world. What kind of boundary is shown in each photo at left? Describe what is happening there.

1.4 Check Your Progress

1 Why do we use models when we study the earth?

2 Describe one of the patterns that scientists found in this Big Idea. What did it tell them about the earth?

3 What does the Theory of Plate Tectonics say about:

a) what causes the plates to move on the earth's surface?

b) the ridges on the ocean floors?

4 Name the following types of boundaries.

a) At an ocean trench, one plate is forced to move down below another one.

b) Plates move apart at mid-ocean ridges.

c) Plates slide past each other.

d) Plates push up against each other and create mountains.

try this at **HOME**

Cake Plates

Make a cake model that demonstrates how plates move.

Procedure

1 Make a chocolate cake. Bake it on aluminum foil inside a cake pan. Let it cool and take it on the aluminum foil out of the pan.

2 Now, use a knife to make a straight cut across the middle of the cake, but only part way down to the bottom of the cake.

3 Then try using it to model movement of the earth's plates at convergent, divergent, and transform boundaries.

Things to Think About

- What happens when you push the two halves together? when you pull them apart? when you slide the two halves past each other?
- How well does your cake model movement of the earth's plates at the three kinds of boundaries?

BIG IDEA

2.0 Processes within the earth cause natural events.

Long before humans walked this planet, volcanoes were erupting and earthquakes were shaking up the emerging land. Mountain ranges grew slowly toward the sky. Huge oceans surged across the earth's surface. This activity still goes on today. Why does it happen? The Theory of Plate Tectonics tells us that the earth is in constant motion. Most of the time we don't notice the motion, but sometimes it shows up in dramatic and devastating ways as earthquakes and volcanoes.

2.1 EARTHQUAKES

Armenia, Colombia, January 1999 (6.0 on the Richter scale)

Explore

You wake up suddenly from a deep sleep feeling as though your bed is on a ship in a bad storm. You have trouble reaching the light to turn it on. When you do, you can see the walls of your bedroom changing shape in front of your eyes. And the noise! The whole building sounds like it's being pulled apart board by board. Everything on your shelves crashes to the floor.

Cleaning up in Armenia, Colombia, January, 1999.

Suddenly all the lights go out, but you can see flashes of light out in the street as sparks fly from electrical wires. Just as you think "earthquake!" your bed stops moving. But you can hear buildings collapsing and people shouting outside.

Have you ever felt an earthquake? Where were you when it happened? What was it like? Share your description with your class. Now imagine that you have just moved to an area with a high risk of earthquakes. As you work through this section, note information about earthquakes that you would put into a newsletter. At the end of this section, you can use this information to create your newsletter.

Develop

What Causes Earthquakes?

The description above is an example of what happens in a strong earthquake. An **earthquake** is a shaking of the earth caused by a sudden breaking of large blocks of rock in the earth's crust.

Earlier in this chapter, you learned that earthquakes happen at the boundaries between tectonic plates. The plates are constantly moving, but earthquakes don't happen everywhere along every plate boundary all the time. Why not? Scientists think that earthquakes occur at plate boundaries mainly where two plates become locked together or "stuck." The plates are still being pushed along by convection currents but they can't move. Look at the following diagrams. You can see how the continuing pressure gradually deforms the rocks. Eventually the rocks can't withstand the pressure, and they break apart suddenly. Earthquake!

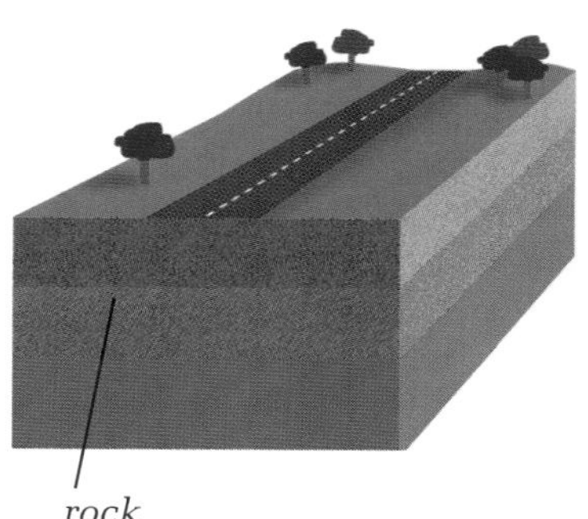

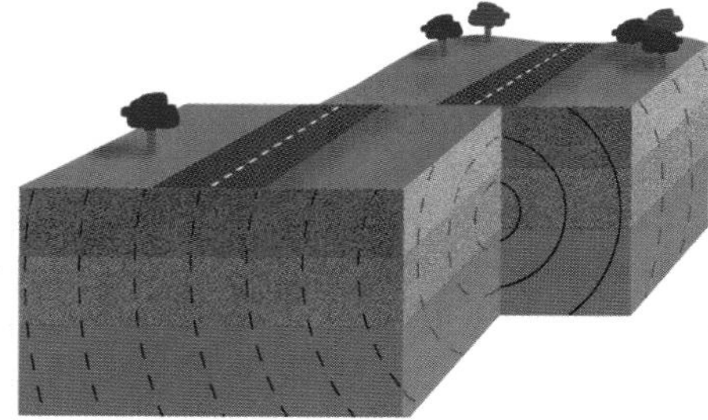

Pressure forces the rocks first to change shape and then to break.

Earthquakes Far from Plate Boundaries

Plate boundaries are not the only places at which earthquakes happen. In other places, sometimes right in the centre of a plate, cracks called faults can form. **Faults** are cracks in the earth's crust where movement occurs. Faults may be so deep inside the earth that they can't be seen at the surface. Earthquakes happen at faults in the same way they do at plate boundaries. Pressure on the rocks forces them to change shape until they suddenly break apart and shake the earth. This can happen when the fault first forms, or later when pressure deep in the earth's crust causes movement along an existing fault.

That First Break

The first place that the rocks break below the surface in an earthquake is called the **focus**. The sudden breaking of rocks at the focus releases energy that spreads as waves through the earth. Earthquake waves are called **seismic waves** (from the Greek word "*seismos*," meaning "earthquake"). Scientists use these waves to study the earth's interior because the waves travel right through the earth's layers. These waves also cause damage and changes on the earth's surface. The shaking you feel in an earthquake is caused by the waves moving through the earth.

Because of the effect an earthquake can have on the surface of the earth, scientists look for its **epicentre**. This is the point on the surface directly above the focus ("*epi-*" means "above"). Officials need to know where the epicentre is to provide disaster relief. It helps them determine if the earthquake was in a location where it would harm people, buildings, transportation systems, or communications. The diagram on this page shows how the focus and the epicentre are related.

reSEARCH

Earthquake waves are valuable tools for scientists who are interested in the structure of the earth. Find out how scientists use these waves to look inside the planet.

- What are the different kinds of earthquake waves?
- How do they show up on a seismograph?
- What effect do they have on the earth's surface?

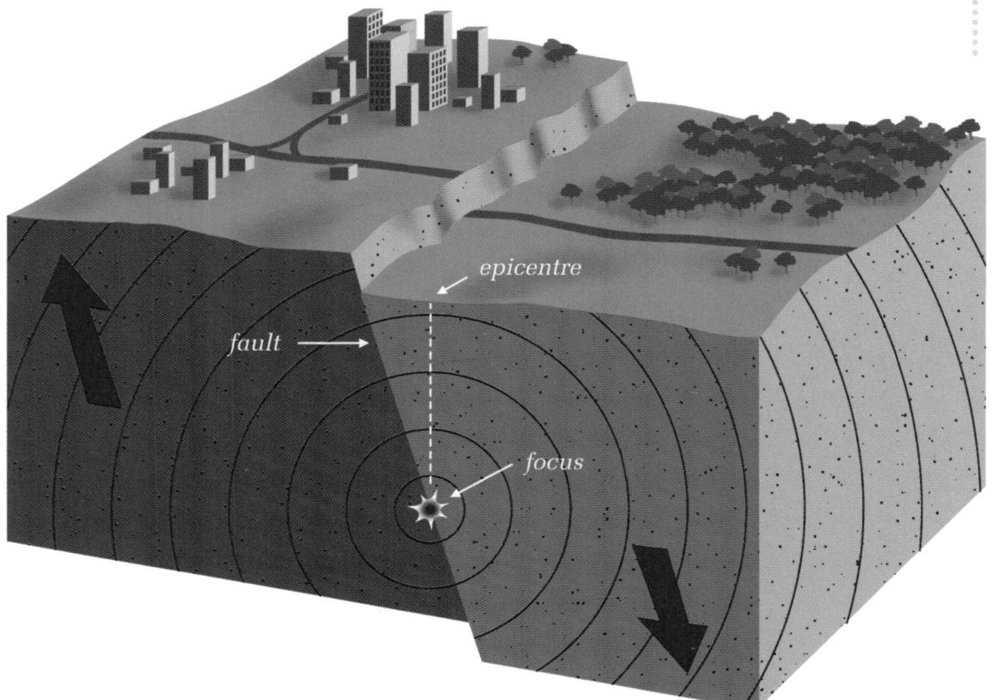

A **seismograph** is a device that detects the waves of energy that spread through the earth from the focus of an earthquake. Scientists can read the **seismogram** produced by the seismograph to determine the strength of the earthquake and where it occurred.

*info***BIT**

Some Canadian Earthquakes

Date	Richter Scale	Place
1663	?	St. Lawrence region
1700	~9	off coast of B.C.
1918	~7	Vancouver Island
1946	7.3	Vancouver Island
1949	8.1	near the Queen Charlotte Islands, B.C.
1990	4.9	Fraser Lowland, B.C.

Measuring the Strength of Earthquakes

Scientists use seismograms like the one in the picture above to determine the strength or magnitude of an earthquake. When you hear reports of the magnitude of an earthquake, it's usually given as a number on the **Richter scale**. Charles Richter, an American, developed the scale in 1935. The scale starts at 0, and each increase of 1 means an increase of 10 times the magnitude of an earthquake. For example, an earthquake that measures 2 is 10 times stronger than one that measures 1. One that measures 3 is 10 x 10 or 100 times stronger than one that measures 1. Look at the illustration below. What was the magnitude of the earthquake reported there? Was this a strong earthquake or a mild one?

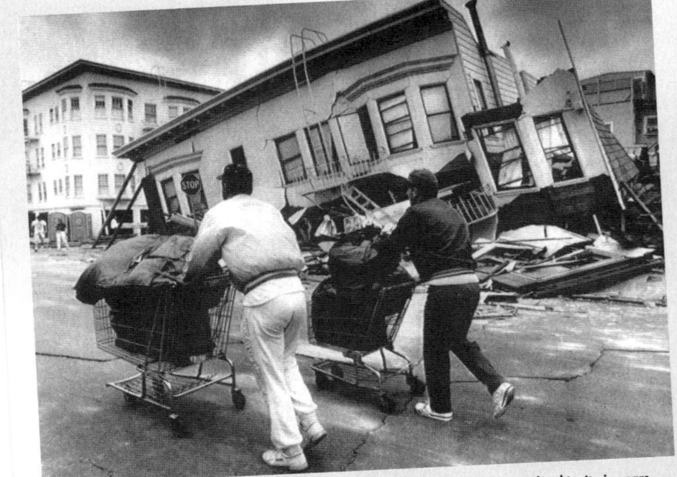

October 17, 1989—Residents flee crumbling buildings in one of the worst quakes to hit this city in years.

Quake hits bay city

SAN FRANCISCO—An earthquake measuring 7.7 on the Richter scale struck the city of San Francisco today, damaging freeways and many buildings. Unconfirmed reports give the death toll at over twenty, and fires are burning out of control in many parts of the city.

Rescue work has been

Why do you think some buildings are still standing, while others are completely destroyed?

Time is another important factor in how much damage an earthquake causes. The longer an earthquake lasts, the more damage it will cause. Most earthquakes last less than a minute. The Alaska earthquake of 1964 was 8.4 in magnitude, one of the strongest ever recorded. It lasted for four minutes—a very long time for an earthquake.

Predicting Earthquakes

In section 1.2 of this chapter, you looked at patterns in the earth's structure and earthquake occurrences. From studying those patterns, scientists know the areas where large earthquakes are most likely to happen. But they can't yet predict the exact location or the exact timing of the next earthquake. Prediction is an important subject of earthquake research. It involves looking at all the little events that can happen just before an earthquake, such as minor land movements and changes in water flow in streams. Scientists hope that by studying these signs and the frequency of earthquake events, they can develop an accurate earthquake prediction system.

Predicting earthquakes isn't just an interesting scientific exercise. In western and central Canada, several large cities are located in major earthquake zones. If we could predict exactly when and where a major earthquake was going to happen, people could be evacuated from the most dangerous areas when necessary. Thousands of lives would be saved.

reSEARCH

On September 25, 1998, an earthquake measuring 5.4 on the Richter scale rumbled through southern Ontario. The National Earthquake Hazards Program of Natural Resources Canada records and researches all earthquakes felt in Canada. Check their Web site at **www.seismo.nrcan.gc.ca** to find out more about this earthquake.

- How long did it last?
- What caused it?
- Did it cause any damage?

PROBLEM SOLVER

CHECKING UP ON EARTHQUAKES

Check the Internet (or other resources) for recent earthquakes and plot them on the map you used in Big Idea 1.0.

- Did these recent earthquakes cause much damage? Why or why not? (Hint: Were they near populated areas?)
- What do you think caused the largest quakes? Explain your answer.
- Try to find out if scientists were able to predict any of the larger earthquakes.
- Research the types of devices scientists use to predict earthquakes.

Communicate

1 At the beginning of this section, you were asked to gather information for a newsletter. Look over your notes and organize the information in an outline. Use your outline to write the feature in your newsletter. Include diagrams or other pictures that would help the reader understand the information.

2.2 Building Mountains

*info***BIT**

What is the Highest Mountain in the World?

If you said Mt. Everest, you're right—sort of! Mauna Kea in Hawaii starts on the ocean floor. If it's measured from its base under water, it's higher than Mt. Everest, nearly 10 203 m high. Everest is 8850 m high.

These mountains are in the Rocky Mountains of western Canada. The rocks in them were originally deposited as flat-lying layers. You can still see the layers in this photograph, but they are no longer flat. How would you describe them now? The layers are thousands of metres above sea level. If you investigated the rocks here, you might find fossils of animals that originally lived at the bottom of an ocean. Fossils are the preserved remains of once-living things. How did they get so high up on these mountains?

Explore

Think about the landscape where you live. What's the highest point of land in your area? Would you call it a mountain? Why or why not? In your Science Journal, explain in your own words what a mountain is. Have you ever visited any mountains? Describe those mountains in words and drawings.

Develop

What Is Mountain Building?

A mountain is a part of the earth's surface that is much higher than the land around it. A **mountain range** is a series of mountains. Mount Rundle at Banff, Alberta, is a mountain, and it's in a mountain range called the Rocky Mountains. Mountains are the result of several processes that scientists call **mountain building**. These processes include folding, faulting, and volcanic activity. Most mountains were created by a combination of folding and faulting. In the next activity, you can model how mountains are built by folding.

FORMING FOLDED MOUNTAINS

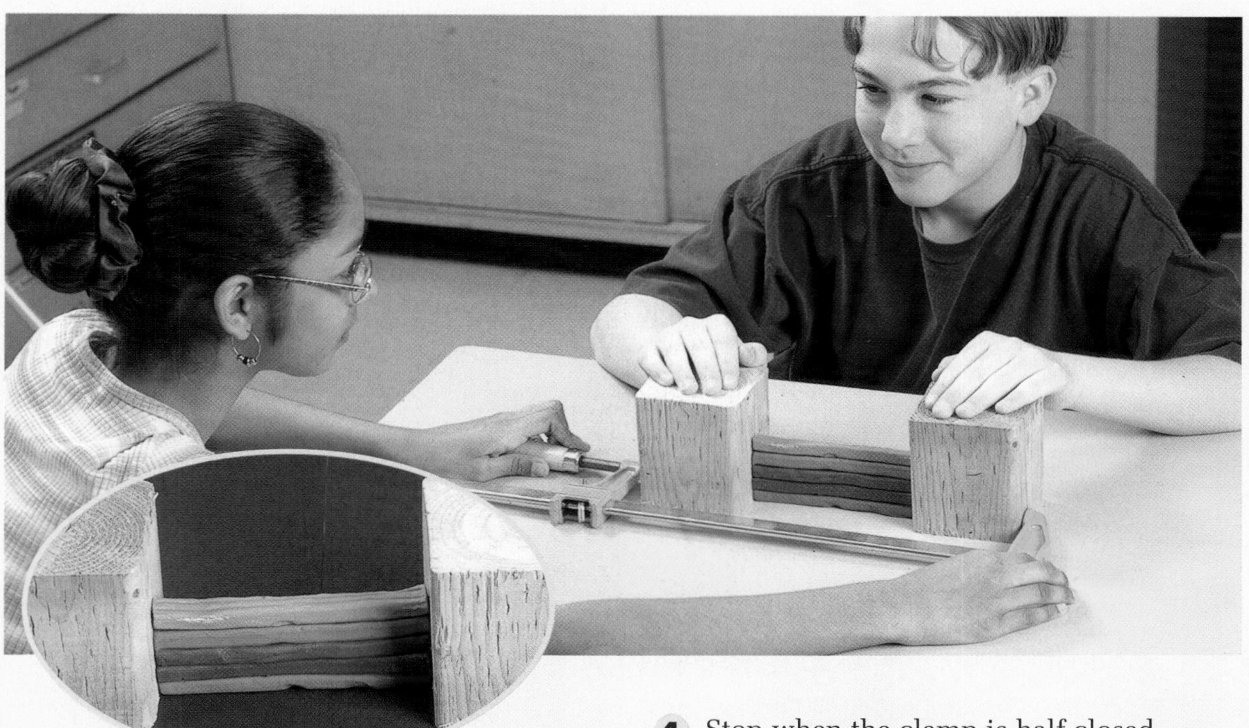

The Question

- How can mountains form by folding?

Materials & Equipment

- *5 rectangular strips of modelling clay, each a different colour and the same size*
- *2 pieces of wood, each 10 x 8 x 8 cm*
- *bar clamp, longer than 50 cm*

Procedure

1 Place one piece of modelling clay on your desk. Lay the other pieces one by one on top of each other to form a pile.

2 Put a block of wood at each end. Place the clamp so that the modelling clay and the blocks of wood are within the clamp.

3 One person holds both ends of the clamp as another person slowly screws the clamp shut.

4 Stop when the clamp is half closed.

5 Clean up after you have completed the activity.

Keeping Records

6 As you slowly close the clamp, stop from time to time to record your observations in words and diagrams.

Analyzing and Interpreting

7 What does the clamp represent in this model?

8 What does the modelling clay represent in this model?

9 What happens to the modelling clay as you close the clamp?

10 Why doesn't the clay break from the pressure of the clamp?

Forming Conclusions

11 Write a summary statement that answers the question: "How do mountains fold?" Include a diagram with your answer.

5 EARTH'S CRUST

Where Does Folding Happen?

The modelling clay you used in the previous activity may seem much too soft to be a good model for layered rocks. Rocks are hard. How can they fold? Rocks can fold only when they have been softened by heat and pressure within the earth's crust. The heat and pressure are not enough to melt the rocks, just enough to soften them. These conditions are most likely to happen where powerful forces are at work in the crust.

Think about the Theory of Plate Tectonics that you studied earlier in this chapter. Go back to the map you made showing the patterns of earthquakes, volcanoes, mountains, and tectonic plates. Can you see a connection between the location of the mountains and the plate boundaries? Colliding plates in the lithosphere provide the heat and pressure needed to soften the rock. As the plates push against each other, the rock "wrinkles" into folds and is forced upward.

This fence was one straight piece when it was built. Why do you think it has this gap in it now?

The Himalayas are still rising at a rate of 1 cm each year.

- Look on your map. What two plates are colliding to form the Himalayas?
- If the Himalayas keep rising, how much taller will they be in 1 000 000 years?

Mountains with Faults

Another powerful earth process that can build mountains is faulting. In section 2.1, you learned that earthquakes can sometimes happen at faults far from plate boundaries. Faults can be so deep in the crust that we can't see them. Some faults, however, are visible on the earth's surface. Have you ever noticed a fault? How could you tell it was a fault?

One place that faults are easy to see is in layered rocks. Where is the fault in this picture? What evidence do you see of movement along the fault?

reSEARCH

Use library resources or the Internet to research what major fault (or faults) is in North America.

The Rocky Mountains: were these mountains built by a fault?

Communicate

1. You have been asked to join a scientific expedition to investigate a remote mountain range in the Antarctic. Your team wants to discover how these mountains formed. Describe the evidence you will look for.
2. Find the definition of a mountain you wrote in your Science Journal earlier. Would you add anything to that definition from what you learned in this section?

reSEARCH

Have you ever heard of a volcano erupting in Canada? Probably not recently, but there are volcanoes here.

- Where are Canada's volcanoes?
- Why are they located there?
- When was the last eruption?
- When and where is the next eruption likely to be?

Create a colourful, interesting brochure to attract tourists to Canadian volcanoes.

2.3 Volcanoes

Explore

A deep rumbling in the earth and a fiery flash in the night sky—the volcano is about to erupt! Run for your life!

How accurate do you think that is as a description of a volcanic eruption? What really happens when a volcano erupts?

Scientists have generally been more successful predicting volcanic eruptions than they have been predicting earthquakes. They can't say exactly when an eruption will happen but they can usually tell if one is about to occur. As you read through this section, think about what people could watch for so they could tell when a volcano is going to erupt. Jot down notes as you go along, which you will use at the end of this section. Here are some questions to keep in mind.

- What evidence could people living near the volcano watch for?
- What other evidence could scientists look for?
- What technology could scientists use to monitor the volcano? (Hint: Think about the evidence you suggested in the previous answer. What devices might be useful for recording and measuring that evidence?)

Develop

What Happens when a Volcano Erupts?

A **volcano** is an opening in the earth's crust through which solid and molten rock, ash, and gases escape. In the next Problem Solver activity, you can use the Internet to learn about recent volcanic activity around the world.

PROBLEM SOLVER

Checking up on Volcanoes

Check the Internet (or other resources) for information on recent volcanic activity, and plot the locations on your map. You may already have some of these volcanoes marked.

- Did the activity cause any damage? Why or why not?
- Look again at the locations of the volcanoes. Why do you think these volcanoes are located where they are? (Hint: Think about the Theory of Plate Tectonics from Big Idea 1.1.)
- Try to find out if any of the communities affected by the volcanoes were warned about the eruptions. If a community did receive a warning, what did the people there do?

A Volcanic Eruption

The following diagram shows what happens when a volcano erupts.

1 *The molten rock in the magma chamber is lighter than the surrounding rock because solid rock expands when it melts. As it expands, the molten rock moves upward.*

2 *The molten rock forces its way upward through a weakness in the earth's crust.*

3 *The eruption begins. Lava either flows from the vent down the volcano's sides or shoots violently into the air as a cloud of rock fragments and* ***ash****.*

4 *The finest ash particles settle at the bottom of the slope or are carried many kilometres by the wind. If ash mixes with heavy rain, it can cause mud flows that race down mountainsides, causing enormous damage and loss of life.*

5 *Larger rock fragments fall near the vent; smaller ones fall farther away.*

6 *Lava and rock fragments move downhill because of gravity.*

7 *The magma activity inside the volcano shows up on the outside as changes to the shape of the mountain. It also causes small earthquakes around the volcano.*

*info*BIT

Volcanic ash can be carried by winds far from the volcano that produced it. The ash is so fine it can stay high up in the atmosphere and even affect the weather.

- Why do you think volcanic eruptions can affect weather?

Soufrière Hills on the island of Montserrat, fall 1997

Communicate

1 At the beginning of this section, you were asked to look for clues that people could use to determine if a volcano was about to erupt.

a) What other information might be useful for predicting volcanic activity that was not mentioned in this section?

b) Working with a small group, use your information to create a poster, a television program, or a brochure to tell people in a volcanic area how the volcano is being monitored and what the signs of an upcoming eruption are. If you need more information to complete your task, use reference books or the Internet.

reSEARCH

One of the most well known volcanic eruptions of all time happened in A.D. 79. Pompeii was a thriving city on the slopes of Mount Vesuvius in Italy when the mountain suddenly erupted. Volcanic ash buried the city and many of the people in it. Find out more about Pompeii.

- Why is Pompeii a famous tourist attraction?
- Why didn't the people of Pompeii just close their windows and doors to keep the ash out, or just run away?

This figure is a plaster cast of a body found buried in the ash at Pompeii.

2.4 Check Your Progress

1 a) What is the difference between the focus and the epicentre of an earthquake?

b) Why is it important to know where the epicentre is?

2 a) What does the illustration below show?

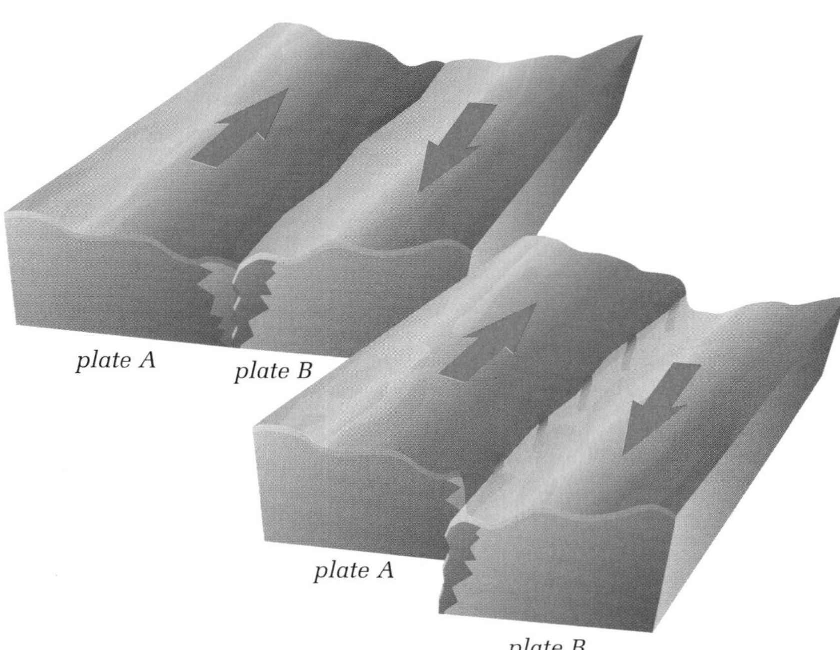

b) What will happen next?

3 a) Explain in your own words how a volcano is caused.

b) Where do most volcanoes occur?

c) Why do they occur there?

4 Why do you think most folded mountains contain some faults as well?

Careers and Profiles

VOLCANOLOGIST

It's Monday, and you're back on the job....but where are you? You're walking over a rocky black mountain and it's rumbling gently under your feet! A few metres away you can see jets of smoke coming from cracks in the rock. Oh no! It's a volcano! But instead of running, you haul out your instruments and set them up. This is your job: you're a volcanologist.

Volcanologists study volcanoes. They measure the movement in volcanoes to see if they're going to erupt. When an eruption occurs, they watch carefully to see how it happens. They also study the way lava comes out of a volcano and how it moves. The most serious part of their job is predicting whether or not a particular volcano will erupt. If they are right, many lives could be saved.

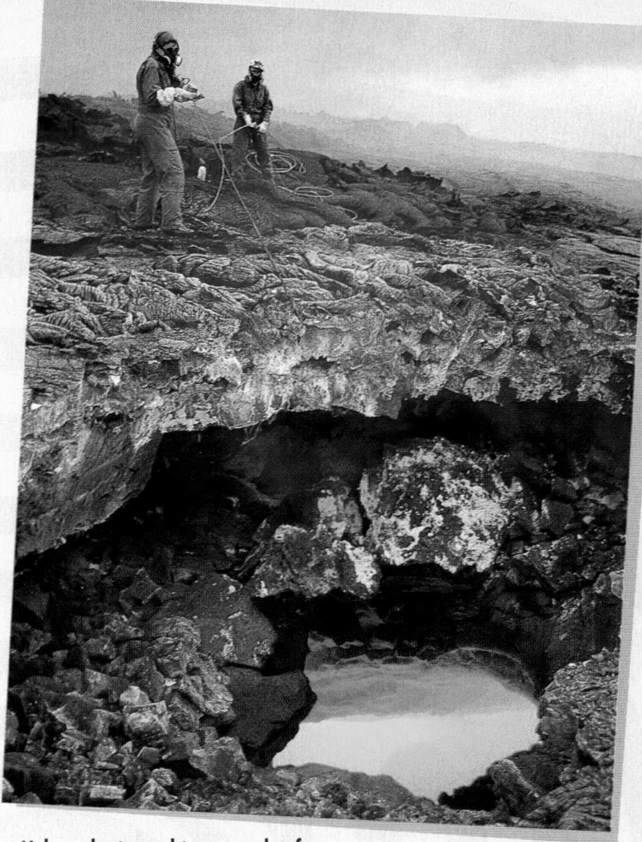

Volcanologists taking samples from a lava tube on the island of Hawaii.

SEISMOLOGIST

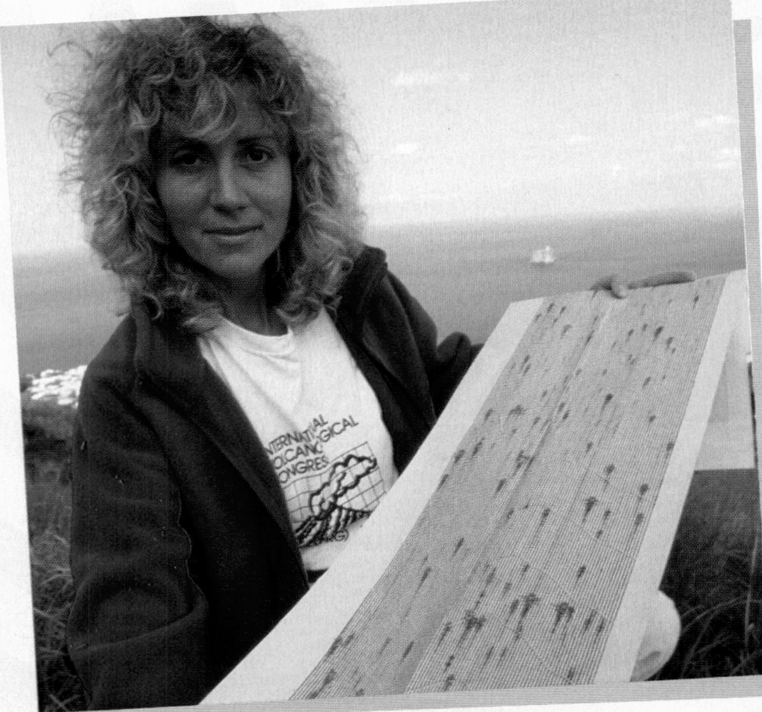

Seismographs record movement deep inside the earth.

Seismologists study earthquakes. They watch carefully for changes in the earth's surface, like the twisting or moving of rocks. Machines like the seismograph are used to record shaking and trembling deep inside the earth. These signs are earthquake warnings! When seismologists know that an earthquake is coming, they can warn the people who live in the area.

Another important part of a seismologist's job is to make sure buildings are earthquake-safe. Buildings made of brick often fall apart in an earthquake. It is better to have a building with a steel or wooden frame. Seismologists teach people in earthquake areas how to be safe in case of danger.

BIG IDEA

3.0 Rocks and minerals can be classified by their composition and by how they formed.

The salt on these chips is actually a rock.

What can rocks tell us about the earth? Geologists can "read" rocks to learn their stories—what they're made of and how they formed. The stories of rocks, combined with what you learned about the earth earlier in this chapter, tell a story of change. You can start to read this story yourself by looking carefully at rocks. What do you see when you look at a rock? Can you tell what it's made of? how it formed?

3.1 WHAT ARE ROCKS AND MINERALS?

Explore

You see rocks everywhere all the time, so you know what rocks are. You walk on them, ride over them, even eat them—when you eat anything salty. But if you had to describe them to someone, what would you say about them? Try it in the next activity.

PROBLEM SOLVER

MISSION CONTROL, THIS IS ...

Imagine that you are a space traveller on a mission to a distant planet. You have just collected some materials from the planet's surface. You now have to transmit a description of the appearance of these materials to mission control back on your home planet.

Use a hand lens to take a close look at the samples your teacher gives you. Describe each one in words and pictures. You can use the following questions to help you with your description.

- What colour is the sample? Is it the same colour all over?
- Does it have a smell?
- What does the surface feel like?
- Is it living or non-living?
- Does it seem to be all one substance or does it seem to be made up of a mixture of different substances? How do you know?
- Are any of the samples similar to others? In what ways?
- What else can you say about these samples?

Minerals in Rocks

To read a rock's story, you have to know what it's made of. When you looked at the samples in the Problem Solver activity, you probably noticed that they are made up of many little grains. These grains are minerals. All **rocks** are made of minerals. A **mineral** is a pure substance that forms naturally as a solid in the earth. Some rocks, such as limestone, are formed of only one mineral. Other rocks, such as granite, are made up of several different minerals.

You may have heard the names of some of the most common minerals, such as quartz and mica. There are thousands of different minerals, and these can combine to form many different kinds of rocks. But you don't have to know thousands of minerals to be able to identify most of the rocks you'll find. Just five minerals combine in different ways to form most of the rocks in the earth's crust. These minerals are:

- calcite
- quartz
- feldspar
- mica
- hornblende

This granite is made of three minerals: quartz, feldspar, and mica. As you can see from these samples, minerals don't have to be part of a rock. They can also occur on their own.

*info*BIT

Quartz

Halite crystal (sodium chloride)

Crystals form when the particles in a mineral line up in a regular pattern that creates smooth surfaces and sharp edges. Most minerals will form crystals if they grow in the right conditions. But the shape of the crystal depends on the type of mineral. Halite (rock salt) forms cubes. Quartz forms long, six-sided crystals, with a pointed end, like the one shown in the photograph above. What kind of conditions do you think a mineral would need to allow it to grow into a crystal?

The *colour* of amber is yellow.

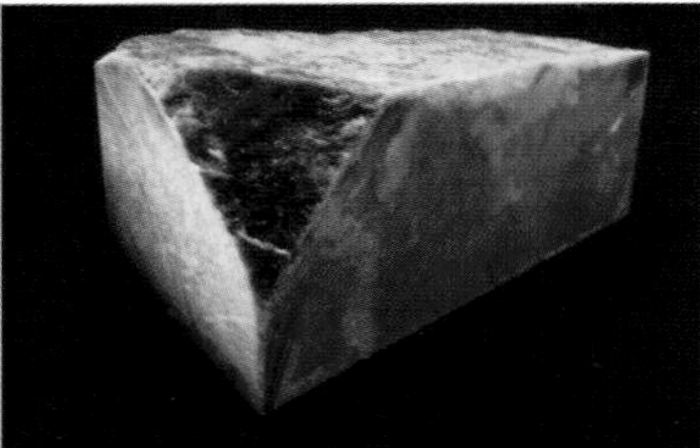
The *lustre* of native copper is shiny.

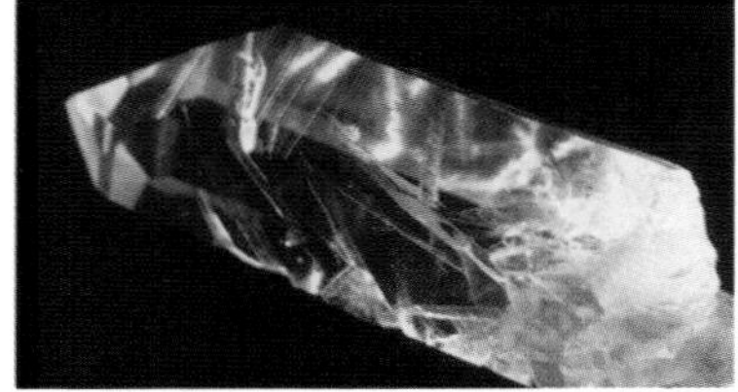
Jade makes a white *streak*.

The *hardness* of quartz is 7.

Using Properties to Identify Minerals

To identify rocks, you need to identify the minerals they contain. To do this, you can use the same techniques that geologists use. Geologists identify minerals by their properties. **Properties** are the features that a material or object has. For minerals, some important properties are:

- colour
- lustre
- streak
- hardness

Knowing only one of these properties isn't usually enough for you to be able to identify a mineral. You need to look at a combination of properties to find out what a mineral is. Think of it as a jigsaw puzzle: one piece doesn't give you the whole picture.

Colour is a useful starting point for identifying minerals because it's the first property you notice.

Next, you can describe the lustre. **Lustre** is the way the surface of a mineral looks in the light. Some minerals have a "metallic" lustre. This means they are shiny like metals such as gold or silver. Two minerals may be the same colour, but their lustre can help you tell them apart. Some of the other words used to describe a mineral's lustre are pearly, glassy, waxy, silky, greasy, and brilliant.

A mineral's **streak** is the colour of the powder that it leaves behind when you rub it across a rough surface. The streak colour is not always the same as the mineral's colour. Usually geologists use a streak plate of unglazed porcelain for testing minerals. This is an unglazed ceramic tile (like the tile used on bathroom walls, but not shiny). They scratch a mineral sample on the plate, and the colour of that streak gives a clue to the mineral's identity.

Hardness is another important property. Minerals can be soft, like chalk, or very hard, like diamond. The illustration on this page shows the hardness scale that geologists use when they test minerals.

The hardness scale is a guide to identifying minerals.

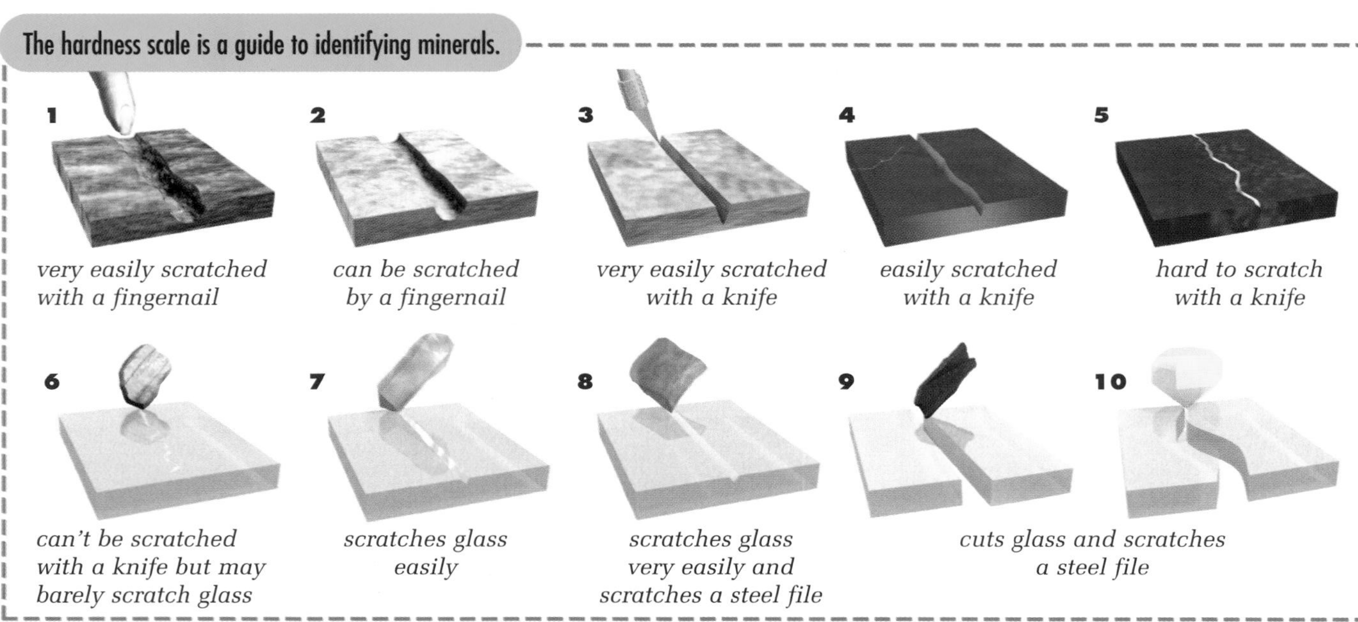

Communicate

1 One of the steps in identifying a rock is to identify the minerals it contains. For example, recall that granite is made of quartz, feldspar, and mica. If you were given an unknown rock, how would you use what you learned in this section to identify it?

2 The properties of minerals are useful for more than just identifying them. Sometimes properties make a mineral valuable. For example, colour is important in gemstones. What other property that you learned about in this section might make a mineral valuable?

3.2 How Rocks Form

Explore

The first step in identifying a rock is identifying the minerals it contains. But to learn the whole story, you need to know how the rock formed. Two rocks can have exactly the same minerals in them, but they may look different because they formed in different ways. The way the minerals are arranged and the sizes of the individual grains can all give clues to how a rock formed.

As you explore the different types of rocks in this section, use a diagram like the one below to keep track of the information. Copy this diagram into your notebook (use a whole page) or get a copy from your teacher. Label your diagram as you go through the text. On your diagram, show where the different types of rock are forming. Add any notes that will help you remember what process formed them. To help you get started, the diagram below shows an example.

*info***BIT**

Treasures in the Earth's Crust

The earth's crust is a treasure house of valuable things. Gold, silver, and precious stones are all found in the earth's crust.

- The Ancient Egyptians were mining for emeralds as far back as 1650 B.C. That's more than 3000 years ago.
- Canada is one of the top 10 gold producers in the world.

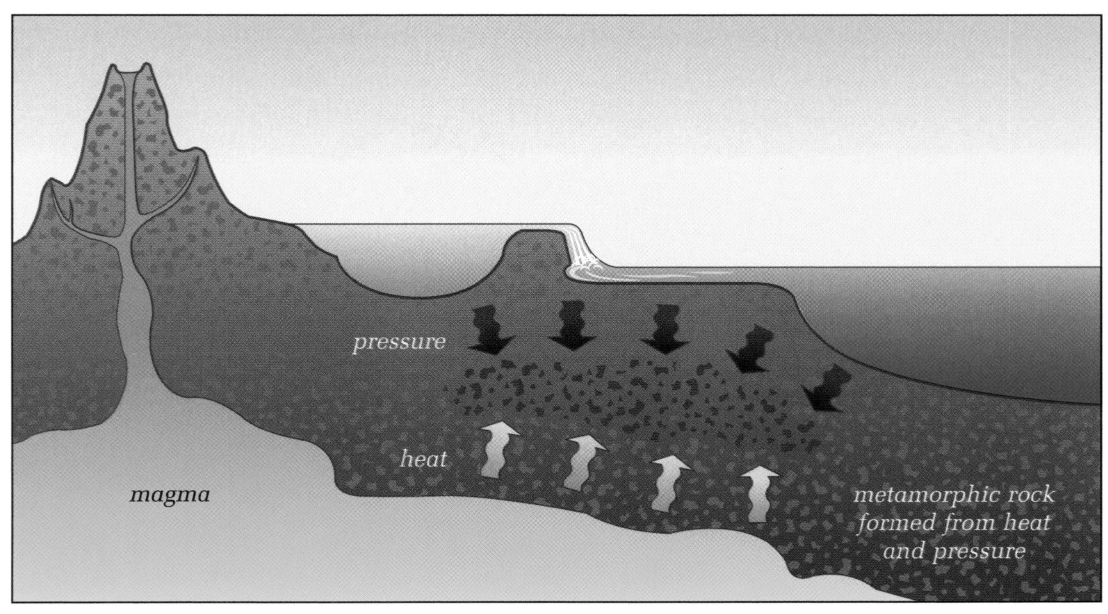

Copy this diagram or get a copy from your teacher.

Develop

Types of Rocks

Geologists classify rocks into three different types, according to how they were formed.

- igneous
- sedimentary
- metamorphic

Kilauea Volcano on the island of Hawaii

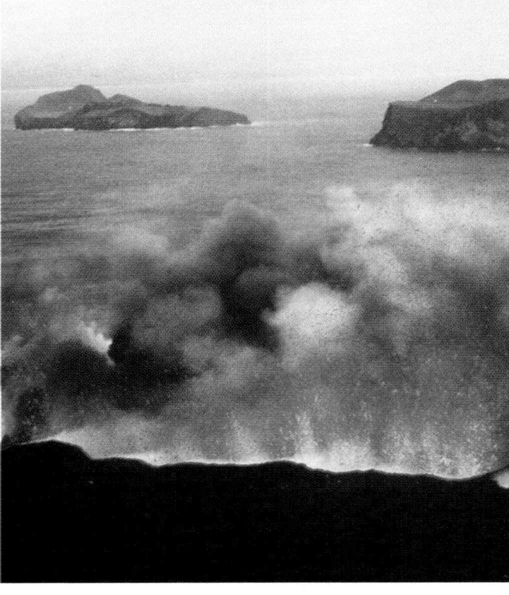

Eldfell volcano on the island of Heimaey, Iceland (1973)

One place where you can watch igneous rock forming is at active volcanoes, like those in Hawaii and Iceland. Why are there so many active volcanoes in these two places? (Hint: Think about the Theory of Plate Tectonics from Big Ideas 1.0 and 2.0.)

Igneous Rocks

The word *igneous* comes from the Latin word "ignis," meaning fire. **Igneous rocks** form from hot, molten rock called **magma**, but by the time you hold them in your hands, they are hard and cold. Magma may cool deep inside the earth, or it may reach the surface before it cools. When it flows out onto the surface of the earth, either on land or beneath the ocean, it's called **lava**. The photographs of pegmatite and basalt show one way that you can tell the difference between an igneous rock that cools on the earth's surface and one that cools deep inside the earth.

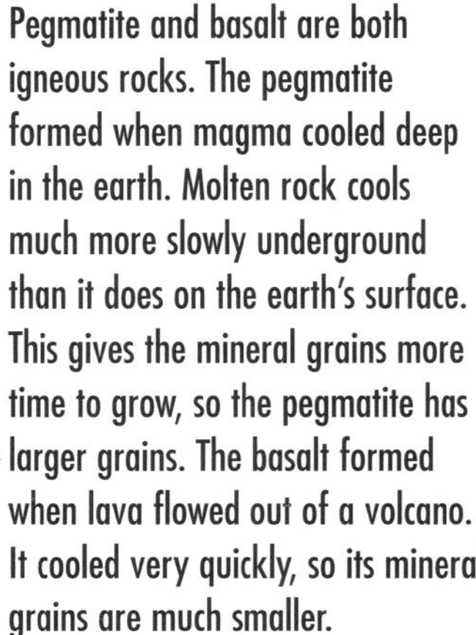

Pegmatite and basalt are both igneous rocks. The pegmatite formed when magma cooled deep in the earth. Molten rock cools much more slowly underground than it does on the earth's surface. This gives the mineral grains more time to grow, so the pegmatite has larger grains. The basalt formed when lava flowed out of a volcano. It cooled very quickly, so its mineral grains are much smaller.

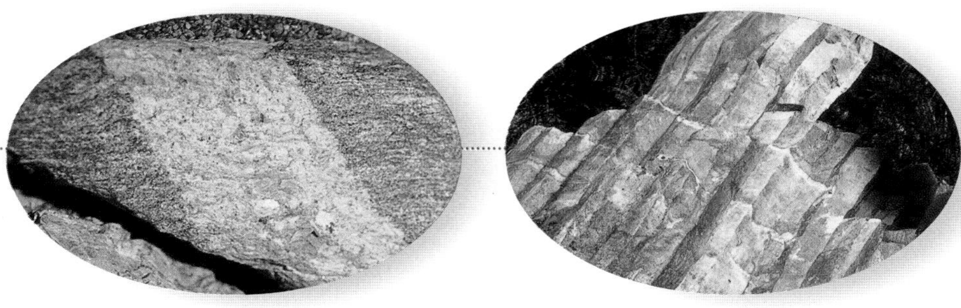

Pegmatite Basalt

Sedimentary Rocks

Limestone (left) and sandstone (right) are two kinds of sedimentary rocks that usually occur in layers.

Have you ever seen rocks that have layers in them, like the ones in the photographs? These are **sedimentary rocks**. Small pieces of rock are carried by water or wind and settle or sink down onto the rocks below them. Sometimes these pieces are made up mainly of tiny shells from dead animals. As more and more sediments pile up, the ones on the bottom are squeezed by the weight of the ones above and by the weight of the water if they are under water. This forces the rock or shell pieces in the sediments closer together. In time, these sediments harden into solid rock. You'll find out more about sedimentary rocks later in this chapter.

infoBIT

Are you a rock hound? A rock hound is someone who collects and studies rocks as a hobby. Some rock hounds specialize in collecting only crystals or only fossils. Every summer, many rock hounds go to the Rock Hound Gemboree at Bancroft, Ontario, to buy and trade minerals from all over the world. The Bancroft area is also famous for the large variety of minerals that occur there.

PROBLEM SOLVER

GRAPH IT!

If you examine this table of the world's top producers, you will probably notice that Canada is among the world leaders in mining. But numbers are difficult to visualize.

- Your challenge is to take the numbers in the table and create a graph (or graphs) that compares Canada with the other countries listed.

Copper (×1000 t)	*China (3200)*	*U.S.(1920)*	*Canada (700)*	*Australia (550)*	*Indonesia (530)*
Lead (×1000 t)	*China (650)*	*Australia (530)*	*U.S. (450)*	*Canada (260)*	*Peru (250)*
Zinc (×1000 t)	*Canada (1250)*	*China (1130)*	*Australia (1100)*	*Peru (770)*	*U.S. (600)*
Nickel (×1000 t)	*Russia (230)*	*Canada (200)*	*New Caledonia (130)*	*Australia (120)*	*Indonesia (90)*
Aluminum (×1000 t)	*U.S. (3600)*	*Russia (2900)*	*Canada (2300)*	*China (1900)*	*Australia (1400)*
Gold (t)	*South Africa (500)*	*U.S. (320)*	*Australia (290)*	*Canada (170)*	*Russia (130)*
Silver (t)	*Mexico (2500)*	*U.S. (1440)*	*Peru (1950)*	*Canada (1310)*	*Chile (1150)*

reSEARCH

Ontario produces about 40% of all the valuable metallic minerals in Canada. A metallic mineral is one that contains a metal such as copper or nickel.

- Where are the major metal-mining areas in Ontario?
- Is there a pattern to their location? (Hint: Look at the types of rocks they are found in.)

Not all sedimentary rocks form from rock or shell pieces. As water flows over and under the earth's surface, it can dissolve substances called "salts" from the rocks. The salt you use on your food is one of these salts. The reason the ocean is salty is that rivers carry so much salt into the ocean. Sometimes, bodies of water that contain dissolved salts dry up, leaving the salts behind. These salts can form thick beds.

Metamorphic Rocks

Metamorphic rocks are rocks that have been changed. The word *metamorphic* is a combination of two Greek words: "meta" means change and "morph" means shape. These rocks started out as igneous or sedimentary rocks but the intense pressure and heat of the earth's interior changed their appearance. It may even have caused the mineral grains to melt slightly and reform. If that happens, the rock becomes harder.

Shale is a sedimentary rock that changes to slate if it's exposed to strong heat and pressure. Slate is harder than shale. If slate is exposed to more heat and pressure, the different kinds of mineral grains in it become larger and separate from each other. The rock is then called schist.

Shale Slate Schist

As the photographs on this page illustrate, sedimentary rocks and igneous rocks can change because of heat and pressure. In the next activity, you can see how pressure alone can change the shape of something.

Granite and gneiss contain the same minerals, but as you can see, the rocks look different. Gneiss is a metamorphic rock that can form from the igneous rock, granite. Heat and pressure cause the mineral grains in the granite to separate into the bands you can see in the photo at right.

Granite outcrop

Gneiss

PROBLEM SOLVER

MORPHING ROCKS

The metamorphic rocks that we see on the earth's surface are the result of a process that takes place deep inside the earth. How can rocks be squeezed and changed without breaking? Heat and pressure soften the rocks so they are similar to modelling clay. You can use modelling clay to show how pressure can change a rock.

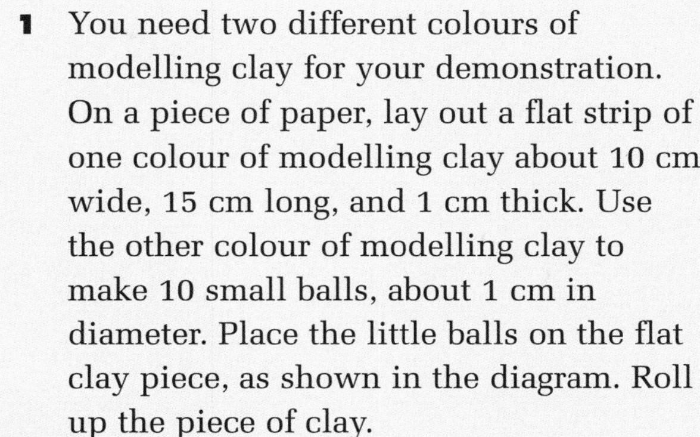

1 You need two different colours of modelling clay for your demonstration. On a piece of paper, lay out a flat strip of one colour of modelling clay about 10 cm wide, 15 cm long, and 1 cm thick. Use the other colour of modelling clay to make 10 small balls, about 1 cm in diameter. Place the little balls on the flat clay piece, as shown in the diagram. Roll up the piece of clay.

2 Place a piece of waxed paper on the clay roll. Then place a flat piece of wood or a book on top of the paper and press down firmly. Remove the wood or book and paper, and cut the compressed clay roll in half. Draw a picture to show what happened to the little balls and the clay roll.

- If your clay roll is a model of a rock, which part represents the mineral grains in the rock?
- What happened to the model mineral grains? Why?

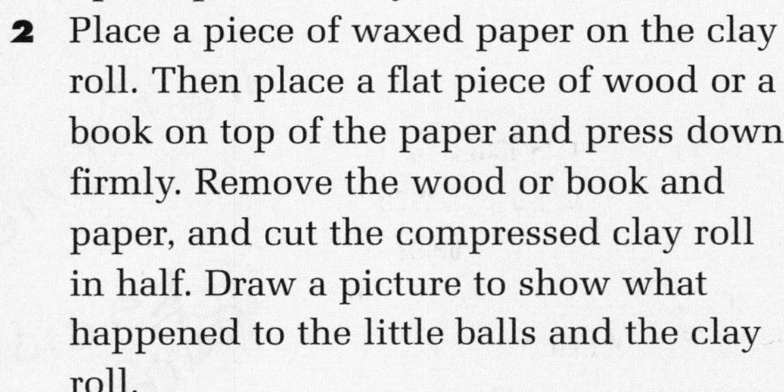

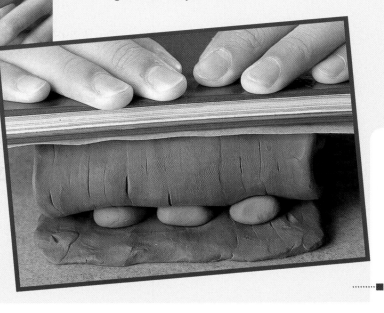

Communicate

1 Using your own words, complete the following sentences.
  a) Igneous rocks form when ...
  b) Sedimentary rocks form when ...
  c) Metamorphic rocks form when ...

2 Lava always forms igneous rocks. But not all igneous rocks are formed from lava.
  a) What is lava?
  b) If an igneous rock didn't form from lava, what did it form from?

3 Now that you've seen how rocks form, how do you think you could use this information to identify them? Look at your diagram that you filled in while you were reading about the different types of rocks. List any information that might be useful for identifying the different rock types. Include information that would be helpful in the field for identifying large areas of rock.

*info***BIT**

The World's Deepest Mines

- Macassa Gold Mine in Northern Ontario (shaft 3): 2202 m (more than 2 km) deep
- Deepest Mine in the World in South Africa, Western Deep Levels Gold Mine: 4 km deep

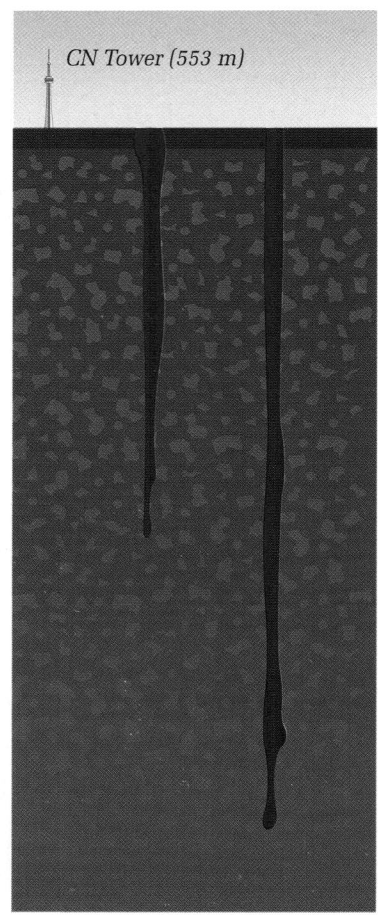

The earth's crust is about 10–90 km deep.

3.3 CHECK YOUR PROGRESS

1 How are rocks and minerals related?

2 Describe four properties of minerals that are used for identification. How is each different?

3 Review the rock samples you examined in the Problem Solver activity in section 3.1 (Mission Control, This Is...). Use a rock and mineral field guide (or other resource) to classify these rocks as either igneous, sedimentary, or metamorphic.

4 Why do some igneous rocks have bigger mineral grains than other igneous rocks?

5 Amal was on a bus that drove past a steep hillside of bare rock. "Look," she said to her friend, "sedimentary rocks!" How did she know?

6 A metamorphic rock is a changed rock.
  a) What did it change from?
  b) What changed it?

7 Why can two rocks look very different even though they are made of the same minerals?

8 Write a song about "rocks" that could be set to "rock" music.

GEOLOGIST—DIGGING DOWN DEEPLY

Nancy Chow studies coral reefs, but not the kind found in tropical destinations like the Bahamas or the Red Sea. She studies coral reefs found in Manitoba, Alberta, and the interior of Australia!

These coral reefs existed 380 million years ago when large parts of North America and Australia were covered in water. Chow is a geologist who analyzes the sedimentary rock layers formed by these ancient reefs.

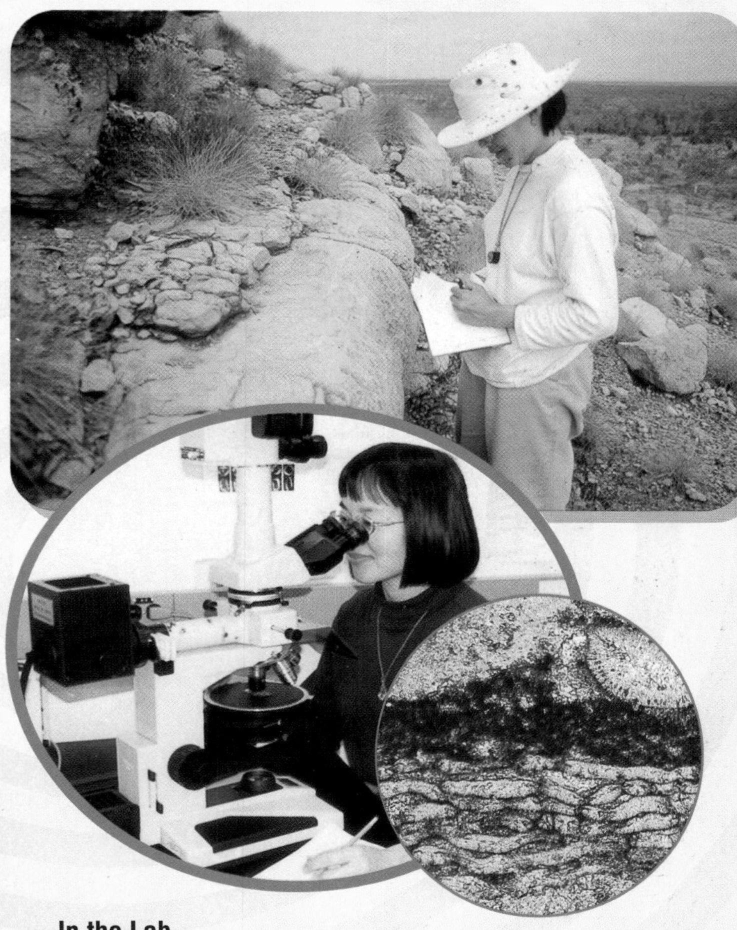

In the Field

Chow spends about a quarter of her time in the field. The rock layers she studies often lie deep underground, buried by thousands of years of sedimentation. To get at the underlying rock, drill core samples are taken. Chow takes careful notes to keep track of where each sample came from.

Investigating modern reefs, Grand Cayman Island

In the Lab

Chow spends the rest of her time analyzing the rock samples in the lab. She cuts the rock samples into paper-thin slices and examines them under a microscope. "Light is transmitted through the samples and we can pick up structures that are too small to see with the naked eye," says Chow.

Does Chow Like Her Job?

"It's been great for me," says Chow. "I've travelled to Australia to work on spectacular rock exposures. I've been to the Caribbean to look at modern reefs. I have no complaints!"

Big Idea

4.0 The rock cycle describes how rocks form and change over time.

5 Earth's Crust

Have you ever seen a rock change? If you sat and watched a rock for a day, you'd probably get bored. You wouldn't see any change at all. In fact, if that rock stayed in your classroom, you could watch it for a million years and probably not see any change at all. Yet many rocks are changing all the time. Some are rocks deep inside the crust—the metamorphic rocks you learned about earlier in this chapter. Others are on the earth's surface, where they are exposed to different kinds of forces.

4.1 What Changes Rocks on the Earth's Surface?

Explore

When this house was built, it had a fresh coat of paint and sparkling windows. A family moved in and grew up there. Children played in the yard. Flowers grew in the front. Vegetables grew in the back. Fifty years later, it looks like this. What happened to it?

With a partner, brainstorm all the factors, both natural and human, that might have caused this house to end up looking like this. Identify which factors you think might also affect rocks. Do you think these factors would have as much of an effect on rocks after 50 years? Why or why not?

As you continue your exploration of the earth, make a list of questions about needs or problems related to changes to rocks on the earth's surface. At the end of the section, you'll use your list to develop investigations into these needs or problems.

Develop

Weathering

Weathering is one of the reasons that rocks change. **Weathering** is the process that wears down rocks and other objects. Think back to the types of rock you studied earlier: igneous, sedimentary, and metamorphic. Even though most of the earth's crust is made of igneous rocks, many of the rocks we see on the surface are sedimentary rocks. Most sedimentary rocks form from tiny rock fragments piling up and being pressed together. Where did these rock fragments come from? Weathering breaks rocks into tiny pieces, which helps to form sedimentary rocks and soil. Later in this chapter, you'll learn more about the formation of soil. Start your exploration of weathering with this next Investigator activity. The photographs and activities that follow it show different types of weathering.

INVESTIGATOR

WHAT'S GOING ON IN THE FREEZER?

The Question

What happens when water freezes inside a solid?

Materials & Equipment

- *plaster of Paris*
- *2 Styrofoam cups*
- *water*
- *stir stick*
- *small balloon*
- *large bowl*
- *freezer*

continued on next page

5 EARTH'S CRUST

Procedure

1. Mix 2 or 3 times the amount of plaster of Paris to water in both Styrofoam cups. Each cup should be about 3/4 full. The mixtures should look like soft ice cream.
2. Put a small amount of water into the balloon so that it's about the size of a cherry tomato. Tie it shut so it doesn't leak.
3. Push the balloon into the plaster in one of the cups. Allow the plaster to harden in both cups.
4. Place the cups in a large bowl and put the bowl in the freezer overnight.
5. Predict what you think the plaster of Paris will look like in each cup after it freezes.
6. Take the bowl with the cups in it out of the freezer the next day.

Keeping Records

7. Record the appearance of the plaster of Paris in each cup before and after it is frozen.

Analyzing and Interpreting

8. What happened to the plaster of Paris without the balloon in it? What happened to the plaster of Paris with the balloon in it?
9. Why did you prepare one cup without a balloon in it?

Forming Conclusions

10. Use your observations from this investigation to explain what happens when water freezes in cracks in rocks.

Mechanical weathering happens when rock is broken apart by physical forces, such as water or wind. In our climate, rock is often broken down by water freezing in cracks. Water gets into cracks in rocks when rain falls or snow melts. If the water freezes at night or on a very cold day, it expands. (This means it increases in volume.)

You can observe this expansion when you make ice cubes. When you pour the water into the ice cube tray, notice where the water level is. After the water has frozen, look where the tops of the ice cubes are. They are higher because the ice has more volume than the water.

The increase in the volume of the water when it freezes in cracks forces the rock to break apart even more. This process can gradually break a rock into smaller and smaller pieces. Where else, besides in rocks, do you think this could happen?

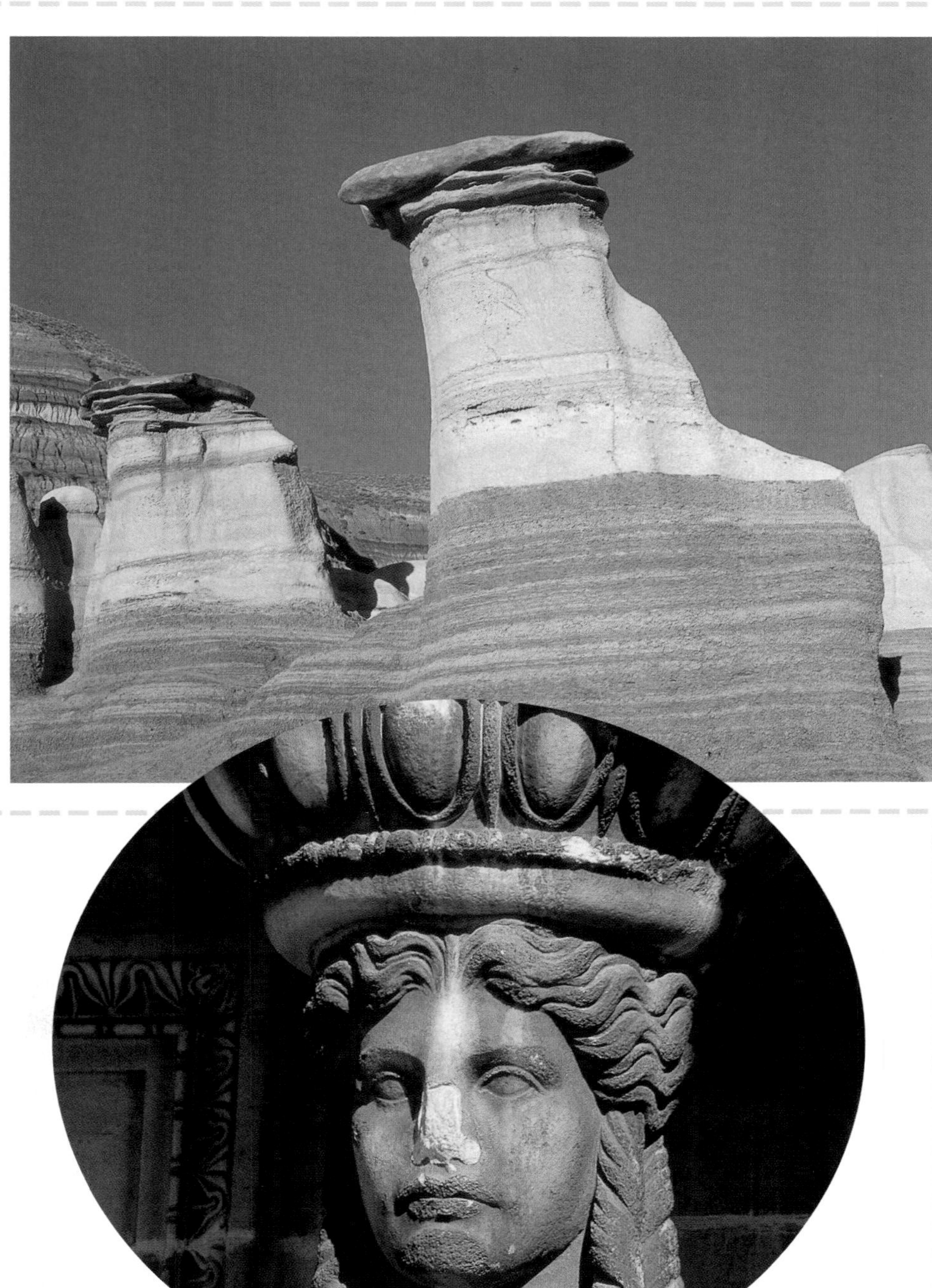

Wind is another cause of mechanical weathering. Wind can pick up pieces of sand or small bits of rock, just as it picks up leaves and blows them around. Have you ever felt little pieces of dust hit your skin on a really windy day? In some places, the wind often blows strongly. If it's a dry climate, the wind can pick up lots of dust and grit and bombard rock surfaces with it. The result is sometimes odd-shaped structures like these, called *hoodoos*. The hoodoos in the picture are in Alberta. How long do you think it would take wind to wear down a rock surface?

*info*BIT

Acid rain can affect more than rocks and statues. It can affect plants and wetlands. Some lakes in eastern Canada have been affected by acid rain so much that the plants and animals that lived in them all died. The water in these lakes is clear and clean looking, but nothing can live in it.

Chemical weathering happens when water in the air combines with chemical substances in the air. Sometimes these substances are in the air naturally. Sometimes they are there because of cars, fires, and smoke from industry. Combined with the rain or snow, the substances form solutions called acids. Rocks exposed to these acids gradually disappear. This is easy to see on statues and stone buildings in towns and cities. There, acid rain caused by air pollution eats away at the surface of stone. Look at older buildings and statues in your community. Have they been affected by acid rain? How do you know?

How strong is a tree? Growing things can be powerful, destructive forces for rocks, sidewalks, and driveways. The need to grow causes plants to force their roots into any small space where a little soil has collected. Then, as their roots and stems get bigger, they put enormous pressure on their surroundings.

Biological weathering is the wearing away of rocks by living things. The tree you see in the picture started growing in a small crack in the rock. As it got bigger, it made the crack bigger. What do you think will happen to the rock as the tree grows? Even small plants can "chip away" at rocks. Have you ever noticed grass growing in cracks in a sidewalk?

Erosion

Weathering is the first step in a larger process that is continually changing the surface of the earth. You may have learned about this process in earlier grades. It's called erosion. **Erosion** is the wearing away and moving of rock materials and soil by water, wind, or ice. These rock materials can be as big as boulders or as small as the grains in soil.

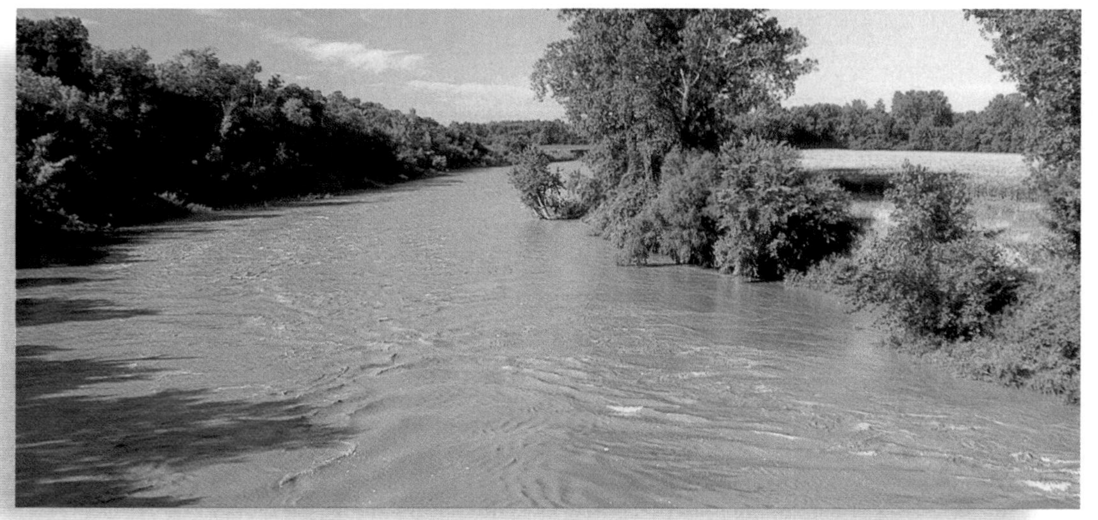

Have you ever seen a river that looks really muddy, like this one? This river flows through soil, not rock. Because soil has such fine grains, the river can pick these grains up easily and carry them along. What do you think happens to the soil in the water when the river slows down or stops flowing?

Think of what you learned about weathering.

- What was "eating away" the rock in mechanical weathering? in chemical weathering? in biological weathering?
- What happened to the rock after it was "eaten" in each type of weathering? Did it stay in the same place?

One of the most powerful forces of erosion is moving water. The small pieces of rock that drop off because of mechanical weathering can be picked up and carried by streams and rivers. These rock fragments then rub against the rock that the water flows over. This gradually wears away that rock, and the water carries those pieces away as well.

This type of erosion takes place very slowly, but sometimes erosion can change the landscape very quickly. **Landslides** usually happen because of water erosion. They can happen when soil on the side of a hill gets soaked with water. The wet soil then slides quickly down the hillside. If any houses or other buildings are built there, they slide too.

*info***BIT**

Landslides and Avalanches

- Avalanches or snowslides are common in western Canada. The biggest avalanche disaster was in 1910, when an avalanche killed 62 railroad workers at Roger's Pass, B.C.
- Landslides are also common in Canadian mountains. A mining town in Alberta, named Frank, was partly buried in 1903 when 90 million tons of rock fell from a nearby mountain. The slide killed 75 people.

Landslides are common in areas with steep hillsides and high rainfall at certain times of the year. If people know that landslides might happen in an area like that, why do you think they build there?

*info*BIT

Disappearing Soil

Because the soil in farmland is turned over or tilled, topsoil is exposed to wind and water erosion. For example, of the 37.7 million ha of cultivated land in the Canadian prairies:

- 36% is prone to severe wind erosion
- 13.5% is in danger of extreme water erosion

Communicate

1 As you read through this section, you wrote down questions about needs or problems related to changes to rocks on the earth's surface. Combine your questions and ideas with other members of your group as you work through the following steps.

a) Choose two of your questions about needs or problems related to weathering.
b) Brainstorm possible answers or solutions to these questions.
c) Select one of these possible answers or solutions and plan an investigation into it. In your plan, identify:
   - a variable that must be held constant to make sure you have a fair test
   - how you will determine if your solution works
d) Share your plan with other groups in your class. Did any other group plan an investigation into the same question that your group did? How was their plan different from yours?

4.2 Tracing Evidence of Geological Change

Explore

Kathy and Mohammed went on a field trip to a local rock quarry. There they found some good fossils in sedimentary beds. Below is a copy of the drawing they made of what they saw, and some of the comments they made. Think of what you know about sedimentary rocks, and answer the following questions related to their comments.

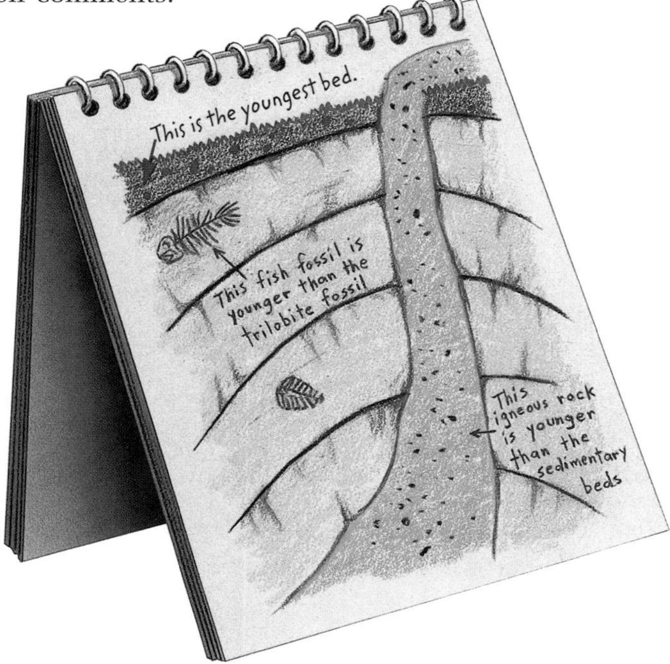

- How did Kathy and Mohammed know that the trilobite fossil was older than the fish fossil?
- How did they know that the top layer is the youngest layer?
- How did they know that the igneous rock is younger than the sedimentary rocks?

Develop

Observing Changes in the Rock Record

Studying sediments is one of the ways that geologists track changes in the geological record of the earth's history. Think back to what you've learned in this chapter about sedimentary rocks and weathering and erosion. What happens when water or wind can't carry rock materials any farther? You can observe what happens to rock fragments carried by water when the water slows or stops moving by using a jar and some rock fragments in this next activity.

PROBLEM SOLVER

SETTLE DOWN!

Get a tall, clear jar with a lid. Fill it about one-third full of a mixture of rock fragments. Use equal amounts of clay or fine soil, sand, and fine gravel.

- Put enough water into the jar so it's two-thirds full. Predict what you think will happen to the different rock fragments after you shake the jar.
- Screw the lid tightly onto the jar, and shake it well. Leave the jar where it won't be disturbed, and look at it later. (You may want to leave it until your next science class.)
- What happened to the rocks in the jar? Was your prediction accurate?
- What did your shaking of the jar represent?

Deposition

In the Problem Solver activity, you saw how sediment settles when water stops moving. As long as you shook the jar nothing would settle. Flowing water behaves the same way. As long as it moves, it can carry sediments. Water that flows rapidly can carry larger rock fragments than slow-moving water. Even a slow-moving river can carry a large amount of rock fragments and soil. But once the water stops moving, the fragments settle out.

The settling of rock materials out of water, wind, or ice is called **deposition**. The material deposited is called **sediment**. These sediments form the sedimentary rock you learned about earlier in this chapter. Sedimentary deposits usually form in layers, called **strata**.

Telling Time Geologically

Strata are useful to geologists because they provide information about what happened in a certain area in the past. Geologists can tell from the kinds of rocks and the grain size in a sedimentary layer what the environment was like when the rocks in that layer were deposited. They can also determine when the rocks were deposited. This information comes from both the position of the rock layers and what they contain.

The sediments at the bottom were deposited first, and then the next layer on top of them, and so on. Any rocks that cut across others, instead of being in layers like the rest of the rocks, are usually younger (newer) than the rocks they cut across. So in Kathy and Mohammed's diagram, the igneous rock was younger because it cuts across the sedimentary rock. These rules make it possible for geologists to study geologic change over time.

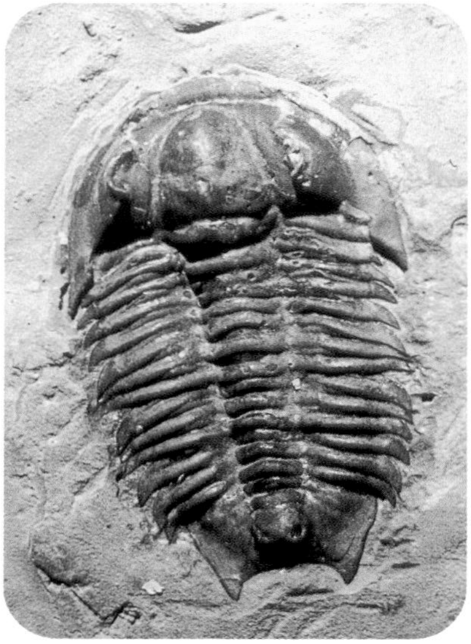

Trilobites lived on the bottoms of oceans 300 million years ago. No trilobites exist today. If you found a rock with a trilobite in it, what could you say about that rock?

Fossils

Geologists also use fossils to study change over time. **Fossils** are traces of once-living things that are preserved in rocks. Fossils form when animals or plants die and fall to the ground or to the bottom of a body of water. There they are buried by sediments. This means fossils are the same age as the sedimentary rock they are found in.

By studying fossils, geologists have discovered that life on earth has changed greatly over time. The fossils that we find in younger rocks show animals and plants similar to the ones we see today. But older rocks often contain fossils of animals and plants that no longer exist. Many of these fossils don't look like the plants and animals we see today. The trilobite in the picture at left is a good example of an animal that once covered the ocean floor, but now, no longer exists.

How a fossil is formed

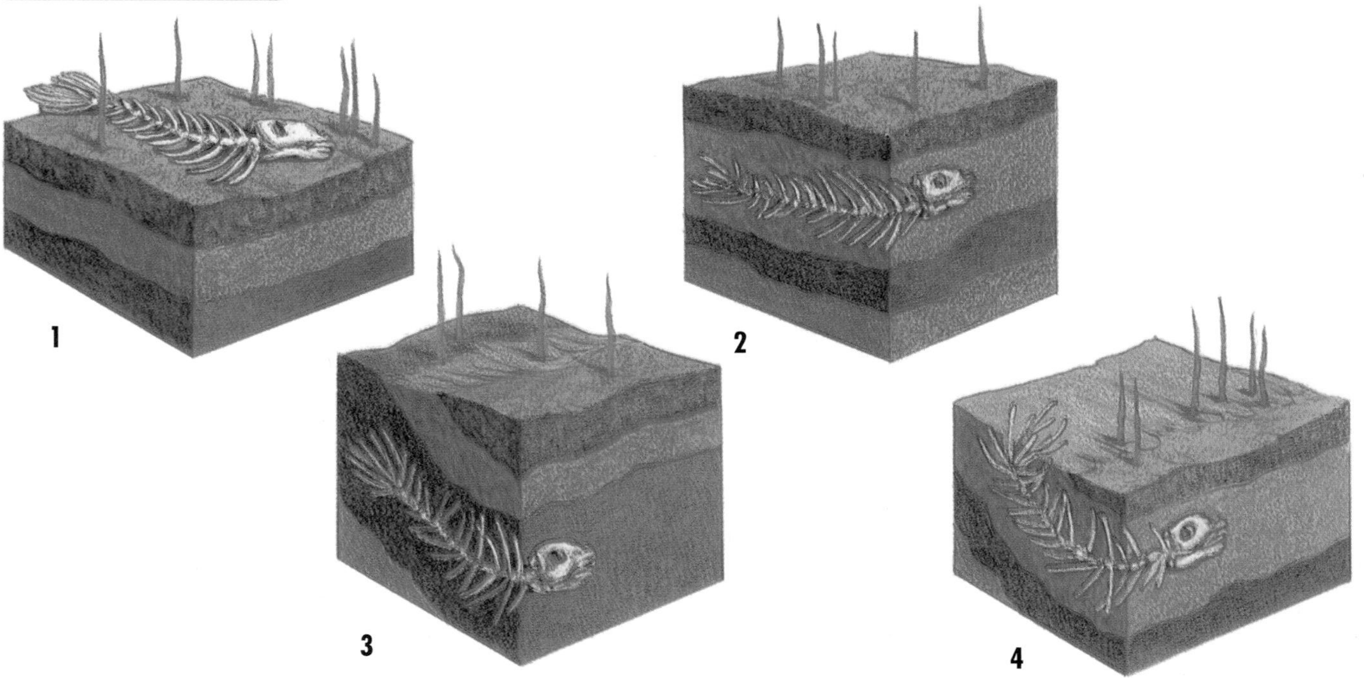

(1) When this fish died, it drifted down to the ocean floor. (2) Sediment gradually covered it. (3) Eventually the sediment, with the fish in it, hardened into rock. (4) When you crack open the rock, you find the impression of the fish's skeleton preserved.

*re*SEARCH

Scientists estimate that the earth is about 4.6 billion years old. To keep track of the events throughout the earth's long history, geologists have developed a time scale. This time scale is separated into the following "eras."

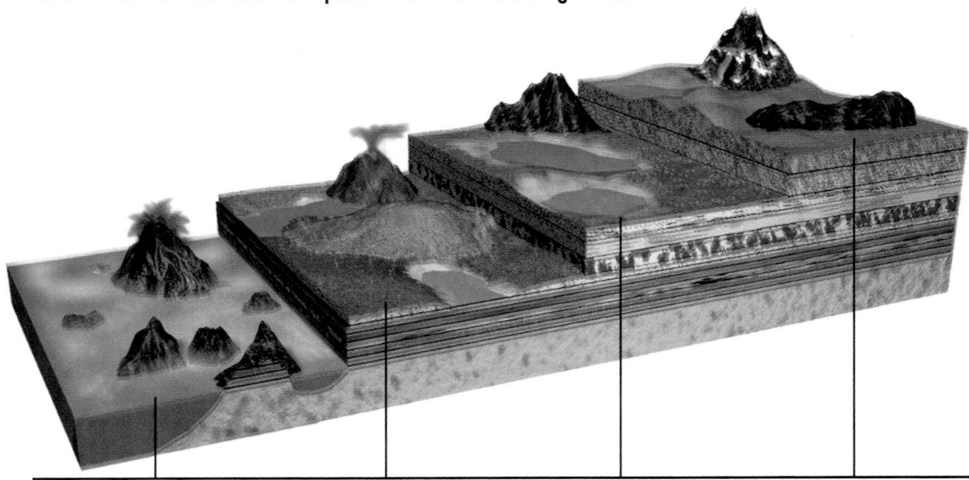

Find out more about the geological time scale.

- Why do geologists divide the scales at those times? (Hint: Find out what happened 600 million, 225 million, and 65 million years ago.)
- What did the earth look like during each era? What changes were happening?
- What forms of life lived on the earth during each era?

Create your own colourful version of the geological time scale, showing what was happening on the earth during each era.

Communicate

1 Imagine that you've been selected to make a video for other Grade 7 students about how to analyze evidence of geological change. Use your notes from this section to decide what information to include in your video. Using this information, prepare an outline for your video script that explains how to analyze evidence of geological change. Include sketches and ideas for locations where you could record evidence on site.
   a) You can present the information in any order you like—you don't have to follow the order in this textbook.
   b) Identify any other information you would like to have to complete your video script. Where would you look for this information?
   c) If you could get anyone at all, who would you get to narrate your script, or host your video? Why would you choose this person?

2 What evidence of geological change do you see in the picture?

4.3 Connecting the Rocks

Explore

You recycle things all the time—cans, paper, and glass and plastic bottles. After you throw them into the recycling bin, they are taken away, broken down, and made into new products. Does that sound familiar? Think of what you've learned about rocks in this chapter—how they form and the processes that affect them. In what ways does the earth recycle rocks?

Develop

Recycling Rocks

The next activity gives you an opportunity to use what you've learned to create a model of how rocks are recycled.

WHAT'S THE CONNECTION?

Think about the three types of rocks—igneous, sedimentary, and metamorphic. What are the different ways they are connected with one another? First, complete this chart to help you recall what you've already learned about these connections.

	sedimentary rocks	igneous rocks	metamorphic rocks
Sedimentary rocks form when. . .			*erosion breaks up and deposits metamorphic rocks.*
Igneous rocks form when. . .	*sedimentary rocks are melted deep in the earth's crust.*		
Metamorphic rocks form when. . .		*extreme heat and pressure act on igneous rocks.*	

On a large sheet of paper, draw and label something to represent each of the three types of rocks, as shown in the illustration.

Working with your group, decide what kind of diagram you want to create to show how rocks are recycled. Be as colourful and creative as you want.

- How will you show the processes that connect the types of rocks?
- How will you show the process that recycles a type of rock into the same type (for example, when a sedimentary rock is eroded and deposited to form a new sedimentary rock)?
- Can igneous rocks form in any other way than those given in the chart? (Hint: What is the interior of the earth made of?)

When you have completed your diagram, exchange it with one from another group.

- Are they able to see all the connections in your diagram?
- Can you see all the connections in their diagram? Tell them what you like about their diagram. Suggest ways, if any, that it could be clearer.
- If you were going to do this again, what changes, if any, would you make to your diagram?

5 EARTH'S CRUST

The Rock Cycle

Geologists call the pattern of events shown in the diagram you just completed the **rock cycle**. A cycle is a series of events that repeats over and over, like the seasons—summer follows spring, which follows winter, which follows fall, and then it starts over. The school year follows a cycle, too. You don't learn the same information every year, but your school year has a pattern. What are the events at school that repeat themselves every year?

Geologists use the rock cycle to show how the changes that happen to rocks follow a pattern over millions of years. We may not be able to see all these changes as they happen but we can "read" them in the rocks when we study them.

Communicate

1 What is the rock cycle a model of?
2 Why do you think the rock cycle is useful to geologists?

4.4 Check Your Progress

1 a) Describe three types of weathering.
  b) Where would you look for these types of weathering in your area? Why?
2 What is the connection between erosion and weathering?
3 The picture at left shows the footprint left behind by one of the astronauts who landed on the moon about 30 years ago. This footprint looks exactly the same today as it did when it was made. What does this tell you about weather on the moon? Explain your answer.
4 Suppose you went to a quarry and found some fossils in sedimentary rocks. Then you visited another quarry 5 km away and found exactly the same kinds of rocks, containing the same kinds of fossils. What could you say about the second set of rocks you found?
5 Write a paragraph explaining the rock cycle.

Big Idea

5.0 Knowing the characteristics of soil can help you understand how it can be used and conserved.

The next time you're standing on some grass, try to imagine what's under your feet. You know what's deep below you—the earth's crust, mantle, and core. But how is all that connected to the soles of your shoes? The soft spongy mat of grass you're standing on is made possible by the soil that connects the rocks of the crust with the world of life and air above. Soil forms the very thin outer surface of the earth's crust and much of it actually comes from these rocks. It may be a tiny part of the earth, but it's important to us and to all other land animals and plants. Our lives depend on soil because plants grow in it, and we can't live without plants.

5.1 What Is Soil?

Explore

If soil is such a thin layer—but such an important one—it must contain some valuable ingredients! In the next activity, you can take a closer look at soil.

Problem Solver

Getting Your Hands Dirty

What's in it?

1 Collect two soil samples, each from a different location. You need a handful of soil per sample. Try to get samples that are different colours and not too wet. Try to collect one sample from a garden or flower bed. The other sample could come from a field, park, or roadside. (Be sure to have permission first, and review any safety concerns with your teacher.)

continued on next page

2 Put each sample in a separate plastic bag. Write on a piece of paper where the sample came from and put the paper in the bag with the sample. Seal the bag so you won't lose any soil before you get to school.

3 In class, put two sheets of white paper side by side on your desk. Place one sample on each sheet and write on top of each sheet where the sample came from. Examine the samples carefully and describe the colour, look, and feel of them in your Science Journal.

- Use a hand lens or magnifying glass to look at the grains in the soil. How big are they? Are they all separate or do they look clumped together? What do you think the grains are made of?
- Rub a bit of each sample between your fingers. What does it feel like? (Wash your hands thoroughly immediately after handling the soil.)
- What else have you observed about each sample?
- How were your samples similar? How were they different?
- Were you surprised by anything you saw in the soil samples?

4 Carefully place your samples back in the plastic bags and return the soil outside.

Where did it come from?

5 You already know something about how soils form from your investigation of weathering and erosion in Big Idea 4.0. Recall that weathering breaks rocks down into tiny pieces that form the beginnings of soil. Discuss with a partner what factors you think are important in soil formation. Then write or draw a short description in your Science Journal of how you think soil forms. The questions below can help with your discussion.

- How can rock break down in small enough pieces to form soil?
- Where does the other material in soil come from?
- How might weather affect soil formation?
- Are living things involved in soil formation?

Develop

A Definition of Soil

When you examined the samples in the previous activity, you discovered that soil is made up of more than one thing. Now you will explore soil in more detail. To prepare for your exploration, start a web diagram with the word *soil* in the centre. Build your web diagram as you read about soil and how it forms.

Soil is a mixture of rock fragments, mineral grains, and organic material. (Organic material includes once-living things and wastes from living things. Decomposers help break down this material.) When the organic material decays completely, it's called **humus**. Humus gives soil a rich, dark colour and helps keep it moist by absorbing water. It also prevents the rock and mineral grains from packing too tightly together. Plants need soil that's loose enough to allow roots to grow easily.

The rock fragments and mineral grains in soil can be as fine as clay or as coarse as sand. The kinds of minerals depend on the type of rock that formed the soil. But soil is more than just humus and rock or mineral grains. The spaces between these components are just as important. They are called **pores**, and they allow air and water into the soil. Plants need both.

The best soil for growing plants is called *fertile* soil. A fertile soil is one that has the right combination of minerals, organic matter, and pores to support healthy plant growth.

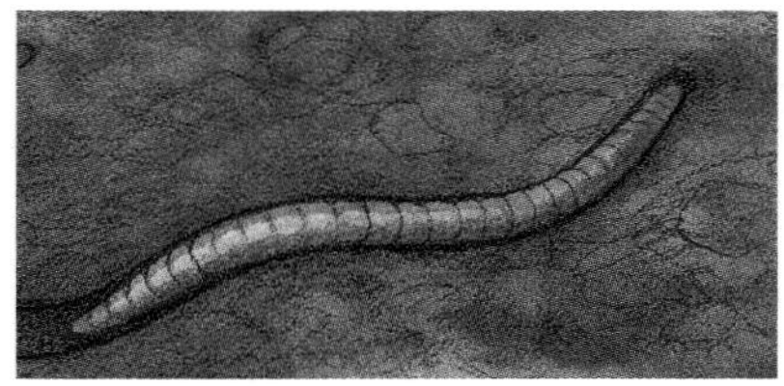

Did you notice any living things in your soil samples? Living things contribute organic matter and help air and water move into the soil. Most living things in the soil are micro-organisms, but you might see earthworms or plant roots.

DECISION MAKER

LOOKING AT LAND USE

The Question

What's the best way to use and preserve our soil?

Background Information

1 Research how the characteristics of soil determine its use. For example:
   a) What soil characteristics are important for farming? for construction? for the forest industry?
   b) What roles do government agencies have in determining land use? (Look at zoning regulations, town plans, etc.)

2 Present your information in chart form.

Type of Soil	Use(s)	Who Decides on Use?

In Your Opinion

3 Do you think farmland should only be used for growing crops?

4 Who should have the most say in determining land use: government officials, people in the surrounding community, or the individual or organization who wants to use the land?

How Soil Forms

Our definition of soil states that it's a mixture of rock fragments, mineral grains, and organic material, with pores that hold air and water. How does solid rock become a loose mixture that provides a home for living things? Look at the diagram below to see the stages of soil development.

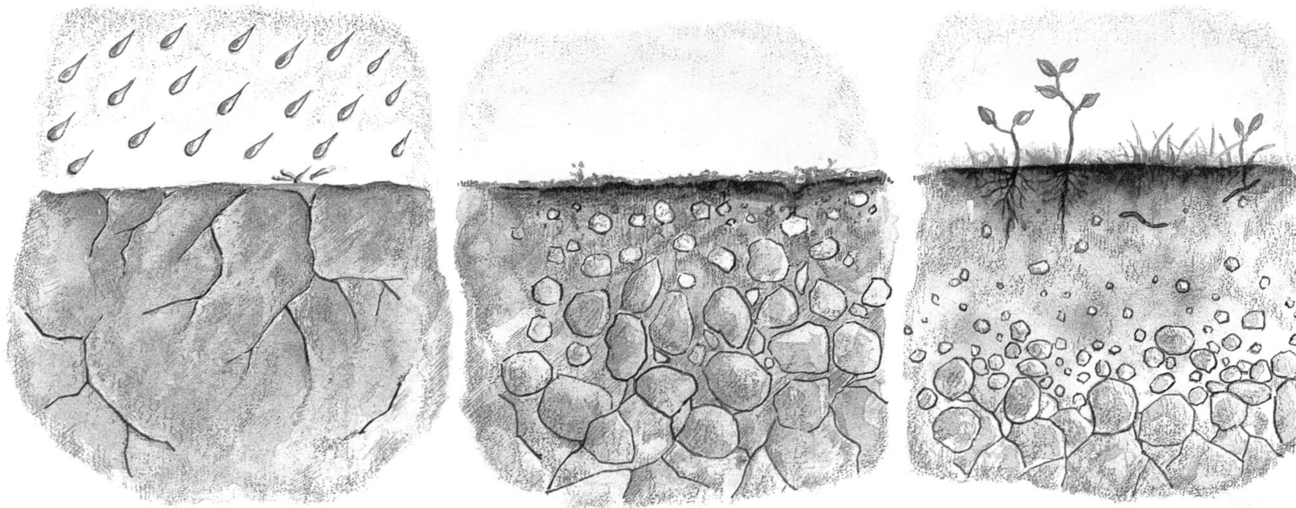

Mechanical and chemical weathering start to break up the bare rock. In the loose grains of rock and minerals, lichens and mosses start to grow. As they grow, they wear down the rock even more. Rainwater enters the spaces in the crumbling rock and dissolves nutrients. Nutrients are the basic materials that living things need to survive. Once the nutrients are dissolved in water, plants can use them to grow.

As the soil starts to develop, more plants of different kinds start to grow in it. Their roots hold the soil in place so it isn't eroded away. The plants die and add organic matter to the soil. Humus forms as bacteria and other decomposers work to break down this organic matter. Meanwhile, the rock is still being broken down.

The soil has developed into three layers: *topsoil, subsoil,* and *parent material*. The topsoil is bound together with plant roots, and is full of micro-organisms, insects, and small animals. All of these help to break down organic matter. Many help to move air and water through the soil. Below the topsoil is the subsoil. It has less organic matter and less air and water in it. The parent material below the subsoil is made up mainly of broken-up rock. This is the rock that originally weathered to form the soil.

Communicate

1. At the beginning of this section, you developed your own description of how soil forms. Look at the web diagram you created as you read about soil. Use it to revise your description to include new information.
2. Imagine you are a small animal digging deep into the soil to make a den. Describe or draw what you would see as you dig down.

5.2 Soil Characteristics

Explore

What do you look for when you shop for a pair of shoes? If you want them for sports, you probably look for good support, soles that grip well, and a comfortable fit. If you want them to wear to school, you're probably more interested in the style and colour. You're looking for certain characteristics in the shoes that suit what you want to use them for.

In the same way, soil characteristics are useful in determining how a soil can be used. For example, an unpaved bike path is easier to ride on if the soil can be compacted (pressed together to form a hard surface). So you wouldn't choose sand for a bike path.

Look at the following situations. Work with a partner to describe in your own words the characteristics that the soil should have for each one.

- You want to plant a vegetable garden.
- A friend says she is going to start making pottery. She plans to use the soil from the banks of a nearby stream.
- A sports field is being put in next to the community centre. (Hint: a layer of sand is being spread on it before the final grass cover is installed.)

What kind of soil characteristics are you likely to find in these locations?

Develop

How to Describe Soil

Scientists use the following characteristics to describe soil: texture, pore size, air and water capacity, nutrient content, and depth. To help yourself keep track of the different characteristics as you read about them here, fill in the following chart as you go along.

Characteristic	What it is	Why it's useful to know
Texture		

Texture

You looked at the texture of two soil samples when you examined them at the beginning of section 5.1. **Texture** is a description of how smooth or sharp the grains of soil are and how big they are. The size of the grains is important because it affects the pore size and how much air and water the soil can hold. From largest to smallest, the grain sizes in soil are referred to as: sand, silt, and clay. Most soils are a combination of grain sizes. The grain size that makes up most of the soil gives it its texture. For example, a soil that is 75% sand, 20% silt, and 5% clay has a sandy texture.

The main types of soil are sandy soils, silty soils, clay soils, and loam. Sandy soils feel gritty and don't hold water well. They are useful where good drainage is needed. Silty soils feel smooth, and clay soils feel slippery. Both can hold a lot of water, but clay soils are also sticky, which is useful for making pottery and bricks. Plants do not grow well in heavy clay soil because it holds too much water. If it dries out, it hardens and cracks.

Loam is an important soil for agriculture because it's a well-balanced soil. It's called "well-balanced" because it's made up of 40% sand, 40% silt, and 20% clay. It contains humus and holds the right amount of water for plants. Loam is a fertile soil in which plants grow well. It's also easy to plough and plant in. A sandy loam is one that has a higher percentage of sand than that given above. What do you think a clay loam is?

PROBLEM SOLVER

HOW DOES IT FEEL?

- You can test soil texture yourself. Examine a sample of dry soil carefully. Rub it between your fingers. Do you think it's a sandy, clay, or silty soil?
- Put a spoonful of soil in the palm of your hand. Mix just enough water into the soil so it's wet but not liquid. Roll the wet soil into a ball. What happened to the ball of soil? Clay soil holds the ball shape. Silty soil falls apart even though it feels like clay soil. Sandy soil also falls apart.
- To check your conclusion about what kind of soil you have, spread the wet soil into a thin layer on your palm. If it's slippery and smooth, with no shine, it's a clay soil. If it looks dull and feels gritty, it's a sandy soil. Wash your hands thoroughly immediately after handling the soil. Was your prediction about this soil sample correct?

Pore Size

The **pores** are the spaces between the soil grains. The size and number of pores depend on the sizes of the grains in the soil. Pore size is important because it affects how easily air and water move through the soil. It also affects how much air and water a soil can hold. Look at the diagrams below of two samples of soil seen through the same microscope. Are the pores the same size in both diagrams? How is the size of the grains related to the size of the pores?

Fine-grained soil such as clay has more pores than a coarse-grained soil because there are more grains in the same volume of sample. More grains mean more spaces between them. However, the spaces are smaller. The smaller the pores, the harder it is for the water to move easily. So clay soil holds more water than sandy soil.

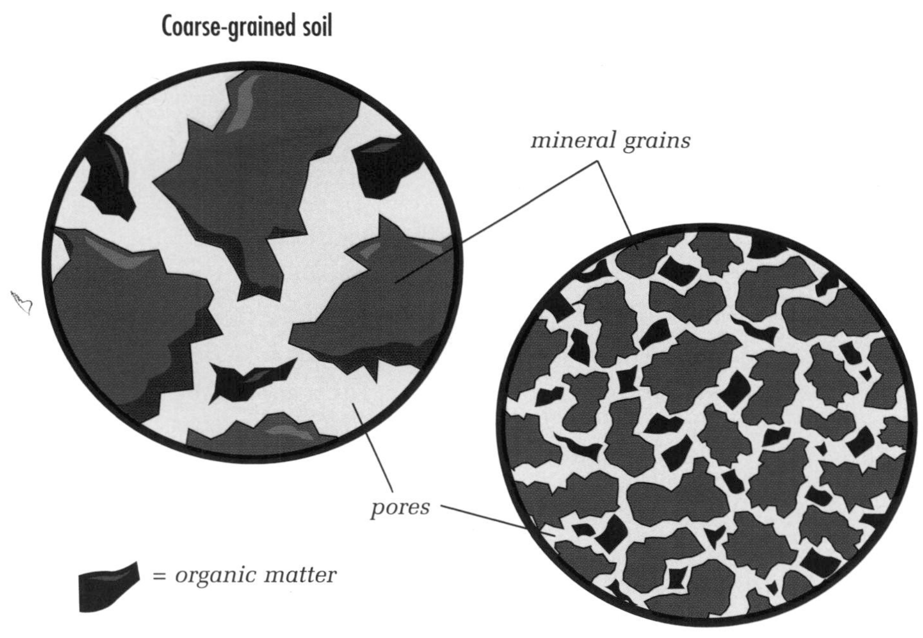

Air and Water Capacity

A good soil for plants is one that contains air and water. Air provides oxygen, which plants need for growth. Water dissolves nutrients that plants need from the minerals and organic matter in the soil. *Capacity* is the amount of something that a material or object can hold. So the air capacity is the amount of air that soil can hold. As you read above, air capacity is affected by pore size. The water capacity of soil is affected by both pore size and the amount of humus in the soil.

*info*BIT

Soil that holds too much water is as bad for most plants as soil that dries out too quickly. Too much water means that all the pores are full of water, so there's no room for air. Without oxygen from the air, plants can't survive. Why do plants need oxygen?

This plant has had too much water!

What soil characteristics can you see in this photo?

Nutrient Content

Nutrients are the basic materials that living things need to survive. For plants, nutrients include large amounts of substances such as phosphorus, and small amounts of minerals such as copper. But plants can absorb these nutrients only if they are dissolved in water. That's why water capacity is an important characteristic of soil. Nitrogen, a major plant nutrient, is provided by decomposer organisms in the soil.

Depth

The *depth of soil* is determined by measuring the distance from the surface down to the rock on which the soil lies. Depth is important because it affects how the soil can be used. You may have a fertile soil, but if it's only a few centimetres deep, it may not be able to support the roots of crops. An area with shallow soil on bare rock is usually expensive to construct buildings on. Where there is a deep layer of soil, it's easy to dig basements. Where there's only a thin layer on solid rock, excavation has to be done by blasting out solid rock.

Communicate

1 Match the following statements with the soil characteristics listed below.

Characteristic	Statement
a) texture	*1) The size of the spaces between the soil's grains affects how quickly water drains out of the soil.*
b) pore size	*2) Soils that are only a couple of centimetres thick cannot be used to grow trees.*
c) air capacity	*3) Plants grow well in soils rich in nitrogen.*
d) nutrient content	*4) Plants need oxygen, so soil for cultivation must contain enough air to satisfy a plant's needs.*
e) depth	*5) The grain size of soils can vary from coarse to fine.*

2 Add information on soil characteristics to the web diagram you began in the previous section.

3 At the beginning of this section, you thought about the importance of soil characteristics. Describe what you think would be ideal soil characteristics for the following situations.
   a) a reforestation area
   b) a landfill site
   c) a vegetable garden

5.3 Soil Conservation

Explore

Now that you've taken a close look at soil, let's step back and look at its importance as a natural resource. How important is soil to you? In your Science Journal, jot down your favourite foods. Now jot down the clothes you're wearing and what they are made of. Working with a partner, combine your lists.

Which items are made from plant or animal products? Which of these items depend on soil for their production? Mark an "S" beside each of these items. (For example, wool comes from sheep that graze on grass that grows in soil.) Share your results with the rest of the class. What percentage of your list relied on soil? Were you surprised by this number?

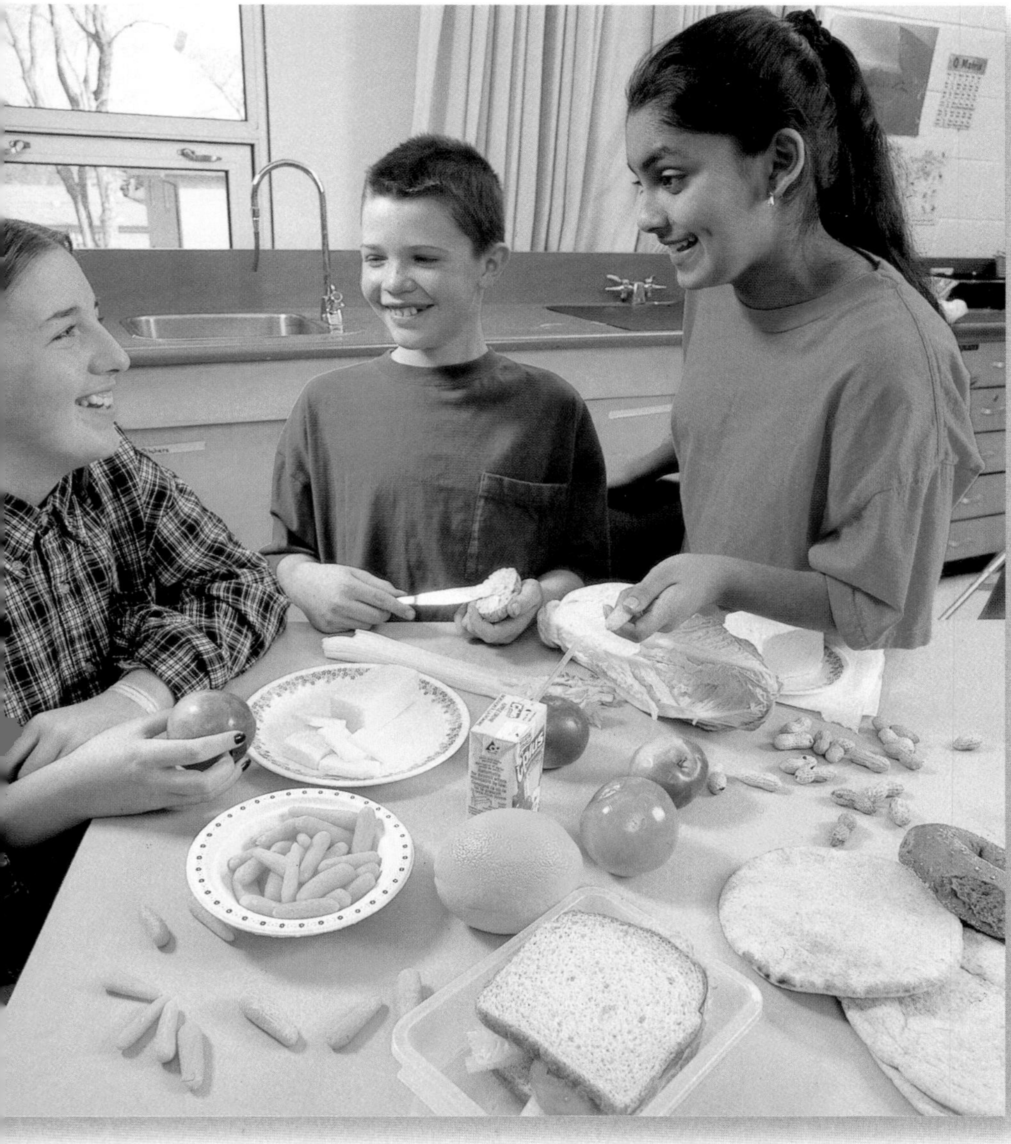

How is your lunch connected with soil?

infoBIT

If you look at a map of Canada, you see a huge land area. But only 7% of this area is suitable for farming. And not all crops can grow in all these areas. Peach trees, for example, need long, dry, hot summers to produce tasty fruit.

Where in Canada are peaches grown?

Develop

Soil Is a Natural Resource

*info***BIT**

A natural resource is a natural material, such as water, minerals, or petroleum, that can be used to meet human needs.

As you saw from listing your own food and clothes, soil is an important resource for food and fibre production. And you weren't even looking at furniture (wood), building supplies (wood, brick), or other items such as pottery! But soil is also important for other reasons. It supports habitats for wild plants and animals, and it provides protection from the effects of flooding by absorbing rainwater. However, soil must have a proper balance of organic materials and mineral content to support crops, wild plants, animals, or absorb rainwater. What happens when soil is eroded, polluted, or over-irrigated?

The photographs shown here help explain how soil can be damaged or destroyed. Using the information on this page and the next, add the different factors that cause soil problems to your web diagram.

When farmers clear land to plant crops, the soil's natural cover is removed and it's exposed to the weather. As long as the soil has a crop growing on it, it's protected. That's because plant roots help keep soil together.

But what happens after the crop is harvested? In dry climates, the soil dries out and the wind easily carries it away. Some farms have lost so much topsoil, they can no longer grow crops. Also, in areas where soil is exposed to rapidly flowing water, large amounts of soil can be carried away quickly.

Artificial pesticides and fertilizers were developed to help improve crop production. Pesticides are designed to kill harmful insects, but they often kill "good" insects as well. Too much fertilizer can harm the soil. Overuse of pesticides and fertilizers can pollute soil and destroy organic matter. The result is that the soil is no longer as fertile as it once was. Then, when it rains, these chemicals are washed out of the soil into local waterways, where they can damage those ecosystems as well.

Irrigation in very dry areas can poison the soil with salt. The salt occurs naturally in some subsoils. When extra water is added by irrigation, it dissolves the salt. In hot areas where there is little rainfall, the water on the soil's surface evaporates, drawing the water from the subsoil upward into the topsoil. This water contains salt, which is left behind on the soil's surface when the water evaporates. Most plants can't grow in topsoil that contains too much salt.

Conserving Soil

Soil is important to all of us. It's an important support to Canada's economy. It provides a living for farmers. It provides all of us with a wide range of products. And it's an important part of our environment, providing habitat, nourishment, and protection for plants and animals. Soil conservation is important, but what do most people know about it?

Communicate

1 Indicate which of the following statements are true, and which are false. For each false statement, correct it to make it true.
   a) Soil conservation is important only to farmers.
   b) Using lots of fertilizer is always helpful.
   c) Plants can help to prevent wind erosion.

2 Below are two examples of actions people have taken to conserve soil. Explain how each one will help the soil.

3 Write a poem, paragraph, or story expressing how you feel about soil conservation.

4 If you haven't already done so, add information on soil conservation to your web diagram.

*info***BIT**

One of the biggest threats to farmland in Canada is urban growth. Our most productive farmland is in the south, where most people want to live. Once farmland is built on or paved over, it's lost forever.

5.4 CHECK YOUR PROGRESS

1 Suppose you collected a soil sample from a flower bed in a local park. What would you expect to see in it if you looked at it through a hand lens? Draw and label a diagram of what you would see.

2 How is weather involved in soil formation?

3 An old service station in your neighbourhood will be torn down and the property turned into a park. What problems with the soil might need to be fixed before it can become a home to trees, other plants, and animals?

4 a) Name two characteristics that are used to describe soil.
   b) Explain how you would use these two characteristics to help you determine if a soil is good for growing plants or crops.

5 Explain in your own words why soil conservation is important.

Guilty or Innocent?

Before You Start...

In this section, you learned how the characteristics of soil can determine how it's used. For example, soil rich in nutrients that holds the right amount of water is good for growing plants. A sandy soil is useful where good drainage is needed. Knowledge of the characteristics of soil also comes in handy for crime investigators. Sometimes soil can give clues to help solve crimes. Try this activity to see how soil can help you solve a mystery. (First, review what you've learned about soil characteristics.)

The Situation

A millionaire who grows exotic plants has reported that two of her large prized plants have been stolen from her garden. She estimates the value of the plants at about $100 000. They grow only in a few places in the world.

A police investigation has discovered a similar plant in a large pot at a local nursery. The owner of the nursery claims that he has recently imported the plant from Uruguay. He says it's still in the original pot and soil.

Police have collected soil from around the roots in the pot at the nursery and from the holes where the plants were removed on the millionaire's estate. They have just received a sample of soil from Uruguay.

The Question

How could soil characteristics help you determine if the plant in the nursery came from Uruguay?

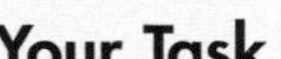

Your Task

1. Work in a group to develop a strategy for determining if the plant came from Uruguay.
2. Decide what materials and equipment you'll need to carry out your strategy. How will you examine the soil samples? What kind of test or tests will you do on them?
3. Plan your procedure. Consider the evidence you are looking for, how you will collect the data you need, whether the test you're planning is fair, and so on.

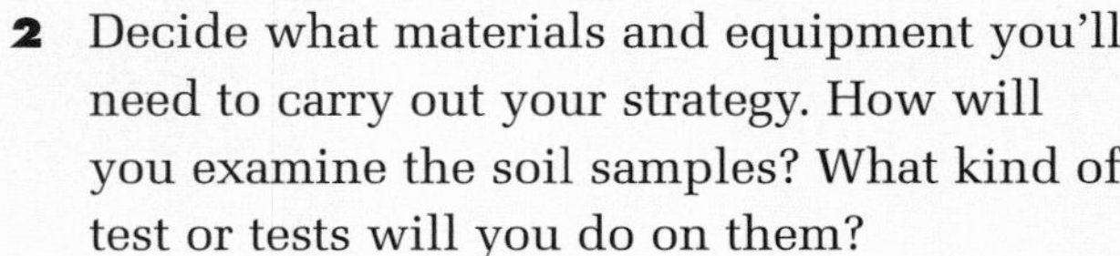

4. Write up your procedure, and show it to your teacher.
5. Discuss in your group how you would carry out your investigation.

Analyzing and Interpreting

6. Do you think your strategy would be successful? Would you be able to determine if the nursery's plant came from Uruguay?
7. Share and compare your experimental plan and findings with your classmates. How do your results compare with theirs?

Big Idea

6.0 We can make informed decisions about how our actions might affect the landscape.

Throughout this chapter, you've been thinking about change on the earth's crust. You learned how processes both inside and outside the earth have altered its surface. The powerful movements of tectonic plates and the constant wearing down caused by weathering and erosion are changing the earth's surface even today. Most of these changes happen very slowly. But there are other changes that we can observe—and even influence. These are the changes caused by humans.

6.1 How We Affect the World Around Us

Explore

Think about your neighbourhood. Have you noticed any changes over the past year? In your Science Journal, write down all the changes you can think of. Maybe a new building or house went up in the next block. Maybe one of your neighbours moved away, and a new family moved in. Did any of these changes affect how the land was used? For example, was something built on an empty lot? Was an old building torn down and a new one put up in its place? Make a note beside those changes that affected how the land was used.

As you read through this section and do the activity, look for examples of land use changes in your neighbourhood or in the larger community (town or city). Maybe 20 townhomes are being put in where there used to be one family home. Maybe a new shopping centre is being built on what used to be farmland. Maybe a new arena is going in where there used to be warehouses. Describe these changes and any debate or controversy that they might cause. You may want to keep clippings from the newspapers about them or take notes from television or radio reports. You might also find information on the Internet. You'll have an opportunity to use the information you collect at the end of this Big Idea.

Develop

Making an Impact

A long time ago, this was a farmer's field, but no one has farmed it for many years.

Roheena, David, and their friends used to use an empty lot near their homes as a gathering place. It was a great place because it had trees and a stream running through it. When they were little, they'd play there for hours. As they got older, it was a good place to sit around on a summer day. There were always lots of birds and squirrels. Sometimes a fox would sprint into the bushes. In the evenings, frogs would sing. Now a sign like the one in the photo has gone up stating that a housing development has been proposed. Their community is about to change. It's turning into a new subdivision.

*info*BIT

People don't always take green space and turn it into pavement or buildings. Sometimes they take former industrial areas or built-up areas and turn them into green space. This photo is of the world-famous Butchart Gardens near Victoria, British Columbia. These gardens used to be a limestone quarry. Are there any parks in your community on land that was once used for industry or buildings?

Roheena and David wondered how this development might affect the land and the people who live in the community now. They watched as the land was cleared and levelled for the construction of the houses, a playground park, and streets. The trees and other plants that had been on the vacant lot disappeared, exposing the soil to the weather. Roheena remembered learning that soil is affected by wind and water when its cover of plants is removed. She wondered what would happen to the animals that used to live in this area.

During construction, a lot of traffic from large trucks and other heavy equipment passed through the neighbourhood.

Workers brought in and buried a culvert for the stream to flow through. (A culvert is a large pipe, usually made of metal.) Other drain pipes were put in the ground under the new streets to prevent flooding during heavy rains. When Roheena and David heard about this, they were surprised. There was never a problem with flooding before. They wondered why special drains were needed under the paved streets now.

Once the houses were built, new soil was trucked in, and grass and other decorative plants were planted. Roheena and David questioned why new soil was being brought in when plants used to grow on the soil that was there. They wondered if the new grass and plants would be the same kinds that used to grow in this area. If they were, why not use the same ones?

With all the new houses going up, Roheena and David knew there would be a lot of families with children moving in. They learned that portable classrooms would be added to their school.

Then they saw an announcement that a new shopping mall would be built on the other side of the subdivision. David's older brother was happy about that—he hoped to get a part-time job there. Roheena's parents wondered how much more traffic there would be on their street after all the houses and the shopping mall were finished. But at least, they said, the bus service would improve.

What do you think?

In the next activity, you can take a close look at the development and express your opinion.

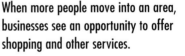

When more people move into an area, businesses see an opportunity to offer shopping and other services.

PROBLEM SOLVER

WHAT HAPPENED?

Look back over the description of the building of the new subdivision and Roheena's and David's questions and speculations. Make two lists of the changes that resulted from the new subdivision. In one list, put all the changes that affected the land. In the other list, put all the changes that affected the community.

- Are there any other changes that probably happened that were not mentioned in the text? Add these to your lists.
- What were the environmental effects of the housing development?
- What were the economic effects of the housing development? (Hint: How did it affect people's jobs and businesses?)

Discuss with a partner whether the housing development was a good change for the community. Share your opinion with your classmates. Would your opinion change if you knew that there was a shortage of housing in the town before the new houses were built?

Communicate

1 For each of the following situations, list the ways in which the landscape might be affected.
   a) a large office building and warehouse built in a swampy area
   b) a multi-lane highway built through a residential neighbourhood
   c) an old factory site turned into a park

2 Look at the list you made at the beginning of this section about changes that happened over the past year in your own neighbourhood. Select one change and answer the following questions.
   a) In what ways did this change affect you?
   b) In what ways did it affect the rest of the neighbourhood?

3 You may have heard people say that it's important to make informed decisions about issues such as land use. What do you think the expression "informed decision" means?

6.2 Using the Earth's Resources

Explore

Housing, shopping malls, schools, and parks are just a few examples of the ways that humans affect the landscape. They are all part of urban development, which means city development. When you studied soil, you also considered the impact of farms on the land. Farms are part of rural or country development. Another important human impact is industrial development. Industry creates the products and services we use every day. All the clothes you wear and appliances you use—even simple things like pencils—have to be manufactured.

What industries are in your area?

Take a look at an ordinary pencil. What is it made of? Probably more things than you think. First, there's the wood. The trees have to be harvested, transported, and processed into pencil shapes. Those activities use metal for vehicles and machinery, and petroleum for transportation. The "lead" in the pencil is the mineral graphite, which has to be mined, processed, and transported. That also uses metal and petroleum products. Then there's the paint on the pencil. It's manufactured from other ingredients that also have to be manufactured. Does your pencil have an eraser? Where does that come from and how was it made? What about the metal strip holding the eraser to the pencil?

harvesting of wood from forest
mining of metal ore
manufacturing of cardboard
processing of ore into metal
collecting of raw material for eraser
warehouses and stores
packaging
manufacturing of metal strip
manufacturing of eraser
processing graphite
manufacturing of pencil
manufacturing of paint
manufacturing of paint colours
mining graphite
harvesting of wood from forest

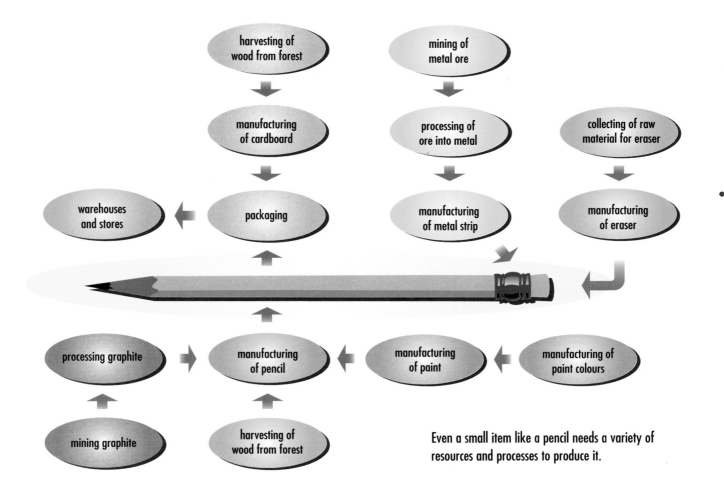

Even a small item like a pencil needs a variety of resources and processes to produce it.

Develop

From Raw Material to Final Disposal

In the next activity, you will investigate what goes into some common products that you use, and what happens to these products when they are no longer useful.

INVESTIGATOR

A Product's Story

Before You Start ...

Human impact on the earth often starts with the process of taking minerals out of the ground. The impact continues when materials are processed and transported. Finally, it ends with the disposal of products. For this activity, you will take a common, everyday product and look at the human impact resulting from its use.

The Question

Where do the earth resources come from to manufacture products and what happens to these products when they are no longer useful?

continued on next page

5 EARTH'S CRUST

Materials & Equipment

- *a common, everyday product, such as a stapler, a pen, a computer disk, or a pop can*
- *reference books*
- *Internet access*
- *presentation materials*

Procedure

1. With your group, decide what product you want to analyze. Make sure it's different from those chosen by other groups in your class. Read the activity all the way through before you start, so you and your group can decide how you're going to collect and present the

information to the whole class. You can act it out, write about it, draw it, project it from a computer, or present it in some other way. Once you have decided upon your presentation, get your teacher's approval before you go ahead.

2 Start by listing everything that was used to make the product. (Remember to include paints, dyes, glues, and anything else used for fastening, colouring, or strengthening the product.) Then find out what it's made of and where each material and its ingredients come from and how they are processed. (Don't forget to indicate wherever transportation is needed, since this uses resources as well.)

3 Once you have identified what goes into making the product, consider how it's sold. What kind of packaging is used? Think about how the product gets to you.

4 In your research, don't forget to include what happens when the product's useful life is over. How is it disposed of? Can it be reused or recycled? Does it just go into the garbage? Where does the garbage go? What effect does the garbage disposal have on the landscape?

5 Present your information to the rest of the class.

Keeping Records

6 Decide how your group will keep track of all the information being collected. You may want to use charts, graphs, photos, drawings, or other techniques.

Analyzing and Interpreting

7 How many different materials were used to make the product you analyzed? How many of these were minerals?

8 What were the main impacts on the land of mining the minerals used in your product?

9 Would using your product have an impact on the environment? For example, if you chose a computer disk, using that disk requires a computer and electricity to run it. The electricity may be produced by hydroelectric generation or by oil- or gas-fired generating stations.

10 Can you suggest any changes that could be made to your product to reduce its impact on the environment?

Forming Conclusions

11 Write a paragraph that answers the question: "Where do the earth resources come from to manufacture products and what happens to these products when they are no longer useful?" Use a flowchart or other type of diagram with your answer.

What materials went into making this computer monitor?

1 What is the connection between a mine in a wilderness area in Canada and the products you buy?
2 Why do we need landfill sites?

6.3 CHECK YOUR PROGRESS

1 At the beginning of section 6.1, you were asked to look for any land use changes happening now in your community (town or city). Answer the following questions about one of these changes.
   a) In what way is the land use changing?
   b) Who is asking for this change? Why do they want it?
   c) Is anybody objecting to the change? Why are they objecting?
   d) Write a letter to your town or city council explaining why you are for or against the change.

2 a) List three factors that people should consider when making decisions about land use.
   b) Explain why each of these factors is important.

3 Choose one of the items from the photos below.
   a) List at least four materials that are used in manufacturing the item.
   b) Choose one of these materials and explain what impact you think it has on the environment.
   c) What happens to the item after you finish using it? Can it be reused or recycled in any way?

Living with the Power of Nature

Meteorologists can use satellite photos of major storms like this hurricane to help predict how and when the weather will affect people.

Most of the time we aren't aware of the effects that natural events have on our lives. But when a major event hits, like a snowstorm or an earthquake, it makes the news. It also makes us aware of the powerful forces of nature. Humans can't change these forces or prevent them, but we have learned to cope with them in a variety of ways.

Prediction is one of the keys to dealing with natural events. If a natural event can be predicted, people can prepare for it. For example, satellites allow meteorologists (scientists who study weather) to observe storms from space and determine what these are likely to do.

In the spring of 1997, the Red River running through Winnipeg flooded its banks. This 2000-km^2 "lake" forced 28 000 Manitobans to leave their homes.

For events that can't be predicted—such as earthquakes, volcanic eruptions, floods, and landslides—people in high-risk areas can still prepare for them. One strategy is to try to reduce the damage such events may cause if they happen. In some cities, building codes require people to use special techniques and designs that make buildings safer in an earthquake. In areas where floods can be a problem, people may not be permitted to build in the most dangerous spots.

Natural events affect all of us, even when we don't realize it. Technology helps us cope with these effects and understand their causes.

People involved in relief efforts after natural disasters rely on communications technology to make sure they get the help they need. They also rely on transportation technology to bring that help to them.

In Your Opinion

1. Planning for disasters is important for saving lives and property. List as many things as you can think of that a community should consider in planning to deal with a severe snowstorm.
2. What kind of technology do you rely on in your life to help you adapt to the climate? List as many items as you can think of. For each one, describe how it helps you.

PROJECT

5 EARTH'S CRUST

Getting Started

In this chapter, you have explored the different processes that create features on the earth's surface. Forces inside the earth, such as the movements of tectonic plates or movements along faults, can create mountains. Forces on the earth's surface, such as ice and wind, can wear down and move mountains through weathering and erosion. For this project, you can use what you've learned about the earth's processes to create models and simulations of the features in your landscape, showing how they formed and why they look as they do today.

Making the right choices about land use requires good information. If an area is covered in buildings or thick forest, it's hard to see what the land really looks like. Models and simulations can help people understand their local landscape better. By understanding it better, people can see how their activities will affect the environment.

These hills formed millions of years ago as mountains. When they first formed, they were tall and jagged. Now they are worn down and rounded. What processes do you think could have changed them?

The soil in this valley is very fertile, as you can see from the many farms. How do you think this soil was deposited here?

Niagara Falls flows over a cliff made of shale and limestone, both sedimentary rocks. The falls originally formed 11 km north of their location today. Why have the falls moved along the river?

Imagine that you are a designer who designs and builds models and simulations for science centres and other museums. Your community is building a new science centre. Your job is to provide a display that shows how the local features in your landscape began, and how they became the way they are today.

Think about the features that you would include in a display of your community. To help your thinking, look at the pictures on the previous page, and see if you can answer the questions in the captions.

The features in those pictures are just examples of what you might see. Your community may be completely different. You may not have any mountains or deep valleys. Your major features may be large areas of flat fertile soil beside a large body of water. Or you may have large swampy areas between low rocky hills. Whatever the features in your area, you can apply the ideas about the earth that you developed in this chapter. Your task is to use models and simulations to help yourself and others better understand your local land features.

Before You Start ...

You and your classmates are partners in Time Travel Designs Inc., a company specializing in displays that show the origin and history of features on the earth's surface. For your assignment, as described, you can use any information you gathered as you worked through this chapter. You will need to collect additional information about your local geology and geography from reference books, the Internet, and other resources.

CONTRACT

This document is a formal statement of an agreement between

Discovery Science Centre

and

Time Travel Designs Inc. (herein called "the Contractor")

To design and construct a display showing major features of the community and its local area.

The Contractor will:

- select the appropriate features to represent
- research the information on the origin and history of the features
- design and construct models and simulations to explain the features to the general public

Discovery Science Centre agrees to provide the Contractor with the space for the display and the materials to construct it.

continued on next page

Your company has found that the best way to develop these displays is for all the partners to work together to determine which features to model and simulate. Then you divide up the features among smaller teams. Each team is responsible for modelling or simulating one feature. When they are completed, all the features are combined in one large display.

Materials & Equipment

- *reference books, maps, aerial photos, Internet access*
- *paper and pencils*
- *materials for models and simulations (these will depend on what you decide to display)*

Procedure

1 With the other members of your class, brainstorm the answers to the following questions.
   a) What features of your local landscape do you want to include?
   b) How will your class decide who builds which models?
   c) How will you show both the origin and history of the local landscape in these models and simulations?
   d) Where will you get the materials you need to build your models?
   e) Add any other considerations you can think of.

2 Once you know what part of the display your team will be doing, brainstorm how you will plan, design, and build your model or simulation. Think of what you already know about the part of the landscape you will be modelling or the process you will be simulating.

3 Design your model or simulation, and give the design to your teacher for approval before you start building it. Include these items in your design.
   a) a drawing of your model
   b) a diagram showing how you will simulate the processes
   c) a list of materials
   d) a procedure for building your model
   e) your schedule
   f) safety considerations

4 Build your model or simulation according to the design and plan that your teacher approved.

5 If you find you have to change your design while you're building it, write down the changes you made. (If they are major changes, check with your teacher before you make them.)

6 Decide how you will explain your model or simulation to the rest of the class. You may want to have different team members explain different parts of the model or perform different parts of the simulation.

Share and Compare

7 Explain your model or simulation to your class. As you watch other teams, write down:
   a) what you liked best about their models or simulations
   b) any ideas or materials that you could have used for your model or simulation

8 Combine your model or simulation with those of your classmates to create the display. Invite other classes to see your display.

Observations and Reflections

9 Prepare a project completion report so your company has a record of the project and its results. Decide in your group what information should be part of your report.

CHAPTER REVIEW

Using Key Terms

1 Write a short story about the earth's crust using the following key terms.

Theory of Plate Tectonics
weathering
landscape
volcano
earthquake
rock cycle
resources
lithosphere
epicentre
mineral
erosion

Reviewing the Big Ideas

2 a) Describe the earth's crust.
b) Is the crust the same as the lithosphere? Explain your answer.

3 How is the strength of an earthquake measured?

4 a) What is a mountain?
b) Describe one way in which mountains can form.

5 Describe what happens inside and outside a volcano when it erupts.

6 Mohammed found a white mineral. With just that information, can you tell him what mineral it is? Why or why not?

7 What can happen to rocks deep within the earth's crust? Why?

8 a) In your own words, explain what weathering is.
b) Describe how ice can weather a rock.

9 a) What are strata?
b) How can geologists use strata to learn about the geologic history of an area?

10 Explain how soil forms.

Connecting the Big Ideas

11 Why do scientists want to be able to predict earthquakes and volcanoes?

12 a) What model do geologists use to show how igneous, sedimentary, and metamorphic rocks are related?
b) Why is this model useful to students?

13 The Theory of Plate Tectonics states that the surface of the earth is made up of moving plates. Earthquakes occur at the boundaries of these plates. If the plates are always moving, why aren't earthquakes happening all the time, along every boundary?

14 Will all rocks eventually become sedimentary rocks? Why or why not?

15 Agree or disagree with the following statements. Give reasons for your answers.
a) Soil is just dirt.
b) Because soil is forming all the time, we don't have to worry about conserving it.

Using the Big Ideas

16 You're looking at two earthquake reports on the Internet. Both earthquakes took place in populated areas. One measured 5.2 and lasted for 2 min. The other one measured 5.9 and lasted for 15 s. Which one probably caused more damage? Why?

17 Imagine that you live near a volcano that hasn't erupted for 100 years. One day you feel a small earthquake. The next day, you notice a bulge on the side of the mountain.

a) What do you think is causing these events? How is it causing them?

b) What will you do? Why?

18 The illustration shows a section of strata. Use the letters printed beside the layers in your answers to the following questions.

a) Which layer is oldest?

b) Look at the fossils in the bottom layer and the top layer. What can they tell you about the environment where these sediments were deposited?

c) Can the grain sizes in the different layers tell you anything about how the environment has changed in this area? Explain your answer. (Hint: Think about how and when water can carry rock fragments of different sizes.)

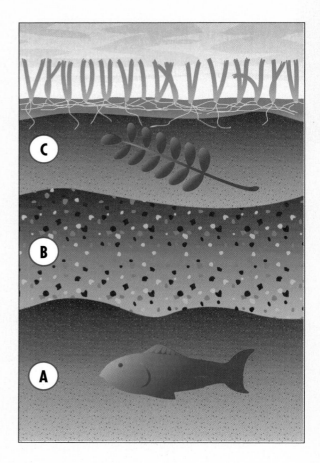

Self Assessment

19 Describe three things you didn't know before the chapter started.

20 What did you like best about this chapter?

21 List three questions you still have about the earth's crust.

Toolbox

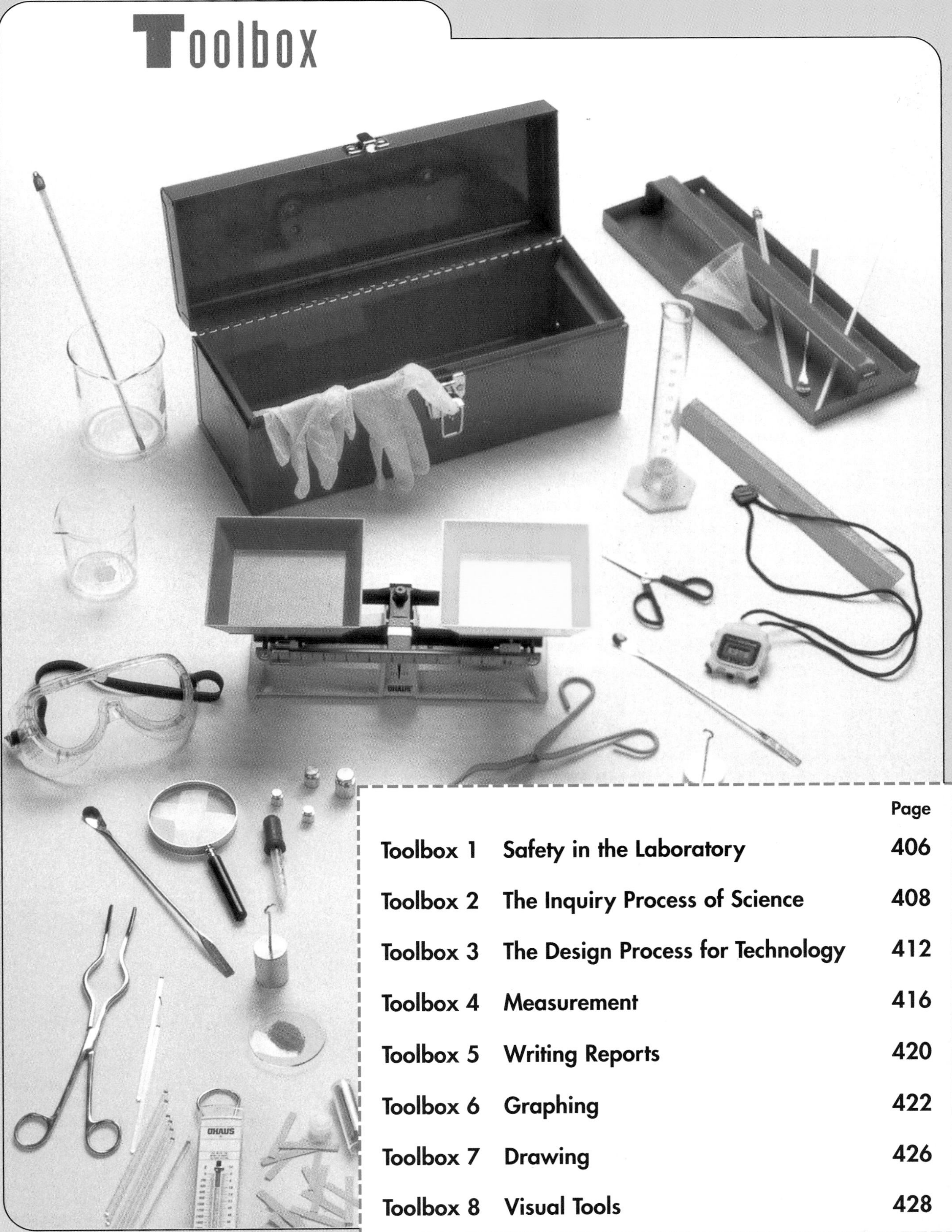

Toolbox 1

Safety in the Lak atory

Safety Wins

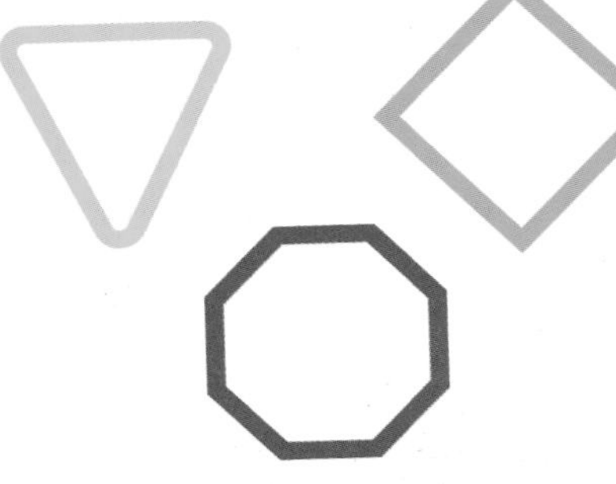

You have probably en some of the hazard symbols below on produc at home. They are a warning that many substances an be harmful or dangerous if handled improperly.

Each hazard symbol c come in either a yellow triangle (which means "caution") n orange diamond (which means "warning"), or a red octa n (which means "danger").

Here are some of the ore common symbols.

Flammabl lazard: Materials could ignite (cat on fire) if exposed to flames, sp ks, or friction.

Explosive azard: The materials or equipmer could explode.

Irritant I zard: The material may cause irritation o eyes, nose, throat, skin, or lungs.

Toxic Hc ard: The material is very poisonous and cou have immediate and serious effects.

Corrosive Hazard: The material may corrode ("eat away at") clothing, skin, or other materials.

Biological Hazard: Be alert to the possibility of poisoning or infection from microscopic and other organisms.

Electrical Hazard: Be alert to the possibility of an electric spark or shock.

Here are some other symbols you might see on the materials you use in your classroom. These symbols are called Workplace Hazardous Materials Information System (WHMIS) symbols. They are placed on hazardous materials used at job sites and school laboratories.

compressed gas

dangerously reactive material

oxidizing material

poisonous and infectious causing immediate and serious toxic effects

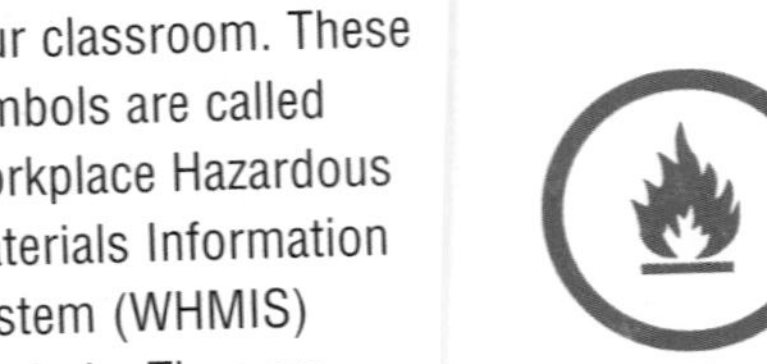

flammable and combustible material

biohazardous infectious material

corrosive material

poisonous and infectious causing other toxic effects

Can you identify the symbols that are similar to the household symbols above? Discuss with your teacher what some of the other symbols mean.

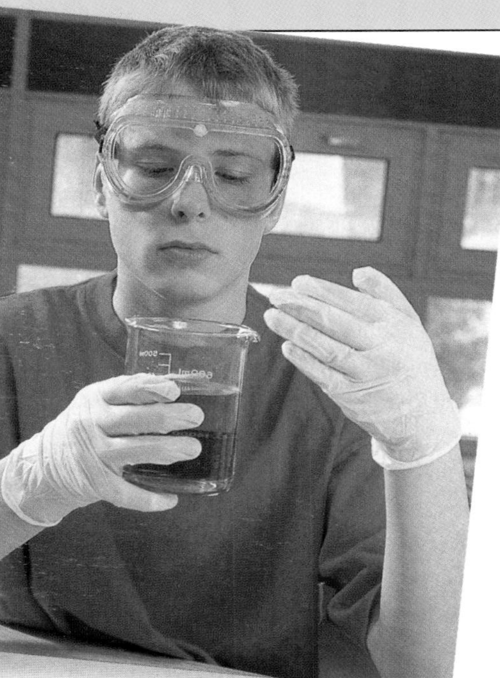

Common-Sense Safety Checklist

Your teacher may have safety instructions to add to the list below. Discuss or jot down your ideas about why each of these is an example of common-sense safety.

- Learn to recognize the warning symbols shown on the previous page.
- Keep your work area uncluttered and organized.
- Know the location of fire extinguishers and other safety equipment.
- Always wear safety goggles and any other safety clothing as requested by your teacher or this book.
- If you have long or loose hair, tie it back. Roll up long shirt sleeves.
- Don't wear any jewellery when doing laboratory activities.
- Inform your teacher if you have any allergies or medical conditions.
- Report any safety concerns you have, or hazards you see (such as spills) to your teacher.
- Handle all glassware carefully. If you see broken glass, ask your teacher how to dispose of it properly.
- Never smell any material or substance directly. Instead, gently wave your hand over it to bring its vapours toward your nose.
- Heat solids and liquids only in heat-resistant glass beakers and test tubes.
- When you heat test tubes, make sure that the open end is pointing away from you and anyone else in the room.
- If heating a substance, make sure the container does not boil dry.
- Follow your teacher's instructions to safely dispose of all waste materials.
- Always wash your hands well with soap, preferably liquid soap, after handling chemicals or other materials.
- Make sure you close the containers of chemicals immediately after you use them.
- Make sure that any water or wet hands are kept away from electrical outlets or sockets.
- When you have finished an experiment, clean all the equipment before putting it away. Be careful with hot plates and equipment that have been heated as they may take a long time to cool down.

Say "Yes!" to Safety

Are you willing to:

- ✔ follow the safety instructions outlined by your teacher and this book?
- ✔ keep an eye open for possible hazards, and report them immediately?
- ✔ show respect and concern for your own safety and the safety of your classmates and teachers?

Toolbox 2

The Inquiry Process of Science

Scientists are always asking a lot of questions. They are always inquiring. They want to understand why the things they observe, and wonder about, happen. Experiments are important tools scientists use to help them answer their questions.

When scientists plan experiments, they usually follow a simple set of steps.

Hints

- Answers always lead to additional questions. New questions often lead to new hypotheses and experiments. Don't be afraid to ask questions, or to re-think the ones you've already asked.
- Science grows when scientists ask questions, answer them, and are willing to question those answers. Scientific knowledge is always growing and changing.

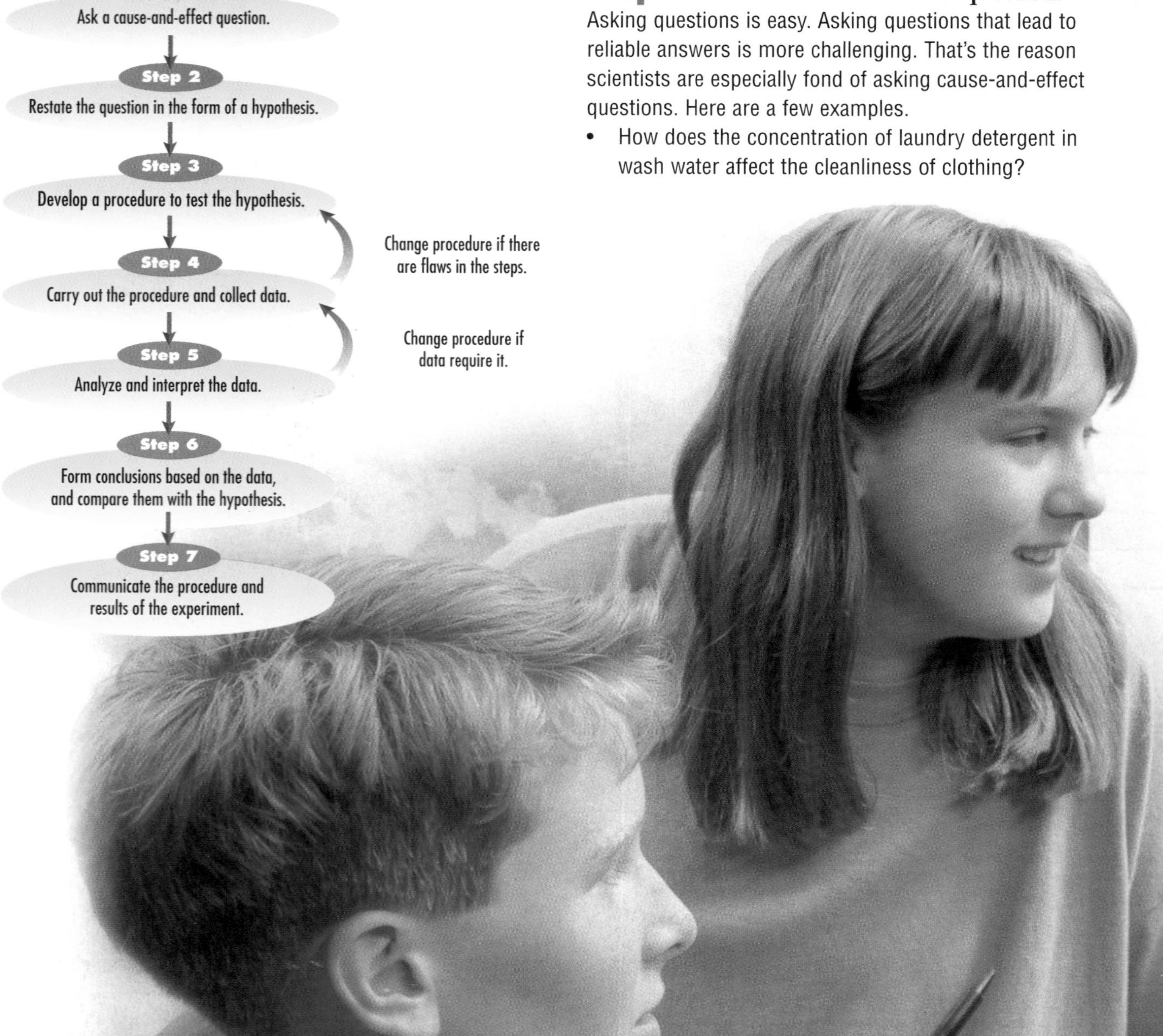
Step 1
Ask a cause-and-effect question.
Step 2
Restate the question in the form of a hypothesis.
Step 3
Develop a procedure to test the hypothesis.
Step 4
Carry out the procedure and collect data.
Step 5
Analyze and interpret the data.
Step 6
Form conclusions based on the data, and compare them with the hypothesis.
Step 7
Communicate the procedure and results of the experiment.
Change procedure if there are flaws in the steps.
Change procedure if data require it.

Step 1 Ask a cause-and-effect question.
Asking questions is easy. Asking questions that lead to reliable answers is more challenging. That's the reason scientists are especially fond of asking cause-and-effect questions. Here are a few examples.

- How does the concentration of laundry detergent in wash water affect the cleanliness of clothing?

- How do different temperatures affect the growth of seedlings?
- How does the amount of moisture affect the growth of mould on bread?

Notice how the causes—the detergent, temperature, and moisture—are things that are changeable. For example, you can have different concentrations of detergent, different temperatures, and different amounts of moisture. Causes are *variables*. They are factors that can change.

The results are changeable, too. For example, some clothes may become cleaner than others, or not clean at all. Some seedlings may grow better than others, or some might not grow at all. Some bread samples may have lots of mould, some may have less, and some might not have any. Results are variables, too. They are factors that can change.

Step 2 Restate the question in the form of a hypothesis.

A hypothesis is a way of restating a cause-and-effect question so that it gives a reasonable, possible answer. Basically, a hypothesis is an intelligent guess at the solution to a problem or question.

Here are hypotheses for the questions outlined in Step 1.

- If the concentration of the detergent is high, then clothing will become cleaner.
- If the temperature is decreased, then the seedlings will not grow as well.
- If the amount of moisture is increased, then the bread will get mouldier.

Hints

A hypothesis is an early step in the experiment-planning process. Your hypothesis can turn out to be "right," but it doesn't always. That's what the experiment is for—to test the hypothesis.

Step 3 Develop a procedure to test the hypothesis fairly.

When you develop a procedure, you need to ask yourself some questions. Here are some questions you should think about. These questions are answered for the seedling example.

- **Which "cause" variable do you want to investigate?** For the seedling experiment, the "cause" variable is temperature.
- **How will you measure this variable (if it's measurable)?** You can measure temperature with a thermometer.
- **How will you keep all other variables constant (the same) so they don't affect your results?** In other words, how will you *control* your experiment so it is a fair test? To control the seedling experiment, these variables should be kept constant: the amount of light the seedlings receive; the amount and temperature of water applied to the seedlings; the kind of soil the seedlings are planted in.

- **What materials and equipment will you need for the experiment?** For the seedling experiment, the materials would include the seedlings, soil, growing pots or containers (same size), water and a watering can, a light source, a thermometer, and a ruler or other measuring device.
- **How will you conduct the experiment safely?** For the seedling experiment, some of the safety factors you should consider include putting the seedling pots in a place where they would not be disturbed, washing your hands after handling the materials, and making sure you don't have any allergies to the soil or seedlings you use.
- **How will you record the data you collect?** You could divide your seedlings into groups and grow each group at a certain temperature. You would keep track of how much each seedling in a group grew over a specified amount of time and calculate the average for the group.

Step 4 **Carry out the procedure and collect data.**
Depending on the kind of experiment you have planned, you may choose to record the data you collect in the form of a chart or table, a labelled sketch, notes, or a combination of these. For example, a good way to record the seedling data would be in tables like the one below.

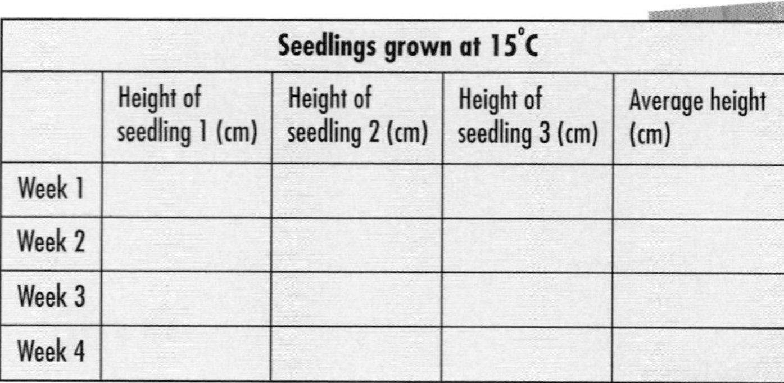

Seedlings grown at 15°C				
	Height of seedling 1 (cm)	Height of seedling 2 (cm)	Height of seedling 3 (cm)	Average height (cm)
Week 1				
Week 2				
Week 3				
Week 4				

Hints

Analyzing the data you collect is the only way you have to assess your hypothesis. It's important that your record keeping be organized and neat.

Step 5 **Analyze and interpret the data.**
Scientists look for patterns and relationships in their data. Often, making a graph can help them see patterns and relationships more easily. (Turn to Toolbox 6 for more about graphing.)

A graph of the seedling data would show you if there were any relation between temperature and growth rate.

Hints

If you have access to a computer, find out if it has the software to help you make charts or graphs.

Step 6 **Form conclusions based on the data, and compare them with the hypothesis.**
Usually, this is fairly straightforward. Either your data will support your hypothesis or they won't. Either way, however, you aren't finished answering your cause-and-effect question.

If your data support your hypothesis, you need to repeat your experiment several times to see if you get the same results over and over again. Doing your

experiment successfully many times is the only way you and other scientists can have faith in your data and your conclusions.

If your data don't support your hypothesis, there are two possible reasons why.

- Perhaps your experimental plan was flawed and needs to be re-assessed and possibly planned again.
- Perhaps your hypothesis was incorrect and needs to be re-assessed and modified.

For example, if the seedlings did not grow as well in cooler temperatures, the hypothesis could be a good one. If the seedlings grew better in the lower temperatures, you would have to re-think your hypothesis, or look at your experiment for flaws. Do certain seedlings grow better at lower temperatures than others? Do different types of soil have more of an effect on growth than temperature? These are some of the questions that could be asked after doing the seedling experiment. Every experiment is different and will result in its own set of questions and conclusions.

- If you don't have in-class time to repeat your experiment several times, you could ask your teacher about scheduling after-school time.
- You could also enlist the help of your classmates. If other scientists get the same results, the conclusions are usually reliable. If not, the hypothesis must be modified.

Step 7 Communicate the procedure and results of the experiment.

Scientists always share the results of their experiments with other people. They do this by summarizing how they performed the first 6 steps. Sometimes, they will write out a formal laboratory report stating their purpose, hypothesis, procedure, observations, and conclusions. Other times, they share their experimental results verbally, using drawings, charts, or graphs. (See Toolboxes 5, 6, and 7 for hints on how to prepare your results.)

When you have finished your experiment, ask your teacher how he or she would like you to prepare your results so you can share them with the other students in your class.

Toolbox 3

TOOLBOX

The Design Process for Technology

When you plan an experiment to answer a cause-and-effect question, you follow an orderly set of steps. The same is true for designing a product that solves a practical problem.

When designers try to solve practical problems, they usually follow a simple set of steps.

Recognize a need or opportunity, or be willing to respond to a design challenge.

Identify the specific problem to be solved.

Set or consider the criteria that limit the nature of the solution.

Generate a list of ideas, possible solutions, materials, and equipment.

Plan and construct a working model or prototype.

Test, evaluate, and modify (if necessary) the model or prototype.

Communicate the procedure and results of your design.

Change ideas if criteria change.

Adjust ideas if model has design problems.

Modify model based on test results.

Step 1 Recognize a need or opportunity, or be willing to respond to a design challenge.
This involves recognizing what the problem is, or a need that exists, or a challenge that has been offered. For example, suppose you observe that a rope bridge across a ravine at a local park is very unstable and swings back and forth when crossed. This might be fine for people who want a thrill, but you find that most people are not comfortable crossing the bridge and don't get to enjoy one of the nicer areas of the park. You wish there were a way to make the bridge more stable so more people would use it. That is the situation or context of the problem.

Step 2 Identify the specific problem to be solved.
When you understand a situation, you can then define the problem more exactly. This means identifying a specific task to carry out. In the situation with the bridge, the task might be to build a new bridge or add support to the existing bridge.

Step 3 Set or consider the criteria that limit the nature of the solution.
Usually, there are factors that set limits on the possible solutions to a problem. For example, there may be limitations of time, of available materials, of the number of people needed, of cost, and of safety. If you are building a product for your own interests, you may set these criteria for yourself. Often in class, your teacher will outline these criteria.

For the bridge example, one factor might include cost. It might be too expensive to build a new bridge so the existing bridge would have to be modified.

Hints

Always consider safety. This includes safe handling and use of materials and equipment, as well as being aware of possible environmental impacts of your ideas. Discuss with your teacher and fellow students how your designs might affect the environment.

Step 4 Generate a list of ideas, possible solutions, materials, and equipment.

Brainstorming, conducting research, or both, are key components of this step. When you brainstorm, remember to relax and let your imagination go. Brainstorming is all about generating as many ideas as possible without judging them. Record your ideas in the form of words, mindmaps, sketches—whatever helps you best.

Conducting research may involve reading books and magazines, searching the Internet, interviewing people, or visiting stores. It all depends on what you are going to design.

One idea for the rope bridge would be to anchor the bridge with strong rope or thick metal wire to large rocks or to the hillside at either end of the bridge. Sketches and diagrams would help to generate different ideas for the bridge design.

Hints

Humans have been inventors for tens of thousands of years—so take advantage of what's already been developed. When you're solving a problem, you don't have to "reinvent the wheel." See how others have solved the same problem before and use their efforts as inspiration. You can also look for ways to "build upon" or improve on their ideas.

Step 5 Plan and construct a working model or prototype.

Choose one possible solution to develop. Start by making a list of the materials and equipment you will use. Then make a working diagram, or series of diagrams, on paper. This lets you explore and troubleshoot your ideas early on. Your labels should be detailed enough so that other people could build your design. Show your plans to your teacher before you begin construction work.

A simple model of the bridge could be made to show how and where components such as stabilizing wires could be added.

Hints

If things aren't working as you planned or imagined, be prepared to modify your plans as you construct your model or prototype.

TOOLBOX

Step 6 **Test, evaluate, and modify (if necessary) the model or prototype.**
Testing lets you see how well your product solves the problem. Testing also lets you know if you need to make modifications. Does it meet all the established criteria? Does it solve the problem you designed it for?

Invite your classmates to try your product. Their feedback can help you decide what is and isn't working, and how to fix anything that needs fixing. Perhaps the stabilizing wires on the bridge model could be anchored elsewhere. Maybe more wires could be added.

Step 7 **Communicate the procedure and results of your design.**
Inventors and engineers create things to meet people's needs. When they make something new, they like to show it to other people and explain to them how it works. Sometimes they will use a carefully drawn diagram of the new device and write about how they performed the first 6 steps. Other times, they will show the device to people and explain verbally how it works and how they built it. Your teacher will tell you how to prepare your results so you can exhibit the new device you make.

Hints

For every successful invention or product, there are thousands of unsuccessful ones. Sometimes it's better to start over from scratch than to follow a design that doesn't meet its performance criteria.

Here's an old saying you've probably heard: "If at first you don't succeed, try, try again." Remember, there can be many possible solutions to a practical problem.

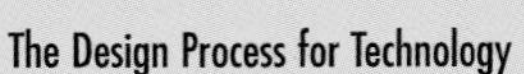

Toolbox 4

Measurement

Measuring helps everyone answer questions such as how far away something is, how massive it is, and how much space it takes up. Here are some types of measurements you might come across every day.

Length

Length tells you:

- how long or short something is
- how far or near something is
- how high or low something is
- how large or small something is.

Common units used to measure length include millimetres (mm), centimetres (cm), metres (m), and kilometres (km). All these units are based on a single standard: the metre.

Check It Yourself

Which length unit would you use for each of the following? Why?

- the height of a table
- the depth of a lake
- the width of a dime
- the length of a skating rink
- the distance from Kitchener, Ontario, to Kamloops, British Columbia
- the distance from the earth's core to its surface

Hints

When you use a ruler, tape measure, or metre stick, always start from the 0 measurement point, not the edge of the measuring tool.

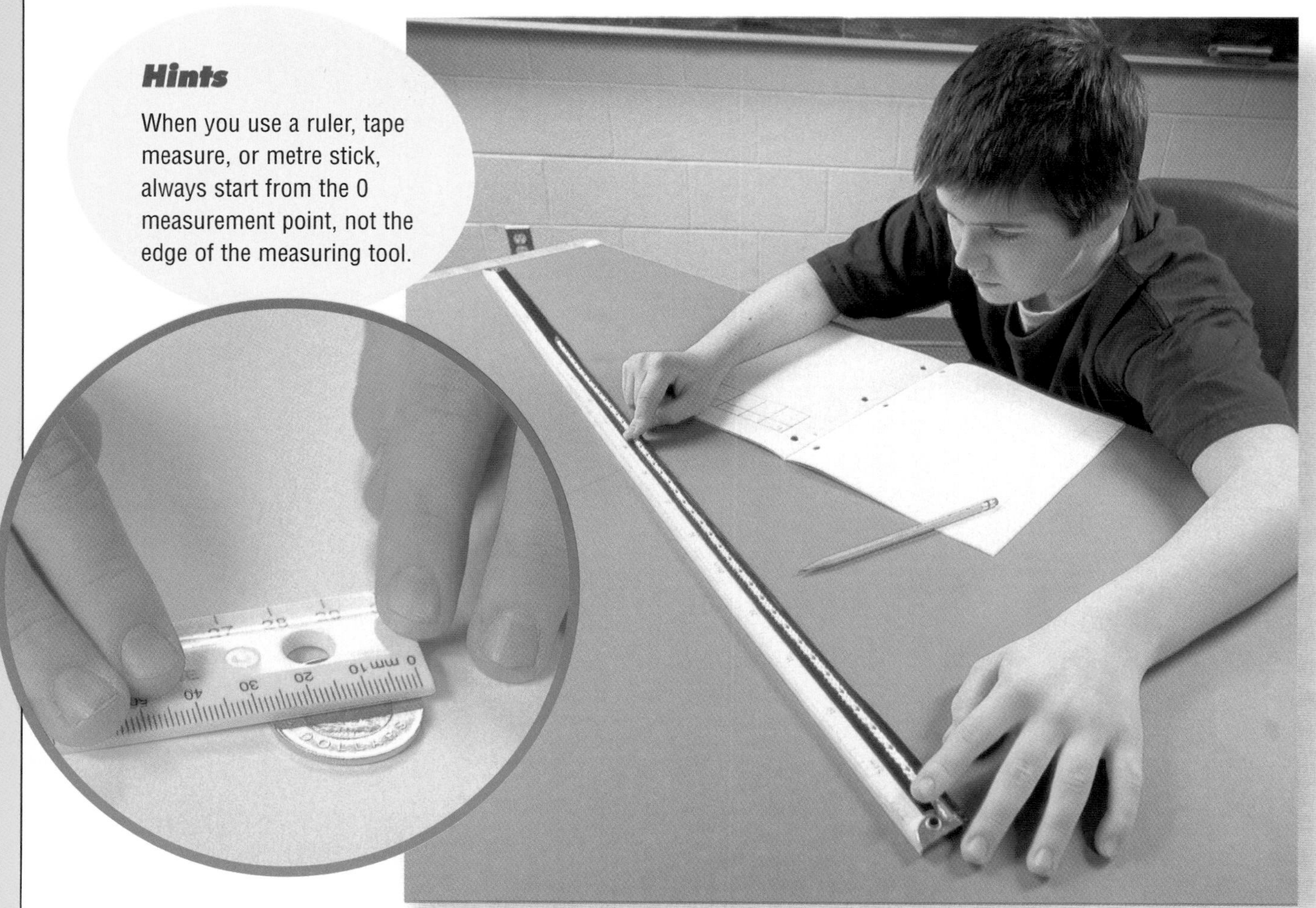

When you use a measuring tool such as a ruler, look directly in line with the measurement point, not from an angle.

Volume

The volume of something tells you the amount of space that it takes up (occupies). Common units used to measure volume include litres (L) and millilitres (mL). Remember, 1 mL equals 1 cm^3.

At home, you often use a measuring cup to determine the volume of something. At school, you usually use a graduated cylinder. Here, "graduated" means a container that has been marked with regular intervals for measuring. For example, a measuring cup, a beaker, and a thermometer are all graduated.

Check It Yourself

1 Which of the following tools could you use to measure volume? Why?
- a spoon
- a test tube
- a balance

2 How could you transform an empty can into a volume-measuring tool? Describe, step-by-step, how you would do it.

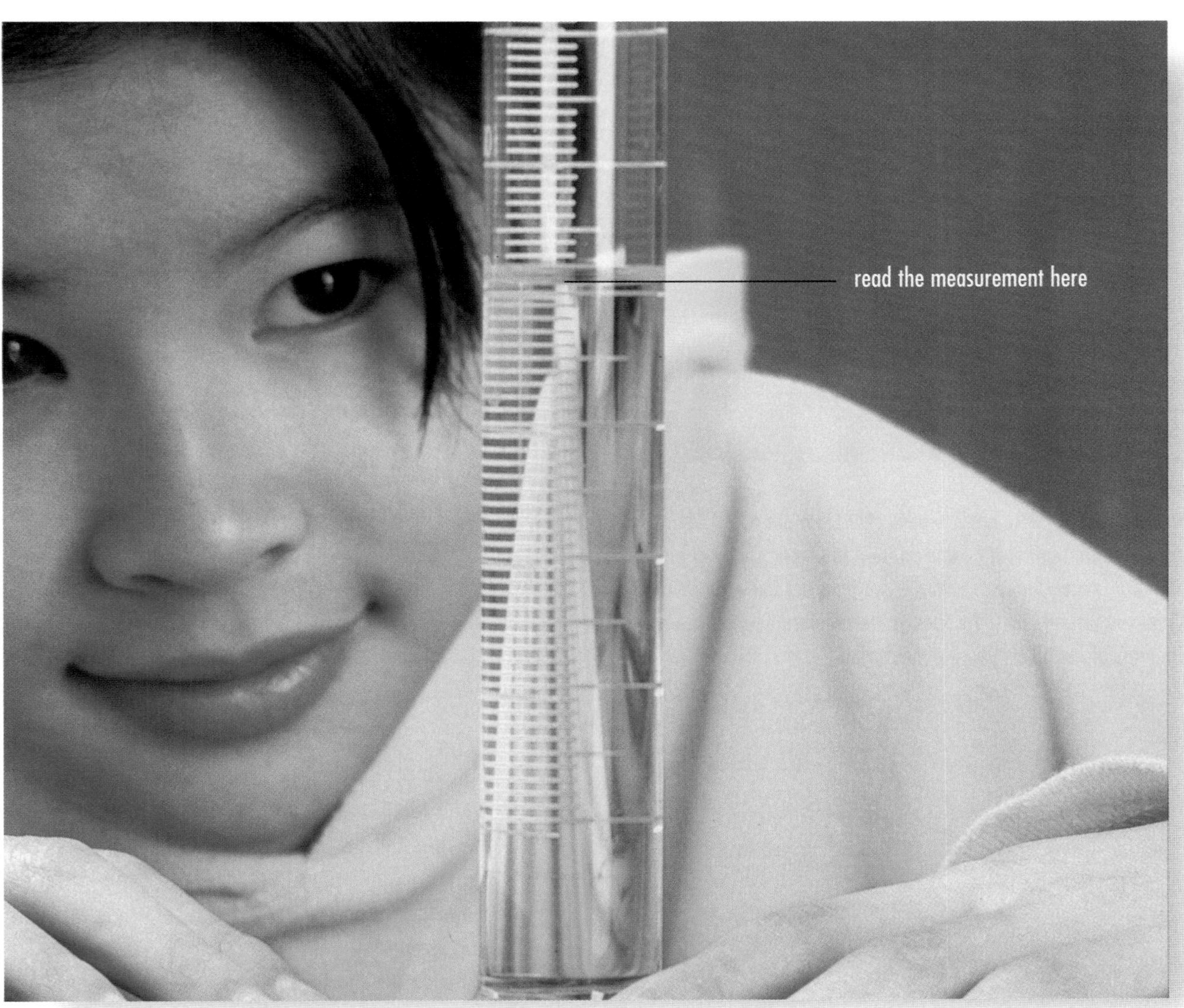

When you add a liquid to a graduated cylinder, the top of the liquid is curved near the sides of the cylinder. This curve is called a *meniscus*. To measure the liquid's volume properly, you need to observe the liquid's surface at the flat, bottom portion of the curve and ignore the sides.

Mass and Weight

In science, the mass of an object and its weight mean different things. The mass of something tells you the amount of matter it has. The weight of an object is the measure of the force of gravity acting on it. We more often use mass in science. Common units used to measure mass include grams (g) and kilograms (kg).

You usually measure mass with a balance. Your classroom probably has an equal arm balance or a triple beam balance like the ones shown here.

The equal arm balance and triple beam balance basically work in the same way. You compare the mass of the object you are measuring with standard or known masses, or their mass equivalent values on the triple beam.

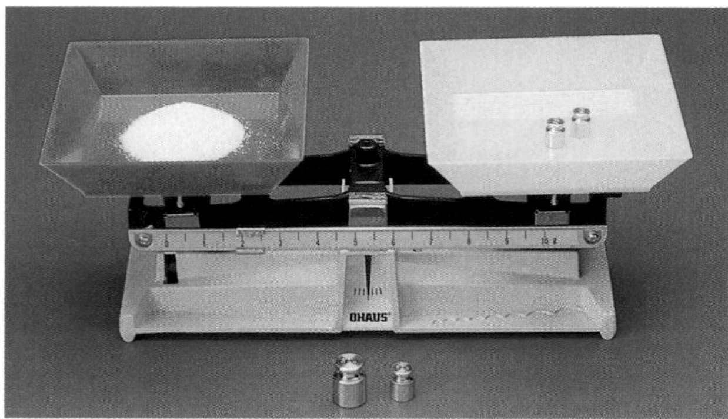

equal arm balance

An equal arm balance has two pans. You place the object whose mass you want to know on one pan. On the other pan, you place standard (known) masses until the two pans are balanced (level). Then, you just add up the values of the standard masses. The total is the mass of the object you are measuring.

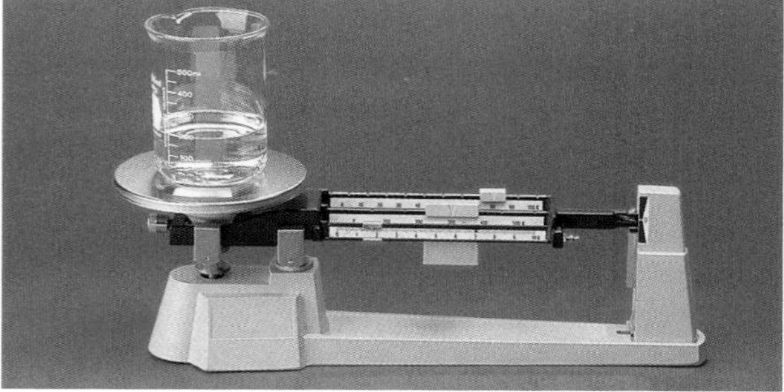

triple beam balance

A triple beam balance has a single pan. You place the object you are measuring on the pan. You adjust the masses on the beams until the beam assembly is level. Then, you add up the mass equivalent values of the beam masses from the scales on the beam.

Some businesses, such as grocery stores, use electronic balances to measure the weight of an item. When you place an object on top of the balance, it will calculate the weight of the object. The next time you're at the supermarket, ask the person at the deli or meat counter to show you how an electronic balance works.

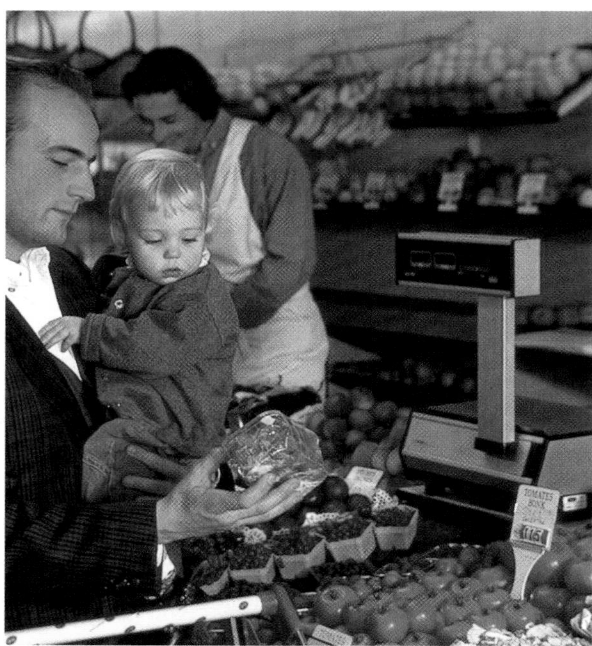

electronic balance

Before you use an electronic balance, you have to press the reset button so it starts at zero. Then, you place the object you are measuring on top of the balance. It will then produce an electronic display of the object's weight.

Check It Yourself

1. The object on the triple beam balance is a water-filled beaker, so the balance is measuring the mass of the water plus the mass of the beaker. What if you wanted to measure just the mass of the water in the beaker? Describe, step-by-step, how you would do it.
2. How would you measure the mass of an apple? How would this be similar to and different from measuring the mass of a pile of salt?

Estimating

When you estimate, you use your imagination to guess the length, volume, or mass of an object. Sometimes, you can estimate by comparing one object with another object that has known measurements. For example, if you are asked to estimate the volume of your drink, you could estimate by comparing it with a large jar of mayonnaise in your fridge (which has its volume marked on the label).

For a large object or distance, you might divide it up into portions in your imagination and guess the length, volume, or mass of one portion. You then multiply that guess by the number of imaginary portions to estimate the measurement of the whole.

Sometimes, it's useful to estimate the measurement of an object before you actually measure it. You might do this to help you decide which units of measurement and which measuring tool to use. In other cases, you might not be able to measure an object at all. In this case, an estimate of its length, volume, or mass might be the best you can do.

Try to estimate the measurements of the items listed below. Include the measurement units that you think should go with your estimates. Then, measure them to see how close your estimates were to the real values. Did you choose the correct measurement units? If you don't have some of these items in your classroom, check at home.

Object	Length	
	estimate	actual value
pencil		
height of your teacher's desk		
length of your classroom		

Object	Mass	
	estimate	actual value
this textbook		
banana from someone's lunch		
piece of chalk		

Object	Volume	
	estimate	actual value
amount of water poured into an empty jar		
marker cap		
drink thermos		

Toolbox 5

Writing Reports

Toolbox 2 shows you how to plan a science experiment, and Toolbox 3 shows you how to do technological design. This toolbox will help you write a report so you can communicate the procedure and results of your work.

Here is a list of things you should try to do when writing your science reports.

- Give your report or project a title.
- Tell readers why you did the work.
- State your hypothesis or describe the design factors.
- List the equipment and materials you used.
- Describe the steps you took when you did your experiment or designed and made your product.
- Show and explain your experimental data or the results of testing your product.
- Make conclusions based on the outcome of the experiment or success of the product you designed.

Give your report or project a title

Write a brief title on the top of the first page of your report. Your title can be one or two words that describe a product you designed and made, or it can be a short sentence which summarizes an experiment you performed.

Tell readers why you did the work

Use a heading such as "Introduction" or "Purpose" for this section. Here, you give your reasons for doing a particular experiment or designing and making a particular product. If you are writing about an experiment, tell readers what your cause-and-effect question is. If you designed a product, explain why this product is needed, what it will do, who might use it, and who might benefit from its use.

State your hypothesis or describe the design factors

If you are writing about an experiment, use a heading such as "Hypothesis." Under this heading you will state your hypothesis. Remember, your hypothesis is your guess at the solution to a problem or question. Your hypothesis makes a prediction that your experiment will test.

If you are writing about a product you designed, use a heading such as "Design Challenge." Under this heading, you will describe why you decided to design your product the way you did. Explain how and why you chose your design over other possible designs.

List the materials and equipment you used

This section can come under a heading called "Materials and Equipment." List all the materials and equipment you used for your experiment or design project. Your list can be in point form or set up as a table or chart. Remember to include the exact amounts of materials used, when possible (for example, the number of nails used in building a model or the volumes and masses of substances tested in an experiment). Include the exact measurements and proper units for all materials used.

Also include diagrams to show how you set up your equipment or how you prepared your materials. Remember to label the important features on your diagrams. (See Toolbox 7 for drawing tips.)

Describe the steps you took when you did your experiment or designed and made your product

Under a heading called "Procedure" or "Method," describe, in detail, the steps you followed when doing your experiment or designing and making your product. If you made a product, describe how you tested it. If you had to alter your design, describe in detail how you did this.

Show and explain the data of your experiment or the results of testing your product

Give this section a heading such as "Data" or "Observations." In this section, you should show the data you collected while performing the experiment or testing your product. Use graphs, tables, diagrams, and any other visual aids that show the results of your tests. (See Toolbox 6 for graphing tips.) If you performed your experiment a few times, give results for each trial. If you tested different designs of your product, give results for each design.

Make conclusions based on the outcome of the experiment or success of the product you designed

This last section of your report can be called "Conclusions." In one or two paragraphs, explain what your tests and experiments showed. If you made a product, explain if your design did what it was supposed to do, or worked the way it was supposed to work. If you changed the design of your product, explain why one design is better than another.

If you did an experiment, explain if your results were predicted by the hypothesis. Describe how you might adjust the hypothesis because of what you learned from doing the experiment, and how you might test this new hypothesis.

Describe the practical applications your product or experiment might have for the world outside the classroom.

Toolbox 6

Graphing

Science and technology often involve collecting a lot of numerical data. This data may be recorded in tables or charts. Sometimes, however, it's difficult to see if there are any patterns in the numbers. That's when it's useful to reorganize the data into graphs.

A graph is similar to a picture or diagram that shows more easily how numbers are related to one another. You have probably drawn a lot of graphs over the years in your studies of mathematics, geography, and, of course, science and technology.

What Do You Recall about Line Graphs?

Line graphs are good for exploring data collected for many types of experiments. Using line graphs is a good way to analyze the data of an experiment that are continually changing. For example, here are some data collected by a group of students investigating temperature changes. They poured hot water into a large container (container A) and cold water into a smaller container (container B). After recording the starting temperatures in each container, they placed Container B inside Container A and took measurements every 30 s until there were no more temperature changes.

Here are the data they collected shown as a chart and as a line graph. How are they similar? Which one can you interpret more easily and more quickly?

Temperatures of Container A and Container B

Time (s)	Temperature (°C) of water in Container A	Temperature (°C) of water in Container B
0	51	0
30	45	7
60	38	14
90	33	20
120	30	22
150	29	23
180	28	24
210	27	25
240	26	26
270	26	26
300	26	26

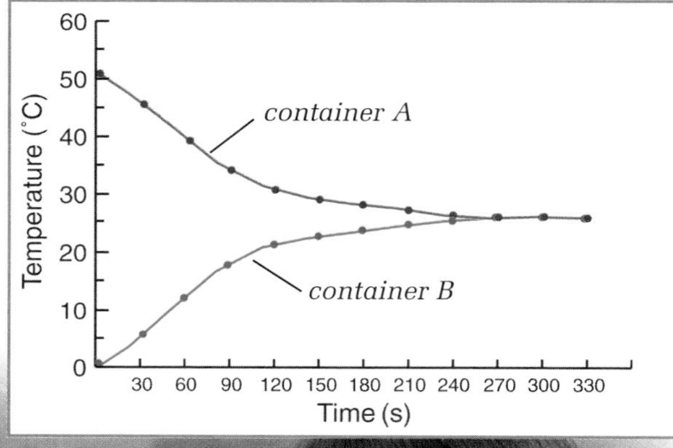

TOOLBOX

Check It Yourself

1. The axes are the two number lines that run horizontally and vertically. Which is the x-axis and which is the y-axis? Which axis is used for the independent (cause) variable? Which is used for the dependent (effect or result) variable?
2. Why would you use a sharp pencil and a ruler to draw the axes and plot the graph lines?
3. How was the scale for each axis chosen?
4. Do you see how each point on the graph was plotted (placed on the graph)?
5. Do you understand how the graph lines were drawn?
6. Is there anything missing or anything else you would add to this graph?

What Do You Recall about Bar Graphs?

Bar graphs are useful for displaying comparisons. For example, the chart in the next column shows the total average monthly precipitation (both snow and rain) for a city in Ontario. Compare the data in this chart with how they "look" when they are reorganized in the form of a bar graph. Which can you interpret more easily and more quickly?

Month	Total Average Precipitation (mm)
January	50.4
February	46.0
March	61.1
April	70.0
May	66.0
June	67.1
July	71.4
August	76.8
September	63.5
October	61.8
November	62.7
December	64.7

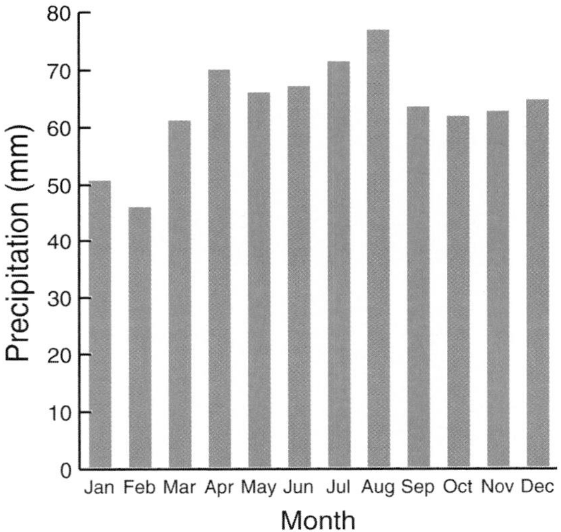

Hints

Scales for bar graphs are often rounded off to the nearest whole number.

Check It Yourself

1. Which axis is used for the independent (cause) variable? Which is used for the dependent (effect or result) variable?
2. How was the scale for each axis chosen?
3. The yearly average precipitation for this city is 761.5 mm. How would you modify the bar graph to include this additional information?

TOOLBOX

What Do You Recall about Circle (Pie) Graphs?

A circle graph is useful when you want to display data that are part of a whole. For example, in this circle graph, the "whole" is the total land area on the earth. The "parts" are the approximate percentages of land made up by each continent.

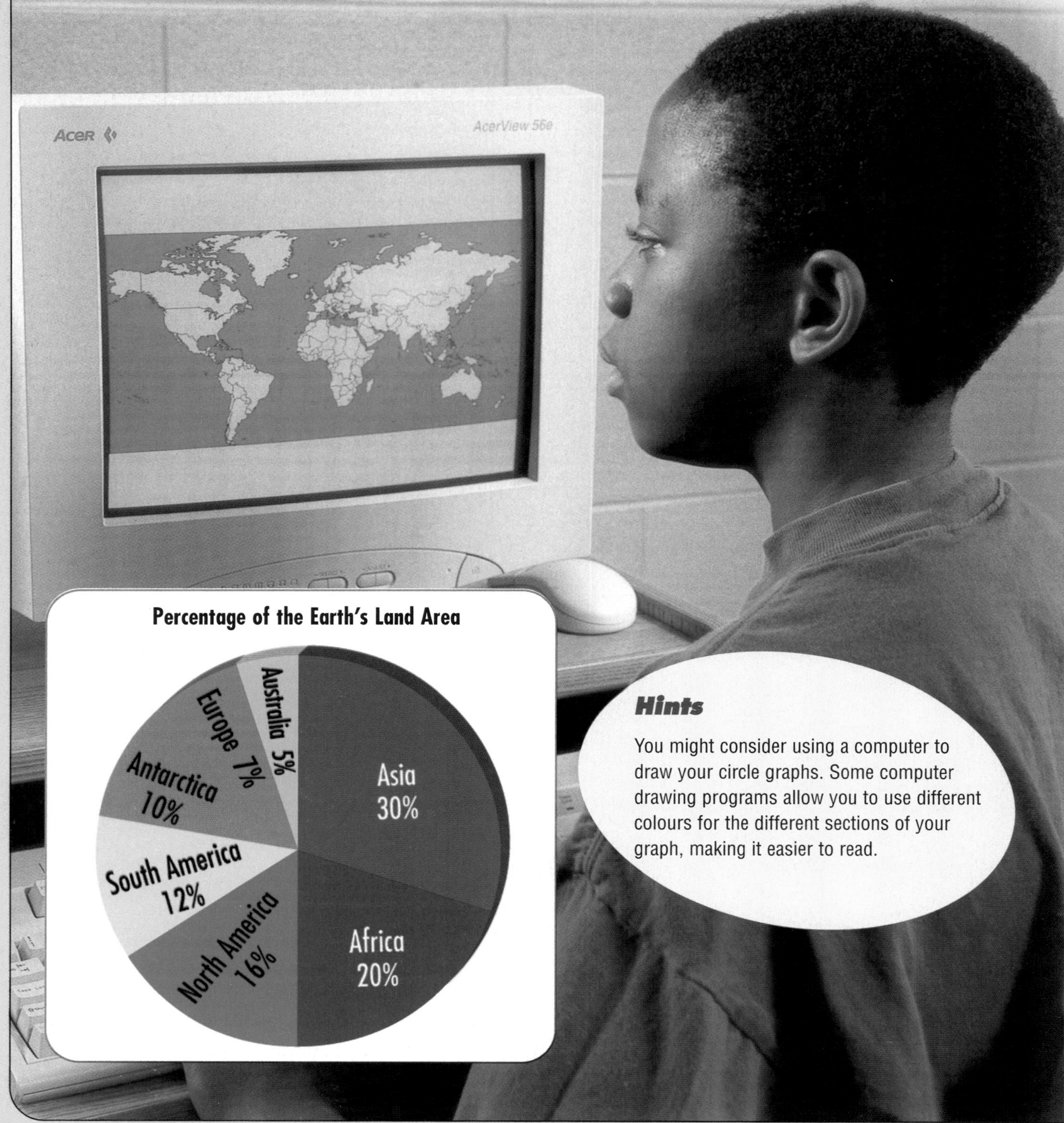

Hints

You might consider using a computer to draw your circle graphs. Some computer drawing programs allow you to use different colours for the different sections of your graph, making it easier to read.

Compare the data in this chart with how they "looked" when they were organized in the form of a circle graph on the previous page. Which can you interpret more easily and more quickly?

Continent	Percentage of the Earth's Land Area
Asia	30%
Africa	20%
North America	16%
South America	12 %
Antarctica	10%
Europe	7%
Australia	5%

TOOLBOX

CHECK IT YOURSELF

1 How were the angles in the circle graph determined? Use the Hints information below if you would like some help to start.

Hints

- The angle at the centre of a circle is 360°.
- To calculate the percentage for Antarctica, for example, you need to determine what 10% of 360° is. 10% is the same as 10/100, which is the same as 0.1. So $0.1 \times 360° = 36°$.

2 How could you use this information to hand-draw your own circle graph?

Toolbox 7

Drawing

Have you heard the saying, "a picture's worth a thousand words"? In science, a picture can be worth even more. A carefully done drawing can help you express your ideas, record important information, and experiment with designs.

Four types of drawings you can use include: a Simple Sketch, a Technical or Scientific Drawing, an Orthographic (Perspective) Drawing, and a Computer-Assisted Drawing (CAD). Examples of each type of drawing are shown. A side view and a top view for a simple sketch are also shown. These different views can be made for each type of drawing.

Practise the four types of drawings on your own.

This photo appears in Chapter 3, Heat. Practise drawing it using one or several of the drawing styles presented here. What labels would you include? Would your labelling choices change depending on the style of drawing you make?

A Simple Sketch

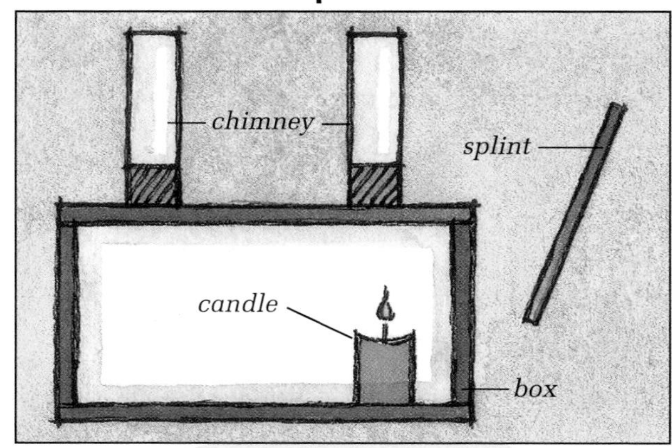

Tools of the Trade

You will need the following equipment for each type of drawing.

Hand-drawing tools
- a sharp pencil or mechanical pencil
- a pencil sharpener or extra leads
- an eraser
- a ruler

For simple drawings
- blank, white paper

For technical and orthographic drawing
- blank graph paper

For computer-assisted drawing
- blank diskette
- access to computer and software

A Simple Sketch (Side View)

Hints

If you're going to use your drawing to help you design a structure, include a top, side, and front view.

TOOLBOX

REMEMBER!

- Give your drawing a title at the top of the page.
- Use the whole page for your drawing.
- Include only those details that are necessary, keep them simple, and identify them by name.
- If you need labels, use lines, not arrows. Place your labels in line with the feature being labelled, and use a ruler to keep your lines straight.
- Don't use colour or shading unless your teacher asks you to.
- Include notes and ideas if the sketch is a design for a structure or an invention.

A Simple Sketch (Top View)

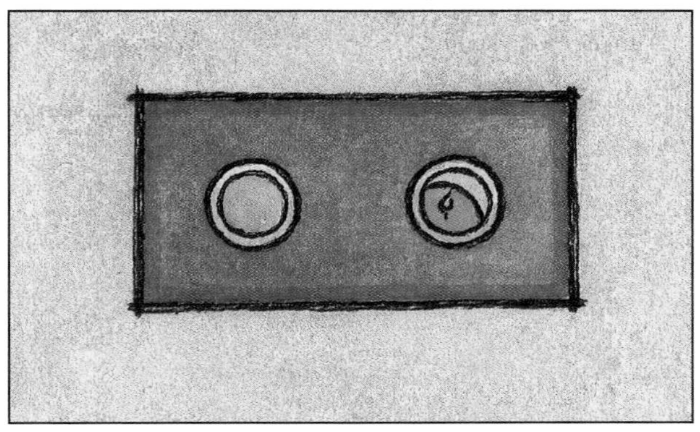

A Technical or Scientific Drawing

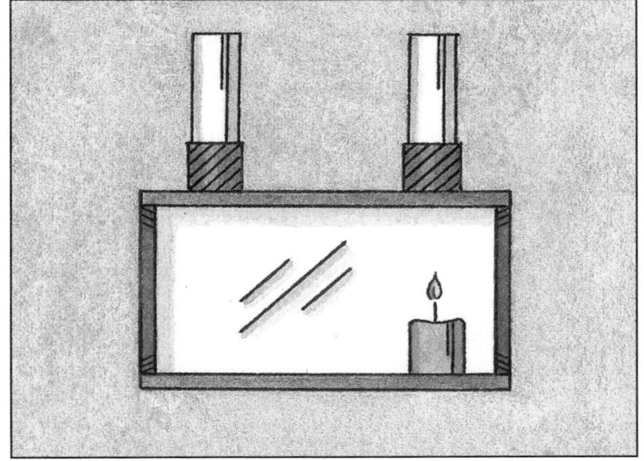

Hints

Use graph paper to help you with the details of your drawing if you don't have a ruler handy.

An Orthographic (Perspective) Drawing

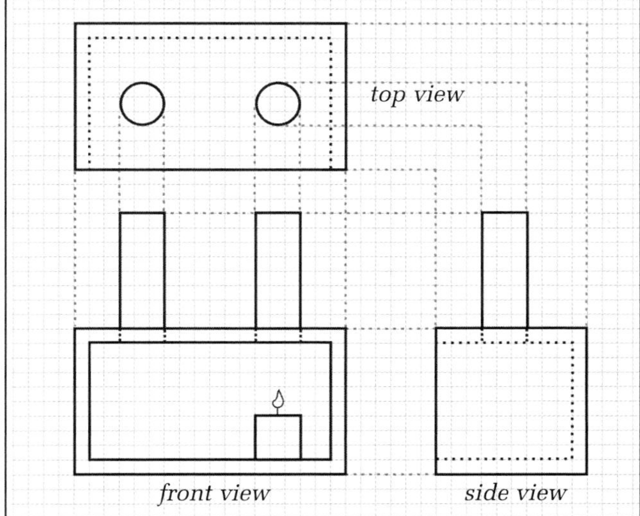

Hints

You can use the squares of your graph paper to make the scale of your orthographic drawing accurate. For example, suppose that each square stood for 1 cm. If what you're drawing is 14 cm long, you would use 14 squares to represent its length.

A Computer-Assisted Drawing (CAD)

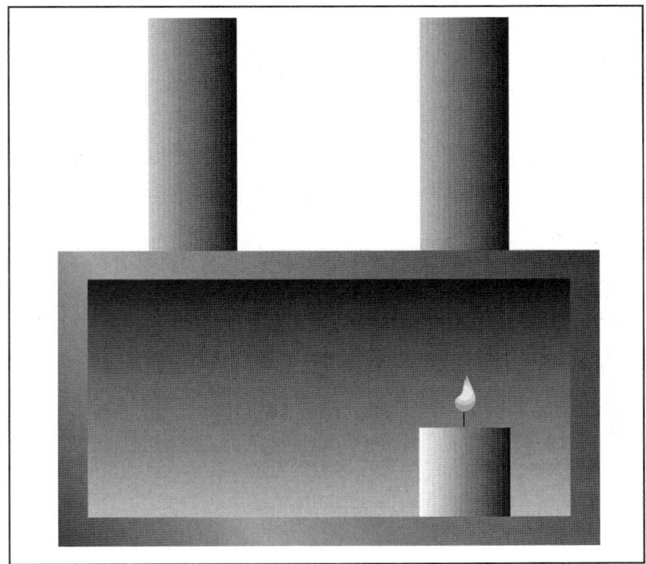

Hints

One advantage of using a computer is that you can easily change your work. After saving your original, practise making changes and moving the image around.

Toolbox 8

Visual Tools

Many people find it helpful to view, share, gather, and explore information in the form of pictures or diagrams. You have probably learned and used several of the techniques shown here. Try out the ones that are less familiar to you. You may find that some help you open up your thinking to new and creative ways.

Comparison Matrix

Comparison Matrix Chart

Things to compare	Characteristics: walk	use food	talk	swim
goat	X	X	X	
tree		X		
rock				
person	X	X	X	X

This is often used to compare the characteristics or properties of a number of things. To use a comparison matrix, ask yourself questions such as:

- What things do I want to compare?
- What characteristics will I choose to compare?
- How are the things I'm comparing similar and how are they different?

Hints

This technique can be useful for brainstorming.

Venn Diagram

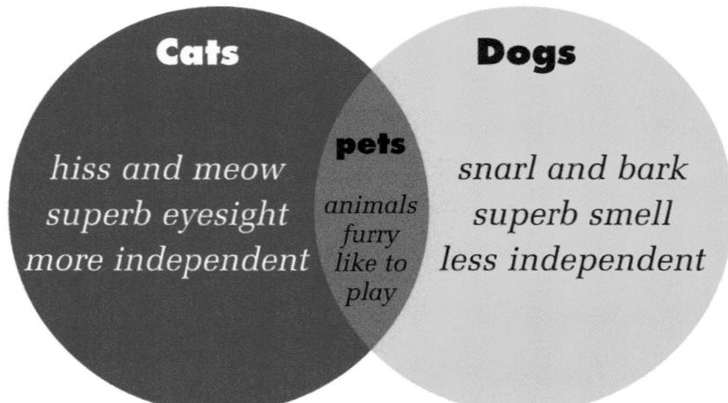

This is often used to compare two things. To use a Venn diagram, ask yourself questions such as:

- What things do I want to compare?
- What do they have in common?
- In what ways are they different?

Hints

You can use Venn diagrams to compare more than two things. Try it and see!

Concept Map

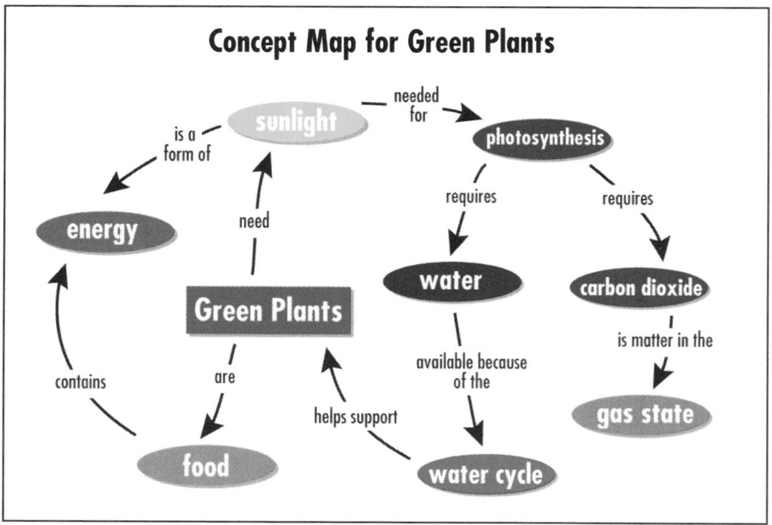

A concept map, or a mindmap, is a kind of web diagram with many uses. For example, you can use it to:

- review something you already know
- gather information about something you don't know
- explore new ways of thinking about something

- outline plans for an essay, a song, an experiment, a design challenge, a science project, and multimedia presentations

To use a concept map, ask yourself questions such as:

- What is the key idea, word, question, problem, or issue to build the map around?
- What words, ideas, objects, or questions come to mind when I think about the item at the centre of my map?

Tree Diagram

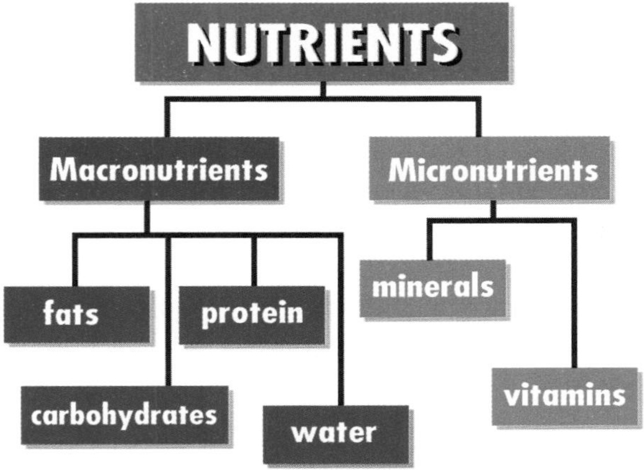

Tree diagrams allow you to see how things originate or how larger things can be broken down into their smaller components. Tree diagrams also allow you to organize or group concepts and things. Knowing about the parts of something helps you to better understand the concept or thing you are studying.

Stem-and-Leaf Plots

Are they graph-like charts, or are they chart-like graphs? Either way, a stem-and-leaf plot helps you summarize numerical information. For example, these numbers are the marks a group of students got on a recent science test.

97 75 69 80 61 69 67 75 81 72
70 58 94 77 66 87 72 80 75 55

To summarize this information with a stem-and-leaf plot, you do this.

1. Ignore the last digit of each number, and list the first digits in order in a vertical column.

Stem	Leaf
5	
6	
7	
8	
9	

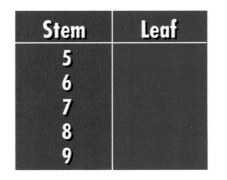

2. The first number is 97. Since the last digit is 7, write a 7 beside the 9. The second number is 75. Write a 5 beside the 7.

Stem	Leaf
5	
6	
7	5
8	
9	7

3. Repeat step 2 for the remaining numbers.

Check It Yourself

1. Based on the stem-and-leaf plot you just made, how many students got a mark of 75? How many got a mark of 80 or more? Which mark occurred most often?
2. Could you have answered these questions as quickly or as easily without a stem-and-leaf plot?

TOOLBOX

GLOSSARY

A

abiotic refers to the non-living components of an ecosystem
aesthetics study or appreciation of beauty
alloy one or more metals blended in a homogeneous mixture usually used to improve special properties
arch curved structure used in bridges and gateways
arch bridge bridge supported by an arch or a series or arches
ash smallest rock particles blown out of an erupting volcano

B

beam flat structure supported at both ends
beam bridge bridge supported by a beam or several beams
biodegradable able to be broken down by living things; usually releasing nutrients and non-toxic materials into the ecosystems
bioinvasion accidental or planned introduction of a non-native species into a community
biological weathering wearing down of rocks by living things
biome large area with a similar climate that supports the same type of vegetation
biotic refers to the living things in an ecosystem
boiling point temperature at which a substance changes from liquid state to gas state
boundary *in plate tectonics*: edge of a plate
box beam long structure in the shape of a hollow rectangular prism
bridge structure carrying a road, railway, or path across a river or valley

C

cantilever structure that is supported at only one end or point
carbon cycle the circulation and recycling of carbon in nature
carnivore animal that feeds on other animals or animal parts
cellular respiration process that releases the chemical energy stored in food
centre of gravity imaginary point in an object where the force of gravity (the weight of the object) acts
centrifuge fast-spinning tool used for the separation of mixtures where parts have different densities
change of state change in matter from one form to another by either adding or removing heat energy
chemical change process in which new substances with new properties are formed
chemical weathering wearing down of rocks by the combined action of water and chemical substances in the air
chlorophyll green pigment in plants that traps light energy during photosynthesis
clear cutting forestry practice that removes all trees in a large area
climax community generally stable community that has a wide range of species; the temporary end of succession
cogeneration technology of producing two or more forms of energy from a single energy generator
coke fuel used in the production of iron and steel; made by heating coal in an air-tight container
colonization first stage in succession when a pioneer species establishes itself in an area
column solid, upright support structure in the shape of a cylinder
community all populations of different species living and interacting in the same place
complementary forces two or more forces acting together
compression squeezing or pressing force
computer-aided design (CAD) computer program for making technical drawings
computer-aided manufacturing (CAM) use of computers to control the operation of machines during production
computer-integrated manufacturing (CIM) use of computers to control the processes of manufacturing

concentrated solution solution that has a large amount of solute

concentration mass of solute (usually in grams or kilograms) dissolved in a certain volume of solvent (usually in millilitres or litres) in a solution; written in g/mL or kg/L

condensation change of state from a gas to a liquid by removing heat energy

condense change from gas to liquid state

conduction flow of energy between substances that are in contact

conductor material that allows heat energy or electricity to flow easily

consumer living thing that relies on other living things for food; all animals are consumers

contract decrease in volume; matter contracts when heat energy is removed

convection *heat*: flow of heat energy that involves moving liquid or gas particles
plate tectonics: upward movement of hot molten rock in the earth's mantle

convection current pattern of moving liquid or gas particles when heat energy is added at one spot

converging boundary colliding edges of the earth's plates

core metallic centre of the earth

corrugated cardboard/metal cardboard or metal shaped into a series of grooves and ridges to increase strength

crust solid outer layer of the earth

cycle circulation of materials in nature; repeating pattern of growth or actions

D

data facts or information

database organised or sorted data usually generated by a computer

decomposer living thing that breaks down dead animals and plants or animal and plant wastes

deposition settling of rock material carried by water, wind, or ice

detergent cleansing agent other than soap

dilute solution solution that has a small amount of solute

dissolving mixing a solute completely with a solvent to form a solution

distillation technique for the separation of solutions involving boiling and condensation

diverging boundary two edges of the earth's plates that are moving apart

ductility ability of metals to be stretched without breaking; it allows metals to be drawn into wires or flattened into thin sheets

dynamic load moving or changing force acting on an object

earth material anything made of rocks or minerals

earthquake rapid movement of the earth's surface as a result of the sudden release of stress built up in the crust

ecosystem place on earth where living things interact with other living things as well as non-living things

energy transformation change of one form of energy into another

epicentre point on the earth's surface directly above the focus of an earthquake

erosion process of wearing away and removal of parts of the earth's surface by the action of water, wind, or chemicals

evaporate change from liquid to gas state

evaporation change of state from a liquid to a gas by adding heat energy

expand increase in volume; matter expands when heat energy is added

external force force applied to an object from the outside

fault crack in the earth's crust where there is movement along the two sides

filter substance (such as a membrane) with many tiny holes that traps solid particles

filtration technique to remove suspended solid particles from liquids or gases by means of a filter

focus place below the surface where the rocks break first, releasing the energy of an earthquake

food chain pathway of energy flow from one living thing to another in an ecosystem

food web link-up of all possible food chains in an ecosystem

force any push or pull acting on an object; forces will either cause a change in movement of the object or a change of shape

fossil preserved remains of living things, usually found in sedimentary rocks

fractional distillation technique for the separation of mixtures of several liquids by making use of their different boiling points

frame structure structure consisting of a rigid arrangement of parts fastened together

freezing point temperature at which a substance changes from liquid state to solid state

friction rubbing between surfaces which produces heat energy

function use or purpose of an object

girder box beam; long structure in the form of a hollow rectangular prism

glass clear solid that has many of the properties of a liquid

graduated cylinder container in the shape of a cylinder that measures volume

gravity natural downward pulling on an object by the earth

H

habitat place where an organism lives

hardness resistance of a mineral to scratching

hard water water that contains mineral salts; it is difficult to make soap lather in hard water

heat capacity heat-holding ability of a material

heat energy energy that flows from matter at a higher temperature to matter at a lower temperature

herbivore animal that feeds on plants or plant-like living things

heterogeneous term used to describe a mixture in which the different component parts are visible

homogeneous term used to describe a mixture in which the component parts appear to be the same throughout

humus soil component that consists of decayed organic matter

hypothesis possible answer to a question or possible explanation for a situation or phenomenon

I-beam beam that has a cross-section in the shape of an I

igneous rocks rocks formed from cooled lava

insoluble not capable of dissolving

insulation material used to limit the flow of heat energy

insulator material that does not allow heat energy or electricity to flow easily

internal force force that one part of a structure exerts on other parts within the same structure

inuksuk person-like stone structure built by the Inuit to mark important locations

kinetic energy energy of movement; particles that make up matter have kinetic energy

landslide sudden flow of large masses of rock or soil from a slope

lava magma that reaches the earth's surface, usually by means of a volcanic eruption

lithosphere solid outer layer of the earth that makes up the pattern of the earth's plates which move in the process of plate tectonics; formed from the crust and the upper portion of the mantle

load external force acting on an object

lustre brightness of the surface of a mineral

magma hot, molten rock deep inside the earth's crust

mantle massive zone of the earth that lies between the crust and the core

manufacturing process by which raw materials are made into finished products

market research gathering and evaluating information about people's likes and dislikes of products

mass amount of matter in an object; given in units such as grams

mass structure solid structure

matter anything that occupies space; all pure substances and mixtures are matter

mechanical mixture heterogeneous mixture; mixture in which the component parts are clearly visible

mechanical weathering wearing down of rocks by physical forces from water or wind

melting point temperature at which a substance changes from solid state to liquid state

meniscus curved shape of the top surface of a liquid in a narrow tube

metamorphic rocks rocks that have undergone changes caused by intense heat and pressure of the earth's interior

mineral naturally formed non-living substance, often occurring as crystals

mixture combination of two or more different pure substances

mountain building result of plate movement that may cause folding, faulting, thrusting, and volcanic activity which in turn lead to the formation of mountains

mountain range a series of mountains

nutrient component of food that supplies energy or building material to a living thing

omnivore animal that feeds on both animals and plants

packaging wrapping or container for goods

patent legal document that proves the ownership of an idea for a product

paper chromatography a method of separating a solution into its components using paper; used to determine if a liquid is a pure substance or a solution

Particle Theory of Matter theory that explains the behaviour of solids, liquids, and gases; it states that all matter is made up of tiny moving particles that attract each other and have spaces between them

pH number between 0 and 14 that indicates how acidic a solution is; the lower the number, the more acidic the solution

phosphate component of fertilizers and some detergents; too much phosphate in lakes and streams is one cause of water pollution

photosynthesis process by which plants use light energy, carbon dioxide, and water to make their own food

physical change change in which the make-up of a substance remains the same; changes of state are physical changes

phytoplankton microscopic plants living in the oceans

pig iron crude iron made from iron ore and coke in a blast furnace

pioneer species first species to be established in a certain habitat

plasticity ability to be easily shaped or moulded

plate *in plate tectonics*: one of the large slabs of rock that form the lithosphere

plate tectonics theory to explain the formation of the major surface features of the earth; it states that the earth's crust is made up of a "jigsaw" of large and small plates that are moving in various directions, colliding or moving apart at their boundaries

pollution contamination of the environment

population all individuals of one species living in a certain place at the same time

population cycle relationship of two or more species in an ecosystem

pores tiny spaces in soil between rock fragments, mineral grains, and humus

precipitation water vapour that condenses and falls to earth as rain, snow, etc.

primary succession formation of a new community in what was once a barren habitat

producer living thing at the beginning of a food chain capable of making its own food; all green plants are producers

properties features of a material or object

pure substance matter that has one type of particles throughout

radiation flow of heat energy in the form of waves

raw material material from which manufactured goods are made, for example, coal, trees, and petroleum

resource useful materials from the earth such as metal ores, minerals, oil, coal, and gas

Richter scale scale for measuring the strength of an earthquake based on the seismic waves caused by the earthquake and recorded by a seismograph

ridge underwater mountain range formed at a divergent boundary of plates

rock material of the earth's crust consisting of mineral particles

rock cycle diagram showing the connections between the different types of rocks as they change over long periods of time

room temperature temperature of about 20°C

R-value number that indicates the ability of an insulating material to stop or limit transfer of heat energy

S

saturated solution solution in which no more solute can be dissolved at a certain temperature

scavenger organism that feeds off the remains of dead animals that are killed by other consumers

secondary succession formation of a new community in a destroyed or greatly changed community

sediment deposited rock materials that came from an area of erosion

sedimentary rock hardened layers of sediment

seismic waves energy waves released by an earthquake

seismogram graphic illustration of the energy waves generated by an earthquake

seismograph device that detects and records the energy waves that spread through the earth from the focus of an earthquake

sewage liquid waste

shear two forces that act on an object in opposite directions along the same line or plane

shell structure hollow structure

slag waste material from producing steel

soap common substance used with water for cleaning

soft water water that contains few mineral salts; easy to make soap lather

soil mixture of rock fragments, mineral grains, organic materials, air, and water that allows plants to grow

solid structure structure containing a solid piece of material

solubility ability to dissolve; the mass of solute that is able to dissolve in a given amount of solvent to form a saturated solution

soluble able to dissolve

solute substance that dissolves in a solvent to form a solution

solution homogeneous mixture; mixture of two or more pure substances that looks like one substance

solvent a liquid substance that dissolves a solute to form a solution; water and alcohol are common solvents

species living things of the same kind which are able to reproduce

spreadsheet computer program that organizes data, using rows and columns

stability ability of an object to maintain its position

stable being balanced, difficult to topple over

states of matter forms in which matter can exist (solid, liquid, or gas)

static load weight of a structure

steel alloy of iron and up to 1.7 % of carbon and often other substances; steel has improved properties compared with iron alone

strata layers of sedimentary deposits

streak coloured line of fine particles a mineral leaves when rubbed along a rough surface such as an unglazed tile

structural failure breakdown of a structure due to the external and internal forces acting on it

structural fatigue weakening of a structure due to the external and internal forces acting on it

structural stress effect of all the forces acting on a structure at one time

structure any large or small object that provides support

sublimation change of state from a solid directly to a gas without melting first

succession a predictable pattern of change in the make-up of an ecosystem

supersaturated solution a solution that has more solute than it would normally be able to dissolve at a certain temperature

surfactant part of a detergent that clings to dirt and grease particles in the cleaning process

survey collecting of information by interviewing people or by asking people to answer questions on paper

suspension bridge bridge having its roadway hung from large cables supported between tall towers

sustainable development capable of being used indefinitely, often referring to the use of resources

symmetry balanced arrangement on opposite sides of a line or plane, or around a centre or axis

temperature measure of the average kinetic energy of the particles in a substance

tension force that stretches an object

texture feel of a soil sample

theory collection of ideas to explain many observed facts; these facts can be supported by repeated experimental results

Theory of Plate Tectonics *see plate tectonics*

thermal pollution heating of large bodies of water by unused heat energy that comes from industrial processes

thermometer instrument for measuring temperature

thermostat device to control temperature; it automatically switches a heating or cooling system on or off according to the temperature setting

torsion force that causes an object to twist

transform boundary edges of two plates that slide alongside each other

trench deep valley on the ocean floor

truss framework of beams that form triangles

truss bridge bridge supported by trusses

unsaturated solution solution in which more solute can be dissolved at a certain temperature

volcano opening in the earth's crust through which solid and molten rock, ash, and gases escape

volume amount of space occupied by matter; millilitres (mL) and litres (L) are common units of volume

waste discarded, unneeded, or unwanted materials from households and industries

water cycle the natural circulation of water from the surface of the earth to the atmosphere and back to the surface again

weathering mechanical, chemical, and biological processes that wear down rocks

weight force of gravity on an object

WHMIS short for Workplace Hazardous Materials Information System; a system of standard symbols used to identify dangerous substances in workplaces and schools

INDEX

I

K

L

M

N

PHOTO CREDITS AND ACKNOWLEDGMENTS

The publisher wishes to thank the following sources for photographs, illustrations, and other materials used in this book. Care has been taken to determine and locate ownership of copyright material used in this text. We will gladly receive information enabling us to rectify any errors or omissions in credits.

Photography

(Cover) Corel Stock Photo Library/ **p. 1** (top) CNRI, Science Photo Library/Photo Researchers/ **p. 1** (centre) Bill Ivy/ **p. 1** (bottom) Darryl Torckler, Tony Stone Images/ **p. 2** Stella Snead, Bruce Coleman Inc./ **p. 3** (top left) Emory Kristof, National Geographic Image Collection/ **p. 3** (bottom, left to right) Desmond Burton, Tony Stone Images/ Corel Stock Photo Library/ Wilfried Krecichwost, Tony Stone Images/ Bill Ivy/ **p. 4** (top, left and right) Corel Stock Photo Library/ **p. 4** (bottom left) Corel Stock Photo Library/ **p. 4** (bottom right) Bill Ivy/ **p. 5** (main) Emory Kristof, National Geographic Image Collection/ **p. 5** (inset) James Sugar, National Geographic Image Collection/ **p. 6** (top and centre left) Bill Ivy/ **p. 6** (bottom left) Corel Stock Photo Library/ **p. 6** (centre) Bill Ivy/ **p. 6** (top and bottom insets) Corel Stock Photo Library/ **p. 11** (top) Corel Stock Photo Library/ **p. 11** (centre) Ian Tomlinson, Spectrum Stock/Ivy Images/ **p. 11** (bottom) Ray Boudreau/ **p. 12** (top left) Corel Stock Photo Library/ **p. 12** (top centre) Kennan Harvey, Tony Stone Images/ **p. 12** (bottom, left and centre) Corel Stock Photo Library/ **p. 13** (all) Bill Ivy/ **p. 14** Corel Stock Photo Library/ **p. 15** (centre) David Prichard, First Light/ **p. 15** (inset) Dr. Dennis Kunkel, First Light/ **p. 16** Andrew Syred, Tony Stone Images/ **p. 17** Corel Stock Photo Library/ **p. 18** (top right) Christy Hayhoe/ **p. 18** (centre and bottom left) Toronto and Region Conservation Authority/ **p. 19** (right) Stuart McClymont, Tony Stone Images/ **p. 20** (top, left to right) Corel Stock Photo Library/ **p. 20** (bottom, left to right) Bill Ivy/ Corel Stock Photo Library/ Corel Stock Photo Library/ Will Crocker, The Image Bank/ Corel Stock Photo Library/ **p. 21** Ray Boudreau/ **p. 22** (centre) Corel Stock Photo Library/ **p. 22** (bottom left) Bill Ivy/ **p. 24** (top left) Eric V. Grave, Photo Researchers/ **p. 24** (top, centre and right) Corel Stock Photo Library/ **p. 24** (bottom left) Corel Stock Photo Library/ **p. 25** Douglas P. Wilson, Frank Lane Picture Agency/Corbis/ **p. 27** Bruno Dittrich, Tony Stone Images/ **p. 28** Corel Stock Photo Library/ **p. 29** (top left) Ron Erwin, Spectrum Stock/Ivy Images/ **p. 29** (top, centre and right) Corel Stock Photo Library/ **p. 29** (bottom, left and right) Corel Stock Photo Library/ **p. 29** (bottom centre) Bill Ivy/ **p. 30** (top) Biophoto Associates, Photo Researchers/ **p. 30** (centre left) Dr. Linda Stannard, UCT/Science Photo Library, Photo Researchers/ **p. 30** (centre right) Dr. Kari Lounatmqa, Photo Researchers/ **p. 30** (bottom left) Manfred Kage, Spectrum Stock/Ivy Images/ **p. 30** (bottom right) Dr. Jeremy Burgess, Science Photo Library, Photo Researchers/ **p. 31** (left) David M. Phillips, Visuals Unlimited/ **p. 31** (centre) Jim Zipp, The National Audubon Society Collection/ Photo Researchers Inc./ **p. 31** (top right) Corel Stock Photo Library/ **p. 32** (all) The Municipality of Metropolitan Toronto, Works Department/ **p. 33** Bill Ivy/ **p. 34** (all) Corel Stock Photo Library/ **p. 38** Corel Stock Photo Library/ **p. 39** Norbert Wu, Mo Yung Productions/ **p. 41** Ray Boudreau/ **p. 44** (top centre) The Jack Miner Migratory Bird Foundation/ **p. 44** (top right) Kenneth Love, National Geographic Society Image Collection/ **p. 44** (bottom left) Dr. Nancy Turner/ **p. 44** (bottom centre) Dawn Loewen/ **p. 46** Corel Stock Photo Library/ **p. 47** (top, left and right) Corel Stock Photo Library/ **p. 47** (bottom left) Ralph A. Clevenger, First Light/ **p. 47** (bottom right) Corel Stock Photo Library/ **p. 48** Corel Stock Photo Library/ **p. 49** Ray Boudreau/ **p. 50** Corel Stock Photo Library/ **p. 51** Corel Stock Photo Library/ **p. 52** (left) Corel Stock Photo Library/ **p. 52** (centre) Rick Frishman, Tony Stone Images/ **p. 52** (right) Phil Degginger, Tony Stone Images/ **p. 53** (from top to bottom) Corel Stock Photo Library/ W. Cody, First Light/ Corel Stock Photo Library/ Norman Piluke, Spectrum Stock/Ivy Images/ **p. 54** Corel Stock Photo Library/ **p. 55** (all) Corel Stock Photo Library/ **p. 56** (all) Corel Stock Photo Library/ **p. 57** Corel Stock Photo Library/ **p. 58** (top) Doug Wilson, First Light/ **p. 58** (bottom left) Corel Stock Photo Library/ **p. 59** Glenbow Archives, Calgary, Alberta/ **p. 60** (all) Corel Stock Photo Library/ **p. 61** (all) John Grunewald/ **p. 62** (top left) H1/Fonds Hydro-Québec, Centre d'archives Hydro-Québec/ **p. 62** (top right) Corel Stock Photo Library/ **p. 62** (bottom left) F5/Fonds Société d'énergie de la Baie James, Centre d'archives Hydro-Québec/ **p. 62** (bottom right) Corel Stock Photo Library/ **p. 67** (all) Corel Stock Photo Library/ **p. 68** V. Wilkinson, Valan Photos/ **p. 69** (centre left) S.C. Delaney, US Environmental Protection Agency/ **p. 69** (bottom left) Phillip Norton, Valan Photos/ **p. 69** (right, top to bottom) J.A. Wilkinson, Valan Photos/ City of Guelph Wet-Dry Recycling Centre/ V. Wilkinson, Valan Photos/ The Municipality of Metropolitan Toronto, Works Department/ **p. 70** Corel Stock Photo Library/ **p. 71** Recycling Council of Ontario/ **p. 72** Corel Stock Photo Library/ **p. 73** (top) Larry Ulrich, Tony Stone Images/ **p. 73** (bottom) Mike Abrahams, Tony Stone Images/ **p. 75** (left) Bill Brooks, Masterfile/ **p. 75** (right) Michael Wallace, Tony Stone Images/ **p. 76** (top) Corel Stock Photo Library/ **p. 76** (centre right) Winston Fraser, Spectrum Stock/Ivy Images/ **p. 83** (top) Corel Stock Photo Library/ **p. 83** (centre) Yoav Levy, First Light/ **p. 83** (bottom) Ken Graham, Tony Stone Images/ **p. 85** Ray Boudreau/ **p. 86** Ray Boudreau/ **p. 87** Corel Stock Photo Library/ **p. 88** Ray Boudreau/ **p. 90** Ray Boudreau/ **p. 91** Corel Stock Photo Library/ **p. 92** Ray Boudreau/ **p. 93** Corel Stock Photo Library/ **p. 94** (top, left and right) Corel Stock Photo Library/ **p. 94** (bottom left) Kevin Anderson, Tony Stone Images/ **p. 94** (bottom right) Corel Stock Photo Library/ **p. 95** Ian Crysler/ **p. 96** (top left) John Cancalosi, Valan Photos/ **p. 96** (top right) Alan Sirulnikoff, First Light/ **p. 96** (centre left) John Cancalosi, Valan Photos/ **p. 96** (centre right) Trevor Bonderud, First Light/ **p. 96** (bottom left) John Cancalosi, Valan Photos/ **p. 96** (bottom right) Joyce Photo, Valan Photos/ **p. 97** (centre right) Corel Stock Photo Library/ **p. 97** (bottom, left to right) Ian Crysler/ Ian Crysler/ Corel Stock Photo Library/ Ian Crysler/ Brent Bear, First Light/ **p. 98** Ian Crysler/ **p. 98** (bottom centre) Ray Boudreau/ **p. 99** Ray Boudreau/ **p. 100** Ray Boudreau/ **p. 101** (top left) Ray Boudreau/ **p. 101** (top right) Ian Crysler/ **p. 101** (centre) Corel Stock Photo Library/ **p. 101** (bottom left) Ian Crysler/ **p. 101** (bottom right) Ray Boudreau/ **p. 102** Ray Boudreau/ **p. 105** (top right) Jessie Parker, First Light/ **p. 105** (centre left) Ian Crysler/ **p. 105** (bottom left) Corel Stock Photo Library/ **p. 105** (bottom right) Ian Crysler/ **p. 106** Ray Boudreau/ **p. 107** (left) The Farm Museum (Milton, Ontario)/ **p. 107** (right) Chuck O'Rear, First Light/ **p. 108** Ray Boudreau/ **p. 109** Ray Boudreau/ **p. 110** Walter Urie, First Light/ **p. 111** Ray Boudreau/ **p. 114** NASA/ **p. 117** (all) Corel Stock Photo Library/ **p. 118** Ray Boudreau/ **p. 119** Ian Crysler/ **p. 119** (bottom right) Ray Boudreau/ **p. 120** Ian Crysler/ **p. 121** Ray Boudreau/ **p. 123** (left to right) Ian Crysler/ Corel Stock Photo Library/ Ian Crysler/ Ray Boudreau/ **p. 124** Corel Stock Photo Library/ **p. 126** Ray Boudreau/ **p. 128** Ray Boudreau/ **p. 129** Ray Boudreau/ **p. 130** Corel Stock Photo Library/ **p. 131** Ray Boudreau/ **p. 133** Ian Crysler/ **p. 134** Pat O'Hara, Tony Stone Images/ **p. 135** Corel Stock Photo Library/ **p. 137** Ray Boudreau/ **p. 138** Corel Stock Photo Library/ **p. 139** Ray Boudreau/ **p. 140** Greig, Greenpeace/ **p. 141** Ray Boudreau/ **p. 142** Ray Boudreau/ **p. 143** (top) Keith Lennox/ **p. 143** (bottom) Gail Mooney, Corbis/ **p. 144** (all) Corel Stock Photo Library/ **p. 145** (top) Charlie Westerman, Liaison International/ **p. 145** (bottom right) Royal Ontario Museum/ **p. 148** Ray Boudreau/ **p. 150** (left) Ron Watts, First Light/ **p. 150** (bottom centre) Ben Osborne, Tony Stone Images/ **p. 151** (top right) Corel Stock Photo Library/ **p. 151** (centre) Christensen, Greenpeace/ **p. 152** Ray Boudreau/ **p. 153** (top left) Derek Hunt, courtesy of Agriculture and Agri-Food Canada, reproduced with the permission of the Minister of Public Works and Government Services Canada 1999/ **p. 153** (top right) Ian Crysler/ **p. 153** (bottom right) John Edwards, Tony Stone Images/ **p. 154** (bottom) Dan Roitner, Spectrum Stock/Ivy Images/ **p. 155** (top) Bali, Greenpeace/ **p. 155** (centre) The Municipality of Metropolitan Toronto, Works Department/ **p. 155** (bottom left) Phillip Norton, Valan Photos/ **p. 155** (bottom right) Greg Pease, Tony Stone Images/ **p. 156** Corel Stock Photo Library/ **p. 157** Doug Wilson, First Light/ **p. 158** (all) Forensic Identification Research Services, Royal Canadian Mounted Police/ **p. 159** (all) Forensic Identification Research Services, Royal Canadian Mounted Police/ **p. 161** Edwards, Greenpeace/ **p. 162** Gerald & Buff Corsi, Visuals Unlimited/ **p. 163** (top) The Image Bank/ **p. 163** (centre) Richard A. Cooke, Tony Stone Images/ **p. 163** (bottom) Kevin Anderson/ Tony Stone Images/ **p. 164** Canadian Forces photo/ **p. 165** Ray Boudreau/ **p. 166** National Interagency Fire Center/ **p. 167** (top right to bottom left) Corel Stock Photo Library/ Ray Boudreau/ Gilbert Duclos/ Corel Stock Photo Library/ Antonio Rosario, The Image Bank/ Corel Stock Photo Library/ **p. 169** (left) Charles O'Rear, First Light/ **p. 169** (centre) Arnulf Husmo, Tony Stone Images/ **p. 169** (right) Tom Mareschal, The Image Bank/ **p. 170** (all) E.R. Degginger, Color-Pic, Inc./ **p. 171** (top left) Michael Holford Photography/ **p. 171** (bottom left) Ray Boudreau/ **p. 171** (right) Ray Boudreau/ **p. 172** Ray Boudreau/ **p. 173** Stratford Perth Archives/ **p. 174** Ray Boudreau/ **p. 175** Ray Boudreau/ **p. 176** (top left) Larry Mishkar, PictureSmith/ **p. 176** (top right) Thomas Moore, First Light/ **p. 176** (bottom left) Gilbert Duclos/ **p. 176** (bottom right) SunPac Foods Limited/ **p. 177** John Cancalosi, Valan Photos/ **p. 178** Ray Boudreau/ **p. 179** Ray Boudreau/ **p. 181** Ray Boudreau/ **p. 182** G. Brad Lewis, Tony Stone Images/ **p. 184** Wayne Sheils, Valan Photos/ **p. 185** Ray Boudreau/ **p. 190** Ray Boudreau/ **p. 191** Ray Boudreau/ **p. 192** Ian Crysler/ **p. 195** (top and centre) Robert L. White/ **p. 195** (bottom) Daniel Abriel, Dalhousie University/ **p. 197** (top) Sunbeam (Canada) Corporation Ltd./ **p. 197** (centre) Ray Boudreau/ **p. 197** (bottom) Philips Electronics Ltd./ **p. 198** (top) Ray Boudreau/ **p. 198** (bottom) David Willey, Physics Instructor, University of Pittsburgh at Johnstown/ **p. 199** Ray Boudreau/ **p. 201** Ray Boudreau/ **p. 203** Ray Boudreau/ **p. 204** Corel Stock Photo Library/ **p. 205** Ray Boudreau/ **p. 210** Woody Blackford/ **p. 211** NASA/ **p. 212** (top left) Corel Stock Photo Library/ **p. 212** (top right) Paul Chesley, Tony Stone Images/ **p. 212** (centre) Corel Stock Photo Library/ **p. 212** (bottom left) Ralph H. Wetmore II, Tony Stone Images/ **p. 212** (bottom right) Cameron Davidson, Tony Stone Images/ **p. 213** (top left) David Madison, Tony Stone Images/ **p. 213** (top right) Corel Stock Photo Library/ **p. 213** (bottom left) Corel Stock Photo Library/ **p. 213** (bottom right) Cameco Corporation/ **p. 214** Corel Stock Photo Library/ **p. 215** (top left) Andrew Farquhar, Valan Photos/ **p. 215** (top centre) Ray Boudreau/ **p. 215** (top right) Andy Sacks, Tony Stone Images/ **p. 215** (bottom left) Stephen Johnson, Tony Stone Images/ **p. 215** (bottom centre) Jeffrey Coolidge, The Image Bank/ **p. 215** (bottom right) Corel Stock Photo Library/ **p. 216** (top left) Ray Boudreau Black & Decker Canada Inc./ **p. 216** (top centre) Camco, GE Appliances/ **p. 216** (top right) Francis Lepine, Valan Photos/ **p. 216** (bottom left) Camco, GE Appliances/ **p. 216** (bottom centre) Corel Stock Photo Library/ **p. 216** (bottom right) John Mitchell, Valan Photos/ **p. 218** Ray Boudreau/ **p. 219** (left) Gilbert Duclos/ **p. 219** (right) Marc Romanelli, The Image Bank/ **p. 223** (top) David M. Doody, The Stock Solution/ **p. 223** (bottom) Robert W. Ginn, The Stock Solution/ **p. 223** (right) Alfred Pasieka, Science Photo Library/ Photo Researchers/ **p. 225** Francis Lepine, Valan Photos/ **p. 226** John Edwards, Tony Stone Images/ **p. 229** (top) Corbis-Bettmann/ **p. 229** (bottom) Corbis-Bettman/ **p. 230** (top) Mansell Collection, Time Inc./ **p. 230** (bottom) Al Harvey, The Slide Farm/

p. 231 (background) Bruce Hands, Tony Stone Images/ **p. 231** (inset left) Daniel Hummel, The Image Bank/ **p. 231** (inset right) Roberts Awnings and Signs/ **p. 232** Al Harvey, The Slide Farm/ **p. 233** Ray Boudreau/ **p. 237** (top) Billy Hustace, Tony Stone Images/ **p. 237** (centre) Ron Watts, First Light/ **p. 237** (bottom) Norman Hallendy, Tukilik Foundation/ **p. 238** Corel Stock Photo Library/ **p. 239** (left) Walter Schmid, Tony Stone Images/ **p. 239** (centre and right) Corel Stock Photo Library/ **p. 241** Ray Boudreau/ **p. 243** (centre, left to right) Corel Stock Photo Library/ Derke & O'Hara, Tony Stone Images/ Corel Stock Photo Library/ **p. 243** (bottom, left to right) Corel Stock Photo Library/ Kennon Cooke, Valan Photos/ Corel Stock Photo Library/ **p. 244** (left) Roland Seitre-Bios, Spectrum Stock/Ivy Images/ **p. 244** (centre) Sylvain Grandadam, Tony Stone Images/ **p. 244** (right) Corel Stock Photo Library/ **p. 245** (top left) Ian Crysler/ **p. 245** (top centre) John Fowler, Valan Photos/ **p. 245** (top right) Corel Stock Photo Library/ **p. 245** (centre left and centre) Corel Stock Photo Library/ **p. 245** (centre right) W. Cody, First Light/ **p. 245** (bottom left and centre) Ian Crysler/ **p. 245** (bottom right) Dr. A. Farquhar, Valan Photos/ **p. 247** (top left) David Madison, Tony Stone Images/ **p. 247** (top centre) J.R. Page, Valan Photos/ **p. 247** (top right) Corel Stock Photo Library/ **p. 247** (centre left) Corel Stock Photo Library/ **p. 247** (centre) Corel Stock Photo Library/ **p. 247** (centre right) Dennis W. Schmidt, Valan Photos/ **p. 247** (bottom right) Yann Arthus-Bertrand, Corbis/ **p. 248** (top left) First Light/ **p. 248** (top centre) Canadian Space Agency/ **p. 248** (top right) Sunrise Medical Home Healthcare Group/ **p. 248** (centre left) Ian Crysler/ **p. 248** (centre and bottom right) Corel Stock Photo Library/ **p. 249** (top left) Corel Stock Photo Library/ **p. 249** (top centre) Jeff Smith, The Image Bank/ **p. 249** (top right) Ian Crysler/ **p. 249** (centre left) Corel Stock Photo Library/ **p. 249** (centre) J.A. Wilkinson, Valan Photos/ **p. 249** (centre right) Rich LaSalle, Tony Stone Images/ **p. 249** (bottom right) Al Harvey, The Slide Farm/ **p. 250** Ray Boudreau/ **p. 251** (top) Corel Stock Photo Library/ **p. 251** (bottom) Ray Boudreau/ **p. 252** Ray Boudreau/ **p. 253** Ray Boudreau/ **p. 255** (top) Stephen Wan, C.W. Tse Architects Ltd./ **p. 255** (centre left) Stephen Wan, C.W. Tse Architects Ltd./ **p. 255** (centre right) Jim Dow, Wood O'Neill O'Neill Architects Ltd., Edmonton/ **p. 255** (bottom right) Corel Stock Photo Library/ **p. 256** (top left) Tom Hanson, CP Picture Archive/ **p. 256** (bottom) Didier Charre, The Image Bank/ **p. 258** (top left) Ray Boudreau/ **p. 258** (all) Corel Stock Photo Library/ **p. 259** (top and bottom) Ray Boudreau/ **p. 259** (centre right) Corel Stock Photo Library/ **p. 261** Ray Boudreau/ **p. 262** Corel Stock Photo Library/ **p. 263** Ray Boudreau/ **p. 265** Ray Boudreau/ **p. 266** Ray Boudreau/ **p. 267** (top) John Higginson, Tony Stone Images/ **p. 267** (bottom) Corel Stock Photo Library/ **p. 268** (top) Corel Stock Photo Library/ **p. 268** (bottom) Oliver Benn, Tony Stone Images/ **p. 269** Ray Boudreau/ **p. 272** Corel Stock Photo Library/ **p. 274** (left) Corel Stock Photo Library/ **p. 274** (right) Eve Smith, First Light/ **p. 275** (left) Glyn Kirk, Tony Stone Images/ **p. 275** (right) William Sallaz, The Image Bank/ **p. 276** (centre left) Andrea Pistolesi, The Image Bank/ **p. 276** (bottom) Ray Boudreau/ **p. 277** (centre) Ray Boudreau/ **p. 277** (bottom) Robert Galbraith, CP Picture Archive/ **p. 278** Corel Stock Photo Library/ **p. 280** CP Picture Archive/ **p. 281** Ray Boudreau/ **p. 282** Ray Boudreau/ **p. 283** Kennon Cooke, Valan Photos/ **p. 284** (left) Corel Stock Photo Library/ **p. 284** (bottom) Jean B. Heguy, First Light/ **p. 287** Ray Boudreau/ **p. 290** (left) Art Wolfe, Tony Stone Images/ **p. 290** (right) Canada Mortgage and Housing Corporation/ **p. 291** (top and bottom left) Bill Ivy/ **p. 291** (centre) Gilbert Duclos/ **p. 291** (top right) Trex Company, LLC/ **p. 294** Corel Stock Photo Library/ **p. 296** Ray Boudreau/ **p. 297** (top right) Bill Ivy/ **p. 297** (centre and bottom) Corel Stock Photo Library/ **p. 299** (top) Corel Stock Photo Library/ **p. 299** (bottom left) Zigy Kaluzny, Tony Stone Images/ **p. 299** (bottom right) Corel Stock Photo Library/ **p. 300** Norman Hallendy, Tukilik Foundation/ **p. 301** (top left) Physics Department, University of Toronto/ **p. 301** (centre right) Jeol USA, Inc./ **p. 301** (bottom left) Bill Ivy/ **p. 301** (bottom right) Fisher Space Pen (Canada) Inc., www.spacepen.ca/ **p. 302** (top left) J.Armand Bombardier Museum/ **p. 302** (top right) Bombardier Recreational Products/ **p. 302** (bottom left) M. Mitchell, First Light/ **p. 302** (bottom right) Ray Boudreau/ **p. 303** (top inset) Ian Crysler/ **p. 303** (centre left) Ian Crysler/ **p. 303** (centre right) Val Wilkinson, Valan Photos/ **p. 303** (bottom left) L. Thomas, Spectrum Stock/Ivy Images/ **p. 303** (bottom right) Inglis Ltd. Photography Library/ **p. 304** (left) Alan Marsh, First Light/**p. 304** (centre) Darwin R. Wiggett, First Light/ **p. 304** (right) Ian Crysler/ **p. 305** (top left) Ian Crysler/ **p. 305** (top centre) Canadian Space Agency/ **p. 305** (top right) Ian Crysler/ **p. 305** (centre right) Al Harvey, The Slide Farm/ **p. 306** Black Creek Pioneer Village (Downsview, Ontario)/ **p. 307** (top) Ray Boudreau/ **p. 307** (bottom) Churchill & Klehr, First Light/ **p. 308** (left) Romilly Lockyer, The Image Bank/ **p. 308** (centre) Peter Tang, First Light/ **p. 308** (right) John Cancalosi, Valan Photos/ **p. 311** (top left) Ken Straiton, First Light/ **p. 311** (top right) Rudi Christl, Spectrum Stock/Ivy Images/ **p. 311** (centre left) Andrew Sacks, Tony Stone Images/ **p. 311** (centre right) Lonnie Duka, Tony Stone Images/ **p. 311** (bottom right) Phillip Norton, Valan Photos/ **p. 313** (centre) Bay Generator Power Products Canada/ **p. 313** (bottom) Gilbert Duclos/ **p. 314** Bill Ivy/ **p. 315** (all) Rocky Mountain Bicycles (Delta, British Columbia)/ **p. 317** Bill Ivy/ **p. 318** (all) Peter Rankis, The Architects Circle (Toronto, Ontario)/ **p. 321** Ray Boudreau/ **p. 322** (left) Gilbert Duclos/ **p. 322** (centre) Corel Stock Photo Library/ **p. 322** (right) Chris Baker, Tony Stone Images/ **p. 323** Associated Press, CP Picture Archive/ **p. 324** Vince Streano, Corbis/ **p. 325** (top) Corel Stock Photo Library/ **p. 325** (centre) Corel Stock Photo Library/ **p. 325** (bottom) David Hiser, Tony Stone Images/ **p. 326** (left) USGS, MSH-7-22-80 Eruption 41ct/ **p. 326** (right) CP Picture Archive/ **p. 327** (left) D.C. Lowe, First Light/ **p. 327** (centre) Corel

Stock Photo Library/ **p. 327** (right) Phillip Norton, Valan Photos/ **p. 328** Jessie Parker, First Light/ **p. 329** Paul Almasy, Corbis/ **p. 330** Ray Boudreau/ **p. 331** Ray Boudreau/ **p. 333** (left) Michael Philip Manheim, First Light/ **p. 333** (centre) Steve McCutcheon, Visuals Unlimited/ **p. 333** (right) Corel Stock Photo Library/ **p. 334** NASA/ **p. 335** Ray Boudreau/ **p. 336** (left) Ontario Science Centre/ **p. 336** (right) Tony Stone Images/ **p. 338** The Boeing Company, Satellites and Ground Control Systems/ **p. 340** (top) James Balog, Tony Stone Images/ **p. 340** (bottom) Mats, Icelandic Photo/ **p. 341** Javier Cassella, CP Picture Archive/ **p. 342** Ricardo Mazalan, CP Picture Archive/ **p. 344** (top) USGS, HVO 375 ct/ **p. 344** (bottom) Frederic Larsen, CP Picture Archive/ **p. 346** Bob Gurr, Valan Photos/ **p. 347** Ray Boudreau/ **p. 348** (left) Corel Stock Photo Library/ **p. 348** (right) USGS, Gilbert, G.K. no. 2485/ **p. 349** (left) Albert Copley, Visuals Unlimited/ **p.349** (right) World Perspectives, Tony Stone Images/ **p. 350** Corel Stock Photo Library/ **p. 351** Chris Brandis, CP Picture Archive/ **p. 352** Roger Ressmeyer, Corbis/ **p. 353** (top) G. Brad Lewis, Tony Stone Images/ **p. 353** (bottom) Roger Ressmeyer, Corbis/ **p. 354** Ray Boudreau/ **p. 355** (left background) Doug Sokell, Visuals Unlimited/ **p. 355** (top inset) Arthur R. Hill, Visuals Unlimited/ **p. 355** (centre inset) John D. Cunningham, Visuals Unlimited/ **p. 355** (bottom inset) Arthur R. Hill, Visuals Unlimited/ **p. 355** (top right) Corel Stock Photo Library/ **p. 355** (bottom right) Albert Copley, Visuals Unlimited/ **p. 356** (all) Corel Stock Photo Library/ **p. 357** Corel Stock Photo Library/ **p. 358** (top left) D. Peebles, First Light/ **p. 358** (top right) Mats, Icelandic Photo/ **p. 358** (bottom left) Albert J. Copley, Visuals Unlimited/ **p. 358** (bottom right) Tom W. Parkin, Valan Photos/ **p. 359** (left) E. Foutz, Visuals Unlimited/ **p. 359** (centre) Mark Newman, Visuals Unlimited/ **p. 359** (right) Ray Boudreau/ **p. 360** (top left) Pam Hickman, Valan Photos/ **p. 360** (top centre) V. Wilkinson, Valan Photos/ **p. 360** (top right) Tom W. Parkin, Valan Photos/ **p. 360** (bottom left) V. Wilkinson, Valan Photos/ **p. 360** (bottom right) A.J. Copley, Visuals Unlimited/ **p. 361** Ray Boudreau/ **p. 363** (all) Nancy Chow, University of Manitoba/ **p. 364** Ian Davis-Young, Valan Photos/ **p. 365** Ray Boudreau/ **p. 366** John Eastcott and Yva Momatiuk, Valan Photos/ **p. 367** (top) James R. Page, Valan Photos/ **p. 367** (bottom) Valenti, Tony Stone Images/ **p. 368** (top) James R. Page, Valan Photos/ **p. 368** (bottom) A.J. Copley, Visuals Unlimited/ **p. 369** CP Picture Archive/ **p. 370** Corel Stock Photo Library/**p. 371** Ray Boudreau/ **p. 372** A. Kertstich, Visuals Unlimited/ **p. 374** Corel Stock Photo Library/ **p. 375** Ray Boudreau/ **p. 376** Corel Stock Photo Library/ **p. 377** Ray Boudreau/ **p. 378** Ray Boudreau/ **p. 381** Corel Stock Photo Library/ **p. 382** Ray Boudreau/ **p. 383** Ray Boudreau/ **p. 384** Corel Stock Photo Library/ **p. 385** (left) Ray Boudreau/ **p. 385** (right) Corel Stock Photo Library/ **p. 386** (top) W.A. Banaszewski, Visuals Unlimited/ **p. 386** (bottom) Dr. A. Farquhar, Valan Photos/ **p. 387** (top) Inga Spence, Visuals Unlimited/ **p. 387** (bottom) Science Vu, Visuals Unlimited/ **p. 388** (left) Al Harvey, The Slide Farm/ **p. 388** (centre) John Sylvester, First Light/ **p. 388** (right) Corel Stock Photo Library/ **p. 390** Deborah Vanslet, Valan Photos/ **p. 391** (top) Phillip Norton, Valan Photos/ **p. 391** (bottom) Jeannie R. Kemp, Valan Photos/ **p. 392** (left) D. Wiggett, First Light/ **p. 392** (right) Steve Strickland, Visuals Unlimited/ **p. 393** (left) Andrew Farquhar, Valan Photos/ **p. 393** (right) Bill Kamin, Visuals Unlimited/ **p. 394** (top) Corel Stock Photo Library/ **p. 394** (bottom) Ray Boudreau/ **p. 396** (top) Ray Boudreau/ **p. 396** (bottom) Gilbert Duclos/ **p. 397** Gilbert Duclos/ **p. 398** (left) Ray Boudreau/ **p. 398** (centre left) Phillips Electronics Ltd./ **p. 398** (centre right) Camco, GE Appliances/ **p. 398** (right) Ray Boudreau/ **p. 399** (top) NOAA/ **p. 399** (centre) Raul Gavidia, CP Picture Archive/ **p. 399** (bottom) Tom Hanson, CP Picture Archive/ **p. 400** (top) William J. Weber, Visuals Unlimited/ **p. 400** (bottom left) Harald Sund, The Image Bank/ **p. 400** (bottom right) Corel Stock Photo Library/ **pp. 405-418** Ray Boudreau/ **p. 418** (right) David De Lossy, The Image Bank/ **pp. 419-422** Ray Boudreau/ **p. 423** Greg Henkenhaf, CP Picture Archive/ **pp. 424-426** Ray Boudreau

The Publisher wishes to thank the following teachers and schools and their students for their participation in photograph sessions:
Andrea Delatory, Lincoln Alexander P.S., Ajax, Ontario
Derek Totten, Parkland P.S., Markham, Ontario
Lynn Williams, Buchanan P.S., Scarborough, Ontario

Illustrations

Crowle Art **2, 24** (bottom), **25, 50, 53, 55, 77, 116, 117, 130, 132, 146-147, 152, 168, 170, 180, 187** (right), **188** (right), **199, 206, 208, 220, 221, 222** (top), **241, 269, 270, 287, 292, 303, 314, 317, 337, 357, 383**
John Fraser **54, 89, 110, 149, 279, 282, 298, 370, 373** (top)
Gefen Group, KnowledgeMedia Designs **90, 112-113, 122, 356, 373** (bottom)
Brian Hughes **all icons**
Bernadette Lau **45, 59, 188** (left), **196, 207, 210, 235, 257, 273, 313**
Dave McKay **143, 164** (background), **186, 187** (left), **193, 194, 209, 222** (bottom), **224, 227, 232, 334, 336, 351, 352, 404**
Al Moon **23, 37, 39, 183, 184, 202, 214, 264** (top), **265, 267-268, 295-296, 310**
Josée Morin **10, 33, 48, 63, 66, 379**
NSV Productions **84, 90, 95, 97, 135, 136, 160, 254, 271** (bottom left and right), **274-275, 289, 309, 319-320, 332, 338, 339, 342, 343, 401, 406, 422, 423, 424, 427** (top and bottom right), **428, 429**
Carole Péloquin **8, 16, 157, 240, 286, 288, 308, 389**
Dusan Petricic **285**
Pat Stevens **380**
Angela Vaculik **26, 35-36, 43, 64-65, 215, 264** (bottom), **272, 426, 427** (top and bottom left)